PROVIDENTIAL BEGINNINGS

"...stand still, and consider the wondrous works of God."

Job 37:14

PROVIDENTIAL BEGINNINGS

by

J. ROSALIE HOOGE, Ph.D.

Providential Beginnings
by J. Rosalie Hooge

Printed in the United States of America

ISBN 1-594672-09-1

Unless otherwise indicated, Bible quotations are taken from the King James Version. Published by the Syndics of Cambridge University Press, in Great Britain.

Xulon Press
www.XulonPress.com

Xulon Press books are available in bookstores everywhere, and on the Web at www.XulonPress.com.

DEDICATION

Marvin E. Hooge

This book is dedicated to my husband Marvin E. Hooge. Without his encouragement this book would have never been published. He was a constant encouragement and help in finding all the old sources I have used and in all the research work. He also did all the setup and prepared the manuscript for publication. He heard a lot of, "Listen to this" as I proceeded to tell him all the wonderful things I had just learned. Though he was probably bored to death by all my 'discoveries' he just kept on listening and encouraging and has my greatest thanks for allowing the Lord to use him in all he did.

ACKNOWLEDGMENTS

My thanks must go to Verna M. Hall and Rosalie J. Slater who have had such a profound influence in my life in teaching me to see the hand of God in history - His Story. Since I began working with them through the Foundation for American Christian Education in 1977, my whole understanding of history has changed. Instead of seeing all events as a series of bits and pieces, they taught me to see everything as a complete picture of God's working through men and nations to accomplish His purpose and complete His plan for this world. Their superb Christian scholarship taught by example that those who followed them should have the same Biblical philosophy of research, reason, relate and record, always beginning with the Word of God.

This book is a direct result of their challenge to see and demonstrate "his marvellous works among all nations." My prayer is that it might be a blessing to all who read and study it and apply its truths to their lives. Because of these ladies my life has been changed and I can truly say with the Psalmist, "O how love I thy law! It is my meditation all the day." Psalm 119:97.

TABLE OF CONTENTS

SECTION I- FROM CREATION THROUGH THE FLOOD 1-70

AUTHOR 2
THE ACTS OF CREATION 3
COMMON THEORIES ABOUT THE TEXT 4
  THE GAP THEORY 4
  THE THEORY OF EVOLUTION 6
GOD'S LAWS OF NATURE 9
UNIFORMITARIANISM 10
DAY-AGE THEORY 11
THE STEPS OF CREATION 12
  GOD FORMED 13
    THE LIGHT 13
    THE DARKNESS 13
    CREATION OF ANGELS 13
    AIR-ATMOSPHERE 21
    THE VAPOR CANOPY 23
    THE SEA 25
    THE LAND 26-27
    PLANTS 27
  GOD FILLED 28
    THE MOON 28
    THE SUN 28
    THE STARS 29
    THE YOUNG AGE OF THE UNIVERSE 31
    SEA CREATURES AND BIRDS 33
    LAND ANIMALS 35
    THE CREATION OF MAN 36
    THE CREATION OF WOMAN 40
  DAY SEVEN
    GOD CEASED HIS LABOR 41
    THE SABBATH 41
  THE RECAP OF CREATION 43
  THE FALL 43
  DIVINE SOCIAL INSTITUTIONS ESTABLISHED AS A RESULT OF THE FALL 48
  THE FIRST MURDER AND ITS CONSEQUENCES 49
  THE FLOOD 51
  COMPARISON OF THE ORIGINAL CREATION AND THE FALL 54
  FLOOD CONDITIONS 56
    GEOLOGY OF THE FLOOD 60
    THE FOSSILS 62
    THE FORMATION OF MOUNTAINS 64
    FORMATION OF LIMESTONE 65

THE ICE AGE 66
ANTHRACITE COAL 67
PETROLEUM 67
POLITICAL RESULTS OF THE FLOOD 68
NOAH'S SIN 68

SECTION II - DISPERSION CHART 71-74

SECTION III - HAM AND HIS SONS 75-124

CUSH 75
NIMROD 77
BABYLON 77-82
THE TOWER OF BABEL 80
THE TEMPLE OF BELUS 81
CONFUSION OF LANGUAGES 82
SEMIRAMIS 82-87
BABYLONIAN RELIGIOUS MYTHS 87
THE FUTURE OF BABYLON 88
THE KINGS OF BABYLON 90-98
MIZRAIM 98-112
THE EGYPTIAN PEOPLE AND THEIR DEVELOPMENT 99
CALENDAR 99
WRITTEN LANGUAGE 99
LUXURIES AND SOCIAL STANDING 100
RELIGION 100
MONUMENTS 104
CONTRIBUTIONS OF EGYPT 106
EGYPTIAN GOVERNMENT 106
KINGS OF ANCIENT EGYPT 107
THE ISRAELITE BONDAGE IN EGYPT 110
THE FALL OF EGYPT 111
SONS OF MIZRAIM 111
PHUT 112-117
THE PHOENICIANS 112
PHOENICIAN ASHKELON 115
PHOENICIAN RELIGION 115
CANAAN 117-122
SONS OF CANAAN 118
CONCLUSIONS 122
CHART OF EGYPT AND ISRAEL 124

SECTION IV - SHEM AND HIS SONS 125-264
ASSHUR 125
ASSYRIAN RELIGION 126

ARPHAXAD 129
    RELIGION OF THE CHALDEANS 130
    SONS OF ARPHAXAD 133
LUD 136
ARAM 136
THE ASSYRIAN KINGS 136-156
THE CHRONICLE OF THE BEGINNINGS OF THE NATION OF ISRAEL 156
    ISRAEL IN THE MIND OF GOD 156
    HEBREW LANGUAGE 157
    UR OF THE CHALDEES, FIRST HOME OF ABRAM 157
        INHABITANTS 157
        GOVERNMENT 159
THE HISTORY OF ABRAHAM 160-
    THE PROMISE OF GOD 162
    DEPARTURE FROM UR 164
    THE PILGRIMAGE 166
    GOD'S COVENANT WITH ABRAM 168
    BIRTH OF ISHMAEL 169
    CIRCUMCISION - THE EXTERNAL SIGN OF THE COVENANT 170
    THE PROMISE OF A SON MADE CERTAIN 171
    THE DESTRUCTION OF SODOM AND GOMORRAH 172
        MOAB AND AMMON 175
    ABRAHAM AND ABIMELECH 176
    THE BIRTH OF ISAAC 177
    THE DEPARTURE OF ISHMAEL 178
    THE SACRIFICE OF ISAAC 178
    MARRIAGE OF ISAAC 180
    ABRAHAM REMARRIES 181
    DEATH OF ABRAHAM 181
THE FORMATION OF A NATION 181
    JACOB AND ESAU 182
    THE STOLEN BIRTHRIGHT 182
    ISAAC AT GERAR 183
    THE STOLEN BLESSING 184
    IN THE HOUSE OF LABAN 187
JACOB'S WEALTH AND ESCAPE 189
    PREPARATIONS FOR MEETING ESAU 192
        ENCOUNTER WITH GOD 193
        BROTHER MEETS BROTHER 194
    A NEW HOME IN CANAAN 194
        DINAH AND SHECHEM 195
        JACOB AT BETHEL 196
        DEATH OF DEBORAH 197
        DEATH OF RACHEL 197
        REUBEN'S SIN 197

DEATH OF ISAAC 197
ESAU AND HIS FAMILY 197
JOSEPH'S DREAMS 199
JUDAH AND TAMAR 201
JOSEPH
JOSEPH IN THE HOUSE OF POTIPHAR 203
PRISON DREAMS 204
PHARAOH'S DREAM 206
JOSEPH'S BROTHERS 209
THE SILVER CUP 212
THE REVELATION 213
JOURNEY TO EGYPT 214
THE CULTURE OF EGYPT 215
PRESENTATION IN PHARAOH'S COURT 216
THE LAST FIVE YEARS OF THE FAMINE 217
JOSEPH'S PLEDGE TO HIS FATHER 218
MANASSEH AND EPHRAIM 218
THE BLESSING OF JACOB'S SONS 218
DEATH OF JACOB 220
DEATH OF JOSEPH 222
THE BEGINNING OF OPPRESSION 223
NEW OPPRESSION 224
THE YEARS IN BONDAGE 225
MOSES 226
MOSES' PREPARATION 227
RELIGION IN ISRAEL AT THE TIME OF THE EXODUS 230
MOSES BEFORE PHARAOH 231
THE TEN PLAGUES SENT BY GOD 232
THE PASSOVER 234
THE EXODUS 235
THE DEPARTURE 236
CONSECRATION OF THE FIRSTBORN FOR RELIGIOUS SERVICE 236
THE JOURNEY 236
MANNA AND QUAILS, AND WATER 239
BATTLE WITH THE AMALEKITES 239
INSTITUTION OF JUDGES OVER THE PEOPLE 240
ARRIVAL AT SINAI 241
GOD'S ANGEL 243
THE PROMISED DEFEAT OF THEIR ENEMIES 244
THREE FESTIVAL TO BE OBSERVED EACH YEAR 244
THE AGREEMENT 245
THE TABLES OF STONE 245
THE GOLDEN CALF 246
THE SECOND TABLET OF STONE 249
GOD'S COVENANT 250

ISRAEL'S HISTORY 251
    THE UNITED KINGDOM 251
        SAUL 251
        DAVID 252
        SOLOMON 253
            THE TEMPLE 253
            JERUSALEM 254
    THE DIVIDED KINGDOM 254
        THE NORTHERN KINGDOM 254
        THE SOUTHERN KINGDOM 256
    CHART OF THE DIVIDED KINGDOM 259
CONCLUSIONS 262

SECTION V - JAPHETH AND HIS SONS 265-344
    MIGRATION IMPULSE 265
    LANGUAGE OF THE SCRIPTURES 265
    GOMER 266
        MIGRATION OF THE SONS OF GOMER 266
        RELIGIOUS BELIEFS OF THE GOMERITES 267
    MAGOG 267
        POLAR NATIONS 268
            MIGRATIONS OF THE UGRIANS 268
            RELIGIOUS BELIEFS 269
        MONGOLS AND MALAYS 270
            GEOGRAPHIC DIVISIONS OF THE MONGOLS 270
            LANGUAGE CHARACTERISTICS 270
            THE CHINESE 270
                GEOGRAPHIC CHARACTERISTICS 270
                CHARACTERISTICS OF CHIN 271
                EARLY CHINESE CONTRIBUTIONS 272
                EARLY ENEMIES 272
                RELIGIOUS BELIEFS 272
                CHINESE LANGUAGE 273
                GOVERNMENT 274
                DIFFERENT CULTURES 274
                LATER RELIGIONS 275
                HISTORIC PROGRESSION 276
                ADVANCES OF THE DYNASTIES 277
                CHINESE INVENTIONS 278
        MALAY 278
            MIGRATIONS 279
            CONTRIBUTIONS FROM OTHER NATIONS 279
            RELIGIOUS BELIEFS 279
            TRIBAL RESEMBLANCE 280
        CHILDREN OF THE NEW WORLD 280

ORIGIN OF THE AMERICAN TRIBES 280
RELIGIOUS IDEAS 280
ARCHITECTURE 281
MEXICO 281
MIGRATION 282
RELIGIOUS BELIEFS 282
PECULIAR CHARACTERISTICS 283
EVIDENCE OF THEIR MIGRATIONS 283
MADAI 283
KINGS OF THE MEDES 284
INDIA 286
RELIGIOUS BELIEFS 287
MIGRATIONS 287
THE PERSIANS 287
RELIGIOUS BELIEFS 288
GOVERNMENT 289
KINGS OF THE PERSIAN PERIODS 289
TUBAL 297
MESCHECH 297
TIRAS 297
JAVAN 297
RELIGIOUS BELIEFS OF THE IONIANS 298
THE GREEK NATION 298
RELIGION 299
THE GEOGRAPHY OF GREECE 302
THE FOUR DIVISIONS OF GREEK HISTORY 302
THE ORIGINAL TRIBES OF GREECE 302
THE WAR OF THE HERACLIDAE 303
GRECIAN IDEAS OF THEIR BEGINNINGS 304
TIME PERIODS OF IMPORTANCE 305
THE FALL OF TROY 305
THE OLYMPIAD 305
FORMS OF GREEK GOVERNMENT 306
THE CITY-STATES 307
SPARTA 307
ATHENS 308
PHILIP OF MACEDON 310
ALEXANDER THE GREAT 312
EARLY LIFE 312
REIGN OF ALEXANDER 313
THE CONQUEST OF THE EAST 313
THE CHARACTER OF ALEXANDER 315
GOD'S PURPOSE FOR ALEXANDER 316
THE DIVISION OF ALEXANDER'S EMPIRE 316
THE KINGDOM OF THE SELEUCIDAE 318

THE MACCABEES 319
THE ROMANS 321
THE ROMAN METHOD OF NATION-MAKING 323
ADVANTAGES OF THE ROMAN DOMINATION 324
PREPARATION OF THE WORLD FOR COMING OF CHRIST 325
INFLUENCE OF THE GREEKS ON THE ROMANS 325
RELIGION 326
ROME AS A REPUBLIC 327
PROVINCIAL GOVERNMENT 327
CIVIL STRIFE 327
FIRST TRIUMVIRATE 328
CONTRIBUTIONS OF CAESAR 329
OCTAVIUS CAESAR, AUGUSTUS 330
AUGUSTUS' PART IN GOD'S PLAN 331
THE BIRTH OF CHRIST 332
ROMAN BOUNDARIES 332
CONDITION OF THE EMPIRE UNDER CAESAR 332
ROMAN SUPREMACY 333
RELIGION AT THE TIME OF CHRIST 334
PLACES OF WORSHIP AT THE TIME OF CHRIST 337
PHILOSOPHY OF ROME 337
ROME'S VIEW OF CHRISTIANITY 338
BEGINNING OF PERSECUTION IN PALESTINE 338
RULER'S OF ROME 338
CONCLUSIONS 342

SECTION VI - CONCLUSIONS 345-348

APPENDICES 349-352

BIBLIOGRAPHY 353-358

MAPS 359-368
ASSYRIAN EMPIRE 359
CHALDEA 360
ROUTE OF THE EXODUS 361
MAP OF ANCIENT EMPIRES 362
THE PERSIAN EMPIRE CONQUERED BY ALEXANDER 363
THE PERSIAN EMPIRE AND BORDERLANDS 364
THE MACEDONIAN EMPIRE 365
TERRITORIAL EXPANSION OF ROME 366
THE ROMAN EMPIRE 367
GREECE AND HER COLONIES 368

INDEX 369-372

SECTION I

FROM CREATION
THROUGH THE FLOOD

INTRODUCTION TO GENESIS

Genesis = origins/generations/beginnings

The purpose of all Scripture is to reveal God to man and bring man back to God. History - His-Story - is the divine revelation of the story of human redemption. In the first chapters of Genesis is introduced the creation and the fall, the failure of man. From Genesis 3:15 onward the Scripture deals with the redemption and restoration of man.

The book of Genesis can be said to contain the history of the world. In it are all the histories of all the nations of the world. To study this book is to study all of history in its germinal form. Through it we gain an understanding of God's plan for each individual and nation and how He will accomplish the purpose of that plan. It is important to remember that all of history deals with the nation of Israel. All Old Testament history looks *forward* to the coming Messiah from the nation of Israel. All New Testament history and all the histories of the world look *back* to the birth, death, and resurrection of the Messiah from Israel.

The book of Genesis is the most important book of the Bible. It forms the foundation of all the remaining books of the Bible. If this book is not true then the remainder of the Bible is also untrue and we are without hope. We know the entire Bible is inspired by God and has to be true because God cannot lie, "...which God, that cannot lie,...." (Titus 1:2.)

It provides us with the records of:

- the origin of the universe,
- the origin of man,
- the beginning of sin,
- the promise of a coming Savior,
- the first Gospel,
- the first death,
- the first record of human civilization,
- the first city,
- the end of the first world with the Flood,
- the emergence of a second world after the Flood, and
- the beginning of a new nation, created expressly by God, from which the Messiah was to come.

Our belief about the book of Genesis will affect all other beliefs in our lives. Our philosophy of life reveals whether we accept a divine creation based upon the Scriptures or if we reject the creation account and accept the theory of evolution. The two books most attacked by liberals, whether religious or profane, are Genesis and the Revelation. This should remind us of the importance of these books to our fundamental belief system, (Hebrews 11:3; Romans 1:20,21).

Our philosophy of life influences our understanding of history. If we believe man has evolved through a series of outward, upward changes during millions or billions of years, our interpretation of the events of history will have to agree with our philosophy and we will see all history as a series of accidental events without relation. But if we, as believers, see the Hand of God working in history in every circumstance, and understand the final plan God has for man, we will be able to see the thread that pulls together all of these events; the thread which instructs us in the common relationship of one to another, and more importantly to a great redeeming work.

The purpose of this study is to see this thread and better understand the events which have occurred in our world and affect us today.

Chapters one through eleven give us the general beginnings of the history of all the nations of the world, as will be seen in the study of the dispersion. This allows us to have a better understanding of the place of each of these nations in God's plan for the ages.

THE AUTHOR

The author of the book is believed to have been Moses. He is the author accepted by the Jewish scribes and by the fathers of the church. He was accepted by Christ also as seen in Luke 24:27,44. *And beginning at Moses and all the prophets, he expounded unto them in all the scriptures the things concerning himself.* (44) *And he said unto them, These are the words which I spake unto you, while I was yet with you, that all things must be fulfilled, which were written in the law of Moses, and in the prophets, and in the psalms, concerning me.*

When the Law is spoken of in this sense it always refers to the first five books of the Bible, the Pentateuch. The Torah of the Hebrews contains the first five books of the Bible; Genesis, Exodus, Leviticus, Numbers, and Deuteronomy; and the word "Torah" means "The Law."

"According to Exodus 17:1; 24:4-8; 34:27; Numbers 33:1,2; Deuteronomy 31:9, 22,24, Moses was commanded to write specific things by the Lord. Other books of the Old Testament allude to the "law of Moses" (I Kings 2:3); "the book of the Law of Moses" (II Kings 14:6); and "the book of Moses" (Ezra 6:18; Nehemiah 13:1, etc.). The New Testament also speaks of Moses, and the law of Moses (cf. Matthew 19:8; Mark 1:44; 10:4,5; Lk. 5:14; 16:31; 20:37; Acts 3:22; 13:39; 15:5; 26:22; Romans 10:5, 19; I Corinthians 9:9; 2 Corinthians 3:15; Revelation 15:3)." (Introduction to the first book of Moses, Santa Biblia, [Holy Bible], Editorial Caribe, San Jose, Costa Rica, 1980.)

Since the creation was already completed at the time of Moses, it is probable that Moses, under the inspiration of the Holy Spirit, penned the oral and written traditions of those times. (For example, that which Adam saw and knew from God he told to his son Seth, Seth in turn told them to his son, etc., etc., until the time of Moses.) This gives more authenticity to the occurrences that are recorded because this history came from the people who actually saw it happening. Moses was guided by God in his selection of the material to be included in the book of Genesis, (2 Timothy 3:16).

GOD

The book of Genesis begins with the incontrovertible fact that God exists and the author does not feel it necessary to "prove" it, (Psalms 90:2; 93:1,2; 102:25; Proverbs 8:23). It is accepted and understood that those who will read this book will also understand that fact. Only those without understanding would doubt the existence of God, (Psalm 14:1 *The fool hath said in his heart, There is no God...*).

In that primitive time no evolutionary system existed and it was not necessary to combat its falsehood; that philosophy appeared many years afterwards to try to disprove the divine creation of God in Genesis 1:1, (Colossians 1:16-18). However, its roots were certainly present in Genesis 3 when Satan approached Eve and said, "Yea, hath God said?"

God reveals Himself through His Word, through nature, history, conscience, and reason, but He must be accepted by faith.

THE ACTS OF CREATION

Genesis 1:1, *In the beginning God created the heaven and the earth.*

If God created everything, then He controls everything and can do everything, (Luke 1:37; Matthew 19:26; Mark 10:27).

In Hebrew the first phrase is translated "in the beginning" and indicates what the rest of the book contains. It tells us the beginning of everything is God, but it does not explain when God began to exist because He has no beginning, (Romans 1:20; Deuteronomy 33:27).

The first verse speaks of the work of God in reference to creation - it is a finished work. Verse two begins to explain *how* God created.

When did this occur? In the Beginning

Verse one tells us the universe had a beginning. One moment it did not exist and when God spoke it began to exist. Nothing existed; not matter, nor time, nor space in which to put them. Here the word speaks only of beginnings, nothing of how everything will terminate; there are no endings here. Upon this foundation of truth, (that everything had a beginning and that beginning was God), all the future revelation of God to man is based.

We know, and all scientists agree, that the universe had a beginning. The Bible tells us the earth "grows old like a garment" and science has added its proof to this truth. The sun is wearing down as are the stars. If we understand that everything is growing old, logic tells us that these same things, at one time, had to be new.

Psalm 102:25-27 *Of old hast thou laid the foundation of the earth: and the heavens are the work of thy hands.*

26. They shall perish, but thou shalt endure: yea, all of them shall wax old like a garment; as a vesture shalt thou change them, and they shall be changed:

27. But thou art the same, and thy years shall have no end.

Isaiah 51:6 *Lift up your eyes to the heavens, and look upon the earth beneath; for the heavens shall vanish away like smoke, and the earth shall wax old like a garment,....*

Who did it? *"In the beginning God..."*

Everything was made by God. The word used here is **Elohim**, the Hebrew name for God. "El" means "the strong God." The ending of the word is "-im" which is a plural ending. This ending is sometimes used in reference to the pagan gods, (Psalm 96:5). In this reference it is used in the singular in one sense and speaks of the majestic name of God, the Creator. But it is a plural name with a singular meaning, suggesting the uni-plurality of the Deity. He is One, yet Three, (1 John. 5:7). The three persons of the God-head were present at the creation. (John 1:1-3,10; Hebrews 1:1,2; Ephesians 3:8,9; Psalm 33:6; Job 26:1-14.)

All was made by Him Who has always existed, Colossians 1:17 *And he is before all things, and by him all things consist.* Consist: "To stand together; to be in a fixed or permanent state, as a body composed of parts in union or connection. Hence, to be; to exist; to subsist; to be supported and maintained." (*Noah Webster's First Edition of an American Dictionary of the English Language*, reprinted by Foundation for American Christian Education, Anaheim, California, 1967; hereafter referred to as Webster's 1828.) (Psalm 136:5-9; Isaiah 45:12,18.)

John 17:5 *And now, O Father, glorify thou me with thine own self with the glory which I had with thee before the world was.*

Acts 17:24,25 God that made the world and all things therein, seeing that he is Lord of heaven and earth, dwelleth not in temples made with hands; *(v. 25)* Neither is worshipped with men's hands, as though he needed any thing, seeing he giveth to all life, and breath, and all things.

How was it made? *In the beginning God created....*

When the Scripture speaks of creating it means to create from nothing, "ex nihilo". Only God can create - man can only manipulate that which God has already created.

The Hebrew word used here is "bara" and means to create from nothing. It is used three times in Genesis 1, one time each in verses 1, 21, and 27. There was no material to use; there was nothing. God made everything from nothing. Only an omnipotent God could do that, (omni = all; potent = powerful). Material is not eternal and had to be created.

Where did the energy come from?

Every philosophy in the world has its origin in some form of already existing energy. From this energy man begins to form his theory of what happened, but he can never explain where the energy came from. (For example in the 'big bang' theory - where did the energy originate to cause such a massive explosion?) Genesis 1:1 tells us that *nothing* existed, but God spoke and by His power everything came into existence. God is the source of all energy.

What was made? *...the heavens and the earth.*

THE HEAVENS

The Hebrew word used here is "shâmay-in" and refers to all of space and not to just the sky or heavens which we can see. It does not mean the stars, which were not created until the fourth day. It seems to refer to the space-mass-time universe, the three parts God used to bring all things into existence.

THE EARTH

This refers to the components of matter in the universe - the basic elements of material of which the earth and all the universe are composed. The Hebrew word is "erets" and can mean either "ground" or "land". It can refer to some land in particular as the 'land of Canaan' or to material in general.

First, the earth 'was void' or empty.

Second, it was 'without form', without object.

Third, it was 'dark', until God began to act upon it.

COMMON THEORIES ABOUT THE TEXT

The Gap Theory or Restitution Theory

The teaching of the gap theory began with Thomas Chalmers, a Scottish theologian, in the early 19th century and was popularized in the Scofield Bible notes, by Harry Rimmer. It was also taught by Robert Milligan in *The Scheme of Redemption,* and by Arthur Constance in *Without Form and Void,* by Clarence Larkin in *Rightly Dividing the Word,* and by others. Many well-meaning theologians have taught this theory for many years. The reason for teaching this theory was to try to accommodate all the so-called geological ages (See Appendix I) necessary for scientists to be able to prove the 'old earth' theory, which in itself is not provable.

It is based upon the theory that between verses 1 and 2 of Genesis 1, Satan was cast out of heaven (or at least some terrible catastrophe occurred) and many millions or billions of years transpired before the final restoration of the earth in a new creation.

Some have also suggested that a falling meteor or comet striking the earth could have caused a great cataclysm at this point and could account for a recreated earth. This does not seem likely since there is no evidence that meteors and comets fell to earth before the period of the Flood.

Problems with this view:

There is no indication in the Bible that there was any time-lapse between verses 1 and 2. Verse two begins with the conjunction 'and' which indicates a continual progression of time. The verb used is indicative of a fixed and completed state. The original matter was created in an unordered state and then God put it in order from verse 2 and forward. Most Hebrew scholars agree there is no 'gap' between verses one and two.

Geological ages do not exist, they are periods of time imagined by evolutionists to have existed, and we do not use geology or any other science to interpret the Scripture - it must interpret itself, (2 Peter 1:20).

Who could possess the knowledge of how long a time-gap of this kind would have lasted? Would it have been long enough to accommodate the epochs of time necessary to "prove" the theory of evolution or the existence of geological ages? How many billions of years are needed?

If a catastrophic event had actually taken place between verses 1 and 2 the earth would have been so changed that none of the evidence to support these geological ages would have remained. The entire original creation would have been obliterated and nothing would remain from which these assumptions could be made. With no traces of a former world it would be impossible to try to assume it had even existed. Therefore, what proof would it be built upon?

Even the basis of the philosophy of uniformitarianism would have been destroyed if this catastrophe had occurred. That philosophy is based upon the assumption that all physical conditions have remained the same since the beginning of what we call time. If there were a time when conditions were altered then this philosophy is incorrect. To some degree conditions do remain the same today as they have in the past, if we exclude times of Divine intervention, (the Curse, the Flood, the time changes in Joshua, etc.). Future changes will also occur which have never occurred in the past; for example, the physical changes which will take place during the Tribulation period, (e.g. Revelation 16).

Evolution is based upon the assumption that fossils must appear in a rigid order so that upward changes can be seen. If some cataclysmic event occurred between verses one and two there would have been no fossils and no evidence of any previous life would exist. Again, there are no proofs.

Dr. Morris reminds us of another important consideration in reference to the gap-theory. If this theory were true it would mean God had created a world before ours in which sin, death, sickness, and suffering existed. These conditions would have existed billions of years before Adam; and God would be a liar because Romans 5:12 and 1 Corinthians 15:21,22 say that sin entered the world through the sin of Adam. It would mean God allowed suffering and death with no Savior to make a way of escape for that civilization.

Fossils are the remains of "dead" things. The fossils which have been discovered to date speak of conditions different from our own - yet it would have been a world without hope even before the fall of Satan from heaven. This is not possible. Henry Morris, *The Genesis Record*, (Grand Rapids: Baker Book House, 1976), pp. 46,47.

1 Corinthians 15:45 speaks of the <u>first</u> man, not the continuation of some long-dead civilization.

When God finished His creative acts He said in Genesis 1:31 "...it was **very** good...." The creative act was <u>very</u> good. This verse, however, does not preclude the existence of Satan and his presence already in the world. We are not told explicitly when Satan was cast out of heaven so no absolute date nor time can be assigned to this event. He was cast out to dwell in the 'air' (prince of the power of the air, Ephesians 2:2) with complete liberty of movement and access to the throne of God, (Job 1:6; 2:1, etc.).

There is no reason to try to put a large block of time between these verses to give Satan a time span in which to fall when the Bible is totally silent about that time. (See section on Satan under "Angels".) Also, the beginning and fall of Satan is clothed in mystery and it is useless to speculate about these events. The gap theory people assumed a great deal in trying to place the fall of Satan between verses one and two. There is nothing in the Scripture to support this view.

Many feel this great time span is necessary in order to accommodate the dinosaurs and other prehistoric creatures, but as seen later in the section on the Flood, there is no reason for this either.

This theory makes no sense and God always makes sense. He is never the God of confusion, (1 Corinthians 14:33).

THE THEORY OF EVOLUTION

The theory of evolution is man's attempt to exclude God from all creative acts in the universe. The premise of evolution is: all things, including man, evolved over eons of time through a process which is unobservable and unprovable.

It is the theory that one or more simple, single-celled organisms gradually changed into the many complex species that do or have ever existed. This process is supposed to have taken millions or billions of years and this organism was believed to have begun spontaneously from the inanimate material which made up the earth. After the 'big-bang' took place, it is supposed that many millions of years passed while rain fell continuously upon the earth's surface. From this 'primordial slime' the single-celled organisms were supposed to have formed. In other words they came from a rock. Even the slightest bit of common-sense tells us this cannot occur.

Most of these evolutionary changes were supposed to have been brought about by random changes called 'mutations'.

Mutations are in fact a result of the law of increasing disorder, not order. They are random changes in a gene. Those who lived from the mutations supposedly were better able to adapt to the next step up the evolutionary ladder through natural selection. (This is not possible in the genetic code of DNA molecules, because it would ultimately destroy itself.)

Those which died out after the mutation were not adaptable (survival of the fittest) and their fossil remains are the only trace of their existence. (Though as noted, the fossil remains speak of the same species with no great differences from those found today.) Mutations do not produce new raw material and a mutation is not the cause of evolutionary change.

In the 19th century, Gregory Mendel, an Austrian monk and botanist, conducted scientific studies in heredity. He discovered that hereditary characteristics were transmitted from parents to children according to fixed laws which are so unchanging that he could predict, as exactly as an astronomer can predict a solar eclipse, what characteristics children would receive from which parents. He formulated the Mendelian Law of Heredity.

Later Thomas Morgan discovered, in the

reproductive cells of all living beings, the factor known as 'genes' which determine heredity.

According to these discoveries, it is impossible for a person to receive a characteristic which was not passed down to him from his ancestors through the genes he inherited. If a characteristic were acquired because of something in the environment it would not be transmitted because the change was not produced by the genes. None of these changes come about because of mutations.

Evolution is based upon the assumed universal principle of (upward) change in nature. This is just the opposite of the proven second law of thermodynamics which is deterioration and disorder. This is a total paradox in science.

Though man has tried again and again to 'prove' that all life comes from a single cell, there has never been found any intermediate form between species that might indicate any kind of change from one species to another. Fossil records show that frogs have always been frogs, mice have always been mice, and on and on.

Darwin himself said: "There are two or three millions of species in the world, enough room, one would think, for observation; but it can be affirmed that despite all the efforts of educated observers, no change has ever been observed in any species."

There is no evidence of even one organism that has evolved from a simple to a complex form. All fossil forms appear suddenly in the geologic column. They are fully formed and complex without any transitional fossils to prove they have evolved from simpler forms. Darwin said, "Geology assuredly does not reveal any such finely graduated organic change, and this is perhaps the most obvious and serious objection which can be urged against the theory."

No help comes from the fossils, and most honest scientists recognize this problem. The early Cambrian fossils include seven of the 11 to 13 more complicated primary groups (fish and plants) and no protozoa appear. Interestingly, there is no sign of any change in species, though scientists continue to frantically search for these changes.

In the lower four-fifths of the earth's crust (5000 feet thick of sedimentary rocks) no fossils at all are found. Could these be the foundation stones placed there by God when He laid the foundation of the world? (Job 38:4-6; Psalm 104:5), etc. All historical evidence of evolution is based upon fossils. To date, 80 to 85% of the earth's land surface does not appear in the right geologic order to prove the theory of evolution.

The theory of evolution was popularized by Charles Darwin, an English biologist, with the publication of his book, *The Origin of the Species,* in 1859. Its actual beginnings were present in the Garden of Eden when Satan cast doubt upon the work and Word of God. Throughout the ages man has continued to imagine more and more complicated processes to explain the appearance of all creation.

Darwin said before his death: "I was, in that time, a young man with unformed ideas. I propounded questions and suggestions, I doubted everything; to my surprise, my ideas spread like a fire in the forest. People changed them into a religion." (Source - the Internet.)

It is actually based upon man's refusal to accept the fact that God created everything by processes which are no longer in operation and which cannot be repeated today.

Is evolution science? The theory of evolution is the great lie of the devil which forms a delusion in the minds of ignorant men. It is blasphemy against God. It degrades man to an animal, and so man begins to behave like the animal he is supposed to be.

Man was created in the image of God, and this theory robs him of his dignity and honor. Sin does not enter into this theory and this in turn takes away the importance of the atoning death of Christ for sin because according to this theory, sin does not exist. It is Satan's most effective tool and it is used to lead men away from the Savior and unless they repent it will lead them to hell with Satan, (see 2 Thessalonians 2:10-12).

This theory claims that man is the most advanced of all the animals, but is really only a highly organized form of matter.

Evolution says because of natural selection all organisms should evolve defense mechanisms to protect themselves for their own survival, however, this is not true in the real world. Lions still attack antelope, cats still attack mice, and man still attacks man. None of these have evolved a protection mechanism, nor will they.

Evolution requires much more 'faith' than does the belief in a divine Creator. In evolution nothing is 'provable'; neither in the laboratory nor in reality. The words noted again and again in evolutionary articles are "probably", "might", "much is not understood", "could be", "we assume", none of which give us much concrete evidence for this belief.

It is true, however, that our belief in divine creation is also a matter of faith. We cannot 'prove' what God did because no one was there to see His creative acts that first morning of time. We do have, however, a Book which tells the story, a Savior who gives evidence of the truthfulness of that Book, and the Holy Spirit dwelling in us who gives witness of His mighty acts.

In the last years of the 19th century, experiments by Pasteur and other scientists convinced the world that life only proceeds from existing life and can never come from an inanimate form. But the teaching of the theory of evolution continues to be taught as truth because it is not a scientific theory, but, in reality, is a religion of the 'fool' who says in his heart there is no God.

This theory has influenced the teaching of nearly all subjects in our schools, and is taught at every grade level. Beginning with the smallest child it is subtly taught in children's television programs, cartoons, and modern literature. There is hardly a person alive today who has not been influenced by this theory, though it has been disproved again and again, (Romans 1:21,22,24; 1 Timothy 4:1,2; 2 Thessalonians 2:11; Jeremiah 17:9).

Reasons why man accepts this theory:

It's easier than fighting the world's philosophy - we believe what we want to believe.

He wishes to get rid of God and remove individual accountability to Him. If there is no higher power, then we are not accountable to it and can make our own decisions based on our own self-interest; the "Eat, drink, and be merry, for tomorrow you die," philosophy of life. Alfred M. Rehwinkel, *The Wonders of Creation,* (Minneapolis: Bethany Fellowship, Inc., 1974), p. 102.

The teachings of evolution have drastically changed the value system of the world. Today we live in a world where nothing is wrong, nothing is right, everything is controlled by 'situation ethics'. Whatever is right (for me) at this moment is my measure of right and wrong.

Man becomes his own god, and in fact becomes a god. Satan told Eve in the temptation, *For God doth know that in the day ye eat thereof, then your eyes shall be opened, and ye shall be as gods, knowing good and evil,* (Genesis 3:5). Today, with the revival of Eastern mystical religions in the New Age Movement, man is again trying to become his own god and this fits well with the teaching of evolution.

It is a delusion of Satan, (Romans 1:20,22,24) and to believe this theory is a matter of will. Men's eyes are blinded because they voluntarily choose to believe the lie either through ignorance or through personal, individual choice.

We either accept a theory as fact or we accept the Word of God as Truth; there is only one path, not two.

GOD'S LAWS OF NATURE

All modern science is based upon two basic laws: the First and Second laws of Thermodynamics, (thermodynamics: the relationship between heat and energy).

- The first law is the law of energy conservation: though energy can be changed from one form to another, this does not decrease the amount of energy in the universe. Today no energy is being created; no energy is being destroyed, it simply changes form.

- The second law is the law of disorder: though there may be the same amount of energy in the universe, that energy becomes less available for useful work.

This law is a result of the cursed earth. All goes from perfect to imperfect, (Genesis 3:17-; Romans 8:20-22), everything dies.

In itself this law refutes the very philosophy it is supposed to proclaim and prove. If there is always less energy available for use, it stands to reason there was a time when there was more energy available. If there was more energy available at a previous point in history, then the universe had to have had a beginning. Evolution requires natural processes to move from simple to more complex and ordered, yet

the opposite must take place if this law is true.

If we use the example of a perpetual motion machine this truth is obvious. Though the machine is made with the best materials available and though it is structurally sound and engineered to the best of man's ability, it will only continue its movement for a limited time period. It begins to slow down (disorder) and will eventually stop altogether. This is an example of the progression of the second law of thermodynamics.

Example of deterioration, second Law of Thermodynamics.
Photo by M. Hooge

Any building left by itself will eventually crumble and fall to the ground. Machinery must be maintained or it becomes useless for work (e.g. an automobile). These are examples of less order and less energy available for useful work. Natural forces cannot premeditate or self-generate order; disorder is always the result of natural processes.

The cursed earth, after the sin of Adam, put the second law into motion. God made everything perfect, but because of sin and the curse, creation has continually deteriorated.

All parts of creation now tend to greater disorder; teeth decay, eyesight is lost, hair falls out, batteries lose power, clothes wear out, etc. Death itself is a result of the curse and is in accord with the second law of thermodynamics.

"The sun is slowly but surely burning out, the stars are dying embers and everywhere in the cosmos heat is turning into cold, matter is dissolving into radiation, and energy is being dissipated into empty space. The universe, thus progresses to an ultimate 'heat death' ...And there is no way of avoiding this destiny. For the fateful principle known as the second law of thermodynamics, which stands today as the principle pillar of classical physics left intact by the march of science, proclaims that the fundamental processes of nature are irreversible. Nature just moves one way." (Lincoln Barnett, *The Universe and Dr. Einstein,* p. 102, source, the Internet.)

The unchanging laws of God

When God created the world in six days He did not use processes which are in operation today, though He did set in motion certain Laws which are unchanging. The philosophy of uniformitarianism cannot apply to the special creative acts used by God to begin time itself and bring into existence every part of creation from nothing. When God completed His creation at the end of day six, He had done something no one would ever be able to do again. These creative acts were unique, unchangeable, orderly, complex and <u>finished,</u> (Genesis 2:1-3).

Examples of God's unchanging laws:

1. the water cycle: water vapors, lightnings, wind (weather patterns), (Psalms 135:7; 147:8,17,18; Jeremiah 10:13; Job 26:8; 28:25,26; 37:11,16; 38:22-27, 34,35; Ecclesiastes 11:3; Zechariah 10:1)

2. the limits of the sea, (Job 38:8-11; Isaiah 54:9; Psalm 104:6-9; Proverbs 8:29)

3. the earth hangs on nothing, (Job 26:7)

4. there is fire in the earth, (Job 28:5)

5. the migration of birds, (Job 28:7)

6. eagles nest in high places, (Job 39:27,28)

7. the earth is a circle, (Isaiah 40:22; Job 22:14)

8. there are 'paths' in the sea, (Psalm 8:8; Isaiah 43:16; 2 Samuel 22:16; Psalm 77:19)

9. times and seasons are constant, (Genesis 1:14; Psalms 104:19; 74:16; Genesis 8:22)

10. the day/night cycle is constant, (Genesis 1:18; Psalms 104:20; 74:16; Job 26:10; Jeremiah 33:20)

11. precious minerals are found in the earth's surface (outer crust); (Job 28:1-6; Deuteronomy 8:9,13)

All these and many others are unchanging Laws instituted by God at creation. Though they may vary because of His intervention, they do not change.

Uniformitarianism

The theory of evolution is supposedly supported by the philosophy called uniformitarianism - which means all physical processes have always functioned the same way - nothing has changed since the beginning of time. This includes cataclysms (or their absence), rates of erosion, sedimentary deposits, movements in the earth's surface, etc.

While it is basically true that present processes are more or less the same, there are always exceptions to the rule. For example Joshua asked God to cause the sun and moon to stand still, (Joshua 10:12-14.) This was at least a partial suspension in the natural process of time.

God is able, through supernatural power, to change even natural processes. He has done this in the past and will do so again in the future, for example in Revelation 8:12. The Creation has remained constant only because God sustains it, Colossians 1:17, *And he is before all things, and by him all things consist.*

The laws of thermodynamics are based on randomness: disorder, disorganization, disarrangement - as opposed to God's creative act of order and organization. The processes used by God in creation were totally different from those which are in operation today and this destroys the philosophy of uniformitarianism. In Genesis 2:1-3, the words used are "finished", "rested", "all His work", "rested from all". The work was completed at the time of creation and cannot be repeated.

TWENTY-FOUR HOUR DAYS

DAY-AGE THEORY

In the 19th century difficulties occurred because scientific theories about the age of the earth needed more time in which to fit the immense ages necessary for the evolution of all living things, whether by natural or theistic evolution. Therefore, the 'days' of the first two chapters of Genesis were lengthened by some scholars and students to accommodate the ages of evolutionary geology.

Some problems associated with this theory are:

It would not help to interpret 'days' as long periods of time in order to accommodate the enormous geologic ages needed for the theory of evolution because the order of events related in Genesis are in reverse order to that required by evolution (for example: the creation of earth before the creation of the sun - which would do away with the big bang theory - whales before the beasts of the earth, birds before reptiles, etc.). In evolution the order is: organisms of the sea, plants, birds, etc. Nothing seems to fit. As the Bible tells us: "In the beginning God".

The fossils are out of order. No fossils of simple protozoa are found in the Cambrian system (see Appendix on Geologic Ages), yet it is purported to be the oldest system and should contain the simplest forms of life.

As before stated the fossils speak of the existence of death before sin and that is inconsistent with God's word.

Literal days

The Hebrew word used in Genesis 1:5 for 'day' is *yôwm*. Here it refers to a literal 24 hour period of time. Zodhiates says that Genesis 1 'portrays time as linear and events occur successively within it.' (Zodhiates Bible notes).

Time could be reckoned in the Bible from morning to night, (Deuteronomy 28:66,67); or from evening to morning, (Esther 4:16).

When the plural form 'days' is used it usually refers to a time period as 'one's life', (Genesis 26:1, in the days of Abraham). The word can also be used for an indefinite time as 'on some particular day", (John 8:56), and usually in the future, as in the 'day of Jesus Christ', (Philippians 1:6). It is not used for a long period of time, but for a period of natural light, (Genesis 1:5; Proverbs 4:18; Mark 4:35; 1:13). It is used 2355 times in the Hebrew Old Testament. (Zodhiates).

When the word 'day' is used with a specific number in the Scripture it always means a 24 hour day, (Exodus 2:13;12:3; Leviticus 7:17; Numbers 1:1,18, etc).

It takes the earth 24 hours to make a complete rotation on its axis and the term used in Genesis 1, 'evening and morning', indicates a 24-hour day. Even before the creation of the sun this was the same.

In Exodus 20:9-11 the commandment speaks of 24-hour periods of time in which God created the heaven and earth. If God did not mean a 24-hour day then we cannot understand this commandment. He compares His week of creation to our week of work, both of which are 6 days of 24 hours each, and one day of 24 hours in which to rest.

The creation of plants, (Genesis 1:11,12), on the third day before the creation of the solar system on day four, (1:14-18), would be a tremendous problem if 'day' meant anything other than a 24-hour day. It would be impossible for plant life to be sustained for millions of years without the sun. (There was a source of light before day four, [1:3,4], and it was an energy source. We can understand this source when we compare Revelation 21:23 in the New Jerusalem where there will be no need of sun or moon. *God is light and in Him is no darkness at all,* (1 John 1:5).

Many have problems with the text of 2 Peter 3:8 in reference to a 24-hour day, *But, beloved, be not ignorant of this one thing, that one day is with the Lord as a thousand years, and a thousand years as one day.* This is a prophetic text, but it is also a present-time text in that it is telling us that our time and God's are not the same. Though He does not do things according to our time schedule, He is always on time. Since He limited Himself at the moment of creation to deal with man in the present time-space-continuum this indicates He deals with us according to a measure of time understandable to us - or 24 hour periods. His prophetic timetable may seem to lag but He has seen the entire picture and is working according to His plan.

This text is prophetic and has no reference to creation and its time period of 24-hour days and should not be confused by trying to put it within that time-frame.

THE STEPS OF CREATION

Beginning of order (Genesis 1:2)

And the earth was...

The significance of the conjunction "and" is that it connects in order and time that which has just preceded it and immediately follows the creative act of verse 1.

The word "was" is the Hebrew word *hayetha* which is a 'being' verb and does not suggest any change in state. It is used through-

out the King James Version of the Bible 98% of the time to mean 'was', (Hebrews 11:3).

without form and void

- The initial creation was of the basic elements and was not yet an ordered system.

- The Hebrew word for void is *bohu* which signifies **emptiness** - meaning it was uninhabited.

- All elements were prepared and were ready to be "formed" by God.

Darkness was upon the face (presence) *of the deep* (Hebrew *tehom*), (Psalms 42:7; 107:24; Isaiah 51:10; Habakkuk 3:10).

- The physical universe was not yet "energized". Light is a form of energy and it was not yet present.

- The deep refers to "the presence" of the water as referred to in 2 Peter 3:5 and Proverbs 8:23,24,27.

- There was darkness: there was no form, no motion, no light.

- The face of the waters - the presence referred to again here.

"...And the Spirit of God moved upon the face of the waters," (verse 2). The Spirit of God starts to move beginning His performance in the creative process. He hovers over the water, and order and life begin, (Psalm 104:30).

- The word "spirit" is the Hebrew word *rûwach* which is the same word used for 'wind' and 'breath' (In the primitive African languages the word spirit is the same word as wind.) The same word is used for spirit in: (Numbers 11:17; Nehemiah 9:20; Job 26:13; 33:4; Psalm 104:30; Isaiah 48:16; Ezekiel 11:19; 36:26,27).

- This Hebrew word, *rûwach*, has several different meanings. It is used 387 times in the Hebrew Old Testament. When the Holy

Spirit 'moved' upon the face of the waters, He was causing the waters to roll or vibrate in motion. Some of the word meanings are: 'to undulate', 'move', 'quake', 'to shake', 'to vibrate'. This is consistent with the action taking place here. This back and forth motion caused friction which forms energy. It is much like when you rub your palms together rapidly then put them on your face. You feel heat which comes from the energy you have produced through friction. The Holy Spirit literally 'energized' the creation.

This same word is also used in Deuteronomy 32:11 (fluttereth); Jeremiah 23:9 (shake), and Nehemiah 5:13 (shook, shake), with these slight differences of meaning.

• Scientists say the combination of chemicals (carbon, hydrogen, oxygen, nitrogen and phosphorus combined with liquid water), brought together by God, are the only possible chemical framework for all life forms.

GOD FORMED

DAY ONE (Genesis 1:3-5)

The Light - day, (Revelation 21:23)

In verse 3 God speaks for the first time. The Holy Spirit has already energized in verse 2, now the **Word** of God brings light.

God the Father is the **source** of all things, verse 1, (Acts 4:24; 14:15; 17:24, etc.; the Spirit is the energizer of all things, verse 2, as He moved or hovered over the face of the waters, and the Word is the **sustainer** of all things, verse 3 (Psalm 55:22; Colossians 1:17; 1 Corinthians 8:6).

The Darkness - night, (Psalm 104:20; Job 3:4-6; 38:19; Amos 4:13)

God divided the light from the darkness. Nothing new took place between the evening and the morning of each day; they were cyclical successions of days and nights, light and darkness. The earth was rotating on its axis and there was a source of light outside the sun.

All types of forces were now in effect:

1. nuclear forces,
2. gravitational forces and
3. electromagnetic forces.

Light waves in all their forms existed from the first day of creation.

THE CREATION OF ANGELS

Sometime prior to day three the angels were created. Job 38:4-7 says they were present 'when the foundations of the earth' were laid (or its solid land surfaces), which took place on day 3. Job says 'all the sons of God shouted for joy' in verse 7. The angels are called the 'sons of God', and 'stars of the morning', (Job 1:6; 2:1; 38:7). The creation of the angels in a position of great authority and in great numbers was one of the greatest events which took place in the creative process, (Psalm 148:2,5). Whenever this creation took place, whether in eternity past or during the six days of creation, it was before the foundations of the earth were laid. When they saw this act of creation the angels were so over-awed by the might and power of their Creator that they joined in a wonderful shout of praise to Him, as seen in the 38th chapter of Job. (Rehwinkel, *Wonders of Creation*), p. 50.

There is an extensive Biblical basis for believing in angels. They are mentioned 100 times in the Old Testament and 165 times in the New Testament. They are mentioned from the beginning to the end of the Bible, and in 34 books of the 66. The teachings of Christ speak of their existence. They are not illusions, and their work is specifically that of messengers.

1. They are created a special order, separate from man, (1 Corinthians 6:3; Hebrews 1:13;) they are spirit beings, (Psalm 104:4), but are not omnipresent.

2. They are **holy**; all were created holy and those who did not rebel against God are called 'holy' in Mark 8:38. They are the elect angels in 1 Timothy 5:21. They were surrounded by holiness. This was the holiness of God and of the atmosphere in which they lived, until sin entered in.

3. They are to operate in this universe, but have their dwelling in heaven, (Mark 12:25; Luke 12:8; 15:10; Hebrews 12:22; Revelation 7:11; 8:2).

4. Their purpose is to minister to believers, and to praise God, (Hebrews 1:14; Genesis 16:7; 19:16; 22:11; Matthew 4:11; Psalm 148:1,2). They do not sing, but are capable of speaking in unison, (Luke 2:14; Isaiah 6:3).

5. Names used for them: they are called the 'host of heaven', not the 'heaven' of the world, but the heaven of God, (Luke 2:13; Deuteronomy 4:19; 1 Kings 22:19; 2 Chronicles 18:18); 'God's host', (Genesis 32:1,2; Psalm 148:2); 'sons of the mighty', (Psalm 89:6); 'sons of God', (Job 1:6; Job 2:1; Job 38:7); 'men', (Genesis 18:2); 'princes', (Daniel 10:13); and 'angel of the Lord'; (Psalm 34:7).

6. Some are to execute judgment, (Genesis 19:13; Judges 5:23; 2 Samuel 24:16; 1 Chronicles 21:15; 2 Chronicles 32:21; Isaiah 37:36; Acts 12:23; Matthew 13:49; Revelation 16:1).

7. They are without number, (thousands of thousands), (Hebrews 12:22; Revelation 5:11; Daniel 7:10).

8. Characteristics of angels:

They are characterized by intelligence and power, (but limited power; they are not omnipotent), (2 Peter 2:11; Psalm 91:11; Isaiah 63:9; Daniel 10:18; 1 Peter 1:11-12; Revelation 7:1; 2 Samuel 14:17,20).

They serve as messengers from God to man. "Angel" in both Greek and Hebrew means <u>messenger,</u> (Genesis 32:1,2; Numbers 22:31; Judges 2:1; 6:11; 13:3,13; Zechariah 1:9,12; 2:3; Matthew 1:20; 2:13; 28:2; Luke 1:11, 2:9; John 20:12; Acts 8:26; 10:3).

The light they radiate marks them as coming from heaven, (Acts 12:7).

Their gaze is fixed on God, not man; they do their job and return to heaven, (Matthew 18:10 and Judges 13:8-21).

Their bodies are assumed but are not truly organic as man's, and must be dispensed with when they return to heaven. They are not limited by their bodies as man is, (they can pass through walls, etc.); they are capable of taking on the essence of light as in Judges 13:20 when the angel ascended in the flame. He told Manoah his name was *secret,* (verse 18); (they are spirit - *pneumata*, Matthew 8:16; Luke 7:21; 8:2; 11:26; Acts 19:12; Ephesians 6:12; Psalm 104:4).

They are higher than man in all ways, (Hebrews 2:7; 2 Peter 2:11).

They can influence the operation of the human intellect by affecting the bodily organs of sense and imagination, (1 Peter 1:13). This is the reason Satan first attacks through the mind, (James 4:4-8; Ephesians 4:17, 23).

Angels are not eternal but are **aeviternal,** meaning they had a beginning, but have no end, (Luke 20:36). They do not propagate, (Matthew 22:30; Mark 12:25). (Procreation brings new individuals into existence and replaces those taken by death. Neither of these necessities exists in the case of angels. They were created but they do not die physically nor cease to exist in their spirit form.)

They can speak, (1 Corinthians 13:1; Judges 13; Luke 1,2; Genesis 19, etc).

Angels had free choice, (Luke 8:28-31; Revelation 12:9).

They are moral agents with moral will and intelligence; angels are obedient (except for those who rebelled) - their entire frame and makeup is to obey God - 'thy will be done...as it is in heaven', (Matthew 6:9,10).

They are capable of serving God, (Isaiah 6:2).

They were capable of rebelling against God, (Revelation 12:4-9).

Angels are not created in the image and likeness of God, only man was created in this way.

They are subject to judgment, (1 Corinthians 6:3; Matthew 25:41; 2 Peter 2:4).

Angels can show emotion, (Luke 2:13, 14; Revelation 18:2).

They are limited by the will of Christ, (Luke 8:28-31; Job 2:6).

Angels have their own language, (1 Corinthians 13:1).

Angels are the royal armies of God, (Psalm 68:17; 2 Kings 6:17, chariots of fire; (they have powers of flight unknown to man and they do not need wings to fly).

They have great strength, (Matthew 28:2; Mark 16:3,4; Revelation 10:1-11).

Their powers are limited, (2 Peter 2:11; Matthew 24:31).

They are able to move with great speed, (Daniel 9:21).

They have power to appear suddenly, (Luke 2:13; Acts 1:10; Acts 12:7).

They can control certain elements of nature at God's bidding, (Revelation 7:1; 14:18, 16:4,8,10,12,17).

Angels should not be worshipped, (Colossians 2:18; Revelation 22:8,9).

9. There are seven organized governmental orders of angels mentioned in the Scripture which are set apart for special rank and service, (Revelation 12:7; 9:11; Ephesians 1:21; 6:12).

Archangels (chief angels) (1 Thessalonians 4:16; Jude 9)

These seem to be the first or highest angel rank, the leaders of the angels. Their name indicates superiority and predominance and has to do with 'force' and strength.

The word 'archangel' is not mentioned in the Old Testament and only in two verses of the New (1 Thessalonians 4:16 and Jude 9), where it speaks of Michael, who is called 'one of the chief princes', (Daniel 10:13); and 'the great prince', (Daniel 12:1). Michael is named in Revelation 12:7 as the leader of the angels who stand against Satan and his demons.

Although the Scriptures do not name any other archangel, it is possible that there are more because of the words 'one of the chief princes'. In Romans 8:38; Ephesians 1:21 and Colossians 1:16 the word translated 'principality' is *arche* in the Greek. This is the same prefix as contained in the word archangel. In 1 Thessalonians 4:16 the idea seems to be that the voice of the Lord will be like the shout of the archangel, but it could also mean that Paul did not have to mention the name of the archangel because there is only one mentioned by name.

Cherubim (called 'living creatures')

They are first seen in Genesis 3:24-their ministry is defensive. They are only found in heaven after the Flood, (Psalm 80:1).

Theirs is a throne ministry, (Psalm 99:1).

Seraphim (Isaiah 6:2,3,6)

The word seraph in Hebrew means *love.*

The seraphim were above the throne of God and were distinguished by their heavenly chanting, and their glory is in their voice.

These are celestial beings who are before the throne of God. They are also consuming beings who are impressed with God's attribute of holiness and spend their time chanting "holy, holy, holy". They adore Him and execute His plans for holiness in the world as messengers of His grace. They are mentioned only one time in the Scriptures.

Thrones (those who rule); (Colossians 1:16)

Angels of dignity and authority used by God in His government.

Dominions (power to direct or control)

(Ephesians 1:20,21; 3:10; Colossians 2:15; 2 Peter 2:11)

Principalities

(Ephesians 6:12; Colossians 2:15; 1:16; 2:10), angels who govern the universe, (Ephesians 3:10).

Powers

Super human authority over the occurrences in the world, (Ephesians 1:21; 3:10; 6:12; Colossians 1:16; 2:10; 2:15; 1 Peter 3:22, etc).

Angels

(Romans 8:38) (fallen angels seem to have the same divisions of offices)

10. the work of angels

- They are sent forth to minister to the saved, (Hebrews 1:14; Acts 27:23,24; Psalm 91:11,12).

- The angels witness our salvation, (Luke 15:10).

Christ personally reports our confession or denial of Him before all the angels, (Luke 12:8,9).

- Angels see what is written in the Lamb's Book of Life, (Revelation 3:5). (Two books are mentioned in the Bible: [Psalm 69:28], The Book of the Living, [Psalm 139:16; Revelation 20:12; Exodus 32:32], which refers to all who are born into this world; The Book of the Righteous, or the Lamb's Book of Life, which lists all who are saved, (Philippians 4:3; Revelation 13:8; Daniel 12:1; Revelation 17:8; 20:12,15; 21:27; 22:19).

- Angelic bodyguards

They are mentioned in:

Acts 5:19, on this occasion they delivered the apostles from prison.

Acts 12:7-9, Peter was delivered from prison by an angel.

Paul, Acts 27:23,24, Paul is delivered from a shipwreck.

Daniel 6:22, the mouths of the lions are shut and Daniel is safe.

Daniel 3:28, the Hebrew children are saved from the fiery furnace.

Angels were sent specifically to guard certain individuals or nations, (Genesis 24:7; Exodus 23:20; Psalm 91:11).

- The ministry of angels in Christ's life:

Angels were with Him at creation, (Job 38:7).

They predicted His birth, (Matthew 1:20; Luke 1:26-33).

They were present at His birth, (Luke 2:8-15).

They announced His birth to the shepherds, (Luke 2:9-15) (spoke in unison), while in Isaiah they would have spoken Hebrew, in this instance they would have spoken Koine Greek under the Roman Empire so the shepherds could understand them.

Angels worshipped at His birth, (Hebrews 1:6).

Angels warned His parents of the danger of Herod, (Matthew 2:13); they delivered Him at various times during His ministry (e.g. when He disappeared from their midst in Luke 4:30, by some supernatural means He 'passed through their midst').

Angels ministered to Him in His temptation, (Matthew 4:11).

They were in the garden when He prayed to minister ('make inwardly strong') to Him, (Luke 22:43).

They were present at the Crucifixion, (Matthew 26:53).

(The legions referred to are representative of the numbers He could have called to His defense; a legion=6000 foot soldiers, the number of angels was 12 X 6000 which equals 72,000 royal bodyguards; He **laid down** His life, it was not taken from Him.)

They announced His resurrection, (Matthew 28:5,6).

Angels rolled the stone from His tomb, (Matthew 28:2).

Angels were present at the Resurrection, (Matthew 28:2-4), (three angels witnessed the resurrection), (John 20:12).

They stand ready to destroy His enemies; (Matthew 26:53; 4:6).

- Guardian angels (as opposed to bodyguards)

Matthew 18:10, for children

Psalm 34:7, for those that fear the Lord

- Angels in the ministry of prayer

angels have brought prophetic visions and messages from God to men: (e.g. Cornelius, Daniel, Mary, etc.)

angels are seen in relation to prayer "when the safety and future ministry of one of God's chosen vessels is at stake," (e.g. Peter, Acts 12)

- Angels give the world's last call of the Gospel, (Revelation 14:6-8):

the call to fear God,

the call to give glory to God,

the announcement of the hour of Judgment - the Day of the Lord,

the call to worship/the King shall reign/men will not hear.

All heaven witnesses "the building of the church of God", (Luke 15:7,10).

- That principalities and powers in heavenly places might know, God gave them a revelation of His wisdom,

angelic theater, (1 Corinthians 4:9) /spectacle =Greek *theatron*, Roman theater or Coliseum - angels are watching; (1 Corinthians 11:10; 1 Timothy 5:21),

they are greatly interested in the work of redemption, (1 Peter 1;12; Luke 15:10; Acts 8:26, 10:3),

angels witnessed Timothy's ordination, (1 Timothy 5:21).

- Christ shall come with all His holy angels, (Matthew 16:27; 25:31; 2 Thessalonians 1:7-10/all the heavenly host; Mark 8:38).

- Angels will separate the nations, (Matthew 13:49,50; 13:39; 13:41,42).

- Angels carry the saints to God at their death, (Luke 16:22).

- An angel will declare the end of time as we know it, (Revelation 10:5,6), when he stops the clock of time; (Matthew 13:39-43).

Description of the angel in Daniel 10:5,6

- He was clothed in fine linen, and girded with fine gold; he was of a sinless and pure nature.

- His body shone like beryl, a rare, precious stone, greenish-blue and a symbol of royalty. Many times angels are described as being greenish-blue in color.

- His face was like lightning with a dazzling brilliance, (Luke 24:4).

- His eyes were like lamps of fire which see all things and radiate holiness and power.

- His arms and feet were like polished brass. Brass equals judgment and angels are agents of God's judgment.

- His voice was like the voice of a multitude: a long, low rumble, powerful and forceful.

- They were called 'watchers' in Daniel 4:13,17,23 (Compare this to the vision of Revelation 1:9-14.)

Only three angels are mentioned by name in the Scriptures:

Michael: "who is like unto God" (the archangel)

In Daniel 10:13 he is called Chief or the first, (Jude 9; Revelation 12:7).

- He is the commander of heaven's armies.

- He is the guardian of Israel, (Daniel 10:21).

Gabriel: "mighty one", (Luke 1:19,26; Daniel 9:21)

- He is the bearer of messages from the throne of God.

- He was sent to interpret the vision of Daniel 8:16, and to give him wisdom concerning the prophecy of the last 70 weeks, (Daniel 9:21-27).

- He announced the birth of John the Baptist, (Luke 1:11-22), and the birth of Christ, (Luke1:26-31).

- He is continually in the presence of God, (Luke 1:19).

Satan: "the accuser, the devil, the adversary, the enemy"

At some time in the distant past he was cast from heaven with one-third of the angels, (Revelation 12).

The Scripture is silent as to the situation which brought about this serious judgment, so we must be silent also.

Some teach that Isaiah 14 and Ezekiel 28 refer to Satan and his consequent fall, but there are many difficulties in these passages if they refer to Satan. The language used is consistent with that used in connection with an Oriental potentate who claimed divine origin and proclaimed himself to be God. The personage here is referred to as a cherubim. If this were Satan he would not be a cherubim because the ministry of cherubim is defensive and is a throne ministry as has already been mentioned. The Scriptures never give any reference to the 'fall' of the cherubim because they are never mentioned as having sinned at any time. It is more likely the writers were referring to the spirit of wickedness behind the throne of these 'princes' which would certainly be satanic, and not to Satan himself. Care must be taken to not attribute more power and glory to Satan than the Scriptures do. He is a despicable, loud-mouthed liar; not an anointed cherub; not a prince. He is a fallen creature whose doom is already sealed, (Matthew 25:41).

The names given for Satan in the Bible never include the name Lucifer and this is the only time (Isaiah 14:12) the word is used. It means 'son of the morning', (14:12). The names for Satan in Revelation 9:11 are Abaddon and Apollyon; in Revelation 12 they are the Devil, Satan, and the old serpent. In other places he is called the dragon, (Revelation 12:9), the deceiver, the liar, the murderer, the accuser, Beelzebub, Belial, the angel of the abyss, the god of this age, (2 Corinthians 4:4), the prince of the demons, (Matthew 12:24; Luke 11:15), the prince of the power of the air, (Ephesians 2:2), etc. But he is never referred to as Lucifer. This word has to do with the pagan worship of the heavens and the worship of the goddess Ishtar.

Satan's choice was to rebel against God, but he had to have had knowledge that his decision was irrevocable.

Satan is called the "prince of the power of the air", (Ephesians 2:2); he has access to the earth and to heaven at this point in history.

He can transform into an angel of light in his role as deceiver, (2 Corinthians 11:14).

The work of Satan:

- He is a murderer and a liar, and the father of lies, (John 8:44; Acts 5:3).

- He is the accuser of the saved before God, (Job 1:6-9,12; 2:1,3,4,6,7).

- By free choice he opposed God.

- He is the deceiver of the world, (Revelation 12:9).

- He blinds men's minds, (2 Corinthians 4:3,4).

- He works through signs and lying wonders, (2 Thessalonians 2:9; in Matthew 12:39, Christ rebukes the people for seeking a sign).

- He resists the servants of God, (Zechariah 3:1; 1 Thessalonians 2:18).

- He stands with the wicked, (Psalm 109:6).

- He seeks to destroy the saved, (1 Peter 5:8).

- He is the tempter, (Matthew 4:1,5,8,10; 16:23; Mark 1:13; Luke 4:8; 1 Corinthians 7:5, etc.).

- He takes away the Word of God sown in the hearts of the unsaved, (Mark 4:15), so they will not believe.

- Some illnesses are caused by him, (Luke 13:16; Acts 10:38).

- He can afflict and can destroy the flesh, (Job 2:7; 1 Corinthians 5:5).

- He has a certain power over death, (Hebrews 2:14).

- He has power to oppress the saved and possess the unsaved, (Acts 16:18; Colossians 1:13; Matthew 4:24; 8:16; 9:32; Acts 16:16; 10:38, etc.).

- The Anti-Christ will receive his power from Satan and will be the incarnation of Satan, (Revelation 13:4).

- He is a king and has a kingdom, (Matthew 12:24-30).

- Some of his princes control certain nations of the world, (Daniel 10:10-14).

- Satan does not have irresistible power to cause man to sin; man's free choice can bring pressure to bear through incitement of passions (the world, the flesh, and the devil).

- Satan cannot read the mind of an individual, but he can read the actions, much as we 'read' another person's reactions, and he does work through the mind. Because of this the Bible tells us the battle is for the mind of the believer, (Ephesians 4:23; 2 Corinthians 10:3-5; Philippians 4:7).

- He works through false teachers to deceive man, (2 Peter 2:1-3; Jude 8; 2 Corinthians 11:15; Galatians 1:6-9; 1 Timothy 4:1 [doctrines of devils], 2 Peter 2:1,2); these false teachers deny the virgin birth of Christ; deny the deity of Christ; deny the return of

Christ before the tribulation, (1 Thessalonians 5:9); deny salvation by grace only; deny the millennium and teach that the world is getting better each day and thus Christ will return to earth; they teach a doctrine of self-healing and many other false doctrines.

- He will be cast out of heaven, (Luke 10:18 future, he has access now to the throne to accuse, but he does not have access to all of heaven as he did before, this will end as seen in the next point).

- He will no longer have access to heaven, (Revelation 12:9-12).

- The angel of God will bind and imprison Satan, (Revelation 20:1-3).

- He will be bound 1000 years, (Revelation 20:2); and be released for a short time in verse 7.

- He will ultimately be cast into the lake of fire, (Revelation 20:10).

There is only a limited amount of information about Satan (or the devil) in the Scriptures. In the last part of the 19th century when the gap-theory people were trying to show a time-lapse between verses one and two of Genesis 1 the teaching of the fall of Satan in this time gap was reintroduced from the fourth century A.D. This teaching is as false today as it was then and the Bible does not lend credence to this belief.

Fallen angels

There is only one Satan, but there are many demons.

One third left their 'first estate' and followed Satan, (Jude 6; 2 Peter 2:4; Revelation 12:4.)

All sinned, (2 Peter 2:4), either by open rebellion or by their choice to follow Satan; Jude 6 refers to only 'some' of the fallen angels; Job 4:18, *and his angels he charged with folly.*

They will be judged, (2 Peter 2:4).

The dwelling place of the fallen angels:

- some are reserved in chains for a special judgment, (Jude 6; 2 Peter 2:4),

- some are in heavenly places, (Ephesians 6:12),

- some are in the abyss, (Revelation 9:11),

- some are on the earth, (Revelation 9:14).

Satan and the remaining angels have complete liberty

- Satan has access to the throne of God at this time to accuse the saved, (Job 1:6,7; 2:12; Revelation 12:7-11).

- Hell was prepared for Satan and the fallen angels, 'Everlasting fire, prepared for the devil and his angels', (Matthew 25:41).

- The same hell serves for fallen angels and fallen men.

- Satan, their leader, has *his* angels, (Revelation 12:7).

- Because of the sin of the fallen angels their intellect was darkened; this was not the loss of knowledge, but the loss of **supernatural** knowledge which is always a gift of God's grace.

- They cannot be saved, (Jude 6).

- They oppose the people of God, (Ephesians 6:12).

- They support the work of Satan, (Revelation 12:4,9).

- Angelic war will come, (Revelation 12:7,9).

Their destiny, (Matthew 25:41; Luke 8:31), punishment - separation from God; the lake of fire with their master.

DAY TWO

The creation of the Firmament, (Genesis 1:6-8).

The Air - the heavens, (Psalm 104:2; Isaiah 40:12,22; 42:5; 44:24; Job 9:8; Proverbs 8:27)

The earth is prepared for the habitation of man.

God speaks - *"Let there be a firmament in the midst of the waters...."* The word *firmament* comes from the Latin *firmamentum* meaning something made solid.

The Hebrew word is *râqîya* - an expanse; referred to in Psalm 104:2 as a tent curtain, and in Isaiah 40:22 as a veil. It is our word used for 'space'. It is the sky, the vault of heaven (space), (Daniel 12:3). The Hebrew Scriptures say 'God stretched out the heavens like a gauze'. In Ezekiel 1:22 the word firmament means 'transparent' and describes the heavens as such.

There are three heavens mentioned in the Scripture:

- the atmospheric heaven, (Jeremiah 4:25), where birds fly,

- the heaven of the stars, (Isaiah 13:10), (the sidereal heaven), and

- the heaven of God's throne, (Hebrews 9:24; Romans 8:34). (Morris, *Genesis*), p. 58.

The heaven referred to here means the atmosphere.

The atmosphere is a belt of air surrounding the earth to a thickness of from 60-100 miles or more, consisting mostly of 78% nitrogen, 20% oxygen and 2% other gases. The gases which make up the atmosphere are proportioned exactly to maintain a proper balance. If there were even a small percentage more of nitrogen it would be impossible to sustain human or animal life on the planet. Today, if the oxygen were increased from 20% to 30% the slightest spark of fire or flash of lightning would ignite all combustible material and everything would go up in flames. Under the vapor canopy this was not possible, though the oxygen level was greatly increased, because of the moisture maintained on the earth at a constant level. (Rehwinkel, *Wonders of Creation*), pp. 74,75.

Oxygen is a dormant gas which only releases its great power with a slight change in temperature. Once combustion occurs the law of nature demands that the whole combustible mass be consumed and combustion is sustained until this is accomplished or another agent intervenes. The heat generated by one portion heats the second portion to the ignition point. Each substance has a distinct ignition point. The combustion continues on and on, just as we see in a forest fire. If you take away the source - oxygen - the fire will be extinguished. A gas fire will continue as long as there is a source of gas to combine with the oxygen. Once the gas is heated to ignition it continues to heat the flow of gas as it reaches the air and burns until the gas is shut off. If God had not placed oxygen and nitrogen in a proper balance the earth would be consumed by fire. Josiah Parsons Cooke, *Religion and Chemistry*, (New York: Charles Scribners Sons, 1880), pp. 78-86.

The atmosphere is matter with all the essential properties of matter:

- it cannot be condensed,

- it penetrates all matter,

- it fills the cavities of all organized beings,

- its particles allow perfect freedom of motion, but yield to the slightest pressure,

- it holds up birds and flying insects of all sizes,

- it is held by gravity,

- it is heated by the sun,

- it is dense in its makeup,

- approximately 30% of light coming through the atmosphere is absorbed by it,

- light is diffused because of the atmosphere, making vision more uniform,

- it diffuses heat,

- if the atmosphere were less dense by one-half, the heat extremes would be so great most organic life could not exist.

Air is a mechanical mixture of oxygen, nitrogen and aqueous vapor existing at the same time in the same space, but each one entirely distinct from the other. Nitric acid is composed of these elements, but forms only under certain conditions. Nitrogen is a basically inactive gas, but if it were suddenly given active affinities it would form nitric acid in the atmosphere which could be fatal to <u>all</u> organic life, but strangely, this same nitric acid when diluted properly both nourishes and sustains plant life. It is usually formed in the atmosphere in minute quantities by lightning when an alkaline substance is present. It then falls to the earth in the rain to nourish the plants. (Rehwinkel, *The Wonders of Creation*,) p. 83.

Oxygen forms eight-ninths of all water; three-fourths of the human body; four-fifths of every plant, and one-half of solid rocks. In a glass of water there are 6 cubic feet of oxygen gas in liquid form. Though oxygen tends to expand like other gases, it does not obey the laws of hydrostatics (the way fluids should act under normal circumstances). The heavier oxygen should sink to the ground and the lighter nitrogen should float above it, but it does not. This is caused by diffusion (the gradual mixing of the molecules of two or more substances due to random thermal [heat] motion). Gases have this property which allows them to occupy the same space. This mixture of gases is important to the transmis-

sion of sound. (Cooke, *Religion and Chemistry*), p. 74.

Because the air is constituted as it is, there is constancy of pitch. Loudness changes with distance, but pitch remains the same. If the mixture of air were different, pitch would change as it passed through each layer or combination of layers and would be heard in an entirely different way. What we know as music would be nonexistent. Only God would have known this and would have caused the components of air to combine in such a way as to give man the pleasure of sound. (Rehwinkel, *The Wonders of Creation*), p. 75, and (Cooke, *Religion and Chemistry*), p. 76.

Space is a complete vacuum and gases are spread to 16 molecules each cubic inch. The electromagnetic charges of radiation (cosmic rays, gamma rays, ultraviolet rays, etc.) do not occupy any physical space, but they are continually passing through space.

Makeup of the earth's atmosphere:

The mesosphere, thermosphere and exosphere together form the ionosphere.

ASCENDING ORDER	
	5. exosphere - 500 km. up
	4. thermosphere - above 129 km. - 1500° 1500° to +3000°C temperature, is necessary to maintain a large quantity of water vapor.
	3. mesosphere - 80 km. - 1500° C
	2. stratosphere 55-75° C - 50 km.
	1. troposphere - 10 km.

The Waters (Psalm 104:3,6; Genesis 1:6-8; 7:11; 8:2; 2 Peter 3:5-7)

Two bodies of water were now in existence: 'the waters <u>above</u>' in a vaporous state - above the clouds which we see, because they were above the 'firmament' and there was no rain, (Genesis 2:5). The other body was the seas, evidently all interconnected to be called by one word, 'seas'.

Water absorbs more than twice as much

heat as any other substance and holds that heat. When the surface temperature of a lake or pond reaches 39° F the surface water becomes lighter and remains on top. The water below will remain at 40° F even though the surface water may be frozen. Unlike other substances, as water becomes colder it rises to the top instead of sinking. (Note the ice in a glass of liquid.) The surface water is cooled and sinks to the bottom as the temperature falls, but when it reaches 40° F it ceases to sink; just 8° above freezing. Ice is a poor conductor of heat and thus protects the water under it from losing heat and it remains at 40° F. If water did not act this way it would freeze solid in winter and all animal and plant life in it would die. The summer sun could not thaw out large bodies of frozen ice and its lack of heat conduction (the ice) would prevent melting except for a few feet on the surface. Because the soil is saturated with water it too would freeze to a depth sufficient to kill the roots and seeds of plants in it. God's wisdom keeps this planet habitable. (Cooke, *Religion and Chemistry*), p. 149.

THE VAPOR CANOPY

Some believe that the vapor blanket could have been in the upper troposphere, *below* the stratosphere. The additional water vapor would have warmed not only the earth's surface but also the atmosphere more uniformly to a distance of four or five miles above the surface of the earth.

The result would be a vapor canopy over the earth which was invisible, and allowed the heavenly bodies to give light when they were created.

This thick blanket of air would make life possible on this planet which was made expressly for the habitation of man. The earth should therefore be considered the true center of the universe; the sun, moon and stars were made to serve the earth and make it habitable for man. (Though it is certainly not the physical center of the universe.)

Results of the canopy:

1. The basic temperature on the whole earth would have been uniformly warm, but not hot.

2. There would have been little wind activity and no 'fronts' would have existed. The spinning of the earth on its axis from west to east causes the winds we see today on any weather map. The earth was spinning the same way it is today but the vapor canopy would have influenced temperature changes. Changes in temperature and the mixing of cold and warm air cause the weather systems which form tornadoes, severe thunderstorms, etc. Wind movements would not have occurred because these conditions did not exist and the temperature remained fairly constant at all times.

It is known today that land areas are more quickly heated by the sun than is the sea. At night or when the sun is hidden, the land cools faster than the sea and during the day there is a current of heated air rising from the surface of the earth near the ocean and a current of cooler air flows in from the ocean to take its place. At night the current is reversed. This causes the land and sea breezes especially noted on sea islands. A vapor canopy would have prevented this phenomenon to a great degree and therefore very little wind would have been present. (Cooke, *Religion and Chemistry*), p. 51.

3. Rain would not fall because moisture would not be condensed. (Salt particles cause condensation from bodies of salt water.)

4. The absence of wind would keep dust particles from moving and would also keep the upper air turbulence from disturbing the

atmosphere so the water vapor in the canopy would remain stable.

5. The mist (Genesis 2:6) which rose from the earth would have kept the humidity levels constant and comfortable.

6. The mists combined with the warm temperatures would have caused profuse vegetation to cover the whole earth.

7. X-rays, UV radiation and infrared light would have been stopped by the layer of water. Good health and long-life would have been the result and for men to live up to 900 years or more would have been normal.

8. At least part of this water vapor would have fallen as rain at the time of the Flood. That water, combined with the waters from the fountains of the deep and the oceans, would have been enough to cover the earth to the depths noted in Genesis 7:20. Some say the canopy would have been about 40 feet (12 meters) thick and if this were true it would have been very easy for rain to fall 40 days and 40 nights from this water source.

9. The absence of high mountain ranges also kept condensation from occurring. Mountain ranges cause condensation of water from winds.

10. According to fossil footprints which have been found, humans would probably have grown to be much larger than today because the canopy would filter out the different harmful rays from outer space which tend to affect the genetic code. Fossil footprints found in Texas and in other areas, indicate that men could have normally been at least 9-11 feet tall.

11. Increased air pressure would have helped dinosaurs breathe because their nostrils were very small and increased oxygen in the atmosphere would have been neces-sary to maintain their lives. Those that are still living are much smaller than those which lived before the Flood and they have been able to adapt to present conditions.

12. There was twice as much oxygen under the canopy. Pre-Flood amber contains twice as much oxygen as is found in the atmosphere today. Today there is only about 20% oxygen in the atmosphere.

13. Healing would have taken place at a faster rate because of increased oxygen. Hyperbaric oxygen chambers contain pure oxygen and are used today for healing. The time period for healing is less than half of the usual time when the person is put into a hyperbaric chamber. This would have been the common time frame before the Flood.

14. Plants would grow faster and larger because of increased CO_2. Trees which formed the major part of coal deposits were much larger and much more profuse than at the present time as seen from the fossil evidence. Henry M. Morris, *The Genesis Record*, (Grand Rapids: Baker Book House, 1982), excerpts, pp. 59-61.

The present day water cycle was not in effect until after the time of the Flood. Job 36:27, *For he maketh small the drops of water: they pour down rain according to the vapour thereof:* (28) *Which the clouds do drop and distill upon man abundantly.*

Under the water vapor life would have been much more enjoyable physically, but that did not keep man from continuing in his sin. External conditions do not change man's heart.

DAY THREE

(Genesis 1:9-10) Land and sea and the beginning of life on earth:

First: separation of the original liquid from solid matter;

Second: seas and continents appear;

Third: vegetation covers the dry land.

THE SEA

The surfaces of solid earth appeared with channels and reservoirs to receive the dividing waters.

It is believed the underground reservoirs were all connected by hollow channels so that 'they were all gathered together in one place', (verse 9).

The waters were collectively called 'Seas', (Ecclesiastes 1:7). There are 197 million square miles of space on the planet:

*   139 million square miles are sea and

*   58 million square miles are land.

*   There is enough water to cover the entire earth to the depth of one and one-half to two miles of water if it were all level.

The content of the seas:

*   three-fourths of the minerals are salt and this combined with the other minerals, if extracted, could cover the earth with 120 feet of solid minerals. (Rehwinkel, *Wonders*,) exerpts above.

The tides:

*   Tides are the daily regularity of rising and falling waters in the oceans, they are due to the relationship of the moon to the earth and the proper distance of each (and to a lesser degree to the sun).

*   The tides are sensitive to the phases of the moon (they are higher at full moon).

Paths in the sea: ocean currents, (Psalm 8:8; Isaiah 43:16; 2 Samuel 22:16; Psalm 77:19);

*   these are rivers in walls of water,

*   they stretch from the equator to the poles,

*   and from the poles to the equator.

*   There are other streams crisscrossing these.

The Gulf Stream is the largest river in the world (1500 feet deep, 50 miles wide, 4000 miles long).

*   It is warm water flowing through walls of cold water.

*   It runs from the Gulf of Mexico north to Iceland, east towards Europe, and merges with another river which flows into the Bay of Biscay north of Spain.

*   This stream keeps temperatures moderate in Northern Europe and Iceland.

*   It deposits seeds and plants from the tropics in Scotland and Norway.

*   It makes Great Britain habitable. Britain is the same latitude as Labrador and only the warm waters of the Gulf Stream make it fruitful.

*   If our continent were only slightly different in configuration, (which causes the Gulf Stream to pass by them), Wales and Scotland would be frozen with Arctic cold.

*   Northern Europe, Sweden and Norway all owe their temperate climates to the Gulf Stream. At this same latitude on the North American continent all is frozen.

*   In 1966 Russian scientists discovered another ocean current 9,000 feet below the Gulf Stream which is traveling in the opposite direction at 8 miles per day.

Another current was discovered under the Pacific Equatorial Current, flowing easterly at 2 1/2 miles per day and under this another current was discovered which was going in the opposite direction.

The Japanese Stream in the Pacific keeps Vancouver and the southern Alaskan climates habitable. It also affects the weather in southern Alberta, Canada and Montana by means of the Chinook winds. These winds occur suddenly and melt the snow and moderate the frigid temperatures. (Rehwinkel, *Wonders of Creation*), p. 113.

Psalm 95:3-7 says the seas are in God's hands because He is their Creator.

THE LAND

The word for **land**, in the Hebrew is *eretz,* the same word as is used in Genesis 1:1,2, and refers to the same components, and the same matter, (Psalms 104:5; 102:25; Job 38:4; Zechariah 12:1; Isaiah 48:13; Jeremiah 31:37). The 'dry land was divided from the lower waters'; this was the separation of the liquid from the solids of the original matter to form the first planet.

The earth was given a spherical shape (Isaiah 40:22 a circle or sphere), and the dry land was covered with vegetation. It was hung in space without cables or beams (Job 26:7 *...and hangeth the earth upon nothing*).

The sorting of primeval surface materials in accordance with weight began; this is the principle of 'equal weights' in geology and geophysics, (Isaiah 40:12 *...and [God] comprehended the dust of the earth in a measure, and weighed the mountains in scales, and the hills in a balance*). The deep granite rocks were probably formed at this time - in the so-called Proterozoic Era, Algonkian period on the geologic scale. There are no fossils in these rocks and they are probably part of the original creation of 'the world that then was' (the world before the Flood).

The land area was much larger at creation than it is today after the Flood, (Psalm 104:5-9). Evidence for this is:

- large areas of the original continents were submerged as the water level rose;

- the continental shelf of North America extends 100 miles into the Atlantic;

- each continent has an extensive shelf giving indications of having previously been a dry land area;

- much of the present sea-bottom was once dry land as demonstrated by the great depth of some of the submarine canyons, by the presence of some flat-topped sea mountains, and by fresh water and shallow-water deposits in deep-sea sediments, (more plant life would have caused more carbon dioxide which would have caused higher temperatures - the result of more land area in the pre-flood period).

- Erosion and excavation by the waters of the Flood would decrease land area and increase water area.

The structure of the earth, (Proverbs 8:29), the foundations of the earth:

- It is 25,000 miles in circumference at the Equator and its radius is 3959 miles (6371 km.).

- Its crust is 20-25 miles in depth; it is solid rock above the Mohorovic Discontinuity. (This was named by seismologist Andrija Mohorovic in 1909. He noted that when earthquake waves passed into the mantle they suddenly increased speed. It is called the Moho for short.) This discontinuity has a pronounced change in density which affects earthquake waves. The crust is thicker under the continents and less so under the oceans.

- The mantle is 1800 miles in depth; it is divided into two parts, the lower mantle is believed to be in a plastic state; with the upper part more or less floating on the lower level.

- The core is 2100 miles in radius with densities of materials (iron and nickel), and temperatures which increase with depth to the core and then stay comparatively constant at 2500° C.

- Its weight: approximately 6,588,000,000, 000,000,000,000 tons, (6,666,225,819,600, 000,000,000 weight in pounds with atmosphere added).

- It is hanging in space, whirling on its axis at 1000 miles per hour.

- It is orbiting the sun once a year at a distance of 580 million miles at 1000 miles a minute. (Rehwinkel, *Wonders of Creation*), p. 93.

The miracle of the earth's precision:

- It maintains an accurate course in time and space.

- It has no engineer to guide it, and has no ground crew to give it directions.

- It carries a cargo of over 6 billion people plus plants and animals.

- It has not varied in 6000-10,000 years.

- It has not deviated from its course and has maintained the same distance from sun, moon, stars, and planets.

- No collisions have occurred with other planets (1983 example).

- No refueling has been necessary,

- nor have repairs been necessary.

- No parts have worn out.

- The rotation of the earth on its axis causes wind motion from west to east.

- The velocity at the poles is 0.

- The velocity at the equator is 1000 m.p.h. (Rehwinkel, *Wonders of Creation*), p. 93.

- Only a great Creator could be responsible for such a feat, (Romans 1:20,25).

- Scientists have now determined that the

earth is slowing at a rate of 1/1000 of a second per day.

This is in accord with the Scripture which says the earth is growing old like a garment and points to the soon coming of the Savior for His bride, (Psalm 102:26; Romans 8:22).

The creation of Plants (Genesis 1:11-13), the soil is prepared to receive plants.

There are three main orders of plants:

-grasses - which are spreading, ground-covering vegetation,
-herbs - which include bushes and shrubs,
-trees - which are woody plants and fruit-bearing trees.

All plants were created full-grown to provide food for man and animals.

They all contained 'seed' and were to procreate after their 'kind': species, genus, family. Variations could take place within the 'kind' horizontally, but no changes could be made vertically, (1 Corinthians 15:38,39).

For example, Luther Burbank was able to produce better varieties of potatoes, but the new varieties were still potatoes. He crossed peaches and plums and produced a new fruit called nectarines, but botanically peaches and plums are the same species and so is the new fruit. He tried to cross peaches and pears, but was unable to do so because they are different species.

The mule is a cross between a donkey and a mare, or a stallion and a female donkey. Here two species are crossed. The mule, however, is not a new species, it is a crossed species and is unable to reproduce to form a new species. Each one dies without offspring.

Plants have never failed in their function to provide food for men and animals.

The food supply on earth has never been exhausted, though there have been times of drought in one area of the world, other areas continue to produce and provide the food necessary to maintain life.

Only plants are capable of absorbing the inorganic through photosynthesis and converting it into its own nourishment which in turn becomes nourishment for men and animals.

Plants help to maintain the needed balance of gases in the atmosphere (i.e. carbon dioxide to oxygen; and man does the opposite by changing oxygen to carbon dioxide).

Plants provide beauty and shelter.

Because of the Flood they have provided anthracite coal to advance industry.

GOD FILLED

DAY FOUR

Creation of the sun, moon, and stars, (Genesis 1:14-19).

(Names of the Planets: Earth, Mercury, Venus, Mars, Jupiter, Saturn, Uranus, Neptune, Pluto; all the planets except Earth were named for Greek gods.)

THE LIGHTS IN THE FIRMAMENT.

Here God says 'let there be lights plural, (i.e. light-givers).

Their Purpose:

1. to give light upon the earth, (Psalm 19:1-6),

2. to divide light from darkness as in the first three days, (Jeremiah 31:35),

3. to be for 'signs, seasons, days, years':
   -evidence of 24 hour days;
   -evidence that the earth's axis was as at present;
   -provided for the slight seasonal changes in temperature under the canopy;

4. to serve the earth.

THE MOON, SUN, AND STARS:

THE MOON

Lunar gravitation produces important tidal circulation effects in the oceans and makes conditions much more suitable for sea life in the shallow zones along shores and in estuaries, (the moon is the nearest object to us, 238,857 miles away).

The moon also affects cycles of planting and harvesting.

THE SUN

The sun is the physical center of the solar universe. Ptolemy, (a Greek king of Egypt), advanced the theory that the earth was the physical center of the universe. This theory was adopted by the Roman Catholic system and not until men like Copernicus and Galileo advanced their belief that the sun was the center of the universe and set out to prove this, was the theory questioned and ultimately disproved.

The sun provides warmth and light to the earth so man, animals, and plants can be sustained here. Its diameter is 866,000 miles, compared with only the 8000 mile diameter of the earth. The heat at its core is estimated at 35,000,000° F. On the surface it cools to 11,000 ° F.

The production of energy by the sun is not understood but without its energy the earth would become a frozen wilderness in a matter of hours. The sun is not another 'star'. It is a special creation of God destined to remain effective until the plan of God is fulfilled. Revelation 8:12 tells of a future time when, at the beginning the Tribulation period, a third of its light will be extinguished.

Its distance from the earth is 93,000,000 miles, the exact distance to maintain proper temperature and light. To increase the distance by a few thousand miles would result in a frozen earth; to decrease it by a few thousand miles would result in an earth as hot as a furnace in which nothing could survive.

This proper distance also controls the amount of radiation reaching the earth and divides the earth into climatic zones in which beneficial crops can be grown to provide life for man and animals. Only an Omniscient God would know the effect of these slight variations and exactly provide for them at the time of creation. He has never had to make any adjustments in His original creative acts.

The sun has continued as God created it except for two special occasions which took place in the Bible. In Joshua 10:13,14 daylight was extended in central Palestine by God. The other event took place in 2 Kings 20:8-11. Hezekiah asked for a sign from God and the sign was that the sun would go backward by 10°.

THE STARS

Stars are considered to be composed of hot luminous gases.

Before the creation of the sun, moon, and stars, there was light. This dispels the myth of 'power' ascribed by astrologers to the stars. In Hebrew they are called 'lamps'. They have certain functions to perform - they are to separate night and day and 'declare His glory'.

Is it possible to account for the enormous lengths of light-years attributed to the stars?

Geometric methods for measuring astronomical distances can only reach about 330 light-years - all greater distances are uncertain. In their book *Binary Stars and the Velocity of Light*, Moon and Spencer say, "The acceptance of Riemannian space [Riemannian space: a type of curved pathway in a mathematical framework in space which would decrease the amount of time needed for light to reach earth from vast distances.], allows us to reject Einstein's relativity and to keep all the

ordinary ideas of time and all the ideas of Euclidean [three dimensional] space out to a distance of a few light years...In this way the time required for light to reach us from the most distant stars is only 15 years." And these men are evolutionists who believe in uniformitarianism.

In other words, God created the stream of light which reached the earth at the same time He created the star - billions of light-years did not have to pass before the light was seen on earth. The closest star to our Solar System is Alpha Centauri which is supposed to be about 30 trillion miles from us. If it were so distant its light stream would still have been created at the same moment it was, and could immediately be seen on the earth.

It would seem logical that God would create photons of light energy at the same instant He created the stars. Because of this Adam and Eve were able to 'see' the stars as soon as they themselves were created. (Photon: A measurement of electromagnetic energy; ...a discrete particle having a zero mass, no electric charge, and an indefinitely long lifetime.) *(Webster's II New Riverside University Dictionary*, 1984 edition.)

Numbers of Stars

There are so many stars that they fill the whole sky from side to side, but because of dust and gas in space they cannot all be seen. Our galaxy, the Milky Way, is one of the smallest in the universe. As more high powered instruments are invented, astronomers discover more galaxies at farther distances - it appears that there is no end to the stars; (Genesis 15:5; 22:17; Jeremiah 33:22; Judges 5:20; Job 38:7; Psalm 8:3; 1 Corinthians 15:41; Revelation 22:16; Isaiah 14:13).

For 'Signs"

God is understood by His creation, (Romans 1:20). The 'signs' here represent something besides stars. A 'sign' represents something else, much as our language represents something else. When you see a stop sign for example, there is nothing in that sign to cause you to stop, but the sign represents a power behind it that causes you to stop because of the consequences it can bring if you don't. By this we understand that when God says the lights of heaven would serve as 'signs', He was saying that they would represent and teach something else. They would, in fact, teach the story of the Gospel.

Man has allowed the paganistic practice of astrology and superstition to mask the Divine teaching of God through the stars. The learned of times past saw a connection between the stars and the Gospel - and we know that many religions did and still do worship the stars, (Deuteronomy 4:19; 2 Kings 17:16; 21:5; 2 Kings 23:5).

The Babylonians seem to have been the first nation which developed an organized study of the stars and their movements and they were able to accurately predict eclipses of the sun. When Alexander the Great conquered the Persian Empire and entered Babylon, he found in their libraries tabulations of future eclipses which extended many years into the future, and the tabulations were very carefully and accurately done.

Only through Christ can we see the moral attributes of God and His offered redemption, but through the stars we can see the faith and hope of those first men in a Promised Savior.

From ancient times God gave man the promise that He would send a Savior into this world. For the four thousand years of the Old Testament man lived with this knowledge and hope, (Genesis 3:14,15).

Legends and myths concerning the dragon and Destroyer and the wounded Savior who would crush him out, date from that period.

Names of the Stars (Psalm 147:4; Job 9:9; 38:31,32)

In the early days after Creation man was aware of the names of the stars. The Scripture says that God named the stars, but someone had to have passed on those names to a person who was knowledgeable in astronomy and observation for him to be able to study and classify them into the groups of constellations which are familiar today.

These names and groups included certain significant and symbolic 'figures'. Most of the nations of the world have used these same names and many continue to use them. These names and figures have been continued in all astronomic records of all the ages and nations since that time. They are founded on astronomical observations and form the basis of all maps and any other publication having to do with stars and star movements, (e.g. almanacs, books, records, etc.). The names are being changed today to eliminate all spiritual references.

Groups of Stars

A group of stars is called a Constellation and there are 48, which include the principle constellations. These appear in a line which the sun travels as it progresses through the year

The Ecliptic

and is called the Ecliptic. The Ecliptic is a belt about 16° wide, extending around the heavens, half the year north and half the year south of the equator on which eclipses occur.

The Zodiac

As the sun makes its annual course from west to east through the Ecliptic, the moon makes twelve complete revolutions around the earth, dividing the belt into 12 sections of 30° each, (12 X 30 = 360). This belt with the twelve moons or months is called the Zodiac. (Zoad = a walk or way, going by steps.)

The Twelve Signs

Each section includes a number of fixed stars making up a constellation with its own specific figure or 'sign' which gives it its name:

1. Virgo, the Virgin: the figure of a young woman lying prone, with an ear of wheat in one hand and a branch in the other.

2. Libra, the Scales: the figure of a pair of balances, with one end of the beam up and the other down, weighing something.

3. Scorpio, the Scorpion: the figure of a gigantic, deadly insect, with its tail and stinger uplifted in anger, as if striking.

4. Sagittarius, the Bowman: the figure of a horse with the body, arms, and head of a man - a centaur - with a drawn bow and arrow pointed at the Scorpion.

5. Capricornus, the Goat: the figure of a goat falling down as though it were dying. The back part of its body ends in the flipping tail of a fish.

6. Aquarius, the Waterman: the figure of a man with a large pitcher from which he is pouring a great stream of water onto the sky.

7. Pisces, the Fishes: the figures of two large fish swimming, one to the north, and the other with the ecliptic.

8. Aries, the Ram, by some nations called the Lamb: the figure of a strong sheep, with powerful curved horns, lying down comfortably, and peacefully looking out with great strength at its surroundings.

9. Taurus, the Bull: the figure of the shoulders, neck, head, horns, and front feet of a powerful bull, in the attitude of rushing forward with head lowered and pushing forward with great force.

10. Gemini, the Twins, or a man and woman sometimes called Adam and Eve: usually, two human figures closely united, and seated together in an affectionate embrace. In some of the older representations the figure of this constellation consists of two goats, or kids.

11. Cancer, the Crab: the figure of a crab holding on with its strong pincer claws. In Egyptian astronomy the scarabaeus beetle, grasping and holding onto the ball in which its eggs are deposited, takes the place of the crab.

12. Leo, the Lion: the figure of a great angry lion, leaping up to tear and destroy with his feet over the writhing body of Hydra the Serpent who is in the act of fleeing.

These constellations constitute the Solar Zodiac.

Each of the twelve signs also has three Decans (or smaller constellations) which accompany it to the north and south of the constellation. For example: "Virgo, or the Virgin has her three Decans; 1. Coma, the Infant, the Branch, the Desired One; 2. Centaurus, a Centaur with a dart piercing a victim; 3. Boötes, or Arcturus, the great Shepherd and Harvester, holding a rod and sickle, and walking forth before his flocks (erroneously called *Bears*)." Joseph R. Seiss, *The Gospel in the Stars,* (Grand Rapids: Kregel, 1972), p. 18.

Each of the constellations with its decans gives the story of the Gospel and the ultimate defeat of Satan.

THE YOUNG AGE OF THE UNIVERSE

The young age of the solar system can be seen by observing natural occurring phenomena:

Comets

Comets consist of chunks of rocks, dust

and frozen gases. Each time they pass close to the sun warming causes parts of the comet to fall off. The short-term comets should be totally destroyed in a matter of 10,000 years. But there are still many comets of this class orbiting the earth, therefore 10,000 years must not have elapsed yet. John D. Morris, Ph.D, *The Young Earth,* (Colorado: Creation Life Publishers), 1994. (Science *of Evolution,* pp. 80-84, source-the Internet.)

Meteors

Meteors are constantly falling to the earth in the form of meteoritic dust. From 14-50 million tons of dust are deposited each year on the earth. In a period of 4-5 billion years this layer would be 150 feet deep and would contain large quantities of iron and nickel. These quantities do not exist either on the earth's surface or on the ocean floor where it should have accumulated on the average of 600 pounds of nickel per square foot. Dense meteoritic dust was not found on the moon by the astronauts, though according to the old-earth theory, it should have been there. Henry M. Morris, Ph.D., *Scientific Creationism,* (San Diego: Creation Life Publishers, 1974), pp. 152, 153. (Ibid., the Internet.)

Age of Rocks

Presently rocks are dated by the fossils found in them because sedimentary rocks in which fossils are found cannot be dated by carbon dating or by radioisotope methods. These methods can only date to the last few thousand years and even then are not totally reliable using the assumptions on which they are based. The assumption is that since the fossil must be millions of years old, because of the geologic column, the rock must be too old to date by these methods and therefore the fossil type is used to date the rock, and evolution has already dated the fossil.

This is a prime example of circular reasoning. It assumes the fossil is a certain age because the supposed order of evolution requires them to be a certain age. The rocks in which they are found must also be that age or how could the fossils have formed in them otherwise? (J. Morris, *The Young Earth),* pp. 13-16.

"There has been in recent years the horrible realization that radio decay rates are not constant as previously thought, nor are they immune to environmental influences. This could mean that the atomic clocks were reset during some global disaster, and events which brought the Mesozoic to a close may not be 65 million years ago but, rather, within the age and memory of man." (Frederic B. Jueneman, *Industrial Research and Development,* p. 21, Tune 1982, source- the Internet).

Genealogical Records

Scripture genealogies do not allow for enormous periods of time even given a few thousand years error margin. John Morris gives this time line:

	Min.		Max.
From Creation to the Flood	1956	to	2400
From Flood to Abraham	300	to	4000
From Abraham to Christ	2000	to	4000
From Christ to Present	2000	to	2000
Total Range of Dates	6000	to	12,000

(Morris, *The Young Earth),* p. 39.

And Morris believes the 6000 year number is the most accurate.

Human Fossils

There are not enough human bone fragments to allow for long periods of time. In fact, there are very few skeletal remains of humans dating from the previous centuries and probably none before the Flood.

Rates of Erosion

Erosion by both wind and water takes place at a rapid rate and this would preclude attributing large periods of time to the earth.

In observing erosion on mountains, by both wind and water, the rate is so rapid that after only a few hundred years they would be markedly changed and diminished. If the earth were billions of years old we would be living on a flat plain.

Helium

The concentration of helium 4 in the atmosphere should be 30 times greater if the earth had existed for 4 billion years. (Dr. Stansfield, *Biblical Age of Earth*, source- the Internet).

Population Rates

Population rates should be much greater if man has been here 2.5 million years. It should be 10 to the 2700th power, but is actually only 2 times 10 to the 9th power. Henry M. Morris, *The Biblical Basis for Modern Science,* (Mich: Baker Book House, 1984), pp. 415-420.

There are many more sources which could be quoted, but these should suffice to show that, contrary to evolutionary teaching, the solar system is young just as the Bible indicates.

DAY FIVE

The birds and sea creatures; the beginning of animal life on the earth, (Genesis 1:20-23).

Day five begins the creation of conscious life - unlike the plants. With the creation of animals conscious life begins; starting from the lowest forms and ending in the highest. The difference between plants and animals is that an animal is conscious of his existence and of his surroundings. He has sense organs (feel, see, hear, etc.), he feels heat and cold, and he feels hunger and thirst. He can select his food and recognizes and provides for his young.

These creatures were to produce 'abundantly'; to 'fill' the sea. "Let the waters bring forth" "let the waters swarm with a swarm of living creatures", all brought about by the spoken word of the Creator.

In considering the great deposits of petroleum found in all parts of the earth and even in the sea, it is necessary to take into account the enormous number of oceanic fossil remains needed to form this petroleum. The first oil well was drilled in 1859 in the state of Pennsylvania. Since that time billions of barrels of oil have been extracted from the earth in all parts of the world. This gives new meaning to the words, "bring forth abundantly" when one considers the astronomical number of sea creatures which were buried by a catastrophic event and led to the formation of the vast oil deposits found today. (See section on the Flood.) (Rehwinkel, *Wonders*), pp. 156-157.

God immediately provided for the continuation of the species: "Be fruitful and multiply" (verse 22).

Both fish and birds continue the species by procreation through eggs. These eggs contain the seeds of life and each one procreates only 'after his kind'. (1 Corinthians 15:38,39).

- The eggs of both these species are fertilized, some before, and some after laying them. However, they must be kept warm in order to germinate and this is done either by the mother setting on them, or by the warmth of the sun in the case of fish eggs and some species of birds like the ostrich. Otherwise they will not hatch and bring forth new life.

- The shell of the egg is manufactured by the female by changing the minerals in her food into the product that forms the shell and she must have the proper food in order to do this.

- Each fish and each bird needs a predetermined amount of time to hatch its eggs. The bird parents understand when this time has elapsed and if the eggs do not hatch, they abandon the nest or they roll the eggs out of the nest and begin a new nest if there is still time in the season to incubate the eggs.

- The mother birds prepare their nests (sometimes with the help of the males) before they feel the desire to lay the eggs. Each nest is different from all others and is made according to the needs of each bird species. Some birds steal the nests of others, but most will only use their own particular kind of nest and each year they make a new nest instead of using the old one.

- Each variety of bird lays a certain size and color egg, as do fish.

- Each bird knows where to put his nest and knows the shape of its particular nest. Sometimes birds will build on a porch or patio of a house seeking a secure place for their young. If those nests are destroyed, the birds frantically seek a new site and the female will return to the destroyed nest if a new one has not been completed in a few days time. She will lay her eggs at the old destroyed site, dropping the eggs to the ground where they break. The nesting impulse is so strong in the spring or summer of the year that if there is not an adequate nest the female lays her eggs anyway in an attempt to obey the nesting impulse. (Personal observation.)

- Each variety of bird eats a specific food. Sometimes this food is hard to find, and this confines it to a specific area of the country in which it can live.

- The sand grouse which lives in the Nimbia Desert in South Africa is so suited to its environment that although there is no water nearer than 50 miles, the father grouse will make the round trip daily in order to provide water for his young. His breast feathers are specially made to absorb water. He soaks himself in the watering hole until his breast feathers are completely wet. After making the return trip he approaches the chicks and they immediately know where to find the water. They drink the water from his feathers until each has had his fill. The desert is desolate and dry, but God has provided both food and water for the animals which live there. (National Geographic Channel program, September 1, 2003.)

- Every variety of bird and fish has an individual covering of scales or feathers which are different in style and color, some quite strikingly beautiful, others very plain.

- Certain varieties of birds and fish have the unexplainable migratory impulse which takes them far distances from their homes and brings them back (or their descendants) again to the same place.

- Different varieties of birds can fly from 30 to 180 miles per hour; they are the fastest creatures in the world.

- God recognizes every creature He has made, (Matthew 10:29,31; 6:26).

- Both birds and fish have bodies specifically suited to their particular environment. (Rehwinkel, *Wonders of Creation*), pp. 155-171, excerpts above.

NUMBERS OF SPECIES

Birds and fish appeared in about the same number of specific species. There are estimates that in North America alone there are 5 billion birds. There are about 9000 species of both birds and fish and hundreds of subspecies under each of these. No species has ever dominated the world; no species has ever crossed over the lines of 'kind' instituted by God. (Rehwinkel, *Wonders of Creation*), pp. 155-162 excerpts.

CREATURES OF THE DEEP

God created great whales, (i.e. sea monsters). This word is used for dragons, (i.e. dinosaurs), (Isaiah 27:1); for serpents, (Exodus 7:9); and for other sea monsters, (Psalm 148:7). This is consistent with the different kinds of dinosaurs and lizards which lived or still live in the sea. Job 41 describes what the Scriptures call 'leviathan', and in verse 31 it says, *He maketh the deep to boil like a pot: he maketh the sea like a pot of ointment.* This would certainly come under the category of a sea monster, probably a Plesiosaur.

Psalm 74:13, *Thou didst divide the sea by thy strength; Thou brakest the heads of the dragons in the waters.*

Psalm 104:26, *There go the ships; there is leviathan, whom thou hast made to play therein.* (referring back to verse 25 - 'the great and wide sea').

Isaiah 27:1, *In that day the Lord with his sore and great and strong sword shall punish leviathan the piercing serpent, even leviathan that crooked serpent; and he shall slay the dragon that is in the sea.*

Marine reptiles of the Plesiosauridae and the Pliosauridae families fit these descriptions found in the Scriptures. These animals were called *dragons* because at the time the King James Version of the Bible was translated the word dinosaur was unknown. It was not introduced until 1841, and means 'terrible lizard'.

DAY SIX

The creation of animals and man, (Genesis 1:24-31; 2:7,18-25).

ANIMALS

There are three basic divisions of animals:
1. Beasts - four-footed animals that eat grass
2. Serpents - all that crawl on the ground
3. Beasts of the field - ferocious animals, usually carnivores

The number of species of beasts and serpents is from one million to more than three millions. They are divided into six categories: amphibians, reptiles, insects, spiders, worms, and mammals.

These groups contain:

Amphibians: frogs, lizards, salamanders

Reptiles: snakes, frogs, turtles, crocodiles, dinosaurs

Insects: they are a varied number between 6-10 millions

Spiders: 2500 species

Worms: they form the lowest form of life

Mammals: they form the highest form of life in the animal kingdom; there are approximately 5000 species besides the subdivisions and subspecies.

Distinctions of Mammals:

1. They give birth to their offspring;

2. the newborn is fed from the mother's milk;

3. the brain and nervous system of the newborn is highly developed;

4. they breathe through their lungs;

5. almost all are covered with hair;

6. almost all are four-footed;

7. their vital organs are similar to those of man, and distinct from those of other animals;

8. in their habits of eating they are divided into herbivore, carnivore, and omnivore (those which eat both vegetable and animal products);

9. those which have been associated more with man from the beginning: cattle, sheep, camels, horses and donkeys, dogs and cats. (Rehwinkel, *Wonders of Creation*), pp. 201-203, excerpts.

THE CREATION OF MAN

Man is the culminating glory of the whole creation, made in the image of God, but a little lower than the angels.

Man is not a mammal and should not be classed as such, because human flesh is different from the flesh of animals, (1 Corinthians 15:38,39), and animals were not made in the image of God.

Man was created with a spirit as well as a soul, (1 Thessalonians 5:23), and he possesses a spiritual nature. He also has a spiritual purpose, (1 Timothy 2:3,4; 2 Timothy 2:2; 4:2; Hebrews 12:1, etc.).

Man is a special creation. He was made in God's image to distinguish him from the physical world of nature.

He was created an intelligent, free, responsible being; he was not developed from mere matter as the rest of creation had been. Because of this special creation he was bound to love and obey his Creator, but, he did not.

Man was made in the moral image of God. God is a Spirit, (John 4:24), man could not, therefore, be made in His physical image. We understand different things from the word 'spirit' depending upon our experiences in life. The essence of the word used here is defined in Webster's 1828 as, "An immaterial intelligent being", (1 Thessalonians 5:23).

Man was created to resemble God in his moral attributes of character, but even at that, man in his finite state can never hope to understand the infinite mind of God or fully comprehend His ways, (Isaiah 55:8,9).

God took council with Himself: "Let us make man", (Genesis 1:29).

Because man was made in God's moral image, God gave him an importance and dignity above all creation. He was, in his original state, capable of God-likeness. He could never become God, but he could become more like God if he was willing to observe and obey God's one command to him.

After man sinned this was no longer possible, 1 Thessalonians 5:23, *And the very God of peace <u>sanctify</u> you wholly; and I pray God your whole spirit and soul and body be preserved blameless unto the coming of our Lord Jesus Christ.*

2 Timothy 2:21, *<u>If</u> a man therefore purge himself from these,* (false doctrines and sin) *he shall be a vessel unto honour, <u>sanctified</u>, and meet for the master's use, and prepared unto every good work.*

He could, after salvation, be sanctified (or made more perfect each day as he yielded himself to God), through the truth of the Word, (John 17:19), but he was now severely limited by his sin nature. Though the Scripture is very clear that after salvation man is a new creature in Christ, it is also clear in saying that the habits of the sin nature are difficult to break and man's sanctification depends upon his learning to understand the truth of the Word. He is no less saved; he is no less made in the image of God, but he is in a battle in this world with sin, the world, and the devil, (Romans 6 and 7).

Man was created an extremely intelligent being. He was capable of naming all the animals already in existence; he was capable of conversation with God, and he was given dominion over all creation. Only man, not some apelike creature, was given this position by an all-knowing God.

The assumption of an understanding of man's mental and emotional state based on 'animal psychology' is one of the greatest lies of modern science. Man is not an animal, never has been, never will be, and cannot be understood from this perspective. Lamentably, many so-called "Christian" psychologists have fallen into the Freudian trap and use the world's definitions and methods in trying to counsel God's handiwork. Tacking a Bible verse onto a lie, does not make it truth.

When God began the creation of this mortal being, everything stopped. Until this moment God had spoken everything into existence by His Word, "Let there be light" etc., but this was a special, unique creation and God would demonstrate for all time the importance of this man.

He begins to form a creature of surpassing beauty from the dust of the ground. That he (and she) were beautiful should be clear to us because God is a God who loves beauty, (e.g. the tabernacle and the temple). The word "formed" used in the Bible is the same word used for potter. The material used was *adamah* translated ground and used to mean 'red earth'. Adam's name comes from this word meaning 'red'. *Gesenius' Hebrew-Chaldee Lexicion to the Old Testament,* translated by Samuel P. Tregelles, LL.D., (Michigan: Baker Book House, 1979), p. 13.

When God had finished forming this being, he was perfect physically, but he was not a living creature. He was a beautifully formed piece of clay, but clay he was! Not until God breathed His breath, the very breath of God, into this creature, did he become a living soul. This is a good picture of natural man without God. He is dead until touched by the breath of God. (The word used for spirit is breath; man must be touched by the Spirit (breath) of God if he wishes to live.)

In that moment man's miraculous physical body began to function and certain processes began which have continued with every individual who has ever lived on this earth:

- "Man's brain began to function, sending thousands of 'messages' each second from its 10 billion neurons through the body's nervous system to every part and every organ in the body.

- "Man's heart began to pump, sending 10 1/2 pints of blood to 60 trillion cells throughout the body. The blood (wherein is life) began coursing through the 60,000 miles of arteries and veins and capillaries in Adam's body.

- "The 375 million tiny air sacs in each of the lungs began expanding and contracting inhaling and exhaling, taking in oxygen and giving off carbon dioxide and other poisonous gases. Man makes 18 inspirations a minute equaling 18 pints of air. An adult male inhales and exhales 3000 gallons of air each day.

- "Adam's digestive system began to function; some 700 enzymes took on the task of converting food to energy, thus fueling and sustaining the life processes." Rus Walton, *Fundamentals for American Christians*, (Plymouth: Plymouth Rock Foundation, n.d.), pp. 246,247.

- Adam's ear began to function transforming vibrations into sound. (See Appendix II)

- The Eye, the window of the soul, began to process the information which entered it. The eye began to function allowing light to enter the pupil where the retina turns the light into electric nerve messages which are carried to the optic nerve and then to the brain allowing man to 'see' the world around him which God had designed. (See Appendix III)

- Man's physical body is made up of many of the elements of the earth: calcium, carbon, iron, phosphates, magnesium, nitrogen, sulfur, zinc, etc. This is another indication of his humble beginnings from the dust of the ground.

The Spirit of Man Separates him from the rest of Creation

Before the creation of man the spirit did not exist, (this does not refer to the Spirit of God which has always existed). It is not present in animals; they are possessed with a soul, meaning they are breathing creatures, from the Hebrew word *nephesh.* The spirit part of man exalts him above all the creatures of the universe and gives him an eternal presence (Genesis 2:7; Job 27:3; Zechariah 12:1). Everything on the earth will pass away, but man's spirit will live forever, either in heaven or hell. Each individual must make this personal decision. God's image in man gives him the opportunity to be saved. Only man can be saved; not angels, not animals, nothing but man, because of his God-breathed spirit, (Ecclesiastes 12:7). (The word spirit [rûwach] also means 'breath' but in a different context. In Ecclesiastes 3:21 it is used to refer to both man and animals, but in that text means 'the element of life'. The 'spirit' has to do with a rational being, not an animal.)

God breathed His breath into man and man became a living soul with a spirit capable of communion with God. Nothing would ever be the same in the just created universe. All the creative acts which preceded the creation of man were made for this being and given to him in trust, (Genesis 1:26,28 and Isaiah 45:18). God had determined before the foundation of the world that all would be made for him, and through him God was to be glorified, (Isaiah 43:7; Ephesians 1:5,11). This was the ultimate purpose of man. Only the possessor of a spirit was capable of this.

When man sinned his spirit was darkened and could no longer fellowship with a holy God. Man began to be governed by his fallen soul - the part of him which is inclined to follow his 'feelings', his 'emotions', his carnal desires. When an individual accepts Christ as Savior his spirit is restored and is again capable of communion with God. As the spirit takes preeminence in the life of the individual the soul part of man is controlled by the Holy Spirit who indwells him, and the beauty of the soul, as it was intended to be, begins to be seen. He is indeed a 'new creation'. 2 Corinthians 5:17, *Therefore if any man be in Christ, he is a new creature: old things are passed away; behold, all things are become new.* Ephesians 4:22-24, *That ye put off concerning the former conversation* (your way of life) *the old man, which is corrupt according to the deceitful lusts; And be renewed in the spirit of your mind; And that ye put on the new man, which after God is created in righteousness and true holiness.*

The Basis of Man's Individuality

Man began to function physically, but he also began to function spiritually.

Since man was made in God's image he is a triune being of body, soul, and spirit, 1 Thessalonians 5:23, *And the very God of peace sanctify you wholly; and I pray God your whole <u>spirit</u> and <u>soul</u> and <u>body</u> be preserved blameless unto the coming of our Lord Jesus Christ.*

God's spirit became a part of man, (Job 33:4; Proverbs 20:27; Isaiah 42:5). Man was created to live forever, as noted in Genesis 2:17. He had a beginning but no end. He was to live in a perfect environment, in a perfect body, with a perfect God.

It is necessary to understand the difference between the spirit and the soul in order to distinguish the message of the Scriptures.

The soul of man has to do with his emotions and will; it is the part of man which is concerned with self-consciousness. By means of the soul, he experiences, he reacts to situations, he relates outside events and circumstances to himself.

The spirit of man is that part of him which is God-conscious. It is only the spirit part of man which is capable of communion with God and can be totally restored to him when his fallen condition is exchanged for the new man in Christ Jesus. It is the spirit which will live forever, not the soul, (1 Corinthians 15:52-54).

ADDITIONAL DISTINCTIVES:

God talked with Adam and Eve.

Man is the only creation of God capable of verbal communication with Him.

Job 32:8 *But there is a spirit in man; and the inspiration of the Almighty gives them understanding.*

When God created man He gave him the gift of speech. There was not a time of learning like a baby experiences. It was fully developed speech and man was capable of carrying on a meaningful conversation with God.

Man was also given the gift of writing so he could record his thoughts and his history. (There is no history of a people learning to write by themselves when the gift has been lost - therefore it is certain Adam was also enabled by God to write.)

His mental capacities were such that he could reason through complex problems and find solutions. When Adam named the animals he needed complex speech patterns and reasoning ability. Man is able to begin with an hypothesis and reason through a problem by considering all the possible consequences, then reach a plausible solution. From the solution he can then build the next hypothesis and find its solution. His memory is such that he can recall what he did or thought in the past and continue from that point without having to relearn everything again each day.

He has an imagination which allows him to form original ideas and carry them to fruition through his reasoning ability.

Unfortunately an imagination unchecked by the Word of God can also lead man into gross sin. Because of the Fall it (the imagination) was no longer 'very good', (Jeremiah 3:17; Proverbs 6:18; Romans 1:21).

But without imagination the world would not have had a Da Vinci, a Michelangelo, a Galileo, or a Kepler, etc. Even the imagination demands a choice - each individual has to choose good or evil, God or Satan.

The Gift of Man's Hands

When God created man He gave him a most extraordinary gift in his hands. By the use of his hands man is able to do things no other part of God's creation can do. The design was so good that even certain animals were also given a decided measure of manual dexterity, but not to the extent man has. Mentally God gave man the ability to ponder, to imagine, to investigate, and then to write down what he had learned. Then he could design, and build (construct), so that he could use his manual dexterity as God's steward.

Because of the dexterity of his entire hand and wrists, he is able to change his surroundings physically. He can build himself a shelter; he is able to till the soil to provide food, and he is able to care for animals which provide him meat and dairy products. He is able to operate complex machines in industry, and with them continue to change his physical environment. Without his manual dexterity none of this would be possible. (Ibid.), p. 247.

But, amazingly, those same hands can be used to dishonor the Lord and the individual himself. Hands can build a home or a place of dishonor; hands can be used to write a song or lesson to praise God, or a pornographic novel. Again, there is an individual choice to be made.

Capital Punishment

"Because God made this man in His own

image He gave him many of His own attributes. The importance of man in the eyes of God gives him his worth and importance. God instituted His laws to preserve and show the value of human life based on this first individual. Capital punishment is one of those laws which gives worth and accountability to each person. Because we are important to God, we should be equally important to our fellow man." (Walton, *Fundamentals for American Christians)*, pp. 252.

Dominion and Duties

God delegated to him special dominion over the earth and its beasts, fowls, and fishes, (Genesis 2:28-30).

The earth was made for man and entrusted to him, (Job 15:19; Psalm 115:16), but Christ is still the King of all the earth, (Psalm 47:2; 24:1).

He was given duties and service to perform, (Genesis 2:15), to "dress and keep" the Garden, his home provided by God (local self-government). God provided his home but he was responsible to maintain it in order. This provided an understanding of local self-government and personal responsibility.

He was given responsibility and accountability, (Genesis 2:16-17).

Accountability distinguishes the law-abiding citizen from the lawless individual. God gave Adam certain authority and power, but He did not give him total nor absolute power and authority because God knew he was not capable of that.

Adam was accountable to God and based upon his obedience was life and death. If he chose to rebel against God and disobey, then death would be the result. This was clearly outlined to him by God, (Genesis 2:15-17), but man had to make the individual choice to obey or disobey.

Adam was granted the greatest liberty, with only <u>one</u> law of restraint. He had perfect freedom within the restraints of the law. He could eat from the thousands of trees in the Garden, he could do anything he wanted to do except <u>one</u> simple thing. (Law for the lawless.)

CREATION OF WOMAN (Genesis 2:18-25)

God created woman *from* man and *for* man, (1 Corinthians 11:8-12). Though Adam could name all the animals, (2:19), in the whole of creation there was nothing found that could be a companion for him. Genesis 2:18, *And the Lord God said, It is not good that the man should be alone; I will make him an help meet for him.*

Willmington says the word 'rib' should be translated side. The Hebrew word used here is *tsela* and is almost always translated *side*, (Exodus 25:12; Job 18:12). H. L. Willmington, *Willmington's Guide to the Bible*, (Illinois: Tyndale House Publishers, 1984), p. 23.

God took woman from the 'side' of man; she was a part <u>of</u> him so that she could be a completer <u>for</u> him. (In English grammar there is a 'complement' which completes the sense of the sentence and either renames the subject noun or describes the subject noun,(e.g. John is a boy. John and boy mean the same person, they complement each other.) In the creation of woman God made woman to complement the man; for this reason the command is given *Therefore shall a man leave his father and his mother, and shall cleave unto his wife: and they shall be one flesh.* (Genesis 2:24.) They become 'one flesh', each complementing or completing the other.

Each human has two chromosomes which contain the DNA responsible for determining and transmitting hereditary characteristics. The female has two X chromosomes and the male an X and a Y chromosome. God created Adam first and took the woman from him and not vice versa because the woman did not have the Y chromosome needed for the man and God would have had to supply this chromosome from another source. The first couple would not have been related to one another in the same way and this is important because the result of sin was that all sinned in Adam and they had to be from the same seed. From the X and Y chromosomes of Adam God created a woman with two X chromosomes and they were truly of one flesh. Robert E. Kofahl, *Handy Dandy Evolution Refuter*, (San Diego: Beta Books, 1977), p. 82.

DAY SEVEN

Thus the heavens and the earth were finished, and all the host of them.

*And on the seventh day God ended his work which he had made; and he rested on the seventh day from **all** his work which he had made.*

And God blessed the seventh day, and sanctified it: because that in it he had rested from all his work which God created and made. (Genesis 2:1-3).

After the creation of man God did no other creative act. Man was the culmination of all creation, (Hebrews 4:3,4,10; Ephesians 3:9).

By the wording in verse 2 it is understood that God had at this time made everything - **all**- there was nothing else to make; all the hosts of heaven were made, all the things of the earth were made, all the things of the sea were made, and man was made; there lacked nothing to be made. Since that time there has never been another creative act. He is the Sustainer of the universe, Colossians 1:17, *And he is before all things, and by him all things consist* (are held together), because He created all of it and continues to care for it.

The word used for 'rest' in this passage carries the sense of 'cease', not physical rest because God does not need physical rest. It was the celebration of completion, the kind of joy we might feel when we complete a difficult task.

God then sanctified the seventh day as a day set apart for a ceasing from labor, (Exodus 20:10; Deuteronomy 5:14). It is a sign of the covenant which He made with Israel when they were liberated from Egyptian bondage; it is also a sign of the eternal rest promised to those who are His in Christ, (2 Thessalonians 1:7; Hebrews 4:9,10; Revelation 14:13; Jeremiah 6:16). This rest for the believer is promised when Christ comes to take His church with Him at the Rapture, (1 Thessalonians 4:15-18; 1 Corinthians 15:51-53).

A weekly day of rest is unknown in other cultures; only through Christ does a nation or individual find 'rest' for his physical body and rest for his soul.

It is important to remember that the Old Testament Sabbath was a cessation of labor, not a day of worship. Worship in the Old Testament was observed daily in the home and until the Tabernacle there was no 'place of worship' except the individual homes of those who believed God. For this reason in Deuteronomy 6 instructions are given to the father of the household to 'teach the commandments of the Lord, in the house, in the way, when thou liest down, and when thou risest up' etc., and refers to the daily hour by hour instruction in the ways of the Lord, promising a blessing if they are observed. It was a sign of total dependence upon the 'work' of the Lord and thus man, as a sign of this dependence, rested and confided in God's ability to provide his needs. It also was a time to let God work in the individual sanctifying him into 'the image of God' as he drew closer to Him and trusted in His provision. Deuteronomy 5:12-15 states clearly that the Hebrew Sabbath was to remind them of their deliverance from Egypt.

When Christ came in the flesh, died and was resurrected, He did away with the responsibility of the Old Covenant and gave us a new commandment; to come together and worship Him on one day of the week set apart for that purpose, the first day of the week, not the Sabbath, (Matthew 28:1; Mark 16:2, 9; Luke 24:1; John 20:1,19; Acts 20:7; 1 Corinthians 16:2; Colossians 2:16,17). The Christian celebration of the resurrection of Christ is on the first day of the week and is clearly taught in the New Testament.

Some activities were forbidden on the Sabbath:

- no work was to be done, (Exodus 34:21; Deuteronomy 5:12-15; Exodus 20:8-11; Leviticus 23:3; Jeremiah 17:22),

- the gates were to be shut, (Nehemiah 13:19),

- every man was to remain in his own place, (Exodus 16:29),

- no beast of burden should be loaded, (Nehemiah 13:15),

- no burdens were to be carried, (Jeremiah 17:21,22),

- no fires were to be kindled, (Exodus 35:3),

- no harvesting should be done, (Nehemiah 13:15),

- no wood (for fire) should be gathered, (Numbers 15:32-35),

- nothing was to be bought, (Nehemiah 10:31),

- nothing was to be sold, (Nehemiah 13:15).

Only certain kinds of responsibilities could be carried out on the Sabbath:

- life could be saved, (Mark 3:4; Luke 6:9),

- the sick could be healed, (Matthew 12:10-13; Mark 3:2; Luke 14:3-5; 6:8-10; John 7:23),

- an animal could be rescued from danger to life or limb, (Matthew 12:11; Luke 14:5),

- the hungry could be fed, (Matthew 12:1-8; Mark 2:23-28; Luke 6:1-5),

- a thirsty animal could be taken to water, (Luke 13:15).

It is obvious that the Sabbath could not have always fallen on a Saturday and we do not find that teaching in the Scriptures. The following, quoted from *Institutes of Biblical Law* illustrates this point:

"The Hebrew calendar began its dating from the deliverance from Egypt...the Hebrews retained the Egyptian calendar of 12 months of 30 days, but, instead of adding the five supplementary days at the end of the year, they added three at the end of the sixth month, and two at the end of the twelfth month. The 15th day of Abib, the first month, had to be a Sabbath every year, which meant that the first and eighth of Abib were fixed Sabbaths, as were the seven Sabbaths following the 15th of Abib (Leviticus 23:6,7,11,15-16). The 50th day would then be Pentecost.

"Now the Sabbath of Abib 15th being fixed by date, it follows that these seven successive Sabbaths must also have been on fixed dates and would fall as follows: Abib 22,20; Iyar 6,13,20,27; and Sivan 4. By no possibility can there be seven Sabbaths complete from Abib 15 to Sivan 4th unless those Sabbaths came on fixed dates of the month every year." Rousas John Rushdooney, *The Institutes of Biblical Law*, (U.S.A: The Presbyterian and Reformed Publishing Company, 1973), p. 134.

Mr. Rushdooney says we can liken this to our birthday which falls on a different day each year. In a seven year cycle our birthday will fall on every day of the week, which could not happen on the Hebrew calendar.

The date of the month remains the same, however, and the days of the 10th, 14th and 16th of Abib could not have been Sabbaths because they were specified as special work days, (Exodus 12:3,5,6,24; Leviticus 23:15). If Saturday had been the Sabbath these dates would have fallen on Saturday every seven years and this could not be because it would be contrary to what God had commanded.

The length of a Sabbath varies in the Scriptures, it was not always just a period of 24 hours.

In Exodus 20:8-11 and Deuteronomy 5:12-15, it is a rest of 24 hours. In Leviticus 23:15,16,21, it is a rest of two days of 48 hours. In Leviticus 25:4,8, it is a rest of one year. In Leviticus 25:8-12, it is a rest of two years and in 2 Chronicles 36:21, it is a rest of 70 years.

The Sabbath meant a <u>cessation</u> or <u>rest</u> whatever may have been its length. It was not always man who was to rest, it was also the land which rested every seven years. Every 50 years the land was to rest two consecutive years, the 49th and 50th years.

This means that it would be incorrect to define the Sabbath as Saturday. The Sabbath was given to the Hebrews as a reminder of their deliverance from Egypt and was not given to the Gentiles. It was a day of rest and celebration for what God had done for them as a nation.

THE RECAP OF CREATION (Genesis 2:4-25)

This was not a new creation. God takes this opportunity to instruct man as to the process used to form man and woman and to describe the beautiful Garden He had provided in which Adam and Eve were to live.

In verse 8 God 'plants' a garden; an act which implies forethought and planning. He was making a beautiful, perfect place in which man was to live. It is somewhere east of where the man was at that time, but we are never told where that place was, and it is useless to conjecture since we have nothing to go on. It is certain that all signs of it were destroyed at the time of the Flood.

No rain fell upon the earth as noted in verse 5, *for the Lord God had not caused it to rain upon the earth.* The earth was watered by a mist which rose from the earth in evaporation, (verse 6). Until the time of the Flood there was no rainfall, nor was the water cycle with which we are familiar today in operation. H. Morris believes the Garden was watered by a mist which occurred naturally (as an artesian spring) from the river which went out from it, (verse 10). If there were a source of heat below the earth's surface (and there is) the mist would naturally rise from it and water the area with a mist.

The rivers mentioned here (the Pison, the Gihon, the Hiddekel, and the Euphrates), do not exist today; the name given to the present Euphrates was given by those who still retained a knowledge of the original creation after the Flood. All the original rivers were destroyed when 'the waters of the deep' broke up.

God caused every tree 'that was pleasant to the sight and good for food' (verse 9) to grow in the garden. Even the tree of the knowledge of good and evil was pleasant to the sight and good for food. The fruit itself was not evil; it was Adam's disobedience which caused the evil to occur. God would not have created evil; as He Himself says, *And God saw **every thing** that he had made, and, behold, it was very good....* (1:31). Nothing was intrinsically evil; all was good, but the prohibition was given so that Adam would have an opportunity to prove his love for his Creator by obedience to Him.

THE FALL (Genesis 3)

Was evil already in the world?

How can 'sin' be understood governmentally outside of the Fall? Government in its basic definition is the flow of force and power, and if there was no flow of force and power in action, then there was no sinful act to disrupt the perfection of the world. But God had put limits of force on Adam and Eve through the one law He had given. He had established His government over them that they might choose whether to obey that government or reject it.

Until this time there had been a very special relationship between God and man. Vertically there could be no greater fellowship between Creator and created; horizontally, the external manifestation of the relationship was at its highest point. The fellowship shared by Adam and Eve was one of perfect love; love untainted by base desires or selfishness. Governmentally, Adam and Eve were under a pure Theocracy - God was in control and they could speak freely and face-to-face with Him. There was no need for any intermediary.

As before stated, the particular sin of Satan is not mentioned in the Bible, but for some just reason he was limited in his access to heaven and his dwelling place is in the 'air' of the earth. His punishment caused him to try to destroy this man whom God had made who was capable of having communion with God. Satan now directed his attention to God's supreme creation in order to bring them down to his own level and destroy God's government over them.

It has been thus since the beginning of time - to the genuine article there has always been a counterfeit to be passed off as the real article. To the true church of God, there is the counterfeit of the false church; to the Savior of mankind, there is a counterfeit (the idolatry of Mary in the Roman Catholic system, or Mohammed in the Islamic system, etc.). To the true Biblical form of government, a Republic, there is the counterfeit of a Democracy. Satan always has a ready counterfeit that is 'almost' the same as God's genuine article. It is no less true at this time in history.

When God said in Genesis 1:31, "...every thing that he had made...was very good"

this does not preclude the presence of evil in the world. God is referring here to His just completed creation, and it was *very good*. This would seem to indicate that Satan and the angels were created sometime before the creation of the world as previously taught in the section on angels.

The Scriptures never say when Satan and his angels rebelled against Heaven, but by the information presented here it can be safely assumed to have occurred at a previous time, probably in eternity past, (John 14:30 ..*the prince of this world*; Ephesians 2:2 ...*prince of the power of the air, the spirit that now worketh in the children of disobedience*; John 16:11 ...*the prince of this world is judged*; John 12:31 ...*now shall the prince of this world be cast out*). But at this time evil was certainly present in the world. Whether Satan was cast out before or after the creation is not important; what is important is that when he came to Eve in the Garden he was the same despicable enemy he is today.

One thing is certain, Satan and his followers will be destroyed in the future, (Revelation 20:1-3, 7-10). In the meantime, our battle is not against *flesh and blood, but against principalities, against powers, against the rulers of the darkness of this world, against spiritual wickedness in high places*, (Ephesians 6:12). (See section on angels for a more complete explanation of the government of angels.)

Satan came to Eve in the form of a serpent. It is interesting to note that she had no fear of the serpent and was not surprised when the serpent began speaking to her.

The Progression of the Fall

Eve begins to speak with the serpent: (Genesis 3:1-9).

The **Serpent:** (3:1), *Yea, hath God said, Ye shall not eat of every tree of the garden?*

Eve: (3:2,3), *We may eat of the fruit of the trees of the garden: But of the fruit of the tree which is in the midst of the garden God hath said, Ye shall not eat of it, neither shall ye touch it, lest ye die.* (Definitions: lest=that not; for fear that.) (Perhaps God really had told them not to touch it. He knew the power of physical touch to stimulate one emotionally. 2 Corinthians 6:17, *Wherefore come out from among them, and be ye separate, saith the Lord, and TOUCH not the unclean thing; and I will receive you.*)

What had God said?

God: (2:16,17), *And the Lord God commanded the man saying, Of every tree of the garden thou mayest freely eat: But of the tree of the knowledge of good and evil, thou shalt not eat of it: for in the day that thou eatest thereof thou shalt surely die.*

Then the **Serpent** continued: (3:4), *Ye shall NOT surely die.* (John 8:44, *When he speaketh a lie, he speaketh of his own; for he is a liar, and the father of it.*) Satan is a liar. Not only would physical death begin, but spiritual death would be the result of sin. Spiritual death began when Adam and Eve disobeyed God and continues today.

The **Serpent:** (3:5), *For God doth know that in the day ye eat thereof, then your eyes shall be opened, and ye shall be as gods, knowing good and evil.*

Eve: (3:6), *And when the woman saw that the tree was good for food, and that it was pleasant to the eyes, and a tree to be desired to make one wise, she took of the fruit thereof, and did eat, and gave also unto her husband with her; and he did eat.*

Satan lied three times when he approached Eve:

1. verse 5, *For God doth know that in the day ye eat thereof, then your eyes shall be opened, and ye shall be as gods, knowing good and evil.*

Satan slandered God's character by saying God did not want Adam and Eve to be as He was.

Eve knew nothing of evil. (Definitions: evil: Hebrew *rah*-bad, evil, adversity, affliction, calamity, and displease (-), distress, evil ([favored -ness)].)

What did she know of other gods? The word translated 'gods' here is the word *Elohim.* He was the only God she knew anything about, and she would certainly want to be like Him because she loved Him. But this was not the problem. The problem was disobedience. Satan counterfeits his lies well by drawing a parallel line so close to the truth that unless we are reading and studying the Word we will be fooled into thinking they are the truth.

2. *ye shall not surely die* (verse 4). Satan denied and rejected God's Word and principles by this lie.

3. Satan intimated that the *fruit is good for food.* Satan wanted Eve to doubt God's provision for them.

The fruit in itself was not bad. It was harmful internally because it demonstrated a heart condition of disobedience. They had no lack of food, so this was not even a valid consideration.

God had given Adam and Eve an intellect, a mind with which to make moral decisions and they were now called upon to use their intellect to make the right choice.

The lie had been planted in the woman's mind by Satan. It only needed a little false reasoning to bring her to the wrong conclusion. Satan works through the mind today in the same way. We respond, not from a perfect nature as she did, but from a fallen nature. How can we hope to stand against the 'wiles of Satan' by ourselves? The only way we can stand is through the Word of God, (James 4:7).

It could not have been a matter of lust to take the fruit because she was an innocent creature. She had a moral choice to make. Upon what was this moral choice based?

- Was it based upon her hunger? She was already provided for.

- Was it based upon the fact that the tree was pleasant to the eyes? Weren't the other trees pleasant to the eyes? (2:9)

- Was it based upon wanting to be as 'gods'? What did she know of other gods?

- Why was it suddenly desired (longed for) to make one wise? She was already intelligent.

- Was it based upon a physical need? She lacked for nothing.

In considering these first humans, it is difficult to understand their innocence. Looking from this side of the fall it is natural to try to compare them to us today. It was not possible for Satan to appeal to the pride of life, the lust of the eyes, or the lust of the flesh because Eve possessed none of these since she was a sinless creature at this point. She was perfect in her creation. (Perfect: complete, finished, consummate, not defective, having all that is requisite to its nature and kind. Fully informed, completely skilled; complete in moral excellencies.)

Man was created a moral being. He was the only part of creation able to make a moral decision under the obligation of moral law. He might accept or reject that law to follow moral ideals. This one factor elevated man above the merely material and animal.

Satan appealed to man's intellect: his mind.

2 Corinthians 11:3, *But I fear, lest by any means, as the serpent BEGUILED Eve through his subtlety, so your MINDS should be corrupted from the simplicity that is in Christ.*

Definitions of the verse from Webster's 1828:

(beguiled: to delude, deceive, to impose on by artifice or craft, to elude by craft [elude by stratagem])

(delude: to lead from truth or into error; to mislead the mind or judgment [deception in opinion])

(subtlety: trickery or sophistry [cunning craftiness])

(minds: intellect, disposition, device, thought, consider, perceive, think, understand).

God had said *'Do not eat of this one tree'*. Her own desires were more important to her at this point than obeying God's command. When she took the fruit, her eyes were opened and she immediately knew the difference between good and evil because she was now acquainted with evil in all its forms. She did not desire to sin, but she willfully sinned because God had given her a choice to make and she chose badly. God still gives us a choice to make, do we choose badly?

Eve's sin was a transgression, being beguiled and deceived, (2 Corinthians 11:3).

Milton wrote: "She plucked, she ate; Earth felt the wound, and nature from her seat, Sighing through all her works, gave signs of woe, That all was lost." And truly all was lost as far as man's perfect communion with God was concerned.

Adam's sin was deliberate, a decisive consent and yielding to Eve over God.

When Adam chose to sin he brought condemnation upon the entire human race and not only to himself. He was no longer fit to stand before a holy God; he was no longer fit to be called a son of God; his heirship was disallowed. He became a man without a country.

But the Scriptures tell us God already had a plan. Because He is Omniscient, God knew how man would handle his most important decision. He is a God of 'demand and supply' and when the demand came He already had prepared the supply.

To repair the breach would cost God His greatest treasure - His only begotten Son. Our Lord Jesus Christ was willing to come to this earth and pay the price for sin that we might be restored as "heirs of God and joint heirs with Jesus Christ", (Galatians 4:4,5). How can it be that the God of the universe could care so much for this creature made of clay that He would make the ultimate sacrifice to redeem him to Himself? This is love beyond comprehension.

Physical death was the material result of sin, but Christ will destroy even death when He returns to reign, (1 Corinthians 15:25,26; Revelation 21:4).

God created man with a free will; with responsibility for his own actions. Today we hear much rhetoric about 'rights' and 'freedom', but little about **responsibility**. Man places the responsibility for the wrongs in the world on society and the environment, but God places it on the individual. Only the individual was created in the image of God. Society was not. It is the individual who is responsible to God for his actions, not society in general.

Human nature has no power to overcome evil. To discern between bad and good presents man with a moral decision. All things are now not 'good' and man, when he meets evil has no power over it. Since Adam the human race has lived for evil. In the light of divine judgment, the state of the human soul is desperate, (Ephesians 4:18-20; Romans 5:12).

The animosity and lack of harmony between God and man is reflected in nature and in human government. The fact that man was not suited for a holy place is seen as Adam was prohibited from entering the Garden - a perfect place requires a perfect inhabitant. This idea argues the point of socialistic government that a perfect environment is the answer for all social problems. Only as long as Adam was without sin and was governed by the will and the law of God was he able to stay in Paradise.

When Adam sinned, the earth was cursed. Adam's rebellion against the authority of God was causative; the cursed earth was the effect of the fall of Adam, (Genesis 3:17-19).

Outward manifestations of man's internal spiritual depravity and their effect upon his Social institutions

External Results of Man's Sin:

ADAM (Genesis 3:17-19)

- The ground was cursed for his sake, 'in sorrow shall he eat of it'; man was now at the mercy of a fallen world.

- Man shall eat bread by the sweat of his face; he had to labor against the thorns and thistles to secure his food. This does not pertain just to agriculture, but to all honest work in whatever category it might be.

- Man shall return to dust, (Job 10:9; 17:16; 34:15; Psalm 104:29).

- He was banned from the Garden and was forced to seek his own way, (Genesis 3:23,24).

- He had to find his own dwelling place now because he had rejected what God had provided. The light and clear vision of God was darkened. He who had been his friend, now became a stranger to him.

- The penalty of death must be paid to the fullest, but while announcing this awful penalty God promised the remedy which would pay for the transgression of the law and would restore the blessing which man had lost.

EVE (Genesis 3:13-16)

Her sorrow and conception were multiplied. Interestingly she had never conceived and only after the Fall did she give birth.

She was put under the authority and subjection of man for her protection, (1 Corinthians 7:3,4; 11:3; Ephesians 5:22). She was not to be a slave, but the final authority in her life would come from her father or her husband as long as it was not contrary to the Word of God.

She would bring forth children in sorrow; this was probably not so much referring to the physical sorrow of childbirth, but to the emotional sorrow experienced by a mother when a child goes astray, (e.g. Cain).

Her sentence was merciful and mingled with blessing. Love would be her reward as she looked forward to the Promised one who would come through the woman and would restore all that was lost through sin.

The Messiah was promised and He would come through the women - the redemption of fallen man was a future reality, as if it had already happened.

GOD'S SOVEREIGNTY OVER EVIL

The forces of Satan are still at war with the forces of Christ, (Revelation 12:10).

Man would be redeemed by God, (Genesis 3:15).

Through redemption man would be restored to God.

Man would again have communion with God, but on a new level; the Holy Spirit would dwell in his heart, (John 14:17; 1 John 2:27, etc).

God drives man from His presence (Genesis 3:24)

Since man now knew he was naked, God clothed him, but only after the shedding of blood, (Hebrews 9:22). God seeks out the sinner and provides him with a covering for sin and promises a Savior. He did not leave man to seek his own salvation.

Man was banned from the Garden to prevent a greater sin. He had proved that he was incapable of obedience and God loved him too much to allow him to eat of the tree of life and live forever in his condition.

Some believe that man's life span was shortened as a result of the removal of the vapor canopy after the Flood, and we believe this to be true, but there is another consideration here. God loved man too much to allow him to suffer for hundreds of years in the wickedness of this world, and for this reason his years were shortened. God's mercy shortened his life-span.

DIVINE SOCIAL INSTITUTIONS ESTABLISHED AS A RESULT OF THE FALL

These divinely established systems for society are given by God, never to be changed or done away with without causing the destruction of all mankind.

Marriage and family (Genesis 2:21,22)

The Primary cause for marriage: *It is not good that man should be alone,* and the woman was to be his partner.

The importance of the woman in the marriage relationship: (Ephesians 5:22; Colossians 3:19)

- She is a proper, suited helpmeet for man.

- She is man's complement, counterpart, and companion.

- They are equal before God and His law.

- Her children would renew her own life.

The ordinance of marriage was established: *Therefore shall a man leave his father and his mother, and shall cleave unto his wife; and they shall be one flesh.* This means both of them, man and woman. When this law is practiced many problems in marriage are avoided.

Marriage is to be a perfect picture of unity and diversity and a reflection of an attribute of a Holy God. Both, man and woman, were to rule over the creation, (Genesis 1:26,28).

The Establishment of Civil Government: Man's authority over man.

According to the Scriptures fallen man has no limits to the depths of sin into which he can sink, (Isaiah 5:11-15; Jeremiah 17:9).

God instituted civil government so that man's natural sinful inclinations would be controlled, and when not controlled, would be punished by established laws. (Kathy Dang, unpublished manuscript), excerpts.

THE FIRST MURDER AND ITS CONSEQUENCES: Genesis 4:1-24

As evidenced by the bringing of a sacrifice Adam and Eve had evidently taught their children that a blood sacrifice was necessary to demonstrate their faith to God.

Cain chose to be a tiller of the ground, but it was still possible for him to exchange his product, the fruit of his labor, for an animal from the flock of his brother had he desired to do so. There is no sign of discord between them until Genesis 4:5.

Abel's offering was accepted because of his faith in the Creator and Sustainer, (Hebrews 11:4), and his obedience in offering a blood sacrifice.

Cain brought the 'works' of his hands, and offered to God his best 'works', but man's works are never sufficient for salvation, (Ephesians 2:8,9). It is as Martin Luther said when he realized the folly of working one's way out of Purgatory, 'how many works are necessary, how much money is enough, when will a person know he has paid the full price?' The same principle applies to the disobedience of Cain. How many fruits or vegetables were enough? The price could never be large enough to pay for the sins of Cain, let alone the sins of the whole world.

When Cain became angry with Abel, (Genesis 4:5), he 'gave place to the devil', (Ephesians 4:26,27) and Satan took quick advantage of the situation. James 1:13-15, *Let no man say when he is tempted, I am tempted of God: for God cannot be tempted with evil, neither tempteth he any man: but every man is tempted, when he is drawn away of his own lust, and enticed. Then when lust hath conceived, it bringeth forth sin: and sin, when it is finished, bringeth forth death* (lust: a longing for what is forbidden, an evil desire).

When his offering is rejected, God speaks to Cain, *Cain, Why art thou wroth? and why is thy countenance fallen? If thou doest well, shalt thou not be accepted* (to have regard)*? and if thou doest not well, sin lieth at the door....* (Genesis 4:6,7). Cain's sin was that he knew what was good, he knew the right way, but refused to follow God's instruction and it became sin to him. (*Therefore to him that knoweth to do good, and doeth it not, to him it is sin.* James 4:17).

Cain had the rights of the firstborn, and God reminded him that those rights were lawfully his and he could claim those rights by obedience, (verse 7). But Cain determined to continue in his own way and that led to the death of Abel.

From the passage it is understood that neither of them were children, therefore Cain had to have overpowered Abel during a 'talk' or he slipped up on him and struck him in a cowardly manner. The result was the same.

We do not know how much time elapsed between the offering of the sacrifice and the death of Abel, but they were both adults at the time.

God banished him from his country and from his kin, as sin banishes the sinner from those who love him best. Sin is a great separator.

When Cain was born Eve doubtless believed that this baby was the promised Messiah because she says in 4:1, *I have gotten a man* (or the man) *from the Lord.* In a matter of years she saw that not only was this child not the Messiah, but he became the first murderer. When Adam and Eve found their second son murdered by his brother the magnitude of their sinful deed began to impress itself upon them as never before. They had not known wickedness or terror in their lives; they had no experience upon which to fall back in this situation. They not only lost Abel in death, they also lost Cain, and it is doubtful he ever returned to his home. He was branded as an outcast by God and sent out to a life of wandering far from his parents, and farther still from God.

Though it seems a moot point, many have problems with the wife of Cain; there can be no other explanation than that she was his sister. (After all Adam married his own 'rib'.)

Until after the Flood with the coming of the Mosaic Law, it was not uncommon to marry within the family. Adam lived 800 years after the birth of Seth and 'begat sons and daughters'. Many children would have been born during this time period. There were no deformed chromosomes and close marriages would not have resulted in birth defects at that time.

Though Abram married his half-sister this was not a common practice and today these marriages result in genetic changes for the worst because of the close blood relationship. In Russia, for example, during the time of the czars it was common to marry within the royal family circle and the results of these marriages were many times children who were mentally or physically deficient. In most 'royal' families the same custom was observed with the same results. The descendants of Philip II of Spain give ample evidence of these genetic changes, both physically and mentally.

The Results of Cain's Sin on the World's System of Government, (Genesis. 4:16-24):

- Polygamous marital relationships are first seen, (Genesis 4:19).

- Musical gifts were given. These gifts are amoral, neither good nor bad; our usage of them determines their effect, but Satan has made good use of them in capturing men's minds, (i.e. Rock and Roll, New Age music, 'Christian' rock, etc.), (verse 21).

- Cain began religious corruption - the desire of man to be his own god and offer his own works instead of putting his faith in an Almighty God is as old as the Fall.

At least one of Cain's sons practiced commerce as a cattleman and lived the life of a vagabond in tents, (Genesis 4:20). This indicates meat was eaten long before the Flood because all this cattle was certainly not raised for milk and hides alone. After the Flood God only prohibited the eating of blood and raw meat, not meat itself, because it was already a common practice to eat meat.

THE PROMISED SEED

Though the firstborn was condemned by his own hand, God is merciful and sent another son to Adam and Eve.

Their son Seth, (Genesis 4:25), was born and was given his name by Eve, meaning "appointed or put" in place of Abel.

Seth became the progenitor of the Savior mentioned in the genealogy of Mary, the mother of Jesus, (Luke 3:38).

His was also the godly line through which some men continued to believe in the promises of God and remembered and taught them to their sons. Though man's sin is great, God is merciful. Seth's line continued through Noah by preserving him from the Flood, and through the son of

, Shem to Arphaxad, to Abraham and the nation called out by God to be His special treasure.

Through 4000 years of waiting God continued to remind His people that:

the Messiah would come
and would 'take away the sins of the world'
and would 'restore Israel'
and would 'be their God'.

The Messiah did come, and now all history looks backward or forward to that date when the Savior of the world became flesh and 'dwelt among us'. In the darkest times of history God is still working out His purpose for those who love Him, (Romans 8:28).

THE FLOOD (Genesis 6-8), approximately 2300 B.C., God's judgment on man's sin.

The condition of the world, (Genesis 6), caused God to send His righteous judgment upon His creation:

- "the wickedness of man was great in the earth",

- "every imagination of the thoughts of his (man's) heart was only evil continually",

- the earth was totally rotten in the eyes of God,

- the earth was full of violence,

- all the ways of man were evil.

There are those who believe the Flood was a local occurrence and not a worldwide flood. But in these verses God says evil was great over the *whole world*. This means *all* the earth. (For this reason the people were afraid to leave the plain of Shinar after the Flood - they did not want this condition of evil to exist again. They wanted to stay together and try to guard against this occurrence, but they went about it the wrong way and disobeyed God's command for them to disperse and repopulate the earth.)

In the last years archaeological discoveries have given evidence that man was dispersed over the entire world even before the Flood. The conditions existing before the Flood; different atmospheric conditions and different continental divisions, made travel easier and men did travel in all directions. The Flood had to be universal to be able to destroy man and with him, this tremendous evil from the face of the earth.

There are several current and historical beliefs in reference to verses one and two of Genesis 6, each will be discussed in turn:

And it came to pass, when men began to multiply on the face of the earth, and daughters were born unto them, That the sons of God saw the daughters of men that they were fair; and they took them wives of all which they chose, (Genesis 6:1,2).

THE FIRST BELIEF

The first belief considered is that the 'daughters of men' were the people of the earth, and 'sons of God' were angels.

Evidence For or Against:

As seen earlier in the study of angels, angels are sexless and do not procreate having no reason for doing so since they do not die physically nor spiritually.

The angels are called 'the sons of God' but they are also called 'men' in Genesis 18:2;

Luke 24:4, and Acts 1:10. John calls them 'angels' in John 20:12, so they are the same beings referred to as 'men'.

In Philippians 2:15; John 1:12, and Romans 8:14, men are called 'the sons of God", so it is not an exclusive term used only for angels.

Angels cannot be saved. What would be the condition of the descendants of this kind of union? God is not a God of condemnation, how could He allow this situation to develop (if they were descendants of angels and humans) knowing that there would be no way these creatures could be saved?

THE SECOND BELIEF

The second belief is that the 'daughters of men' referred to the line of Cain, and the 'sons of God' referred to the descendants of Seth.

Evidence For or Against:

What about the "sons of men" were they all corrupt before God, or was it only the "daughters" who were bad?

Were all the "sons" of Seth godly? Surely not, knowing man is born in sin and is by nature a sinner. In looking at the genealogy in chapter 5 it can be observed that only one of the sons of Seth is included in this godly line and his progress is followed through the generations to Noah. What happened to all the rest of the sons of Seth and their descendants? They also perished in the Flood.

Some believe the giants referred to in verse 4 came into being because of the crossing of these two genetic lines (Seth and Cain). The reasoning is that because of the inbreeding of the two lines there would have been a recessive genetic change which would have become dominant when the two lines crossed thus giving birth to giants. It is not impossible that these two lines had already crossed by this

time as not all of the line of Seth were good and could have very easily crossed with some of the children of Cain.

At the time of David there were still giants, (i.e. Goliath, the Anakim). When the Jewish nation entered the Promised Land (and before, in the lives of Moses and Joseph, etc.), and crossed lines through intermarriage with other nations (Canaanites, Moabites, Philistines, Egyptians, etc.), they did not produce a line of giants or monsters. The Jews were, doubtless, one of the most inbred nations at this time in history, but no giants are recorded among their ranks so this reasoning is at best without any scientific or Biblical basis.

God mentions both lines, the 'sons of God' and the 'daughters of men' perhaps to teach us that both lines were corrupted, as both perished in the Flood, (Genesis 6:12).

THE THIRD BELIEF

The third belief presented is that they were spirits of fallen angels (demons) who took control of the bodies of willing men and through their state of total wickedness copulated with as many women as they wished. The Scripture says, "they took them wives (or women) of all which they chose", (Genesis 6:2).

Evidence For or Against:

The result of these unions would be children who were also controlled by demonic spirits and would continue in the evil ways of their parents.

Demonic control is almost always played out in some form of sexual aberration - constant sexual thoughts, pornography, homosexuality, increased sexual appetite and greater wickedness. This would certainly account for the great wickedness mentioned in Genesis 6:5, and the 'wickedness of man (not angels) was great in the earth, and every imagination of the thoughts of his heart was only evil continually'.

God said he would visit 'the iniquity of the fathers upon the children and upon the children's children, unto the third and to the fourth generation,' (Exodus 34:7; 20:5; Numbers 14:18; Deuteronomy 5:9; 1 Corinthians 10:20). These cases refer to demonic idol worship. Though this was certainly written to Israel it still applies to all nations and peoples that forget God and has been witnessed repeatedly by missionaries who deal with pagan cultures where demonic activity is unrestrained.

The item associated with idol worship becomes the dwelling place of demons. (Neil Anderson, in *The Bondage Breaker*, says demons don't care what you call them. You can address them as Jesus (a crucifix) or Mary (any emblem bearing her likeness) or Elmer Fudd, they just want to be worshipped under whatever name you care to use.) Neil T. Anderson, *Rompiendo las Cadenas (The Bondage Breaker)*, (Oregon: Harvest House Publishers, 1990). The succeeding generations of children would continue in the wickedness of their parents and would doubtless find new ways of expressing iniquity, much as we see today in the philosophy of the 'free sex society'.

Since God is 'not willing that any should perish' it is understood that the wickedness was so great that even a long-suffering God gave them up and found no remedy but to destroy the whole civilization; babies, children, teenagers, adults, middle-aged, and old people - everyone. The entire creation would be forever changed because of God's judgment on a reprobate world.

What better way for Satan to try to destroy God's promise of a coming Savior brought into the world through a woman, than to corrupt all the peoples of the earth through demonic control and bring forth children of great wickedness through the woman. This certainly shows us that Satan does not know the future, as all occult religions claim, because the Messiah was coming and nothing Satan tried could prevent His coming.

The Scripture says in Matthew 24:37-39, *But as the days of Noah were, so shall also the coming of the Son of man be. For as in the days that were before the flood they were eating and drinking, marrying and giving in marriage, until the day that Noah entered into the ark, And knew not until the flood came, and took them all away; so shall also the coming of the Son of man be.*

Luke 17:26-30 says, *And as it was in the days of Noah, so shall it be also in the days of the Son of man. They did eat, they drank, they married wives, they were given in marriage, until the day that Noah entered into the ark, and the flood came, and destroyed them all. Likewise also as it was in the days of Lot; they did eat, they drank, they bought, they sold, they planted, they builded; But the same day that Lot went out of Sodom it rained fire and brimstone from heaven, and destroyed them all. Even thus shall it be in the day when the Son of man is revealed.*

These texts seem to tell us two things about His coming. In the case of Noah, he warned the people for 120 years, but they did not listen. They continued on with their everyday affairs unconcerned by the coming disaster. In the case of Lot there was no warning given because Lot had not been faithful in proclaiming his faith in the true God, so this presents another scenario. In looking at these two occasions of God's judgment, a pattern can be seen and that pattern is a civilization given over completely to Satan and satanic activity. We are seeing the same pattern today around the world. Can His coming judgment be far off?

God's reaction to the situation in the world was consistent with His holy character:

- He repented that He had made man; meaning He sorrowed or pained over man.

- He grieved in His heart over the sin of man.

As an omniscient God He already had the remedy for the problem and had prepared a man to carry out His plan and purpose.

Noah was called out. He was one man who was unique in his generation.

- He found grace in the eyes of the Lord.

- He was a just man.

- He was perfect in his generation (perfect in the sense of being complete in moral excellencies, not sinless).

- Because of his character and his good government of his own household, God could spare Noah's family.

- God ordered him to build an ark of great dimensions to save his family and a pair of each 'kind' of animals on the earth plus other 'clean' animals to be used later as sacrifices.

- Shem, Ham, and Japheth were born before Noah was five hundred years old.

- He went into the ark when he was 600 years old, and lived 350 years after the Flood, (Genesis 9:28,29).

After the flood God made a covenant between Noah's seed and Himself:

God's part was never to destroy the earth again by water.

Man's part was the continuance of a form of civil government which was designed to restrain evil in the world and punish those who refused to abide by the laws of God.

- Man is responsible to check violence and judge it in other men.

- Authority was delegated to man over another's life, in the ultimate offense - murder. Capital punishment was instituted by God after the flood, (Genesis 9:6).

- A system of civil government was instituted by which minor and major offenses to human life are checked and condemned.

- Murder is the supreme abuse, judged by the supreme power over another - taking of his life; while minor abuses are judged in lesser degrees.

- Civil government is designed to secure the life, liberty, and property of the individual.

- Our evaluation of man is directly proportionate to our estimation of God. Because man was made in the image and likeness of God, this image could not be destroyed indiscriminately without judgment falling upon the perpetrator. If the proper value is placed upon man, then when a murder is committed the murderer must pay the price by giving his own life. (Dang, unpublished manuscript.)

- But when man is considered nothing more than a higher form of animal, no restitution is required because the evaluation of man is so inferior that he has no more importance than another fallen animal. Society's evaluation of God is directly manifested in its evaluation of man within that society and capital punishment is looked upon as the ultimate cruelty to man when proper values are not placed on God's most noble creation.

Noah, through his sons, was to repeople the earth.

COMPARISON OF THE ORIGINAL CREATION AND THE FALL

The Original Creation

After the original creation the earth was beautiful. There were no great mountains as we have today, but evidently some hills did exist. The earth was rich in minerals which fed the plant-life which grew profusely in all regions. There was no rain, but the earth was watered by a vapor which rose from the earth every night. There was no thunder or lightning, no hail and no times of drought because no weather systems formed. The vapor canopy kept the movement of winds to a minimum though the earth was rotating on its axis and caused some wind movement. The whole earth was fruitful and plants were much larger than today. Multitudes of animals existed including dinosaurs and malamutes and they were scattered over the whole earth. Though evil was present, there was no sin to disturb a perfect place until after the Fall.

It would seem that the continents were joined, at least in places, before the Flood and if this were the case this would have helped to disperse both animals and man over the whole earth. The fossils of the Flood tell an interesting story of conditions before and after the Flood. They show that conditions were very different from those that exist today.

The Fall

When Adam sinned, the earth was radically changed. Thorns and weeds began to grow but they did not affect the quantity of plants. Plants existed, then as now, that man did not desire. He had to struggle to destroy them in order to obtain his food. These plants probably came from mutations of existing plants since God created nothing new after the sixth day and we know that all mutations are bad.

Before the Fall all animals appear to have been herbivores; after the Fall some became carnivores. The Scripture tells us of the son of Cain who became a worker in metal - no doubt part of this work was to fashion spears and other implements to protect man and domestic animals from the wild animals. Animals don't seem to have been afraid of man until after the Flood when God said 'the fear and dread of you shall be upon every beast of the earth, and upon every fowl of the air, etc.'

(Genesis 9:2). During the millennium animals will return to their former state, (Isaiah 65:25; 11:6-9), these verses describe the beautiful kingdom of the future.

Degeneration began and affected all of creation. The second law of thermodynamics was in effect. Sickness, bacteria, and parasites had an effect on both humans and animals and their lives were shortened because of this. Man's shortened life-span kept him from having to live so many years on a cursed earth.

It was necessary to work hard in order to live. This helped to keep man occupied and kept him from multiplying his sin, (Genesis 5:29). (When man has too much time on his hands in his sinful state it is easier to fall into sin. He has more time to think of evil and carry out his sinful desires.) God said, *'cursed is the ground for thy sake'*, (Genesis 3:17). God in His mercy was going to do a work which would benefit man, though man did not understand this at this time.

In Romans 8:19-22 is found a description of the earth today as a result of the curse which came about because of the fall of man. These conditions are still in effect and will not change until 2 Peter 3:10 when God's 'big bang' will take place and Revelation 21 when God will create a new earth.

Death passed upon all creation because of man's sin. It is not known how much time elapsed between the creation and man's sin, but it is possible death existed in the animal world before the Fall. We do know Romans 5:12 says, 'death passed upon all men because of sin', (Romans 5:14; 1 Corinthians 15:22).

There were no radical geologic changes in the surface of the earth because of sin as the earth continued to be very fertile. The radical changes came as a result of the Flood.

The changes in man took place immediately. Man had to work continually and woman suffered in child birth. The word 'sorrow' here means physical and mental pain, or extreme anxiety. It is possible this included a physical change in the woman's body. As a result of sin she was to suffer and be subject to the authority and government of her husband, (Ephesians 5:22), though both were individually accountable to God just as today.

The serpent, instead of walking on all fours, would have to crawl on its belly. This was a physical change in the serpent's design. We do not know if the serpent walked differently than other animals but it is very possible, (and scientists have found traces of what could have been legs on the serpent). Dust would now become his food, (Micah 7:17; Isaiah 65:25). In the Scriptures dust is used as a type of humiliation and the serpent would be humiliated because he allowed Satan the use of his body. During the millennium he will not be changed as the other animals because he will continue to eat dust, (Isaiah 65:25).

The vapor canopy affected the entire earth. Men lived to great ages (900+ years) and this allowed the population to increase to a size which could have easily covered the earth in such a period of time.

FLOOD CONDITIONS

Biblical testimony of a worldwide Flood: (Genesis 7:10-8:12; Job 22:15,16; Isaiah 54:9; Matthew 24:37,39; 1 Peter 3:20; 2 Peter 2:5; Psalm 104:5-9; 2 Peter 3:3-7; Luke 17:26,27).

There are at least 300 legends from the nations of the world which give an account of the Flood. Each legend deals with a large boat and a group of people and animals who were saved and replenished the world. Some are local floods and some are worldwide floods.

Reasons for believing in a Universal Flood:

God commanded Noah to build a very large ark.

Since men seem to have been much larger before the Flood this would make a cubit much larger than formerly thought because the measurement from a man's elbow to the tip of his fingers would be much larger, and the cubit was determined by this measure. The ark would possibly even be 1/3 to twice as large as the dimensions usually given.

If there had not been a universal flood it would have been easier for them to move to another location and it would have been unnecessary to save men and animals in an ark.

The Bible says Noah was to cover the ark inside and out with pitch, (Genesis 6:14). The word here is the same one used for sap from trees and this would have served to waterproof the boat. The immense number of trees in the prediluvian world and the time span Noah had to collect the sap (120 years) would make this easily attainable, (and petroleum was not formed until after the Flood).

The size of the ark indicates a worldwide flood even when present measurements are used.

Dimensions of the ark

- 130 meters long

- 22.44 meters wide

- 13.46 meters high, which would be equal to about 13,960 tons of space, and be comparable to ocean-going ships of today.

- Using a cubit to equal 45 centimeters it would be a little larger than 20 university basketball courts. (H. Morris, *Genesis Record)*, p. 181.

Noah had 120 years in which to build the ark and would have had help not only from his sons but from the people who lived around him, as hired laborers.

Deducting the oceanic creatures, Noah would only have needed to put 35,000 vertebrates in the ark. There were fewer 'kinds' before the Flood so fewer animals were required to continue the species afterward. The animals taken into the ark were probably babies or at least young adults and would require less room. It is not surprising that all of them would fit into a boat of that size.

The space in the ark would have been equal to 522 railroad cars which equal 8 trains with 65 double-stacked cars. The 35,000 "kind" would fit into 73 double-stacked cars, but the ark had 522 cars so there was plenty of room for animals and their food, plus whatever other supplies were needed. (Ibid.), p. 181.

To have eight people caring for this many animals for over a year seems to be an impossible task. It is possible God caused them to hibernate, either totally or partially, and if so, they would require much less food, water, and attention. The Scriptures do not say whether the principle of hibernation was in effect before the Flood because conditions at that time were much different. This possibility does give us an explanation of the conditions during the 371 days. Since that time animals have not ceased to hibernate. In Genesis 8:22 God put the cycles of the earth into effect and these included animal habits of hibernation and migration. In Genesis 9:1,2 there is a change in the condition between animals and man, and animals began to fear man. (Ibid.), pp. 186,187.

God also put the desire to go into the ark in the animals and Noah did not have to hunt for them. Everything was done supernaturally. God continued to care for them during the entire time of the Flood and afterward, (Genesis 8:1).

If evolution were really true, why would God have instructed Noah to build an ark to preserve life, when 'life' would have regenerated through the evolutionary process after the Flood?

The depth of the waters indicates a world-wide flood.

Genesis 7:19,20, *And the waters pre-*
vailed exceedingly upon the earth; and all the high hills, that were under the whole heaven, were covered. Fifteen cubits upward did the waters prevail; and the mountains were covered.

All of the mountains were covered. Fifteen cubits equal 6.77 meters. This refers to the position of the ark in the water. The ark was 30 cubits high and sunk down into the water 15 cubits or half its height because of its weight. If the water was at least 15 cubits high above the mountains, this gave plenty of clearance room for the ark during the five months the water continued over the earth.

The duration of the Flood is too long to have been a local Flood:

- 40 days of rain

- 110 days the waters increased, (Genesis 7:24), (150 days), because of the fountains of the deep

- 74 days of receding waters

- 40 days more before Noah released the raven

- 7 days more before Noah released the dove, (8:8)

- 7 days more before Noah released the dove again, (8:10)

- 7 days more before Noah released the dove the third time, (8:12) (285 days)

- 29 days between 7:11 and 8:13

- 57 days between 8:13 and 14

- total days 371

(H. Morris & Whitcomb, *The Genesis Flood*), p. 63.

Since the Flood lasted 371 days it is impossible that it was a local flood.

The waters increased for 21 weeks. The waters receded for 31 weeks more. After forty more days the tops of the mountains became visible and Noah opened the window of the ark, (Genesis 8:6), and sent the raven from the ark. It did not return because it had evidently found some dry places or carcasses or logs upon which to land and had found food from the carrion left from the Flood on which to feed.

After 150 days of rain, the waters started receding and diminishing. It had rained 40 days and nights from the vapor canopy and continued 110 days more, evidently from the subterranean water shooting into the atmosphere and falling as rain.

The ark came to rest on the mountains of Ararat the 17th day of the seventh month. (Mt. Ararat in Armenia is an extinct volcano and probably did not exist in the days of Noah. It is not known where the ark landed, but the Scriptures say it came to rest on the 'mountains of Ararat' and it had to be somewhere in this mountain range. In Turkey the name given to an area of the Ararat mountains means 'Noah's big boat'.)

The waters continued to diminish and on the first day of the 10th month (after 74 days) the tops of some of the mountains became visible. Each day the waters diminished 5 or 6 meters, at least during the first days or weeks after the Flood.

For 40 days more the waters continued to lower and Noah left the ark, after 371 days.

Because mankind was scattered over the face of the earth a worldwide flood was necessary.

Approximately 1600 years had passed since the creation and during this time the population of the world would have reached several millions or several thousands of millions, taking into account the many hundreds of years men lived and the numbers of children which would have been born during these years. Genesis 6:1 says, *...when men began to multiply on the face of the earth....*

The Mesopotamian region could not have supported the enormous numbers of people who were born during this time.

Historically the most pagan nations are very prolific and this time period lends credence to this fact. Some examples of this would be Mexico, the Arab nations, some of the nations of Africa (as witnessed in the famines of recent years), and some of the South American nations.

All men died:

Genesis 6:7, *And the Lord said, I will destroy man whom I have created from the face of the earth: both man, and beast, and the creeping thing, and the fowls of the air; for it repenteth me that I have made them.*

Genesis 7:22, *All in whose nostrils was the breath of life, of all that was in the dry land, died.*

Genesis 7:21, *And all flesh died that moved upon the earth...and every man.*

God said He would destroy all men because of their degenerate state and the only way he could have kept His word was to destroy them all except Noah and his family.

Sin was not confined to only one area, it was universal.

Only Noah and his family (8 people) escaped the judgment of God. God said Noah was 'perfect' in his generation - meaning he sought after God. (See definition for perfect under section on the Fall.) (Genesis 6:8-9, 17-18, 22.)

In Luke 17:26,27 Christ refers to the destruction of all humanity.

The fact that no pre-Flood human fossils have been found also indicates a total destruction of the human race. Some incomplete human fossils have been found, though as yet there is no proof they were pre-Flood and indications are that they are post-Flood.

In the fossil remains there are a few fish, amphibians, reptiles, birds and mammals. Most fossils are of marine creatures (95%), algaes, and plants and trees which formed anthracite coal and invertebrate fossils including insects (5%). In the Flood sediment few mammals are found. When fossils are found they are incomplete and include only a bone or a tooth and from these evolutionists form their conclusions of the ages of fossils, from 8-10 millions of years ago or more, depending on the mind set of the 'scientist'.

Men are supposed to appear in the Geologic Chart in the Cenozoic era - but the fossilized remains of men do not appear in this era. Those which have been found in the past few years have been of very recent ages and are found to be like men today.

Some reasons why no human fossils are found:

- Dead human bodies rise to the surface in water and would have been destroyed by the turbulence of the water as the sand, mud, and rocks were washed back and forth by the rapid currents as the surface of the earth was in a liquid state.

- If the dead bodies were deposited in the last few layers of sediment they would have been totally saturated with water and this water would have served to oxidize the organic molecules of the bodies and destroy them. The chemicals in the water at this time were also capable of dissolving human bones without leaving a trace.

- The deeper the bodies were deposited the more likely they would be to be changed and destroyed by the great pressure and high temperatures in combination with the chemicals and minerals in the water and in the earth. Many of the fossils in the origi-

nal sediments were destroyed in this way.

- Volcanic action would have destroyed many fossils because of the tremendous heat and liquid rock.

- Many remains would have been eaten by flesh-eating birds and animals.

- When human remains stay in water for an extended period they begin to decay and fall apart before they can be buried.

- If there are several hundreds or even thousands of human fossils in the Flood sediment it would be very difficult to locate them in such a large world, and to have them recognized and identified as human remains would be even more difficult.

- The most important reason by far is the consideration of God's purpose for sending the Flood. In Genesis 6:7 God said He was going to 'destroy' man from the face of the earth and that is exactly what He did. Allen P. Ross, *Creation & Blessing,* (Grand Rapids: Baker Book House, 1988), p. 194,

With the Flood waters God destroyed all the evidences of man and his civilization so men would understand, then as now, that He keeps His word.

The death of all the animals of the earth speaks of a universal flood:

Genesis 6:7, ...*both man, and beast, and the creeping thing, and the fowls of the air....*

Genesis 7:21-23, *And all flesh died that moved upon the earth, both of fowl, and of cattle, and of beast, and of every creeping thing that creepeth upon the earth, and every man: All in whose nostrils was the breath of life, of all that was in the dry land, died. And every living substance was destroyed which was upon the face of the ground, both man, and cattle, and the creeping things, and the fowl of the earth: and Noah only remained alive, and they that were with him in the ark.*

It is evident that God promised to destroy all men and all animals, and He did.

Some prediluvian animal fossils do exist. Animals are not morally responsible for the sin in the world. The fossils cause us to remember the price of sin and the character of God. He cannot <u>look</u> on sin. The fossils tell us of a world very different from our own which was destroyed because of the sin of man and they speak to us of death and judgment.

Peter's testimony speaks of a worldwide flood:

1 Peter 3:20, *Which sometime were disobedient, when once the long-suffering of God waited in the days of Noah, while the ark a was a preparing, wherein few, that is, eight souls were saved by water.*

2 Peter 2:5, *And spared not the old world, but saved Noah the eighth person, a preacher of righteousness, bringing in the flood upon the world of the ungodly.*

2 Peter 3:3-8, *Knowing this first, that there shall come in the last days scoffers, walking after their own lusts, And saying, Where is the promise of his coming? for since the fathers fell asleep, all things continue as they were from the beginning of the creation* [uniformitarianism]. *For this they willingly are ignorant of, that by the word of God the heavens were of old, and the earth standing out of the water and in the water: Whereby the world that then was, being overflowed with water, perished: But the heavens and the earth, which are now, by the same word are kept in store, reserved unto fire against the day of judgment and perdition of ungodly men. But, beloved, be not ignorant of this one thing, that one day is with the Lord as a thousand years, and a thousand years as one day.*

Peter says God created the world and destroyed it by water. The text refers to God's promises. To us they seem to take forever, but God is always on time. When we consider that God has willingly limited Himself to our 'time' for a short period, we can better understand this reference to a thousand year period. It's only a little while in God's measure of time.

If God kept His word and destroyed the original world it's sure He will do what He said about the future. He will return and He will destroy the world by fire in His time, not ours.

The Testimony of the Rainbow is Universal.

God made a covenant between Him and Noah and his descendants. The symbol of this covenant is the rainbow. The covenant is explicitly between God and Noah and <u>his</u> descendants, making it clear there were no other people in the world at that time.

The covenant extended to all men who would be born and also to the animals and to the earth itself, (Genesis 9:12,13).

God would never destroy the world again by a universal flood, (but this does not mean there would be no local floods which would destroy many people).

This is an eternal covenant, (Genesis 9:12).

The covenant is God's - the rainbow was to remind Him of the covenant, (Genesis 9:14,15). When God sees it He is reminded of His promise and when we see it we are reminded that He is faithful and always does what He says He will do, (Isaiah 54:9).

GEOLOGY OF THE FLOOD

THE FIRST CHANGES

Genesis 7:11, *In the six hundredth year of Noah's life, in the second month, the seventeenth day of the month, the same day were all the fountains of the great deep broken up, and the windows of heaven were opened.*

The word 'deep' *tehom*, (Psalm 104:6),

used here, is a word which refers to the ocean and underground waters which opened up because of earthquakes as the water from subterranean caverns poured forth.

Surface water can only seep to five miles in depth because of the immense pressure on the rocks. At this point the pressure closes all the channels in the rocks and water cannot pass through them. Drilling has been done to only about a depth of 7.5 miles. At this depth the water is extremely hot with double the salt level found in the ocean. Water temperatures were so hot that these drilling projects had to be abandoned. The pressure at even this depth was enormous and gives an understanding of the tremendous explosion that would have occurred when the fountains of the deep broke up.

One scientist has propounded this plausible theory of the breakup of the 'fountains of the deep'. He says when the subterranean water pressure built up because of heating (there are several reasons why heating could have occurred: increased pressure in the rocks because of a slight shift, a meteorite striking the earth, radio active heat from the rocks, etc.), it would soon reach a point at which it could contain no more pressure. At this point it opened a small crack in the surface of the earth. On each side of this crack, because of the stress from the opening, it continued to open at a speed of about two miles per second. This means it was going in two directions at the same time, either north and south or east and west. (Some scientists believe this is demonstrated by the Mid-Atlantic Ridge running north and south which they believe to be the break line.) In a few hours, following the course of least resistance, it would have circled the earth. The rocks would have been torn open like a cloth and the water would explode violently from the 10 mile deep opening. At supersonic speeds, from the pressure deep in the earth, the water would have reached

the atmosphere above and caused torrential rains to fall on the earth. Because of the extremely cold temperatures in the atmosphere, at least part of the water froze and fell as large hail. This would have killed and rapidly frozen large numbers of animals, (e.g. those found in Siberia today). These animals would have been quickly covered by the muddy waters in the first phases of the Flood.

When the waters from the 'deep' combined with those falling from the heavens they covered the earth in only 150 days. He says it would have been an explosion equal to more than 10 billion hydrogen bombs as the water shot to the surface and into the atmosphere. (Walt Brown, Center for Scientific Creation, www.creation science.com).

Other scientists believe that the floor of the ocean was uplifted and the waters overflowed the earth. Both of these events could have occurred simultaneously since it is evident that the ocean floor was certainly uplifted in order to deposit so many marine creatures from the ocean depths all over the earth's surface. Since these creatures make up 95% of the fossil remains, something catastrophic had to have precipitated their upheaval.

Since we weren't there it is not possible to determine what actually occurred. But we do know there was a tremendous upheaval because of the remaining signs.

We can only try to imagine the conditions which existed when the waters began to cover the earth. Great earthquakes occurred, volcanoes erupted with smoke and fire and lava, and earth movements began in the earth's mantle. Great waves formed in the depths of the sea and covered the earth. Tidal wave after tidal wave covered the land as a result of the great storms taking place. The earth was having convulsions, and much of this action continued for many years after the Flood ceased and some of it (particularly volcanic action) continues today.

The earth literally melted, (Psalms 46:6; 114:8). This refers to the earth's surface becoming a liquid because of the action of the water, wind and volcanic movement.

What happened to all the water that then covered the earth?

Some was absorbed into the atmosphere, but most was carried into the sea because of the wind which passed over the earth during this time, Genesis 8:1, *And God remembered Noah, and every living thing, and all the cattle that was with him in the ark: and God made a wind to pass over the earth, and the waters assuaged.* The temperature changes after the Flood caused the movements of the winds. The air masses near the poles cooled and those near the equator began to heat up causing atmospheric motions which formed the winds. This wind was something new in the earth and helped to remove the waters from the earth. Today wind movements cause the 'fronts' which form the weather systems affecting us daily.

Genesis 8:3, *And the waters returned from off the earth continually: and after the end of the hundred and fifty days the waters were abated.* This does not say that all the water disappeared after 150 days, but only that the earth was visible in some places.

Great changes continued for many centuries afterwards, possibly even for about a thousand years, as the water made tremendous changes on the earth's surface. Some of the waters filled the seas, which became much larger than before the Flood. The continental shelf extends into the ocean for some 750 miles to a depth of from 300 to 1500 feet. It appears that the continental plates were raised or the depths of the sea were lowered or both events occurred. (The continental plates should move from west to east because movement from north to south would be very difficult because of the shape of the earth.) There are many is-

lands in the sea that show evidence of having been formed above sea level but are now submerged. And fresh water streams in sediment deposits have been found in the bottoms of the oceans. Scientists have no explanation for this. It is generally accepted that the seas have increased their capacity by 30% or more. The topography of the earth changed and the ocean's deep basins were formed to receive the waters. (Whitcomb, Morris, *Genesis Flood),* pp. 324,325.

Immediately after the Flood the sea was more shallow than at present because of the subterranean waters, the ice caps, and the waters which were still <u>on</u> the earth and <u>in</u> the spongy ground. The more shallow sea provided wide land bridges between the continents which facilitated the migration of men and animals for many centuries, (e.g. the Behring Strait). The waters which continued to diminish from the earth, the sedimentation from the waters, and the great quantities of rain which fell after the Flood helped to fill the oceans to their present depths.

Some of the waters froze and fell as snow over the high mountains and is still there as ice caps.

Some of the waters returned to the subterranean caverns where they remain today.

The construction of the surface of the earth was changed in several ways: the location of the continents was changed, the temperatures of the earth's surface were changed, rainfall began, and plants and animals were also changed. It was a catastrophe so great it would be impossible to begin to imagine all that happened as a result.

THE FOSSILS

The fossils were formed during this time, but granite and basalt which form the foundations of the earth, (Genesis 1:9; Psalm 104:5), do not contain fossils. Not all granite and similar rocks are the result of igneous fusion; some were formed from loose beds of mud and clay and the effect of water. This is consistent with the original creation. Some maintain that granite and basalt are igneous rocks, formed by volcanic heat, and it is possible that some of them are. But it is more consistent to see that the foundation rocks were formed by God from the mud, clay and water present as He separated the land from the water in the first days of creation.

Modern geologists teach a rigid order for the appearance of fossils in order to 'prove' the theory of evolution and the great age of the earth. However, this order does not exist in the rock strata formed by the Flood waters.

Fossils of elephants and whales have been found in England, crocodiles from Egypt have been found in Germany, and even the Egyptian pyramids are constructed of a kind of rock formed from marine and coral fossils from the sea.

There is an enormous quantity of elephant fossils buried in Siberia. There are so many elephant fossils there that in a period of 20 years during the 19th century, at least 20,000 elephant tusks were taken from the fossil 'mines' and sold in Europe. Since 900 A.D. many merchants have traded in tusks from Siberia which were sold in China, Arabia and Europe. There are still today untold numbers of fossilized animals buried in the northern regions. Along every streambed they are uncovered after the stream has flooded. There are entire islands made up of fossilized bones and tusks, (e.g. the Island of Laikav off the Siberian coast in the Arctic Ocean). Bryon C. Nelson, *The Deluge in Stone,* (Minneapolis: Bethany Fellowship, Inc., 1968), p. 121.

Most of the frozen earth of Siberia is formed of animal remains. Buried frozen animals have been found still with flesh on their bones and so well preserved that the dogs use them for food. This should not be a surprise since bacteria cannot function in frozen meat. The animal remains that have not yet been found can continue for thousands of years in their present frozen state just as they have since the Flood. Some mammoths are still found with identifiable food in their mouths and stomachs. This would certainly be possible if the rain had fallen as hail in those regions and had frozen the animals very quickly in the first days of the Flood as indicated.

How can we explain how this happened? Water could certainly have drowned the animals without mutilating their bodies. It killed without respect to their strength, age, or size. The same water covered their bodies with mud and dirt - this is the only element capable of such wholesale death. Only a universal flood could have done this.

"...it is reasonable to postulate a very rapid rate of deposition; that is a single lamina [layer] would probably be deposited in a period of seconds or minutes rather than a period hours...there is factual evidence from both field observation and experience that laminae composed of bed material are commonly deposited by current action within a period of seconds or minutes." (Allan V. Jopling, Department of Geology, Harvard, "Some Deductions on the Temporal Significance of Laminae", *Journal of Sedimentary Petrology*, Vol. 36, No. 4, pp. 880-887, source-the Internet).

The fossils never appear in the right order for the evolutionary 'proofs' needed. There are marine fossils buried with land animals. 'Young' fossils appear in 'old' strata where they should not appear. 'Old' fossils appear in 'young' strata, and evolutionists cannot explain these problems. Marine fossils abound on the tops of mountains. On the Texas-New Mexico border there is a high mountain covered with marine fossils and there is no sea near to provide an explanation other than the Flood.

Elephant fossils have been found on the mountains in Tibet as high up as man has gone, but elephants do not climb mountains. Their remains have been found all over the world from the Equator to the poles, and at every elevation. (Nelson, *Deluge,*) p. 93

The fast-flowing waters would have picked up the animals later deposited as fossils and carried them far from their original sites. They could have been picked up and redeposited many times before they finally came to rest permanently.

It is difficult to imagine how fossils could be used to "prove" the theory of evolution when many have been moved from one area to another so many times and cannot give a complete picture of their order of deposition.

It has been reported that in 80-95% of the earth's surface there are not even three geological periods in the necessary order for evolutionists.

Some animals are now extinct because the conditions which existed before the Flood no longer exist. Some of these animals found in areas such as Siberia, both large and small, still have their eyes fixed in a frozen stare. All give evidence of being buried rapidly while still living. There are both old and young animals and many different types are mixed together in the same graves in the same areas. Leakey, an evolutionist, found the fossil remains of an ancient pig as large as a rhino; a six foot sheep, and a 12 foot bird.

There are, however, marine animals whose fossils have been found and which probably still exist in the depths of the sea where man has not yet penetrated.

In the last few years there have been more and more discoveries of both living and dead marine animals which are supposed to have been extinct for millions of years.

In his book, *Dinosaurs by Design*, Duane

T. Gish tells of a dead creature caught in the net of a Japanese fishing boat near New Zealand in 1977. It came up from a depth of over 900 feet. They supposed the creature had been dead for at least a month and it still weighed more than 4000 pounds. Scientists thought it was probably a Plesiosaur from the descriptions given by the crew. And sightings of unknown sea monsters continue to be reported. Duane T. Gish, *Dinosaurs by Design*, (China: Master Books, 1998), p. 86.

Most honest scientists will admit that though some fossils may be 'bigger and bumpier', no changes in the species have taken place. An hundred and twenty years after Darwin and a quarter of a million fossils later there are still no intermediate fossils of any species. But as one scientists said, 'If you don't find evidence for your idea, just make up a story to fit.'

THE FORMATION OF MOUNTAINS

During the Flood and the centuries after the mountains were formed. Because of the great earth movements, lakes and valleys were also formed; some of these disappeared and some were changed. Some of the mountains were formed by uplifting and erosion; others by uplifting of thick strata because of pressure and expansion or by pressure of igneous rocks from below forcing the strata upward, doubling and breaking them. It is possible that the core of some of the mountains are formed of prediluvian rock. Below the strata of nearly all the earth exists the granite and basalt which represent 'the earth that existed before'.

When the Flood ceased the great earth movements of the earth began. This was partly due to earthquakes. The uplifting of some areas and sinking in others caused the formation of some mountain ranges. The continental plates moved (up and down) because of the waters and the great pressure they caused. Erupting volcanoes deposited magma in some places as mountains. These have been eroded and are now much lower. We also know that many mountains still exist which were made by volcanic deposits. Many of those volcanoes are still 'live' and continue to spew out magma and sulfur around their cones.

After the Flood the turbulent conditions continued for several centuries. When the rains began to fall the water cycle was not yet in effect and profuse rains continued over the earth forming great rivers and lakes. There is sufficient evidence to prove those rivers were

Photo by R. Hooge

Strata doubled and broken, near Saltillo, Coah., Mex.

much deeper in times past. The runoff of immense quantities of water has cut large terraces in the sides of the rivers' former courses which can be seen today. Many lakes were also much more extensive than they are today.

The whole of France lies on a level plain sloping slightly to the west. The Seine River which runs across the plain gives evidence of having been an immense stream at some previous time. The different levels of horizontal terraces tell the story of fast-moving, receding water. Even the evidences around the Potomac near Washington, D.C. tell that it was at one time 256 feet higher than its present level. There are evidences all over the world of the same thing happening. This phenomenon has been observed in Washington State in the Spokane River, in the Thames in En-

gland, in Lake Bonneville in Utah, and in Lake Texcoco in Mexico; it could only have occurred from a world wide flood. (Nelson, *Deluge)*, p. 98.

The almost liquid state and sponginess of the earth's surface would have affected the way the fossils were deposited, and also the way the river beds were cut out.

There is a great deal of discussion about how the Grand Canyon of Arizona was cut out. Some believe it was during the first fast-moving waters of the Flood and some believe it came about as a result of lakes which were deposited by the Flood runoff. A natural dam breaking far above the canyon and spilling all the water into the canyon could have cut out the tremendous rock terraces which are found there, some of them more than a mile from top to bottom. It is obvious that it was cut by a tremendous amount of fast moving water. There is no way the present Colorado River running through the canyon could have accomplished this. (Some information from an ICR video on the Grand Canyon, and Steven A. Austin, Ph.D., *Grand Canyon, Monument to Catastrophe,* California: Institute for Creation Research, 1994.)

Most deserts of the world give testimony that they were formerly lakes during the long period of surface changes in the earth after the Flood. The climatic changes would have been sufficient to allow for the rate of evaporation needed to dry up all the water in areas like the Sahara, and the Sahara itself shows evidence of having been covered by deep waters.

During this time the earth's surface was more liquid because of the water it contained. It was thus easier to move, cut, and redeposit the surface contents.

FORMATION OF LIMESTONE:

There are two basic types of limestone: one is made of calcite which is a mineral form of calcium carbonate. The second is formed by the shells and bones of different kinds of sea organisms.

Water (both fresh and sea) contains dissolved calcium carbonate. When water evaporates it leaves calcium carbonate crystals which form limestone.

When sea water first evaporates it forms a white 'lime' mud which is deposited on the sea bottom. This slowly hardens into limestone.

When fresh water evaporates the calcium carbonate forms a crust over the plants and ground in the immediate vicinity. This accumulates into a mound or terrace called 'tufa', a kind of limestone.

The limestone formed in caves is another type called travertine. It forms the stalactites and stalagmites from the calcium carbonate in the water dripping into the cave.

The limestone formed by organisms is formed from deposits of marine shelled creatures and bones. The sea creatures (oysters, clams, snails, corals, etc.) draw calcium carbonate out of the sea water and use it to form their shells. When they die the shells and bones are pulverized by the action of the water and form coral sand and mud. "Most of the limestone layers in all parts of the earth were once shell or coral sand and mud...." (Robert W. Charles, Ph.D., University of California, Los Alamos National Laboratory, the Internet.)

The above explanation was not written by a Christian, but by a scientist who, however unwittingly, backs up the formation of limestone deposits after the Flood. Walt Brown gives another view of limestone formation during the activity of the Flood waters:

"From the subterranean waters, the most significant gas that came out of the solution was carbon dioxide. About 35% of the sediments were eroded from the basalt below by escaping water; up to 6% of basalt is calcium by weight. Calcium, which was in the escaping water, along with dissolved carbon dioxide gas (carbonic acid), caused vast sheets of limestone ($CaCO_3$) to precipitate as the pressure dropped." (The Internet.)

And marble is formed when the limestone is under pressure and heat for an extended period, thus explaining its hardness and softness at the same time.

The earth's sedimentary rocks are formed of 65% granite and 35% basalt.

THE ICE AGE

After the Flood rain continued to fall in large quantities. In regions higher than 1846 meters, which had probably not existed previously, the rain fell in the form of snow. This snow would have fallen in immense proportions in the higher mountains and on the Poles - possibly 100 times more than falls today. The upheaved continents (which would have required many years to find their counterbalance or equilibrium) were much colder than now.

The volcanic dust and clouds which covered the sun for much of the year would have produced a nuclear winter and would have prohibited the regular water cycle from operating. In the higher altitudes and elevations profuse precipitation and low temperatures would have produced great amounts of snow. The hot sea and the cold earth would have generated winds high in the atmosphere which would have transported humid air to higher regions and snow would have resulted. It is not the cold, but the snow which produces an ice age. The snow forms ice when it does not melt during the summer and snow begins to fall again in the winter. (Walt Brown, the Internet).

Since the proportion of water and land was changed after the Flood, these great quantities of snow helped to dissipate the water which had fallen during this time. It is possible the ice cap extended over parts of the northern continents for a long period. To say the ice cap extended over the whole earth, even in the equatorial regions, is not provable. There are other, more plausible, explanations for the scratches and gouges found on the earth's surface in those areas. Rock movements can leave the same prints as glaciers. Glaciers have never been found in areas lower than 1846 meters and as many of the equatorial zones are below sea level, they never rise to altitudes where snow could fall. Only the Flood could have caused those conditions.

Today, ten percent of the earth is covered by glaciers which move from a few inches to 100 feet per day depending on the time of year. Though they are constantly 'calving' (breaking off large chunks which fall into the sea), they continue to exist. Sometimes they are smaller because of melting, but as the warm cycle changes they again freeze and cover more area.

ANTHRACITE COAL

There is evidence that coal was formed in deep flood waters. In the United States of America there are areas where there are found various layers of tree bark scraped from uprooted trees which formed coal because of the heat and pressure above them.

While the waters of the Flood remained on the earth they were subject to the tides of the oceans. We know there are four tidal movements of the sea each day; two coming in, two going out. The different strata were being formed during this period of decreasing water, and plants, including trees, were being buried. Because they remained in the water so long their consistency became pulpy and they were deposited in more-or-less flat layers or strata. We know coal is formed of vegetable substances, especially trees. The world before the Flood was covered with enormous quanti-

ties of plants which formed the coal and this begins to give an understanding of the profuseness of the pre-Flood vegetation. When the lower strata were being formed, plants were still floating on the surface of the water. As the land began to dry out and the mountains were forming, the plants began to be deposited. They were mixed with other heavier components and everything was deposited together. There are strata of lighter material below and above the heavier coal stratum. Nowhere on the earth has there been found a rigid line of coal deposition.

Large coal deposits have been found in Antarctica containing fossilized tree trunks 24 feet long and two feet thick. Some of the coal layers are 3-4 feet thick, and there were 30 layers of anthracite coal in one area.

Most scholars are in agreement that these deposits were made when the waters had become tranquil. This left the plants in place during the moving tides and the decreasing waters. Deposits of coal are found in most of the world and there are, no doubt, still many undiscovered deposits. Coal formed because of the tremendous pressure of the covering strata deposited afterwards, the change of temperature, and time.

There is no evidence of coal formation taking place today though the uniformitarians would like us to believe it is happening. They refer to a formation of peat in the state of Virginia and hope it will ultimately change to coal, but there is no evidence of this occurring. (Nelson, *Deluge*), pp. 69-81.

PETROLEUM

There is still much discussion among uniformitarians concerning the formation of petroleum. From what has been seen and studied it appears to have been formed from deposits of marine animals (fish and others) which were created in great numbers the fifth day of creation. When the waters covered the earth these creatures were deposited over the whole earth; on the highest mountains, and below the sea. (It is also possible that some of the deposits were made when the land was still level and when the mountains were uplifted the marine fossils ended up on the tops of mountains.)

Great quantities of petroleum are found today in the earth's crust. Taking into account the enormous quantities of petroleum which have been taken from the earth since the first oil well was dug in 1850, God's command to 'be fruitful, and multiply, and fill the waters in the seas' begins to take on a whole new perspective; (Genesis 1:22). Petroleum had to have been formed by means of a great worldwide catastrophe - the universal Flood. It is still not known just what processes combined to form petroleum; but it is believed to be formed by heat, pressure, bacterial action, radioactivity, and by catalytic reactions, but no one is sure. We only know it was formed by deposits of marine fossils and by the pressure and the time periods involved after the Flood. (Whitcomb, Morris, *Genesis Flood*), pp. 429-438. (Nelson, *Deluge*), p. 89.

CONCLUSION

A certain amount of faith is required to believe all that has been presented in reference to the Flood. It is not blind faith, however, because there is no physical evidence of the Flood which contradicts the information we have in the Word of God, and we can trust that Word.

POLITICAL RESULTS OF THE FLOOD,

Genesis 9

When Noah and his family left the ark after the Flood, he built an altar and taking the clean animals, which were kept for this purpose, he offered a sacrifice to God in thanksgiving for their salvation from the Flood.

God's acceptance of Noah's offering put into effect certain unchanging principles and the following were the result of His acceptance:

- God said He would never curse the earth again because of man's sin (because the heart of man is wicked and it is not possible to hope he will do good).

- He would never again destroy all living things from the earth.

- The seasons, and the rhythm of day and night will continue as long as the earth exists.

- God blessed Noah and his sons, giving them instructions to 'be fruitful, and multiply, and replenish the earth'.

- There would be enmity between man and animals. God gave man the animal kingdom and gave him dominion over it.

- Permission was given to continue eating meat and all the 'fruit' of the earth.

- Prohibition of eating blood and raw meat was given, (9:4).

- God gave instructions for civil government: a life for a life, (verse 5) (capital punishment); the reason: man is made in the image of God.

- The rainbow was given as a sign of God's promise between Him and Noah and his descendants and the earth, (verse 17).

NOAH'S SIN

When Noah left the ark he planted a vineyard and drank the wine made from its fruit.

Some writers think he did not know he would become drunken because the grapes would not have fermented under the vapor canopy. This does not make sense when we read Luke 17:27 where Christ is speaking of the prediluvian civilization, "they did eat, they drank...". This speaks of alcoholic beverages not of drinking water or other non-fermented liquids.

Wine is a beverage which must be made by a specific complicated process. If grape juice is left to itself it will never change into wine; it will change into vinegar. The air contains wild-yeast spores which enter the juice and change it into vinegar and no one can drink straight vinegar and be drunken. The conclusion is that Noah knew what he was doing and sinned, even though he believed in God and was 'perfect' in his generation. We will never come to a sinless state and Noah was no exception; he had a choice to make and he chose badly.

When he was drunken he was uncovered in his tent. The abuse of alcoholic beverages always leads to wickedness in one form or another.

Noah's son Ham was a man of low morals. He had seen the sin of the prediluvian world and it seems he was at least somewhat in favor of that sin. (If we do not separate ourselves from the world a certain amount of its evil will influence us.)

It is evident that Ham had believed in God since he was included in those who entered the ark. It is also known, though, that not all the members of a family follow the moral teachings of their fathers. In this case, the youngest son of Ham, Canaan, followed the wicked example of his father and when his father told him about the condition of Noah, he entered the tent. What follows afterward leads to the belief that he did something 'to' his grandfather in his drunken state. In Genesis 9:24 the Scripture says: *And Noah awoke from his wine, and knew what his younger son had done unto him.* He had done something physically to his grandfather and it was something so horrible that Noah remembered it when he came to his senses. Noah cursed

Canaan, not Ham. (But the fathers always suffer for what the children do.)

In the Bible it is common to call the grandson, 'son', as seen in Ruth 4:17; Genesis 31:28, etc. Here Noah calls Canaan his younger son. This cannot refer to Ham because he is always second in the list of the sons of Noah, (9:18; 10:1). (Also, in 9:18 Ham is mentioned as the father of Canaan and this is what gives him his distinction. It does not mention the other sons of Ham, only Canaan.) The youngest son of Ham is Canaan, (Genesis 10:6).

The curse begins in Genesis 9:25 and falls only upon Canaan. Noah continues with the blessing of Shem and Japheth, but does not mention the name of Ham in the blessing nor in the curse. Canaan was to be the servant of both Shem and Japheth. For Ham's carnality his family received no blessing and since that time has suffered because of it.

When God told Canaan he would be a 'servant of servants' he was telling him about the part this line was to play in the plan of God.

In one sense each son of Noah was to be a servant of the others. The Shemites were to serve the others in giving the Gospel to the world, in guarding the Word of God, and in providing the line from which the Savior would be born.

The Japhethites were to give the intellectual impulse which would advance the discoveries and inventions of the world to help all mankind.

In the same sense the Hamites served the others by means of their physical inventions (mathematics, medicine, astronomy, etc.). They took their inventions to a certain point and there they stayed. It took Japheth to continue with them and refine them for their best use.

None was to be the exclusive servant of the other. This is the only occasion in the Bible where the phrase 'servant of servants' is used and it speaks here of the 'stewardship' of a steward, who would care for the physical things of others, exactly what Ham and his descendants did.

Canaan took for himself the region God promised to the Hebrews. It was a great and fearful nation the Israelites encountered when they entered the Promised Land, (Genesis 12:6). All the Canaanites were idolaters and God told the Jews to destroy all of them. Because of their disobedience Israel had to suffer and God used the Canaanites to judge them, (Judges 2:21,22; Numbers 33:55; Judges 3:3,4, etc).

God gives us the genealogy of each of the sons of Noah in chapter 10 of Genesis. Each will be followed through the dispersion of the nations after the Tower of Babel.

SECTION II

DISPERSION CHART

SONS OF NOAH

Shem   Ham   Japheth

SONS OF JAPHETH

(Gomer Magog Madai Javan Tubal Meshech Tiras)

1. **Gomer:**

CELTS
Scotch
Irish
Manx
Welsh
Britons
Cornish

Other
Turkey (Togarmah-Ez. 38:6)
Indians of India

GERMANS
(Ashkenaz & Riphath)
East Germanic
    Burgundians
    Alemani
    Vandals
    Franks
    Lombards
    Suevi
North Germanic
    Danes
    Norwegians
    Swedes
    Icelanders
West Germanic
    High German
    Swiss
    Low German
        Flemish
        Dutch
        Platt Deutsh
        Frisians
        Angles {
        Saxons {   English
        Jutes   {

2. **Magog (and Meshech included)**
    SCYTHIC TURANIANS
            Polar Nations-Finno-Ugrians
        Mongols
                (northern oriental)
                Indians of the New World
        Malays
            (island people)
        Turks
    SCYTHIANS (Slavs)
        Russians   Croats
        Bulgarians   Slovaks
        Bohemians   Bosnians
        Polish   Montenegrans
        Serbians   Slovenians
        Czechs   Hungarians
        Basques

3. **Madai**

    Indian (of India)
    Iranic Nations
            Medes
            Beluchi
            Afgans
            Persians

4. **Javan**
    (Elishah, Tarshish, Kittim, Dodanim, Ez. 38:13)

    Greeks
    Romans (Gauls, Etruscans, Iapygians, Italians)
        Romance Nations
            Italians (Latins, Umbro-Sabelleans)
            French
            Spanish
            Portuguese
            Provence
            Roumanian

5. **Tubal**

    Some western European nations

6. **Tiras**
        Dacians
        Goths
        Thracians

SONS OF HAM

(Cush Mizraim Phut   Canaan)

1. **Cush**
     Ethiopians
          Seba (India - aboriginal)
          Havilah
          Sabtah
          Raamah
          Sabtekah
               Raamah
                    Seba or Sheba
                    Dedan   Ez. 38:13
          Nimrod

2. **Mizraim**

     Egyptians
          Ludim
          Anamim
          Lehabim
          Naphtuhim
          Pathrusim
          Casluhim   { The
          Caphtorim - Crete{ Philistines

3. **Phut-N. Africa**
     Libyans
     Phoenicians

4. **Canaan-Palestine**

     Canaanites
          Sidon - the Mediterranean coast
          Heth - Asia Minor
               Hittites
               Hurrites
          Jebusites - Jerusalem
          Amorites - Syria, Palestine
          Girgasite
          Hivite-Asia Minor and Syria
          Arkite - north of Sidon
          Sinite - sea coast
          Arvadite
          Zemarite
          Hamathite - on the Orontes River

SONS OF SHEM

(Elam Asshur Arphaxad **Lud** Aram)

1. **Elam**
   Elamites
   Elymeans
2. **Asshur**
   Assyria
   Kurds
3. **Arphaxad**
   Chaldeans
   Babylonians
   Hebrews
   Saleh
   Eber
   Peleg
   Reu
   Serug
   Nahor
   Terah
   Abraham
   Ishmael - combined Arab nations
   Isaac
   Jacob - Israelites
   Shemite **Arabs**
   Joktan

   Almodad
   Sheleph
   Hazormaveth
   Jerah
   Hadoram
   Uzal
   Diklah
   Obal
   Abimael
   Sheba
   Ophir
   Havilah
   Jobab

4. **Lud**
   Lydians - **Asia** Minor
   Armenia - went to Lybia, northern Africa, Canary Islands, and possibly to Brazil

5. **Aram**
   emigrated to **Ur** of Chaldees
   Uz - Syro-**Arabs**
   Syria
   Hul
   Gether
   Mash

SECTION III

HAM AND HIS SONS -

The Nation of Invention

His sons were: Cush, Mizraim, Phut, Canaan, (Genesis 10:6-20).

Ham's name is related to 'heat' and means 'dark'; thus he is the father of the dark-skinned division of the human race. Ham's genealogy is listed to the third generation, but Shem's to the fifth. The reason for listing any of the genealogies was in order to be able to follow the tribal divisions after the Dispersion, (Deuteronomy 32:8,9).

God gave Ham the first opportunity to rule the world, and he took his brother Shem captive through the enslavement of the Israelites in Egypt. The rest of the Japhetic line was still wandering around at the time of Ham's rule, and were all unsettled except for Madai who was established in Media.

The architectural achievements of the line of Ham often became objects of worship, (e.g. the temples, pyramids, etc.).

Today, some of the Hamitic tribes who live in deepest Africa demonstrate the moral and intellectual degradation of the man who has no knowledge of the true God, and many of the descendants of Ham ruled (and rule) in darkness and in the power of darkness. Paganism has been an integral part of the religion of Ham and his descendants. This they exhibited clearly in Babylon, Nineveh, Canaan, etc.

Shortly after the Flood, Ham separated physically from his brothers because of the confusion of languages, but he had been separated from them spiritually for some time.

The cause of this spiritual separation is not given. There are only intimations of his carnal nature which give some indication of the road he had chosen.

Even in the best of families every individual must make his own choice and it is not always the choice his parents hoped for.

Though this man believed God and was saved from the destruction of the Flood, he later chose to follow his own way and leave God out of his life. The words of Ephesians 4:17-19, seem to describe the life of Ham: *This I say therefore, and testify in the Lord, that ye henceforth walk not as other Gentiles walk, in the vanity of their mind,* [the moral depravity of thought, feeling, will], *Having the understanding darkened, being alienated from the life of God through the ignorance that is in them, because of the blindness,* [the unwillingness to see], *of their heart. Who being past feeling have given themselves over unto lasciviousness,* [wickedness], *to work all uncleanness with greediness.*

Evidently Ham chose to follow the 'vanity of his own mind', always a dangerous choice, and gave himself over to sin.

His brightest epoch was in Egypt, and though very advanced both culturally, and economically, he was spiritually bankrupt. The literature dating from this period is mostly connected with paganism, but there are glimpses of morality and a longing for a belief in a higher Being.

THE SONS OF HAM:

CUSH - Babylonia, Ethiopia, Egypt, Arabia, Africa.

His sons: Seba, Havilah, Sabtah, Raamah, Sabtecha, Nimrod, (Genesis 10:7,8).

The first city built by Cush was probably called Seba or Saba, from the name of his eldest son.

Several of his sons crossed into the Arabian peninsula, and established settlements as far east as Raamah and Dedan on the Persian Gulf, and eventually crossed the Red Sea into the area known as Abyssinia or Ethiopia. Both Sheba and Dedan were in the eastern part of the Arabian desert near the Persian Gulf. When they moved west and north they intermarried with the tribes of the descendants of Joktan, a Shemite, and with those of Abraham from his six sons by Keturah, and possibly with some of the descendants of Ishmael.

The first people who moved into Northern Nubia were probably Egyptian, but other sons of Ham quickly displaced them. They were more like the black nations of today. They were from Cush as shown by their color and their facial features of thicker lips and woolly, kinky hair. Many of the hieroglyphics from Egypt picture this nation of people, some of whom became their priests and their kings. The Cushite black was mixed with the fellaheen (peasants) of Egypt from the beginning, and somewhat with the Semitic Arabs from the coast of the Arabian desert. The Semitic Arabs were at times the rulers of Ethiopia. The native population served them in various capacities. They attained high official prominence in the Shemite government, but the people were mostly uninterested in governmental positions, preferring to live their life in a more nomadic manner.

The Abyssinians were from the Semitic Arabs and were described thus, 'well formed and handsome, with straight and regular features, lively eyes, hair long and straight or somewhat curled and in color dark olive approaching brown'. They were mixed with the people of Sheba (the Sabaeans), who were descendants of Shem.

The Bible says it was the 'queen of Sheba' who went to see Solomon and seek his wisdom. This has been seen to be true in the past few years as Sabaean inscriptions found in Abyssinia which go back for 2,600 years, refer to her as 'a queen of Ethiopia', which would have been consistent if she were a Sabaean who ruled over the country of Ethiopia.

There are two great African kingdoms after Egypt: Ethiopia and Abyssinia.

Ethiopia vanished from world-view for many centuries after the conversion of the Ethiopian eunuch.

Abyssinia grew under the Cushite Arabs, (who came later than the Semitic Arabs), descended from Seba and Dedan. They were a mixed people with a mixed speech, among them the Amaara, remnants of the first Cushites.

The Cushites built famous and wealthy cities. They were a warlike people who made many alliances with Egypt. Many times the Ethiopian king also became the king of Egypt. They worshipped Ammon and his kindred deities.

The name Cush means *burnt-one* or *blackened*, and the inhabitants of Ethiopia were colored men, mostly black.

Their migration took place from Ethiopia down the Southeastern coast of Africa. The further south the people traveled the more degraded in ideas and morals they became. They eventually lost their culture and architectural genius, and became wandering tribes.

All the tribes of Africa are descendants of three or four great families. The most northerly have a small amount of Hamitic blood, (because of intermarriage), being of Syro-Arabian stock. The true descendants of Ham are the Galla family and their related tribes, to the east and south of Abyssinia. The next family is in South Africa, from the equator to the Southern tropics. Another line of families is in Sudan, Guinea, and Senegambia. There is a fourth family around the Cape of Good Hope and the Orange River. (Wright, *Bricks*), p. 72.

There are in North and South America areas of black natives; the Charruas or Guavans of Brazil, the Jamessi in Florida, the Black Carribees of St. Vincent, and some on the Isthmus of Darien in Panama. Many South American carvings depict Negroid faces. (Ibid.), p. 73.

Religious beliefs

All nations of Africa retain traces of the early religious faith learned before the confusion of languages. Only the sons of Japheth would sink so low as to deny the existence of God.

They acknowledge one great God who dwells beyond the sky; they believe in a malicious evil deity, capable of harming them, who must be appeased by offerings. They believe in the immortality of the soul and two states after death. They believe in charms, spells, witchcraft, and astrology, as do all false religions.

Most African tribes believe themselves, and all created things, to be the handiwork of the good God to whom they pray. They believe their troubles come from the evil being to whom they sacrifice. Some have the tradition of an evil Serpent, others of the Son of their Great God, who is their friend and Mediator with his Father.

Over a 4000 year period the sons of Cush have been wandering over the plains and mountains of Africa. They were divided into many tribes with many dialects, but their speech had degenerated. Because they rejected the teaching of God, they came to have fewer and fewer noble ideas and ideals and needed fewer words to express their thoughts.

THE SON OF CUSH, NIMROD: The Mighty Hunter, (Genesis 10:8-12)

The most famous, or infamous, son of Cush was Nimrod, founder of the first great world empire - the Assyrian Empire, (Assyro-Babylonian Empire).

Genesis 10:8, *And Cush begat Nimrod: he began to be a mighty one in the earth.* The name Nimrod means "let us rebel!" Nimrod's whole life was spent in fomenting rebellion against God and His purpose for man.

...he began to be a mighty one in the earth. Those who had lived before him had been content to be on the same level as their neighbors. Each one ruled his own house, but did not concentrate his energies in trying to rule others. Nimrod was determined to be raised above his neighbors and rule over them or 'lord it over them.' He reinstituted and embodied the spirit of those who lived before the Flood, (Genesis 6:4), who were also determined to be supreme rulers. His spirit was so fed with ambition and pride that it seemed impossible to satisfy it.

He was a mighty hunter before the Lord.... (verse 9).

"The simple meaning of this statement is that Nimrod was the exact opposite of the divine ideal of a king - that of a shepherd (cf. II Samuel 5:2; 7:7). Whereas a hunter gratifies himself at the expense of his victim, the shepherd expends himself for the good of the subjects of his care." Merrill F. Unger, *Unger's Bible Dictionary*, (Chicago: Moody Press, 1957), pp. 794,795.

Under the pretense of hunting, he gathered men under his command and trained them as warriors. He then 'violently invaded his neighbor's rights and property' and persecuted innocent men until, by force, he became their ruler. Matthew Henry says he thought himself a mighty prince because of his power, but to the Lord he was just 'a mighty hunter'. God's estimation of usurped power is not the same as man's. Nimrod's plan was to establish a centralized government with himself as the head so he could control the movements of every individual, which is the goal of all centralized governments.

Babylon

And the beginning of his kingdom was

Babel...., (verse 10). Either by force or by making himself indispensable to the people as a protector, he became a sovereign ruler. (Though he had no blood claim to rulership, nor had he been anointed by God to rule.) When the surrounding nations saw this king in power, they would, for protection and prestige, have instituted their own kings. In I Samuel 8:5 the Israelites also demanded a king 'like all the nations' and began what became known historically as the 'divine right of kings'. This philosophy of government caused trouble from that time until the institution of the Constitution of the United States which brought about the end of man's "right" to rule over man, and protected it by law.

Nimrod's name signifies 'rebellion'. He tried to defy God Himself; *'Tyrants to men are rebels to God'*, (e.g. the former Soviet Union). He instituted Totalitarianism as a governmental philosophy, and formed the first Imperialistic Empire. This fact alone serves to introduce him into the genealogy of the tribes.

Nimrod entered the land of Shinar *'being made strong'*, or when he had been made strong, (Asshur), and built cities, (Genesis 10:10). These were: Erech, Accad, Calneh, and Babel in the land of Shinar, (Babylonia). (Erech [Uruk] is one hundred miles southeast of Babylon. Accad was just north of Babylon and gave its name to the Akkadian empire [or the Sumerian empire]. In Daniel 1:1 the area is identified as Babylonia.) Babel or Babylon was the capital. Hislop says verse 11 of Genesis 10 is usually misunderstood, in that Asshur is said to be Assur the son of Shem, and so states Rollin, and the Assyrians became the masters of it during the Assyrian Empire. (Hislop, *Two Babylons*), and (Rollin, *Ancient History*.)

Assyrian Cylinder, with Fish-God.
(Ragozin, Assyria)

However, the Chaldean word signifies "to make strong" and should be interpreted, "He, (Nimrod), having been made strong (Asshur) went forth and builded Nineveh." This seems to be the most logical explanation since it was Nimrod who built Nineveh, (Micah 5:6). Nineveh means "the habitation of Ninus" another name for Nimrod, as Ninus or "Son" is clearly identified in history as Nimrod. The Assyrian legends speak of "Ninus" as the founder of Nineveh. (The ruins of Nineveh are today called Nimroud.)

In Assyria he also built Rehoboth, Resen, and Calah. (Resen was said to be between Nineveh and Calah, so that the entire complex of cities was called 'a great city', that is, a large metropolitan area. It took three days journey by horse to cover all the complex.) Erech, one of the cities of Nimrod, was one of the chief centers of the worship of Ishtar; prostitution was compulsory in that city. The symbol of Nineveh was a pregnant woman with a fish in the womb who represented the goddess of the fish-god Ea or Dagon.

Clay Images of Ishtar
(Rawlinson, Vol. I)

Accad, another city of Nimrod, was a library center. Sargon I was from that city.

The book of Jonah gives some indication of the paganistic roots of Nineveh. The people were so wicked that Jonah refused to go there, preferring rather that they all perish for their sins. His attitude seems to have been, "Good enough for them, let them all die!"

Nineveh was situated on the upper Tigris River, roughly two hundred miles north of Babylon and later was the capital of the great Assyrian empire. Nimrod built Nineveh and desired to make it the largest and noblest city in the world so that no city built after it would ever equal it. Jonah 3:3 describes it as 'an exceeding great city of three days journey. It was 18 3/4 miles in length, 11 1/4 miles in breadth, with a circumference of 60 miles. The walls were 100 feet high and so thick that three chariots could go upon them side by side with ease. It was fortified and adorned with 1500 towers, 200 feet high. Emma Willard, *Ancient Geography*, (Hartford: Wm. Jas. Hamersley, 1852), p. 34.

In a 17 year span Nimrod conquered a vast area from Egypt to India and Bactriana. He first entered Shinar and then went to Assyria, (Micah 5:6). The Assyrians looked to Babylon as their original home and as the center of their worship. Their form of writing was also taken from Babylon. (Babylon was built 115 years after the Flood, Genesis 10).

Nimrod built great cities to make himself greater and to feed his pride, but the end of his kingdom is foretold in Revelation 18, during the Tribulation period.

Nimrod realized the need for unification through religious worship. (cf. I Kings 12:26-33). This unification then took form in the Tower of Babel. The tower was not designed to 'reach' heaven in a physical sense, but to be the center for worship of the heavenly bodies which would embrace astrology in all its demonic forms. From this rebellious beginning came the Babylonian mystery religion which would later be carried into the emerging nations in all its corrupted forms.

In Babylon, the worship of Baal, and the worship of the moon first began. The people were a mixed nation, but it was a learned nation, "a head of gold."

They excelled in agriculture, war, and the arts and sciences which were led by the Chaldean Magi. They had legends about the beginning of the world and the Flood, though they only concerned their own nation. They began as monotheists - the worship of one God, but soon added many other gods.

Willard describes the city of Babylon: "Babylon was long the most celebrated city of the world. The walls built of large bricks, cemented by bitumen, were 350 feet high, 87 feet thick, and 60 miles in circumference. The form of the city was a square, its sides subtending the four cardinal points. The towers on the walls were only 250 in number, several places being surrounded by marshes, and therefore sufficiently secure without towers. There were 100 gates - 25 on each side, all of solid brass. From these ran straight streets intersecting one another, and dividing the city into squares. Around these squares stood the houses, separated by certain intervals, and three or four stories high. The space in the middle of each square was generally laid out in gardens, but pasture grounds for cattle were reserved. In the centre of the city stood the Temple of Belus, a massy square edifice, half a mile in extent every way. The river Euphrates flowed through it, and over this river was a bridge more than half a mile in length. At the end of the bridge were two palaces that communicated with each other by a vault built under the channel of the river. Before the bridge and vault could be built, a lake 37 miles square and 35 feet deep, was dug to receive its waters. After this was completed, the river was again permitted to flow in its ancient channel." (Willard, *Ancient Geography*), p. 33.

"The hanging gardens were works scarcely less stupendous. They are said to have contained a square extending 400 feet on each side. They consisted of terraces rising one above another, like the seats of a theatre, and carried up to the height of the walls of the city. These terraces were supported on arches, and were watered from the Euphrates by means of engines. Large trees grew upon them, and they had, at a distance, the appearance of a woody mountain, intermixed with the most beautiful flowers and plants of all kinds." William Channing Woodbridge, and Emma Willard, *Universal Geography,* (Hartford: Wm. Jas. Hamersley, 1852), pp. 33,34.

The basis of Classical Mythology finds its roots in the Chaldean religious system. The Greeks received the foundations of their religious ideas at Babylon.

Nimrod began post-diluvian idolatry and Babel was the mother of harlots. Historically Bel-Cush, (Genesis 10:8), (meaning the son of Cush, or Nimrod), as well as Cush himself was preeminent in leading mankind into apostasy.

Cush, as son of Ham, was known as Hermes or Mercury. Hermes is the Egyptian synonym for "the son of Ham". *Her* - in Chaldean is synonymous with Ham or Khem "the burnt one." Ham was deified as the "Sun". *Mes* signified the "son of" or Hermes - the son of Ham, or Chus (Cush). "For many ages men lived under the government of Jove (Hebrew Jehovah) without cities and without laws, and all speaking one language. But after that Mercury interpreted the speeches of men (whence an interpreter is called Hermeneutes - from Hermes), the same individual distributed the nations. Then discord began." Alexander Hislop, *The Two Babylons*, (New Jersey: Loizeaux Brothers, 1959), p. 26. In other words he caused the languages to be divided and the people to be scattered through his idolatrous leadership. He was called Nebo by the Babylonians and was said to have led the movement at the Tower of Babel and caused the division of tongues.

Bel was the name of Cush in Chaldean and meant the *Confounder,* and as the father of Nimrod, and Ninus, (Jeremiah 50:2), "Bel is confounded"; the Confounder is brought to Confusion. In pagan antiquity he was called Chaos, the god of Confusion, equivalent to Chus or Chush, Khûs or Khus pronounced

Khawas or Khaos. He was first given the name Merodach as Bel which means: merod - "to rebel", dakh - 'that' or 'the great'. His name also meant "to break in pieces, or scatter abroad." He broke apart the previously united earth. His symbol was a club which breaks in pieces, (Jeremiah 50:23).

To conquer a people is bad, but that which followed was much worse. Nimrod instituted idolatry to confirm his usurped empire and for this reason constructed the Tower of Babel, and there began the most terrible wickedness and idolatry in the history of the world. That idolatry became the scourge of the earth and continues today. The people deified him as a god; his name is synonymous with Baal. They offered sacrifices to him and gave him all the honor God had reserved for Himself alone. He was called the Horned or Mighty One, Kronos or Saturn, 'the Father of the gods'.

The Tower of Babel

The Tower of Babel was a symbol of rebellion against God, which sought to destroy individuality, and denied the diversity of the individual. It was built to make a name, manifesting human pride and ambition. It was also to keep the people from scattering in defiance of God's command to 'people' the earth. But most importantly it was to defy God's government of, and designs for, man, and effect a world empire.

It was built to replace and usurp God's authority over man with another man's authority, and was a beginning of "future mischief". Genesis 11:6, *...and this they begin to do: and now nothing will be restrained from them which they have imagined to do.*

This was another attempt by man to try to make his own way to heaven. Though God had given him the instructions, he was not willing to follow them. Man always thinks he has a better way, (Genesis 11), and it always fails.

The Tower was one of the results of the work of Cush and Nimrod. As before stated one of the names of Cush was 'the Confounder' and by his influence all the world was confused. Nimrod wanted to be a universal monarch with all peoples under his control, and to accomplish this he wanted everyone in one place where he could keep watch over them. It is God's exclusive privilege to be the universal Monarch, Lord of Lord, and King of Kings and He will permit no one to take that honor from Him.

The Temple of Belus

The Tower was actually a monument to the heavenly bodies. The seven stages of the ziggurat were each dedicated to a different wandering star (planet) and in the uppermost part the constellations were painted on the ceiling. Here began the study of astrology and the worship of the host of heaven.

It was half a mile in circumference, and one-half mile high. It had eight towers, one above the other, decreasing gradually at the top, called a pyramid by the ancient historians, and was much higher than the greatest pyramids of Egypt in height. Its construction was of bitumen and bricks; believed to be the same tower as the Tower of Babel.

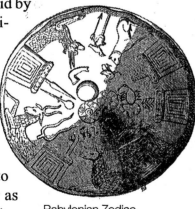

Babylonian Zodiac
(Rawlinson, Vol. 2)

It is described as having stairs on the outside, in a spiral ascending line eight times around. There were large rooms, and arched roofs supported by pillars. The top of the tower was an observatory, and the Babylonians became more expert in astronomy than all other nations. The main use of the tower was the worship of the god Belus,

or Baal (Nimrod) and several other lesser deities, and because of this there were a multitude of chapels in different parts of the tower. All statues, tables, censers, cups and other sa-

Restoration of a Ziggurat.
(Ragozin, Chaldea)

cred vessels were of gold. One statue was 40 feet high and weighed 1000 Babylonish talents of gold. The combined riches in the temple equaled 6300 Babylonish talents of gold, on today's market worth more than $441,000,000, (which the Persians took).

"According to Strabo the tower was a stade (606 feet 9 inches) in height; but this estimate, if it is anything more than a conjecture, must represent rather the length of the winding ascent than the real altitude of the building...About half-way up the ascent was a resting-place with seats, where persons commonly sat a while on their way to the summit. The shrine which crowned the edifice was large and rich. In the time of Herodotus it contained no image; but only a golden table and a large couch, covered with a handsome drapery. ...Previously, if we may believe Diodorus, the shrine was occupied by three colossal images of gold - one of Bel, one of Beltis, and the third of Rhea or Ishtar. Before the image of Beltis were two golden lions, and near them two enormous serpents of silver, each thirty-talents in weight. The golden table—forty feet long and fifteen broad—was in front of these statues, and upon it stood two huge drinking-cups, of the same weight as the serpents. The shrine also contained two enormous censers and three golden bowls, one for each of the three deities." George Rawlinson, M.A., *The Seven Great Monarchies of the Ancient Eastern World,* Vol. II, (New York: A. L. Burt Company, 1875). pp. 174,175.

The temple was destroyed by Xerxes after having plundered it of its treasures.

Alexander purposed to have it rebuilt on his return from India, and put 10,000 men to work on it to clear away the rubble, but he died two months later and the work was never completed.

Confusion of Languages

God confused the languages and scattered the people because of their rebellion against Him. Nimrod was the leader in the endeavor, but no people can be enslaved against their own will. They gave their consent, either overtly or tacitly, for him to be their leader. It is always a matter of choice how we will be governed.

Men were divided into language groups. Where men had planned a permanent center of the race, God caused the parting-place of nations.

There are three great language divisions: Aryan or Japhetic, Semitic, and Hamitic. God predetermined the regions to be inhabited by each one, Acts 17:26, 27, *And He has made from one blood every nation of men to dwell on all the face of the earth, and has determined their preappointed times and the boundaries of their habitation, (27) so that they should seek the Lord, in the hope that they might grope for Him and find Him, though He is not far*

from each one of us. (N.K.J.V.) In this verse is also seen God's purpose in locating the nations around Israel - that they might have knowledge of Him.

The confounding of language was a sign of the confusion of man's heart. The significance of the confusion is seen in the direction each tribe took in leaving the plain of Shinar. God had already placed in man the necessary gene-code to develop all the different characteristics of all the nations of the world. All they needed was to be physically isolated by high mountains, streams and lakes, and through intermarriage those genes would surface and form a people of almond-shaped eyes, or slanted eyes or round eyes, etc. The color was also pre-programmed as were all the particular facial features for each tribal group. The language also formed the basis of their culture and had an impact on their understanding of religious thought.

(See section on Distinct Characteristics, and Assyrian Empire for the remainder of the information on Nimrod.)

Semiramis: The beginning of the mother-child religion

Semiramis was a Syrian princess who was taken from her husband (who then committed suicide), and given to Nimrod as his wife.

Semiramis
(Hislop, Two Babylons)

After the death of Nimrod, Semiramis continued with his empire, but added more to its idolatry. She was deified as the 'goddess of fortification', and called Rhea. She was worshipped at Ephesus as Diana with a tower as a crown. She had Nimrod worshipped as 'Zero-ashta' - the woman's promised seed. He was presented as having died voluntarily for the good of mankind, and to have 'bruised the serpent's head', but as having died because his own heel was bruised. (Zoroaster was the first to invent magic arts and study the motions of heavenly bodies, this came from the Zodiac because of its association with astrology.)

She began the religion of "Mother and Child" which is practiced today in the Roman Catholic system. She told her subjects that by a miracle her husband had been born again as her child and her husband at the same time. This child's name was Ninus, a name synonymous with Nimrod, and Adonis, Zoroaster, etc. She was represented with a child in her arms, an image that can be seen in any Roman Catholic temple today.

She was called the Mother-goddess, and at the beginning of the religion in Assyria, she received her glory from the child in her arms. In the Scripture he is called Tammuz, (Ezekiel 8:14), and among classical writers he is called Bacchus, the Lamented One. "Though represented as a child in his mother's arms, he was a person of great stature and immense bodily powers, as well as one of most fascinating manners... To the ordinary reader the name of Bacchus suggests nothing more than revelry and drunkenness, but it is now well known, that amid all the abominations that attended his orgies, their grand design was professedly 'the purification of souls', and that from them the guilt and defilement of sin. This lamented one, exhibited and adored as a little child in his mother's arms, seems, in point of fact, to have been the *husband* of Semiramis, whose name Ninus, by which

An Egyptian goddess piercing the serpent's head.
(Two Babylons, Hislop)

he is commonly known in classical history, literally signified 'The Son'.

"As Semiramis, the wife, she was worshipped as Rhea, whose grand distinguishing character was that of the great goddess 'Mother', in conjunction with her husband...." (Hislop, *Two Babylons)*, pp. 21,22.

Soon she became more the object of worship than her son-husband. She was always presented in beautiful attire and said to be the embodiment of everything beautiful in the female. She was raised to a position of divinity in order to justify this worship and <u>she</u> was to bruise the serpent's head, herself. She is represented as the goddess Diana in Greece carrying a serpent without a head. (See the painting *The Immaculate Conception* by Tiepolo in the collection of the Prado Museum in Madrid, Spain.)

She was called 'the hope of the whole world' and the 'Alma Mater' or the Virgin Mother, both Hebrew terms which would have been carried to Babylon during the Jewish captivity and bestowed upon her as a new title. However, the Roman Catholic name of 'Virgin' does not mean the same thing we understand by the term. It means she was a virgin, and is a perpetual virgin, contrary to the Scriptural teaching about her that other children were born to her after the birth of Christ, (Matthew 13:55; Acts 1:14). She was called the 'Queen of Heaven', 'the Habitation of God' and on one of her temples in Egypt was this inscription:

"I am all that has been, or that is, or that shall be. No mortal has removed my veil. The fruit which I have brought forth is the Sun."

She was represented as a dove with an olive branch, identifying her with the "spirit of all grace," and was adored as the incarnation of the Holy Spirit. To her were attributed all the qualities of tenderness and mercy, and when she died, the legend says, she was changed into a dove, and as such was adored

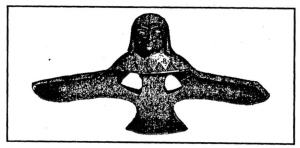

Semiramis changed into a dove. (Bronze ornament bent to fit the shape of a drinking cup and serve as a handle.)

(Ragozin, Assyria)

by the Babylonians. She was taking the place of the Holy Spirit who is represented as a dove. The Assyrians and the Africans use the word

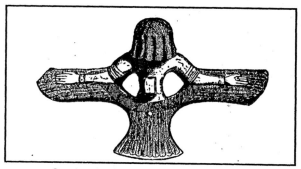

Semiramis changed into a dove. (back view)

(Ragozin, Assyria)

'wind' to describe the Holy Spirit and the Chaldean word for 'air' indicates the Holy Spirit. But Semiramis was adored as the incarnation of the Holy Spirit, the spirit of peace and love. This worship was universal, as she was worshipped as the mother of the gods by the Persians, the Syrians, and the kings of Europe and Asia. The Jews, as noted in Jeremiah 44:16-19, continued to worship her, though God chastised them for following this religion.

Mother and child from India

(Hislop, Two Babylons)

From Babylon this religion spread to the ends of the earth. In Egypt she was worshipped as Isis, her husband/son was Osiris (Horus) who was transformed into a young bull or calf with the name Apis. This symbol was the pattern used for the golden calf of the Israelites.

Osiris, her son/husband, was the dying god who resurrected, and was a picture of the coming Messiah who would die to take away the sin of the world and would rise from the dead with the promise of eternal life in him. Though the Egyptians did not understand this concept Satan did, and tried to pass off Osiris as the savior.

Mother and Child from Babylon

(Rawlinson, Vol. 2)

The mother and son were called different names in different places, for example: in Phrygia: Cybele, and Adonis; and among the Hittites: Kubaby and Attis, who were represented by a sculptured lion over the door. The fertility goddess was symbolized by triumph of life over death - the hope of everlasting life. She was called the Mother of the gods by the Greeks whose name was Aphrodite or Venus.

They were worshipped as Ator 'the habitation of God', the greatest and most powerful of all the divinities. In India they were Isi and Iswars; in Asia, Cybele and Deoius; in pagan Rome as Fortuna and Jupiter puer or Jupiter, the boy, and as Venus and more anciently as Astarte. They were worshipped in Greece as Ceres, the Great Mother with a babe at her breast or as Irene, the goddess of peace, with the boy Plutus in her arms and as Aphrodite. In Tibet, China and Japan, the Jesuit missionaries found a mother-child counterpart of the Madonna and Child called Shing Moo or Holy Mother with the child in her arms, and with "glory" around her. She was also called Virgo, or the Virgin Mother.

The Babylonian word was Beltis, which in English means "My Lady", and in Latin, "Mea Domina". In Italian the word is corrupted to "Madonna" leaving the child out of the name. The goddess Mother, and the Son as a helpless infant or dead on a cross, have become the objects of worship. (Hislop, *Two Babylons*), p. 20.

After paganism began to extend, instead of being destroyed, the name of the goddess was changed to the Virgin Mary and the three persons of the Trinity were purported to be; God the Father, the Virgin Mary, and their Son, Messiah. This renaming took place at the Council of Nicea, 325 A.D. by the Roman Catholic hierarchy. The mariolatry practiced in the Roman Catholic system has its origins in Babylon - not in the Bible. She is called the "Queen of Heaven", in Jeremiah 7:18; 44:17-19, and Israel is rebuked sternly for following after her. Today we see a resurgence of this Mother-goddess religion in the New Age movement. Nothing has changed in the pagan religion, it just has a new following under a different name.

In this paganism the divinity of Christ is based upon the divinity of His mother. The Virgin Mary is called 'the consecrated house of God,' 'the mansion of God', 'the tabernacle of the Holy Spirit', and the 'temple of the Trinity'. (Ibid.), pp. 21-64.

There is also a circle or halo over the head of the Virgin which comes directly from Babylon through Zoroastrianism which

Goddess of Fortification.
(Hislop, Two Babylons)

holds the circle or 'zero' as the symbol of the 'seed'. This symbol came originally from the Chaldeans who worshipped as the Zoroastrians. There is nothing similar in the Scriptures. Christ is never described with a crown of light surrounding His head, so He cannot be the source of this custom. But in the gods of Babylon, especially the gods of the sun, is found the halo which surrounds Mary's head.

It is evident that the same goddess who receives all this glory and honor is the same queen of Babylon who tried to pass off her son as the replacement for Jesus Christ. In Babylon he had the peculiar name Zoroaster meaning 'the seed of the woman', but from the Scriptures we know that Christ was the only seed of a woman without an earthly father. This is just another of Satan's counterfeits. Since before the Garden of Eden, Satan has tried to fool the world as to the promised Messiah and this religion is the fulfillment of his project. He has fooled more people, sending them to hell, through this means than by any other method. It has been a vicious plan against humanity and it is obvious that this religion has its roots in the most vile paganism in the world.

The history of the Roman "Church" took the place of ancient paganism and though paganism 'died outside of her' it appeared 'inside of her'. Gibbon says: "As soon as the doors of the church were thrown open, they [the Christians] must have been offended by the smoke of incense, the perfume of flowers, and the glare of lamps and tapers, which diffused, at noonday, a gaudy, superfluous, and, in their opinion, a sacrilegious light. If they approached the balustrade of the altar, they made their way through the prostrate crowd, consisting, for the most part, of strangers and pilgrims, who resorted to the city on the vigil of the feast; and who already felt the strong intoxication of fanaticism...Their devout kisses were imprinted on the walls and pavement of the sacred edifice; and their fervent prayers were directed, whatever might be the language of the church, to the bones, the blood, or the ashes of the saint, which were usually concealed, by a linen or silken veil, from the eyes of the vulgar...The same uniform original spirit of superstition might suggest, in the most distant ages and countries the same methods of deceiving the credulity, and of affecting the senses of mankind: but it must ingenuously be confessed that **the ministers of the catholic church imitated the profane model which they were impatient to destroy** [emphasis mine]." Edward Gibbon, *The History of the Decline and Fall of the Roman Empire*, Vol. III, (London: The Folio Society, 1985), p. 355. In other words, everything found in a pagan temple was transferred to the temples of the Catholic system. Called by any other name it was still a pagan temple with all its rites and practices.

Since the time of the first Pontificate Maximus the Roman system has presented its paganistic worship as the worship of Christ, though the rites, pomp and ceremonies have all come directly from ancient Babylon. Daniel 11:36-39 seems to indicate that the papacy is fulfilling and will fulfill the prophecy of Daniel referring especially to the end times, which says, *And the king shall do according to his will; and he shall exalt himself and magnify himself above every god, and shall speak marvelous things against the God of gods, and shall prosper till the indignation be accomplished: for that that is determined shall be done. Neither shall he regard the God of his fathers, nor the desire of women, nor regard any god: for he shall magnify himself above all. But in his estate shall he honor the God of forces: and a god whom his fathers knew not shall he honour with precious stones, and pleasant things . Thus shall he do in the most strong holds with a strange god, whom he shall acknowledge and increase with glory: and he shall cause them to rule over many, and shall divide the land for gain.*

Many scholars believe this refers to the Roman Catholic system, and that is certainly a distinct possibility, but it can also refer to the Mohammedan religion which is sweeping the world in its most militant form. When many of the commentaries were written the influence of this religion had not made itself felt as yet on the world scene, but no one can deny that this text can as well refer to Mohammedanism as to Roman Catholicism. There has never been a religion that abhors women and treats them the way these men do. The 'god of forces' is certainly honored in Jihad, their 'holy war' against anyone not professing their faith. The 'God of their fathers' would be the God of Abraham and they certainly do not honor Him, believing their god, Mohammed to be the supreme god above all others. Only God knows to whom this prophecy refers, but further study needs to be made before making a blanket statement in reference to one religion or another.

At the end of the fourth century, as today, the pope was the only representative of Nimrod on the earth and the pagans have accepted him as such. He also became the legitimate successor of the Roman 'dragon of fire'.

Figure of Nin, The Fish God
(Rawlinson, Vol. I)

When he was given the title of Pontificate he began to propagate the doctrine of Babylon of baptismal regeneration. He, and those who cooperated with him, prepared the way for the civil and spiritual tyranny which took place in Europe in 606 A.D. when the pope of Rome was made the universal bishop. At that time also the ten European empires recognized him as the vicar of Christ in the earth, the only center of unity and the basis of the stability of their thrones. The power of the pope, at that time, cannot be denied, because it is an historical fact. This does not, however, settle the question of the future prophecy. The pope became the representative of the fish-god, Dagon, and today wears the mitre of Dagon. (Hislop, *Two Babylons*), p. 215.

Governmentally, Nimrod usurped God's authority with his own, and then Semiramis carried this same usurpation to a blasphemous degree. When man refuses to be governed by God, Satan will always impose his own rebellious authority over him. Any individual or nation which rebels against God or His principles as manifested in His Word, takes his stand with Satan, and becomes in essence another Nimrod. All of this comes from the line of Ham and reveals both his character and that of his descendants.

Babylonian Religious Myths

Their myths were borrowed from the Sumerians whom they displaced.

The Babylonian "Poem of Creation" was a blending of cosmological themes of the Occidental Shemites and Sumerian myths. All Semitic myths formed an integral part of a specific ritual.

Their particular gods:
- Marduk - the head of the Babylonian pantheon
- Nippur - center of the cult of Enlil
- Ur-Sin - the moon-god
- Uruk - Anu - the god of the sky
- Tiamat - the goddess of the sky and earth

Their Story of Creation:

The goddess Tiamat was conquered by the demiurge, Apsu, (the creator of the material world), and her body was given to be used for the sky and the earth.

The waters contained the seeds of life and brought into existence the divine couples (or divine generations) with eons of time between. Each was more powerful than the last until the birth of *Anu* (sky-god), then *EA* (Enki-Ea who ruled the primeval abyss), whose wife *Damkina* appeared later.

Tiamat and Apsu were disturbed by the noise of other gods and determined to destroy them by a Flood.

Tiamat was reluctant to destroy her offspring (the sky and earth) so Ea 'poured sleep' over Apsu, bound him in chains and killed him. He bound Mummu (the advisor of Apsu) and put him in the apsu (abyss). Ea and Damkina, his wife, still live there in majesty.

In the deep waters of apsu *Marduk* was born. Anu (the sky-god) made the winds rise and created waves and disturbed Tiamat so she prepared a fresh attack on the younger gods.

Tiamat, the Abyss-Mother, chose one of her firstborn gods, *Kingu*, and he became her husband, (i.e. Semiramis and Ninus). Her husband then led the 'forces of chaos' into battle against the champion of the gods, the demiurge.

Tiamat created monsters to aid her, and Ea and Anu were instructed to confront the monsters but refused, so Marduk was instructed (by the gods) to defend them. He did so on the condition that he be given supreme power.

Marduk defeated Tiamat's army of demons and then bound and imprisoned them and took their leader, Kingu, captive. He was bound and put in the ranks of the dead gods.

He destroyed the body of Tiamat (sky and earth) and then created the world after having overcome the forces of chaos. (This seems to be part of the basis for the teachings of the Gap-Theory, showing that it is completely pagan in all its roots.)

The Creation of man:

The creation of man was attributed to Ea. The man was made from the blood of Kingu (husband of Tiamat), who was sacrificed to the gods.

"They bound him, holding him before Ea.
They imposed on him his guilt and severed his blood (vessels)
Out of his blood they fashioned mankind."
                              -Poem of Creation

Pierre Grimal, Editor, *Larousse World Mythology*, (New York: Prometheus Press, 1965), p. 68.

He (Marduk) then gave the gods their respective places in heaven and earth. The gods built him the great Esagila temple to show their gratitude.

Myth in ritual:

Marduk was symbolic of the cosmic order. The sun, by its warmth, dispersed the mists of the sea which are represented by Tiamat who symbolized the forces of spring.

The spring equinox marks the rebirth of the year in which the sun and winter have been at conflict. The conflict was symbolized by Tiamat and Marduk. The sea-monster symbol of chaos comes from the Semitic pantheon.

The Babylonian new year was the most solemn moment in their religious life.

Ulligarra and Zalgarra were created to serve the gods.

"The goddess they called...the Mother,
The most helpful of the goddesses, the wise Mami:
Thou art the Mother-womb,
The one who creates mankind...."
(Larousse, *Mythology*), p. 69.

The importance of the 'son' in the Babylonian system:

The emphasis on the 'son' came by means of the zodiac. The sun-god, was the heavenly original of earthly rule. The earthly king was put in place of the sun-god, the sun of Babylon or the sun of all peoples. The royal insignia and robes were decorated with celestial emblems, (the sun, moon, planets, zodiacal constellations, etc.). The sun became the symbol of political order.

The solar summodeism, (worship of the sun), was continued by Constantine. In the fourth century, the Roman Catholic system shifted the birthday of Christ, the "Sun of Justice", to December 25, in the pagan belief that this was the birthday of the sun; the day when it began to rise again. The calendar has retained the name Sunday (the day of the Lord) since the time of Constantine.

"...in all of these respects the sun-king assumed the character of a Soter, of a savior, of the herald of a new age, of a representative sufferer for the community who carried the burden of its sins and redeemed them, and incidentally redeemed himself in order to resume his unsullied kingship." Eric Voegelin, *Order and History*, Vol. I, (Louisiana State University: Vail-Ballon Press, Inc., 1956), p. 34.

The Future of Babylon

The Bible predicts a reborn Babylon and mentions it 280 times, while other references speak of the future city of Babylon. Isaiah 13:19, *And Babylon, the glory of kingdoms, the beauty of the Chaldees' excellency, shall be as when God overthrew Sodom and Gomorrah.* This has not happened yet. The city was conquered by the Medes and Persians and declined, but it was not destroyed by fire as were Sodom and Gomorrah.

Isaiah 13:16, *Their children also shall be dashed to pieces before their eyes; their houses shall be spoiled, and their wives ravished.* According to Dyer this destruction has to occur during the time of the Tribulation before the second coming of Christ.

Isaiah 14:1-4,7, verse 4, *That thou shalt take up this proverb against the king of Babylon, and say How hath the oppressor ceased! the golden city ceased!* When this destruction occurs Israel will be in a period of peace, (verse 3). Israel has had no peace since the Babylonian captivity and certainly not since being granted a homeland in 1948, though this was only a political move and did not in reality give them a homeland. They have been fighting ever since to secure what that declaration was supposed to have granted them.

Babylon was a 'house made for iniquity'. Zechariah 5:5-11, *Then the angel that talked with me went forth, and said unto me, Lift up now thine eyes, and see what is this that goeth forth. And I said, What is it? And he said, this is an ephah that goeth forth. He said moreover, This is their resemblance through all the earth. And, behold, there was lifted up a talent of lead: and this is a woman that sitteth in the midst of the ephah. And he said, This is wickedness. And he cast it into the midst of the ephah; and he cast the weight of lead upon the mouth thereof. Then lifted I up mine eyes, and looked, and, behold, there came out two women, and the wind was in their wings; for they had wings like the wings of a stork: and they lifted up the ephah between the earth and the heaven. Then said I to the angel that talked with me, Whither do these bear the ephah? And he said unto me, To build it an house in the land of Shinar: and it shall be established, and set there upon her own base.*

Zechariah saw a basket in the form of a barrel with a lid of lead on the basket. In the basket was the representation of all the wickedness in the world and this woman was the personification of all that wickedness. The lid of lead was put in place so that she, the wickedness, could not escape.

After the angel showed him this scene he cast the woman into the basket and shut the lid. This does not mean that God had taken evil out of the world, but that He had limited it so that it did not have the power to completely fill the earth.

The basket was carried by two women (representations of Assyria and Babylon according to most scholars), to the land of Babylon, the city of Babylon. The wickedness was deposited in the land where man had rebelled against God and where the rebel Nimrod had led men to build a tower whose 'top may reach to heaven'. Babylonia was the empire that burned the city of Jerusalem and constantly threatened the Promised Land.

The angel said that wickedness would reside again in Babylon. But, how? Zechariah had seen the land of Babylon fall to the Medes and Persians, could it rise again? Yes. The vision of Zechariah shows that Babylon will rise again when all 'is prepared'. The time is fast approaching when God will bring all these things to pass.

In all the centuries since its destruction Babylon has never been totally abandoned. It has continued to be a religious center and the adoration of Marduk and other Babylonian gods has continued there. The judgment of Babylon is still future. It must come 'in the day of the Lord', (Isaiah 13:6,9; Matthew 24:21,22; Isaiah 13:10,13). Many nations will come against Babylon, in Isaiah 13:4,5; Jeremiah 50:9, 41-42, those of the north come against her. The Medes will come against Babylon, (Jeremiah 51:11,28), and the Kurds from the northeast of Iran and the northeast of Iraq. The destruction will be swift and will be a destruction that cannot be healed, (Jeremiah 50:44; 51:8,9). Jeremiah 51:53-58 says the destruction will not come from a natural disaster but from battle.

When this occurs Babylon will never be inhabited again, like Sodom and Gomorrah, Isaiah 13:20, *It shall never be inhabited, nei-*

ther shall it be dwelt in from generation to generation: neither shall the Arabian pitch tent there; neither shall the shepherds make their fold there.

This prophecy was not fulfilled in 539 A.D. when Cyrus captured the city, (Jeremiah 50:15; 51:30). It will be totally desolate, (Jeremiah 51:43); not one brick will be used in other sites, (Jeremiah 51:26). Those who wish to save their lives should get away from Babylon, (Jeremiah 51:6).

The Historical Character of Babylon and her Character today

- The state is autocratic, and is an absolute dictatorship, (Daniel 5:19).

- Babylon rejected the true God when she had both spiritual light and opportunity, though God longed to save and spare her, (Jeremiah 51:9).

- The deification of man. The Babylonian kings demanded and received worship as gods, (Daniel 5:22,23).

- The claim that their chief god had the right to universal dominion, and the attempt to extend the sovereignty of this god territorially by military force, fed her lust for military conquest which was limitless, (Habakkuk 19; 2:5).

- The priestly hierarchy maintained their claim to superiority over the civil authority. This title to superiority was indicated by the fact that the king was crowned by the priest. Even an Assyrian emperor, when he became the king of Babylon, "took the hands" of the god Bel, and was crowned by his priest; thus acknowledging the supremacy of Bel, and his own dependence upon the god for his authority as king of Babylon.

- Its religious system was and is a persecuting religious system and sorcery plays a large part in the Babylonian religion and by it her evil purposes are accomplished, (Isaiah 47:9,12). It is a system which rejoices in cruelty and slaughter, (Habakkuk 1:14,15).

- It sought to achieve and to maintain the monopoly of the commerce of the world, as it does today through the sale of oil.

- Pride is the determining trait of Babylon and is based on her great wealth, luxury and ostentatious displays. The Word of God described their proud independence of God which was a trait of the Babylonian leaders when He said, *Their judgment and dignity shall proceed of themselves,* (Habakkuk 1:7), and *they shall scoff at the kings,* (Habakkuk 1:10). (Cf. Isaiah 13:11; Jeremiah 50:29,31.)

- There was social, moral and commercial corruption coupled with high intellectual achievements and culture, just as there is today.

- So great has been her indulgence in luxury and display and everything that the flesh desires that the commerce of the world will be impoverished by her fall, (Revelation 18:9).

- Babylon is not an exception. Babylon furnished an example of the principles by which God deals with nations. The nation which shares her sins will share her judgment.

THE KINGS OF BABYLON BEGINNING FROM THE LINE OF HAM:

At the fall of the Assyrian Empire three kingdoms were formed from the ruins:

- The Medes - which Arbaces restored to its liberty.

- The Assyrians of Babylon - given to Belesis, governor of the city.

- The Assyrians of Nineveh - the king took the name of Ninus the Younger.

The Second Babylonian Empire, both of Nineveh and Babylon, lasted 210 years to the edict of Cyrus, issued by his father-in-law, Cyaxares. The Jews were permitted to return to their own country after 70 years of captivity at Babylon.

Kings of Babylon

Nimrod (see previous notes in this section on Nimrod)

Hammurabi 1955-1913 B.C.

Hammurabi was one of the kings of the first dynasty of Babylon. He extended the territory of the Babylonian Empire by conquest. His administration was noted for its written law and the order it maintained. The law Code of Hammurabi was discovered in 1901. The laws of Hammurabi resembled those of Moses.

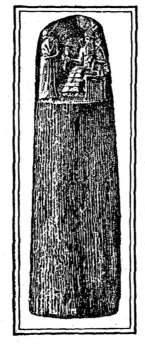

Monument of Hammurabi, a contemporary of Abraham.

(Ploubets, 1913)

Achievements of Hammurabi

"Hammurabi, the exalted King, the King of Babylon, the King renowned throughout the world, conqueror of the enemies of Marduk, the King beloved by his heart am I.

"The favor of god and Bel gave the people of Sumer and Accad unto my government, Their celestial weapons unto my hand they gave. The canal Hammurabi, the joy of men, a stream of abundant waters, for the people of Sumer and Accad I excavated its banks, all of them I restored to newness; new supporting walls I heaped up; perennial waters for the people of Sumer and Accad I provided.

"The people of Sumer and Accad, all of them, in general assemblies I summoned. A review and inspection of them I ordained every year. In joy and abundance I watched over them, and in peaceful habitations I caused them to dwell.

"By divine favor I am Hammurabi, the exalted King, the worshipper of the supreme deity.

"With prosperous power which Marduk gave me, I built a lofty citadel on a high mound of earth, whose summits rose up like mountains, on the bank of Hammurabi river, the joy of men."

Laws of Hammurabi

If a man bring a accusation against a man and charge him with a capital crime, but cannot prove it, he, the accuser, shall be put to death.

If a man in case (pending judgment) bear false witness, or do not establish the testimony he has given, if that case be a case involving life, that man shall be put to death.

If a man steal the property of a god or palace, that man shall be put to death; and he who received from his hand that stolen (property) shall also be put to death.

If a man aid a male or female slave of a freeman to escape from the city gate, he shall be put to death.

If a man practice brigandage and be captured, that man shall be put to death.

If the brigand be not captured, the man who has been robbed, shall in the presence of god make an itemized statement of his loss, and the city and the governor, in whose province and jurisdiction the robbery was committed, shall compensate him for whatever was lost.

If a son be too young and be not able to conduct the business of his father, they shall give one third of the field and of the garden to his mother, and his mother shall rear him.

A woman, merchant or other property holder, may sell field, garden or house. The purchaser shall conduct the business of the field, garden or house which he has purchased.

If outlaws collect in the house of a wine-seller, and she do not arrest these outlaws and bring them to the police, the wine-seller shall be put to death.

If a man be in debt and sell his wife, son or daughter, or bind them over to service, for three years they shall work in the house of their purchaser or master; in the fourth year they shall be given their freedom.

If a man take a wife and do not arrange with her the proper contracts, that woman is not a legal wife.

If a son strike his father, they shall cut off his fingers.

If a man destroy the eye of another man, they shall destroy his eye.

If one break a man's bone, they shall break his bone.

If one destroy the eyes of a man's slave or break a bone of a man's slave, he shall pay one half his price.

The laws of Hammurabi kept the land in order and followed the Scriptural mandates of the Jews. It was a government of laws, just laws which acted externally on the people, though internally their hearts were not changed. (From George Willis Botsford, *A Source Book of Ancient History*, New York: The Macmillan Co., 1912.)

Belesis - same as **Nabonassar,** 747 B.C.

Some famous astronomical epochs at Babylon were named for him. In scripture he is called *Baladan*.

He reigned 12 years, and was succeeded by his son, (2 Kings 20:12).

Merodach-baladan - a Chaldean, 721 B.C.

He sent ambassadors to King Hezekiah to congratulate him on the recovery of his health. He rebelled against Assyria and was taken prisoner by Tiglath-Pileser II, King of Assyria.

There were several kings afterward, but little information has been transmitted on them.

The Babylonians were replaced in 538 B.C. by the Persians under Darius. The Persians, under Cyrus the Great, allowed the Jews to return to their land and to rebuild their Temple, (Ezra 1:2-4, 6:3-5).

Middle Babylonian Period

Saosduchinus (669 B.C.) Called Nebuchadnezzar I, he began the Pashe Dynasty, and was contemporary with Sargon of Assyria.

His was a common name for the kings of Babylon and he was distinguished by the name Nebuchadnezzar I. The defeat of Nineveh was foretold by Tobit under his reign. It was to be destroyed because of its great wickedness.

Saracus (626 B.C.)

He succeeded Saosduchinus and was contemptible to the people, very effeminate, and took no care of his dominions. Nabopolassar took over Babylon from him and reigned over it 21 years.

Later Babylonian Empire 626-539

Nabopolassar (626-605 B.C.), was a Chaldean general in the Assyrian army. (2 Kings 24:1).

He made an alliance with Cyaxares, king of the Medes and together they blockaded and took Nineveh, in 612 B.C. They killed Saracus and destroyed the city, (Nahum 3:1-3; 2:1-4). Babylon then became the only capital of Assyria. The king of Egypt, Necho, became alarmed at their power and marched against them towards the Euphrates, taking Carchemish. Syria and Palestine then revolted, and because of his (Nabopolassar's) age and health, he could not recover them. He made his son his partner and sent him with an army to regain the territories. From this time the Jews began to reckon the years of Nebuchadnezzar; from the end of the third year of Jehoikim, king of Judah. He reigned 21 years. He received Babylon for helping the Medes in battle.

Nebuchadnezzar II (605-562 B.C.)

Under this king Babylon reached its greatest glory; he was the son of Nabopolassar. (Jeremiah 46:2; 2 Kings 24:7-25:30.) He married a princess from Media, named Amihia, and built the Hanging Gardens in Babylon for her.

Daniel was taken to Babylon during his reign, (Daniel 1:1-7). Jehoiakim, son of Josiah, became king under the Babylonian power.

Nebuchadnezzar defeated the army of Necho, king of Egypt, near the Euphrates and retook Carchemish. He then reunited Syria and Palestine. He entered Judea and took Jerusalem and put Jehoiakim in chains and was to send him to Babylon, but was moved by his repentance and restored him to the throne. Great numbers of Jews, including children of the royal family, were carried to Babylon, with all the treasures of the king's palace and part of the sacred vessels of the temple, (Daniel 1:1-7). This was God's judgment pronounced by Isaiah to King Hezekiah. The captivity of the Jews at Babylon is dated from this time, (the fourth year of Jehoiakim, king of Judah). Daniel, only 18 years old, was carried into cap-

tivity, (587-586 B.C.), and Ezekiel was taken some time afterward.

This king took possession of all the dominions of his father: Chaldea, Assyria, Arabia, Syria, and Palestine. He reigned 43 years and rebuilt Babylon to five times the size of London. The walls were 338 feet high, 85 feet thick, and studded with towers. The town was accessible through bronze gates. Its palaces and hanging gardens became one of the seven wonders of the ancient world.

Coin of Nebuchadnezzar
(Rawlinson, Vol.1)

In the fourth year of his reign he had a dream which terrified him, but which he could not remember, (Daniel 2:1). When the wise men and diviners couldn't tell him his dream, he became very angry and condemned them to death, including Daniel and his three companions. Daniel prayed to God first, then asked to be introduced to the king to whom he revealed the meaning of the dream. "The thing thou sawest," said he, "was an image of an enormous size, and a terrible countenance. The head thereof was of gold, the breast and arms of silver, the belly and thighs of brass, and the feet part of iron and part of clay. And, as the king was attentively looking upon that vision, behold a stone was cut out of a mountain, without hands, and the stone smote the image upon his feet, and brake them to pieces; the whole image was ground as small as dust, and the stone became a great mountain, and filled the whole earth." Daniel related the dream and gave the interpretation showing him that it signified the three great empires which were to succeed the Assyro-Babylonians; the Persian, the Grecian, and the Roman. "After these kingdoms," continued Daniel, "shall the God of heaven set up a kingdom, which shall never be destroyed; and this kingdom shall not be left to other people, but shall break in pieces and consume all these kingdoms, and shall stand for ever." By which Daniel plainly foretold the kingdom of Jesus Christ.

The king declared that the God of Israel was the God of gods, advanced Daniel to the highest offices of the kingdom, made him chief of the governors over all the wise men, ruler of the whole province of Babylon, and one of the principal lords of the council.

Jehoiakim revolted from the kingdom of Babylon, but the generals who were still in Judea marched against him and ravaged the country, (2 Kings 24:1,2). "He slept with his fathers, is all the Scripture says of his death. Jeremiah had prophesied that he should neither be regretted nor lamented; but should be buried with the burial of an ass, drawn and cast forth beyond the gates of Jerusalem: this no doubt was fulfilled, though it is not known in what manner." (Rollin, *Ancient History*, Vol. I), p. 289.

Jechonias, (Jehoiachin), (2 Kings 24:6-18), succeeded his father and was as wicked as he. The city of Jerusalem was taken after three months by Nebuchadnezzar himself. He took the riches from the temple and the king's palace and sent them to Babylon, including all the golden vessels remaining which Solomon had made for the temple. He carried away large numbers of captives, including Jechonias, his mother, his wives, and the chief officers and great men of his kingdom. Nebuchadnezzar set up Jechonias' uncle, Mattaniah, also called Zedekiah, on the throne of Judah, (2 Kings 24:17-20).

Zedekiah made an alliance with the king of Egypt, breaking the oath of fidelity to the king of Babylon, who defeated the king of Egypt and blockaded Jerusalem for nearly 12 months. The city was taken by storm and a terrible slaughter took place. The two sons of the king were killed before his eyes by order of Nebuchadnezzar. He (Nebuchadnezzar) had the king's eyes put out, loaded him with chains, and took him to Babylon, where he was kept in prison as long as he lived.

The city and temple were pillaged and burned and all their fortifications were demolished.

When Nebuchadnezzar returned to Babylon he ordered a golden statue to be made ninety feet high, and called all the great men of his kingdom to worship at the dedication. He commanded all his subjects to worship it, threatening to cast those who refused into a burning fiery furnace. Here are found Ananias, Misael, and Asarias, (Shadrach, Meshach, and Abednego), the three Hebrew youths who refused to obey the king's command, and were delivered miraculously by the hand of God. The king himself witnessed this miracle and published an edict saying that the people were forbidden, punishable by death, to speak against the God of Ananias, Misael, and Asarias. They were promoted to the highest honors and given the best in government positions, (Daniel 3).

In the twenty-first year of his reign, Nebuchadnezzar marched into Syria and blockaded Tyre, ruled by Ithobal. Tyre was a strong and wealthy city which had never been conquered. It was noted for its commerce and many of its citizens were like princes in wealth and magnificence, (Ezekiel 26:1-21). It was built by the Sidonians, two hundred and forty years before the temple of Jerusalem. When Sidon was taken by the Philistines of Ascalon, many of its inhabitants escaped in ships and founded the city of Tyre. In the Scripture it is called by Isaiah, "the daughter of Sidon", (Isaiah 23:12). For 13 years she had resisted the monarch to whom all the rest of the East had submitted.

During the siege of Tyre Nebuchadnezzar's troops suffered incredible hardships and the words of the prophet were fulfilled: "every head was made bald, and every shoulder was peeled." Before he finally took the city, the inhabitants took most of their riches and escaped to an island half a mile from shore, where they built a city which far surpassed the former. When Nebuchadnezzar took the city he found nothing to reward his labors, but God promised, by the mouth of Ezekiel, to give him in return the spoils of Egypt, and not long afterward he conquered Egypt.

Another disturbing dream filled Nebuchadnezzar with great anxiety. He dreamed, *I saw, and behold a tree in the midst of the earth, and the height thereof was great. The tree grew, and was strong, and the height thereof reached unto heaven, and the sight thereof to the end of all the earth: The leaves thereof were fair, and the fruit thereof much, and in it was meat for all: the beasts of the field had shadow under it, and the fowls of the heaven dwelt in the boughs thereof, and all flesh was fed of it. I saw in the visions of my head upon my bed, and, behold, a watcher and an holy one came down from heaven; He cried aloud, and said thus, Hew down the tree, and cut off his branches, shake off his leaves, and scatter his fruit: let the beasts get away from under it, and the fowls from its branches: Nevertheless, leave the stump of his roots in the earth, even with a band of iron and brass, in the tender grass of the field; and let it be wet with the dew of heaven, and let his portion be with the beasts in the grass of the earth: Let his heart be changed from man's, and let a beast's heart be given unto him; and let seven times pass over him. This matter is by the decree of the watchers, and the demand by the word of the holy ones; to the intent that the living may know that the most High ruleth in the kingdom of men, and giveth it to whomsoever he will, and setteth up over it the basest of men.* (Daniel 4:10-17.)

Again he consulted his wise men, who could tell him nothing, and he was forced to call for Daniel who told him the meaning of the dream. Daniel told him he would be driven from the company of men for seven years, would be reduced to the condition of a beast of the field, and would eat grass like an animal. His kingdom nevertheless would be preserved for him, and he would repossess his throne, after he learned to know and acknowledge that all power is from the God of heaven. Daniel then pleaded with him to forsake his sins and live a righteous life by showing mercy to the poor. All of which he refused to do.

At the end of twelve months, he was walking in his palace, admiring all the beauty and wealth, and said, *Is not this great Babylon, that I have built for the house of the kingdom by the might of my power, and for the honor of my majesty?* A voice cried from heaven, *O king Nebuchadnezzar, to thee it is spoken: The kingdom is departed from thee,* (4:31). The same hour his understanding went from him; he was driven from men, and ate grass like the oxen, and his body was wet with the dew from heaven. The hair of his head and body grew like eagles' feathers, and his nails like birds' claws, (4:33).

When the appointed time had passed, he recovered his senses, and the use of his understanding: *He lifted up his eyes unto heaven,* says the Scripture, *and blessed the most High; he praised and honoured him that liveth for ever, whose dominion, and whose kingdom is from generation to generation:* confessing, *that all the inhabitants of the earth are as nothing before him, and that he doeth according to his will in the army of heaven, and among the inhabitants of the earth; and none can stay his hand, or say unto him, what dost thou?* (Daniel 4:34.)

He returned to his former physical condition and was restored to his throne, becoming greater and more powerful than ever. He published a solemn edict throughout his dominions telling what miraculous things God had done for him.

He died a year later, after reigning forty-three years from the time of the death of his father.

Nebuchadnezzar sent his armies against Israel three times during his reign:

- 605 B.C., he occupied the city. He took some of the treasures from the Temple, and took the king's sons and those of the royal families captives.

- 597 B.C., he took the rest of the Temple treasures and Ezekiel was carried away prisoner. Jehoiachin, son of Jehoiakim, the princes, and all the valiant men, some 10,000 captives were taken, (2 Kings 24:14-16, etc).

- 586 B.C., he came to judge Zedekiah for his rebellion. He destroyed Jerusalem, the Temple and the walls. He killed the sons of Zedekiah, put out Zedekiah's eyes, and carried him prisoner to Babylon where he died.

The captivity was the judgment of God on Israel which had been announced by Isaiah and Ezekiel. But God would judge Babylon for her part against Israel.

Nebuchadnezzar was one of the greatest Eastern monarchs, and was succeeded by his son.

DANIEL'S PROPHECY OF THE TIMES OF THE GENTILES
Daniel 2:31-35

The Dream		The Interpretation 2:36-45
Parts	Interpretation	Suggested Fulfillment
Head of gold	Nebuchadnezzar's Kingdom of Babylon	Neo-Babylonian Empire 606-538 B.C.
Breast and arms of silver	An inferior kingdom	Medo-Persian Empire 538-333 B.C.
Belly and thighs of brass	A world kingdom	Grecian Empire 333-63 B.C.
Legs of iron	A kingdom strong as iron. It breaks in pieces - subdues.	Roman Empire 63 B.C.-476 A.D.
Feet of iron and clay	Division of iron kingdom and mingling with other nations. Parts fall apart.	Romance, Germanic and other nations 476 A.D.
Destroying stone: Great Mountain	God will set up a kingdom. It will not be destroyed. It will not pass on its sovereignty. It will break up and consume all other kingdoms. It will stand forever.	God's kingdom is now being preached to all nations and entered by repentance and faith. The stone has not yet been cast. Christians are to pray for the coming of God's kingdom.

The Jewish Captivity

3 major deportations: 606, 597, 586 B.C.

606 B.C. _____ 536 B.C.

Decree of Cyrus

597 B.C _____ 527 B.C.

586 B.C. _____ 516 B.C.

Completion of rebuilding Temple

Evil-Merodach, (Amel-Marduk- 'man of Marduk'), (561-560 B.C.) (2 Kings 25:27-30; Jeremiah 52:31-) (See Kings of Assyria)

Son of Nebuchadnezzar

Some of the clay tablets found in Babylon mention Jechonias, king of Judah, and five of his sons in reference to property of the captives, and the Babylonians always accepted him as the legitimate king. Because of this they took great care of him and his family and Evil-Merodach released Jechonias from prison where he had been for 37 years.

During the reign of Evil-Merodach Daniel was delivered from the lion's den. He reigned only two years, and was so wicked that his relatives plotted against him, and put him to death.

Neriglissar (560 B.C.) Nergal-sarezer, (Jeremiah 39:3,13)

He was the husband of Evil-Merodach's sister and one of the chief conspirators against him.

He made preparations for war against the Medes, which caused Cyaxares to send for Cyrus out of Persia, to come to his assistance. Neriglissar was slain in battle in the fourth year of his reign.

Naborosoarchod (555 B.C.)

He was a wicked prince, who was so cruel that he was put to death by his own subjects, after a nine month reign.

Labynit or Nabonid (555-539 B.C.)

He shared the rule with his oldest son **Belshazzar,** (Daniel 5).

He was an elderly scholar who lacked the physical energy and competence to direct the empire, thus it was left to his son Belshazzar.

He was supposed to be the son of Evil-Merodach, grandson of Nebuchadnezzar, to whom, according to Jeremiah's prophecy, the nations of the East were to be subject, as also to his son, and his grandson after him: *all nations shall serve him, and his son, and his son's son, until the very time of his land shall come.* (Jeremiah 27:7).

In the first year of Belshazzar's reign, Daniel had the vision of the four beasts, which represented the four great monarchies, and the kingdom of the Messiah, which was to succeed them, (Daniel 7). In the third year, he had the vision of the ram and the he-goat, which prefigured the destruction of the Persian empire by Alexander the Great, and the persecution which Antiochus Epiphanes, king of Syria, would bring upon the Jews, (Daniel 8).

While Belshazzar's enemies surrounded Babylon, he gave a grand party for his whole court. During the festivities the handwriting on the wall appeared and was interpreted by Daniel. God said the kingdom was to be taken from him and given to the Medes and the Persians. That very night the city was taken, and Belshazzar was killed.

Belshazzar and the handwriting. (Peloubet, 1922)

Thus ended the Babylonian empire, after existing 210 years from the destruction of the great Assyrian empire. Cyrus, (the Medo-Persian Empire), took control of this region at this point, 539 B.C.

MIZRAIM and **SONS** (1 Chronicles 1:8,11; Genesis 10:6). Egypt

His sons were: Ludim, Anamim, Lehabim, Naphtuhim, Pathrusim, Casluhim, Caphtorim.

When the Bible refers to Egypt it usually calls it the 'land of Ham', (Psalms 105:23,27; 106:22; 78:51), and therefore of Mizraim as his son.

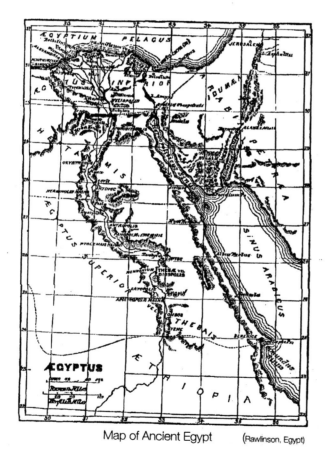

Map of Ancient Egypt   (Rawlinson, Egypt)

When Ham left the plain of Shinar, Mizraim was evidently with him and stopped in the area later known as Egypt. Whether Ham remained there for a time, or continued on south is not known.

Some writers believe the name Menes is the same as Mizraim, but since he (Menes) was a legendary figure, no one can be sure of this.

Egypt, along the Nile River, was and is, very fertile and because of the crops which could be grown there, it was a good area in which to found a nation.

Mizraim was the father of the Egyptians, who were also known as the Ural-Altaic Nation because of the area from which they migrated to Egypt. (The Altai and Ural mountains.)

When he went to Egypt he built great altars to the sun, and the old empire of Babylon under Nimrod, was replaced by the world empire of Egypt.

He was the genius of the age and instituted a reign of culture. He used papyrus and stone for writing materials upon which he recorded his history. He had knowledge of gold, silver, and copper; lead and flint were common during his reign.

His buildings and monuments have lasted through the ages, (e.g. the pyramids); his language and realm grew equally, but have not endured like his physical structures.

The kingdom he built would slowly degenerate, but the world would continue to come to his land to read his history in his tombs and writings.

He built boats and ships, and made trading expeditions on the Mediterranean to Phoenicia, Syria and Ophir.

His civilization was taken from Babel, and his religion came from his brother Cush. The earliest Egyptian monuments show scenes of religious exchanges between the Cushite Ethiopians and the Egyptians. The Cushite priests are always superior in these scenes.

The Egyptian People and their development

The people were described as having a "high, well-filled forehead, short beard, upright profile and wavy brown hair. He was short of stature and slender...His head was large in proportion to his size. His complexion was dark...His hair was dark brown or black. His hands and feet were small. He was good tempered, lighthearted, hospitable and affectionate...." Dorothy Ruth Miller, *Ancient History in Bible Light,* (New York: Fleming H. Revell Co., 1937), p. 72.

Rawlinson describes them as "slight in figure, wanting in muscle, flat in foot, with limbs that are too long, too thin, too ladylike." George Rawlinson, *Ancient Egypt,* (New York: G. P. Putnam's Sons, 1887), p. 25. He says there were two types of Egyptians as seen in the portraits of Rameses III, and Rameses II.

"A moderately high forehead, a large, well-formed aquiline nose, a well-shaped mouth with lips not over full, and a delicately rounded chin. The other is comparatively coarse - forehead low, nose depressed and short, lower part of the face prognathous and sensual-looking, chin heavy, jaw large, lips thick and projecting." (Ibid.), p. 25. This difference can be easily accounted for because of the mixing of the descendants of Mizraim with those of Cush in Ethiopia.

The early Egyptian colonists were cultivated and observant men. Shortly after the Flood, when they migrated to that area, they were found to be a very cultured people. They appear to have taken their culture from the pre-Flood civilization which was evidently quite advanced. There is no evidence to assume man has ascended gradually from a 'savage state'; he had a great heritage of established culture and great inventors before the Flood destroyed the world.

This can be demonstrated by the finds of textile fabrics in the earliest graves which are finer than those of later periods, and by the carved animal skins and glazed pottery also found in those graves. The pottery was red and glazed with white clay patterns. This same pottery is still made in the mountains of Algeria. It was made in many forms and was evidently either poured into a mold, or made by master potters as it was so uniform in shape.

The Egyptians used copper, gold, silver and lead at the beginning of their history, as evidenced by the artifacts found in recent years. This is consistent with the knowledge they would have brought with them from the Ural-Altai region.

They lived in towns instead of leading a pastoral life. Their homes were furnished with items of wood and stone. They wore jewelry of shells, ivory, precious metals and glass. Cosmetic containers have been found from this period in the shapes of men and animals.

Calendar

The calendar was introduced in the predynastic period. It remained unchanged until the end of Egyptian history. The calendar divided the year into twelve months of thirty days each and added five extra feast days plus six hours at the end of the year. An extra day was not added every four years so they had no leap year.

Written language

The early Egyptians possessed a system of writing which was carried down to those of the historic period. It was made up of an alphabet of twenty-four letters. The writings were in the form of characters called *hieroglyphics,* or sacred carvings, or priestly writings. These writings remained a mystery until the time of Napoleon when a French engineer discovered the 'Rosetta stone' which allowed scholars to finally decipher the sacred carvings. Because it was partly in Greek, due to the period of Grecian rule over Egypt, they were able to use those comparisons to the Egyptian writing and discover the alphabet used. Manuscripts were written on papyrus made from the leaves of an aquatic plant (our word for paper is derived from papyrus).

Egypt had some of the first libraries and also used parchment, made from the skins of sheep, and calf-skin or vellum, as writing material.

Rosetta Stone
(Enciclopedia de la Biblia)

In the Temple of Seralit in Sinai the oldest alphabetic writing in the world has been found, telling us that man has always been able to write; the ability did not evolve, it was God-given.

Luxuries and social standing

From the earliest ages the Egyptians surrounded themselves with all the comforts and luxuries of a cultivated life. Artisans of all kinds abounded. Monogamy was the rule and women in Egypt held high positions and were equal to their husbands. They were unveiled and could hold and dispose of real property. They could also become rulers in their own right as Cleopatra did.

The wealthy owned chairs in which their guests were seated at dinner parties when most of the world was sitting on blankets on the floor or the ground.

The homes of the wealthy were works of art and demonstrated the love the Egyptian had of beauty and light in his surroundings. All his useful items were made to be beautiful. He was surrounded by beauty. His spoons had handles of lotus blossoms. His wine was served in blue vessels of the same flower. Ivory

chairs, carved in the form of lions or oxen, were upholstered with soft leather cushions. Many of the chairs were overlaid with gold and silver or inlaid with ebony and ivory.

Thirteen hundred feet of copper drain pipe were found in one of the pyramids, indicating that the plumbing trade was thriving in this early period. Also in the Fourth Dynasty portrait sculptures carved in wood or stone were done. They were done in real life colors and the eyes were inlaid with rock crystals. They were the most lifelike portraits ever produced though they are the earliest kinds of portraits in art history. (Rawlinson, *Ancient Egypt*), excerpts from various parts.

Religion

The Egyptian had an intense fear of the supernatural. This terror, coupled with superstition, formed his religion. He was not capable of understanding the pure religion of Noah because of his own lack of spiritual insight. The sun became a god to him as well as the moon and the stars. He was one of the first to observe the courses of the planets and the heavenly bodies and this, like his forefathers in Babel, caused him to make them an object of worship. He felt compelled to worship these deities so that another catastrophe like the Tower of Babel wouldn't occur. He seems to have had some remembrance, however, of the True God and His command against graven images, because his first temple was smooth, square, and undecorated. His altar was the same - the teaching that it was a sin to make an image of God was still remembered by the primitive Egyptians.

"The sacred texts, known only to the priests and to the initiated, taught that there was a single Being, 'the sole producer of all things both in heaven and earth, himself not produced of any,' 'the only true living God, self-originated,' 'who exists from the beginning,' 'who has made all things, but has not himself been made.' This Being seems never to have been represented by any material, even symbolical, form...He was a pure spirit, perfect in every respect—all-wise, almighty, supremely good. It is of him that the Egyptian poets use such expressions as the following: 'He is not graven in marble; he is not beheld; his abode is not known; no shrine is found with painted figures of him; there is no building that can contain him;' and, again: 'Unknown is his name in heaven; he doth not manifest his forms; vain are all representations;' and yet again: 'His commencement is from the beginning; he is the God who has existed from old time; there is no God without him; no mother bore him; no father hath begotten him; he is a god-goddess, created from himself; all gods came into existence when he began'." (Rawlinson, *Egypt*), p. 38.

The remembrance, however dim, still remained in the minds of some of the people of the pure religion they had learned in Shinar after the Flood. But without the continued revelation of that light they were unable to see the personal connection, and 'men love darkness rather than light'.

The first city of importance was On or Heliopolis which was dedicated to the sun-god. E. Willard describes the city: "Heliopolis had also a most magnificent temple of the Sun, the ruins of which form the most conspicuous object, amidst the gloomy remains of its ancient grandeur." (Willard, *Ancient Geography*), p. 43.

When Mizraim died he became a god to them, as did all the succeeding pharaohs.

As new cities were built, new gods were required to guard them, and polytheism soon filled the land. Symbols were made in wood, stone and metal, to represent the gods.

The Egyptian held sacred a whole list of animals: goats, sheep, hippopotami, croco-diles, vultures, frogs, shrew-mice, cows, cats, dogs, ibises, hawks and apes. (Rawlinson, *Egypt*), p. 31. If one was killed or eaten, even by a person who did not know the law, the offender was immediately put to death because the Egyptian believed in reincarnation and the animal eaten might be his relative.

Some of these animals were changed into deities and worshipped as gods, (e.g. the sacred bull at Memphis, Hapi or Apis). The sacred bull had his own temple and priests and a harem of cows. He was given meals of the finest food, and had grooms and currycombers. A cup-bearer brought him water and during festivals he was led through the main streets of town as a god.

At his death he was embalmed with jewels and placed in a granite tomb. The calf Mneus was worshipped at Heliopolis.

Their religion remained unchanged for centuries. They worshipped the "Queen of Heaven", and believed in self-justification, and ritual. They represented God's unity and trinity in their god Thoth or Hermes, the guide of the soul. "Ham, ...was deified in the god Min, also called Khem, a very exact Egyptian equivalent for 'Ham' (Spanish 'Cam').

"That Ham, the son of Noah, should be deified in the Egyptian pantheon is not surprising. The sensuality of this god Min or Khem also accords well with the reputation for licentiousness borne by Ham, the son of Noah. These facts suggest very strongly a trace in Egyptian mythology of the actual history of the movements of the Hamitic people." (ISBE, Vol. III), p. 2069.

They believed in a future state, in the immortality of the soul, and in rewards and punishment of deeds done in the body. These beliefs had to have come from God to Adam to Noah and Shem, and are another proof of the common beginnings of man.

The embalming of dead bodies was part of the religious beliefs of the Egyptians. The body was thought to be reunited with the soul on judgment day so it was to be preserved from corruption. They believed that even in death, the body was not totally unconscious, and this was one of the reasons for putting eating utensils, food, servants, etc., in the tombs.

Each man was judged after his death to determine what kind of person he had been. Even the kings could not escape this judgment. If the person was judged to have been responsible and worthy of emulation, he was allowed an honorable burial. If he was not found to be an honorable person, he was not allowed to be buried. In the books of Kings and Chronicles, are found the histories of kings who were not honorable, and they were not allowed to be buried in the 'sepulchres of their fathers'. This custom was brought from Egypt by the Israelites and continued during the times of the kings.

Egyptian Mythology

The idea of life after death is one of the most important considerations in religion.

The Pharaohs, as before stated, became greater gods at their death, but they were considered gods during their reign also, and were known collectively as 'sons of the gods'. Each Pharaoh was supposed to be the actual incarnation of the sun - the living Horus. They were responsible for all religious practices and the *ritual* of the religion was more important than what one believed. They built the temples for the gods and maintained them after their construction.

Deities were associated with an animal which was the soul (Ba) of the god. The bull was a popular animal used in this regard, as were eagles, hawks, fish, etc. A sacred bull, kept at Heliopolis near the temple, was said to be the living soul of the god he represented.

It was common to bury these 'sacred' animals in a necropolis (a cemetery). In Phoenician Ashkelon, 'sacred' dogs were buried in great numbers. ("Why were Hundreds of Dogs Buried at Ashkelon?" by Lawrence E. Stager: BAR, May/June 1991, Vol. XVII, No. 3).

Sixty-four Apis bulls were found buried at Memphis.

Sometimes the animal's head was retained as an object of worship of that particular god, and special temples were built for them. The physical layout of these temples was similar to that seen in the Tabernacle and Temple. First, there was the courtyard where only the privileged could enter, second, was the stateroom where fewer still could enter, and last, was the sanctuary, which was limited to the few because the 'god' was enshrined there.

Rituals were to take place at certain times of the day, month, year and seasons. These rituals were performed by the highest priests, and included prayers, hymns, moving the god from one location to another, parades, etc.

When the god was paraded through the temple and the city, he was carried in a shrine by the priests who stopped by wayside chapels with him. Offerings were given and sacrifices were offered to the god. It was a totally pagan and godless religion.

Though the Pharaoh was the supreme priest of the gods, he relegated his position to the local high priest and to those under the high priest; thus forming the 'sacerdotal hierarchy'.

Divine families and myths:

The local god was considered the universal god who was eternal, and was the organizer and creator of the world.

The belief in a triad was common, consisting of:

- god the father,
- the goddess mother, and
- the divine son.

The god of the ruling house became the god of the people. When the capital of the Old Kingdom was transferred to Thebes, *Amun* became the god of the kings.

The Heliopolitan Religious System

In this system *Atum* was the primeval god - meaning 'the whole', 'the complete'.

Through self-fertilization he produced the first divine couple: *Shu* and *Tefnut*.

Shu means *air, the void* and *life-giving air*. Tefnut means *moisture in the atmosphere*. From them came *Geb* or Seb, the earth god, and *Nut* the sky goddess.

Two more couples were born from Geb and Nut; they were *Osiris* and *Isis,* and *Set* and *Nephthys*.

The gods were nine in number - a divine ennead.

Atum is associated with Re who represented the sun, and with Horus, the falcon-god. Horus was one of the most prominent figures in the Egyptian celestial and solar pantheon.

The Memphite Religious system

In Memphis the god *Ur* ('Great') was equated with Atum, who had brought about creation by the two abilities of his fundamental nature: heart and tongue, which represented thought and speech. The heart conceived the idea, and the tongue-commanded and uttered the creative word. He brought all things into existence: the divine college, other gods, men, animals, plants, minerals, all that exists, and the principles of law and justice. He was called *Ur-Atum.*

The Theban Religious System

In the Theban System the god *Amun* became the god of the royal house during the Middle Kingdom. *Mut,* meaning Mother, became his goddess. She was originally the Vulture-goddess.

Khons, the moon-god, was his son. He was associated with Re, therefore the name, *Amun Re,* King of the gods, Master of Thebes. He was recognized by the Greeks as *Zeus.*

Osiris was god of the dead, the flood and vegetation.

The legend:

Geb, was the representative of the royal establishment founded by Atum who transferred his powers to his son Osiris. The sister-wife of Osiris, Isis, spread knowledge. Osiris was slain by his brother, Set or Sutekh.

Isis, and her sister Nephthys, looked for the remains of Osiris which were found on the Syrian shore at Byblus. As Isis was taking them home to bury them, Set stole them from her and cut them into fourteen pieces which he hid in different places.

She hunted until she found all the pieces and buried them honorably.

She escaped to the marshes of the Delta and gave birth to a son, Horus. He was brought up in secret and fought Set to avenge his father Osiris' death. The god Thoth healed both of them after the battle, (Horus had lost an eye), then they were taken before the divine court and Set had to restore the eye to Horus. Horus then gave his eye to his father, Osiris. Osiris replaced it with the divine serpent, which became one of the symbols of royalty. Osiris transferred the earthly kingdom to Horus and retired to the kingdom of the blessed. (Horus, the god of kingship, was represented by a hawk. He was replaced by the sun-god Ra or Re.)

Isis released Set from prison, (he was her brother), and Horus was so angered by this that he tore the crown from her head and replaced it with a cow's head - or horns.

Osiris was a prototype of the dead king who conferred his titles on his son, and then came to life in a beautified form; all Pharaohs went through the same transformation. He was Horus during his reign, then became Osiris at his death and was worshipped as such by his sons and successors.

This transformation was also represented by the god of vegetation which was buried in the Nile, (a seed), and resurrected, (a plant comes forth).

The Eye of Horus, or Eye of Re was the solar eye and was initially called the morning star. It was connected with Osiris after he had been brought back to life by his son, Horus.

The monstrous serpent *Apophis*, was the demon of darkness and evil who tried to keep Re from completing his daily journey of bringing back the sun each morning.

The Eye of Horus - Solar Disk
(Rawlinson, Egypt)

Hathor, meaning "house of Horus", was depicted by a cow or a woman with cow's horns. She was the goddess of music, dancing, and love and the protector of infants. The Greeks identified her with *Aphrodite*, one of the names of Semiramis.

The Divine Birth of the Pharaoh

The god Amun decided he wanted a son who would become king. The queen (wife of one of Re's [Amun's] priests) was taken into the nuptial chamber. He told her the name the child would have and his fate. The potter-god, Khnum, fashioned a body, and the god Ka, fashioned the material of the soul of the child.

Hathor, (the mother goddess), was present with her fairies or "Hathors" who cared for infants.

It was quite a fanciful belief system with just a few signs left of the true God. From them came the belief in the 'eye of Horus' or the 'third eye' of the New Age religion through which communication takes place between the seeking party and his demonic guide. Many satanic beliefs came from the Egyptian pantheon of gods.

Monuments

The earliest monuments were the pyramids, which existed during the time of Abraham, c. 1920 B.C. The first were built during the Fourth Dynasty. The Egyptians began building at Babel and continued after the dispersion, and the pyramids were similar to Babylonian and Asian construction. Many believe the religious idea prevailing when the pyramid was built was a belief in one God as demonstrated by the Egyptian king's response to Abraham - he believed in God in almost the same way Abraham did, (Genesis 12).

The pyramid builders were: Khufu (Cheops, Shufu), Khafre (Kephren) and Mankara who belonged to Manetho's fourth dynasty. Khufu was the builder of the Great Pyramid and one of Egypt's greatest rulers. The pyramids were designed as sepulchers for the kings. There are as many as 70 on the left bank of the Nile near Memphis. The greatest is the pyramid of Khufu.

The Pyramid of Khufu.

The Great Pyramid is the greatest structure that the world has ever known; "the greatest mass of masonry that has ever been put together by mortal man." Sir Wm. Dawson describes the Great Pyramid as 'a miracle of skillful masonry in the construction of its internal passages'.

"This pyramid covers thirteen acres. The sides of the pyramid at its base are 755 feet long and its height was 482 feet. About 2,300,000 blocks of limestone went to make it. Single blocks weigh over fifty tons. The

Great Pyramid   (Rawlinson, Egypt)

passages and interior chambers are built with such skill, that, notwithstanding the stupendous weight supported, after more than four thousand years there is no perceptible settling of the walls. Blocks weighing tons show joints of less than one thousandth of an inch. So skillful was the cutting and polishing of these immense blocks of stone that their surfaces and edges, though involving acres of material, are equal to an optician's lens." (Miller, *Ancient History*), p. 75.

Pyramidal Tomb
(Rawlinson, Egypt)

It is 200 feet higher than the Capitol in Washington, D.C.

"Its cubic contents would build a city of 22,000 houses...[if] laid in a line of cubic squared would reach a distance of nearly 17,000 miles, or girdle two-thirds of the earth's circumference at the equator. Herodotus says that its construction required the continuous labour of a hundred thousand men for the space of twenty years, and moderns do not regard the estimate as exaggerated." (Rawlinson, *Egypt*), p. 75.

The stones, some weighing 1600 tons, were dragged for hundreds of miles on sledges. In one instance it was said to have taken 2000 men three years to take one stone from the quarry to where it was to be used.

"In all ages travellers have felt and expressed the warmest admiration for them [the pyramids]. They impressed Herodotus as no works that he had seen elsewhere, except, perhaps, the Babylonian. They astonished Germanicus, familiar as he was with the great constructions of Rome. They furnished Napoleon with the telling phrase, 'Soldiers, forty centuries look down upon you from the top of the pyramids.' Greece and Rome reckoned them among the Seven Wonders of the world. Moderns have doubted whether they could really be the work of human hands. If they possess only one of the elements of architectural excellence, they possess that element to so great an extent that in respect of it they are unsurpassed, and probably unsurpassable." (Rawlinson, *Egypt*), p. 89.

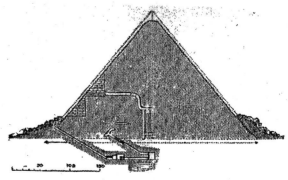

Section of Great Pyramid   (Rawlinson, Egypt)

"The Great Sphinx is also assigned to this period. This human-headed Sphinx is the largest statue in the world. The head is said to be a portrait of Khafre, the Pharaoh who built the second pyramid." (Miller, *Ancient History*), p. 76.

There was little art, only sculpture on a massive scale, but it was massive, not beautiful. Painting was limited to frescoes in the sepulchers and in some private homes of the wealthy. All art forms were dictated by religion and the artist was never allowed to develop his individual skills.

Contributions of Egypt

- Architecture
- History
- A settled government
- An organized body politic
- Science (primitive geometry, arithmetic,
- astronomy and medicine)

Egyptian government

The government was a hereditary monarchy which continued because of the power of the priestly class which was the power behind the throne. The power of the monarch over the lives and property of his subjects was limited by law-but he had the right to make the laws.

The government consisted of the king (or Pharaoh) with an assembly of thirty judges who came from the higher orders of the people from the principal cities of the nation. These judges were chosen by the monarch for their honesty and knowledge. They were well-versed in the laws of the country and the common-man was guaranteed a certain amount of personal liberty. In one of the temples built by King Osymandyas was found a picture of the judges, the president of whom was wearing on his breast a picture of Truth, with her eyes closed. This seems to be one of the earliest portrayals of justice being blind and impartial in the administration of the laws. The business of the judges was conducted in written form to avoid any miscarriage of justice because of the eloquence of one person over another. They judged the poor and the rich equally without partiality. Children were taught the laws of the land from infancy and were expected to become law-abiding citizens. Because of this the Egyptians preserved their laws and customs longer than any other ancient nation.

The laws were very strict and even the food and liquid consumed by the monarch were decreed by the law. Food was of the most common variety. They ate to live, but did not live to eat. They lived an austere life in order to prepare them for hardships and keep them from becoming lazy and soft.

Murder was punished with death regardless of the position of the individual.

Perjury was punished with death because it was a crime against the gods and the state.

The false accuser was to suffer the punishment which the accused person was to suffer had he been found guilty.

If a person failed to save another's life when that person was attacked, and it was in his power to save him, he was punished in the same way the attacker was punished.

No one was allowed to be useless. Each person had to register with the government and state his means of support. If he lied he was put to death.

No one was allowed to borrow money without pawning his father's body to the creditor. (His father was mummified and kept in a box in the house of the son. This was moved to the house of the creditor until the debt was paid. If the son refused to honor his debt and redeem his father before he died, [the son], he was not allowed an honorable burial.)

Polygamy was allowed to all except priests, who could only have one wife.

The aged were held in great esteem.

The highest virtue was gratitude.

A caste system existed which kept each individual in his family's occupation. The three broad divisions were: priests, soldiers, and lower orders. No slave nor foreigner was admitted into the court service of the monarch. (This is interesting in connection with Joseph who arrived in the country as a slave and a foreigner. God was in control as he took Joseph from his position with Potiphar to his position as second in the kingdom under Pharaoh.)

Priests were not confined to religion. They were the only officials who could read and write and possessed both medical and scientific knowledge. They were in control of the entire country because they dictated the religious life of every Egyptian, including the king.

Every soldier (about 400,000 of them) was given 6 1/2 acres tax free, but he could not be involved in any art or trade. These lands were 'privileged property'. Both soldiers and priests possessed land. All other lands belonged either to the nobles or to the king. He rented the land to the people and received 1/5 of the produce. (See Section IV under Joseph.)

The lower orders included husbandmen, artificers, and herdsmen, with many other divisions of each. The lowest order were the swine herders who were not allowed to enter the temples. No caste below priests and soldiers had any political rights and could not own land. Charles Rollin, *Ancient History*, Vol. I, (New York: World Publishing House, 1875), pp. 112,113 excerpts.

When Jacob entered Egypt he was given an area far from the other Egyptians because of the stigma associated with anyone who was a shepherd. He and his family had always been shepherds and were given great honors by the Pharaoh and a special place to live to be able to continue their way of life in peace and comfort because of Joseph, not because they were shepherds, (Genesis 46:34).

Ancient Egypt is believed to have had a population of 5 millions or more. As before mentioned, the abundance of food led to a rapidly growing population.

There were 20,000 inhabited towns; Memphis and Thebes being the most famous.

KINGS OF ANCIENT EGYPT

Menes or Mizraim

As before stated, he was the founder of Egypt, and was the son of Ham, the son of Noah.

Osymandyas

This king was one of the great builders of Egypt. He built a mausoleum for himself which was said to have been surrounded by a circle of gold.

Uchoreus

He built the city of Memphis. There are very few ruins to give evidence of the great city it was.

Moeris

He had Lake Moeris built.

Thethmosis or Amosis

This king expelled one of the invasions of the Hyksos who had ruled in Lower Egypt. Rollin believes that Joseph was brought into Egypt during his reign

Head of Thethmosis II
(Rawlinson, Egypt)

Rameses-miamum

He reigned 66 years and was the oppressor of Egypt, (Exodus 1:11,13,14).

Amenophis - son of Rameses

Sesostris - son of Amenophis

One of the most powerful Egyptian kings, he was a great conqueror who invaded Arabia and Libya and subdued most of the African continent. He advanced further into India than Alexander would centuries later. It is said he subdued the countries beyond the Ganges and reached the ocean.

He was supposed to have conquered the Scythians, and his empire extended from the Ganges to the Danube in Europe.

He had many monuments constructed to honor his exploits, but also built great earth-enworks to protect the country from flooding by the Nile.

In his old age he became blind and killed himself.

Pheron - son of Sesotris

He was a cruel prince who only reigned a short time and became blind.

Proteus

During his reign Helen of Troy was supposed to have been left in his care until her husband came to rescue her.

Rhampsinitus

A king who gathered great wealth for Egypt.

Cheops and **Cephrenus**, these two were brothers who reigned one after another for 56 years. They were both cruel and used forced labor to build great monuments to themselves. The Egyptian kings had always used captured peoples to build their monuments, but these two forced the Egyptians to labor for them in this endeavor. They were, naturally, hated by their subjects.

They had the great pyramids built as monuments to their own importance.

Mycerinus, son of Cheops

He was a good king who dealt justly with his subjects, and was not at all like his father. His reign was of short duration.

Asychis

This king enacted the law of giving the body of the dead father as collateral for a loan.

INTERVAL

Here there is a 300 year lapse before there is information of another king. This king was Sabachus, king of Ethiopia.

During this time-period the Scriptures mentioned several other kings:

Pharaoh, king of Egypt

He gave his daughter to be Solomon's wife, and through this made an alliance with Israel, (1 Kings 3:1).

Shishak or **Seconchis**, (1 Kings 11:40; 12:2)

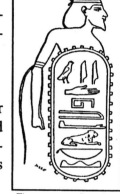

Figure recording the conquest of Judea by Shishak.
(Rawlinson, Egypt)

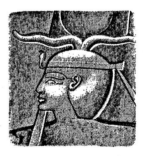

Shishak
(Rawlinson, Egypt)

Jeroboam fled to him when Solomon sought to kill him. He was supposed to be from Lybia.

He marched against Jerusalem in the fifth year of Rehoboam's reign, (2 Chronicles 12:1-9).

He took treasures from the house of God and made Judah (the southern kingdom) his vassal.

Zerah

This man was the king of Ethiopia and of Egypt.

He made war on Asa, king of Judah and God defeated his army of a million men, (2 Chronicles 14:9-15).

Amysis

He was blind, and under him the kingdom was taken by Sabachus.

After the 300 year period the list of kings begins again:

Sabachus (Shabaka), called **So,** in the Scriptures

He was also the king of Ethiopia and reigned 50 years in Egypt.

Hoshea, king of Israel, sought his help against Shalmaneser, king of Assyria, (2 Kings 17:1-6).

Sethon, or Sevechus

He ruled 14 years, and was also an Ethiopian.

He was more interested in being a priest than in being a king.

Tharaca (Taharka), **Tirhakah** in the Scriptures, (2 Kings 19:9)

He joined with Sethon to try to protect Jerusalem. He was an Ethiopian, and after Sethon, he became king and reigned 18 years.

Two years of anarchy followed his reign.

Psammetichus

During his reign the Greeks began to have an influence on Egypt as teachers of their children.

He warred against Assyria, and died in the twenty-fourth year of Josiah, king of Judah.

Nehcao or Pharaoh-Necho, son of Psammetichus

He attempted to join the Nile with the Red Sea. An hundred and twenty thousand workers died in trying to complete this project.

He stopped the work after he was told it would open up a road for other nations to conquer Egypt.

During his reign there was great maritime activity. It is believed that Phoenicians in his service sailed from the Red Sea, went around the coast of Africa and returned through the Strait of Gibraltar three years later. If this feat is to be believed as reported by ancient historians, the

Pharaoh-Necho
(Rawlinson, Egypt)

Cape of Good Hope had been passed twenty-one centuries before Vasco da Gama attempted to sail around it and at a time when there was no compass to guide sailors.

He warred against Assyria and passed through Judah on his way to the Euphrates River. King Josiah was afraid of him entering his territory and fought him at Megiddo where he (Josiah) was mortally wounded in the battle and his subjects returned him to Jerusalem. Necho continued on and defeated the Assyrians and the Medes, (2 Kings 23:29,30; 2 Chronicles 35:20-27).

While Necho was in Assyria Jehoahaz had proclaimed himself king in Jerusalem. Necho took Jehoahaz prisoner to Egypt where he died, and made Jehoiakim, (Eliakim) his brother, king over Judah and Jerusalem, (2 Kings 23:31-35; 2 Chronicles 36:3,4).

Jerusalem was taken and Judah again became vassal under tribute to Egypt.

Nabopolassar, king of Babylon, sent his son Nebuchadnezzar at the head of a large army against Necho, and Necho was defeated near the river Euphrates, (Jeremiah 46:2). By defeating Necho, he took for Babylon all the country which formerly belonged to Egypt.

Psammis, (Psammetik), son of Necho (See sections on Assyrian and Babylonian kings.)

Psammetik
(Rawlinson, Egypt)

He reigned six years.

Apries (Pharaoh-Hophra), son of Psammis

Reigned 25 years, (Jeremiah 44:30).

Zedekiah, king of Judah, made an alliance with him against Babylon. God had forbidden these alliances and God told Ezekiel to prophesy against Egypt, (Ezekiel 29:2-32:16), because of this alliance.

God had promised Egypt as a spoil to Nebuchadnezzar. When Tyre was finally taken by him, he received no spoil because everything of value had been moved from the city to the island in the sea, (Ezekiel 29:18-20). But in a few years God gave him Egypt as his spoil for having taken Tyre.

Egypt was fighting internally at this time and Nebuchadnezzar took advantage of this and made it a part of the Babylonian empire.

Apries was taken prisoner after Nebuchadnezzar had left and was strangled in his own palace, (Jeremiah 44:30).

Amasis

He reigned 40 years in Egypt. He was one of the officers of Apries who had been left as king by Nebuchadnezzar, and was the one who took Apries prisoner and had him killed.

He built many temples for the gods; he conquered the island of Cyprus and married a Cyrenian wife.

Psammenitus, son of Amasis

He reigned six months before becoming a prisoner of Cambyses, son of Cyrus the Mede.

This was the end of the Egyptian kings until the Ptolemies began to reign after the death of Alexander.

(No dates are given for the Egyptian kings because there is so much confusion concerning the different dynasties.)

The reign of those kings lasted about 300 years to the reign of Cleopatra.

The Israelite Bondage in Egypt

Israel's bondage did not begin immediately upon the death of Joseph, (1805 B.C.), but occurred with the rise of power of a new king 'who knew not Joseph'. This king seems to have been Rameses-Miamum. He reigned 66 years and oppressed Israel during his entire reign. Some have indicated that this bondage took place under one of the Hyksos kings, (in Egyptian meaning - "rulers of foreign countries"), also called 'Shepherd Kings' because they may have been at least partially of Semitic origin and invaded and subdued the Delta area for a least a century (1675-1570 B.C.).

Rameses II
(Rawlinson, Egypt)

The Hebrew phrase translated "arose... over Egypt", (Exodus 1:8), might better be rendered "arose against Egypt".

The reason stated for fearing the Hebrews given in Exodus 1:9,10, is that they have become "more and mightier than we." It is improbable that the Israelites could have ever outnumbered the natives of Egypt, but it is very possible they could have become more numerous that the Hyksos ruling minority.

According to archeology, the Biblical statement that the Hebrews labored at the city of Rameses fits the Hyksos Period. At the time of the oppression the city was called Avaris and later renamed Rameses after Pharaoh Rameses II. Charles F. Aling, *Egypt and Bible History*, (Grand Rapids: Baker Book House, 1981), pp. 65,66.

The date of the Exodus was c. 1446 B.C.

The Exodus occurred in the 18th Dynasty during the rule of Pharaoh Amenhotep II (1453-1415), son of Thutmosis III, perhaps the greatest of all the Pharaohs.

Thothmes III
(Rawlinson, Egypt)

Amenhotep II was born and raised in the delta region. He built estates there, and in all probability resided there at times, at least in his early reigning years. (Aling, *Egypt*), p. 100.

Amenhotep II waged two wars early in his reign (1450 and 1446 B.C.) and a lesser war in 1444. After this there is no other record of military activity. This sudden end of military campaigns by a king who went out of his way to boast of his talents can best be understood in Bible light. When he pursued Moses into the Red Sea, he lost an army including 600 chariots (Exodus 14:5-28). The Scriptures do not say that Pharaoh drowned, just his army.

Also in favor of this theory is the fact that Amenhotep II had three sons who preceded him in death. Webensenu was probably the firstborn son since he was granted the privilege of burial in the royal tomb of his father. It is reasonable to regard this prince as the son of Amenhotep II killed in the tenth plague, for he never lived, as far as history records, to marriageable age. (Aling, *Egypt and Bible History*), p. 105.

The Fall of Egypt

Because Egypt continued to war against Israel during the monarchy, God sent judgment on the nation, (Ezekiel 29; Isaiah 19:20; Jeremiah 25:19-33), and it ceased to exist as a powerful nation.

In dealing with the Pharaohs it is important to note that Egypt was divided into at least four different kingdoms at the time the Israelites had contact with them. Not until later was Egypt united under one Pharaoh. The list of the Pharaoh's given is only for the kingdom that had an influence on the history of Israel.

(See Chart, End of section.)

All dates before 650 B.C. are approximate and since we believe the Flood account to be true there would have been approximately 2300 years of the B.C. period remaining after the Flood and the dates need to fit within this framework.

The National Geographic Society has a good map called "Egypt's Nile Valley" which helps to put into focus some of the different kingdoms of Egypt.

Sons of Mizraim

Ludim

These were the people who inhabited the country of the same name in northern Africa. They are mentioned as bowmen in the armies of Egypt and Tyre, (Ezekiel 27:10; 30:5). They are not the same as the Lydians from the Semitic line.

Anamim

Nothing is known of them, (Genesis 10:13; 1 Chronicles 1:11); some place them in the Nile Delta, but no proof can be found.

Lehabim

Also called Lubim. "A people known as Libyans (but not of the great tribe of Phut) dwelt on the southern shore of the Mediterranean, west of Egypt. The Twenty-Second Dynasty of Egypt was Libyan in origin. Its founder was Sheshonk, Biblical Sheshak; who invaded Jerusalem and Judah during the reign of Rehoboam (2 Chron. 12:2-9)." John D. Davis, *Davis Dictionary of the Bible*. (Tennessee: The Varsity Company, 1973), p. 551.

Naphtuhim

"...mentioned between the Libyans of Lower and the Pathrusim of Upper Egypt (Genesis 10:13; 1 Chronicles 1:11). Ebers derives the name from *na-ptah*, the [people] of Ptah, or inhabitants of Middle Egypt, in the district about Memphis, the seat of Ptah's worship." (Davis, *Dictionary*), p. 551.

Pathrusim

Inhabitants of Pathros in Upper Egypt. Ezekiel 29:14-16, *And I will bring again the captivity of Egypt, and will cause them to return into the land of Pathros, into the land of their habitation; and they shall be a base kingdom. It shall be the basest of the kingdoms; neither shall it exalt itself any more above the nations: for I will diminish them, that they shall no more rule over the nations. And it shall be no more the confidence of the house of Israel, which bringeth their iniquity to remembrance, when they shall look after them: but they shall know that I am the Lord God.* This indicates that Pathros was the land of the origin of the Egyptians. Studies in Egyptology indicate that the earliest Egyptian civilization was in Upper Egypt.

Casluhim

From Mizraim came a family of the Casluhim who settled east of the Nile in the Suez region. From them came a family known as the Philistines. They were described as 'fierce, bloody, worshippers of many gods', and eventually 'possessors of cities walled up to heaven'. They were destroyed by the Shemites and became extinct as a nation (except for those who intermarried with the Israelites). They probably kept their family together with that of Caphtorim, who is also identified with the Philistines, (Amos 9:7; Jeremiah 47:4).

"Perhaps they were the inhabitants of Casiotes, a district on the Mediterranean Sea extending from the eastern mouth of the Nile to Philistia." (Davis, *Dictionary*), p. 125.

Caphtorim

These two (Casluhim and Caphtorim), as before stated, kept their families together and both are identified with the Philistines. The ancestors of the Philistines seem to have gone from the Egyptian delta from Kapethor to Crete and later to Philistia on the western coast of Palestine, (Jeremiah 47:4; Amos 9:7). The Philistines as a whole were Cherethites, probably Cretans (1 Samuel 30:14; Ezekiel 25:16; Zephaniah 2:5). (Davis, *Dictionary*), p. 125.

PHUT and his sons

Josephus and the Septuagint place Phut in Libya, in the area known as Tripoli.

Kalisch puts him on the Delta in Egypt; Rawlinson between Abyssinia and Egypt, in Nubia. Research indicates that the original Libyans were related to the Egyptians, Ethiopians, and Canaanites, in other words, to Phut.

Eight centuries before Christ the Ludites (Lud), fourth son of Shem, invaded the people of Phut. The Ludites had lived in the Armenian mountains above Asshur. They were warlike, energetic, and were renowned horsemen. They left their former home and established themselves between Phut and Mizraim. They took over the nation of Phut and gave them a strong Semitic culture, though they also took much of the Egyptian culture as their own, (see Lud under Shem).

The Phoenicians, from the tribe of Phut

Ragozin puts the Phoenicians near the Persian Gulf in present day Yemen, and coming from the Hamitic line. Their name was *Punt* or *Puna,* coming from Phut, and later corrupted by the Greek influence to *Phoenicians.* They spread from Arabia to the corner of eastern Africa known as Somali because of its strategic commercial position near the Red Sea, the Arabian Sea, and access to the Indian Ocean. They took the territory of the displaced Canaanites and through intermarriage with those who were left, took the name "the sons of Canaan." Zénaïde A. Ragozin, *Assyria, From the Rise of the Empire to the Fall of Nineveh,* (New York: G. P. Putnam's Sons, 1901), pp. 68-70.

Genesis 12:5,6 says when Abram and his family arrived in Canaan 'the Canaanite was *then* in the land.' They had not been there long, as indicated by the word 'then'. This migration was possibly caused by the Elamite conquest which sent both Canaanite and Shemite from the area of the Persian Gulf. The same invasion sent the Hyksos (Canaanite Hittites and Shemites) into Egypt 2200-2000 B.C. When the Canaanites entered Palestine it was already inhabited by other tribes (mostly Hamitic), and by forcing them to leave or destroying them, the Canaanites took possession of their lands and cities. Some of the original inhabitants still occupied the land when the Israelites came into Palestine after the exodus. The Anakim and Emim ('the terrible', 'the formidable') were there as evidenced in Numbers 13:22,28,33 and Deuteronomy 2:10-11, 20-21.

Numbers 13:28-29, *Nevertheless the people be strong that dwell in the land, and the cities are walled, and very great: and moreover we saw the children of Anak there. The Amalekites dwell in the land of the south: and the Hittites, and the Jebusites, and the Amorites, dwell in the mountains: and the Canaanites (Phoenicians) dwell by the sea, and by the coast of Jordan.* (verse 31), *But the men that went up with him said, We be not able to go up against the people; for they are stronger than we.*

Deuteronomy 2:10,11, *The Emims dwelt therein in times past, a people great, and many, and tall, as the Anakims:*

Which also were accounted giants, as the Anakims; but the Moabites call them Emims. (verses 20, 21), *That also was accounted a land of giants: giants dwelt therein in old time; and the Ammonites call them Zamzummims; (because of the sound of their speech), A people great, and many, and tall, as the Anakims; but the Lord destroyed them before them; and they succeeded them, and dwelt in their stead.*

These were the people the Israelites feared and Goliath was a descendant of these peoples. (Some scholars believe the children of Anak were Turanians from the Japhetic line of yellow nations.)

The Phoenicians were the great merchant-adventurers of their day and conquered the then-known world by commerce - all the way to the Atlantic. They established commercial cities all along the Mediterranean; Gades (Cadiz) in Spain, was established in 1100 B.C. Their principal cities were Sidon, Tyre, and Arvad. They had established Carthage on the northern coast of Africa by the 9th century B.C. They were noted for their embroidered work and for the blue and purple dye they produced.

The name Phoenicia came from the Greeks and it meant 'purple'.

Their greatest prosperity came during the fourth and fifth centuries of Hyksos rule in Egypt. Sidon became their principal city and they were referred to also as 'Sidonians'.

Sidon was the first place to begin trafficking in the shellfish from which the purple dye was taken. This dye was the greatest export item they possessed and they were its only source.

When the supply in one area was exhausted they extended their boundaries in search of the precious material. They expanded their range of territory to all the countries bordering on the Mediterranean Sea and the islands in it, especially Cyprus and Crete. The search for both shellfish and copper took them further and further afield. This led them to southern Spain which they called Tarshish and later Tartessus. From there they extracted the precious ores - silver, copper, lead, and some tin. Tin was the most sought-after ore at the time (because of its malleability) and the Phoenicians found a more abundant supply in England - which they reached as the outer border of their territory. The Greeks called England the 'Tin-Islands', (this was the area of Cornwall).

They traded through the Arabian and Persian Gulfs with India, Ceylon and the coasts of Africa. Theirs were the merchant-caravans which covered the East by sea and by land; they became the wealthiest peoples of their day. (See Zechariah 9:3 and Ezekiel 27 & 28 in reference to the riches of Tyre.) Ezekiel 27:13 says they were also slave traders and part of their wealth came from that traffic.

They were the money-makers of the ancient world; their goal in all life was to become wealthy. There were no statesmen, no soldiers, no poets, no writers, no works of science or speculation - only businessmen. (There were some artists, however, as seen in the use of the men from Tyre to adorn Solomon's Temple.) They were happy to pay tribute rather than fight as long as they were allowed to continue their commerce unhindered.

Development of phonetic alphabet
(Swinton, Outlines)

The phonetic alphabet was adopted and advanced by them in order to further their business. They used it only for bookkeeping purposes. The Greeks took this alphabet and advanced it; then the Romans took it and changed some of it, making it the basis of our modern alphabet.

Their greatest period was the 500 years from the 11th to the 6th century B.C. They were subject to the Assyrians in the 9th century; to the Babylonians under Nebuchadnezzar at the close of the 7th century; to the Persians under Cambyses at the close of the 6th century; to the Greeks under Alexander in the 4th century B.C., and were absorbed by Rome in 63 B.C. During the Middle Ages all Phoenician power was lost and Tyre became a 'place for the drying of nets', (Ezekiel 26:14).

"Thus as each one of the great nations that have in succession played prominent parts on the historical stage of the world seems to

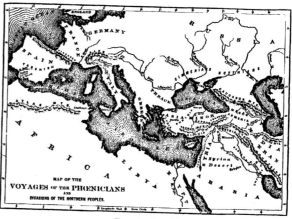

(Ragozin, Assyria)

have had allotted to it a special mission, in accordance with its own particular powers and gifts, we really might define that of the Phoenicians by entitling them, in a certain sense, without disrespect, and without undervaluing their immense importance, the Peddlers of the Ancient World. It was in its time undoubtedly a most necessary, most beneficent mission; yet one would hesitate to call it either noble or glorious, as those epithets can never apply to a pursuit so entirely selfish and grossly material as that of wealth for its own sake." (Ragozin, *Assyria*), p. 102.

"In this respect," says François Lenormant, ..."it is impossible ever to overrate the part which the Phoenicians played in the ancient world and the greatness of their influence... There was a time, of which the culminating point may be placed about twelve centuries before the beginning of our era, when the counting-houses of the sons of Canaan formed an uninterrupted chain along all the shores of the Mediterranean to the Strait of Gibraltar, while another series of similar establishments were stationed along the sea route that stretched from the southern extremity of the Red Sea to the shores of India. These counting-houses exercised an immense influence on the countries wherein they were established. Every one of them became the nucleus of great cities, for the natives quickly rallied around the Phoenician commercial settlement, drawn to it by the advantages it offered them and the attractions of civilized life. Every one, too, became a centre for the propagation of material civilization. A barbarous people does not enter into active and prolonged commercial relations with a civilized one without gradually appropriating the latter's culture, especially in the case of races [nations] so intelligent and capable of progress as were those of Europe...New needs make themselves felt: the native covets the manufactured products which are brought to him, and which reveal to him all sorts of refinements of which he had no idea. Soon the wish arises in him to find out the secret of their fabrication, to master the arts which create them, to profit himself by the resources his own country yields, instead of giving them up in the shape of raw material to the strangers who know so well how to make use of them...." (As quoted in Ragozin, *Assyria*), p. 100.

Phoenician Ashkelon

In 538-332 B.C. Persia ruled the area where the Phoenician city of Ashkelon was located. The Persians allowed their conquered peoples to continue their lives basically the same way as always. The Phoenicians were especially good allies because they gave the Persians naval power and the wealth it brought. The Phoenician settlements were mostly on the shores of the Mediterranean.

That Ashkelon was a Phoenician settlement is evidenced by inscriptions and symbols referring to their religion - especially to Tanit their goddess, and to Phoenician pottery found there. (Stager, "Why were Hundreds of Dogs Buried at Ashkelon?")

Phoenician religion

The Phoenician religion was based in 'Dualism': light-dark, heat-cold, good and evil, etc. It came from the Babylonians and was polytheistic in scope. Their god was the sun whom they called Baal or 'Lord', the same as the Babylonian 'Bel', and Moloch: 'king', (Baalim - gods in plural, and only refers to sun-gods). The female deity was Ashtoreth (Astarte in Greek), who was called Ishtar, Mylitta or Belit - 'lady', by the Assyro-Babylonians. She had the same attributes in both religions: goddess of love and war, goddess of fertility and pleasure; she was associated with the moon and wore the symbol of the crescent. "We have a Phoenician cylinder of cornelian, representing the Baal in the shape of a tree or post, the rays which surround it characterizing it as the symbol of the sun-god, and accompanied by the Crescent. The cylinder which so clearly brings before us the joint

Phoenician Cylinder (Ragozin, Assyria)

worship of Sun and Moon, the male and female principle, is supposed...to represent the Baal of Aphaka...." (Ragozin, *Assyria*), p. 108.

Symbols associated with the Canaanite goddess:

- the sacred groves, which represented her eternal youth and productiveness

- the cypress: the emblem of everlasting life

- the pomegranate: its many seeds were the symbol of fertility

- the fish: the symbol of fertility, represented in Ashkelon as the form of a woman to the hips and ending in the body of a fish, her name there was *Derketo*

- the white dove: a holy bird representing the Holy Spirit, but referring to her

- the sacred tree-(or grove), the *Asherah* - it was planted near the altar (see 2 Kings 23; Jeremiah 7:31; 19:5,7, and others, Israel was rebuked for this worship)

Assyrian Portable Altar
with Asherah
(Ragozin, Assyria)

The masculine and feminine counterparts always represented as husband and wife are seen under different names in various places: in Tyre as: Baal = Melkarth, and Ashtoreth or: Milkath (queen); in Ashkelon as: Baal = Dagon, the fish-god, Ashoreth = Derketo, the fish-goddess already mentioned. (Dag = fish in the Semitic language which was spoken by the Phoenicians.) The fish-god had the face and hands of a man, the body of a fish and the feet of a man, the same as Oannes, the Babylonian fish-god. Adonis-Thammuz, from the Chaldean *Dumuzi* was the holiest god and his goddess was Baalath, the Greek *Beltis*.

The divine group of the Phoenicians consisted of the Seven Kabirim - meaning Mighty Ones. They were all said to be the sons of *Sydyk* or Justice. The two most famous of these gods were Melkarth and Astoreth, then came the *Orderer* who invented the art of working in iron, and the other, *Law*. The other sons were named for the planets and don't seem to have had as much importance as those already mentioned.

An eighth son was added named *Eshmun* who was supposed to be the 'great god'. The divine group were the guardians of the nation's political and social organization and the inventors of economic arts, (e.g. shipbuilding, navigation, iron works). They were the religious teachers, also. The Phoenicians believed their sacred writings came from the Kabirim, but there remains no record of any literary writings today other than their bookkeeping records.

Their religion was taken with them to their commercial settlements and was accepted in the Greek and Italian islands and by the Greek nation. The Greeks added their own ideas and restated the crude beliefs in a poetic form, adding their own pagan ideas and names to the worship.

The Phoenicians, as well as most other early religions, including Israel, offered human sacrifices to obtain favors or to appease their gods, (2 Kings 23:10; Jeremiah 7:31; 19:5). They especially offered children as sacrifices and the sons of Canaan continued this practice to the first century A.D.

In 2 Kings 3:26,27 is an account of child sacrifice which came directly from the Canaanite culture. *And when the king of Moab saw that the battle was too sore for him, he took with him seven hundred men that drew swords, to break through even unto the king of Edom: but they could not. Then he took his eldest son that should have reigned in his stead, and offered him for a burnt offering upon the wall. And there was great indignation* (meaning to become so demoralized emotionally that they could not continue the battle) *against Israel: and they departed from him, and returned to their own land.*

"In 1978, a cuneiform tablet from the Syrian city of Ugarit was published, the text of which indicates that Mesha's seemingly unprecedented, as well as morally outrageous, act was in fact carried out in accordance with ancient Canaanite laws of 'holy war'...It follows that Mesha's sacrifice of his son, rather than unprecedented, was in fact an integral, if seldom implemented, part of an age-old Canaanite tradition of sacral warfare." (Baruch Margalit, as quoted in Biblical Archaeology Review, [BAR], November/December, 1986), pp. 62,63.

In an excavation by archeologists from BAR, Lawrence Stager discovered a burial site in Ashkelon containing many dogs. He believes the dogs were part of the healing cult associated with the Phoenician god, Reseph-Mukol.

Deuteronomy 23:18 says, *You shall not bring the hire of a harlot, or the wages of a dog into the house of the Lord your God in payment for any vow; for both of these are an abomination to the Lord your God.* This could refer to such a paganistic practice as the healing cult.

Since Ashkelon was under Persian rule at that time it is significant to note that the Zoroastrians of Persia believed dogs to be second only to humans. In the death-rites of the Zoroastrians a dog is given an egg to eat as a symbol of immortality. The dog is then taken to the home of the deceased where he views the corpse and eats three pieces of bread from the chest of the corpse.

The dead body is then washed and clothed and for three days the dog eats three meals a day for the dead person. For the next forty days the dog is given three pieces of bread and a mashed egg each day at the home of the dead person.

This seems to be a rite associated with most of the Canaanites who dwelled in the land of Israel and would be the reason God forbids this practice to the Israelites.

Stager says further: "Recently a temple dedicated to the goddess of healing (Gula/ Ninisina) was partially excavated at Nippur, in modern Iraq...In cuneiform texts the temple of this goddess of healing (Gula) is sometimes referred to as the 'Dog House' *(E-ur-gi-ra)*, and her emblem is the dog." (Ibid.), p. 42.

Since the Phoenicians didn't write down their myths and religious beliefs, it has been difficult to understand their religious system. For the most part the myths and beliefs have been taken from stamps and coins and a few pieces of their monuments. They told some of their stories to the Greeks who wrote them down and claimed them as their own and thus kept them for the world.

In the Scriptures, cities which were 'devoted' to God by the Israelites were utterly destroyed. This meant the Israelites were to take nothing from the cities because of their great wickedness in serving pagan gods, (Numbers 21:2,3). Many of the cities Israel took over, including some Phoenician cities, were destroyed in this way and certainly no records remained.

CANAAN (Genesis 10:14-18; 1 Chronicles 1:8, 13-16, and more than 150 Old Testament references to them.)

His sons were: Sidon, Heth, Jebus, the Amorite, Girgasite, Hivite, Arkite, Sinite, Arvadite, Zemarite, and Hamathite.

Canaanite legends say they came from the Persian Gulf to the Mediterranean coast, and that they were the sons of Phoenix and Agenor (mythology) and were related to Egypt and Babylon.

They were fierce, merciless warriors and between them and the Hebrews there was intense hatred. The Canaanite tribes came from Canaan and were mixed by intermarriage with the Phoenicians (from Phut), who also became known as the 'sons of Canaan'. They were the inhabitants of Syria and Palestine.

Canaan migrated only as far as the land which bears his name - Canaan, near Jordan, but he does not seem to have migrated immediately after the Dispersion. Canaan was called the "Land of Purple" from the shellfish (murex) from which the purple dye was extracted. It was very expensive and difficult to obtain and was only used for the wealthy.

There were eleven tribes of his descendants, each spread out in the fertile valley. They were:

Sidon, (Genesis 10:15)

Sidon, the firstborn, founded the city on the coast that bears his name. The name Sidon means "firstborn of Canaan."

In the Old Testament it is sometimes spelled with a 'z,' Zidon. It is the modern city of Saida. Ethbaal, the father of Jezebel (who became Ahab's wife), was a king of Zidon, who came from that city, (1 Kings 16:31). Solomon married a woman from the Sidonians whose goddess was Ashtoreth, (1 Kings 11:4,5). The people of Israel were forbidden to marry with them because of their idolatry.

Heth, (Genesis 23:10)

He was the ancestor of the Hittites, also called KAETAS. They were "a great and powerful people, spreading over an immense territory...who were reaching the height of their glory just as Assyria began to emerge from insignificance. It is always the Khetas against whom the Pharaoh's expeditions are principally directed, and from whom they occa-

sionally treat on equal terms, and whom they mention with respect, as foes worthy of themselves... [they were] in very early possession of the greater part of Canaan (Syria) in compact masses or scattered tribes." (Ragozin, *Assyria*), p. 31.

Kadesh was the Hittite capital on the Orontes River.

They were from the Taurus mountains in Armenia, and even after they left the mountains for the hot plains of Canaan, they never gave up their boots and close-belted tunics from the mountains. In Egyptian wall-paintings they are pictured in this attire. "The Hittites were a sturdy race of men. They are generally represented as beardless. They wore pointed hats and loose tunics. Their shoes were tilted up at the tips and fastened by a large bandage round the foot and ankle. They are like the shoes still worn by the peasantry of Asia Minor, and are the best preservative for the feet when the country is covered with snow. [They] also wore long gloves, covering the forearm, with one compartment for the thumb and another for the four fingers, (remnants of their days in the Taurus mountains)." John D. Davis, *Dictionary of the Bible*, (Nashville: The Varsity Co., 1973), p. 132.

There were many groups of them and the capital of the eastern group was Karkhemish. The king of Karkhemish (Carchemish) is mentioned in the Bible, and became the most powerful of the Hittite kings and could call the Hittites to war or for whatever services he required. The king of Kadesh was second in command.

The Hittite empire extended all the way to the boundaries of Egypt and some scholars feel that one of the Hyksos dynasties was Hittite.

They were present in the land of Canaan at the time of Abraham, (Genesis 15:19-21), and reached the height of their power sometime later in Asia Minor, (c.1400-1200 B.C.) Abraham purchased the cave of Macpelah from them for a quantity of silver - their medium of exchange, (Genesis 23:1-20; 25:9). This tribe lived near Hebron, west of the Dead Sea, and were called 'the children of Heth'. Esau took

Ancient Hittite god.
(Ragozin, Assyria)

wives from the Hittite women against the command of God not to marry with the idolatrous tribes around them, and the Bible says they were "a grief of mind to Isaac and Rebekah," (Genesis 26:34,35).

In the Assyrian monuments they are called *Hatti* and are called *Keteioi* in Homer's Odyssey. For 500 years they struggled with the Egyptians, and for 400 years they fought the Assyrians (1100 -717 B.C.), and were finally defeated by Sargon. Their kingdom had endured about 3000 years, no small feat compared to the length of existence of its conquerors.

Geographical Location: N. Syria and Anatolia

Tribes from Heth:

Hittites

These were Indo-European invaders who settled in Asia Minor in the 18th century B.C.; their last years were about 1300 B.C.

They paid tribute to Egypt in silver and precious stones. They were treated with respect by the Egyptians because they considered them equal opponents.

The Hittite religion came from Chaldea. Their highest god was Sutekh, "King of heaven and earth". Ishtar was worshipped under the name of Atargatis in Karkhemish and in her temple lived large groups of girls and women who were her 'sacred' priestesses.

They had their own form of writing which included hieroglyphics they had invented and which was unlike the Egyptian writing.

They were the foes of Assyria, and the Assyrian king, Asshur-Uballit was one of the first who tested his men and weapons against the Hittites.

Hittite Inscriptions, Hieroglyphics
(Ragozin, Assyria)

They were replaced by the Aramaeans, (Shemites) who took Syria, and its capital Damascus, as their own possession.

Hurrites

They were located east of the Tigris River before 2000 B. C. of the Aryan dynasty. In the 15th century B.C. they made the same Hurrite states into one vast empire from the Tigris to the Mediterranean.

The Hittite king Hattusil I, (c. 1650-1620 B. C.), wrote in his annals that the Hittites brought back prisoners and spoil from their campaigns against the Hurrites; priests and statues of stolen gods were included. The Hurrite religion influenced the Hittites, as they also did socially.

Hurrite religion

Their religious thought developed in Upper Mesopotamia from the beginning of the second millennium; the religious ideas came from Sumer and northern Syria.

The father of the gods was called Kumarbis, who was not considered the creator and organizer of the world.

The Hurrite text of the Song of Ullikummis refers to a primitive creature,

Uppelluris, upon whose shoulders the ancient gods raised the sky and earth, (the Greek Atlas).

The fathers of the gods and the ancient gods were displaced by new gods and cast into the underworld

They believed the creation was not perfect, but was in a chaotic state and one day the moon "fell from the skies."

Background to the myths

Kumarbis - was the father of the gods

Teshup - was the storm-god (also called King of Kummiya), and his son was Sharma

Khepat - was his consort, and was a goddess
   • Sheri and Khurri -were bulls of the storm-god
   • Ishtar - the goddess from Nineveh
   • Some of the Sumerian couples gods were also adopted by them:

   Anu-Antu, Enlil-Ninlil, and Ea

They believed that there was a continual coming and going between heaven and earth.

At one time a divine seed fell on Mt. Kanzuras (location unknown), and became Ullikummis. In this belief there are parallels between the birth of Christ and the birth of Ullikummis.

Also, there are references to a rebellion and of Satan and of him being cast from heaven to earth.

Ullikummis refers to a diorite-man or a stone-god. He was made of stone and was born of Kumarbis as a great invincible stone.

Ishtar, the goddess, tried to charm him with song. She was told to find him before he became all-powerful and his appearance became terrifying.

He continued to grow to 9000 leagues high, and 9000 leagues around. He caused

Khepat to leave her temple in the city of Kummiya because she could no longer receive the messages of the gods.

The conflict between Ullikummis and the storm-god (Teshup) threatened world order and Ullikummis wanted to also destroy all mankind as well as the storm-god.

Ea argued against the destruction of mankind because they were the ones who offered sacrifices to the gods. He was angry with Kumarbis, father of the gods.

Ea was instructed by Upelluris (the ancient god who holds up heaven and earth) to take the copper cleaver with which the heaven and earth had been separated, and cut off the feet of Ullikummis. The gods then got together to fight against Ullikummis and the storm-god leaped upon his chariot and went down to the sea to fight the diorite-man, (Kumarbis).

Ullikummis challenged him and said [In the heavens] I shall assume the kingship. [I shall destroy] Kummiya. I shall take over the Kuntarra (the temple) [I] shall [drive] the gods [from the heav]ens.' Ullikummis was then defeated.

Myth of the serpent Illuyanka

The storm-god fought against the serpent and was overcome at first, but then defeated him with the help of a human being.

Myth of Telepinus

When the god of vegetation disappeared all vegetation ceased. A bee found him sleeping in a meadow and he was awakened by the bee's sting, (folklore: the bee's sting cures paralyses). He ultimately returned to his temple and everything returned to normal.

The analogy here with the Sumero-Babylonian myths was: Ishtar descended into hell and all reproduction on earth ceased; in the Canaanite and Syrian myths: Tammus-Adonis disappeared and life ceased. This has to do with the seasonal cycles of spring, fall and winter.

Jebusites

Jerusalem takes its name from this Canaanite tribe. They later dwelt with the tribe of Benjamin as "strangers" when the Hebrews took possession of the land. (Joshua 15:63)

Amorites

Their land extended from the Arnon River to Mount Hermon and from the wilderness to the Jordan. They were conquered by the Hebrews, and made bondservants by Solomon. There were two Amorite kingdoms referred to in Deuteronomy 3:8, which occupied the area from the Arnon River to Mount Hermon. Their rulers, Sihon and Og, were defeated in their battle against Israel in Numbers 21:34-35. The Amorites were incorporated into the Canaanites when they moved into western Palestine. There were also some Amorite tribes which settled in Mesopotamia and some believe that Hammurabi, one of the kings of Babylon, was from this tribe.

Girgashites

The boundaries of their habitation are unknown.

Hivites

Their principal settlement was at the foot of the Lebanon, from Mt. Hermon to Hamath.

In Genesis 33 at Shalem, (Genesis 33:18), it is a Hivite prince who speaks to Jacob about his daughter Dinah asking for her hand in marriage for his son and offering the Hivite daughters for wives of the Israelites and vice versa. This could not be done because of God's command to them in reference to the gross idolatry of the people of Canaan, of whom one tribe was the Hivites.

The Hivites of Gibeon were made 'hewers of wood and drawers of water', (Joshua 9), because of their deceit in a treaty made with Joshua.

Arkites

They founded the Phoenician city of Arke, modern Arka, about 12 miles north of Tripoli in Syria. "This town is mentioned as Arkatu by Thothmos III, about 1600 years before Christ." (Davis, *Dictionary*), p. 54.

Sinites

This tribe probably gave its name to the origin of Sin, the moon-god. From the number of names referring to the word 'sin' it is possible that this tribe had an influence over a large territory which retained its name; the wilderness of Sin, Mount Sinai, Sinim, etc.

One of the most important Assyrian gods was 'Sin.' The particular son of Canaan named Sin, thus, may have been prominent enough in his time not only to give his name to a wide region in the land of Canaan but also to exert great influence in the Sumerian-Assyrian homeland of the Canaanites. The deified 'Sin' was said in the monuments found in Ur, to have established "laws and justice" among men.

Although some feel that the Chinese line came from this son of Ham because of references to the word 'Sino' and others from the same root referring to the Chinese, it is more probable that it came from the worship of the moon-god which was taken from Babel by the Japhetic tribe which later formed the nation of China.

Arvadites

The city of Arvad was built on an island about two miles from the mainland and 125 miles north of Tyre. Their island was called Aradnus, now called er-Ruad. It was the northernmost city of the Phoenicians. The warriors from Arvad were used for the defense of the city of Tyre, (Ezekiel 27: 8,11). (Davis, *Dictionary*.)

Zemarites

The inhabitants of Simura, Sumura, now called Sumra, were on the coast between Arvad and Tripoli.

Hamathites

The inhabitants of Hamath, "a city on the Orontes, north of [Mt.] Hermon, about 120 miles north of Damascus." It is now called Hama or Hamah. It was conquered by the Assyrians and some of the Hamathites with their god, Ashima, were taken to Syria as captives. Their history became merged with Syrian history. (Davis, *Dictionary*), p. 299.

The Scriptures mention them many times, usually in reference to being an idolatrous nation, (2 Kings 17:30; Isaiah 10:9). The boundaries of their territory are also mentioned in reference to Israel, (Numbers 13:21; Joshua 13:5). And as having sent tribute to David because he had defeated the king of Damascus, Hadadezer, (2 Samuel 8:9).

CONCLUSIONS OF THE SONS OF HAM:

The empire of Ham encompassed a wide territory. He and his descendants were content to live in areas of heat where food could be provided with little effort. The majority of the Hamites were not concerned with 'lofty achievements' but were content to live their daily lives with as little effort as possible.

However, there also were among them some of the greatest builders the world has ever known. Some were traders who trafficked with the East and shared the area of Arabia with the sons of Shem. Their ability for world-rule was clearly manifested in Babylon and Egypt.

Ham received the first kingdom in Chaldea (Babylonia). His descendants received part of Arabia and most of Africa. They settled in Palestine and maintained their foothold there until the Israelites entered and either destroyed them, drove them out, or intermarried with them.

Another group left Babylon and journeyed east to India. There, some of them formed the indigenous black peoples of that nation, and others of them were pushed down the coast to Malacca by the Japhethites who were entering the Indian continent in great numbers. These Hamites mixed with a group of Japhethites (the Malays) and traveled to the Polynesian Islands and most of the other habitable sea islands. Together they formed a dark-skinned nation which had lost most of its knowledge of the true God and lived in terror and superstition.

The Libyans, on the north coast of Africa and the islands of the Mediterranean Sea were the lightest in color of the Hamites. They also mixed with the native Iberians (Spain and Portugal) on the European coast of the Mediterranean.

When 'Egypt, Ethiopia and Babylonia perished, the reign of Ham was ended'. Julia McNair Wright, *Bricks From Babel*. (New York: John B. Alden, Publisher, 1885).

"It is to the Saracens (Arabs) that the world of today owes much of its science — mathematics, astronomy, navigation, modern medicine and surgery, scientific agriculture — and their influence led to the discovery and exploration of America." Henry Grady Weaver, *The Mainspring of Human Progress,* (New York: Foundation for Economic Education, Inc., 1953), p. 105.

"In the case of Ham and his descendants, history shows that they have rendered an extraordinary service to mankind from the point of view of the physical developments of civilization. All the earliest civilizations of note were founded and carried to their highest technical proficiency by Hamitic people. There is scarcely a basic technological invention which must not be attributed to them." (Noah's Three Sons, Dr. Arthur Custancs, as cited in *Willmington's Guide to the Bible*.)

EGYPT AND ISRAEL

Ancient Kingdom
Old Kingdom (2800-2200)
Dynasties II - VI
Pyramids
Re, the sun-god of Heliopolis

First Intermediate Period (2200-2100) Dynasties VII-XI (2090) Politically weak	Abraham enters Egypt Genesis 12:10-20

Middle Kingdom (2100-1786) Dynasty XII, Imperial period Foreign trade, built monuments Classic Age of Art & Literature Sesostris II (1897-1878) (Senusert II) Sesostris III (1878-1840) Amenemhet III (1841-1797)	Joseph in slavery (1897) Joseph made Vizier (1884 B.C.) Jacob enters Egypt (1876 B.C.) dies 17 yrs. later at 130 Joseph dies (1805 B.C.)

Second Intermediate Period (1786-1570) Dynasties XIII & XIV -vassal rulers Dynasties XV & XVI -Hyksos "Shepherd Kings"	First Oppression (Exodus 1:8-12)

18th Dynasty
Early New Kingdom (1570-1304)
Ahmose, queen (1584-1560)
Amenhotep I (1560-1539)

Thutmosis I (1539-1514) Thutmosis II (1514-1504) Hatshepsut "Female King" (1504-1482) Princess who adopted Moses(?) Thutmosis III (1504-1450) The Greatest Pharaoh(1486) The Largest Empire Amenhotep II (1453-1415) Webensenu, firstborn dies young No major campaign after 1446 Thutmosis IV (1415-1414) Amenhotep III (1414-1378) ———— Akhenaton (1364-1347) Tel-el-Amarna Tablets	Orders Infanticide (Exodus 1:15-22) Moses born (1526) Moses flees to desert Plagues & Exodus 10th plague: death of firstborn (1446) Army drowned in Red Sea Conquest of Canaan Invasion of *Habiru*, not to be confused with the Hebrews.

SECTION IV

The Nation of Dissemination and Order

Shem and his Sons

In the genealogy of Genesis 10, Shem lists his own family last. He knew from the prophecy of 9:26 that his nation would be the one God would use to preserve and transmit the knowledge, both written and verbal, of the true God, (Romans 3:2).

He continued his genealogy for more generations than the other two because he realized the importance of being able to trace their line to the Messiah who was to come from them.

In verse 21 Shem is called 'the father of all the children of Eber', from whom most scholars believe the name 'Hebrew' is taken. If the genealogy of Abraham is followed it will come from Shem, and Abraham is called 'a Hebrew' in Genesis 14:13, which is the first use of the name in Scripture.

Genesis 11 again gives the genealogy of Shem but is only concerned with the line of Arphaxad from which Abram would come. The true Hebrew line comes through Arphaxad to Abraham and from Abraham to the actual Hebrew nation.

As the names of Ham and Japheth mean respectively 'dark' and 'fair', so Shem has the connotation of 'dusky'; and thus is the father of the dusky-skinned branch of the human family.

Location of the Sons of Shem: Central Zone

   -the Middle East (Asia)
   -part of Asia Minor
   -parts of the Arabian Peninsula
   -parts of Europe

Skin color: white to black

The sons of Shem: Elam, Asshur, Arphaxad, Lud, Aram.

ELAM

He was the father of the Elamite nation which joined with the Japhethite Persians at a later period.

These people settled on the eastern banks of the Tigris at Susa. They were overrun by the Cushites after several centuries, but retained their own nationality. Elam is the progenitor of the Elamites. In the Scripture their most famous king was Chedorlaomer who was the leader of the group of kings who invaded Canaan during the time of Abram, (Genesis 14:4,5) and took Lot prisoner. Their ancient capital was Susa or Shushan, which is northeast of the Persian Gulf.

It is now part of the country where Iran is located.

Since that time there has been a combining of different people to form the nation living there today. The Elamites intermarried with the Persians and the Medes and then some of the Arabs from the Arabian peninsula emigrated into the area and mixed with those already living there. Those Arabs took with them their religion of Islam which became the controlling factor both in religion and politics.

ASSHUR

Asshur was the founder of the Assyrian nation, (Genesis 10:22; 1 Chronicles 1:17; Numbers 24:22,24; Psalm 83:8; Ezekiel 27:23; 32:22; Hosea 14:3 and 140 + Old Testament references).

They were the people from whom the Assyrian Empire took its name. They seem to have migrated from Babylon, taking their religious ideas and culture from there. Though Nimrod controlled the area for a time and built great cities there, the Assyrians were a Semitic people, and this was expressed in their physical and mental makeup. They also spoke a Semitic language. In appearance they resembled the Jews, though they were a more muscular people. Their descendants in Kurdistan preserve this appearance. Their religion was also Semitic.

Asshur was located north of Babylonia,

Nin's symbol - Man-Bull
(Rawlinson, Vol. 1)

between the Tigris and Euphrates, south of Armenia, and northeast of Syria. It was a dry, barren desert, made productive only by irrigation. Through conquest the land area increased to at least 75,000 square miles; this is more than almost all contemporary nations.

Its most ancient city was Aushar, which appears to mean "well-watered plain", and was later changed to Asshur, (Genesis 10:22). It was governed by king-priests called *patesis*, as were those of Chaldea. The bricks of their temple ruins bear the names of Ishmi-Dagan and his son, Shamash-Ramân who lived approximately 1800 B. C. The first colonies were Semitic. Both the region and the people shared the name of 'Asshur' and it was the cradle of the great Assyrian Empire. They were a people of vigorous and aggressive character. Zénaïde A. Ragozin, *Assyria, From the Rise of the Empire to the Fall of Nineveh,* (New York: G. P. Putnam's Sons, 1901), p. 2.

Their three great cities were Kalah, Nineveh, and Arbela. Dur-Sharrukin (the city of Sargon), was added much later and known as Arturia or Assyria proper, (Genesis 11-12).

The Assyrians were intensely religious and expressed a love of beauty like the Hebrews. The sensuousness of the Hebrews was refined by their belief in Elohim, but the sensuousness of the Assyrian was unchecked by higher motives and revealed itself in gross wickedness. They accepted a Divine Unity, but added to it the Babylonian pantheon of gods.

The Assyrian monarchy was to be God's tool of judgment against Israel, (2 Kings 17:6, 23,24; 18:11; 15:29; 1 Chronicles 5:26).

The northern kingdom of Assyria became more powerful and absorbed the southern Chaldean kingdom, 1250 B.C. From the union of these two went out the conquerors of the then-known world.

Assyria defeated Babylonia and for six centuries was the greatest imperial power of Western Asia.

Babylonia was a political division, including the alluvial plain between the lower waters of the Tigris and Euphrates Rivers (southern Mesopotamia or Shinar) and Chaldea southward to the Arabian desert. (Mesopo = Shinar.)

The independent kingdom of Assyria lasted a thousand years; its empire for seven centuries. It was ultimately conquered by the Medes, (Daniel 5:31).

They were famous for art, inlaying, enameling, overlaying with metals and cut gems; manufactured goods, architecture, sculptures, transparent glass, lenses, principles of the arch, tunnels, aqueducts, drains; pulleys, levers, and rollers.

Assyrian Religion

Their most important god was Asshur, then came Bel, or Baal, the god of the Babylonians; the two religions were almost identical. To the principle idea of divinity they

Assyrian Temple.
(Ragozin, Chaldea)

added the Babylonian ideas of successive emanations, two great triads, five planetary deities, and a host of inferior divinities, but over all one supreme God and Master. They called him 'Asshur', giving him a distinct and individual personality. They identified themselves with this god and called themselves "his people", believing they were under his special protection and leadership in peace and war. His name heads their list of "great gods". He is often invoked alone much as the Hebrews did Elohim.

They attributed their victories and conquests to Asshur and carried his emblem before them into battle. Their reasons for conquests and expeditions were attributed to the desires and commands of Asshur, as the Hebrews attributed theirs to Jehovah.

Assyrian Cylinder, with the Fish-God.
(Rawlinson, Vol. 1)

Note the quote by Tiglath-Pileser I, "Asshur, and the great gods who have exalted my royalty, who have endowed me with strength and power, *commanded me to enlarge the boundaries of their land, and gave into my hand their mighty weapons,* the whirlwind of battle: countries, mountains, cities, and kings, foes to Asshur, I overthrew, and conquered their territories." (Ragozin, *Assyria*), p. 7.

Priest and King before altar.
(Rawlinson, Vol. 1)

Particular instances of unusually cruel punishment are attributed to commands from Asshur to behave in a certain way toward their enemies and this was another parallel to the Hebrew reaction to the command of God to utterly destroy their enemies, (Joshua 8:7,8; 1 Samuel 15, Saul and Agag, etc.). The Assyrian king was also the priest (patesi), who called himself "High-priest of Asshur." He took the place of God, and the priest and king were taken together as one entity which nothing could separate (just as the Egyptians did with their Pharaoh). The national god and national leader were the basis of the importance of the state; they were its security and were in constant communion with each other.

The Hebrew priest was always more powerful than the king. The king was anointed by the priest and was subject to him in spiritual matters. He was not allowed to offer sacrifices as this was a privilege only allotted to the priest, (1 Samuel 15), and was only observed among the Hebrews.

Emblems of the god Asshur

He was a mostly human figure ending in a feathered appendage, like a dove's tail, (the

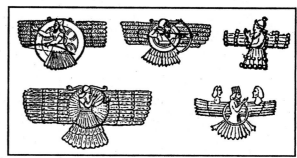

Curious emblem of Asshur.
(From the signet cylinder of Sennacherib)

(Rawlinson, Vol. 1)

sacred bird of the Assyrians and other Semitic and Canaanite nations), from the waist down. The emblem was framed by, or passed through, a winged circle or wheel, and is only seen above the sacred tree or on a sacrificial altar. It only accompanies the king as a protection and consecration of his royalty. In battle this emblem is represented as drawing a bow before the king, portraying protection for the king and destruction on his enemies. In peaceful occasions the bow is lowered and the right hand is lifted, or no bow is present and one hand holds out a wreath. At times the human figure is missing and the emblem is represented as a winged circle or disk with a bird's tail. It resembles the Egyptian symbol of deity which is the sun, and is represented by a winged disk without a tail, with the wings of a sparrow-hawk; the sacred bird of Egypt. (Ragozin, *Assyria*), p. 12.

(Ragozin, Assyria)

The dove is the symbol of Ishtar, goddess of fertility and is the sacred bird of other Semitic and Canaanite nations. (See section on Nimrod, under Section III, Ham.) The symbol is represented together as Heaven -the sun, and Earth -the dove. Inside the disk are sometimes placed five balls, evidently representing the five planets of heaven. On the seal of King Sennacherib there is a small head on each wing, representing the Supreme Triad with its feminine member -Nature, (Heaven and Earth joined, not by Jesus Christ incarnate in the flesh, but by a feminine deity representing Earth, from which comes the title "Mother-Earth").

A ninth century B.C. seal shows the king and two of the "eagle-headed winged-protecting genii" worshipping before the sacred tree with the emblem of Asshur above it. From the circle of the emblem comes a wavy line ending in a fork which is the emblem of Kamân, the god of the atmosphere. The wavy line and fork represent lightning. The kings' costume shows him to be equal with all other gods and subject only to Asshur himself. The king wears the five secondary emblems as a necklace: a sun, a crescent moon, a star, Ramân's lightning fork, Bel's horned cap, adorned with bull's horns, the symbol of divine lordliness and power, worn also by Asshur himself and by the winged bulls and lions who guard the palace, and by the winged good genii. (Ibid.), p. 14.

Eagle-Headed figure before the sacred tree
(Rogozin, Chaldea)

Other Assyrian Deities

Bel-Marduk of the Chaldeans and Babylonians, becomes Jupiter, a secondary god. The father of Bel-Marduk, *Ea*, is hardly mentioned.

The goddess *Ishtar* was highly favored and two great temples were built for her at Nineveh and Arbela. At Arbela she was the goddess of war and battle. At Nineveh she was the goddess of love, nature and all carnal delights. Because of these two distinctions she became two distinct deities with different clothing and different attributes (a perfect example of the distinct 'Virgins' in Roman Catholic countries). She is called Venus and is evidently pictured as the star in the five divine emblems, the star representing the word *deity,* male or female.

"Another interesting detail in the same direction is that, the planet Venus appearing in the evening soon after sunset, and then again in the early morning, just before dawn, was called Ishtar at night and Bêlit at dawn, as a small tablet expressly informs us; a distinction which...tends to confirm the fundamental identity between the two, - Ishtar, 'the goddess,' and Bêlit, 'the lady'." (Ragozin, *Assyria*), p. 19.

ARPHAXAD

The Chaldeans (or Babylonian nation), and the Hebrews.

Behold the land of the Chaldeans; this people was not, till the Assyrians founded it for them that dwell in the wilderness.... (Isaiah 23:13.)

Come down, and sit in the dust, O virgin daughter of Babylon, sit on the ground: there is no throne, O daughter of the Chaldeans: for thou shalt no more be called tender and delicate. (Isaiah 47:1.)

For, lo, I raise up the Chaldeans, that bitter and hasty nation, which shall march through the breadth of the land, to possess the dwelling places that are not theirs. They are terrible and dreadful: their judgment and their dignity shall proceed of themselves. Their horses also are swifter than the leopards, and are more fierce than the evening wolves: and their horsemen shall spread themselves, and their horsemen shall come from far; they shall fly as the eagle that hasteth to eat. (Habbakuk 1:6-8.)

In that night was Belshazzar the king of the Chaldeans slain. (Daniel 5:30.)

Chaldea is located south of the lower course of the Euphrates at the head of the Persian Gulf.

Descendants of Arphaxad of great importance:

Salah

Eber

Peleg - Joktan

The early nation was of Semitic root from Arphaxad, which was overrun by the Hamites, under Nimrod.

The area was sometimes called Shumir

and Accad. Shumir was the same as Shinar, in Southern or Lower Chaldea, and was a flat region.

Accad is Northern or Upper Chaldea which has mountains or highlands. The kings were called "the Kings of Shumir and Accad". Zénaïde A. Ragozin, *The Story of Chaldea*, (New York: G. P. Putnam's Sons, 1909), p. 146.

Geographically, Upper Mesopotamia was ancient Assyria, and Lower Mesopotamia was ancient Chaldea and Babylonia. Babylon was the northern capital of the Chaldean empire at different times.

Mesopotamia means: land between the rivers and is called the Plain of Shinar.

Chaldea became a graveyard of empires and nations because it was considered a holy place and the dead were taken there to be buried. "It appears that the land of Chaldea, because it was the cradle of nations which afterwards grew to greatness, as the Assyrians and the Hebrews, was regarded as a place of peculiar holiness by its own inhabitants, and probably also by neighboring countries, which would explain the mania that seems to have prevailed through so many ages, for burying the dead there in unheard of numbers. Strangely enough, some portions of it even now are held sacred in the same sense." (Ragozin, *Chaldea*), p. 80.

One writer remarked that it is impossible to walk in the area of Chaldea without walking over the remains of someone, even today.

In Daniel 5:30,31, Belshaz-

Captives building Platform-mound.

(Ragozin, Assyria)

zar was called 'King of the Chaldeans', (and 'Babylon', Daniel 4:30). When he was killed, Darius the Mede received the kingdom. Darius was the predecessor of Cyrus (see Medes under Japheth, Section V), who captured Babylon, according to Herodotus, by detouring the waters of the Euphrates and entering the nearly dry riverbed through the gates left open on the night of revelry.

The Chaldeans built mounds upon which they constructed their palaces and temples. They used sun-dried bricks cemented together with mud and slime, and kiln-dried bricks cemented together with bitumen. They had no stone with which to build, only clay and reeds, and straw from grain crops which they used to make their bricks. Their first monuments were crude and simple, but were large and usually square or rectangular.

When the Assyrians moved northward to Upper Mesopotamia they continued to build as the Chaldeans, though the country was full of stone. They even heaped up mounds instead of using the natural hills, (e.g. Nineveh). This is another indication of man's common beginnings. (Ragozin, *Chaldea*), p. 50.

Their educational contributions were mostly contained in the Library of Asshurbanipal. It contained books covering such subjects as science (mathematics and astronomy), astrology, geography, biology, and grammar. There were also dictionaries and school reading books.

Ancient Chaldeans
(Ragozin, Chaldea)

(See History of Israel, this section, for remainder of information on the Chaldeans.)

The area was first inhabited by Shemites then a group of Hamites entered and took over the country, and later there was a Semitic migration to Chaldea, as well as a Turanian element. It was called *Kip-rat-arbat,* "Four Nations", and the peoples of those four nations were called the *Arba Lisun* or Four Tongues. They were Hamitic, Turanian, Semitic and Aramaean, or Syrian. At least for some time the Hamitic people seem to have been the dominant group.

Some identify Arphaxad with a region known as Arraphachitis northeast of Nineveh. "Others consider the word a compound of Arpak and Chesed, i.e., Arpak of the Chesdim (Biblical Chaldaeans)." John D. Davis, *Davis Dictionary of the Bible,* (Nashville: The Varsity Company, 1973), p. 43. The latter theory is supported by Josephus who states that the Arphaxadites "are now called Chaldeans." Therefore making one of the four nations Shemites.

Religion of the Chaldeans

Traditions and beliefs

The Chaldeans worshipped the heavenly bodies as well as their own particular gods and goddesses. Chaldea was a flat area which was particularly suited to watching the heavens. To have developed an advanced astrologically-based religion is not surprising by a people who were constantly concerned with the movements of the heavenly bodies.

They believed the earth was the shape of an inverted round bowl, and its thickness represented the ratio of land and water. The inner part of the earth, beneath the 'Abyss', was the place of the dead and of the 'powers' that ruled their lives. Under everything was the ocean, the watery deep.

Above the convex surface of the earth was the sky which was divided into two regions; the highest heaven or firmament, and the lower heaven. In the highest heaven the fixed stars revolved around an axis, or pivot, of a great high mountain. The sun rose daily out of the ocean through well-guarded gates in the east and set in the west in the same ocean through well-guarded gates. In the lower heaven, the planets continued on their appointed paths. The planets were represented by seven kindly, symbolic animals.

Above these was the Spirit of heaven called *Ai-Ana*, also just *Ana*. He was the great spirit of the highest rank and greater in power than all the others. Between the lower heaven and the surface of the earth in the atmospheric region dwelt *Im* or *Mermer, the Wind*. His job was to drive the clouds through the heavens and cause the storms which poured down the rain. Ea, meaning 'the house of waters', dwelled in the watery deep. He was the great Spirit of the Earth and Waters (*Zi-ki-a*) in the form of a fish, and in that form was called 'Ea the Fish', or 'the Exalted Fish'. At times he rode upon a magnificent fish traveling the earth, guarding and protecting it.

Clay Statuette of the Fish-god.
(Rawlinson, Vol.1)

Their most important gods were Nannar and Sin, both gods of the moon who were honored with a great temple. It was 66 X 45 meters, 21 meters high, and was called the "hill of heaven" and "the mountain of god".

The minor spirits of the earth and heaven are only spoken of as a host or legion.

There were seven spirits of the abyss who lived in the depths of the earth. Their voice could be heard upon the mountains and they could travel through space. They had a bad reputation both in heaven and on earth. These spirits caused disasters in nature. They were born in the abyss, but were not submissive to its ruler nor did they acknowledge Ana's rule over them. They were called the spirits of rebellion. They were originally Ana's messengers, but secretly plotted against him and rose up against the heavenly powers and obscured the moon. (Another pagan reference to the fall of Satan.) They were feared and hated.

There were supposed to be many hosts of demons who attacked man physically and morally by civil upheavals and family problems. Their goal was to bring confusion and everyone was accessible to them. Their dwelling places were the tops of mountains, the disease-producing marshes by the sea, and the deserts. Diseases were brought by them (by *Namtar* or *Dibarra* - the demon of Pestilence or by *Idpa* -the demon of fever and insanity).

Evil Genii contending
(Rawlinson, Chaldea)

The dead were consigned to *Aralû* the dismal region also called *'the Great Land'*; (Kigal), *'the Great City'*, (Uru-gal), and *'the spacious dwelling.'* There was no hope of life after death, only punishment. The after life was ruled by a female divinity called *Allat*, the 'Lady of the Great Land', the 'Lady of the Abyss' (*Nin-ge*), who was Death personified. Namtar (god of Pestilence) was the chief minister.

The Spirit of Earth, Ea, cared for and protected the Chaldeans. He had 'all knowledge and wisdom'; his name was a terror to the evil ones because he knew the spells and words to break their power and make them obey. They felt he was too mighty and exalted to be appealed to for every problem, so they made their appeal to another imaginary spirit called Meri-Dug, the son of Ea and Damkina, (a name for earth). He acted as a mediator between his father and mankind. Meri-Dug took the request to his father using all kinds of wonderful words, and asked for the removal of a 'spell' or the remedy for an illness. Ea gave the answer to him and Meri-Dug related it to the priest who gave it to the victim.

Their temples were built in the form of ziggurats much like the construction of the Tower of Babel. One of the oldest remains is from the period of Abraham and was built by the king Ur-nammu. It was 200 feet by 50 feet by 70 feet high and had the square pyramidal shape of the ziggurats of the day. (Ragozin, *Chaldea*), pp. 159-179, and (Larousse).

The Chaldean king was also worshipped as a deity and all the activity of the city revolved around this cult. It is very possible that Terah, father of Abram, worshipped the god of the moon, (Joshua 24:2).

The Shumiro-Accads also believed in sorcerers, who were wicked men who could cause the powers of evil to do whatever they asked. They could inflict death, sickness, and disaster by a look, (the evil eye). They did this by uttering certain words, and by concoctions of herbs. The 'evil eye' did not always depend on a person's own will and could be innocently inflicted. This belief persists today in Mexico and in other superstitious countries.

The sympathetic magic, (voodoo), was the worst type of all. It consisted of making a small figure of wax, clay or any other material, meant to represent the intended victim. The punishment which was intended for the victim was inflicted upon the figure. It was melted slowly with heat to cause fever or other slow disease; it was thrown into water in order to drown the person; it was buried on the threshold or in a secret place; it was tied up with knotted ropes or stuck through the heart; all of these were symbolic of real injury. These were the roots of the modern-day voodooism which continues today in most of the Caribbean Islands and in Louisiana with the Creoles where Roman Catholicism and paganism have intermingled.

Intent to discourage the influence of evil.

They could not invoke prayers or give offerings since they felt the demons had no good qualities to which to appeal. They used magic (conjuring with words, and rites, incantations, spells) to take the place of worship.

Their ministers were not priests, but conjurers and enchanters.

There were also prayers for protection and help addressed to good beings.

These good beings were above all others. The good beings were:

Ana and Ea

Ana = Spirit of Heaven
Ea = Spirit of Earth

All illnesses were thought to be the result of demons entering the body and could therefore only be dispelled by casting the demon out. If the conjurer was unsuccessful the patient died, otherwise he got well any way he could. Because of this belief the Chaldeans had no science of medicine as late as 400-300 B.C.

The Chaldeans were great believers in talismans as protection against demons. Most of

Inscribed Cylinder
(Rogozin, Chaldea)

their talismans were made of clay or stones. The winged bulls placed at the gateways of the Assyrian palaces were a kind of Accadian guardian spirit called Kirubu, the Hebrew word Kerubim or Cherubim. The cylinder seals found in graves, tied to the wrists of the dead, are also talismans, placed there to ward off demons. The talismans were given their power by the magic words spoken by the conjurer.

Some were placed in their homes to keep them free of evil influences. (Today the same kinds of talismans are seen in many primitive countries. Chains of garlic and objects made of woven palms which have been blessed by the priest, are used over doorways to ward off demons. Century plants are planted near the houses to act in the same way.)

Demons were thought to be most active and most powerful at night in the darkness and the Shumiro-Accadians were very afraid of the night. They made a god of the sun and called it *Utu* or Babbar. The sun was their hero of protection. He was the source of truth and justice and was the supreme judge in heaven and on earth. He knew how to distinguish a lie from the truth and he knew if a man was truthful or not.

As a substitute for the sun when it set, he made Fire his night god and called him *Gibil* (Fire), or *Nusku*, to whom burnt sacrifices were offered. He was able to exorcise demons and to drive away pestilence. This phenomenon does occur from the strong air currents generated by a great blaze. (During a terrible plague in Athens at a much later period, Hippocrates kept great fires going throughout the city to try to get rid of the sickness.) The night god was also hailed as a purifier of metal which indicates their metallurgical skills in the making of bronze by mixing tin and copper. Fire would be indispensable in that process.

The repentant individual cried out to his god or goddess; the priest added his power to the exhortation, and both of them sought to restore the favor of the pagan deity. The goddess was called the Ruler of All, Mistress of Mankind, and the Merciful One. She was appealed to the same as to the god and many times was attributed more power than he.

It is interesting to note that this ancient civilization was acquainted with the signs of the Zodiac and with the movements of the moon. They knew of the 12 divisions of the year into months, and of 24 hours in a day,

which they called *'Kasbus'* or double hours, since they had 12 double hours in their day. They did not do the dividing as some claim. It has been previously seen that it was God who made the divisions and then made man aware of them. (See Section I on the stars). (Ragozin, *Chaldea*), pp. 144-186, excerpts.

Descendants of Arphaxad

Saleh, Salah

The name seems to indicate that they inhabited some part of Babylonia since through Eber he is an ancestor of the Hebrews who migrated from Ur of the Chaldees.

Eber, son of Salah, (Genesis 10:22, 24)

He was the progenitor of Abram, and Josephus says, "...and his son was Eber, from whom they originally called the Jews, Hebrews." He was also the progenitor of the Joktanide Arabs, (10:25-30). Peleg and Joktan form two distinct divisions of peoples.

Peleg, son of Eber.

From Peleg, (whose complete genealogy is given under this section on Israel), came the line that extends to Abraham in the following order: Shem, Arphaxad, Saleh, Eber, Peleg, Reu, Serug, Nahor, Terah, and Abraham, (1 Chronicles 1:24-27).

The name Peleg means *division*. Since this is mentioned twice in the Bible, (Genesis 10:25 and 1 Chronicles 1:19), it must be significant. The word "earth" in 1 Chronicles means "land", which could mean either of two things: either the land itself was divided, or the peoples of the land were divided. Whichever it alludes to it is certain there was a great division in the time of Peleg. Josephus says he was so named "because he was born at the dispersion of the nations to their several countries; for Peleg, among the Hebrews, signifies 'division'." Morris says Nimrod and Eber were in the same generation and were mature men when the dispersion from Babel took place. If, as indicated, Peleg was born shortly after the dispersion, his father, as a reminder of that event, (the division), named him Peleg.

Joktan, son of Eber, brother of Peleg.

The Semitic Arabs from Joktan migrated from Babel to the desert of Arabia and are essentially unchanged today. They were traders, shepherds, and leaders of caravans. They built the granite fortresses of Arabia and traded in fragrant spices and the gold from Sheba and Ophir which were sent to Solomon.

The campfire tales of the Arabian Nights belong to them - they were the <u>pure</u> Arabs - the Semitic Arabs.

As already seen, one group of Arabs also came from Cush, but there is still another branch of Semitic Arabs which was formed from Ishmael and the sons of Abraham and his second wife Keturah.

Under the Saracenic Caliphs, the Arabs dominated much of Africa and Europe. Their language is rich and extensive and they appreciated the arts, sciences and literature. It was due to their influence in Spain that Europe was able to cast off the intellectual imprisonment of the Dark Ages and begin to progress in all the arts and sciences.

The Arabs were without centralized government and because of their individual freedoms they were able to use their talents to advance civilization.

The numbers we use each day came from the Arabs and are called Arabic numerals.

They invented the zero whose importance in advanced math, as well as in the other sciences, cannot be overemphasized. From them also came algebra, geometry, and all advanced math principles. They advanced the study of astronomy and from their observations they understood that the earth was a circle and that it rotated on its axis around the sun. They measured the earth and passed this knowledge on to Europe.

They also invented the compass and the sextant which enabled man to navigate his ships far from the shore.

They studied medicine and built hospitals and universities (e.g. Baghdad and Granada) to further their studies. Until the century of the Americas there would be no greater advances made in medicine.

They discovered local anesthetic and performed the first operations. They were the first to isolate patients with contagious diseases.

They studied advanced methods of agriculture and began systems of terraces to conserve the land, (especially in Europe).

Because of the Crusades, Europeans discovered other inventions of the Saracenic Arabs: mattresses, rugs, curtains, fine cloth, silk, oil lamps, sugar (they thought it was poison), cosmetics, window blinds, glass, bathrooms, coffee; vegetables, rice, spinach, asparagus, lemons, melons, peaches and strawberries - all the result of their agricultural methods. The Crusaders also found porcelain, flatware, ice cream, talcum powder and a mail system which used horses and pigeons. There were two messenger pigeons at the entrance of each city. Excerpts from Grady Weaver, *The Mainspring of Human Progress*, (New York: The Foundation for Economic Education, 1974), pp. 113-116.

Because of their Semitic root they were monotheistic, but were superstitious and began to worship the heavens. The Cushite Arabs were idolaters.

Sons of Joktan (son of Eber, brother of Peleg)

This group of people are called Kachtan by the Arabians. They were thought to be the first of the primitive tribes of Arabia. There are still places and districts in Arabia which continue the use of some of their names.

Almodad

They settled in the south of Arabia.

Sheleph

This name is common in Yemen, and is also identified in southern Arabia with an old Arabian tribe, Salif or Sulaf.

Hazormaveth -meaning 'village of death'

"A region in Arabia Feliz, in the south of the peninsula, is still called by Arabs Hadramâut, which corresponds etymologically to Hazarmaveth. The place is mentioned in the inscriptions of the ancient Sabaeans, the people of Sheba." (Davis, *Dictionary*), p. 306. Its modern name may be Hadramawt.

Jerah, 'moon', 'month'

Location not known.

Hadoram

Probably in Yemen.

Uzal

"The kindred name was, according to Arabian tradition, the ancient name of Sana, the capital of Yemen, in Arabia." (Davis, *Dictionary*), p. 841, (southwest of Mareb).

Diklah - 'a palm tree'

They evidently lived somewhere in Arabia where palm trees abounded and from which they were named. Unger puts him in Yemen to the east of the Hejaz.

Obal - 'corpulence'

"Obil is the name of one of the oldest tribes of Arabia and of a district in Yemen. Bochart suggests Pliny's Avalitae on the African coast, near the straits of Bab el-Mandeh." (Davis, *Dictionary*), p. 572. (The name is spelled Ebal in 1 Chronicles 1:22.)

Abimael

From southern Arabia.

Sheba

The Semitic Sabeans "migrated eastward (Gen. 25:6; Job 1:15; 6:19). They dwelt in the south (Mt. 12:42), and traded in gold, incense, and precious stones (I Kg. 10:1; Ps. 72:10; Isa. 60:6; Jer. 6:20; Ezk. 27:22; 38:13). Sheba was a country and people of southwestern Arabia, well known from its own records and classical geographers. Its capital was Saba, where is now the ruin of Meriaba. The Sabeans were a great commercial people. They traded not only in the products of their own land, but also in those of India and Ethiopia. Their language was Semitic. They spread widely, and have left traces of their name on the eastern coast of Arabia, and in the northern desert along with the Nabathaeans. It is readily conceivable that in their dispersion they became mingled with other tribes by intermarriage or attached to them by political relations, and hence they might trace their descent by different lines and be classed variously in a genealogy." (Ibid.), p. 744.

From this kingdom came the famous Queen of Sheba to visit Solomon. Sheba is represented as the great-grandson of Kahtân (Joktan) and ancestor of all the South-Arabian tribes by the Arab genealogists. He is said to have founded the capital of Saba and built its citadel Marib (Mariaba).

Ophir

This tribe was located in southern or southeastern Arabia; between Sheba and Havilah. The region was celebrated for its gold and Solomon sent there for gold (1 Kings 9:28). "The voyage out and back (by the Red Sea) in the ships of that day, with the peculiar winds of the Red Sea, and including the lying in port, lasted, it may be judged, three years (1 Kgs. 10:22; 22:48)." (Davis, *Dictionary*), p. 582.

The Sons of Ophir

Havilah (sandy?) (bordering on the coast of the Persian Gulf)

"A district of Arabia, peopled in part by a body of Cushites and in part by a body of Joktanites, a Semitic people (Gen. 10:7, 29; 1 Chron. 1:9, 23). The association of Havilah with Hazarmaveth and other places points to a locality in central or southern Arabia... These productions strongly indicate the mountainous district to the north of Yemama; and in this neighborhood Havilah is best sought. How far beyond these mountains the boundaries of Havilah extended is not clear. From the record of Saul's warfare with the Amalekites it may be inferred that the Arabian desert for several hundred miles north of the mountains bore the name Havilah (1 Sam. 15:7; cp. Gen. 25:18). Migrations of the people would also carry the name to distant localities, as perhaps to the coast of Africa near the straits of Bab-el-Mandeb...." (Davis, *Dictionary*), pp. 305-306.

Jobab (shouting, trumpet call, howling, a desert)

Location unknown, somewhere in Arabia.

LUD, (Genesis 10:22)

For sometime the Ludites settled between Phut and Lybia in northern Africa where they learned the culture and customs of the Egyptians.

They then took over the nation of Phut (son of Ham, the Lybians), intermarrying with them, leaving their language and culture imprinted upon them, and pushed on across Africa.

They inhabited the Balearic Islands and several other Mediterranean islands. They spread out into the Sahara and dwelled in the oases, then took possession of the Canaries. They were keepers of flocks.

They had learned from Mizraim how to embalm their dead and their mummies can be found in the rock tombs of Tenerife in the Canary Islands.

The Guarani of Brazil are believed to be the true Guanches (original inhabitants) of the Canaries, who were the Ludites.

The Carthaginians, were called bilingual; they spoke the Libyan of Phut and the Phoenician of Shem or Berber and Hebrew.

There seems also to be a branch in Asia Minor called the Lydians whose culture was Semitic, but there is no conclusive proof that they were descendants of Lud and are more likely of Assyrian roots.

ARAM (Genesis 10:23) (Father of the Syrians.)

The Aramaeans occupied the highlands between the Tigris and the Mediterranean, now called Syria, and their ancient city is Damascus. Unger calls him "the progenitor of the Aramaean peoples, who spread widely in Euphrates and from the Taurus Range on the north to Damascus and northern Palestine on the south." *(Unger's Bible Dictionary)*, p. 76.

Job probably lived there in the land of Uz and he teaches us that for some generations these people held to the belief of a true God. "Ptolemy says that the Uzzites dwelt in the Arabian desert west from Babylon, under the Caucabenes, and adjacent to the Edomites of Mount Seir, who at one period occupied Uz, probably as conquerors (Lam. 4:21)." (Unger), p. 1129.

The Syro-Arabian nation was regarded as the model of physical perfection. His sons were Uz, Hul, Gether, and Mash (also Meschech in 1 Chronicles 1:17. Possibly located above Nisibis in Armenia).

THE ASSYRIAN KINGS

The Assyrian kings were mostly Shemites and therefore will be considered at this time before the history of Israel, because they have a great bearing on Israel's later history.

The first capital of the Assyrian empire was Assur, which is 150 miles north of modern Baghdad on the west bank of the Tigris.

There are two periods of Assyrian history:

1. from the independence of Assyria to the founding of the New Assyrian Empire under Tiglath-Pileser II,
2. from the ascension of Tiglath-Pileser II to the fall of Nineveh in 625 B.C.

(The dates of the kings are not successive because there were some for whom no records remain and the blanks cannot be filled in.)

Nimrod, c. 3000 B.C.

After the Tower of Babel was abandoned Nimrod took control of the entire country around it and subdued his neighbors or drove them out. One of those who was driven out was Asshur, son of Shem. Nimrod then united the different remaining peoples under one authority.

His capital city was Babylon, (Genesis 10:10), which became the metropolis of all the provinces of the 'land of Shinar'.

In the land of Assur he built Nineveh. Though some writers intimate that he used the Assyrians to conquer the Babylonians, the opposite is probably true.

Nimrod married Semiramis, who was born in Syria. As the king "had conceived a violent passion for her" her husband killed himself so he wouldn't be in the way of the king's desires. She was said to have been extremely beautiful. When Nimrod died she became queen. Her conquests extended to include a great part of Ethiopia, and she and Alexander were the only ancients who attacked India. (See notes in Section III, Sons of Ham for complete history on Nimrod.)

Ninyas - the son of Nimrod

(It is highly possible that this person was just a legend among the Assyrians and that this individual never existed - there is no historical fact to support his having lived and ruled, and probably refers to Nimrod himself.)

Ishmi-Dagan, this line was the king-priests, called "*patesis*", and were purely Semitic.

Shamash-Raman, n.d. son of Ishmi-Dagan.

In 1600 B.C. he participated in the Battle of Megiddo against Egypt. He was called 'a chieftain', indicating that he was the builder of the Temple of Anu and Ramân. He extended the Assyrian territory to the 'Snowy Mountains', and to the east to the Zagros Mountains; to the south there was a varying border, depending on their relations with Babylon. It became the most extensive territory of any ancient kingdom, but Assyria had not come into great power at this time.

Shalmaneser I, c. 1300 B.C.

He founded the city of Kalah with the slave labor brought back as captives from their wars with the Khatti or Hittites. It became the third capital of Assyria and the favorite residence of many later monarchs.

Tukulti-Nineb, son of Shalmaneser I.

He was the first Assyrian king to make a conquest against Babylon, then called Kar-Dunyash.

Asshur-Uballit, c. 1200 B.C.

He marched to Babylon to avenge the murder of his kinsman, using this as an opportunity to assert his power and importance. He marched against the Hittites to the west and northwest of Nineveh. He took them captive and they became the slaves used to build the great mounds and palaces.

Asshur-Resisi I, c. 1151-1117 B.C.

Three nations were to play a part in Assyrian history: Babylonia; the Hittites who were waning; and the Jews who were only beginning to appear in the history of the world.

THE FIRST OR OLD ASSYRIAN EMPIRE

Tiglath-Pileser I, B.C., 1100-1000.

During his reign Saul and Jonathan killed two of the Philistine governors and became heroes, (1 Samuel 13,14).

This king embodied the first period of Assyria's greatness.

He conquered the Hittite strongholds called the 'land of Naïri', in the highlands of the upper Euphrates and Upper Tigris into the mountains of Armenia. He defeated their five kings and twenty thousand warriors. "With their corpses," says the king, "I strewed the mountain passes and the heights. I took away their property, a countless booty. Six thousand

Figure of Tiglath-Pileser I
(Rawlinson, Assyria)

warriors, the remnant of their army, who had fled before my arms, embraced my feet. I carried them away and counted them among the inhabitants of my own land." (Ragozin, *Assyria*), p. 47.

In his later years he made a foray into Babylon taking his favorite god Ramân and the consort-goddess, Shala. These were captured by the "King of Accad" and taken to Babylon. Four hundred years later Sennacherib 'brought them forth' and restored them to their temples.

"Forty-two countries altogether and their princes, from beyond the lower Zab, the remote forest districts at the boundaries, to the land of Khatti beyond the Euphrates and unto the Upper Sea of the setting sun" - (the Mediterranean above the mouth of the Orontes) - "my hand has conquered from the beginning of my reign until the fiftieth year of my rule. I made them speak one language, received their hostages, and imposed tribute on them." (Ibid.), p. 57.

He was the first Assyrian king to sail on the sea and from the records, he is said to have killed a large sea animal, probably a dolphin. The sea had been the territory of the Phoenicians, the sons of Ham, and this trip was a demonstration of the power of Tiglath-Pileser in possessing even the 'great sea'.

The area of the Assyrian Empire extended from the Zagros Mountains on the east to the Euphrates on the west, from the Snowy Mountains in Armenia on the north, and to Babylon on the south. It encompassed an area of about 75,000 square miles.

Shalmanasar I, 1028-1017 B.C.

This king moved the Assyrian capital to Nineveh, and reorganized the economy and the army.

There is no Assyrian history for the next one-hundred years.

In the first century after Tiglath-Pileser I, Israel and the Philistines were at war. Saul and his son Jonathan, began their career against the Philistines at this time, and Saul was made king, (1120 B.C.). Then followed the establishment of the Davidic throne. David built the royal city of Jerusalem and made it the only holy place in Israel and thus united the nation.

Until that time there had been many holy places in Israel and this always caused a separation (both physically and spiritually). The national shrine, the Ark, was enthroned in the sanctuary in Jerusalem.

After David, came the reign of Solomon, which began in the middle of the 10th century. "When David's son and successor, Solomon, built the temple on Mount Moriah, and it was proclaimed the only high place at which it was lawful for Yahweh's people to pray and sacrifice, the seal was set on the work begun by his father, a work which endured through all ages down to our own day. But for that command, and but for that memory the Jews might in after times, like all conquered people, have amalgamated with the conquerors and lost their political consciousness...." (Ragozin, *Assyria*), p. 153.

Aram (Aramaeans) had become a powerful and united nation, with the seat of his empire in Damascus, (he was Semitic, and took Syria from the Hamitic Hittites). Damascus is one of the few cities in the world which was never destroyed. "Essentially a Semitic center, it retained its splendor and leading position all through antiquity; in the Middle Ages, when the Arab Semites went abroad conquering land after land as they preached the religion of their prophet, Mahomet, Damascus became one of their chief seats of power and learning, little inferior to Baghdad itself...This sums up for it a continuous existence of 3500 years at least, more, perhaps, than any other living city can boast." (Ibid.), p. 56.

THE NEW ASSYRIAN KINGDOM - 911-605 B.C.

This kingdom brought about the submission of all of Mesopotamia, including Babylon, all of Syria, and part of Asia Minor. Even Egypt felt the pressure of the Assyrian kingdom during this period.

Adadnirari II, 911-890 B.C.

He took control of Babylon and subdued the Aramaeans.

Tukulti-Ninêb II, 890-883 B.C.

He extended his frontiers to Armenia, to the northwest of Assyria.

Asshurnazirpal II - son of Tukulti-Ninêb, 884-859 B.C.

He revived the Assyrian empire and continued battling to subdue the 'land of Naïri' (the Hittites). He was a cruel king and the accounts of atrocities practiced against the conquered Khatti (Syria) are both cruel and very repulsive. He said of himself, "I am the king, the lord, the exalted, the strong, the revered, the gigantic, the first, the mighty, the doughty, a lion and a hero - Asshurnazirpal, the powerful king, the king of Asshur." (Ragozin, *Assyria*) p. 159. He made ten campaigns in six years.

The Hittites appear to have been vassals of Assyria and because of their remote mountainous home they rebelled at times and brought their Assyrian masters to war against them.

The king restored Kalah, his favorite residence and the second capital of the empire, by the labor of his captives. He was a great hunter of wild beasts, especially lions, which were kept for that purpose in royal reserves. He seems to be the first Assyrian king to use bas-reliefs for the decoration of his palaces. "The evidence of the sculptures alone is quite sufficient to show that the Assyrians were already a great and luxurious people; that most of the useful arts not only existed among them, but were cultivated to a high pitch; and that in dress, furniture, jewelry, etc., they were not very much behind the moderns." (Ragozin, *Assyria*), p. 168. He said, in recording his acts of cruelty against his enemies, "after taking another stronghold which 'hung like a cloud in the sky' he built a pyramid of the heads of the slain defenders. The 'prince of the city' he took home with him to his city of Arbela, and there flayed him alive and spread out his skin on the city wall...." (Ibid.), p. 161.

"He seems to have been in the habit of cutting off prisoner's hands and feet, noses and ears, and making piles of them, putting out captives' eyes, [and] burning boys and girls in the fire." (Ibid.), p. 162. There is an instance of something similar to this in Judges 1:7, *But*

Lion Hunting

(Ragozin, Assyria)

Adoni-bezek said, Threescore and ten kings, having their thumbs and their great toes cut off, gathered their meat under my table: as I have done, so God hath requited me. And they brought him to Jerusalem, and there he died.

His kingdom extended to Syria (Khatti), to the border of Lebanon and the seashore, Tyre, Sidon, Gebal, Arvad, (wealthy cities which purchased their safety with their wealth), and the southwest of Turkey where he says he cut wood for himself in the Amano mountains.

He spent his free time in rebuilding and adorning his capital city of Kalah, founded by Shalmaneser I.

He constructed an important canal not only to carry water to the city, but also to irrigate the surrounding area by a series of dams and sluices.

His "Annals" say 'he filled the Land Kaldu with terror'. Kaldu was Biblical Chaldea, and this is the first mention on any monument, Babylonian or Assyrian, of Chaldea. It was separated from Kardunyash (Babylonia) for the first time. Both were fierce enemies of Assyria.

Shalmaneser II, 858-824, B.C. son of Asshurnazirpal. (Shalmanu-usshir)

(Under Shalmaneser II the first direct collision between Israel and Assyria would take place.)

Assyria attained her highest power under this king. The empire extended from the source of the Tigris to the Lebanon and the Mediterranean.

His exploits and reputation were such that the rulers of Lower Syria banded together against him, among them: the king of Damascus, **Hadidri** (or Dadidri), the **Ben-Hadad II** of the Bible, (1 Kings 15, 20 etc.), with 1200 chariots, 1200 horsemen, and 10,000 infantry; the king of Hamath (called Hamath the Great by Amos the prophet), with 700 chariots, 700 horse, and 10,000 infantry, Amos 6:2); and **Akhabbu Sirlai - Ahab** of Israel, (Omri was the father of Ahab who built the great royal city of Samaria and married a princess from Tyre. The fame of Israel reached the Assyrian kings during this time and the whole kingdom was called 'the house of Omri' - Bit-Khumri), with 2000 chariots, and 10,000 men.

Shalmaneser names nine other princes or kings of Arvad and of Ammon, an Arabian, and 1000 men and 1000 camels sent by the king of Egypt. This gives evidence of the fear already invoked by the Assyrian name. They marched out confidently to meet Shalmaneser at Karkar near the Orontes river.

The confederation of kings was defeated, but did not become vassals of Assyria which indicates that his was not a sweeping victory. It was five years before he returned to do battle with them again at Hamath, without Ahab, who had previously been killed.

Another campaign took place in 846 B.C. against the Syrians (the 3rd campaign, still against Benhadad II), the Phoenicians, and possibly the Philistines. They were defeated by Shalmaneser. Benhadad II was murdered by Hazael, the palace officer, (2 Kings 8:7-15).

His fourth campaign (842) against the countries of the south was against Khazailu

(Hazael) who was defeated (the confederation of nations was not continued at the death of Benhadad).

Shalmaneser then subdued Tyre and Sidon and received tribute from both, and from 'Yahua, the Son of Khumri' (Omri), although it referred to Jehu who had in fact destroyed the house of Omri and taken the throne by a military coup, (2 Kings 9-10). To the end of Assyrian history Israel remained 'the House of Omri', to them.

Though the Bible does not record the part of Ahab in the Syrian league and the war against Shalmaneser II, nor the subject of Jehu in the campaigns, both events are recorded in the Assyrian "Annals" and on the bas-reliefs on the Black Obelisk of Shalmaneser. In 2 Chronicles 20:34 there is also mention of a 'book of Jehu' which does not exist at this time.

Shalmaneser lived mostly in Kalah and spent the time in his last years building, repairing, and ministering to the great gods. (Ragozin, *Assyria*), p. 191.

All the annals give his yearly battles and agree with the Biblical truth in 1 Chronicles 20:1 - *at the time when kings go out to battle.* Most of his battles concerned the West instead of the North and South. He does say he went to the land of Naïri as his ancestors had done and reached and invaded Armenia, without success it seems, because they were not enslaved nor is there any record that they paid tribute.

Ragozin says "on another occasion he took the opportunity of a quarrel in the royal house at Babylon to display his powers there, to sacrifice at the great sanctuaries, and to frighten the princes of Chaldea into sending him tribute, 'striking terror unto the sea (Persian Gulf) by the might of his arms'." (Ibid.), p. 177.

The main object of his career was to put

Black Obelisk, side 1 showing servitude of Israel, row 2
(Ragozin, Assyria)

Black Obelisk, side 2 Israel in servitude, row 2
(Ragozin, Assyria)

the roving tribes of the Syrian Desert into subjection and to stop the various wealthy Syrian kingdoms from becoming rivals. Their

Black Obelisk, side 3 Israel in servitude, row 2
(Ragozin, Assyria)

Black Obelisk, side 4 Israel in servitude, row 2
(Ragozin, Assyria)

wealth made them desirable vassals and he took advantage of this.

One of the cities he took was Karkhemish. "...so important both strategically and commercially as to be the key of the great high-road from Egypt to the North. It admitted his sovereignty without a protest, and its Hittite king sent him not only large gifts in herds, gold, silver, iron, bronze, and purple cloth, etc., but his own daughter for his royal harem, with more presents, together with the daughters of a hundred of his nobles." (Ibid.), p. 178.

At the end of his life his eldest son rebelled against him and took at least 16 of his cities as his own. Another son succeeded to the throne.

Shamshi-Raman, 824-810 B.C., son of Shalmaneser II, though not the eldest son.

There is little recorded concerning his reign. He was more famous for having an illustrious son.

Raman-Nirari III, 811-782, son of Shamshi.

He followed in the footsteps of his grandfather, reigning almost as long and going on almost as many campaigns. He especially concentrated on Syria. He took the capital of Aram, Damascus, and imposed a large tribute on the city.

Israel and the cities of the seacoast were not subdued but sent presents, establishing a dangerous precedent, since to the Assyrian, sending presents was tantamount to admitting to being a vassal

He says he subdued the land of Khatti (Hittites), and all the Phoenicians (Akharri), and the cities of the coast, plus Edom and Philistia. He also mentions the Bit-Khumri (Israel) though, as already indicated, this submission only amounted to paying tribute to the Assyrians.

Shalmaneser III, only lived a short time.

There followed two kings under whom a revolt took place and an usurper was placed on the throne. He was Tiglath-Pileser II.

SECOND PERIOD OF ASSYRIAN HISTORY

Tiglath-Pileser II, 745-728 B.C., King at Nineveh (Pul), (2 Chronicles 28:16-21; 2 Kings 15:19), the Bible spells his name Tiglath-Pilneser, (2 Chronicles 28:20, etc).

His kingdom encompassed Babylonia (Chaldea), Mesopotamia, Media, Syria, Phoenicia, most of Palestine, Arabia, and Egypt. The kings paid homage and tribute to the "King of Kings" as he called himself.

Tiglath-Pileser II conquered Babylon and took the Babylonian name Pul. It is still Tiglath-Pileser in Assyrian. 1 Chronicles 5:26, *...Pul king of Assyria,* that is, *Tiglath-Pilneser king of Assyria....* He is supposed to have been the first who reigned at Nineveh after the destruction of the ancient Assyrian empire. He is also called Thilgamus by some historians. He was said to have taken the name of Ninus the Younger to honor and distinguish his reign by the name of the ancient and illustrious prince, whether in a real-life person or in a mythological form.

He took the Reubenites, the Gadites, and the half-tribe of Manasseh into captivity. "Ahaz, king of Judah, whose incorrigible impiety could not be reclaimed, either by divine favours or chastisements, finding himself attacked at once by the kings of Syria and Israel, robbed the temple of part of its gold, and silver and sent it to Tiglath-Pileser, to purchase his friendship and assistance; promising him, besides, to become his vassal, and to pay him tribute. The king of Assyria, finding so favourable an opportunity of adding Syria and Palestine to his empire, readily accepted the proposal." Charles Rollin, *The Ancient History of the Egyptians, Carthaginians, Assyrians, Babylonians, Medes and Persians, Grecians, and Macedonians,* Vol. I, (New York: World Publishing House, 1875), p. 284.

2 Chronicles 28:16-21 tells of Ahaz paying money from the temple treasury for his help.

The second empire was essentially commercial and the form of nation-making was changed to a more consolidated nation where Assyrians governed the conquered whenever possible. The conquered nations became subject provinces and each had a fixed amount to contribute annually to the imperial treasury. Those who refused to be subdued were sent to distant parts of the empire. This was done on a large scale so that a fourth of the population of the subdued nations was transferred to some other province.

The Assyrian empire was greatly increased during the reign of Tiglath-Pileser II.

He extended the empire to southern Syria (the entire valley of the Orontes, and the seacoast). He transferred great numbers of captives to the land of Naïri which he had spent some time in subduing. Peoples from Babylon were sent to take their places in Syria.

Babylon became a vassal state and the king called himself "King of Shumir and Accad" and "King of Kar-Dunyash" (Babylon), all these titles were retained by his successors until the northern monarchy fell.

He went to the land of Israel where Menahem, king of the ten tribes, gave him a thousand talents of silver to help him (Menahem) secure his throne, (2 Kings 15:19,20). (Since Menahem had just received his throne by murdering the former king [Shallum], and had just terminated a civil war, he seems to have felt that 1000 talents of silver was better than another war at that time.)

One hundred years had passed since Jehu had usurped the throne from the sons of Omri and the nation was in a continuing decline, (2 Kings 10:32).

Moab began to rise again and harassed Israel on the southeast, and the kings of Damascus (Syria) on the north. Hazael and his son, Ben-Hadad III, had conquered and annexed most of the country east of the Jordan, (2 Kings 13:3-7). The southern kingdom, Judah, sent gifts to Hazael to keep him from invading Jerusalem, (2 Kings 12:18).

Ahaz, king of Judah, sent messengers to Tiglath-Pileser II and asked for his help against the king of Syria and the king of Israel, (2 Kings 16:7). He sent gifts from the 'house of the Lord' and the king of Assyria vowed to help him.

Pekah, (the son of Remaliah) who had killed Pekahiah, king of Israel, was assassinated by Hoshea. Hoshea, his successor (734 B.C.), acknowledged himself a vassal of Assyria, (2 Kings 15:29). Tiglath-Pileser carried them captive to Assyria.

Tiglath-Pileser then turned to Syria to conquer that kingdom under Rezîn. The blockading of Damascus lasted two years, but finally the army was routed, and Rezîn escaped to the capital city only to be killed later, (2 Kings 15:37; 16:5-9; Amos 1:5).

The Assyrian king then returned to the southern part of his empire to subdue the Chaldeans who were trying to invade Babylon where they intended to establish the Chaldean monarchy. They had made Ukînzir, a Chaldean, king of Babylon. When Tiglath-Pileser entered Babylon he was hailed as a great deliverer and took back most of the territory, but could not unseat Ukînzir and they reigned jointly at Babylon the last four years of Tiglath-Pileser's reign. The capital was at Sapiya.

Tiglath-Pileser took Merodach-Baladan, ruler of a large and wealthy Chaldean principality, vassal and received tribute from him. Merodach-Baladan was a proud and ambitious

Oriental prince who, in a few years, became the 'evil genius of Asshur'. He is supposed to be the king of Nineveh who repented at the preaching of Jonah.

This marked the end of the military campaigns of Tiglath-Pileser II, and the "Annals" record that 730 B.C. was spent 'in the land'. He died in 727 B.C. He is supposed to be the father of Sardanapalus (Sardan - pul=Sardan, the son of Pul).

Sardanapalus, 728 B.C.

He has been described as an effeminate, luxury-loving coward. He spent all of his time in the palace among the company of women, and dressed and painted himself like them. He found his happiness in the possession of immense treasure, feasting, rioting, and in base and criminal pleasures.

Statue of
Sardanapalus
(Rawlinson, Vol. 1)

Arbaces, governor of Media, found a way to get into the palace and formed a conspiracy against Sardanapalus. When he heard of the plot, Sardanapalus ordered wood piled at the door of his rooms, and set fire to it. He burned himself, his eunuchs, his women, and his treasures. The treasures were supposed to have amounted to $6,216,000,000 plus.

Salmanasar IV, (2 Kings 17), B.C. 727-722, (Shalmaneser).

There is no record of his origins. He could have been a son, (as Rollin says) a relative, or a usurper. He made only two important campaigns; one against Tyre and the other against Samaria.

Hoshea, king of Israel, tried to rid himself of the Assyrian yoke by making an alliance with So, the king of Egypt, (2 Kings 17:3-

7), during the reign of Shalmanesar.

So, (Shabaka), king of Egypt, was an Ethiopian Cushite who by his own power, and that of his predecessor, had subdued Egypt. He was then king of Ethiopia and king of Egypt.

Israelites bringing tribute to Shalmaneser
(Rawlinson, Vol.I)

Ragozin says: "There was...a country and race which had to avenge many centuries of oppression and contempt. Ethiopia, the 'Vile Kish' of the inscriptions in the times of Egypt's glory, saw her opportunity and took it...the Kushites of Ethiopia had assimilated the culture of their hated masters and had become a match for them, not only in material strength, but also in intellectual and political attainments. Under able and ambitious leaders their progress was slow, but it ended in the subjugation of all the Egyptian principalities until the Ethiopian king, Shabaka, could call himself, without boasting, king of Egypt also." (Ragozin, *Assyria*), p. 242.

First Hoshea gave presents to Assyria, then conspired with So to rise up against Shalmaneser. Since he 'sent no present' the king of Assyria put him in prison and this is the final information given on the last king of Israel, (2 Kings 17:6).

THE NEW ASSYRIAN DYNASTY - *The Sargonides*

Sargon II, 721-705 B.C., (Isaiah 20).

2 Kings 17:24-33

In the ninth year of Hoshea the king of

Assyria took Samaria. This king was Sargon. Shalmaneser IV had besieged Samaria for three years, but did not take the city. The "Annals" of Sargon say: "In the beginning of my reign I besieged, I took by the help of the god Shamash, who

Captives and plunder

(Rawlinson, Vol. I)

gives me victory over my enemies, the city of Samaria. 27,280 of its inhabitants I carried away. I took fifty chariots for my own royal share. I took them [the captives] to Assyria and put into their places people who my hand had conquered. I set my officers and governors over them, and laid on them a tribute ...." (Ibid.), p. 247.

The Jews were taken 'to Halah, in Habor, the river of Gozan, and put in the cities of the Medes,' (2 Kings 17:6). Hosea was put in chains and imprisoned for the remainder of his life. The ten tribes were destroyed by this Assyrian kingdom as God had foretold through His prophets.

Sargon II

(Peloubet, 1922)

Those who had been sent to Samaria to people the city were nearly overcome by lions and the king was told that the reason for the lions was because the people sent there did not worship the god of the country. He sent them an Israelitish priest from the captivity to teach them the worship of the God of Israel. They incorporated the true God into the worship of their ancient divinities and worshipped

Killing a Lion.

(Rawlinson, Vol. I)

Him with their false gods.

This corrupt worship and the mixed nations that resulted from the mix between Assyrians and Jews was the source of the aversion felt by the Jews against the Samaritans. When Christ speaks with the Samaritan woman in John 4, the disciples are astonished because of their

Sargon

(Rawlinson, Vol. I)

history and the attitude of the Jews toward the Samaritans, (2 Kings 17:41).

Sargon has no written history before his ascension to the throne. He seems to have taken the royal name *Sargon* from the ancient Sargon of Agadê. "The name, in its original Semitic form, *Sharru-Kenu,* is translated 'the established king', or 'the true, faithful king'. (Ragozin, *Assyria*), p. 251. He called himself 'the true' or 'faithful shepherd'.

He extended the territory of the empire and was constantly at war on all sides at once to quell the uprisings in the provinces.

The Egyptian king, Shabaka (So), constantly conspired with the Syrian nations against Sargon. Hezekiah, king of Judah, was the only king in the area who remained neutral on the advice of Isaiah, who kept reminding him that Egypt was a powerless nation against Assyria.

Syria rose against Assyria the second year of Sargon's rule, and the old battles were refought; Damascus, Arpad, Hamath, and Samaria. Not all the Israelites had been taken to Assyria and the remnant that remained retained their national spirit and pride.

The city of Karkar was taken and 63,000 Assyrians were sent to take the places of those who were deported. Their job was to keep peace in those provinces.

Sargon then marched down to meet So, before he could come to the rescue of his co-conspirators, (Joel 1:4-6; 2:3). They met at Raphia, (south of Gaza), in 720 B.C. The king of Gaza had joined So against the Assyrians, but So was defeated and fled to Egypt.

Tyre was also offered heavy terms as vassal at this same time.

Standard of Sargon
(Ragozin, Assyria)

The northern kingdoms (all the lands of Naïri and several neighboring countries) revolted against Assyria, and Sargon was hard pressed to keep them in line, but he could not completely suppress the rebellion in the confederation of nations. The king of Karkhemish was taken into captivity with most of the people from the city, plus an enormous amount of the spoils of war. The Hittite empire ceased to exist with this king, but the conquest of the lands of Naïri continued for many years afterwards.

Sargon made a conquest then of many of the Median tribes, supported by Dalta of Ellip, or Media proper.

The people of Ashdod (Philistines) on the Mediterranean, rose up and killed the king the Assyrians had put on the throne and installed their own king, Yaman. The people of 'Philistia', Judah, Edom, and Moab, joined together against the Assyrian yoke and again sought help from the king of Egypt.

When he (the king of Egypt) heard of the

approach of the Assyrian army he fled to Ethiopia, leaving 'his gods, his wife and sons, the treasures, possessions and precious things of his palace together with the inhabitants of the country to be carried into captivity.' (Ibid.), p. 267. Then the king of Ethiopia (and Egypt), betrayed Yaman and delivered him to the Assyrians, asking for mercy for himself. (See Isaiah 20).

(Merodach-Baladan was at that time ruler of Bît-Yakin, 'the largest and wealthiest of the Chaldean principalities'. His territory extended to the Persian Gulf and gave him great

Capture of a City
(Rawlinson, Vol.I)

advantage for commercial trade. The sons of the House of Yakin went by the flattering designations, 'Kings of the Sea', or 'the Sea-coasts'. (Ragozin, *Assyria*), p. 238. In the peaceful years that followed, Merodach-Baladan used all means to secure himself the crown of Babylon. This was in the same year that Sargon became king of Assyria. His ally was Khum-Banigash, king of Elam. The Assyrians and Chaldeans were divided into two parties and Merodach-Baladan was not accepted wholeheartedly. Sargon had partially defeated the king of Elam, but because of the eastern troubles, had not been able to follow up his victory and therefore left Merodach-Baladan reigning in peace over Babylon for eleven years.)

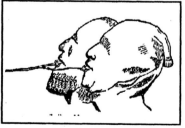

Captives of Sargon
(Rawlinson, Vol.I)

Sargon had been careful through the years to cultivate his friendship with the wealthy

Babylonians and the priests who were displeased with the Chaldean usurper on the throne. Merodach-Baladan kept his friendship with his allies, the Elamites, the king at that time being Sutruk-Nan-khundi. This 'backdoor' escape route was vital to Merodach-Baladan as he knew Sargon would, early or late, be on his doorstep. He had also become allies with the desert nomads and Sargon complains in his "Annals" that Merodach-Baladan had stirred them up against him.

At this time, also, Merodach-Baladan (also called Berodach-baladan), sent an 'embassy' to the king of Judah, Hezekiah, (2 Kings 20:12-19).

Hezekiah had been ill and made a miraculous recovery, the news of which had reached the surrounding countries. Hezekiah had remained neutral in all the intrigues of the surrounding nations and had accumulated a vast amount of wealth. When the embassy arrived they flattered him in such a way and to such an extent, that Hezekiah showed them all his treasures. Isaiah rebuked him for his foolishness, and told him because of his pride, his treasures, his sons, and his people would be taken captive to Babylon. Hezekiah's main concern seems to have been only that it not take place during his own lifetime, (2 Kings 20:19).

In the meantime, Sargon had managed to crush his enemies and the time had come to depose Merodach-Baladan.

Sargon became the champion of the gods of Babylon and proclaimed that they (the gods) had called him to 'prevail against the Chaldeans'. Part of his armies advanced from the north meeting little resistance, and another part of his army was making inroads from the east on the Elamites in order to try to cut off Merodach-Baladan's retreat to that country.

Sargon crossed the Euphrates and set up his headquarters in one of the Chaldean cities.

Merodach-Baladan escaped to Elam by a secret route and asked for help from his ally Sutruk-Nan-khundi who had already fled for his life into the mountains. The king refused to help Merodach-Baladan, who then returned by the secret route to his own country, Dar Yakin, or Babylon.

When Merodach-Baladan left Babylon the dignitaries and priests had asked Sargon to take possession of the capital, which he was only too happy to do.

Meanwhile Merodach-Baladan prepared for Sargon's attack by building a moat around his city which was filled with water from the Euphrates. The city fell to Sargon and Merodach-Baladan escaped into his citadel abandoning his riches and his family and disappeared from the scene. The city was 'made a heap of' by Sargon.

Sargon sent the captive peoples whom he found in Babylon to their own cities; returned the gods Merodach-Baladan had taken from other cities; put back in place the laws and ordinances which Merodach-Baladan had not observed; and put the nomadic tribes back under his own power.

He returned to Babylon as conqueror. Because of his fame and reputation, even people of the 'islands' (Cyprus, and Dilmun in the Persian Gulf), sent him gifts of 'gold, silver, ebony, sandalwood, etc.'

A small uprising occurred in the north, but was immediately put down and a short war with Elam occurred after this, but Sargon's military career actually ended when he took Babylon.

He then set about to construct his own palace and city called Dur-Sharrukin - 'the city of Sargon', unearthed by Botta in 1842 and called Khorsabad. By his own account, and by the excavated ruins, it was a marvel of workmanship and artistic beauty, accomplished in five years (712-707). It is a demonstration of the advanced state of the Assyrian culture. (Ragozin, *Assyria*), pp. 272-294.

Only 15 months after the consecration of the city Sargon was murdered by an unknown assassin. Sargon was one of the greatest and most noble of the Assyrian kings.

Sennacherib (705-681B.C.) Senaquerib - (2 Kings 18:13,19).

Sennacherib was a son of Sargon. He was warlike, as his father had been, but spent a great portion of his reign rebuilding Nineveh, where he resided.

He was quickly called upon to fight against Elam, and Babylon, which was no longer his ally. Merodach-Baladan made his appearance again, and after two years again became king of Kar-Dunyash (Babylon). He was allied with the Elamites and some of the nomadic tribes.

Sennacherib defeated them. After a six month reign, Merodach-Baladan again sought refuge in his Chaldean marshes of Bit-Yakin. He was not found, but Sennacherib placed Belibus, the son of a scribe, on the throne of Babylon. He only stayed a short time and was not worthy of mention.

His second experience was against the northern tribes of the Kasshi who had never been subdued by the Assyr-

Sennacherib
(Rawlinson, Vol.I)

ians. (This appears to have been a tribe of Japhethic descendants called Cossaeans by the Greeks, and possibly were later known as the Cossacks, since most scholars seems to think they were Turanian, or of the yellow-line of Japheth.) The trouble was ended by destroying the capital cities, taking captives, rebuilding the cities, and placing Assyrians in them. Sennacherib mentions that the distant Medes sent a large tribute to him on his return journey and says his fathers had not known of these Medes. (In 100 years they would take Assyria's place.)

Five years into his reign Sennacherib descended upon the nations of the west, along the seacoast, who were conspiring against the Assyrians. He then made his third campaign into the land of Katti.

Egypt was to be the ally of the western nations, which included King Hezekiah. Egypt was under the rule of the third monarch of the Ethiopian line, King Taharka. Against Isaiah's advice, Hezekiah, (Isaiah 36:6), was at first allied with the western nations. He made preparations for war and cut off the invaders water supply, armed the people and repaired the walls to withstand the invaders. The people of the city of Ekron had placed the king, Padî, in chains because of his allegiance to Assyria and had sent him captive to King Hezekiah, who put him in prison. God would not allow the Assyrians to take Jerusalem, (2 Kings 19:35; Isaiah 37:36), at that time.

Meanwhile the Assyrians came down the seacoast to Sidon and received the tribute of other Phoenician kings, (the king of Sidon had fled to Cyprus), and of Ammon, Moab, and Edom.

Sennacherib then proceeded to Ascalon, subduing that city, taking captives, transporting them and placing a new king on the throne. He then turned his attention to Hezekiah, sending a detachment to collect the tribute

Hezekiah had failed to pay.

He, and the rest of the army, marched to Lakhish before the Egyptians could take it. Sennacherib captured Hebrew cities, palaces, and small towns 'without number'. The Egyptians still did not come to their rescue just as Isaiah had warned.

Hezekiah sent messengers to Lakhish to Sennacherib saying, ...*I have offended; return from me: that which thou puttest on me I will bear....* (2 Kings 18:14). Sennacherib's fine was one million dollars in gold and silver. Hezekiah, (2 Kings 18:15), ...*gave him all the silver that was found in the house of the Lord, and the treasures in the king's house.* (verse 16), *At that time did Hezekiah cut off the gold from the doors of the temple of the Lord, and from the pillars which Hezekiah king of Judah had overlaid, and gave it to the king of Assyria.* He also returned Padî, the king of Ekron, whom Sennacherib restored to his kingship. He divided the lands taken from Judah, to Padî and the kings of Ashdod and Gaza.

After taking Lakhish, Sennacherib heard that the Egyptians were finally enroute to do battle with him. The arrived so quickly that Sennacherib retraced his steps to Ekron just in time. In order to avoid having an enemy at his rear, he sent messengers to Hezekiah to tell him to surrender Jerusalem, (2 Kings 18:13-19:37; Isaiah 36-37; 2 Chronicles 32:1-23).

Judah was miraculously delivered by the Lord. God had heard the blasphemy of Sennacherib in calling himself the "King of Kings", and had heard the prayer of Isaiah. In one night God destroyed 185,000 men of the Assyrian army.

History reports that a plague broke out among Sennacherib's troops and they retreated to Nineveh. This was a plague of boils - called 'mice' and was not uncommon among Oriental peoples, (2 Samuel 24:15-17, etc.).

Sennacherib returned to Nineveh in shame, having presumed to insult the supreme majesty of God.

The next year Merodach-Baladan was back on the scene, though not as king of Babylon. Another Chaldean prince, Suzub, took the Babylonian throne. Sennacherib promptly sent him on his way and he disappeared. Then Sennacherib went to Bit-Yakin after Merodach-Baladan, who fled to the sea and was never heard of again. Sennacherib took from Bit-Yakin, 'his brother, (Merodach-Baladan's brother), the seed of his father's house...and the rest of the people of his land.' He destroyed the cities and punished Merodach-Baladan's allies, the Elamites.

A campaign to the Nipus mountains to the north opened up the seventh campaign for Sennacherib.

During Sennacherib's absence, Suzub, called *'the Babylonian'*, reappeared and again made himself king.

Before taking care of this problem Sennacherib led a marine attack on Bit-Yakin and sent all the captive people to Assyria to prevent the conspiracy between them and the Elamites. (His ships were built by the Phoenicians who were captive shipwrights. The ships were constructed in Nineveh and floated by canals and rivers to the Euphrates and down to the Persian Gulf. Offerings of golden ship models and golden fish were offered to Ea [the fish god Dagon] by dropping them into the sea when the ships arrived.)

The king of Elam, Khudur-Nankhundi, had fled again into the mountains and because of the adverse weather conditions, Sennacherib had to retreat. He deposed Suzub and took him as a prisoner to Assyria. King Khudur-Nankhundi died and his brother, Umman-Minan, took his place.

In the intervening six year period Suzub

somehow escaped and returned to Babylon and retook the throne. The people gave him the crown of 'Shumir and Accad'. His allies, the Elamites, joined with him and went to Babylon with armies, chariots, and wagons. Together they went out to meet Sennacherib as he advanced on the city.

In the "Annals" Sennacherib describes the battle: "Then he, the Elamite, whose cities I had captured and made even with the ground, showed that he had no sense: he was unmindful of it. He assembled his army; his chariots and wagons he collected; horses and asses he harnessed to their yokes...A vast host of allies he led along with him...and the road to Babylonia they took...The Babylonians, wicked devils, the gates of their city barred strongly and hardened their hearts for resistance.

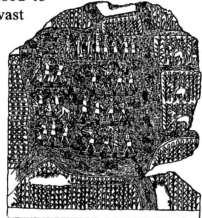
Chaldean Reeds
(From slab of Sennacherib)
(Rawlinson, Chaldea)

"Even as swarms of locusts pass over the country, they hastened onwards, to do battle with me. The dust of their feet rose before me as when a mighty storm-wind covers the face of the wide heaven with rain-laden clouds. By the city of Khaluli, on the bank of the Tigris, they drew themselves up in battle array and called up their forces. But I prayed to Asshur, Sin, Shamash, Bel, Nebo and Nergal, to Ishtar of Nineveh and Ishtar of Arbela, my heavenly helpers, to give me victory over the mighty foe.....My lofty war chariot, that sweeps away the foes, in the wrath of my heart I hastily mounted. The mighty bow I seized which Asshur has given into my hand, my mace, the life-destroying, I grasped. Against

all the hosts of the rebels I broke loose, impetuous as a lion: I thundered like Ramân.....With the weapons of Asshur my lord and the onslaught of my terrible battle, I made their breasts to quake, and drove them to bay. I lightened their ranks with mace and with arrows, and their corpses I strewed around like sheaves... [part of text missing]. Khumbanundash, the king of Elam's general and principal stay, a man of high estate and prudent, together with his attendant lords, - golden daggers in their girdles, armlets of pure gold on their wrists, - I led away like sturdy bulls that are fettered, and ended their lives: I cut their throats as one does to lambs, and the dear lives I beat out....With the bodies of their warriors I filled the valley as with grass...As trophies of victory I cut off their hands and stripped from their wrists the armlets of shining gold and silver; with maces set with sharp spikes I shattered their arms; [see Lamentations 5:12], their golden and silver daggers I took from their hips....Him, Ummanminan, the king of Elam, together with the king of Babylon and his allies from the land of Kaldu, the fierceness of my battle overthrew them. They abandoned their tents, and, to save their lives, they trampled on the corpses of their own warriors; they sped away, even as young swallows scared from their nests....I drove my chariots and horses in pursuit of them; their fugitives, who ran for their lives, were speared wherever they were found." (Ragozin, *Assyria*), excerpts, pp. 298-330.

Counting and Piling up Heads of Captives
(Ragozin, Assyria).

After the battle of Khaluli in 692 or 691 B.C., the Elamites retreated into the mountains and for many years did not fight any battles.

Flocks and Captive Women Carried Away
(Ragozin, Assyria)

Sennacherib went to Babylon with the view of destroying it before it became a political rival and restored the old empire. Thus he describes it in the "Annals": "The city and houses, from their foundation to their upper chambers, I destroyed, dug up, in the fire I burnt. The fortress and outer wall, the temples of the gods, [I destroyed]...In order that, in the course of time, no one may find the place of this city and of its temples, I covered it with water." (Ibid.), p. 321.

He made a successful conquest of Babylon and retrieved the signet ring of Tukulti-Nineb which that king had lost, and the Babylonians had preserved as a sign of his retreat from their city, six hundred years earlier.

When Sennacherib returned to Nineveh he treated his subjects and family cruelly. He was enraged by his disgrace in battle (at Jerusalem), and took out his hatred on the Jews killing great numbers of them each day and refusing to allow them to be buried.

The last ten years of his life he spent in Nineveh. He was so cruel to his own family that his two eldest sons killed him in the temple of his god, Nisroch, as he lay prostrated before him. Those sons promptly fled to Urartu, (Armenia) (2 Kings 19:37; 2 Chronicles 32:21; Isaiah 37:38). His fourth son, Esar-Haddon, took the throne.

Esar-haddon, 681-668 B.C., Asarhadón (Asshur-Asarhadon), (Isaiah 37:38).

He was the son of Sennacherib and the grandson of Sargon.

He built three cities of note: Babylon, (which his father had tried to destroy), Kalah - which was not completed and was destroyed by fire, and built up Nineveh.

Esar-haddon
(Ploubet, 1911)

He annexed Babylon, made himself master, and reigned over the two united empires for thirteen years.

He united Syria and Palestine with Assyria, then entered Israel and took most of the people captive. He sent generals and an army into Judea to take them captive. They were successful in taking King Manasseh, putting him in chains and carrying him to Babylon. Manasseh repented to God and was returned to Jerusalem, (2 Chronicles 33:11,13).

Isaiah 7:8, was fulfilled, *Within three score and five years shall Ephraim be broken, that it be no more a people.* This was exactly the space of time which had elapsed. Israel ceased to be a visible nation and those who were left were mixed and tainted by other nations.

Esar-haddon's first act was to march on the lands of Naïri (part of which is known today as Kurdistan), where his brothers had fled, to try to avenge the death of his father. He was victorious over the armies, but there is no record of whether he killed his brothers or whether they escaped into the mountains.

Merodach-Baladan's son of the Bit Yakin family, (of Chaldea), seized Ur during Esarhaddon's absence and put himself on his father's throne. Esarhaddon sent his armies to overthrow him, but the Chaldean fled to Elam and nothing is known of his fate there. His brother, Nahid-Marduk, went to Nineveh and offered his submission to Esarhaddon and was given the 'inheritance of his brother' meaning the province of the seacoast. He was, of course, required to take yearly tribute to Nineveh.

Esarhaddon restored the city of Babylon and the desecrated temples. He called himself the 'chosen instrument of the god' Marduk to restore the city which was his favorite residence.

He made an expedition to 'distant Media', and captured several 'chiefs of cities, and forgave and reinstated others'. The other Median chiefs took him gifts of horses to Nineveh. He also had a frontier skirmish with Tiushpa the Gimirrai (Cimmerians). This was another of the first mentions of the sons of Japheth in the secular histories.

He made an expedition against the Arabians in their desert dwelling place where no king had been before. He killed eight Arabian sovereigns, two of whom were women, and carried away their riches and their gods.

The countries of the West had been peaceful for 20 years, but an uprising began in Sidon. They removed the king whom Sennacherib had set up and defied Assyria. Esarhaddon 'rooted up its citadel and dwellings and flung them into the sea'. (Ragozin, *Assyria*), p. 339. He built a new city in its place and called it the 'city of Esarhaddon'.

He returned to Nineveh and called together the 'kings of Khatti and of the nations beyond the sea'. (The Khatti were originally Hamitic Hittites, but the name came to signify any nation in control of Syria, and usually referred to the Aramaeans in the last cen-

turies of the B.C. period.) These included Baal, king of Tyre, and Manasseh, king of Judah, twenty-two kings in total - all bringing gifts of tribute to Esarhaddon. The materials which were used to construct his palace at Nineveh were provided by these gifts. Shortly after this, Baal, king of Tyre, joined with Taharka (Tarku), king of Egypt, to rid his city of the Assyrian yoke, (see 2 Chronicles 33 for the involvement of Manasseh).

In the history of Esarhaddon, Tarku is called the King of Kush. When the Assyrians fought against Tyre, Taharka fled to Egypt and then to Ethiopia. Esarhaddon followed him to Egypt, took Memphis, the lower capital and took Taharka's family captive. He then established Assyrian rule over the land, (see Isaiah 19). Esarhaddon left Egypt divided among twenty princes and a few Assyrians. He set Necho, a hereditary prince, over the rest and he called himself 'King of the kings of Muzur (Egypt)'.

Esarhaddon was said to have been 'the noblest and most gracious' of all the Assyrian rulers. He gave the rule to his son Asshurbanipal, April 12, 668 B.C. Asshurbanipal ruled the kingdom of Assyria from his grandfather's, (Sennacherib's), royal palace. (Ragozin, *Assyria*), pp. 331-346.

Esarhaddon became king of Babylon, with his younger son, Shamash-Shumukin, as viceroy and died within the year 668 B.C.

Asshurbanipal, 668-626 B.C. Ashurbanipal (As-Shur-Bânî-Habal).

During his reign the Assyrian empire attained its greatest geographical limits, and then began to disintegrate.

Asshurbanipal received his father's kingdom, which was a prosperous beginning for him. He held Assyria, Babylon, Syria, Palestine, Egypt, and Elam. Egypt revolted c. 660 B.C., and eight years later Babylon revolted, led by Asshurbanipal's brother, Shamash-Shamukin.

He was an intellectual king and literature flourished during his reign. He founded two large libraries at Nineveh which have now been discovered and have given a more precise history of the Assyrian culture and how advanced they were in literature and the arts. The king said the gods had given him 'attentive ears'.

Asshurbanipal was a warrior and conqueror as his father had been. He was also a great lion hunter, and kept a harem equaled only by that of King Solomon. The kings who were his vassals, sent their daughters, those of their brothers, and those of the highest in the kingdom, along with their tribute gifts, and by this means his harem grew to be quite large.

Stele of Asshur-idanni-pal, with altar in front
(Rawlinson, Assyria)

Taharka, the Ethiopian king who had been dethroned by Asshurbanipal's father, Esarhaddon, revolted and took the power from the princes whom Assyria had put in place. He then retook the throne of Egypt at Memphis. Asshurbanipal arrived quickly and Taharka fled to the land of Kush - Ethiopia. He restored the princes to power and returned to Nineveh.

The princes, meanwhile, called Taharka back from Ethiopia and pledged their allegiance to him. The Assyrian generals (who had stayed in Egypt) captured several of the kings (princes) and sent them captive to Nineveh. Asshurbanipal showed them kindness, especially Necho, prince of Saïs, who was men-

tioned in the reign of Esarhaddon. He returned Necho to Egypt with many gifts and with many Assyrian generals as governors, and demanded more tribute from him. Taharka died and his nephew or his stepson (it is not known for sure which), took the thrones of Thebes and Memphis. The Assyrian army returned and in the panic they created, the Ethiopian fled from Memphis, which he had taken from the Assyrians. He then fled to Thebes and finally escaped to his own country and died shortly thereafter, ending the Ethiopian dynasty.

Thebes was destroyed by the Assyrians. It had been a cultural and religious gem of Egypt, but when the Assyrians finished with it, there was nothing left as archeological finds have demonstrated.

Gyges, king of Lydia, a Shemite, (Gugu, King of Ludi to the Assyrians), came to Nineveh and asked help from Asshurbanipal against the Cimmerians (Gimirraï) who were 'robbing and plundering countries', his own included.

The Assyrian yoke proved to be too hard and too costly and after several years Gyges joined forces with the Egyptian king, Psammetik, the son of Necho, king of Saïs, who also wanted to rid himself of the Assyrian yoke.

Asshurbanipal made war on Gyges, and Gyges was killed 654 or 653 B.C., and his country was overrun by the Cimmerians. His son, Ardys, paid tribute to Asshurbanipal. The Lydians didn't receive much help from Assyria because another nation was on the march and demanded their attention.

That nation was the Saki or Scythians - the Magog of the Hebrews. The Assyrian records tell of 'Gôg, king of Mâgôg' a real person, (Ezekiel 38-39), chief of the Scythians in the time of Asshurbanipal. They were defeated by Asshurbanipal and seventy-five of their chief cities were taken and two of Gog's

(Gâgi) sons were taken as prisoners to Nineveh.

However, the most important wars of his reign took place against Elam and Babylon.

Asshurbanipal's younger brother, Shamash-Shumukin, governed the southern country called Babylonia. Elam was under the rule of Urtaki, the second in a line of three brothers who ruled Elam, plus several coastal tribes. He invaded Accad and blockaded Babylon, but the Assyrians drove them out. Urtaki returned to his own country and died shortly thereafter.

Teumman, Urtaki's younger brother became king of Elam in his place. He tried to kill his five nephews, sons of the two previous kings, but they fled to Assyria with a great number of people and sought refuge there. Asshurbanipal granted them his protection and refused to give them up to Teumman.

Teumman took that as a cause for war. Asshurbanipal met him on the banks of the Ulaï River and totally defeated his armies. Teumman was wounded, and he and his son, fled into the woods where they were found

Asshurbanipal's Battle at Ulai (Ragozin, Assyria)

and beheaded; some say by his own nephew Tammaritu, Urtaki's youngest son. The king's head was taken to Nineveh to be exhibited in the triumphal procession of King Asshurbanipal. "The head of Teumman had been tied on

a string and hung around the neck of one of his chief allies and friends, a prince of the marshes who had been captured alive and now walked in the procession." (Ragozin, *Assyria*), p. 391. The captives were tortured and killed, says the "Annals" "...their tongues I pulled out, I tore off their skins." (Ibid.)

Ummanigash, a son of Urtaki, was placed on the throne of Elam; his younger brother, Tammaritu, ruled over another province of Elam, c. 655 B.C.

Meanwhile Asshurbanipal's brother, Shamash-Shumukin, plotted against him and tried to overthrow him by making an alliance with Psammetik, king of Egypt.

Ummanigash was murdered by his brother, Tammaritu, who refused to honor any allegiance to Assyria and denied he had cut off his uncle's head. He was unseated by Inda-Bigash, but escaped to Nineveh again, with 85 of his kinsmen, and asked for asylum, which Asshurbanipal granted, though they were, in reality, prisoners of Assyria.

Since the army was needed to put down the revolt in Babylon, the other vassal kingdoms took advantage of the situation:

- Egypt shook off the Assyrian yoke under Psammetik and established an undivided royalty in Egypt.
- Gyges was left stranded and the Cimmerians went unchecked.
- The Syrian states and the people of the seacoast formed a confederacy which was not challenged by Assyria.

After a lengthy blockade, Babylon was finally conquered. The people in the city were reduced to eating their children because of the lack of food. The city was taken, Shamash-Shumukin was killed, and the tribes were subdued.

Nabu-Belzikri, a grandson of Merodach-

Baladan, one of the Chaldean princes, pretended to be loyal to Asshurbanipal and asked for his help. When the Assyrians went to help him, he captured them and sent them to Elam. Indabigash was king in Elam and did not want problems with Asshurbanipal, so he sent the prisoners to Assyria with offers of alliance. Asshurbanipal wanted more than his alliance, he wanted Nabubelzikri and threatened to overrun the country of Elam if his demands were not met.

When the Elamites heard of the threat, they overthrew Indabigash, then murdered him, and put Ummanaldash II, the son of a general, on the throne. He refused to send Nabubelzikri to Asshurbanipal and also refused to return a goddess, (Nana), which had been taken from Erech many centuries before.

Asshurbanipal used this as an excuse to invade Elam. He was accompanied by the refugee Tammaritu. Assyria was victorious and Asshurbanipal put Tammaritu on the throne at Shushan. Tammaritu rebelled against him again, but since Asshurbanipal had not yet left Elam, he put down the revolt and took Tammaritu prisoner to Nineveh to await his fate.

Shushan was destroyed and their gods were carried to Assyria. The goddess Nana was returned to Erech after an absence of 1600 years. Elam, as a kingdom and as a nation, was destroyed. (It later became mixed with the Medes and formed part of the Medo-Persian empire.)

But Assyria's end was also in sight, Zephaniah 2:13-15, *And he will stretch out his hand against the north and destroy Assyria; and will make Nineveh a desolation, and dry like a wilderness. And flocks shall lie down in the midst of her, all the beasts of the nations: both the cormorant and the bittern shall lodge in the upper lintels of it; their voice shall sing in the windows; desolation shall be in the thresholds: for he shall uncover the cedar work. This is the rejoicing city that dwelt carelessly, that said in her heart, I am, and there is none beside me: how is she become a desolation, a place for beasts to lie down in! every one that passeth by her shall hiss, and wag his hand.* (See also Nahum 2:8-3:19.)

Ummanaldash returned to his destroyed cities and Asshurbanipal again demanded the surrender of Nabubelzikri, the Chaldean. When he heard that, Nabubelzikri commanded his armor-bearer to 'Slay me with the sword', which he did, each killing the other. The corpse was sent to Asshurbanipal who 'cut off the head' and hung it round the neck of a follower of Shamash-Shumukin, who had gone with Nabubelzikri into Elam. After a couple of years, those who were left of Elam revolted against Ummanaldash, and Pakhe took the throne, but was captured and taken captive to Nineveh.

Asshurbanipal made one more campaign against the Arab princes, capturing one of the most powerful chieftains, Vaiteh. The "Annals" say that Asshurbanipal 'struck down his son before his eyes'. On his return he says he destroyed the people of Akko (along the seacoast) because they had not been submissive. These were the last campaigns of Assyria under Asshurbanipal.

When he returned to Nineveh, he organized a large procession or parade. He ordered the 'last three kings of Elam - Tammaritu, Ummanaldash and Pakhe, and Vaiteh, the Arab chieftain, to be yoked to his war chariot, which they were forced draw in state to the gates of the temple'.

The rest of his life was spent in luxurious leisure, and in the restoration of Sennacherib's old palace. His death took place c. 626 B.C.

After his death Assyria declined, (there may have been two or more powerless kings after him) and Nineveh fell in 625 B.C. to a coalition force of Babylonians (Nabopolassor), Medes (Cyaxares), and Scythians. Assyria disappeared from history after this event.

The two principle tasks of the Assyrian kings were to engage in military exploits and build public buildings, and both were considered religious duties.

From records of inscriptions, scenes, and figures, indications are that the Assyrian kings were some of the most cruel people who ever existed. Their atrocities included dismembering, beheading, impaling on stakes, gouging out the eyes, cutting off noses, ears, and eyes, and trampling the captured victims.

The ultimate indignity, because of their religious beliefs, was to expose the bones of their dead kings and cause their 'shades' to walk the earth unable to accept food and water offerings. This was done to the people of Elam, southeast of Assyria.

They justified the cruel treatment of their captives by their religious zeal. As though it were a command from their pagan gods. 'By command of Asshur', Asshurbanipal cut off the king of Elam's head. (Ibid.), pp. 371-410.

"New invasions of the Near East by the Cimmerians and Scythians, and the rise of nationalism in Media and Babylonia saddened the last years of Asshurbanipal and sapped the military and financial reserves of Assyria. A combined force of Medes, Babylonians, and Scythians captured the Assyrian capital of Nineveh in 612 B.C., and thus brought the independence of Assyria to an end." (*Collier's Encyclopedia*, Crowell-Collier Publishing Co., Vol. 3 , 1962), p. 428.

(See Babylonian Kings, Section III, Sons of Ham.)

THE CHRONICLE OF THE BEGINNINGS OF THE NATION OF ISRAEL

From the line of Shem, Matthew 1:1, comes the genealogy of Jesus Christ; the most complete genealogy that has ever existed.

Until Abraham appeared nothing was known of the men whose names form part of the genealogy. Abraham's importance is immediately seen when Christ is seen as 'the Son of Abram', as well as 'the Son of God', (Matthew 1:1; Hebrews 2:16).

From this point until the Gospel is sent to the Gentiles, God dealt almost exclusively with the family of Shem, and the histories of Ham and Japheth must be found for the most part in profane (secular) history.

After the Flood each generation lived fewer years than those before it. Shem reached the age of 600, the next three sons only reached 500, and the next three only 300. Only Terah reached even 200 years. In the time of Moses 70 or 80 was the norm. Natural conditions were not the only factor in these changes. If not for the Providence of God, man would live many years and have more suffering than he could endure. It is the grace of God that shortens man's years, (Genesis 47:9).

Israel in the Mind of God

Isaiah 49:6, *And he said, It is a light thing that thou shouldest be my servant to raise up the tribes of Jacob, and to restore the preserved of Israel:* I will also give thee for a light to the Gentiles, *that thou mayest be my salvation unto the end of the earth.*

The Bible deals with the history of God's chosen people and His promises to them nationally. God cautioned that 'whatever nation blesses them' will be blessed and vice versa. In tracing the nation Biblically and historically, God's prophetic message, in one sense, became a reality when, in the preceding century, Israel again was granted a homeland in 1948. That certainly is not to say that the nation now in existence will be the one with which God will deal during the Tribulation period. They are an ungodly people with no thought for their Deliverer. The in-gathering by God has not yet begun, though a great many Jews have returned to Palestine of their own accord. When God calls them, they will all return, not just a scattered few. And the world will see the ultimate fulfillment of prophecy concerning Israel. (Isaiah 43:5,6, etc.).

The Hebrew language.

The Hebrew language appears to have come from Eber and was created to portray the solemn teaching of the attributes of God and to teach God's laws and judgment. For this reason a language of strength and majesty was required. It was the language of an isolated people, designed to keep them isolated. It was a perfect language for the philosophy and the philosophers of this nation which would control the intellectual history of the peoples of the world. It was designed to give the world the message of the eternal Gospel and the noble truths of God's grace to man.

Physical movements of Shem

Shem was not a traveling individual as were both Ham and Japheth. From his line there are fewer nationalities and greater distinctions between the languages and customs of his descendants. There are also greater differences in their way of life, their politics, and their religion, (e.g. the Kurds in northern Iraq who are Muslims, etc.).

UR OF THE CHALDEES, FIRST HOME OF ABRAM

Location

Ur of the Chaldees was located in Lower Mesopotamia, ('the land between the rivers')

and was one of the largest cities of that period. At the time of Abram it was on the Persian Gulf, though it is now more than 160 miles from there. This is due to the silt deposits from the Tigris and Euphrates Rivers which increase at a rate of 100 feet per year, and accounts for its present distance from the water. It was a city with a large port used for commerce, with a very advanced civilization.

It was a fertile land which is always a necessity for a region to become settled and populous. It is the only country in which wheat is known to be indigenous, but other grain crops were also grown there. Dates, pomegranates, apples, grapes, and other fruits were thought to have first come from Chaldea.

Chaldea was the "cradle of civilization", and from there the nations were dispersed at Babel, taking with them the religious beliefs of the Chaldeans (Habbakuk 1:6; Isaiah 13:19). It was considered to be a holy place, and for many centuries the dead were brought there to be buried. They worshipped a multitude of idols, and were so immoral that archaeological discoveries have revealed a shameless society.

Inhabitants

The first peoples were called the Sumerians. They were joined with the nation of Accad, of Upper Chaldea, (the Sumerians were from Lower Chaldea) and were from the same Turanian (Japhetic) language group.

It is evident that these peoples came from somewhere else as they entered the country with the essential tools of civilization; a written language, and the knowledge of metallurgy.

The name Accad means "mountains" or "highlands" which could not have originated in the flatlands of Chaldea, so must have come with them from their original home. Even their language was extensive in its ability to describe metallurgical processes. The region north of Chaldea is a mountainous area rich in metal ores; a natural place for a people possessing their metalworking ability. It is also the heart of the region from which the nations came. Though it is not certain, the Shumer-Accads probably came from that northern area.

The area was first inhabited by Shemites then a group of Hamites entered and took over the country, and at a later date a Semitic-speaking group of people came into the region. It is thought they came from the area of the Arabian desert (the Semitic Arabs) and ultimately became the rulers, as demonstrated by Sargon, king of the first true empire which reached from central Persia to the Mediterranean. They were known as the 'white people'. The name Shem means 'Glory', 'Renown', and they believed they were the chosen of God.

When they arrived on the plains of Chaldea they were not accustomed to living in cities, but learned quickly. They learned the government and the spoken and written language of the area, but they retained their own peculiar language which was different from all those of the region. They also learned some Assyrian, Aramaic, Syrian, and Arab. (The Phoenicians of the coast and some of the Canaanite nations spoke a Semitic language, and this is the reason they have been erroneously classified as Shemites. They were Hamites who spoke a Semitic dialect.)

The Shemites gradually became the majority in Chaldea. They entered as shepherds, but later formed their own villages and joined with the peoples already living there. When Abram left the city of Ur with his family, he resumed his nomadic pastoral life. Among the Chaldeans, only the Semitic group followed the concept of a Supreme God, instead of worshipping the pantheon of gods in the Chaldean/Babylonian myths. The other Shemites adopted the paganism of the Chaldeans, changing the names of their gods to Semitic names. They gave respect to their temples and offered gifts to their gods. When Joshua speaks to Israel before his death, he tells them their fathers had 'served strange gods', (Joshua 24:2,14,15).

The Chaldean empire took a secondary position to the Assyrian nation in the 13th century B.C.

Writing was practiced, and schools existed for the benefit of the people. Religion and science were the most important subjects studied; science included mathematics and astronomy. They also advanced architecture which was pyramidal in design, and used the wedge-shaped or cuneiform characters. They cut, polished, and engraved gems. They were proficient in metallurgy, in casting arms, ornaments, and implements, and they loomed delicate fabrics for the commerce which they carried on with many nations, by land and sea.

Characteristics of the Sumerians:
- brown skinned
- unrelated language
- large-scale government
- formal state
- formal laws
- large-scale business
- standard weights and measures
- timekeeping
- credit
- literature
- the tale, which was their invention
- proverbs
- epics, and
- technical skill

"Leonard Woolley, who excavated the ziggurat at the city of Ur, reported his amazement at finding that there was not a single straight line in the vast building. Outlines were all slightly curved, walls sloped inward and had slightly convex surfaces - everything was nicely calculated to counteract the appearance of bending or sloping that would be given by actually straight lines; and so to create the optical illusion of perfect squareness and symmetry. Two thousand years before the Greeks, the Sumerians had discovered the secret by which the builders of the Parthenon were to amaze the world." Herbert J. Muller, *The Loom of History,* (New York: Harper and Brothers, 1958), p. 35.

The influence of the Sumerians extended to:

- the Semitic Akkadeans,
- the Babylonians (the Law Code of Hammurabi and the Gilgamesh Epic grew out of Sumerian originals),
- the Assyrians,
- the Chaldeans,
- the Indus Valley,
- China,
- pre-Columbian America,
- Syria,
- Anatolia - Hittites,
- the Minoans,
- the Hebrews,
- the Phoenicians, and
- the Greeks.

Government

Chaldea had a well-ordered society with codified laws (2250 B.C.) very similar to those of Hammurabi. Even their religious ceremonies were involved with maintaining legal justice as demonstrated by the following prayer by a priest in behalf of his penitent believer:

"Has he sinned against god? (small letter)...Has he given too little (in mercantile transactions)? -Has he withheld too much? -For 'no' said 'yes', for 'yes' said 'no' (lied)?...Has he used false weights?...Has he taken an incorrect amount (of interest), -not taken the correct sum? -Has he fixed a false boundary, -not fixed a just boundary? -Has he removed a boundary, a limit, or a territory? -Has he possessed himself of his neighbor's house? -Has he approached his neighbor's wife? -Has he shed his neighbor's blood? -Robbed his neighbor's dress?...Was he frank

in speaking, but false in heart? -Was it 'yes' with his mouth, but 'no' with his heart?" (Ragozin, *Chaldea*), p. 179.

There was a ruling personage, who was a king, instead of a ruler-priest, (a patesi). Under a peaceful government the arts flourish and culture is advanced; Abram grew up in a city of culture and good government. Commerce was carried on with other countries (fabrics were manufactured by them, gems, metals, etc.); this was another sign of peaceful conditions.

The Great Palace of Ur can be dated to the twenty-fourth century B.C.; it is the oldest known edifice set apart as the residence of a king. Michael Grant, *The History of Ancient Israel,* (New York: Charles Scribner's Son, 1984), p. 10.

Kings of Shumir and Accad

Lugal-Zaggisi - a Shemite (*lugal* meaning a great man)
Edin-Gira-Nagin - who defeated the Shemites
Sharru-Kenu - or Sargon of Agade
Naram-Sin, the son of Sargon
Ur-Gur/in Ur
Dungi, son of Ur-Gur, "King of Shumir and Accad"
Gudea - a patesi, priest-king
Khudur-Mabuk - an Elamite
Khudur-Lagamar/Chedorlaomer - a Shemite, from Elam, (Genesis 14)

At some time after Ur-Gur and Gudea, kings of Shumir and Accad, the Elamites came from the highlands of the east and overran the country. During this period they took the moon-goddess Nana from her temple at Erech. This was the short-lived Elamite Dynasty which was ultimately destroyed by the Assyrians. The first rulers in Elam were Turanian (Japhetic) peoples whose language was much like the Shumir-Accadian language. When the Shemites went into Elam and gave it its name, they became the nobility of the land from whom the kings and other rulers were taken. They became the masters of the Turanian peoples and complete separation was evidently kept between the two groups as demonstrated by pictures on the Assyrian sculptures. The Scriptures mention them (the Elamites) in Genesis 10:22 as "a son of Shem, a brother of Asshur and Arphakshad". (Ragozin, *Chaldea*), pp. 197-214, excerpts.

(Arphakshad, probably from Hebrew Aseph-Kasdim, "boundary [or perhaps 'land'] of the Kasdim" [Chaldeans].) (Ibid.), p. 214.

Sargon was the Shumiro-Accad king, a Shemite, who collected the theological works of the former peoples as well as their other literary works, and had them copied on clay tablets with the original texts and the translation in the Semitic language. These books were given to the college of priests at Erech and the city was called the "City of Books".

From this library fourteen centuries later Asshurbanipal collected copies for his own royal library at Nineveh. Because he had restored their goddess Nana (called Ishtar by the Shemites), whose temple was at Uruk (Erech), the priests were especially inclined to be generous with their books.

Khudur-Lagamar, king of Elam, (Chedorlaomer) supported by his allies, the king of Shumir (Shinar), Larsa (Allassar), and of Goim (king of the nomadic tribes in the area), made vassals of Sodom and Gomorrah and three other cities. They paid tribute to him for twelve years and then rebelled. Khudur-Lagamar, with his allies, defeated them in the valley of Siddim and carried away the spoils, including many of the people. Among the people was Lot, the nephew of Abram. This brought Abram into the picture as he pursued them to free his relative, (Genesis 14).

It is believed that at the time Abram lived in Chaldea many Shemites also lived there and professed a pure form of religion. Though the Chaldeans were idolaters, Abram, and at least part of his family, were worshippers of the true God.

It is very possible that Abram, following the voice of God, took his family into the desert to escape the land of the Chaldeans and the city of Ur where paganism was rife. His relatives who remained in Mesopotamia continued to be idolaters as shown in Genesis 24-29, etc., with the brother of Abraham, Nahor. In Genesis 31:19, Rachel took the idols of her father so she would receive the blessing they were supposed to convey, in her own house. She didn't seem to mind removing their influence from her father's house.

Because of the influence of strange gods the Israelites continued in idolatry for most of their history. God continually warned them not to accept the gods of their neighbors. It was prohibited to marry idolatrous peoples because they would lead them into idolatry as occurred with Solomon and many other kings of Israel.

THE HISTORY OF ABRAHAM, (Genesis 12:1), c. 1948 B.C.

Genealogy of Peleg, ancestor of Abraham
Shem
   Arphaxad
     Saleh
       Eber
          Peleg, (Genesis 10:25; 11:16; 1 Chronicles 1:19, 24-27)

            Reu

              Serug (shoot or branch)
              Nahor (breathing hard, snorting), grandfather of Abraham
                Terah (wild goat?) died at Haran, father of Abraham, an idolater. Lived in Ur of the Chaldees until he left

with Abram as he began his pilgrimage.
Abraham (exalted father),
(2 Chronicles 20:7), the friend of God, (James 2:23).
Ishmael-combined Arab nations
Isaac
Jacob - Israelites

Ten generations had passed since the Flood and again men left the true God and followed 'strange gods'. There was danger that the knowledge of the Truth would be lost in the earth. God's purpose in choosing one man, and through him a nation, was to make them a witness to the world. He was going to entrust to them the ancient truths and the Messianic hope until the coming of the Son of Man. Through this family and nation was to come the Redeemer. For this reason God called Abram to leave his land, his friends, and his family and go to a land about which he knew nothing.

"Five hundred years before Abraham's day there was a flourishing import and export trade on the Canaanite coast. Egypt exchanged gold and spices from Nubia, copper and turquoise from the mines at Sinai, linen and ivory, for silver from the Taurus, leather goods from Byblos, painted vases from Crete. In the great Phoenician dyeworks well-to-do Egyptians had their robes dyed purple. For their society women they bought a wonderful lapis lazuli blue - eyelids dyed blue were all the rage - and stibium, a cosmetic which was highly thought of by the ladies for touching up their eyelashes." Werner Keller, translated by William Neil, *The Bible as History,* (New York: William Morrow and Co., 1956), p. 57.

Abram (Genesis 12:1)

Abram was to be God's instrument; through him would come the promised Messiah, and through him would come a nation with singular opportunities and responsibilities for service to God:

- the divine teaching would be proclaimed;
- the chosen people would be entrusted with the Scriptures;
- the Messiah would be born from this line, and
- redemption for all would come with no distinction because of hereditary background.

Edersheim says Abraham was 'elected' and 'selected' by God to form a special nation.

Through the Semitic line of Eber, the witness of the true God continued. Eber lived longer than any other man after the Flood and this was, doubtless, a special blessing from God so he could teach his children and grandchildren of the true God. Someone had to have taught Abraham the truth of God, because his own father was an idolater and the knowledge could not have come from him.

There are two passages which deal with this subject; Joshua 24:2, *"And Joshua said unto all the people, Thus saith the Lord God of Israel, Your fathers dwelt on the other side of the flood in old times, even Terah, the father of Abraham, and the father of Nahor: and they served (worshipped) other gods."* And Genesis 31:53, where Laban is speaking: *"The God of Abraham, and the God of Nahor, the God of their father (Terah), judge betwixt us...."* This is Laban's attempt, as a pagan, to place Abraham's God and Nahor's god on an equal footing. It does not imply that they were the same God, and there are indications to demonstrate he was referring to pagan gods in his case, as demonstrated by the household gods stolen from his house by Rachel.

Though there are no detailed records of worship or of places of worship, there is the knowledge of the results of that worship.

Abram had made an individual commitment to Elohim, and when God spoke to him he was acquainted with that Voice. There is no indication of any surprise or terror when God spoke, signifying that Abraham was either accustomed to the Voice, or was expecting a message at any time. Like Noah, Abram was a just man in his generation, and when God spoke, he obeyed immediately. Part of his family and many servants and herds left with Abram. They moved north of the Euphrates to Haran and stayed there until the death of Terah, his father, who died at age 205.

Abraham was justified by faith as were all who were 'made righteous' in the Old Testament. To presume that anyone was capable of salvation by keeping the Law, is to deny the Word of God, which says that no man is capable of keeping the Law except Jesus Christ, (Romans 4:2-5; James 2:23).

Locke says, "This Faith for which God justified Abraham, what was it? It was the believing God when he engaged his Promise in the Covenant he made with him. This will be plain to anyone who considers these places together, Genesis 15:6. 'He believed in the Lord', or 'believed the Lord'. For that the Hebrew Phrase 'believing in', signifies no more but 'believing', is plain from St. Paul's citation of this place, Romans 4:3, where he repeats it thus: 'Abraham believed God', which he thus explains, vs. 18-22, 'Who against hope believed in Hope, that he might become the Father of many Nations: According to that which was spoken, so shall thy seed be. And being not weak in faith, he considered not his own body now dead, when he was about an hundred years old, nor yet the deadness of Sarah's womb. He staggered not at the promise of God through unbelief; but was strong in faith, giving glory to God. And being fully persuaded, that what he had promised, he was also able to perform. And therefore it was imputed to him for righteousness.' By which it is clear, that the Faith which God counted to Abraham for Righteousness, was nothing but a firm belief of what God declared to him, and a steadfast relying on him for the accomplishment of what he had promised." Verna M. Hall, *Self-Government With Union,* Vol. II, (San Francisco: The American Christian Constitution Press, 1962), as quoted on p. 76, paragraph 2.

God chose one individual to whom He would reveal His plan for the world. Man in general had rejected the Creator and His government; his opportunity had passed and would not be renewed for many centuries.

The name 'Abram' meant 'high or exalted father or ancestor'. Afterward it was changed to Abraham, meaning 'father (ancestor) of a multitude'.

The Promise of God (Genesis 12:2)

The Covenant was evidently made while Abraham was still in Ur - "The Lord <u>had said</u> unto Abraham," all in the past tense, verse 1.

Joshua 24:1-3 says that Abraham's family was idolatrous and he is the only one to whom God speaks and gives the promise of a continued inheritance.

There was a twofold command:
1. leave your home and family;
2. go where God leads you,
and a threefold promise:
1. God would make him a great nation;
2. he would have extensive lands;
3. God would bless him and make him a blessing to <u>all</u> nations.

"I will make of thee a great nation"

Although he did not have children, God

promised to give him a large and complete family. He was already 75 years old and had no child. This promise would not be made manifest in his generation because many generations must pass before a great nation can be formed. It was realized in Israel, but it was spiritually realized in the spiritual children of Abraham, the Christian church, (Galatians 3:29).

"I will bless thee"

This was a temporal blessing having to do with the riches Abram would receive, but it was also a spiritual blessing in reference to what he would receive from God in the future. God gave him the promise of all the blessings he would receive from God's hand. We have the same promise of blessing today.

"I will make thy name great"

When Abram left his country he lost the importance of his name, but God was going to give him a greater name than he already had. Since Abram had no children, his name would be lost at his death, but God was going to give him a name the whole world would know. Mortal man has never received more honor than Abram. Mohammedans, Jews and Christians all honor his name. God says here that He will exalt whomever He wishes if that is His plan, but the fame of the world is unimportant in His over-all plan.

"Thou wilt be a blessing"

You will have a blessing and be a blessing; this was God's promise. Abram would be famous not for what he received, but for what he gave to others.

"I will bless those who bless thee"

The friendship between God and Abram was so complete that God would take Abram's part in every situation. The friends of Abram were the friends of God. If one did something good for Abram it was as if he did something good for God, and he would receive God's blessings according to his acts. Whatever good is done for the child of God receives its reward, even a cup of cold water given in His name, (Matthew 25:35,40).

"I will curse those who curse thee"

Those who injured Abram were cursed by God. It is important to remember that this statement is still in effect in reference to Israel. It also refers to Christians, as it intimates that whoever opposes God's child opposes God Himself, and that person or nation will reap its own reward, (Psalm 33:10-12).

"In thee shall all the families of the earth be blessed", verse 3

This promise has been kept in three ways:

1. By the benefits the world has received from the industry, riches, genius and morality of the Jews;
2. by the benefits the world has received from the Scriptures; the law, the literature, the religious spirit and the monotheism of the Hebrews, and
3. from the greatest blessing in the world - the Messiah who came from the line of Abram. Jesus Christ is the greatest blessing ever to come to this world. All families of the earth are blessed in Him; salvation is for all, (Jude 3).

The name of Abram became great because the Son of Man was to come through him and that was more important than being the father of a great nation, (Genesis 28:14). The first promise of the Messiah was given in Genesis 3:15; here is the reaffirmation of that promise with a better understanding of how God would bring it to pass, (1 Thessalonians 5:24).

The Jews come from Judah, one of the 12 sons of Jacob, grandson of Abraham, 'the Hebrew'. As Jacob had prophesied, (Genesis 49:9-12), Judah became the predominate tribe.

During the Babylonian captivity the word Jew, was used to refer to all the Israelites. Paul referred to himself as a Benjamite and a Jew, (Romans 11:1).

The Jews are the same today as they have always been. Many ancient nations (e.g. the Phoenicians, Philistines, Canaanites, etc.), are lost to mankind, but Israel continues unchanged.

The first empires of the world, the Assyrians, Babylonians, Egyptians and Persians, made their mark on the world and faded into oblivion. The Greeks and Romans filled the earth with the arts and the sounds of war and then were gone, yet the Jew remains. The nations of the world have tried to destroy the Jews and continue to do so today, but the Jew continues. More than six millions of them were slaughtered by Hitler in World War II, and even that number of deaths could not destroy them.

All mortals fade away but the Jew seems immortal because of God's everlasting promise to them through Abraham.

The Jews are united by:
- the same Torah and other books of the Bible;
- the Talmud;
- the same religious festivals;
- the observance of the Sabbath, and
- the same genealogical line.

The promises given to Abraham were not just to him alone, but to all men everywhere. Though the promises were limited for a time to a small group, they would ultimately reach all men and bring the world the Messiah through whom came our salvation.

A great nation is one which has:
- many members,
- unity,
- high moral character,
- a great culture and prosperity,
- a fixed government; a constitution and laws,
- a godly religion,
- noble ideas and ideals, great confidence, and great plans for the future, and
- great influence in blessing others.

Only a nation that obeys and serves God could realize all of these goals and Israel became a great nation when it met these criteria.

The strategic location of the Promised Land was emphasized by God:

Deuteronomy 32:8-10, *When the Most High divided to the nations their inheritance, when he separated the sons of Adam, he set the bounds of the people **according to the number of the children of Israel.** For the Lord's portion is his people; Jacob is the lot of his inheritance. He found him in a desert land, and in the waste howling wilderness; he led him about, he instructed him, he kept him as the apple of his eye.*

Acts 17:26, *And hath made of one blood all nations of men for to dwell on all the face of the earth, and hath determined the times before appointed, and the bounds of their habitation.*

Ezekiel 5:5, *Thus saith the Lord God; This is Jerusalem: I have set it in the midst of the nations and countries that are round about her.*

Departure from Ur

Abraham was seventy-five years old when he was called out of Ur.

He was called by God to leave his home and his family so he could be in the place God had determined for the coming of the Redeemer.

Abram did not know where he was going, (Acts 7:3; Hebrews 11:8), but he immediately left. His faith would have been an offense to the pagan people of Ur and until the death of his father, God would not tell him where he was to settle. God had to separate him from his family and from their idolatrous influence, so Abram would faithfully follow Him. When he was removed from those worldly influences, God was able to teach him the true faith. Acts 7:2 says, *"The God of glory appeared unto our father Abraham"*, calling him to leave for a place yet unknown.

His father accompanied him and was evidently the physical leader of the caravan; true to the patriarchal form of government. Abraham's brother, Haran, had died, (Genesis 11:28), in the land of his birth, in Ur of the Chaldees, before they could leave that idolatrous country, so they took his son Lot with them. Abram married Sarai and he says in Genesis 20:12 that she was the daughter of his father but not the daughter of his mother, or his half-sister. (There is no reason to associate her with Iscah about whom nothing is known.) Sarai was ten years younger than he.

The group consisted of Terah, Abram, Sarai, and Lot, with the servants and herds. The sons of Terah were: Abram, Nahor, and Haran. (From the family of Nahor came the wives of Isaac and Jacob, and possibly the wives of most of Jacob's sons.)

They went as far as Haran and stopped. Later in the Scripture the city of Haran is called the 'city of Nahor', probably meaning that Abraham's brother, and his family, settled there at a later time. And it is to this area the servant of Abraham goes to find a wife for Isaac years later. Edersheim says this district retained the peculiar Chaldean language and worship, for many years even though it was considered to belong to Mesopotamia. Alfred Edersheim, *Prophecy and History in Relation to the Messiah,* (Grand Rapids: Longmans, Green, and Co., 1901 original printers, reprint 1980), p. 75.

Much of the land was still unclaimed and they were able to travel with their flocks without problem. John Locke makes these observations on the aspect of property in the following lines from his *Treatise on Civil Government.* This will help in understanding the condition of the world at the time Abraham made his pilgrimage.

"God and his reason commanded him (man) to subdue the earth, i.e., improve it for the benefit of life, and therein lay out something upon it that was his own, his labour. He that, in obedience to this command of God, subdued, tilled, and sowed any part of it, thereby annexed to it something that was his property, which another had no title to, nor could without injury take from him.

"Nor was the appropriation of any parcel of land, by improving it, any prejudice to any other man, since there was still enough and as good left; and more than the yet unprovided could use. So that in effect there was never the less left for others because of his enclosure for himself. For he that leaves as much as another can make use of, does as good as take nothing at all. Nobody could think himself injured by the drinking of another man, though he took a good draught, who had a whole river of the same water left him to quench his thirst; and the case of land and water, where there is enough of both, is perfectly the same.

"God gave the world to men in common; but since He gave it them for their benefit, and the greatest conveniences of life they were capable to draw from it, it cannot be supposed He meant it should always remain common and uncultivated. He gave it to the use of the industrious and rational (and labour was to be his title to it), not to the fancy or covetousness or the quarrelsome and contentious. He that had as good left for his improvement as was already taken up, needed not complain, ought not to meddle with what was already improved by another's labour; if he did, it is plain he desired the benefit of another's pains, which he had no right to, and not the ground which God had given him in common with others to labour on, and whereof there was as good left as that already possessed, and more than he knew what to do with, or his industry could reach to.

"...The law man was under was rather for appropriating, God commanded, and his wants forced him, to labour. That was his property, which could not be taken from him wherever he had fixed it. And hence subduing or cultivating the earth, and having dominion, we see are joined together. The one gave title to the other. So that God, by commanding to subdue, gave authority so far to appropriate. And the condition of human life, which requires labour and materials to work on, necessarily introduces private possessions.

"The same measures governed the possessions of land, too. Whatsoever he tilled and reaped, laid up, and made use of before it spoiled, that was his peculiar right; whatsoever he enclosed and could feed and make use of, the cattle and product was also his. But if either the grass of his enclosure rotted on the ground, or the fruit of his planting perished without gathering and laying up, this part of the earth, notwithstanding his enclosure, was still looked on as waste, and might be the possession of any other. Thus, at the beginning, Cain might take as much ground as he could till and make it his own land, and yet leave enough for Abel's sheep to feed on; a few acres would serve for both their possessions. But as families increased, and industry enlarged their stocks, their possessions enlarged with the need of them; but yet it was commonly without any fixed property in the ground they made use of, till they incorporated, settled themselves together, and built cities; and then, by consent, they came in time to set out the bounds of their distinct territories, and agree on limits between them and their neighbours, and, by laws within themselves, settled the

properties of those of the same society. For we see that in that part of the world which was first inhabited, and therefore like to be the best peopled, even as low down as Abraham's time they wandered with their flocks and their herds, which were their substance, freely up and down; and this Abraham did in a country where he was a stranger: whence it is plain that at least a great part of the land lay in common; that the inhabitants valued it not, nor claimed property in any more than they made use of. But when there was not room enough in the same place for their herds to feed together, they by consent, as Abraham and Lot did (Genesis xiii. 6), separated and enlarged their pasture where it best liked them. And for the same reason Esau went from his father and his brother, and planted in Mount Seir (Genesis xxxvi. 6).)" John Locke, *Treatise of Civil Government,* (New York: Appleton-Century-Crofts, 1937), pp. 21-26.

The Pilgrimage

Abram stayed in Canaan about one hundred years. God had selected Abram to guard and to fulfill His promise of the coming Savior. God called him to go, then He called him to go even further. Abram had to be willing to go wherever God called without questioning Him.

We love our own country; we love our relatives and our own family, but we have to 'hate' them in comparison to our love for Christ and His work, (Luke 14:26). This world is not our home, we are pilgrims here in transit to our real home. While we are here we have a job to do. God gives each individual an important work to do and it is his responsibility and privilege to carry out that work.

God was proving the faith of Abram by sending him to a place only God could show him. God did not say, "It's a land I'm going to give you", He only said, "It is a land I'm going to show you." Abram had to follow in faith with no security except God's promise. This taught Abram to confide more in God and to depend upon His promises. This is an important lesson for us today. If we could follow Him with eyes of faith instead of with eyes of doubt, we would receive more blessings and would live much happier lives.

Geographical Progression of the Pilgrimage:

From Ur of the Chaldees to Haran. From there to Sichem, (Shechem), (the plain of Moreh), (Genesis 12:6), which was in the land of the Canaanites (see notes on the Canaanites in Section III, Sons of Ham), and from there to Beth-el, (Genesis 12:8). Because of a famine in the land of the Canaanites, Abram went down to Egypt to escape its consequences. This was an accepted way of life for the Canaanites, because it appears there had been many times of famine for many years as the hieroglyphics demonstrate.

It is interesting to note that his wife was 65 years old at this time. He was so worried about her beauty that he asked her to tell a half-truth. She was to say she was his sister instead of his wife, in order to avoid being killed by the Pharaoh who would surely desire her for his own. An occurrence of this type is also portrayed in the hieroglyphics of Egypt. They show a Pharaoh killing the husband and carrying off the man's wife for his harem.

Abram was a wealthy prince and would have been looked upon with favor by the court of the Egyptian prince. It would have been to Pharaoh's advantage to make a political alliance with this wealthy prince by marrying his 'sister'. The Pharaoh was quite taken with her and would have carried out his plan had not God revealed the perfidy of Abram to him. Abram left Egypt accompanied as far as the border by Pharaoh's soldiers, and he left a much richer man. He was given riches in 'sheep, oxen, donkeys, men and women ser-

vants, and camels' by Pharaoh as payment for Sarai; which would have been expected if she were his sister. Genesis 12:16 says, *And he (Pharaoh) entreated Abram well for her sake....* which means because of Sarai, Abraham was given many goods and thus was 'treated' very well and 'made happy and successful' because of his added goods.

From Egypt he returned to Beth-el, and there he and his nephew Lot separated from one another because of their great wealth, most of which was counted in the numbers of their herds. The land was unable to sustain them both while they were together, and for this reason they determined to part. Lot chose the plain of Jordan eastward and settled in Sodom; and Abram went to Hebron where God again renewed His promise to give all the land he could see to him and his seed forever, (Genesis 13:14-18).

Sometime later Abram rescued Lot from the confederation of kings from the area of Assyria which had taken him prisoner.

After the birth of Ishmael; and the destruction of Sodom and Gomorrah, Abram journeyed south between Kadesh and Shur in the land of Gerar. There he again made a serious mistake in saying his wife was his sister. Abimelech, (the name used for the kings of Gerar), wanted to make a political alliance with that wealthy prince and therefore would wish to take Abram's sister as his wife. Sarah was 90 years old at this time and we are not told she was still beautiful, but that because of her position as a wealthy princess, she was to be desired.

After the offering of Isaac Abram returned to Beer-sheba. Sarah died in Hebron (Kirjath-arba), (Genesis 23:2), in the land of the Hittites, so he had gone back there sometime in the interim. Abraham was buried in the cave of Macpelah near Hebron where Sarah was buried.

God's Internal Covenant with Abram
(Genesis 15)

God promised that his descendants were to be *'As the stars of the sky, or as the sands of the seas'*, certainly meaning without number.

God began by assuring Abram that He was his *'shield and exceeding great reward'*, (verse 1).

Abram asked God if his steward Eliezer, who had been born in his house, but whose ancestors were from Damascus, Syria, was to be his heir.

God said no. His heir would be of his own flesh and blood, and his descendants would be without number, as the stars of the sky are without number. Abram believed God's promise and it was counted to him for righteousness, (verse 6).

The Covenant (Genesis 15)

God then reaffirmed His promise to Abram through a covenant which was a sign of agreement between two parties.

The covenant was confirmed by killing a three years old animal, which was considered the age of maturity. The animal was then cut into two pieces lengthwise, and the two parts laid parallel, leaving a passageway between them. The two parties in the agreement then walked between the two pieces of the animal and the covenant became binding. If one of the parties failed to keep the agreement, he could expect the same treatment as the animal had received. Marcus Dods, *Genesis*, (Edinburg: T. & T. Clark, n.d.), p. 71.

Abram prepared the animal and kept watch over it all day and waited, but nothing happened. Then as he slept in the evening hours, God spoke to him in a dream and gave him a prophecy of the history of his people before they were even a 'people' and before they possessed any land:

- They were to be 'strangers' in a foreign land for 400 years (a round figure).
- God would judge the nation that caused them to serve it, (Ezekiel 29-32).
- They would leave that land with great riches, (Exodus 12:35,36).
- Abram would live a long peaceful life and be buried as an old man, (Genesis 25:8).
- Abram's 'people' would return to the land promised to Abram after four generations, (Exodus 12:40,41), when the time of the wickedness of the Amorites was finished. God's judgment would fall upon the Amorites through the Israelites when they entered the 'land', (Joshua 10).
- God gave him the boundaries of his territory, 'from the river Nile to the Euphrates', (Genesis 15:18-21), and he was to possess all the land in between, which was under the control of the Hamites at that time. This land was 150 miles long from north to south, and 60 miles wide from east to west, (Genesis 15:13-21).

God then passed between the pieces as a 'smoking furnace and a burning lamp' and the Covenant was sealed. It was not necessary for Abram to pass through because this was a picture of grace and only one party is needed to extend grace - the Lord Jesus Christ. No part of the Covenant was dependent upon Abram, it was totally dependent upon God, (verse 17).

The Covenant was reaffirmed in Genesis 17:4-8 and circumcision became the physical sign of that covenant. On the eighth day after birth every Jewish male is to be circumcised. Every time this takes place it is a reminder of the promise given to Israel (and has been found to be a very healthful practice for other nations as well).

Abraham had been brought from Ur of the Chaldees by the leadership of the Spirit of God. He and his descendants were to receive all of this area as their inheritance. In the section on the Sons of Ham can be found an explanation of the verse which says, 'and the Canaanite was then in the land'. They did not settle there first, but came there at a later period, before Abraham came into the land. The Canaanites were sons of Ham, and were eventually destroyed by Israel and the nations around them. This area which became known as Palestine because of the Phoenicians or the Philistines who settled there, did not receive its name until a much later period. Though Abraham lived as a pilgrim in this land, it was in fact, his land. It now belongs to his descendants, and the nations of the world may try to give it away to whom they will, but it will always remain the property of the Hebrew nation as promised by God in an everlasting covenant.

This eternal covenant and was reaffirmed to David in Psalm 89:33-37. It is still in effect, regardless of what the Arabs surrounding the Holy Land want to believe.

Birth of Ishmael (Genesis 16)

(In the Code of Hammurabi, c. 1700 B.C., the husband could not take a second wife unless the first was barren. However if his wife gave him a slave as concubine then this law had no effect on him. The husband could take a concubine himself even if his wife had borne him children, but the concubine never had the same rights as the wife, and he could not take another concubine unless the first one was barren.)

Hagar was evidently included in the 'menservants and womenservants' given to Abram while in Egypt, and she became Sarai's servant girl.

When Sarah gave her handmaid Hagar to Abram he, no doubt, felt that God was going to work through her to bring about the promised seed. When Ishmael was conceived, Hagar tried to make herself more important than her mistress. This made Sarai very angry as well as being jealous. For this reason Sarai wanted her sent away.

Sarai blamed Abram for her situation, (Genesis 16:5), and said the Lord should judge who was more at fault for the 'wrong done to her'.

Wherever the blame lay, this was still Abram's child and he would have grieved over Hagar's departure. Abram was willing to follow Sarai's advice in taking Hagar as his wife though he believed God would still keep His promise of a son; in this way he could help God out and get his son by his own means. Not only was Sarai barren, but now the child who was conceived through the Egyptian handmaid was gone.

(Sara didn't actually send Hagar away on this occasion, she just made her life so difficult it was easier to leave than live in the same place with Sarai, [Proverbs 21:19].)

When Hagar ran away from Sarai's presence she took the road that would lead her back to Egypt, and God 'found her by a fountain of water' (16:7) on the way to Shur. He told her to return to Sarai and be submissive to her.

Hagar acknowledged God's presence as 'Thou God seest me'. This was apparently her first real encounter with the God of Abram, and she recognized Him again when she and Ishmael were sent into the wilderness to live, (21:17).

God then promised her that her son would become a great nation, (Genesis 25:16). His name would be Ishmael "the Lord heareth" and he would be a 'wild man'; (Genesis 16:10-16; 17:20; 21:13; 25:16-18). Verse 12 says he was to dwell "...in the presence of all his brethren", meaning both Isaac and the sons of Keturah. Ishmael became the father of one branch of the great Arab nations of the world, but Joktan was the father of the first group and Japheth and Ham also contributed in part to this nation.

(The Ishmaelites were merchants who lived in tents. They were wealthy and were governed by kings. One of their trading caravans took Joseph to Egypt, (37:25). Theirs is a history of lawlessness, but as observed in 1 Kings 10:15 and 2 Chronicles 17:11, they finally became more peaceful and sent tribute to King Solomon and others.)

Ishmael was born when Abram was 86 years old. He had been in the land for eleven years and may well have assumed that Ishmael was to be the promised seed because God had not, at this time, made it clear that Sarai was to be the mother of the one who had been promised. That did not occur until Genesis 17:15-21.

As a natural father Abram would have enjoyed his son Ishmael; seeing him grow into a fine young man would have brought him great pleasure. And who could tell, this <u>might</u> be the fulfillment of the promise.

Another 13 years passed before God spoke to him and explained how the promise was to be fulfilled.

(It is interesting to consider the mothers of Ishmael and Isaac in order to understand the differences between the Jews and the Arabs of today.)

Circumcision - the External Sign of the Covenant (Genesis 17)

In verse 1 Jehovah calls Himself the <u>Almighty</u> God. This is the first usage of the word which is *Shadday*, and is the plural of Majesty, (the Powerful One or Mighty One - God). This was the covenant name of Jehovah until the time of Moses.

Then He said to Abram, *Walk before me and be thou perfect.*

God was beginning a new kind of relationship with Abram; He was now a more personal God. Abram had followed God's voice in leaving his Chaldean home and had demonstrated believing faith in obeying. Now God said, *I am Shadday, the Powerful, Mighty One, walk before me, and be thou perfect.* After believing faith comes the walk of testimony. Some scholars liken this walk to the shepherd who follows his sheep watching over them so they don't come to any harm. This was not a polite request made by God, but was rather an order to be carried out. After the years of silence (13) Abram was probably only too ready to feel God's presence and hear His voice in reaffirming the covenant.

God told Abram his name was now changed to Abraham - the father of a multitude. This was also part of the new relationship between God and Abraham.

God then explained to him the rite of circumcision as an external sign of the everlasting covenant between them.

In verse 17 Abram fell on his face and laughed when he heard God's words reaffirming the promise of a son who would be born to him and who would be the father of kings. This was not a laugh of derision, but a laugh of delight in hearing that the promise was not over, but had only begun. God did not rebuke him for his laughter, He ignored it as though to say, 'Just watch and see how I bring this to pass'.

Sarai's name was changed to Sarah; some say the meaning is 'queen' because she was to be the mother of kings; some say it was just a play on words. Whatever the reason, God knew why He did it. She was named for the first time as the mother of the promised seed. Until this occasion the promise only had to do with Abraham, but now the mother was known.

The child was to be named Isaac (laughter, verse 19), and the eternal covenant was promised to Isaac and his seed. The time of the birth was also given.

The future of Ishmael was declared. Abraham said in verse 18, *'O that Ishmael might live before thee'*. The meaning here is 'O that he might have the right relationship with You, Lord!' Abraham already understood that this son was not interested in walking before the Lord in righteousness, and as a godly father this was his greatest desire for his child.

God again promised, to Abraham this time, that Ishmael would become a great nation and would be the father of 'princes', not kings.

But the covenant was not for Ishmael, it was reserved for Isaac, the promised son.

When God *'went up from Abram'*, (verse 22), Abram immediately carried out God's instructions in circumcising all the males of his household, including Ishmael.

Circumcision had nothing to do with the wishes of the child who was being circumcised, but had everything to do with the parents and their willingness to obey God. It also had nothing to do with any nation which was not included in the covenant, as Paul indicated in the New Testament, (Galatians 5:2-6; 6:15; 1 Corinthians 7:18,19; Colossians 3:11); because in Christ all are made equal as far as salvation is concerned, and circumcision of the flesh 'availeth' nothing; the important aspect in these texts is circumcision of the heart.

If the rite of circumcision was not observed by a Jew, then that person was cut off from Israel because he had broken 'in pieces' the covenant. Therefore, it was necessary that the parents' walk be right so they would carry out God's command in relation to the child. This rite did not save the child, nor was it a symbol of baptism - it was the external recognition of God's everlasting promise to them.

Circumcision is a daily visual reminder that the covenant is eternal and that God can be trusted to keep His word. After the exter-nal sign of the covenant was given, God spelled out more completely the fulfillment of the promise He had made to Abraham.

Physically, circumcision is a sanitary practice which has kept the Jewish people from experiencing outbreaks of genital cancer. It has long been recognized in the United States as having healthful benefits and as such has been practiced extensively. Day eight of the child's life is the best time for circumcision medically because it has been proved to be the day when the baby's antibodies are highest and there is less likelihood of infection.

Gentiles practice circumcision for health reasons; Jews practice it to remind them of God's promise to them nationally.

This rite had nothing to do with women, only men. Many forms of female genital circumcision are practiced today by the Moslem nations in order to further degrade Moslem women. This was never part of God's plan.

The Promise of a Son made certain
(Genesis 18)

Thirteen years had passed since God's promise in chapter 15; thirteen years of quiet until God spoke to Abraham in Chapter 17. He was now 99 years old and though Abraham believed God, he had waited a very long time to see His promise fulfilled.

First the Scripture says, *the Lord appeared unto him in the plains of Mamre....* Not three people, just the Lord. Then *he lifted up his eyes* in verse 2, and there were three men near him. Some writers

Abraham's Oak at Hebron
(Peloubet 1913)

have intimated that all three were a manifestation of the Lord, but looking at Genesis 18:2 it does not seem likely. The two 'men' appear to be angels and are so called in 19:1. God used angels many times in the Old Testament to bring judgment on different nations and peoples. (See Section I on angels.)

When the three men appeared Abraham ran to greet them and in the Oriental custom of a great prince bowed down and addressed one of them as 'My Lord' (adônây). If he recognized the Lord at this point or at least suspected who He was, we are not told, but a little later he certainly knows to Whom he is speaking.

A meal was hastily prepared for the guests and according to custom when entertaining people of importance Abraham stood while they ate and does not appear to have actually eaten with them.

In verse 9 Abraham was surprised to hear them ask the question, *Where is Sarah thy wife?* (How did they know he had a wife named Sarah?) By this time Abraham seems to have figured out who his visitors were and without questioning them says, 'She's in the tent'. She was in the tent where she could see and hear without being seen by strange men.

The Lord, 'he' said, (Genesis 18:10), 'I'll return when the proper gestation cycle has passed and Sarah will have a son.' Now not only is Sarah again named as the mother, but the exact time is given for this child's birth.

And Sarah laughed. An 89 year old woman might well laugh at hearing such news. It is important to remember that Abraham's faith was not her faith. It was she who had suggested he take Hagar as his wife to help God out, and it was she who had watched for 13 years as the boy born of that union received the affection from Abraham that a son of hers should have had. That would have been a bitter daily object lesson for a barren woman who

had been named as the mother of a great nation. No wonder she laughed.

She didn't laugh out loud, but God heard her heart of unbelief and said, 'Why did Sarah laugh?' He already knew why she had laughed, but was teaching them a priceless lesson in faith. *Is anything too hard for the Lord?* (Genesis 18:14). 'No, it isn't, and at the proper time I'm coming back and you will have a son, just as I promised.'

Sarah spoke to the Lord then, denying her laughter. The Scripture says she was afraid. Here was a holy man who knew her name and could read her mind, and make such a promise; she would do well to be afraid.

How often do we do the same thing when confronted with sin. 'No, I didn't do that'. But God, in love, comes to us as He did to Sarah, 'Yes, you did'. He doesn't add to His rebuke. He just leaves her to think about what she had done. The laughter itself was not the problem; the heart of unbelief it showed was the problem, just as it is with us.

The Destruction of Sodom and Gomorrah
(Genesis 18:16-19:38)

The people of Sodom and the plains cities were Canaanites from the line of Ham. They were an extremely immoral people whose archeological remains have been of the basest sort, so much so that it has been extremely difficult for moral people to even look at them.

After the pronouncement of Isaac's birth, the Lord and the two men 'look toward Sodom' which was to be the second phase of their business in the area.

God speaks to Himself, "Shall I tell Abraham what I'm about to do?" (verse 17). Then He continues to logically consider the reasons why he needed to be told:

- Abraham would become a great and mighty nation;

- all nations would be blessed in him;
- he would command his children and his household to:

> keep the way of the Lord,
> to do justice,
> and to bring judgment.

Therefore, Abraham needed to know and recognize the need for justice in judgment for sin. And this was to serve as an example to Israel throughout the ages that sin will be judged. Sodom was used over and over to compare Israel's condition to that of Sodom and remind her of judgment, (Jeremiah 23:14, etc.).

Genesis 13:13 had already stated that the men of Sodom 'were wicked and sinners' so their reputation was well-known in the area. Abraham had rescued them from the Assyrian kings who had taken them captive and he had a vested interest in their welfare.

The wickedness of the city had reached the throne of God and He came again to see the wickedness of man. This was the third time He had come to earth to see man's great wickedness:

(1) the pre-Flood visitation when He repented that He had even made man, (Genesis 6);

(2) the Tower of Babel, (Genesis 11);

(3) and Sodom and Gomorrah. In any of these situations, God would have shown mercy had those involved asked forgiveness, but in none of these occasions were men concerned with their sin. They lived in a state of rebellion, never considering the coming judgment from a just God.

The world today is in the same condition and the concept of judgment is totally foreign to the majority of those who live in moral degradation of the worst kind. But judgment is coming as surely as night follows day, (1 Thessalonians 5:3).

Abraham accompanied his visitors for part of the journey, true to the manner of Oriental custom, and the Lord stopped to speak with him while the other two men (angels) continued on toward Sodom.

Abraham then began speaking to the Lord about what was going to happen and he was touched by the thought of the coming judgment. One writer mentioned how different our reactions are when we hear of coming judgment on a people. Some are happy, feeling that they get what they deserve (Jonah); some are sorrowful because of the lost and the innocent children who will suffer; and some, like Abraham, begin to pray and intercede with God. May God give us such a vision of hell that we will not only pray, but give and go to take the message of pardon before the coming judgment falls upon this lost world.

Abraham knew that God was just and would not allow the righteous to be condemned with the guilty, so he began to bargain with God. Beginning with the possibility of finding fifty just people, only ten in each of the five cities of the plain; he ended up with a total of ten. Each time he approached the Lord with another number, he humbly asked His pardon and begged Him for those people. The Lord never rebuked him, but allowed him to exhaust all the possibilities and finally said, "Yes, even for ten I'll hold back judgment," but He already knew there weren't even five just people in the entire plain.

When their conversation was finished Abraham went home to await the results. He knew his nephew had believed and it was counted to him for righteousness, (2 Peter 2:7,8), but he did not know about Lot's family. What he was totally aware of was the wickedness of those cities and the effect they could have on even a righteous person, let alone on an unsaved person.

As chapter 19 began, the men were now called 'angels'. As they entered Sodom they met Lot sitting in the gate, in a place of honor, but dubious honor in such a city as Sodom. The last time anything was mentioned about Lot he was dwelling in tents on the plain, now he was not only in a city, but was a part of its governing body. How quickly sin calls the believer to 'just try a little' and how quickly the 'little' become a way of life. Satan is not our friend and he uses every trick possible to take us from the narrow path of blessing.

Lot urged the angels to stay in his home because he knew the perversion that took place in the streets of Sodom at night. Oriental custom alone would dictate they not be left in the street, but he knew a more urgent reason to get them inside.

News traveled quickly and before they could go to bed the men of the city showed up at his door and began calling for the men to come out. They were not interested in who they were, they only wanted to use their bodies to satisfy their own perverted lust.

Whenever the Scripture refers to homosexuality it is judged in the harshest terms. Paul gives a progression of this sin in Romans 1. He begins by saying these people forget who their Creator and God is then follow after 'other gods' because their 'foolish heart is darkened'.

From there they progress to a form of idol worship - whatever their particular idol may be, and from there to moral uncleanness (akatharsia) to 'burn in their lust' toward members of the same sex. And because they continue in this lifestyle God gives them over to a 'mind to be abhorred by God and man'. Then they are assured that they will receive their just reward for practicing that lifestyle and doing those things which are not 'fit' for a creature made in God's image to do.

All pagan nations were afflicted with this sin and the United States is no exception today. It would appear that we have become even worse than the pagan nations of old. A more serious judgment must fall upon us nationally because we had and have the Truth, whereas the ancient pagan nations had lost the truth of the One True God.

This is one of the most difficult sins to overcome because Satan forms a stronghold in the life of the individual, and only the power of Christ can break it. Few families today have escaped the tragedy of one or more of its young people becoming involved in this despicable lifestyle, but God is able to deliver them if we, as Christians, are willing to 'go where they are' and help them escape. Our hearts should be broken for those involved in this sin in our country.

Lot tried to appease the wicked crowd by offering his virgin daughters to the crowd instead of the 'men', but they would have none of that - they wanted the men. The angels pulled Lot inside and caused the whole crowd outside to become blind so they couldn't cause any more harm. They then told Lot and his family their reason for being there and sent Lot out to speak to his future sons-in-law so they could all leave.

As he went to the homes of the men who were going to become his sons-in-law and told them the story of coming destruction they laughed in his face. His testimony had been such that he was not a credible witness for God. (The Spanish Bible translates Genesis 19:14, as 'he went to speak to his future sons-in-law who were going to marry his daughters, not who had already married them. The English version gives a reference Scripture in Matthew 1:18 which speaks of the engagement of Joseph and Mary and their espousal, but not their marriage. From this we are to assume that these men were not yet married to his virgin daughters.)

He was back home by morning and the angels were forced to drag him and his family from the city because they hated to leave their sin and comforts behind. The angels took them to the edge of the plain and said, 'Get going and don't look back, get to the mountains because everything down here is going to be destroyed.'

And still Lot lingered and tried to make another deal 'Couldn't we just go up to Zoar, it's just a little city and it's close and I'm afraid to go to the mountains, how about it?' The angel gave him permission and again told him to hurry. As soon as Lot got to Zoar the Lord rained fire and brimstone upon these cities and destroyed them completely.

But Lot's wife turned and looked back with longing at her former home and the wonderful things she had had there, and was turned into a pillar of salt. 'Remember Lot's wife' is an admonition to us to follow God's commands to the letter. He is merciful and He is long-suffering to a point, then His holy justice must be served.

When Abraham got up the next morning and looked toward Sodom and Gomorrah he saw the whole land smoking like a furnace. Most scholars agree that the fire and brimstone were precipitated from an earthquake opening the earth along the fault line that runs through that area, causing an explosion of the flammable sulfur and petroleum that seep through the ground, probably combusted by a bolt of lightning from heaven. Whatever the cause it wiped those five cities off the face of the earth and they still haven't been found, though some think at least some of them are buried in the southern end of the Dead Sea. One thing is certain, the names of Sodom and Gomorrah have never been forgotten through the ages and they always stand for the grossest of moral sin.

Keller says there is no trace of Sodom and Gomorrah because they were covered by the Dead Sea. The eastern shore is a peninsula called el-Lisan ("the tongue") which protrudes like a tongue into the water. It is mentioned in Joshua 15:2 "from the bay" or "tongue". From the peninsula of el-Lison to the southernmost tip was the Vale of Siddim. There is a shallow area in the Dead Sea of 50 to 60' deep where outlines of forests are preserved by the salt content of the Sea.

No other part of the globe lies deeper than 300 feet below sea level. The Jordan Valley is part of a huge fracture line from the foot of the Taurus Mountains in Asia Minor to beyond the Red Sea in Africa and along this line there is intensive volcanic activity; the Vale of Siddim fracture runs through this line. Around 1900 B.C. a great earthquake occurred accompanied by explosions, lightning, issues of natural gas and general conflagration. An occurrence of this kind would have plunged Sodom and Gomorrah into the abyss and submerged them beneath the waters of the Dead Sea. Abraham is thought to have lived around 1900 B.C.

"The Vale of Sidimus (Siddim) sank and became a lake, always evaporating and containing no fish, a symbol of vengeance and of death for the transgressor." (Written by Sanchuniathon, a Phoenician priest.)

God saved Lot for Abraham's sake because he had so earnestly interceded for him and his family. We are not told if they ever met again, but we know how the actions of Lot's daughters at this time would affect Israel in the future.

When the plain exploded Lot decided he needed to put some distance between him and destruction so he left Zoar and went into the mountains and lived in a cave with his two daughters.

Moab and Ammon (Genesis 19:30-38)

How long Lot and his daughters lived in the cave before the next sad phase of Lot's life took place is not mentioned in the Scriptures. It is evident from verse 31 of chapter 19 that the women believed they were the last inhabitants of the earth and so conceived their vile plan. To see their perverseness gives us an indication of how living in an environment permeated with wickedness affects those in close proximity. These women, (not 'girls' at the time), felt no shame in having an incestuous relationship with their father. However, they believed it necessary to get him drunk before carrying out their plans because he would have evidently refused to be a part of such wickedness otherwise.

An interesting question comes to mind here, where did they get the wine? It would have been difficult to carry it out of Sodom because the angels had them by the hand; there is no indication as to how long they were in Zoar, but perhaps long enough to buy some provisions, including the wine, and make for the mountains. Lot does not appear to have been a drunkard because verses 32-34 repeat the phrase, 'let us make him drink wine'. Since most wine today is between 10 and 17% alcohol it would take several glasses of wine to make him drunk especially if he were not accustomed to drinking large amounts at a time, and therefore they would literally have had to keep him drinking until that point was reached.

After committing their disgraceful act they were both expecting a child by their father. What must he have thought when he found they were both expecting a child? In verse 8 of the last chapter, he had offered them as virgins to the men of Sodom and now it's a different story. A father who cares more for comfort and riches than he cares for his family loses contact with them and usually gets a shock when he finds out what they are doing behind his back.

There is never an indication that he knew who the father of the children was, because he didn't know what they had done. What is known is that the children born became a curse to Israel and constantly tried to do them harm. They were mighty warriors of great wealth, and great idolatry. The Moabites sent Balaam to curse Israel after refusing them passage through their land, (Numbers 22-24). The Ammonites were a cruel and idolatrous nation whom God cursed, (Ezekiel 25:1-7), along with the Moabites, (Ezekiel 25:8-11).

The Scripture says, 'do not evil that good may come from it', (Romans 3:8), and the end never justifies the means if it is contrary to God's Word.

With this act the curtain falls on the life of Lot; a sorry end for a man who had chosen the 'well-watered plains' and in so doing had left God behind.

Abraham and Abimelech (Genesis 20)

The Scripture gives us another example here of Satan trying to stop the coming of the Messiah by trying to dispose of the woman who was to be the mother of the promised seed.

God had told Abraham in Chapter 18 that the promised seed would come through Sarah and that seed would be the means of blessing for the whole world. There was no doubt about how these events were to take place, nor when they were to take place, (within the year).

Abraham now leaves the plains of Mamre. If they were as fertile as archaeological discoveries have shown it would be difficult to believe he left because of lack of food for his animals.

It is more likely that after seeing the destruction of the cities of the plains he felt the need to get away from the area for a while. Whatever the reason, we don't see God's name mentioned as directing him to go.

About 25 years had passed since his journey to Egypt. He seems to have forgotten the results of his deception concerning his wife and only remembered how effective it had been in saving his own life.

As before mentioned Sarah was 90 years old, and though she had been a beautiful woman, it is not likely that she was desired for her beauty on this occasion, but for the political power of her princely 'brother'. He was a man of great wealth and it was in Abimelech's favor to make a treaty with him, in token of which, he would take Abraham's sister as part of his harem, and allow Abraham to prosper in his land.

God rebuked Abimelech in a dream for having taken Sarah. He declared Abraham to be a prophet (the first use of the word in the Scripture), and told him that Sarah was the prophet's wife, and he was a dead man if she wasn't returned immediately. Abimelech then rebuked Abraham for his deception and returned Sarah to him.

He wanted to make up for his mistake (he said, I did it in ignorance and in good faith, 'in the integrity of my heart and innocency of my hands'). Therefore he gave gifts to Abraham of livestock and people and gave Abraham a thousand pieces of silver to compensate for Sarah's absence. He said to Sarah, *I have given your 'brother' a thousand pieces of silver....* He could have been using sarcasm to both of them in saying he was her brother, or he could have accepted their explanation and recognized that technically he was her brother.

Abimelech asked Abraham in what way he had not respected his rights *(châtâ)* to deserve this kind of deception.

Abimelech recognized the voice of God though he was a pagan Philistine, a descendant of Ham. It is interesting how even an unbeliever can recognize God's voice and God's workings when they touch his own life.

The shame in this scene belongs to Abraham. He risked the mother of the promised seed to save his own life. He allowed Satan to draw him aside from God's plan in his attempt to stop the coming of Isaac, the progenitor of Christ, by destroying the vessel through which he was to come.

Abraham helped to redeem himself in the eyes of Abimelech by praying for his household. God, who is the lifegiver, had not allowed any of the household of Abimelech to have children. When Abraham prayed God lifted His curse from Abimelech's house and they were again fruitful.

Abraham's personal testimony was destroyed, but because God worked through the prophet, his national testimony was intact and Abimelech offered him any part of his land Abraham wanted to live in.

The Birth of Isaac (Genesis 21)

Abraham continued to live in the region of Gerar and the long-promised birth finally occurred.

When Isaac was born Sarah was 90 years old, well past the natural time of childbearing, but this was a miracle child brought to life by God's direct intervention.

The name Isaac meant 'laughter' and Sarah said, 'God has made me laugh', (verse 6); not the laughter of unbelief now, but the laughter of joy and fulfillment. Not only Sarah would laugh, but all that heard about her son, then and in ages to come, would laugh with her as they saw God's faithfulness.

Isaac's birth had been promised some 25 years before its occurrence. Sarah had doubted, most probably because of her age, and she tried taking things into her own hands with Hagar, but that experiment failed. From what we see of her relationship with Abraham she was a dutiful, obedient wife, but she did not believe the way he did. She was evidently a strong-willed woman because Abraham did as she said in reference to Hagar on two occasions, though he was not in favor of casting out his son.

She did not believe wholeheartedly in the promise of God. Women, in general, are more apt to experience a lack of faith in things they cannot see, nor reason. She was governed by her emotions, which told her, when a women is 90 years old it is not likely she is going to become a mother, and that was a reasonable belief. But God does not operate by the same laws of nature which govern man.

The Departure of Ishmael (Genesis 21:8-21)

When Isaac was weaned, (from one to three years of age), Sarah demanded that Abraham send Hagar and Ishmael away because Ishmael was mocking Isaac. In this case Sarah understood better than Abraham that Isaac should not be under the influence of Hagar's son. This time Sarah and God were in agreement and God told Abram to send the boy and his mother away.

To send them away was a grief to Abraham because Ishmael was his son by blood and he loved the child.

God was faithful even in this. God promised Abraham that Ishmael would become a great nation in numbers because of his blood relationship to Abraham, (Genesis 21:13).

Hagar and Ishmael lived in the wilderness around Beer-sheba with the blessing of God on them, and the promise of God still ringing in their ears.

Ishmael did become a great nation, forming a large branch of the Arab nations which inhabit the Middle East today. There were twelve sons, just as the tribes of Israel would be twelve. The sons of Ishmael were called 'princes' and the descendants of Sarah were called 'kings', (Genesis 17:16); God makes an interesting distinction between them.

His mother took him a wife from Egypt and this emphasizes again the importance of the wife and mother in the family. How different the line of history between Ishmael and Isaac is today. Ishmael became a curse to Israel and the whole world through the Muslim religion. Isaac became a blessing to the whole world through the Lord Jesus Christ who was born of his line.

Ishmael's territory was from Havilah to Shur which would put his descendants from the Desert of Shur, east of the Nile and north of the Red Sea on the Mediterranean, to the tip of the Arabian Peninsula on the Indian Ocean (where Yemen is today). He evidently felt more at home at the beginning living closer to Egypt and later extended his territory to the Persian Gulf.

From this time onward Ishmael is referred to in the Scripture in reference to his sons, and usually in a derogatory manner.

The Sacrifice of Isaac (Genesis 22:1-19)

After the long years of waiting for his birth and the years spent enjoying and loving his son Isaac, God asked Abraham to do the humanly impossible. He asked for Abraham's son in sacrifice.

Abraham knew that the pagan nations around him offered only their best to their gods in sacrifice. They offered their most precious of gifts - their own children. They offered them in vain to gods which were no gods.

His conscience did not convict him about giving a human sacrifice because he knew God could raise up Isaac from the dead, and he also knew God would not ask him to do anything he should not do, (Hebrews 11:19). How could he possibly understand that God was asking him to be totally willing to sacrifice his son, but it would not be required of him.

God does not condone human sacrifice and was teaching the difference between the spirit of sacrifice and the actual offering of a human being. Never was this an accepted practice to God and certainly it was no exception in the case of Abraham.

God was teaching a lesson to the pagan nations that human sacrifice accomplished nothing and only as God provided Himself a sacrifice would the sacrifice of a God-man be efficacious.

He was teaching Abraham to trust - no matter how hopeless the situation seemed. Isaac was learning to not only trust his father and obey his instructions in everything, but also to rely upon God's provision. God proved Abraham in asking him to sacrifice his son, the rightful heir to the eternal promises for a blessed nation. Abraham did not hesitate; he prepared everything, and with the young man, he headed for the place designated by God.

As Abraham and Isaac left the servants behind and continued up the mountain, Abraham's mind must have been in great turmoil. How many questions occurred to him in those hours? As to Isaac, he was a young man seeing new territory and at peace with his father's decisions for him - not really a boy and not yet a man. He followed his father's instructions as far as lying down upon the altar and being tied, or bound, by his father. If Isaac had resisted it is doubtful a man of approximately 117 years of age would have been able to overpower him.

But as the precursor of the Savior, Isaac 'laid down his life willingly'. Not for the sins of mankind, as Christ would do, but in strict obedience to his father, as Christ would do about 2000 years later, *O my Father, if it be possible, let this cup pass from me: nevertheless, not as I will, but as thou wilt.* (Matthew 26:39.)

Isaac was obedient to his father and never seemed to doubt the wisdom in starting out to make a sacrifice without the presence of a sacrificial animal.

God knew Abraham's heart and knew he would do as commanded; God proves us so our own faith will become stronger. Testing and tempting are two distinct words and do not mean the same thing. God never tempts us; He only tests us (or proves us).

And God is faithful. Though He allowed Abraham to lay his son on the altar, to lay the wood in preparation for the consuming fire, and to lift the knife to plunge it into Isaac's heart, God stopped him by providing a substitutionary sacrifice.

The picture is so compelling that one is amazed by the faithfulness of this father, but more so as we think of our Savior becoming the substitutionary sacrifice for each of us individually and laying down His life in place of our own.

When Abraham said to Isaac, *My son, God will provide himself a lamb for a burnt offering* (Genesis 22:8), he was, in effect, foretelling the death of Christ on the cross where God did indeed provide Himself as the Lamb to take away the sin of the whole world. Abraham believed God could bring Isaac back from the grave if it was His will and purpose. His faith did not falter. God proved His purpose in choosing Abraham as the father of a great nation and Abraham proved how his faith had matured through the ensuing years.

Isaac had done nothing to deserve death; neither had Christ. Isaac obeyed his father; so did Christ. Isaac was to serve as a blessing to all nations; in Christ all the world can have the salvation provided by His death. Isaac was ready for the deathblow; Christ received it that man might be restored to fellowship with a holy God.

In Isaac the sacrifice was made in spirit; in Christ it was made in the flesh.

Abraham was to completely yield Isaac to God; to realize Isaac no longer belonged to him but to God. That was the spiritual sacrifice of Abraham.

How many times do we as parents surrender our children to the Lord and then forget that they no longer belong to us but to God. "Make him a doctor, make her a lawyer, but please don't make him be a preacher and especially not a missionary!" Our children are the greatest gift we can offer to the Lord and we can trust Him to be faithful in leading them in the right path.

The sacrifice was completed. They descended from the mountain with a new understanding of God's purpose for them as the founders of a nation which was to serve as an example to all the nations of the world of a coming Savior.

The family was living in Hebron when Sarah died at the age of 127, and Isaac was between 36 and 37 years old, (Genesis 23:1). As before stated she was buried in the land of the Hittites in the cave of Macpelah. Abraham was buried beside her 38 years later, (Genesis 35:8,9; Hebrews 11:13).

Marriage of Isaac (Genesis 24)

It was not unusual at that period of time to marry within the same family. Sarah was Isaac's grandfather's daughter, but not the daughter of his grandmother. Other instances of close marriages continued to occur throughout the Old Testament period, especially until the time of Moses.

After a time of mourning for his mother Abraham believed it was time for Isaac to take a wife. This was no doubt to help him get over his grief for his mother, but was also so Abraham could see his son settled before he died.

Abraham called his faithful servant to his side. Because of Abraham's own advanced age and his fear of dying before the task was completed, he asked the servant to swear that he would not allow Isaac to marry any of the women from the pagan nations around them. When he received this promise the servant was then sent out to find a bride for Isaac from Abraham's own family.

The servant went to Mesopotamia, (the land along the western side of the Euphrates, which is today northwestern Iraq), to the city of Nahor, and asked God to guide him to the right person. This person turned out to be Rebekah, the daughter of Bethuel, who was the son of Milcah, daughter of Haran, and wife of Nahor, Abraham's brother. This would make her Abraham's great niece. (In Genesis 25:20, she is called the daughter of Bethuel the Syrian, but it was because of the Syrian influence from Ur and because of the physical location of her home, not because they were Syrians by birth. They were Shemites from Arphaxad, not from Aram who formed the Syrian nation.)

Rebekah returned to Hebron with the servant and she and Isaac were married and Isaac was comforted by her presence after the death of his mother, (Genesis 24:67). He had grieved for Sarah for at least 3 years, since he was 40 years old when he married Rebekah.

It is interesting to note that Isaac was not a strong man emotionally, and was easily led astray by his physical desires. This weakness is seen, both in his treatment of his wife Rebekah before Abimelech, and in his love of his son Esau's 'savoury meat'.

God knew all about Isaac before he was ever conceived; He knew what kind of man he would become. Isaac was an obedient son as was seen in the occasion of his impending sacrifice to God by his father. He was a loving man, as seen by his mourning for his mother,

Sarah, and by the love he had for Rebekah and Esau. He was an unfair man, as seen by his treatment of Jacob. It proves God can use anyone He wishes to carry out His plan for an individual or a nation.

Abraham remarries (Genesis 25:1-6)

It would appear from the context of the Scripture that Abraham married Keturah (a Hamite) shortly after the death of Sarah and several years before the marriage of Isaac. He was able to father six more sons.

There is no indication that this marriage was approved by God and there is some reason for believing it was not. The sons born through Keturah became a curse to Israel and formed part of the Arab nations which continue to plague Israel today.

Through the Midianites, one of these sons of Abraham and Keturah, Israel was led into Baal worship, (Numbers 31).

Abraham had eight sons, but only Ishmael and Isaac are referred to repeatedly in the Scriptures as the sons of Abraham. The sons of Keturah were wild, idolatrous men who brought grief to Abraham and to the nation of Israel.

When the inheritance was given it was all given to Isaac, (25:5). Abraham gave 'gifts' to the sons of the 'concubines', therefore both Hagar and Keturah were considered concubines and not legal wives. (Concubine: "a wife of inferior condition; a lawful wife, but not united to the man by the usual ceremonies, and of inferior condition. Such were Hagar and Keturah, the concubines of Abraham...." Webster's, 1828.)

The resentment they felt toward both Abraham and Isaac must have been tremendous and may account in part for the way they treated Abraham's descendants. Today this resentment comes from their desire to possess a land that is not theirs nor can ever be theirs -

the root is the same but it is doubtful they understand its complete ramifications.

Death of Abraham (Genesis 25:7-10)

When Abraham died it was made plain that his sole heir was Isaac. The other sons were sent to areas of the country far from Isaac so they would not influence Isaac's obedience to God. God's purpose for Isaac had not been revealed other than that he was to carry out the promise of God to his father Abraham.

Both Isaac and Ishmael were present to bury their father. This gives some indication that they were at least on speaking terms and that Ishmael had some contact with Abraham through the years. They lived in close proximity since the area around Hebron is not far from Beersheba where Ishmael lived at the beginning of his life away from Abraham's home.

The formation of a Nation (Genesis 25:19-34)

Rebekah was barren, as Sarah had been, and as Rachel would be in the future. It was only by the intervention of prayer by Isaac that Rebekah was able to conceive after 20 years of marriage.

Isaac 'entreated' God for Rebekah. This is the Hebrew word *atar* or *áthor* which means 'to assail one with petitions or intercede in prayer': 'to let oneself be entreated' as Genesis 25:21 speaks of God's reply to Isaac. Zodhiates says, "This word for prayer depicts an imploring, beseeching, spontaneous petition of God who is waiting to listen." (Zodhiates Bible notes), p. 1627. Though Abraham prayed for the barren women in Abimelech's household (20:17), there is no record of him praying about Sarah's barrenness. God kept telling him a son would be born and Abraham trusted God's word that it would happen; there was no need to pray about a sure thing.

Isaac knew the fulfillment of the covenant depended upon him having a son and since God had not specifically promised one to him, he 'entreated' the Lord and received his answer from a faithful God.

Jacob and Esau (Genesis 25:19-26)

God intervened and gave Rebekah twin sons, Esau and Jacob. From the beginning there was strife between the two brothers. Part of the problem may have originated with the parents because of their partiality to one or the other. Parents do not realize how important it is for them to treat each child as a special gift from God and other than making allowances for each one's individuality there should be no difference in the way each child is raised. Each child is an individual and has distinct character traits which must be taken into account, but to show partiality to one child over another always leads to resentment from the other siblings and to emotional problems for the chosen child. Esau and Jacob are a classic example of this.

God had foretold that there were two nations in her womb and that the elder would serve the younger, but this did not do away with individual choice which is accorded to all men.

Esau had a choice to make and chose wrongly, but God did not make him choose what he did. Because God is sovereign He knew before his birth what Esau would choose. Esau's name meant "ruddy" or "red" describing his physical looks, and Jacob's name meant 'protect' and did not receive the negative connotation of 'assailant', 'overreacher', 'deceiver' or 'supplanter', until much later.

Even before their birth there was conflict between the two brothers. The word used for 'struggled' in 25:22 is *rasas* or *ratsats* which carries the connotation of 'break (in pieces), bruise, crush, discourage, oppress, struggle

together and to dash one another'. Given the many meanings of the word it is not surprising that Rebekah was alarmed about what was going on in her pregnancy and went to inquire of the Lord. This was not just a little discomfort, but a frightening occurrence. And the oracle of the Lord was:

- 2 nations are in thy womb,
- 2 manners of people shall come forth,
- one will be stronger,
- the elder shall serve the younger.

When they were growing up Isaac loved Esau because of his prowess as a hunter. Esau was a rowdy, outgoing man who loved the outdoors; just the opposite of Isaac.

Rebekah loved Jacob because his spirit was opposite to her own. She was the outgoing member of the pair and her quiet son was a balm to her restless soul. The Scripture says he was a plain man, meaning a 'quiet man', a gentle man of introspection who lived plainly in his tents. It's interesting how God many times uses a quiet, gentle man to accomplish His purposes. The world sees the 'cunning hunter' and applauds him as the hero, but God sees the quiet man who tends to his business and makes no claim to fame, as His instrument to carry out His plan.

The Stolen Birthright (Genesis 25:27-34)

Esau was the firstborn and carried the responsibilities of the firstborn in Jewish society. This meant he was spiritually responsible for the family (in his generation), and was to receive a double portion of the inheritance, (Deuteronomy 21:17).

When everything seemed to be going well, the Scripture tells of Esau, at age 40, marrying two Hittite women, (26: 34).

And they were a 'grief of mind' to his parents. Esau knew better, but his whole life was spent in getting instant gratification without consideration of the consequences.

Sometime after his marriage, (there is no indication here of a time-lapse), and as Esau was returning from the hunt, he was tired and hungry. The exhilaration of the hunter had subsided when he was unable to find his prey, and being a fleshly man concerned only with the desires of the flesh, he felt he was about to die from hunger. That was unlikely to occur since he was well-fed and had received only the best of food all of his life. As he approached the encampment he smelled the seething pot of soup Jacob had cooking over the fire. His desire for a bowl of that soup overwhelmed him and he bartered his desire for food for his most prized possession. If he had been willing to wait a few minutes, his servants would have prepared him whatever he wished, but like most people bent on immediately having their own way, he was not willing to wait even the normal time period of preparation.

Jacob was willing to feed him, but not without a price. He had likely been waiting all day for the return of Esau so he could do his underhanded deed. He had purposely made the soup, a kind which he knew Esau liked, and he had spiced it just right so the smell would be the first thing that met Esau as he returned from the field.

Jacob said, "Sure, you can have some soup, but in order to pay for it, you must sell me your birthright." Esau did not hesitate to sell the possession which he should have valued more than anything, for a bowl of soup. He esteemed lightly the position God had given him; but Jacob asked for something that was not his by right. The birthright belonged to the firstborn, but was taken from him because of his own carnal nature. Food was more important to Esau than the birthright. The Scripture says he 'despised his birthright', (25:34). The word 'despise' means "to disdain, to have the lowest opinion of". The Hebrew word is *bazâ* - 'to make light of', in other words it meant less than nothing to him.

Jacob made Esau swear that he was giving him the birthright. The Hebrew word is *shâba*, "swearing was the giving of one's unbreakable word that he would faithfully perform a promised deed or that he would not harm his partner." In Jewish culture, 'to swear' was a binding agreement that was not to be broken and there is no indication that Esau ever tried to break it though he certainly regretted his decision later in life, (Genesis 27:36).

When Esau finished eating, he left to go to his tent, never giving another thought to what he had just done, or the long-term effects it would have.

Esau was never interested in the things of God and never understood the importance of the promised nation he represented. God knew this before he was ever conceived and for this reason had passed the responsibility to Jacob, the younger of the two. But God would have worked it all out according to His plan and not the way Jacob did it by deception.

Isaac at Gerar (Genesis 26)

Because of a famine Isaac moved his family to the Philistine city of Gerar, whose king was another Abimelech.

The Lord spoke to him telling him not to go into Egypt, but to stay in the land where he was at that time. God reaffirmed the promise to Isaac which He had given to Abraham, and its certain fulfillment.

Isaac lied about his wife as Abraham had lied about Sarah; saying she was his sister, (Genesis 26:7). She was in fact, his second cousin, and he had no basis for calling her his sister. He had, no doubt, heard the story of his father's actions in Egypt, and it had worked so well he decided to try it also.

Evidently Rebekah had not yet been taken into the household of Abimelech because Isaac had access to her presence and was flirting with her when Abimelech saw them and quickly accused Isaac of lying about her. Isaac admitted that she was his wife and excused the lie because he was afraid of being killed because of her beauty.

After settling the problem between him and Abimelech, and feeling more secure in his position, Isaac planted crops near Gerar. Because of the Lord's blessing he received an hundred fold increase. More grain meant more flocks and more flocks meant greater riches. As he began to get more possessions Abimelech told Isaac to move farther from them because the Philistines were jealous of Isaac's possessions and Abimelech was afraid a war might break out.

Isaac left the city area and moved to the valley of Gerar, near the western coast of Canaan.

Because the Philistines had filled in the wells Abraham had dug in the area years before, Isaac began to re-dig them and open them up so he would have water for his household and his flocks.

As the wells were opened the Philistine herdsmen of the area began to argue about the water saying it was theirs.

Isaac moved again rather than have difficulties with them, and dug another well called Rehoboth, *the Lord hath made room for us, and we shall be fruitful in the land,* (Genesis 26:22).

The Lord appeared to him again, and again reaffirmed the promises given to Abraham, (verse 24). Isaac then built an altar and worshipped God in that place and dug another well.

Abimelech, his captain, and a friend, arrived at Isaac's camp. Isaac was surprised because they had treated him so badly before that he assumed they were his enemies. But even a pagan is impressed by God's blessings, and

they saw how God had blessed Isaac and recognized that it was God who had done it.

They asked that a covenant be made between them so neither would harm the other, and the covenant was sealed by a feast prepared by Isaac's household.

When Abimelech and his company left, a servant told Isaac the well they had just dug was successful and water had been found. Isaac called the well, Shebah, (verse 33) and it was then known as Beer-sheba, 'well of an oath'; *beer*, meaning 'well', *sheba*, meaning 'an oath'.

God reminded Isaac five times in this chapter of Abraham's obedience to Him, and two times more He renewed His promise of provision and of the covenant made with Abraham.

The Stolen Blessing (Genesis 27)

When Jacob took Esau's blessing he again took something to which he had no right. A father could bless his son in any way he wished whether it was the first son or the fifth. Isaac was determined to give Esau the blessing of the firstborn though he understood that God had placed Jacob first. He did not place the spiritual above the carnal until after the blessing was stolen by Jacob.

Isaac was an old man as indicated by Genesis 27:1, and he felt his days were coming to an end. He was at this time almost blind and very feeble; he had never been a man with a lot of energy and strength, and less so now as the years continued their steady march. In fact, he lived another 43 years after this event. God had plenty of time to make everything right, but neither Isaac nor Jacob was willing to wait on God and let Him work it all out in the best way. Just as we, so many times, are not willing to wait on the Lord in our lives to work out seemingly impossible problems.

When Rebekah heard Isaac tell Esau he was going to bless him, she immediately formed a plan to deceive him and get the blessing for Jacob.

Jacob knew he was wrong in deceiving his father in connection with the blessing Isaac was going to give to Esau. He kept voicing his objections to his mother but she said, "Listen to me, and do what I say." He said, "Look, mother, how can we make goat taste like venison? How can we fool my father, I'm a smooth man and Esau is a hairy man? My father can't see, but he can still smell, and I don't smell like an outdoors man, there are too many problems to be able to carry out this deception successfully." But Rebekah had an answer for all of his objections. He was not concerned with the deceit so much as being discovered in the deceit by his father.

When Jacob approached his father, he began with a lie and continued to lie during the whole interview and when the whole affair was over he had accomplished his purpose, but not without great personal loss to himself. He had to live with the fact that he had purposely betrayed his father's trust in him.

Isaac was lying down when Jacob entered his tent. He declared himself to be Esau who had been successful in the hunt and had prepared the dish of venison Isaac longed for. He then invited his father to get up and eat. He even got God involved in the trickery by saying he had found the deer so quickly because God had been with him and he called Him 'thy God', words usually not coming from Esau's lips. Isaac felt something was wrong, but just couldn't put his finger on the problem. He and Esau were much alike in their desire for fleshly gratification. He felt the animal skins and heard the voice which seemed to be that of Jacob, but because he desired the meat he accepted his own doubts and sat to eat. Then, after he had eaten his fill of the savory meat, he blessed Jacob.

The blessing once given was binding and could not be changed. When Isaac gave the blessing to Jacob he thought he was giving it to Esau. What he said in giving the blessing to the person he thought was Esau was totally contrary to the promise God had given Rebekah before the twins were born. God said, *Let people serve thee, and nations bow down to thee: be lord over thy brethren, and let thy mother's sons bow down to thee....* Isaac knew there was only one other son, and he knew <u>that</u> son had been promised the position of leadership in the family by God because the blessing of the firstborn gave the heir the right to be lord over his brethren. While he certainly could as well have been referring to the descendants of both Esau and Jacob in the blessing, there was a sense of the present also in his pronouncement. Isaac was determined to place Esau in the number one position, regardless of what God had said. In this instance he loved Esau more than he loved God. He knew the promise of God for the nation because it had been reaffirmed to him in Genesis 26, and when he gave the blessing he did not give the blessing of Abraham to Esau. He only intimated the blessing of Abraham in saying, *cursed be every one that curseth thee, and blessed be he that blesseth thee* (Genesis 27:29). He evidently had enough spiritual insight to realize he had no right to give that particular blessing when God had ordained that it go to Jacob.

Isaac was as much at fault in giving this blessing to Esau as Rebekah was in trying to fool him. For this reason when he discovered he had given the blessing to the wrong son he *trembled very exceedingly* because he knew he couldn't fool God in trying to change His plan for Jacob. He was powerless to change the plan of the Almighty and was found guilty trying to do so.

When Esau became aware of Jacob's trickery he accused him of stealing both his birthright and his blessing. He had willingly sold his birthright and could not blame anyone else for his own lack of discernment. He asked his father if he had not reserved a blessing for him also; this would seem to indicate that it was possible Isaac had not planned to give any blessing to Jacob, and this may have been the reason Rebekah acted as she did. Esau's blessing was purely physical; it had no spiritual reference at all. He was to be wealthy and was to live by the sword and serve his brother until he *broke his yoke from off thy neck* (verse 40), which was finally accomplished when Antipater and Herod, both Edomites, ruled over Israel.

Jacob saw the hatred Esau now felt for him and knew that when Isaac died Esau would try to kill him. His mother, after being told what Esau was saying about killing Jacob, (Genesis 27:41), sent him to her family in Haran until Esau's wrath subsided.

In this also she tricked Isaac by saying she wanted Jacob to go to Laban, her brother, so he would not marry one of the Hittites as Esau had already done. When deception begins it knows no limits in the human heart. She thought it would only be a little while, but there is no indication that she ever saw her beloved Jacob again in her lifetime. And the Biblical narrative passed from Isaac to Jacob at this point.

Jacob was a consistent man, (he worked 14 years for Rachel), a persistent man with dogged tenacity, but he was also a calculating, selfish man; he seems to have been a lot like the rest of us.

Rebekah did not take into account the cunning treachery of her brother Laban, nor could she have imagined that Jacob would find a love so great that it would make him forget his dear mother.

Esau saw the concern of his parents for the wife Jacob was to take so he took another wife. He thought he would get back into their good graces by marrying a wife from the line of Ishmael. He never realized his greatest sin was in not recognizing the God of his father and grandfather; he thought everything could be made right by the external and never considered the internal heart of man.

The trickery of Jacob led to his banishment from his home and from the mother who had been his greatest friend. God had said Jacob would rule over Esau, but they were not willing to allow Him to bring it to pass in His time and in His way.

Why did Esau not understand about God and His promise of a possession in the land and the importance of a personal relationship with Him? Esau could be described as a fickle, capricious man who lived for the moment; a carnal man who never considered the consequences of his acts; a man who was generous but without principles to guide his life.

The actions of parents make a tremendous impression on the hearts and lives of the children. Esau knew of the favoritism in the home and the ever-present undercurrent of trickery. He saw in his father what he perceived to be a weak man, and could not admire that weakness, being a strong man himself. The inconsistencies were too much for him.

How many young people have left home and gone the opposite way of their parents because of the inconsistencies in the home? Hebrews 12:16 calls Esau a 'profane' man (i.e. heathenish, wicked), in other words without knowledge of the truth. He grew up in the same home as Jacob, and heard the same stories of Jehovah God as Jacob, but what made the difference? Again, it goes back to individual choice. Every person has to make his own decision to believe or not to believe. Esau's personal choice was not to believe and his life was affected by that choice. His descendants, the Edomites (the Idumeans), were a wicked irreligious nation that continued in the path of their father Esau.

Jacob reaped a bitter harvest throughout his life because of his attitude toward trickery. He was in turn tricked by Laban, his father-in-law; by his wife Rachel, in reference to the gods of her father; and by his own sons, when they lied to him about Joseph. Had he been willing to wait on God he would have avoided all these problems.

Before Jacob left his home his father gave him the blessing of Abraham, which he had withheld when he thought he was blessing Esau. This blessing confirmed him as the true heir of all the promises of God to Abraham and Isaac, and made him the representative of Abraham, (28:3,4). Jacob did not slip away like a thief; he was sent by his parents to find a wife of his own kin, and his going was for his own sake as well as theirs.

In the house of Laban (Genesis 28-31)

As Jacob journeyed to Padan-aram, the land of Laban (a distance of about 400 miles), God gave him the promise of the eternal covenant when he stopped in his journey to spend the night at Beth-el. This was the first time God had spoken personally to Jacob. He had heard about God speaking to his father and grandfather, but had never experienced firsthand the presence of God. Only the line of Abraham spoke with God, and then only at specific times.

Beth-el was considered to be a holy place; the dwelling place of the Spirit, (Genesis 12:8; 13:4). The peoples of the area were pagans and believed the pagan myths attributed to certain holy places. It was not inconsistent for Jacob to have knowledge of this place from the history of his grandfather and also from the stories told about it by the pagan peoples around him.

As Jacob slept he saw a vision of a ladder or staircase reaching from earth to heaven on which angels were ascending and descending. (Most scholars believe the ladder is a symbol of the Lord Jesus Christ as indicated by John 1:51.) The Lord was standing at its highest point and He began to speak with Jacob. He was again given the covenant first given to his grandfather Abraham - the promise of the land and of a great nation which was to come through him. God also promised to be with him as He had been with Abraham. Though he was now leaving the land of promise, God would care for him and bring him back in His time.

When he awoke from his dream, Jacob said, *Surely the Lord is in this place; and I*

Jacob at Bethel
(Peloubet 1922)

knew it not, (Genesis 28:16). This would cause us to believe he was not aware that the Lord Jehovah dwelt there. He had thought because of what he had heard, that some 'spirit' dwelt there, but now knew it was a dwelling-place of the only God and *that* God had now become **his** God, and he was filled with awe.

Jacob set up a monument at Bethel and poured oil upon it, marking it as sacred, in remembrance of the promise given to him by God in that place. He promised to give God the tenth of his goods because God had promised to be with him wherever he went and because He had become his personal God. As he continued his journey he was a new man with a new heart, but not yet a mature heart in the things of God.

After traveling the 400 miles, Jacob arrived at a well near the home of Laban, his uncle. There he found the shepherds gathered with their sheep, apparently waiting until all the shepherds were gathered before they removed the stone from the well. Jacob asked them where they were from and they replied 'from Haran', so he knew he had come to the end of his journey. He asked if they knew Laban and they replied, 'Oh, yes, we know him.' They doubtless knew of his trickery and underhandedness in his dealings with them. They also told Jacob, Laban's daughter Rachel was arriving at that moment at the well with the sheep. In the custom of the country she would probably have been heavily veiled and Jacob could not see her face. He removed the stone from the well and gave water to Laban's sheep though according to the shepherds it was not yet time to do so.

The shepherd of that time was not a 'sissy'. He had to be strong and tough in order to live under primitive conditions and be able to protect the sheep from bears, wolves, lions, and robbers. They were people of the open-air and their weapons were as much a part of their person as their clothing. They recognized in Jacob a man of their own kind and made no attempt to stop him from removing the stone from the well before the set time.

An Oriental Shepherd
(Peloubet, 1922)

After Jacob had given water to the sheep he made himself known to his cousin Rachel and she ran to tell her father about him. Laban had become more consumed with his desire for riches since the time of his sister's leaving (Rebekah), and he saw in Jacob the arrival of a rich man's son who could be of benefit to him and his house.

Laban went out to meet Jacob and invited him into his home and upon arriving there Jacob told him why he had come. Not to escape his brother's wrath surely, but to find himself a wife of his near kin. It is not often that a man will tell the bad things about himself to a stranger and Jacob was no exception.

Jacob worked for Laban for about a month, (29:14), helping wherever he could, and since he was an industrious man Laban soon saw the advantage of having him around. Jacob had been a shepherd all his life so he was well aware of the business of raising sheep and goats. When Laban asked what he would require for wages, he said, "I'll serve you seven years for your daughter Rachel." In Jewish culture this was the time a bondservant was to serve his master; Laban 'sold' his daughters to Jacob, and for this reason, in 31:15, both women say their father had sold them. From the beginning Jacob had fallen in love with Rachel, and it was a love that endured his entire lifetime. Even when she died he never stopped loving her and mourning her loss.

Laban was delighted with this arrangement. He would get a good worker and not have to pay much for his help. Also, he knew in his treacherous heart he was not going to give Rachel to Jacob because Leah was the oldest and had to marry first, according to their custom.

After seven years (Jacob was at least 77 at the time he arrived in Haran), Jacob went to Laban and said, "All right, my time is up, let me have my wife." Laban acted like everything was in order and the wedding was performed.

According to the custom the woman was veiled during the ceremony and taken immediately after the ceremony to the tent of her husband. The groom went later, after receiving the congratulations of the crowd and taking part in the festivities. When Jacob entered his tent it was dark and he could not see his bride. The next morning his surprise and shock knew no limits when he saw he had been tricked and the woman in his bed was not his beloved Rachel, but her sister Leah. But Jacob recognized that he had received just retribution for his trickery of Esau in stealing the birthright and the blessing. The trickster was tricked.

Leah was not a bad person, nor was she the ugly duckling, but she had weak, dull eyes, the very most important feature on the face of a woman of the Middle-East. It was the most prominent feature because of the veil which only allowed the eyes to be seen. But the most important reason for being rejected was that she wasn't Rachel, and for Jacob she had not even existed because of his love for Rachel.

When he accused Laban of trickery Laban told him, "Nothing can be done about it now! We don't let the younger daughter marry before the elder in this country (evidently a local custom). Stay with her a week according to custom and then you can have Rachel, too, and serve another seven years for her." She was then also sold by her father and Jacob actually served fourteen years for Rachel. Leah was an extra, and he never considered he had served for her since he really had not wanted her in the first place.

God was still in charge and from all indications Leah was the wife He had chosen for Jacob though Jacob never appears to have stopped and inquired of God about his mate. Through Leah came Judah who would be in the direct line of the Savior; she was the chosen one as demonstrated by this very special birth. But Jacob loved Rachel and he never saw Leah. Even in this seeming calamity God was making good come from evil in order to build up the house of Israel.

We can imagine the week Jacob spent waiting for Rachel. It is doubtful Leah enjoyed much of his company. She had, after all, been a party to the deceit and knew Jacob did not love her. It is highly possible she had loved him from the beginning and was a willing pawn in the trickery. With her father everything had to work together for his own good, and whatever was expedient to accomplish that was fair game in his eyes.

After Jacob's marriage to Leah and Rachel, twelve sons were born to him. Their significance is that they form the 12 tribes of the nation of Israel. There was still no name given to this nation - only the promise of its existence.

Jacob's first born was Reuben, then followed, Simeon, Levi, Judah, Issachar, and Zebulun whose mother was Leah, (six sons, one daughter; only one was mentioned but there were probably more daughters). Rachel gave him her handmaid Bilhah and Dan and Naphtali were born to her. Leah then gave him her handmaid Zilpah and she had Gad and Asher. Two sons were born to Rachel, Joseph and Benjamin.

During these years there was undiminished jealousy between Leah and Rachel and many devious tricks were used by both women to obtain the love and attention of their husband, Jacob. In the end both were brought to a personal knowledge of Jacob's God and His place in their lives. Leah was the first to recognize God as Jehovah, a personal God, and finally after the birth of Joseph, Rachel also recognized Him as Jehovah and not only as Elohim, the God of creation.

Jacob's wealth and escape (Genesis 30:25-33)

Jacob served Laban for fourteen years and towards the end of that time Joseph was born. Jacob then asked Laban for permission to return to Canaan. Canaan was his possession and he wanted to possess it. But Laban would not give him permission to leave because he knew that God had blessed him because of Jacob. In 30:27, he said he had 'learned by experience' but this phrase is the phrase 'learned by divination'. It means Laban had by some paganistic magic ascertained that God blessed him because of Jacob. The word for *divination* is the same one used for serpent and this is very significant. Edersheim says all false religions and paganistic practices come from 'that old serpent, the devil'. (Edersheim, *Bible History*, Vol. I), p. 129.

Laban had continued to use trickery with Jacob all the years he was serving him. Later Jacob said Laban had changed his wages ten times - always to the advantage of Laban.

Laban asked him what it would take to make him stay. He meant 'what material possession will convince you to stay here so I can continue to be blessed'.

Jacob asked to make a deal with him concerning the sheep and goats. They were to go through the flocks of sheep and goats and take out all the brown sheep and the speckled and spotted goats. Those were to be Jacob's.

Those flocks were then taken by Laban's sons a three-day journey away so they could not be bred and increase the flocks of Jacob. Whatever sheep were born brown after this were also to be Jacob's and whatever goats were born spotted and speckled were Jacob's. This left only the white sheep and the black goats in the flock.

Laban thought he was getting the best of the deal because there were only a few brown sheep and spotted and speckled goats born in a large herd, so he agreed. Jacob was in charge of Laban's flock of white sheep and black goats.

Jacob had not been a shepherd for years without learning a few things about livestock breeding and he put that knowledge to work for his own benefit. In chapter 31 he told Rachel and Leah how God had appeared to him in a dream and had blessed him with the increase of his herds. Evidently God had also given him some indication of how to do selective breeding in order to get the best results.

He put peeled rods of poplar, hazel and chestnut, (some say storax, almond, and plane), in the watering troughs so the animals would see them when they came to drink. Some writers believe the chemicals released in the springtime by the rods which had been partially stripped of their bark acted as an aphrodisiac and this gives an understanding of Genesis 30:39 which says the 'flocks conceived before the rods'. (It was believed that babies born in the springtime were stronger and this was what Jacob was after.) The more baby animals born, the better the chances of brown and spotted and speckled animals. Jacob separated those born brown and spotted and speckled, from the main flock and by breeding only the strongest animals he increased his flock and his riches. He could not have given a lesson on dominant and recessive genes, but he had observed the principle in operation and used it to his advantage. His real increase, though, came by the hand of God as he himself recognized, (Genesis 31:9).

After six more years he was ready to leave Laban. God had spoken to him in a dream and instructed him to return to Canaan. Though he and Laban had agreed on the animals as just wages for work rendered, Laban could not believe how Jacob's flocks had increased and became very angry with him. Laban's sons were just as angry and accused Jacob of taking their father's riches - or stealing the flocks.

Jacob knew Laban was planning to take back the flocks and possibly take his family also, so he spoke to Rachel and Leah and told them the situation. They met in the field so their conversation would not be overheard and reported to Laban.

He told them of Laban's anger over his good fortune, of his trickery in changing his wages, and of God's protection through all of it.

Rachel and Leah were united in their desire to follow Jacob's leading and leave their father. They also had just complaints against him because he had taken their inheritance, had sold them to Jacob, and then spent the money on himself. When it's God's time everything falls into place. They felt anything Jacob had received from their father was rightfully theirs to begin with, and they weren't taking anything belonging to him.

The plan was made and as soon as Laban left to go shear the sheep, a three day's journey from Jacob's flocks, Jacob took his family and his flocks and left for Canaan. Unknown to Jacob, Rachel had stolen her father's idols (teraphim) and had hidden them in her baggage.

When Rachel stole her father's idols it was more than a pagan desire to have her father's gods with her. The possession of the idols signified the rights of heirship. She wanted Jacob to be the heir of her father instead of Laban's sons, her own brothers, because of the way Laban had treated Jacob for twenty years.

When Laban returned home and found that Jacob had already been gone for three days, he was incensed. He gathered a group of men and set out in pursuit of Jacob. He was angry at being tricked (a dose of his own medicine), but was probably more angry that his gods had been stolen. The whole life of the pagan was wrapped up in his gods; there was the god of flocks, the god of harvest, the god of planting, the god of the household, etc., etc. Each one was a repository for demons and demonic activity, but that was never a concern for Laban; he only wanted to receive the good he thought they might give him. After seven day's journey he caught up with Jacob's company.

The night before Laban was to meet Jacob, God had appeared to Laban in a dream, telling him not to harm Jacob. He knew it was God and he feared Him, but he was not willing to give up his pagan beliefs to follow the true God and serve Him.

His hypocritical character was clearly manifested as he entered Jacob's presence. Laban began to accuse Jacob of sneaking away and stealing his daughters and grandchildren. (Jacob knew the price he had paid for them.) He also said, "If you had just told me, we would have had a party and sent you off with singing and dancing." (He had already refused to give permission before and was planning to take Jacob's possessions.) He presented himself as a loving father and grandfather, but his daughters both saw him as a scheming thief. Then he made his threat, "I have the means to destroy you but - last night the God of your fathers told me to leave you alone. You were this close to dying."

Then comes the real crux of the matter, "Who stole my gods?"

Jacob replied, still politely. He knew nothing of the stolen gods as Genesis 31:32 implies. Had he known he would never have made such a statement, *kill the person with whom you find them*, especially if he had known it was Rachel who had stolen them.

Laban and his men then searched the entire camp and when her father entered her tent Rachel told him she was ill 'after the custom of women'; she was sitting on his gods defiling them by this act, and couldn't get up, but he was welcome to search her belongings. At the time of her monthly period a woman was not allowed to even go near the gods and this shows her contempt for the gods, though she kept them because they were the signs of heirship as before stated. Of course, since she was sitting on the idols he found nothing.

Now the years of abuse Jacob had silently suffered at Laban's hand were over. He was livid and began to speak his mind to Laban. "Who do you think you are chasing after me, going through all my belongings and causing an uproar in the camp? I'm not a thief, I've done nothing wrong to you, on the contrary, you've done plenty of wrong to me. I've worked for you twenty years, I've eaten my own food, I've taken the loss when an animal of the flock was killed by wild beasts or was stolen. I kept the flock in summer and winter; I went without sleep to keep them safe. I served you like a slave for fourteen years for your daughters, and that debt is paid, they belong to me. I served you another six years for the livestock in my possession and you changed my wages for your own benefit ten times in these years. If you weren't afraid of the God of my fathers, Who is also my God, you would have taken everything I have and sent me away with nothing. God has judged between us!"

Laban knew that everything Jacob said was true and he did not attempt to deny anything. He had calmed down considerably, but he knew Jacob's God meant business and he would have to do something to protect himself. He proposed a covenant be made, a kind of boundary marker, so he would not pass over it to do harm to Jacob, nor Jacob to him. Jacob stacked up stones as a witness of the covenant and they ate on the stones to seal the bargain.

Laban called the place Jegar-sahad-utha - 'heap of the testimony', a Chaldean word, and Jacob called it Galeed, a Hebrew word meaning - 'heap of the testimony or witness'. Laban gave it another name, Mizpah, which meant 'the watchtower'. Though he seems to

have been giving a sweet benediction in Genesis 31:49, he was really giving a serious warning to Jacob and using the name of Jacob's God to do it.

Laban blustered some more and made an attempt to equate his gods (the gods of Nahor) with the God of Jacob. As far as Laban was concerned he was finished with his part of the covenant, but Jacob showed the reverence he had learned for his God and offered a sacrifice to Himupon the heaped-up stones.

The next morning Laban and his company left and his daughters and grandchildren never saw him again as far as the record states. He arrived a pagan and went home a pagan.

Jacob had matured in his walk with God in the twenty years since he had left, but he had one more testing ahead which would change his life forever.

Preparations for meeting Esau (Genesis 32:1-21)

God was caring for Jacob every step of his journey and showed him the angels who were guarding his path. They were there all the time, but Jacob could not see them. He called the place 'Mahanaim' - 'two hosts' or 'double-camp'; comparing the host of powerful angels with his own helpless camp.

He traveled in dread of meeting his brother Esau. Jacob had been a trickster, but he had received trickery in kind from his father-in-law. He knew his sin in reference to his brother and he knew what he deserved, but would Esau still be angry after all those years?

Jacob sent a messenger to tell Esau he had enough possessions to share and asked Esau to receive him favorably in his country. The messenger returned and gave Jacob the message from Esau, "We saw your brother and he's coming to meet you with 400 men."

As can be imagined Jacob was extremely fearful. First he divided the people and animals into two groups and separated them so if Esau attacked one group the other could escape.

Jacob also began to pray to his God and ask for help and wisdom in dealing with Esau. He reminded God that He was the one who had told Jacob to go back to his country and he was going to trust Him to deliver him and his family. Though externally things looked pretty bleak, Jacob believed internally that God would keep His word to deliver him and his people and their possessions.

He then prepared a gift to send to Esau to try to soften him up and to give him an idea of his wealth. He sent 580 animals of his flocks to Esau. The animals were divided into various droves and each was driven by some of his servants. Each drove left at a different time and the servant in charge was to tell Esau when he asked to whom they belonged that they were a gift to him from Jacob and that Jacob was also on his way to meet his brother.

Encounter with God (Genesis 32:22-32)

The night before his meeting with Esau, while it was still night, Jacob got up, and after waking the camp, sent his family and servants to the other side of the creek Jabbok, which put them in the land of Canaan. He stayed alone on the other side and laid down to rest awhile before daylight came. While resting he was seized by an unknown assailant.

God appeared to him in the form of a strong man who wrestled with Jacob until daybreak. As before stated a shepherd was a man of strength and Jacob was no exception. He had been accustomed to hardship by his life in the fields guarding the flocks, and expected to make short work of this 'man'. After wrestling with him for some time the 'man' saw that Jacob was a worthy opponent and He touched Jacob's hip socket and broke it, and in so doing the muscle, or tendon, connected to the hip joint drew up, but still Jacob wouldn't let go.

The 'man' told Jacob to let him go because the sun was coming up, but Jacob said, "I won't let go until you bless me." It had dawned on Jacob just Who this 'man' was and he knew He was the Lord God Almighty because He was the only one who had the power to bless Jacob.

The Lord said, "What is your name?" He knew it was Jacob but He wanted Jacob to acknowledge who he was and what his name had come to mean. He was Jacob the supplanter, the deceiver, the overreacher, the assailant. God always forgives confessed sin and Jacob was confessing his sin in giving his name. God was now going to make a totally different man of Jacob.

As soon as Jacob confessed his name, God gave him a new name; he would be called Israel, a prince with God, which meant 'God fights', 'God contends', 'God will rule', 'may God rule'.

All of these names were used to remind Jacob of his fight with God and that God, from then on, would fight his battle for him as He would for the nation of Israel when they obeyed His commands.

He was not Jacob the deceiver from that day forward. He had a new name and he had a limp for the remainder of his life to remind him of his encounter with God. From this change of name the promised nation finally received the name by which it would be called. Jacob asked the man his name, and He said, "Why are you asking me my name? You know Who I am", and He blessed Jacob. Jacob received the assurance of God's blessing on him and his family and called the place Peniel, (Penuel), 'the face of God'.

After this experience with God, Jacob was never the same and was now ready to meet his brother. Victories are won through struggle. Having faced God, he was now ready to face anything. Is God trying to get your attention? Are you struggling with God because of some area in your life you are unwilling to give up? Are you trying to throw off the very thing God is trying to bless you with?

Jacob got up and limped across the creek Jabbok into the Promised Land, a new man with a better vision of God's purpose for his life.

Brother meets brother (Genesis 33:1-16)

Esau and his men could already be seen approaching when Jacob reached the other side. Though he had just 'seen' God he was still a man of little faith; it takes times to mature in the Lord. He divided his family into four parts and put the concubines and their children at the front of the column, followed by Leah and her children, with Rachel and Joseph last.

He put the less valuable people, as far as he was personally concerned, at the front of the column and the most valuable to him in the back. What effect must this have had on the children of Leah and the concubines when they realized their lack of worth in the eyes of their father?

As Esau neared the camp, Jacob went out to meet him, (32:3), bowing himself to the ground seven times, very much in the custom of an eastern court, and showing his acknowledgment of Esau's right to call him into account for the way he had treated him before leaving his father's home.

Esau ran to meet his brother, and also according to custom fell on his neck, kissing him on both cheeks, and both men wept over their reunion. In speaking with Esau Jacob continued to refer to himself as a servant and to his brother as lord. He was not denying the birthright he had stolen so many years previously, but was saying 'I took it through deceit, so please forgive me.' He asked Esau to take his 'blessing' in place of the one he had stolen and to share in the blessing God had given him through those years.

When Esau came to meet him, Jacob expected the worst, but it would be a very small man who could remain angry for twenty long years. Jacob found Esau a wealthy man who refused his gift (or rather bribe) and welcomed him again to his home country. When Esau refused the gift on the basis that he had enough, Jacob said, 'then take it as a token of our reconciliation'. Esau finally took what Jacob called his 'blessing', which was the gift offered, and by this sign of acceptance Esau received his brother, (33:11).

It would have been an insult to refuse the gift of a friend and especially that of a blood brother.

Esau offered to accompany Jacob on the remainder of his journey or at least to send some of his men along, but Jacob knew now that God was with him and he did not need other protection.

Esau returned to his home east and south of the Dead Sea; a home of rocky cliffs and little fruitfulness which is southern Jordan today. Isaac had said Esau would live by the sword and that was what he had been doing when he went to meet Jacob. He came from making an attack on the country of Seir in which the Horites (from Horim) lived and which later became his possession known as the land of Edom where the ancient city of Petra is located, (Deuteronomy 2:12, 22).

A New Home in Canaan (Genesis 33:17-20)

Jacob settled in a place called Succoth meaning 'booth', where 'he built himself a house'. The word used here for house is *bayeth*, which can mean a tent, a hut, a house, a mansion, palace, temple, dwelling-place, etc., and may not mean what our word 'house' today implies. Since he didn't stay very long at Succoth it is doubtful it means a house constructed in the normal sense of the word. He also built 'booths' or some kind of coverings for his livestock. It was autumn when he left Haran and he needed a place to pass the winter both for himself and for his animals.

He stayed there at least through the winter and possibly longer, and then moved to the western side of the Jordan to the Hivite (Hamitic) city of Shechem. He bought a parcel of land on which he had pitched his tent, from Hamor for 100 pieces of money. God surely was not pleased with this since the land already belonged to Jacob through God's promise. When a wandering pilgrim buys land and pitches his tent toward the city he is asking for trouble.

Jacob erected an altar on his land and called it El-elohe-Israel - 'God is the God of Israel'. He also dug a well there which was the well where the Samaritan woman met the Lord many centuries later, (John 4:5,6). This was also the land Jacob gave to Joseph as his inheritance.

Dinah and Shechem (Genesis 34)

The place we choose to live is important because our children are influenced by the people around them. Dinah, (a girl of about 15), Jacob and Leah's daughter, went to a party at the home of one of the Hivite girls of Shechem. She was seen by the prince of the city, Shechem, whose father was Hamor, the leading man of the city. Shechem was captivated by Dinah and seduced her, and then kept her at his house, (34:26). Whether she had returned home and given the news to her family and later returned to Shechem's house after the arrangements were made, we are not told. Somehow the family learned what Shechem had done to Dinah, either by her own mouth, or from another source.

When her brothers came in from the field and heard the news, they were very angry and ashamed *because he had wrought folly in Israel,* (34:7). The word folly is *nebalâ*, which means 'a godless act that polluted the whole family'. This was not a sin which affected only one person; the entire family was made to suffer. Any sin has a radiating effect and always affects many more people than those directly involved.

Shechem's father approached Jacob to try to make some honorable arrangement for a marriage between his son and Dinah. He also wanted to arrange marriages between the people of the city and the children of Jacob. He even tried to sweeten the deal by saying they would be welcome to dwell in the land and trade with them and get as many possessions as they wanted. This was not the story he later told to the city fathers when he made his case to them.

Then Shechem spoke to Jacob and his sons and begged them to tell him the price for Dinah and whatever it was he would pay it. There is no doubt he loved Dinah and wanted to right the wrong he had done to her by now doing the honorable thing. In this he was a much more honorable person than Simeon or Levi. He was not concerned with any other marriages, only with his own.

Dinah's brothers got into the discussion at this point and Jacob remained silent. They told Hamor that it would be impossible to give Dinah in marriage to anyone who was not circumcised. Jacob had at least taught them something, but they didn't understand the full importance of circumcision. By the act of circumcision the individual was brought into a covenant relationship with God, and this was certainly never their intention.

They had observed the deceit and trickery that had taken place in their own household and they were well-versed in its practice.

They had no intention of allowing marriages to a pagan nation and could not allow Dinah to be a part of such an arrangement.

They proposed that all the men of Shechem be circumcised so that the future marriages might take place. Shechem was excited about complying with this request and he and his father returned to the city to speak with the other men who would be involved.

Hamor began by presenting Jacob's family as a peaceable group (they found out too late that was not true) who would continue to dwell in the land and trade with them, making them more wealthy. They would also be able to intermarry if they would all be circumcised. Then all their (Jacob's) possessions would be theirs, (they were probably going to take them forcibly). After hearing of all the advantages, they consented to be circumcised.

On the third day when the wounds were the sorest Simeon and Levi, sons of Leah and brothers to Dinah, went into the city and killed all the men. They took Dinah out of Shechem's house and took all their livestock, their wealth, and their wives and children as slaves. They wiped out the entire city.

When Jacob heard the news he was heartbroken; he had a daughter who had been shamed; he had two sons who had become murderers; and he was certain the Canaanites around them would be coming quickly to kill them all to avenge the city of Shechem.

Jacob never forgot the nature of his sons and in Genesis 49 he again speaks of their treachery and wickedness.

God knew what was happening and He had already worked it all out for Jacob. He spoke to Jacob and told him to go back to Bethel, to the place where God had first spoken to him. He was instructed to build an altar there. Jacob had vowed to return to his father's house and to the God of Bethel, (28:20,21),

and now he was going to fulfill that vow.

Until this occasion there is no indication of Jacob taking the proper role in his family in reference to idolatry. He told his household to *put away the strange gods that are among you, and be clean, and change your garments,* (Genesis 35:2). His servants would have been idolaters and Rachel still had her father's teraphim. They took their gods and their charms, (usually worn as earrings), with which they supposedly warded off evil spirits, and Jacob hid them under an oak near Shechem.

He should have done this much earlier and would have therefore avoided many of the problems which surfaced later on. Evidently little teaching was being done in this family about the true God and His purpose for this tiny group of people. What a difference it would have made had they known God's purpose for them.

Jacob feared the nations living around him and they were doubtless banding together to avenge themselves on him and his family, but God struck terror in their hearts and they stayed away from his family.

Jacob at Bethel (Genesis 35:6-15)

When he arrived at Bethel Jacob built an altar which he called El-beth-el - 'the God of Bethel'; he knew more than ever that God was present in that place. God appeared to him again at Bethel and reaffirmed his new name as Israel, and reaffirmed the Abrahamic covenant to him. He set up a pillar in the place where God had spoken to him and poured a drink offering upon it, (this is the first mention of a drink offering and it was probably of wine, [Exodus 29:40], but the drink offering was never drunk, only 'poured out' and was offered with the burnt offering or sacrifice as a sweet savor unto the Lord, Numbers 15:5-7). He then poured oil on it to emphasize again the sacredness of the spot.

After his time at Bethel Jacob continued on his travels a different man. His deceit was all in the past and God was going to break him so he could be better used as the last patriarch over the now forming nation of Israel.

Death of Deborah (Genesis 35:8)

Jacob had been in contact with his father, Isaac, and since his mother had already died he took her nurse, Deborah, to be a part of his household. Deborah had traveled with Rebekah when she left Haran to become the bride of Isaac. She had been present during all the growing-up years of Jacob and she would have been a source of comfort to him just having her with him. He also hoped she would be a good influence on his own children, and his family in general. She would have been very elderly at this time and it was not surprising when she died. During the time she was with them they had all learned to love her very much, and when she died the oak under which she was buried was called 'the oak of weeping' signifying their feelings toward her. Jacob's sorrows had only begun.

Death of Rachel (Genesis 35:16-20)

Though God had told him to dwell there in 35:1, Jacob left Bethel for some unknown reason. Given the direction he was traveling he was probably going to his father's house in Hebron. They were almost to Bethlehem (Ephrath) when Rachel went into labor with her second son. There was some complication in the birth because Rachel was still a young woman at this time and she died giving birth. Just before her death she named the baby Ben-oni, 'the son of my sorrow', but Jacob called him Benjamin, 'the son of my right hand'.

It would be difficult to imagine the grief experienced by Jacob at the death of his beloved Rachel. The Scripture does not dwell on his sorrow and only says he set up a pillar on her grave. This was a sacred spot to Jacob and there is no indication of how long he remained there mourning her passing.

When the land was divided indications are that the Benjamites removed her bones and buried them in their own territory just north of Jerusalem, (1 Samuel 10:2).

Rueben's Sin (Genesis 35:21,22)

In having sexual relations with Jacob's concubine, Reuben was trying to usurp his father's authority and because of his sin he lost the right of inheritance, (Genesis 49:3,4).

Because Reuben sinned with Jacob's concubine, (35:22), his birthright was taken from him, and ultimately Judah would occupy the place of importance in the lineage of Jacob, (Genesis 49:8-12).

After this event the narrative leaves Jacob and gives a genealogical record of Esau's descendants and then moves on to the next character of importance in Israel's history, Joseph.

Death of Isaac, (Genesis 36)

Isaac died at the age of 180. The death is listed immediately in the Scripture in order to finish up the history of Isaac before moving on to the next narrative. Jacob and Esau were both present to bury their father, (Genesis 35:27-29). This gives some further indication that all accounts were settled between them and they lived in peace.

Esau and his Family (Genesis 36)

After the death of Isaac Esau took his family and moved to the east near Mt. Seir because there were too many possessions for him and Jacob to dwell together. There he founded the kingdom of Edom (meaning 'red'). Esau became a great nation as God had promised.

Esau is listed as having married five women. Some writers believe the first two had died and those listed next were those who followed them. The first Bashemath was the daughter of Elon the Hittite, the second Bashemath is listed as being the daughter of

Ishmael (the tribe of) whose brother was Nebajoth, who was also listed in Genesis 28:9 as the brother of Mahaloth, Esau's wife.

In Genesis 36:2 Adah is listed as the daughter of Elon the Hittite and there is no mention of her sister Bashemath. Aholibamah is listed as the daughter of Zibeon the Hittite. Whether there was an error in copying and they were same people as previously listed, we can only conjecture.

Five sons were born to Esau: from Adah - Eliphaz; from Bashemath - Reuel; and from Aholibamah - Jeush, Jaalam and Korah. Those five sons formed the foundation of the Edomite empire. The Edomites and the Ishmaelites formed the greatest numbers of the later Arab nations.

One of Esau's descendants, Amalek, became a scourge to Israel. During the Exodus, Israel came to their borders and asked to cross their land but was refused permission because of their great number and the fear they caused. God later judged the Edomites for this action taken against His people. The Edomites were also referred to in the Scriptures as Idumeans.

The listing of the Horites in Seir is believed to be because the Edomites, after conquering them, intermarried with them and that would have been considered important information to the nation of Israel.

The information given in verse 31 tells us that the Edomites had a king long before Israel was even a nation.

Several times the Scriptures reiterate that Esau is the father of the Edomites so there will be no mistake about where they came from and who gets the ultimate blame for the way they acted toward Israel.

Joseph

Two hundred years had already passed since God had made the promise to Abraham that all Canaan would be his. The narrative of Jacob is over and that of Joseph continues the story.

The story of Joseph takes up one-fourth of the book of Genesis and he wasn't even in the Messianic line. After the history of Joseph is completed the Scripture will be concerned with the entire nation of Israel, and not just with certain individuals who were to make up that nation.

Jacob remained in the land of Canaan after the death of his father. He had learned little from his own experience and chose his son Joseph as his favorite. Joseph was an obedient, faithful child who also worked as a shepherd along with his brothers. Edersheim describes him as having inherited the best qualities of his ancestors: "like Abraham he was strong, decided, and prudent; like Isaac, patient and gentle, like Jacob, warmhearted and affectionate." (Edersheim, *Bible History*, Vols. I-IV), p. 144.

Jacob had never really reconciled himself to the fact that he had sons born of Leah and the concubines. It was never his intention to marry anyone but Rachel, and to bestow the firstborn rights on Joseph would have seemed right to him. He was Rachel's son and that was enough for Jacob. But God had ordained it otherwise.

Joseph was not only resented; he was hated by his brothers. The Scripture says they *could not speak peaceably unto him*. This means they could not greet him in the Eastern custom of 'Shalom', 'peace to you'. They hated Joseph, not Jacob, but the fault lay in Jacob. Seeing how little importance they had in Jacob's eyes when Esau was going to meet him, would have affected all of them adversely and they were looking for someone to bear the brunt of their resentment.

In reading the account of the 'coat of many colors' given to Joseph by his father, it has more significance than at first might appear. According to early writers it was a white robe with bands of color along the hem and around the sleeve edges. That kind of garment, a robe, was made with long sleeves. Anyone who wore a princely garment with long sleeves was a person who did no physical labor. Philips calls it the 'robe of position, priesthood, and privilege'. John Phillips, *Exploring Genesis,* (Chicago: Moody Press, 1980), p. 295. It meant that the rights of the firstborn were to be transferred to Joseph.

This fact would certainly not endear him to his brothers who worked out in the field with the livestock. They were delighted to cover the robe with blood and rip it up before taking it to Jacob - it had been a sore spot for some time.

Joseph's Dreams (Genesis 37:1-10)

Even before this occasion, dreams had, at times, been used as verbal communication between God and man. Before Jacob left his home country he dreamed a dream at Bethel in which God promised him protection and property in Haran, (Genesis 28:12-15). God appeared to Laban in a dream, (Genesis 31:24), and told him not to harm Jacob. In Genesis 20:3, God appeared to Abimelech in a dream warning him to restore Sarah to her rightful husband. There are many other examples, but the dreams mentioned needed no interpretation and Joseph's dream did. He and his family understood them to mean that they were bowing down to him, which did not please them. They, however, had no way of knowing how circumstances would bring that to pass.

Joseph was 17 years old when his history begins. He first dreamed of a number of sheaves. Evidently Jacob practiced some farming as well as raising livestock because Joseph was acquainted with the harvest custom of binding the sheaves. This knowledge of farming also enabled him to prepare for the seven lean years in Egypt when he became the assistant of Pharaoh.

In his dream his sheaf stood upright and those that represented his brothers bowed down to his sheaf. When he told his brothers the dream and its interpretation, they hated him even more 'for his *dreams*, and for his *words*,' (Genesis 37:8).

His next dream included his father as well as his brothers. The sun, moon and the eleven stars bowed down to him. His father rebuked him because of the dream, but then he 'observed the saying', the Hebrew word *shâmar* - 'to preserve, retain, to take heed, to hear'. He evidently felt there might be something to those dreams and took a 'wait and see' attitude, (Genesis 37:11).

His brothers 'envied' him, *qânâ* - the Arabic root means 'to become very red'. The Hebrew word means 'jealous', 'a very strong emotion which desires some quality of possession of another'. (Zodhiates), p. 1634. They wanted what Joseph had; his position, his coat, and most of all their father's love.

The brothers went north from Hebron to the area around Shechem, about 60 miles north, to allow the flocks to feed. Only Joseph and Benjamin were left at home with their father.

Jacob became concerned about his sons and his flocks up there in an area where they had wreaked so much havoc earlier and sent Joseph to see if they were all right. He knew their character and never knew what kind of trouble they might be brewing. Though they were supposed to be at Shechem they had moved to Dothan, a place of two wells according to the name, about 12 miles north of Samaria. They had probably moved because the pasture was better there.

When the brothers saw Joseph approaching, (Genesis 37:18-23), they remembered all the things that had happened. Joseph had previously taken an 'evil report' about the actions of his brothers, (the word here is *ra'*, which means, 'an unethical immoral activity against other people'), to his father concerning the actions of the sons of the concubines and they would have supposed he was there to take back an evil report of their activities, also. He had dreamed two dreams in which he was the ruler over them, and he was their father's favorite son who was to receive the birthright. They were in a murderous mood that day and determined, as far as they were concerned, to do away with the source of their problems. How quickly the sinner attacks the upright person in order to remove the guilt from himself.

Behold, this dreamer cometh, they said. The dreams had made a very unfavorable impression on the brothers. They weren't about to kneel down to this upstart, the second youngest son in the family.

Why did Joseph tell them his dreams? There is no indication that God told him to, but perhaps as a young person, he was so impressed by a seemingly impossible event, that he told it in amusement the first time. But the second dream was more serious, and in its telling even his father had been disturbed. Joseph had no knowledge that the dreams were prophetic so could not have been 'lording' it over his brothers. Whatever the reason, they were going to do whatever was necessary to keep them from coming to pass, even if it meant killing Joseph.

They joined together to kill him, place his body in a pit, and tell their father that a wild animal had killed him. This would be premeditated murder in any court of the land, punishable by the death penalty. When they finally finished with their wickedness they thought it was all over and they could forget it, but sin doesn't work like that. It always makes its presence known and usually at the most inopportune moments, as it did for them later.

Both Reuben and Judah tried to keep the others from killing Joseph. Reuben told them to put him into a pit which was close by and planned to take him out later and return him to Jacob. No doubt he remembered how his sin of fornication had affected his father, and there remained some sense of right in him. He did not want to put his father through more sorrow than he had already suffered.

Judah said, 'Sell him to the Midianites' (descendants of one of the sons of Abraham and Keturah), who were passing nearby on the Eastern trade route. They pulled Joseph up out of the well in which they had placed him, and

A Desert Caravan
(Peloubet, 1922)

began to haggle over the price he would bring. The price agreed upon was 20 pieces of silver; the price of a common male slave from ages 5-25.

There is no indication given of the shock and dismay Joseph must have felt as his brothers attacked him for no apparent reason. Nor is there any information given of the grief he surely experienced on his journey to Egypt knowing he had been sold by his own brothers as a common slave. He was only a boy and his heart must have been broken by what had so rapidly occurred, and by the knowledge that he would probably never see his dear father again. Where were his dreams now? How could they ever be realized? Had God forsaken Him?

At times it seems God has forsaken us when all our dearest plans are defeated, but the lesson is here for all to learn. God is working. Joseph found the truth of this message when he arrived in Egypt.

Meanwhile the brothers took the coat they had stripped off Joseph, and after killing a baby goat dipped the robe in its blood and took it to Jacob. The deceiver was again deceived. Hadn't Jacob killed a kid to present to his father as venison; hadn't he taken the skins of a kid and covered his arms in order to convince Isaac that he was Esau so he could steal his blessing?

When Jacob heard the news and identified the robe as belonging to Joseph his grief was a terrible thing. He tore his clothes and put on sackcloth - the outward symbols of grief, and mourned inconsolably for his son - the inward symbol of grief. He could not be comforted by son or daughter.

His sons reaped a bitter harvest as they observed the terrible grief of their father who said he would go to his grave mourning for Joseph. One by one they would slink out of his presence, unable to face the omnipresent guilt of the deed they had done out of pure jealousy and spite. They weren't young men at this time and understood the ramifications of a hasty, hateful act as only adults can understand them.

Joseph arrived at the slave market in Egypt. He had never seen such sights as he saw in this new land. God had removed him from Canaan, from a pagan, ignorant, idolatrous people, as He would the remainder of his family a little later, so they could be away from the evil influence of the Canaanites. All historical indications are that they were one of the most base and wicked nations the world has ever seen. While in Egypt Israel would become a mighty nation in number and, because of their isolation in Goshen, their line would be kept pure and their knowledge of the true God would increase. The prophecy given to Abraham would be fulfilled, (Genesis 15:13,14).

The Midianites sold Joseph to a man called Potiphar, who was the head of Pharaoh's military guard. In Joseph, Potiphar saw a handsome young man with great potential. Joseph did not allow bitterness nor a need for revenge to occupy his mind; he just kept trusting God to care for him and lead him in the right path. 'The steps of a good man are ordered by the Lord', though not yet written at that time, was already a reality for Joseph.

Judah and Tamar, a digression (Genesis 38)

Judah was the fourth son of Leah and Jacob. He was given the place of importance by his father in Genesis 49:8-12, in the line of Christ, but Jacob still pointed out the human faults in this son who would be the ancestor of the perfect Savior. His name in Matthew 1:2,3 is called Judas, but he is the same Judah of the Old Testament.

This digression from the history of Joseph tells us how Judah became the father of Pharez and Zarah.

Against his father's instructions Judah left his brethren after the previous events with Joseph, and went into the surrounding area where he met a man who became his close friend. He was Hirah, an Adullamite, one of the Hamitic tribes south of Jerusalem. (See Joshua 12.) While with this friend, and under his influence, he met and married a Canaanite woman, the daughter of Shuah. She bore him three sons: Er, Onan, and Shelah. The influence of this pagan mother on the household cannot be over emphasized, because it accounts for much of what happened later in the family.

In the Oriental custom of the day Judah found a wife for his oldest son, Er, whose name was Tamar. She was from the same area so we can assume that she was also a Hamite. The Bible says Er was so wicked that God killed him. The word used for wicked is *ra'*, meaning to be totally evil with no redeemable qualities.

Then according to custom Tamar was married to the next son, Onan, so he could raise up a child in the name of his dead brother. He refused to have a child which would not be his, but which would be his brother's according to tradition.

Because his brother would have received the inheritance of the firstborn, the child born in his name would also receive those same rights and Onan would be left with a lesser portion of his father's possessions. For this reason he caused his 'seed' to spill on the ground rather than take the chance that Tamar might have a child. God found this so repugnant that He killed Onan also.

There is no doubt that the mother of those boys was their advisor to do evil. God gave a clear command in the New Testament to *be not unequally yoked together with unbelievers,* (2 Corinthians 6:14). The mother has such an important influence on the children for good or evil that one would do well to follow God's command in this regard. How many homes have been destroyed by the evil influence of the mother. To follow the history of the kings during the divided kingdom and see the reference stated, *and his mother was* gives an indication of the importance God puts on mothers.

When it came time to give the youngest son as Tamar's husband, after the custom, (see Ruth 4:1-12), Judah refused to allow the marriage. He said that the boy was too young and she would have to wait until he was older. Of course, this was just a pretext; Judah was afraid Shelah would also be killed by God. His family had become totally wicked and Judah never intended to allow the marriage.

He told Tamar to go home to her father's house where she would be protected, and wait.

Judah's wife died during this time. There is no indication of why, and he is seen again in the company of his friend, Hirah.

In Genesis 38:12 there is an interesting phrase, *the daughter of Shuah Judah's wife died; and Judah was comforted.* This could be taken several ways, as the word, *nâcham,* (comforted) has a positive and negative meaning. The most obvious meaning is that he wasn't very sad when his wife died and it actually was a relief to him.

He and his friend, Hirah, went north to Timnath somewhere between Zorah (Judges 13:2) and Adullam. When the Scripture says someone went 'up' it is usually because they have entered into a mountainous area and physically climb up higher. They were headed for a sheep-shearing where there was bound to be a celebration and they meant to take part in it; not exactly a sign of mourning.

By this time Tamar had understood that Judah was not going to give his last son to be her husband. She heard that he was going to Timnath and hatched her own plot to draw his attention to how badly he had treated her when she was innocent. She had nothing to do with the deaths of Er and Onan, the Scripture plainly says God killed them. Judah was not willing, however, to be accountable for his own part in their deaths. He had not overcome the evil, pagan influence of their mother, and had not taught them the right way himself.

Tamar took off her widows' garments which would have identified her right away, and covered (hid) herself with a veil and wrapped her clothing around her so nothing about her was recognizable. She had two reason for covering herself:

1. Judah wouldn't recognize her, and
2. to avoid being taken as a temple prostitute.

A temple prostitute would not have covered herself. It was her place to be out in the open and partake of the temple rites with those who wished, through her, to become an initiate into the mysteries of the pagan religion and a participant in the fertility rites. The temple prostitute would be found in the temple area, not waiting on the road to Timnath. Tamar presented herself as a common harlot.

She seems to have known her father-in-law quite well; his habits were not of the best, and she set a trap for him so she could give him an unmistakable lesson in right.

Because she was covered Judah took her for the common harlot she seemed to be, and spoke to her about her price for services rendered. She asked for his signet ring (his symbol of power, used on all legal documents, and always recognizable as belonging to its owner), his bracelets, and his staff which marked him as a shepherd (it would have carried some identifying symbol), until he could send her a kid which was to be her payment. She knew him and his trickery well enough by now to have evidence ready to cover herself when she was discovered.

Afterwards, she put her widow's clothes back on and returned to her father's house.

Later, Hirah, Judah's friend, was sent with the required payment of the kid to redeem the articles Judah had left with Tamar. But when he arrived at the spot where Judah had encountered her, no one was there. Upon inquiring about her, the men of the place said, 'there's no harlot in this area and never has been.' No doubt, Judah was relieved, but his pledged articles were missing and in the dark- est hours of the night he; must have asked himself 'where are they and how will this all turn out?' He was soon to find out.

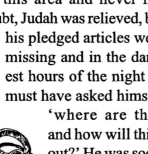

Rings and Seals
(Peloubet, 1922)

- Staff
(Peloubet, 1922)

Three months later she was found to be ex- pecting a child by Judah. When he heard the news he was very angry and said she should be brought forth and killed. It was all right for him to have gone into a harlot, but there was another standard for Tamar. He never stopped to see his own actions in the light of right and wrong. When he went to live with the pagan tribes of Canaan he forgot all about any lessons he had learned in his early years.

Tamar had expected this to happen and for this reason she had demanded the pledge of his personal articles from him. She wanted a child, and whether she understood the importance of Judah is certainly not known, but it is doubtful since she was also a pagan. She was not right in what she did, but neither was Judah.

When she confronted her father-in-law with the items he had given her and said 'the man who owns these is the father', he was left without recourse. He had to admit his own sin and that Tamar was more righteous than he.

Tamar remained in her father's house and when her time to deliver came, there were two babies instead of one. The ascension of the younger over the elder reminds us of the birth of Esau and Jacob.

The second-born put his hand out first and the midwife tied a scarlet thread around it, but the other son was born first. His name was Pharez, 'to break forth', (Numbers 26:20; Genesis 46:12); then the baby with the scarlet cord was born and given the name Zarah, 'a rising of light', (Numbers 26:20; Joshua 7:1; Genesis 46:12).

Thus ended this painfully sad story, inserted here partly to contrast the wickedness of Judah with the uprightness of Joseph, and also to give proof of the direct genealogical line to Christ.

Joseph in the house of Potiphar (Genesis 39)

Joseph remained faithful and obedient in the house of Potiphar and God blessed the house and Potiphar's business because of him. He was a slave, but he was not bound by a spirit of slavery. He did his best under the circumstances in which he found himself and it was duly noted by his Egyptian master.

Potiphar made Joseph the overseer of all his business and his household. He had such confidence in Joseph that by his own testimony he knew nothing of the business and was only aware of what he ate as far as his possessions were concerned.

The wife of Potiphar saw in Joseph a handsome, intelligent young man whom she could pursue and conquer. Like many women of the same character she believed she was able to have any man she wanted. Physical beauty can be a blessing or a curse depending on how it is used. That this was not her first conquest is aptly shown by Potiphar's treatment of Joseph when faced with his wife's accusation.

When Joseph continued to refuse her advances she became more determined to have what she wanted and finding themselves 'alone' in the house, with only the servants, she tried to physically force herself on him.

He told her he could never be so unfaithful to his master and he certainly could not sin against God in that way. Other than Joseph's testimony in the house she would have had no knowledge of the true God and this idea would have been incomprehensible to her.

When he saw she was not to be denied, he left his coat in her hands and ran out of the house to escape her.

Her anger at him was so intense that in order to get vengance for his rejection and make herself look better, she began to scream and yell and called the servants. There she stood with his coat in her hand, and like most humans when caught in sin, she began to blame someone else. She said, 'See the result

of my husband's bringing that Hebrew slave into the house; he just tried to rape me and here is the proof, his coat which he left after I fought him off'. It was her husband's fault, not hers. The servants knew her already and had seen her pursuing Joseph, so they knew the whole story.

When Potiphar arrived home she told him the same tale and though he knew his wife, he became angry at even the possibility that anything of the kind could have occurred as she said it had.

Joseph was taken by Potiphar and placed in the king's prison. If Potiphar had really believed the story about Joseph he would have put him to death. The fact that he was placed in prison shows plainly that Potiphar knew there was a considerable margin of doubt as to Joseph's guilt.

Twice already Joseph had had difficulty over a coat; first over the coat his father had given him and now over the coat he left in the hands of Potiphar's wife.

Joseph conducted himself as he always had, and soon came to the attention of the head jailer who put him in charge of all the prisoners. As before, God blessed everything Joseph did and He showed Joseph He was with him even in his darkest hours. This confirmed the promise given to Abraham, *I will bless thee, and make thy name great; and thou shall be a blessing,* (Genesis 12:2).

Prison Dreams (Genesis 40:1-23)

When two of the king's servants landed in prison they also came under Joseph's care. The Scripture says they had 'offended' the Pharaoh. The word offended '*châtâ*', has several different meanings, but in this case seems to refer to 'a breach of civil law'. They had both been involved in some kind of acts which the Pharaoh took as an offense against his person and his government.

In 40:4, the words *they continued a season in the ward* can be interpreted to mean 'a day', 'a season', or a time period up to a year. They were there long enough for Joseph to get well enough acquainted with them to be able to read their moods by seeing their faces.

As he entered the area of the prison where those servants were kept, (they were in a better area because they were the king's servants), he immediately perceived a difference in the expression on their faces and asked them what had caused them to be so unhappy.

Both of them told him they had had a dream which had upset them because there was no one who could tell them what their dreams meant. And Joseph replied, 'No, there is no one, not magicians, not soothsayers, not even me, who can give the interpretation of dreams, but God can.' He knew that in himself he could never know what their dreams meant, but he also knew that God could speak through him as He had before, and give him the interpretation.

The first to speak was the chief of the 'butlers', who was evidently the chief cup-bearer of the king as demonstrated by his dream. He recounted the dream to Joseph of the three-branched vine on which the clusters of grapes were found and from which he took the fruit and squeezed it into Pharaoh's cup and handed it to him.

Joseph interpreted the dream: The three branches represent the three remaining days before the Pharaoh's birthday on which he would condemn some palace prisoners to death and on which some would be restored. He said, 'in three days Pharaoh will *lift up thine head,* a phrase used to mean the restoration of a person to a former position. Joseph asked the cup-bearer to please remember him when he was restored to his position and to bring his situation before Pharaoh because he was

an innocent man who had been condemned without reason. He told of coming to Egypt as a slave, stolen out of his country and from his father's house; a Hebrew who really didn't belong where he was.

Whether he intended to return to his own land when freed, there is no indication given, but this is the first time he identifies himself in the Scripture with the connotation of a Hebrew, though Potiphar's wife referred to him twice as a Hebrew, (Genesis 39:14,17). There was as yet no nation to be referred to as the *Hebrews* and the root of the word came from Eber (Genesis 10:21), who is considered the father of the line through which the Israelites came. (Why does he at this time identify himself with the term Hebrew? To separate himself from the Egyptians? To claim ancestry from a different line? To help him recall who he was and where his real home was?)

Egyptian Bakers, as Shown in the Tomb of Rameses III

Ploubets, 1887

The chief baker, seeing the good interpretation of his cell-mate's dream, was anxious to receive the same kind of answer and told Joseph his dream. In his dream, as he carried the three baskets of baked goods to Pharaoh, the vultures ate the pastries that were in the top basket. Vultures ate dead bodies and they were the telling sign that very soon they would be eating the flesh from the baker's dead body.

Joseph told him that in three days, on the king's birthday, the Pharaoh would *lift up thy head from off thee,* which meant he would be hanged and his body thrown out on the trash heap where it would be eaten by the vultures.

On Pharaoh's birthday, three days later, everything happened just as Joseph had said. The 'butler' was restored to his office and the baker was hanged. But the chief cup-bearer, under the influence of his own good fortune, quickly forgot about Joseph.

Joseph waited and waited to be called from the prison, but the call never came. Though he never lost his confidence in God's care and His presence, he did despair of ever being able to leave the prison. *God's time is always on time.* This lesson is as hard for us to learn today, as it was for Joseph at that time. If the cup-bearer had spoken to Pharaoh when he first left the prison, he might not have paid any attention to Joseph's request. The Pharaoh had no knowledge of Joseph and would certainly have believed Potiphar's account before he would believe an unknown man in prison. The time was not yet right and God was teaching Joseph to trust even when it seemed there was no reason to trust.

Pharaoh's Dream (Genesis 41)

After two more dreary years in the prison God had brought all the necessary circumstances into alignment to be of benefit to Joseph. In the life of the believer there are no happen-stances, no 'just happened', no coincidences; *the steps of a good man are ordered by the Lord,* (Psalm 37:23).

When Pharaoh had a need no one else could fill, God had the man who could answer the need at the exact time.

Pharaoh's dreams were connected and both had to do with the special circumstances of Egypt. Whenever there was a famine in the land of Canaan there was always food in Egypt because of the great harvest reaped from the land on which the Nile overflowed each year. When Pharaoh dreamed of the seven fat cows (the fat cows were a symbol of Isis, the Egyptian goddess of fertility), which came up out

of the river and fed on the grass on it banks it was nothing new to him because he had seen that happen many times. But when he dreamed again and the seven emaciated cows came out of the river and ate up the fat cows with no physical change in their bodies, it was cause for alarm.

Then he slept again, and the second dream was like the first, only for livestock was substituted corn, or more correctly, sprigs of wheat. That particular kind of wheat was native to Egypt and instead of having only one head, it had several heads coming from the same stalk - thus 'seven ears of corn came up upon one stalk' (called *Triticum compositum,* the common kind with only one head is *Triticum vulgare).* The seven fat 'ears' were consumed by the seven thin 'ears' which had been withered by the east wind.

When the wind blew from the east it brought only dry air and no moisture, a sure sign of drought.

Pharaoh was very disturbed by his dreams. Pagan peoples are always superstitious and part of the superstition was, and is, attached to dream interpretations.

He called all his magicians and soothsayers and told them his dreams and asked for the interpretation, but they were unable to tell him what the dreams meant.

At that moment the chief 'butler' was attending the Pharaoh and saw the inability of Pharaoh's 'wise men' to interpret the dreams. He remembered how Joseph had interpreted his own dream and that of the baker.

He reminded Pharaoh of his time in the palace prison, being careful to put all the blame upon himself for being there. He then said he and the chief baker had both dreamed dreams that had been interpreted by a young Hebrew and the interpretation had been true in both cases.

When the Pharaoh heard that, he immediately called for Joseph to be brought to him.

Joseph could not go before the Pharaoh in his prison raiment nor with a beard, so the chief jailer gave him clothes to wear in which it would be fitting for him to stand before the Pharaoh. The Egyptians associated facial hair with a sign of mourning and it would not be advisable to stand before the Pharaoh unshaved, so Joseph shaved himself and was taken to Pharaoh. (The Jews, however, believed it was a disgrace to be without facial hair.)

For Joseph to appear before Pharaoh was something that had surely never crossed his mind in the years he had spent in prison. But God was still working.

Pharaoh said to Joseph, 'I understand you can interpret dreams'. But Joseph said, 'No, I can't, but God can and it's up to Him whether I will have the answers you seek'.

Pharaoh was considered to be a god himself and was worshipped as such by his subjects. He was seated upon the royal throne with servants to meet his every need, and in comes a young man of the Hebrews who has the audacity to speak to him of the true God who could interpret dreams and give him an answer in his distress. His heart had been made ready by God to receive Joseph's words, or he could have just as easily had Joseph killed.

As Pharaoh recounted his dreams God gave Joseph the interpretation and he was able to show Pharaoh their meaning. As the 'wise men' of the kingdom heard the meaning it became obvious to them, and they couldn't understand why they couldn't see it before. Their eyes were blinded because God's purpose was to be fulfilled by, and for, His chosen people through Joseph.

When Joseph explained the details of the dreams he also had a workable plan in mind which would change the end results of the famine. The situation which God had revealed to Pharaoh would not be long in coming so something had to be done quickly.

He told Pharaoh to quickly find a man whom he could trust, to take charge of the situation. Through the addition of other officers, appointed by Pharaoh, they would take a fifth of the bountiful harvest during the good years which would be stored to be used for food during the bad years. By doing that the whole nation would not perish.

The plan sounded good to Pharaoh and he saw something in Joseph he had never seen before in his own men, as he said, *in whom the Spirit of God is,* (Genesis 41:38). He believed that the spirit of that same God would continue to give Joseph wisdom as He had in interpreting the dreams and in formulating a plan to save Egypt. Joseph was put in charge of Pharaoh's house, (or the entire country), and he was second only to Pharaoh in power.

By waiting until it was God's time, Joseph was exalted to a position he could never have imagined. If the 'butler' had spoken to the Pharaoh when he first left the prison, Joseph might have been freed and in time would have probably returned to his father's house, but God had much bigger plans for him. He was to be the instrument to save not only his own family, but the entire infant nation which was to come from him and his brothers. Joseph's circumstance in going to Egypt was ordained of God. Truly 'men meant it for evil, but God meant it for good' all along.

Joseph did not become annoyed under the circumstances God brought into his life; he quietly yielded to whatever came to pass and trusted God to bring about the best in his life. This is an important lesson for every believer to learn.

When he stood before Pharaoh he was only 30 years old, so he had been in Egypt about 13 years at that time. His had not been an easy road, but it had led to great honor because of his faithfulness to both God and man.

He was faithful in his father's house to obey him. Even when he knew his brothers hated him, he went to inquire about them as his father asked; he was faithful in Potiphar's house, though Potiphar's wife wrongly accused him and he was put in prison; and he was faithful in the prison even when the 'chief butler' forgot him. And God was faithful when He put him into a position of power not sought for nor even imagined by a young man of the Hebrews.

When Joseph was installed in his office as chief minister, or vizier, to the king, Pharaoh gave him his own signet ring, which was a symbol of his power and was used on all royal documents. He also gave Joseph royal robes to wear, (he was somewhat acquainted with wearing princely garments because of the robe his father had given him many years before).

They were robes of 'fine linen', usually white, and only allowed to be worn by those of highest rank. It was linen woven from flax with 140 threads per inch, whereas most linen had 100 threads per inch, and its feel was like the softest silk. It would have been what is called Byssus, fine flax, which was often dyed purple and worn by royalty. Joseph's garment seems to have been the white linen worn by the priests and the highest officers of the land. Pharaoh also put a gold chain around his neck, another symbol of royalty and authority. By

Costumes of the Vizier
(Rawlinson, Vol. I)

these acts Pharaoh passed his authority and power to Joseph. M. A. Peloubet, *International Lessons for 1887*, (Boston: W. A. Wilde and Company), p. 110.

Joseph was then placed in the second royal chariot and driven through the city so all could see their new chief minister and give him honor. Most writers believe the term *'Abreck!'* which was shouted by the herald who preceded the chariot meant, 'bow the knee', which the people would have been required to do as the chariot passed by. Allen P. Ross, *Creation and Blessing,* (Grand Rapids: Baker Book House, 1988), p. 643; F. N. Peloubet, D. D., and (Peloubet, 1887), p. 110.

Pharaoh gave Joseph a new name, Zaphnath-paaneah, 'governor of the Living One' or 'bread of life'. There are other interpretations which also mean 'giver of life' and 'God speaks and lives'. All these names were appropriate for his position and give honor to the One who would bring it all to pass. *(Ross, Creation and Blessing),* p. 643; (Peloubet, 1887), p. 110.

Joseph was also given a wife, named Asenath, meaning 'one who belongs to Naith, the Earth Mother'. She was the daughter of Potiphera, the chief priest of On.

The city of On was about 19 miles north of Memphis in the Delta region. Those who became exalted priests were usually related to the Pharaoh so Joseph became Pharaoh's relative by marriage. The city of On was a place where the sun-god, Ra, was worshipped and his father-in-law was a leader in its cultic rites. The priests from that city were also noted for their great wisdom and learning.

There is some indication that Asenath left her pagan religion and followed the true God of Joseph. When his sons were born he gave them Hebrew, not Egyptian names. Manasseh, the eldest, meant 'causing to forget', and Ephraim meant 'double fruit' or 'doubly fruitful'. Both sons were born during the seven good years. Joseph still felt he was not at home in Egypt because in Genesis 41:52, he called it *the land of my affliction.*

Joseph 'went out from the presence of Pharaoh' (Genesis 41:46); his work was not in the palace, but out in the fields and villages with the farmers whose crops were of great interest to him. During the seven good years the Nile would have overflowed its banks more than usual and left larger, richer deposits of silt in which the farmers could sow their grain, (the seven fat cows). A fifth part of such a harvest would be sufficient to feed the nation during the seven lean years. When the seven years of famine came, Joseph held the land of the people and a one-fifth tax of the annual produce was given to the king to run the central government. This helped to consolidate the kingdom, and took the power away from the independent petty kingdoms under the nobles. That made the country stronger and more stable.

Joseph's Brothers (Genesis 42-45)

If there was a famine in Egypt it was much worse in Canaan. There was little left to eat in Canaan and Jacob heard that Egypt had an abundance of food. He sent his sons, all except Benjamin, to buy food. They traveled with other peoples who were going to Egypt in search of sustenance, some 250 miles from Hebron. Benjamin would have been about 25 years old at this time; Joseph 39, and Jacob was nearing 130.

When the ten older brothers thought of going to Egypt their minds must have recalled the day they sold their brother as a slave and sent him off to that far country. Guilt lays heavily on the heart of a man who knows himself to be at fault, and each knew his own personal guilt, and that of his brothers. Jacob rebuked them before they began the journey by saying, 'Why are you standing around looking at one another? There's work to be done, get on with it!' The years had mellowed their character, and at the command of their father, they laid aside their personal feelings and began the journey to Egypt.

Joseph was the ruling royal governor in charge of all sales of grain in Egypt. When his brothers approached him they bowed down to him, as befitted his station of importance. It was entirely up to him whether grain was to be sold to an individual or not. Dream number one had just been fulfilled.

They were recognized by Joseph, but they did not recognize him. When they last saw him he was a boy; now he was a man in royal Egyptian apparel in a position of power speaking a strange language. They certainly never thought they would ever see Joseph again because they thought he was dead, (Genesis 42:13).

He recognized them because they were grown men when he last saw them. They still wore the shepherd's garments with which he was familiar and his memories of home were still very much alive.

He made sure he was not recognized, by speaking through an interpreter and by speaking harshly to them. He accused them of being spies who had come to see if they could conquer Egypt while she was 'naked', or while there was easy access because of the conditions of the famine.

Joseph had several reasons for treating them as he did; he wanted to see what kind of men they had become; he wanted to find out if his father was still alive and whether Benjamin was well; and where they were all living at that time.

Verse eleven of chapter 42 is significant in refuting Joseph's accusation, 'we are all one man's sons', because no man would risk all his sons by sending them together as spies. It was a good argument in their favor, but Joseph put them in jail for three days anyway.

They admitted in Genesis 42:13 that they were twelve brothers of one father, the youngest of whom had remained with their father and the other one 'is not'. They were finally admitting the probable death of Joseph and recognizing him as their legitimate brother. That was one of the things Joseph was waiting to hear.

He demanded that they send one of their number for their younger brother to prove they were not spies. *By the life of Pharaoh* is a phrase used in verses 15 and 16 of chapter 42 of Genesis, and seems to be a kind of vow meaning, 'it's a sure thing', as we might say, 'It will happen just as I'm telling you', etc., that something or other is true and will happen as stated.

Joseph put them in jail and left them to think about their condition for three days. During that time they realized their situation had been brought about by God because of the sin they had collectively committed more than twenty years before.

When Joseph brought them before his presence after the three days, he told them one of them would have to stay in jail while the rest were allowed to return home and get Benjamin. They were so guilt stricken at this point that they began talking among themselves confessing their guilt, *we are verily guilty concerning our brother* (no one had to ask which brother), *in that we saw the anguish of his soul, when he besought us, and we would not hear; therefore is this distress come upon us*, (Genesis 42:21).

This may have been the first time they had confessed their guilt to one another over their treatment of Joseph. They had seen the terrible effect it had had on their father who *would not be comforted;* they had suffered the guilt individually for over 20 years, and at last the confession came to their lips. How could

they keep their word to this powerful Egyptian and deprive their father again of the son whom he loved? When one comes to the point of seeing himself as God sees him, he must always confess, 'It's my fault'.

Then Reuben said, 'Didn't I try to tell you? But no one would listen, now see what has happened! His blood is required' - payday is here. Joseph may not have known at the time about Reuben's part in trying to save him, but now he relived the whole episode from the lips of the guilty and he was moved to tears, (Genesis 42:24). He was not feeling sorry for himself; he was rejoicing in the change he saw in his brothers.

The second son of Leah, Simeon, was imprisoned and the grain sacks of the others were filled. Their money was put in the tops of their sacks without their knowledge, and they were sent on their way. During the journey one of them opened his sack to feed his pack animal and found the money. He reported this to his brothers and they were all frightened, *what is this that God hath done to us?* they said. Not what the Egyptians had done, but what God had done. In all circumstances they were ready to acknowledge that God was in charge and was working. Looking over their shoulders and hurrying on their way, lest the Egyptians should overtake them before they reached Canaan and accuse them of theft, they finally reached their father's house.

They told him the story of their journey to Egypt and of the demand made to bring the youngest son and of leaving Simeon as the guarantee that they would return. Then as they began to empty the sacks of grain, each one found his money in the tops of the sacks. When they saw that, the whole family was afraid.

Jacob felt something terrible was about to happen and to the nine who returned he began to lament their actions. 'You've taken away Joseph, (did he have some suspicion of their part in his 'death'?), you've left Simeon in Egypt, and now you want to take Benjamin, too! No, he is not going!' Reuben offered his two sons in sacrifice if he was unable to bring Benjamin back, but this was clearly a rash statement without any merit. What good would it do for Jacob to kill his grandsons? Doing that wouldn't bring any of his sons back. Jacob further told them, if anything happened to Benjamin he would die from the sorrow it would bring him on top of all he had already suffered.

But the grain ran out and another trip had to be made in order to survive.

Judah was now the son in charge; (Reuben lost his place because of his sin with Bilhah; Simeon and Levi had lost their places because of their wickedness in Shechem), and Judah was next in line. He reminded his father that they could not go again unless they took Benjamin because the mysterious Egyptian would refuse to see them or give them the grain they needed if he was not with them.

Jacob responded like a petulant child, 'Well, why did you have to tell him you had a younger brother?' At that time Jacob was 130 years old and did not feel he would be able to endure the loss of another son. Judah told him they were forced to tell the Egyptian about Benjamin because the man asked them pointedly about their father and 'another' brother. They had no recourse but to tell him. How were they to know he would demand they bring Benjamin?

Judah offered himself as surety for Benjamin, saying if something went wrong he would bear the blame forever, (Genesis 43:9). Though this was probably not a lot of comfort to Jacob, he seems to have respected the spirit in which Judah spoke and allowed Benjamin to accompany them. He prepared a gift for the vizier which his sons were to take. Evidently, not everything in Canaan was destroyed through the famine and he was able to get together enough fruit and nuts for the gift. For centuries the fruit of Canaan was exported into Egypt as a cash crop, so it was always plentiful.

He also told them to return the money they had found in their sacks, and sent an equal amount to make the new purchase. Jacob came to terms with his lot in life as he sent his sons away as observed by his statement: *If I be bereaved of my children, I am bereaved,* (Genesis 43:14). If they didn't go the whole family would die anyway, so he had no choice but to send Benjamin and trust God's mercy to bring him back.

And when Joseph saw Benjamin with them, he said to the ruler of his house, Bring these men home, and slay, and make ready; for these men shall dine with me at noon, (Genesis 43:16).

Joseph sent them to his own home. It was a great honor for anyone to be invited to dine with the grand vizier, but they interpreted the move as a threat because of the money in their sacks.

They spoke to the man in charge of Joseph's house, telling him about finding the money and their innocence in the affair. They were certain they were about to be put in jail with Simeon, but the steward reassured them, saying he was responsible for their money being returned. He then brought Simeon to them unharmed.

Joseph's testimony was well-known in his own household as demonstrated by the words of the steward, *Peace be to you,* (when Joseph was at home the brothers couldn't even greet him with peace), *fear not: your God, and the God of your father, hath given you treasure in your sacks,* (Genesis 43:23). A Christian's best testimony should be in his own home.

Observing the Oriental custom, the men were taken to Joseph's house where water was provided and they washed their feet before entering. They prepared their gift and nervously awaited the arrival of the Egyptian vizier.

When he arrived they bowed themselves again before Joseph and presented their gift. Joseph inquired about them and especially about their father; then at seeing Benjamin up close, he asked if he was their younger brother. He was unable to maintain his composure after speaking to Benjamin, *God be gracious unto thee, my son,* (Genesis 43:29).

He left the room, no doubt leaving a puzzled group behind, and went into a private area of his house where he could weep. He wept for the wasted years; for the restoration of his own brother, and for the change he observed in his other brothers. And he wept for joy because his father was still alive and he would be able to see him again.

When he had composed himself and returned to the dining room, he seated his brothers according to their ages. They were very puzzled as to how he could have that information. Joseph did not eat at the same table with them because, not only could an Egyptian not eat with an Hebrew (Genesis 43:32), but a man in his position of importance could not eat with commoners.

The food was served and Benjamin was given five times more than the others. The brothers did not exhibit their usual jealous spirit at this occurrence but 'ate and drank and were merry with him', (verse 34). Joseph continued to observe the actions of his brothers to see how they would react to the tests he was giving them. When Benjamin received preferential treatment they did not become upset but continued as before.

The Silver Cup (Genesis 44)

And he commanded the steward of his house, saying, Fill the men's sacks with food, as much as they can carry, and put every man's money in his sack's mouth. And put my cup, the silver cup, in the sack's mouth of the youngest, and his corn money. And he did according to the word that Joseph had spoken. (Genesis 44:1,2.)

The silver cup placed in Benjamin's sack, along with his money, had more significance than the intrinsic value of the silver. As stated in Genesis 44:5, it was a 'divining cup'.

This was a bowl or large cup made of silver, into which water was poured, sometimes over stones. The reflection of the water was then studied and a pronouncement made as to the outcome of the problem under consideration. Most writers agree that Joseph did not practice divination, but that the Egyptians thought God spoke to him and gave him his wisdom through that medium.

Joseph's last test of his brothers had begun. They had not traveled far when Joseph sent his steward (and probably some soldiers) to catch them. He gave his steward instructions as to what he should say to them. When the steward caught up to them, he asked them why they had repaid good for evil in taking the divining cup.

They were all shocked at the accusation. In order to give evidence of their innocence they said if anyone had it that person would be put to death and the rest would become slaves to the governor.

As the search was made the cup was found in Benjamin's sack, exactly where the steward had placed it. Here was their opportunity to get rid of Benjamin, their father's favorite, just as they had rid themselves of Joseph so many years before. But their hearts had been changed and the guilt over their previous deed was still so fresh in their minds that they never thought of committing another act as wicked as they had previously committed.

They tore their clothes (a sure sign of mourning), and loaded their sacks on their pack animals, and returned to the court of Joseph where he accused them of stealing his divining cup.

Judah again took the position of spokesman and offered them all as servants, but Joseph only wanted Benjamin and told the rest of them to go home.

An explanation and an appeal of great pathos follows from Judah. In essence he said, "You demanded that we bring our younger brother, we did as you asked. Our aged father did not want him to come because he was afraid of what might happen to him. I gave him my word that he would return unharmed and that I would stand in his place (bear the blame = sin). I beg you to take me instead of Benjamin. If I return without him my father will die and I cannot bear to inflict any more sorrow upon him."

In testing his brothers Joseph needed to see how they would react in specific situations:

- in the admission of a lost brother,
- about the money returned in the sacks of grain,
- would they become jealous when Benjamin received preferential treatment,
- did they really care for their father,
- what would be their reaction to the stolen cup,
- would they be willing to give their lives for Benjamin, and
- Judah's pledge.

Judah was the most changed of all the brothers, (Genesis 44:33,34) as manifested by his great love for his brother and his great concern for his father.

Joseph could, at last, reveal himself to them with the assurance that they were not the same men who had sold him so many years before.

The Revelation (Genesis 45)

Then Joseph could not refrain himself before all them that stood by him; and he cried, Cause every man to go out from me. And there stood no man with him, while Joseph made himself known unto his brethren, (Genesis 45:1).

He began to weep and sent all the other people out of his presence, leaving only his brothers. And weeping he told his brother he was Joseph and immediately inquired about his father.

They were speechless, as can be imagined, not knowing whether they were about to be imprisoned or killed. Joseph immediately reassured them that his plans held only good for them. 'Yes, you sold me as a slave, but God was in control even in that as you will soon see', he told them.

The sovereignty of God was in control in:

- taking him to Egypt,
- making him ruler over Egypt, and in
- bringing his brothers to Egypt to save them.

He told them, *be not grieved, nor angry with yourselves,* (verse 5). It is always easier to forgive others than to forgive ourselves, and they were having a hard time dealing with themselves at that moment.

There were still five years of famine remaining and Joseph would also care for them during those five years. 'My position in the land,' he said, 'gives me the power to save all of my family at this time'. *So now it was not you that sent me hither, but God: and he hath made me a father to Pharaoh, and lord of all his house, and a ruler throughout all the land of Egypt,* (Genesis 45:8).

(To be 'a father to Pharaoh' was to be second in power to him and be the one who advised him in all things, showing the high regard Joseph enjoyed in Egypt.) Everything he told his brothers he was able to do because of his position.

He said, 'Go get my father and tell him of my position in Egypt. Bring down all the family and I'll give you a place to live and will care for you'. He then embraced his little brother and began again to weep for joy and for the lost years.

His brothers were finally reassured and began to speak with him, (verse 15), no doubt asking his forgiveness and rejoicing because he had been restored to them.

The news spread all the way to Pharaoh that Joseph's brothers had come. He told Joseph to send his brothers for his father and to take wagons in which to carry the children and women on their return journey. Pharaoh said, 'Tell them not to worry about bringing anything else because the land of Egypt is before them and they will have everything they need', (Genesis 45:19,20).

Joseph gave gifts of clothing to his brothers. They could not stand before Pharaoh in their shepherd's clothes and when they returned they were to have an audience with him. He gave Benjamin five changes of clothes and 300 pieces of silver, but the other brothers did not manifest a spirit of jealousy about that either. He sent food and everything necessary to bring his father and his brothers' families to Egypt.

His last instructions to them were, *See that ye fall not out by the way,* (45:24). He was admonishing them to have no hard words with each other by casting blame on one or the other.

They had the ordeal before them of confessing to their father what they had done to Joseph so many years before, and that was enough to cause anyone to start looking for a scapegoat. But they were collectively responsible and had already faced that fact.

They had to acknowledge that Joseph's dreams had meant something after all; they had already bowed to him at least twice.

Arriving home they confessed the whole story to Jacob and told of their experiences on

Ancient Egyptian Cart
(Ploubet, 1913)

the journey. They then told him of Joseph's position as governor (vizier) over Egypt and his request that they move there.

Jacob did not believe them until he saw the wagons (a two-wheeled cart which could only have come from a wealthy, powerful source) which Joseph had sent. He realized something wonderful had happened and announced his intention of going to see Joseph before he died.

Jacob was 130 years old when he left Canaan and lived another 17 years in Egypt, dying at 147, (Genesis 47:28). Joseph lived 54 years after the death of his father and died at 110.

Journey to Egypt (Genesis 46:1-31)

As far as can be seen from the Scripture, God had not given permission for Jacob to leave Canaan. Because of this he stopped to inquire of God at Beersheba, on the southern border of Judea before entering Idumea, (the territory of Ishmael and his descendants). It would have been on the direct route from Hebron to Egypt. Egypt was about 250 miles away, a long, hard trip for an old man 130 years old, and women and children.

Jacob offered a sacrifice to God at Beersheba, and God spoke to him in a night vision. He probably had mixed feelings about going to Egypt because his ancestors had not had a good record in that land. But God told him to go and there He would make of Jacob a great nation. Not only would he become a great nation in Egypt, but God promised to bring him and the nation back to the Promised Land. Jacob did return, but not until after his death.

After that night vision of God speaking to Jacob, there were no more personal contacts in which God spoke to any individual, not even Joseph, for many hundreds of years. There were many years of darkness until God spoke to Moses to lead the people out of Egypt.

There follows in the Scripture a listing of the sons of Israel which were supposed to be those who went into Egypt, but most scholars agree that these were not the actual individuals but the heads of tribes in most cases. For example, in Genesis 46:12 the sons of Judah, Er and Onan, are listed and they were both dead at the time; the sons of Joseph, and Joseph himself, are listed, but they were already in Egypt. Benjamin was a young man of about 25 at the time and for him to have 10 sons at that age would be pretty difficult unless he had several wives or several multiple births.

When Moses wrote the history of Genesis he was looking from the other side of the pilgrimage and included those who became heads of tribes of the nation, about seventy in number.

Joseph had already told them to go to the land of Goshen because it was a good place for shepherds and their flocks. Jacob sent Judah ahead to advise Joseph of their arrival and he immediately went to Goshen to meet his father or *attend to his father.* After 23 years, Joseph was reunited with his father and *fell on his neck, and wept on his neck a good while,* (Genesis 46:29).

Jacob was now ready to die since he had seen Joseph again. This, however, was not God's plan and He allowed him to live to see his grandchildren, the sons of Joseph, become young men, whom he blessed with a special blessing.

It was God's purpose to move them to Egypt in order to isolate them from pagan influences and intermarriage with pagan nations, so He could make them a great nation in number and in character. God wanted them to learn from their culture, but not become a part of it.

The Culture of Egypt

The Egyptians were not a warlike people, but they kept a standing army of 400,000 soldiers to rebuff any invaders. There were many incursions into their territory on the east, by many different nations, as noted by the times of Hyksos rule.

They were a peace-loving people who were governed by good laws and civility which they carried with them as they colonized other parts of the world.

"They triumphed by the wisdom of their counsels, and the superiority of their knowledge; and the empire of the mind appeared more noble and glorious to them, than that which is achieved by arms and conquest." (Rollin, *Ancient History,* Vol. I), p. 131.

Some of the first libraries were in Egypt and those who were allowed their use learned from the most brilliant minds that had ever lived.

They studied the movements of the stars and planets and from them observed the course of the sun and were able to develop a yearly calendar made up of 365 days and six hours.

They developed the science of surveying because of the yearly flooding of the Nile and this in turn led to the development of geometry.

Their doctors were knowledgeable; usually each doctor studied only one disease. This was because he was responsible for the welfare of the patient and if he was not properly cared for the physician could lose his life. Being a specialist in only one disease offered him some protection.

Architecture, painting, sculpture and other arts reached a high degree of excellence in Egypt. Music, however, was considered 'useless and dangerous'. (Rollin, *Ancient History,* Vol. I), p. 122.

They invented paper made from the bark of the papyrus, a plant which grew to a height from 9 to 11 feet. Later were added other sources of writing-material; parchment made from sheepskin, and vellum, made from calfskin.

Wonderful foodstuffs were grown along the Nile and from the Nile came fish of different kinds. The peoples of Egypt were well-fed with a variety of fruits and vegetables, meat and fish, and when the Israelites left there those were the things they mourned for, (Exodus 16:3).

The highest virtue in Egypt was gratitude. Old age was respected and every man was expected to have and practice some profession; no man was allowed to be a slothful character. All were registered with the government, giving name, address and means of support. If anyone lied about any of these he was put to death.

No man could borrow money unless the body of his father was given to the creditor until the loan was repaid, and it was to be redeemed as quickly as possible. (See section on Jacob and embalming.)

"[In Egypt]...they will there observe the perfect polity which reigned in Egypt, both in the court and the rest of the kingdom; the vigilance of the prince, who was informed of all transactions, had a regular council, a chosen number of ministers, armies ever well maintained and disciplined, and of every order of soldiery, horse, foot, armed chariots; intendants in all the provinces; overseers or guardians of the public granaries; wise and exact dispensers of the corn lodged in them; a court composed of great officers of the crown, a captain of his guards, a chief cup-bearer, a master of his pantry, in a word, all things that compose a prince's household, and constitute a magnificent court. But above all these, the readers will admire the fear in which the threatenings of God were held, the inspector of all actions, and the judge of kings themselves; and the horror the Egyptians had for adultery, which was acknowledged to be a crime of so heinous a nature, that it alone was capable of bringing destruction on a nation." (Rollin, *Ancient History,* Vol. I), p. 127.

All these were admirable qualities which could be emulated by the Israelites, but their paganism was not to be emulated and for this reason God put the Israelites in Goshen to keep them separated as much as possible from their religious practices.

Presentation in Pharaoh's court (Genesis 47:1-12)

Joseph instructed his brothers and his father as to what they should say when he presented them to Pharaoh. Joseph wanted them in the land of Goshen where they could continue to care for their flocks and where they would be kept isolated from the Egyptians by their location and their profession.

Joseph took his father and five of his brothers to be presented to Pharaoh, (the rest remained to guard the flocks and the people). First his brothers spoke with Pharaoh and told him they were, and had always been, shepherds. They asked for permission to live in

Goshen because there was no pasture left in Canaan. They indicated they were only there for a while until conditions improved in Canaan, *to sojourn in the land are we come,* (47:4), and would not wish to become citizens, but would be returning to their homeland. Pharaoh gave them a special honor in making them keepers over his herds, a role consistent with their occupation as shepherds.

Pharaoh gave permission to Joseph to place his family in that area of Egypt, calling it 'the best of the land'. Edersheim says, "The land of Goshen lay between the eastern part of the ancient Delta, and the western border of Palestine; it was scarcely a part of Egypt Proper, was inhabited by other foreigners besides the Israelites, and was in its geographical names rather Semitic than Egyptian; it was pasture-land, especially suited to a shepherd people, and sufficient for the Israelites, who there prospered, and were separated from the main body of the Egyptians." (Edersheim, *Bible History,* Vols. I-IV), p. 176.

It was also easier for the Israelites to escape from the area many years later because of its proximity to Canaan. Goshen was later called Rameses. It was an 80 mile fertile strip of land near Memphis; the perfect place for God's people to settle.

Shepherds were looked down upon by the Egyptians because: "(1) Shepherds belonged in Egypt to the fourth or lowest class. (2) The Egyptians often suffered from inroads from the sheep-keeping tribes on their eastern borders, who committed many depredations on persons and property. (3) The foreign shepherd nations were looked upon as a kind of barbarians, living in a wild, uncultivated way, while Egypt was the wealthiest, most learned, and most cultured nation existing at that time. (4) It is probable that most of the shepherd class who came into Egypt were the worst specimens, the banditti, the tramps, who gave a poor impression of those at home." (Peloubet, 1887), p. 121.

Joseph then presented his father to Pharaoh and Jacob blessed Pharaoh when he came in and when he left. *Blessed* is the Hebrew word *barak* which can mean 'to speak peace to a person or bless him in the name of God'. This was a special blessing Jacob could give to Pharaoh because of his faith in God, and few other men of the time were able to do that because few believed in God as Jacob did.

Pharaoh asked Jacob his age, which he gave as 130, (the Egyptians did not reach advanced ages). Jacob went on to say his life had been shorter than that of his ancestors, and it had been a life of adversity which he considered only a pilgrimage leading to a better place, (Hebrews 11:9-13).

Jacob and his family then took up residence in Goshen and were cared for by Joseph.

The Last five years of the famine (Genesis 47:13-26)

And there was no bread in all the land; for the famine was very sore, so that the land of Egypt and all the land of Canaan fainted by reason of the famine, (Genesis 47:13).

When the people had no more money to buy food, Joseph took their livestock in payment. When their animals were gone he took their land as payment and moved them from the areas in which they had lived to other areas of the nation, (verse 21).

After taking their land for Pharaoh he gave them seed so they could raise some crops and from their harvest they were to give one-fifth to the Pharaoh, or the central government, for running expenses. It was a fair arrangement, as they themselves recognized, because without Joseph they would all have died anyway.

He did not take the priests' lands because they were given to them by the Pharaoh and could not be taken from them.

Joseph's pledge to his father (Genesis 47:27-31)

...put, I pray thee, thy hand under my thigh, and deal kindly and truly with me, bury me not, I pray thee in Egypt. But I will lie with my fathers, and thou shalt carry me out of Egypt, (Genesis 47:29b and 30a).

After a period of 17 years had passed, Jacob knew his days on earth were about over and called Joseph to his side to give him instructions concerning his burial and to get a promise from him.

He told Joseph not to bury him in Egypt, but to return him to Canaan and bury him in Macpelah where Abraham and Sarah and Leah were buried, (Genesis 50:13).

Joseph gave his pledge or promise that he would do as his father had instructed him.

Manasseh and Ephraim (Genesis 48)

And it came to pass after these things, that one told Joseph, Behold, thy father is sick: and he took with him his two sons, Manasseh and Ephraim, (Genesis 48:1).

When Joseph was told his father was sick he took his two sons to him so Jacob could bless them. Jacob sat up on his bed at Joseph's coming and recounted to him the promise God had given him at Bethel (Luz).

Zodhiates, (p. 72), in a note, says in verse 5 that Jacob actually adopted Joseph's sons as his own and for this reason they took their place as tribal heads in Israel. Jacob took Joseph's sons in place of Reuben, who lost the birthright, and Levi, and passed on to them the double-portion rights of the firstborn through Joseph. They were Rachel's grandsons and that made them special to Jacob. The sons born to Joseph after Manasseh and Ephraim would be his but these two were Jacob's. He continued to recount the history of Joseph's mother's death and burial, and it seems, just as an aside says, 'Who are these?', referring to Joseph's sons. Joseph told him and asked him to bless them.

They were brought to Jacob and were kissed and embraced by their grandfather who remarked that though he had never thought he would see Joseph again, he was not only seeing him, but his children as well.

Joseph moved his sons away from his father and bowed down before him in an attitude of humility and thanksgiving, then presented the boys to him again in the order of their birth. But Israel laid his right hand on Ephraim, the youngest, instead of on Manasseh, and blessed both them and Joseph. When Joseph saw what his father had done he was upset and took his father's hand from Ephraim's head to put it on Manasseh, but Jacob said, 'I know what I'm doing, Manasseh will become a great people, but Ephraim will be much larger and more powerful'. Ephraim did become one of the largest tribes in Israel and the most powerful next to Judah, just as his grandfather had said.

Jacob then blessed Joseph with a double portion (the blessing of the firstborn) and promised that God would be with him and take him again into the land of his fathers, but again, this did not occur until Joseph had been dead for many years. Joseph was to receive ancient Shechem and the land Jacob had bought from Hamor, (Genesis 33:19). This blessing was looking forward to the fulfillment of God's promise to all Israel, not just to Joseph.

The blessing of Jacob's sons (Genesis 49:1-28)

And Jacob called unto his sons, and said, Gather yourselves together, that I may tell you that which shall befall you in the last days, (Genesis 49:1).

In the blessing given to his sons, Jacob remembers the good and the bad associated with each of them, and his blessing is given accordingly.

Reuben - what he could have been, what he became, and for which he lost the birthright. He was as unstable as water and did not have the character to lead, nor did any of his descendants. There were no judges, nor prophets from his line. He received his inheritance east of the Jordan, (Joshua 13:15-23).

Simeon and Levi - partners in cruelty, (Joshua 19:1-9).

Simeon - (1 Chronicles 4:38-43), the land given to him was east to Gedor, and to Mt. Seir, the country of Ishmael, and he had a small part of Judah's inheritance. His tribe was ultimately absorbed by the tribe of Judah, (Deuteronomy 33).

Levi - was separated from Simeon in the Promised Land so they wouldn't repeat their actions. The Levites received no inheritance in Israel, (Joshua 18:7), and were scattered throughout the tribes. Dod says, "...that the tribe of Levi should have been so used for God's immediate service stands as evidence that punishments, however severe and desolating, even threatening something bordering on extinction, may yet become blessings to God's people. The sword of murder was displaced in Levi's hand by the knife of sacrifice; their fierce revenge against sinners was converted into hostility against sin; their apparent zeal for the forms of their religion was consecrated to the service of the tabernacle and temple; their fanatical pride, which prompted them to treat all other people as the offscouring of the earth, was informed by a better spirit, and used for the upbuilding and instruction of the people of Israel. In order to understand why this tribe, of all others, should have been chosen for the service of the sanctuary and for the instruction of the people, we must not only recognize how their being scattered in punishment of their sin over all the land fitted them to be the educators of the nation and the representatives of all the tribes, but also we must consider that the sin itself which Levi had committed broke the one command which men had up till this time received from the mouth of God...In saying, 'At the hand of every man's brother will I require the life of man,' God had shown that human life was to be counted sacred...To take private revenge, as Levi did, was to take the sword out of God's hand, and to say that God was not careful enough of justice, and but a poor guardian of right and wrong in the world; and to destroy human life in the wanton and cruel manner in which Levi had destroyed the Shechemites, and to do it under colour and by the aid of religious zeal, was to God the most hateful of sins...Very humbling must it have been for the Levite who remembered the history of this tribe to be used by God as the hand of His justice on the victims that were brought in substitution for that which was so precious in the sight of God." (Dods, *Genesis*), pp. 430,431.

Judah - the birthright was transferred to him and the line of Christ was promised through him, (Genesis 49:10,11); (Matthew 1:2,3). His kingship, and his authority over his brothers was recognized. The lion spoken of in reference to him represented the monarchy. His position of ruler would remain until the rightful King (Shiloh-'peace-maker'; 'peace-bringer') came and took His position. (Joshua 15:1-62; Judges 3:9), the first judge came from his line.

Zebulon - his dwelling would be by the sea, (Joshua 19:10-16; Judges 1:30). He represented the commerce of Israel.

Isaachar - his name meant 'reward'. He preferred the abundance of material things and would trade his freedom for them. He had no ambition and no desire to excel as long as he had comfort. He was practical, but lazy. (Joshua 19:17-23), the judge Tola was from his line, (Judges 10:1).

Dan - meaning 'judgment'. He would judge as one of the tribes of Israel. His name also has the connotation of defense, and he would help to defend the tribes. In Revelation 7:5-8 Dan is not listed and Edersheim suggests that the Antichrist may come from this tribe, as the sand adder who hides himself and when least expected bites the passerby, (Edersheim, *Bible History*), p. 184. *Dan shall be an adder in the path, that biteth the horses' heels, so that his rider shall fall backward* (Genesis 49:17), this was to happen because of his idolatry, (2 Kings 10:29; Joshua 19:40-48; 21:23; Judges 1:34).

Samson was from the tribe of Dan, and through Samson the Philistines were defeated for a time and left Israel in peace.

Gad - was to be a valiant warrior, (1 Chronicles 12:8). The Gadites were some of David's valiant men. (Joshua 13:24-28), his inheritance was east of the Jordan.

Asher - he received the most fertile possession, and provided 'delicacies to kings'. (Joshua 19:24-31; Judges 1:32.)

Naphtali - they were mountain people, (Joshua 19:32-39). Thirty-eight thousand of them fought for David, (1 Chronicles 12:34).

Joseph - he received the greatest blessing, a double portion, that of the firstborn, because of the blessing of the Almighty on his life which pointed out his superiority over his brothers. God would bless him: in agriculture, in livestock, and with many descendants.

His two sons were to receive the inheritance of land in Israel because their father had received the blessing of the firstborn, and it was divided between them. Joseph did not raise them to be honored in Egypt and to have places of power. He wanted them to return to Canaan and take their inheritance among their uncles as true sons of Jacob. (1 Chronicles 5:1,2); they took Joseph's place and that of Levi, (Joshua 18:7).

Benjamin - he would divide the spoil, he would have an abundance and would share it with the other tribes. He was known because of his descendants:

> Ehud - (Judges 3:15-30; 5:14), a Benjamite judge
> Saul - (1 Chronicles 8:40; 12:2), first king of Israel
> Jonathan - (1 Samuel 14), son of Saul

In blessing his sons, Jacob gave an indication of the position each would hold in the coming nation. As before stated, a father could bless his sons with any blessing he chose and those blessings were not to be retracted. After the blessing of Jacob's sons was completed there were no more individual blessings given. From that point on the blessings were for the nation, not the individual, until the time of the New Testament when Christ would die for the individual and restore the blessings.

Death of Jacob (Genesis 49:29-33)

When Jacob died Joseph wept for his father and had him embalmed so he could be taken to Canaan and placed in the cave of Macpelah.

In Egypt embalming took about 40 days and mourning lasted from 40-70 days depending on the importance of the person. The embalmers lived in the cemeteries and were divided into three classes:

1. Those who made the incision and took out the organs. After finishing their job they ran away while having stones thrown at them by the spectators.

2. The embalmers who placed the spices in the cavity. The spices were myrrh, cinnamon, spikenard, and many others. The body was then covered with myrrh and Arabic gum which kept the wrappings in place. After the wrappings were put in place they were covered with perfumes. The body was then returned to the family where it was put into an open chest and was ultimately put into a sepulcher if the person

was deemed worthy. The body was kept, many times, in the home of the deceased in a closed casket for many years. When a man borrowed money his father's body was taken as collateral; if the son failed to redeem the body he was not allowed to be buried when he died.

3. The third group was in charge of the ceremonies which took place before the burial.

The Egyptians believed in a trial after death in which the person was judged by the way he had lived, according to the testimony of the public.

Rollin explains it thus: "It was a consolation among the heathens, to a dying man, to leave a good name behind him, imagining that this is the only human blessing of which death cannot deprive us. But the Egyptians would not suffer praises to be bestowed indiscriminately on all deceased persons. This honour was to be obtained only from the public voice. The assembly of the judges met on the other side of a lake, which they crossed in a boat. He who sat at the helm was called Charon, in the Egyptian language...As soon as a man was dead, he was brought to his trial. The public accuser was heard. If he proved that the deceased had led a bad life, his memory was condemned, and he was deprived of burial. The people admired the power of the laws, which extended even beyond the grave; and every one, struck with the disgrace inflicted on the dead person, was afraid to reflect dishonour on his own memory, and his family. But if the deceased person was not convicted of any crime, he was interred in an honorable manner

"A still more astonishing circumstance in this public inquest upon the dead, was, that the throne itself was no protection from it. Kings were spared during their lives, because

the public peace was concerned in this forbearance; but their quality did not exempt them from the judgment passed upon the dead, and even some of them were deprived of sepulture. This custom was imitated by the Israelites. We see in Scripture, that bad kings were not interred in the monuments of their ancestors. This practice suggested to princes, that if their majesty placed them out of the reach of men's judgment while they were alive, they would at last be liable to it, when death should [reduce them to the level of others]." (Rollin, *Ancient History*, Vols. I-IV), p. 119.

After the time of embalming, 40 days in this case, (Genesis 50:3), and the 70 days of mourning, Joseph spoke to the Pharaoh and asked permission to return the remains of his father to his home in Canaan for burial among his relatives, and permission was given.

Pharaoh also sent up a 'great company' of people and chariots, (50:9), as well as all of Joseph's brothers and their families, except the small children. They approached Canaan from the east side of Jordan, (the same route Israel would take 400 plus years later to approach the Promised Land, (Edersheim), p. 187, and together, the whole company mourned Jacob for another seven days.

The entourage accompanying Joseph and his brothers was so great and so impressive that the Canaanites were overwhelmed by seeing their mourning, (50:11), and called the place Abel-mizraim, the 'meadow of the Egyptians' or 'the mourning of the Egyptians'. *Mizraim* referring to their ancestor who founded Egypt.

Joseph and his brothers then continued on to Macpelah with the body of their father and buried him in the cave which Abraham had bought many centuries before.

They then collected the rest of the company and returned to Egypt.

After the death of their father, the brothers were afraid, and feared that Joseph would avenge himself at that time for all they had done to him. They asked Joseph to forgive them because it was their father's wish. But Joseph was so shocked at their accusation that he wept, (Genesis 50:17), and again assured them that he would continue to care for them.

Joseph said, *Fear not: for am I in the place of God? But as for you, ye thought evil against me; but God meant it for good....* (Genesis 19,20a). He would not stand in judgment against his brothers, that was God's job, and though it had been a very difficult situation in which they had placed him, God still used it to bring about their salvation through all of it.

Death of Joseph (Genesis 50:26)

So Joseph died, being a hundred and ten years old; and they embalmed him, and he was put in a coffin in Egypt, (Genesis 50:26).

Joseph had reached the age of 110; he was 17 when he was sold as a slave; for 10 years he was a slave in Egypt; for three years he was a prisoner and for 80 years he was the ruler in Egypt. Genesis 50:23 says he lived to see his great-grand-children.

He asked his brothers to promise him that when they left Egypt they would carry his bones with them and bury him in the Promised Land, and they gave their word. He knew where home was and never became reconciled to being at home in Egypt. But he also knew God would return them to the land He had promised to Abraham and he wanted to be a part of that land, even in death (50:24).

He was embalmed and mourned and placed in a coffin in Egypt. Because of his character and position, the Egyptians would have mourned him for at least 70 days as they did his father. Only the Pharaoh was mourned more than 70 days, usually 72. But the significance is that no matter how important a person may be, nor how he might be viewed by himself or others, all die.

When the Israelites left Egypt, (Exodus 13:19; Joshua 24:32), Moses took the bones of Joseph with them and he was buried in Shechem, which was part of Joseph's inheritance and became the inheritance of his sons.

Exodus 1:6 says, after the listing of Jacob's sons who entered Egypt, that Joseph died and all his brethren of the same generation, as well as all the Egyptians of the same generation.

During the years the Israelites were in Egypt they became a great multitude numerically. The time period of their stay in Egypt is much discussed because of the references given in Genesis 15:13,14; Exodus 12:40,41; and Galatians 3:17. Mr. Peloubet gives an interesting explanation of the years of the bondage which are also in accord with Zodhiates' note on Galatians 3:17:

"In Genesis 15:13,14, Exodus 12:40,41, and Galatians 3:17, the duration of the bondage is given as 430 years. The common chronology, as we have seen, makes it extend from the call of Abraham to the Exodus, one-half of it, or 215 years, being spent in Egypt, and the other half in the wanderings of Abraham, Isaac, and Jacob, as pilgrims and strangers. The others think that the whole 430 were spent in Egypt, and none of it belongs to the previous wanderings of the patriarchs. St. Paul says in Gal. 3:17, that from the covenant (or call of) with Abraham to the giving of the Law (less than a year after the Exodus) was 430 years. But in Gen. 15:13,14, it is said that they should be strangers in a strange land, and be afflicted 400 years, and nearly the same is said in Ex. 12:40. But, in very truth, the children of Israel were strangers in a strange land from the time that Abraham left his home for the promised land, and during the whole period of 430 years to the Exodus they were nowhere rulers in the land. So in Ex. 12:40, it is said that the sojourning of the children of Israel, who dwelt in Egypt, was 430 years. But it does not say that the sojourning was all in Egypt, but this people who lived in Egypt had been sojourners for 430 years." (Peloubet, 1887), p. 126.

There is, however, another view, which has more credence in the Scriptures: Acts 7:34; Genesis 15:13,14.

In Acts 7:34, Steven is recounting the history of Israel to the high priest and quotes the Lord as saying, *I have seen, I have seen the affliction of my people which is in Egypt, and I have heard their groaning....*

Here, the affliction of the people is referred to and 'their groaning' which would be the result of the affliction. In Canaan they had been accepted as a peace-loving people whom God blessed, but they were not afflicted there by any of the tribes around them. When they had difficulties they were of their own making; (e.g. Abraham and Isaac with the kings of Gerar; Jacob and Shechem, etc.).

In Genesis 15:13,14, God spoke to Abraham saying, *...know of a surety that thy seed shall be a stranger in a land that is not theirs, and shall serve them; and they shall afflict them 400 years. And also that nation, whom they shall serve, will I judge, and afterward shall they come out with great substance.*

Not only would his seed be strangers in a land that was not theirs, but they were to serve those of that land and would be afflicted or dealt with hardly by them. That did not happen when they were in Canaan, but did occur in Egypt. God also said the people would return in the fourth generation. Taking only 100 years as a generation, they would be at least 400 years in bondage.

Also, Genesis 15:14 says God would judge that nation which afflicted them and that the Israelites would 'come out' of it with great substance. This was exactly what happened. Israel left Egypt with great herds and flocks; with many servants, and with the jewels of silver and gold and raiment of the Egyptians, (Exodus 12:35).

The number of people who left Egypt could not have been born in less than 430 years.

After Joseph died and the people had multiplied 'abundantly', (Exodus 1:7), they were looked upon as a threat to Egypt.

THE BEGINNING OF OPRESSION

Now there arose up a new king over Egypt, which knew not Joseph, (Exodus 1:8).

This was not just a new king, but a new dynasty of kings, under whom Joseph had never served.

God had carried out His plan through the wicked devices of men, but He knew the end from the beginning. Here again we see the crooked line of man's actions being guided by the Providence of an all-knowing God.

When a king arose *who knew not Joseph,* the Israelites had multiplied and become a formidable group with which to deal, (Exodus 1:9). Here the name "the children of Israel" is attached to the nation, not just to the sons of Jacob, by an Eastern potentate. He recognized this group to be a nation.

The Hyksos kings of the 12th Dynasty would have been those under whom Joseph ruled. They were Senusert II (Sesotris, 1894-1878); Senusert III (Sesotris (1878-1840). Joseph died during the reign of Amenemhet III (1841-1797).

The Hyksos were never in control of the whole of Egypt and their capital was in the north at Avaris, called Zoan in the Hebrew, and Tanit in the Septuagint version. It was north of Goshen on the Tanitic branch of the

Nile. They used the Israelites as laborers to build the city of Raamses which replaced Avaris. They also seem to have built Pithom. This was the first heavy oppression placed on the Israelites and the Hyksos hoped to keep them under control and from uniting with the native Egyptians by taking this measure. However, they continued to multiply at an alarming rate and the Hyksos were afraid they would be overwhelmed by them.

Prisoners of War Making and Carrying Brick

Ploubet 1913

It is possible that they were also working on storage buildings and the Prince's Wall which ran from the Mediterranean to the Red Sea. They did not work on the Pyramids because they were already constructed by this period.

The land of Goshen was just west of Pithom and Raamses. (Pi-Ramses: Meri Amun "The House of Ramses the Beloved of the god Amun"; Pithom: Pi-Tum, "House of the god Tum".) Both places were connected with the pagan religion of Egypt which the Hyksos had adopted as their own.

New Oppression (Exodus 1:15-22)

The Egyptians succeeded in getting rid of the Hyksos in the north and had established the 18th Dynasty. The first king of this period (Ahmose), issued the order to kill all the newborn males in order to keep the population growth under control. By this time the Israelites were becoming an extremely large group and even the native Egyptians were afraid they might rise up against them and try to take over the country.

The Israelites were not bondslaves, but were forced labor. They were allowed to retain their houses, and they continued to work the land and have their own flocks.

Thutmosis I issued the order to have all the Hebrew male babies thrown into the Nile. He was afraid of the Israelites because he was often gone on warring expeditions to gain more territory for Egypt and took most of the army with him. He could foresee the possibility of the Israelites trying to lead a revolt while he was gone.

The daughter of Thutmosis I, Hatshepsut, is believed to be the princess who adopted Moses and raised him in the palace of her father who had issued the decree. She was a strong woman who took the throne from her (half) brother/husband Thutmosis II. When he died she allowed her next half-brother to become her husband, (Thutmosis III), but he was only ten years old at the time and she was the ruler of the kingdom. When she died twenty-two years later he had all of her monuments and temples defaced, removing all evidence of her. He became one of the greatest rulers of Egypt. Leon Wood, *A Survey of Israel's History,* (Grand Rapids, Zondervan Publishing House, 1970), pp. 114-119.

What was the spiritual cause which led Israel to accept slavery? They were a large nation, evidently larger than the ruling party, and could have prevented their own enslavement. But they seem to have accepted it without a word. A nation cannot be enslaved without its consent, whether tacit or overt. It has been said of China's fall to Communism, "It was not that Mao was so strong, it was that the people were so weak." The same situation is seen here with Israel. Why were they so weak? According to Exodus 12:40, they were in Egypt 430 years; almost 400 years of which had been lived in bondage as God had foretold in Genesis 15:13 to Abraham.

A dependent character will always lend itself to slavery - to being controlled by an outside force. The history of the Israelites was worth knowing, but they evidently had little knowledge of it. God had chosen an insignificant family from an insignificant area and had given them the promise of a great nation being formed from them.

They knew about Jehovah, but they had no personal experience with Him. A head knowledge is not sufficient for an individual or nation to arm itself against its enemies. When Moses led them out of Egypt they were still a passive, dependent nation which blamed everyone else for their problems and demanded to be fed and watered. They would not govern themselves so they looked for someone to be their governor.

When an individual or a nation is not taught, or forgets, its own history; where he comes from, what his Gospel purpose is, and what God's plan is for him, then he loses sight of the ultimate goal of his life. In the United States of America many have never known or have forgotten our history. What is our Gospel purpose as a nation? as individuals? Until we determine where we came from and why, we will continue in our downward trend toward slavery, be it intellectual, spiritual, or physical. The more we live in a welfare society of big government, the more enslaved we will become.

To forget our past is to invite anarchy into our future. We need to be vigilant that the same thing that happened to Israel does not happen to us. It can only be avoided as we see that wonderful golden thread that weaves through the actions of men to accomplish God's purpose in our nation and in our individual lives, and are willing to take our place in God's plan individually and nationally.

God used the time in Egypt to teach His people about His care and provision. They should have learned to rely on God and trust Him for all things, but they obviously did not - as seen in the period of the Exodus.

The Years in Bondage - 430 years, (Exodus 12:40)

Israel did not have a national history until they departed from Egypt, c. 1445 B.C.

They were on the border between Egypt and Palestine (in the land of Goshen), and were in a position to aid the invaders if they chose, but they chose to live under the Egyptian oppression because God was teaching them some very important lessons, though they were not aware of this at the time.

By their location they were more isolated and were kept from most of the Egyptian idolatry.

They were united by their isolation into a cohesive nation, and they were forced to look to God because of this isolation.

They were taught the practical arts of weaving, metallurgy, carpentry, pot-making, writing on papyrus and clay tablets, etc., which would be used later in their pilgrimage.

Their simple life-style prepared them to leave Egypt and its luxuries.

They had progressed from a nomadic life to a more agricultural one.

Most importantly, they were to be an example to the world that God could deliver them as a nation.

As before stated when Israel left Egypt, it left with a slave-character. It was dependent, non-reasoning, and in need of a ruler. When the character of a people becomes dependent, they must have a ruler, because they are unable to rule themselves. Moses was not the type of leader to allow them to continue in this servant mode. God had spoken to him and impressed upon him the need for an independent people who would form a strong, godly nation designed to give testimony to the surrounding nations of the power and plan of God for them as a peculiar people. They were not to remain in their oppressed condition.

God granted them a margin of liberty never before heard of in the ancient world. They were not governed by another man; they were governed by God - the God, Jehovah.

When the monarchy began under Saul, it was because Israel had rejected God's government and had chosen to follow the governments of the nations surrounding them. As God said to Samuel, *they have not rejected you; they have rejected Me,* (1 Samuel 8:7).

MOSES

The birth of Israel's deliverer, (Exodus 2:1-10).

Moses' parents were both from the tribe of Levi. They were Amram ('people of the most high') and Jochebed ('the glory of Jehovah'). They kept the boy baby against the command of Pharaoh to kill all the baby boys born. Their fear of the Israelites was so great that the Egyptians were willing to allow only girl babies to live so they would not be able to raise an army of men who could destroy the nation. They didn't seem to realize that after a short time without men they would not have workers for their construction.

God miraculously preserved baby Moses by using the daughter of Pharaoh as His instrument. For forty years he grew up in the luxury and depravity of the court of an Oriental despot. He was educated and privileged, (Acts 7:22, *And Moses was learned in all the wisdom of the Egyptians, and was mighty in words and deeds)*, but he was not content. Because of the importance and character of his adoptive mother, he was educated in their schools and universities (probably the one at Memphis) in the practical sciences and arts:

math, astronomy, music, painting, archery, medicine, history, law, poetry, etc.

He would also have been trained as a military man and all this knowledge was part of God's formal training to become a leader. Living in the court he would have learned the proper protocol connected with people of importance and the rules and regulations which controlled the governing of a great nation.

While his mother cared for him, as an agent of the princess, she no doubt impressed upon him his importance to his own nation, and those lessons were never forgotten. She taught him love, honesty, and compassion. In learning about the plan of God for his nation he knew they were not to remain slaves indefinitely. She taught him the importance of the God of Israel and about their history concerning Abraham, Isaac, and Jacob. He also learned to work with his hands so he knew how to apply the practical sciences he was to learn in Pharaoh's court. He learned about the social virtues of his family; about getting along within the confines of a family unit. The lessons learned at the mother's knee are written in stone in the heart of the child - never to be forgotten.

The princess gave him his Egyptian name, Moses, which was a common Egyptian name, meaning 'drawn out' or 'drawn out of the water'.

At forty years of age Moses killed an Egyptian slave-handler and was forced to escape for his life. This slaying was the result of a decision he had taken much earlier to be counted with the people of God. Even his princess-mother could not save him from the wrath of the Pharaoh. God led him into the desert where a place was already prepared for him. While there he married the daughter of a Kenite priest from northwest Arabia in the land of Midian, (one of the sons of Abraham by Keturah). The Kenites belonged to the coppersmiths of the area because the mountain ranges east of the Gulf of Aqabah in which they lived, were rich in copper deposits.

The name of the priest was Reuel, ('the friend of God'), from which is understood that he was a worshiper of the true God. When Moses arrived in Midian, his father-in-law already had seven daughters who were tending his flocks of sheep and goats. Besides this, he doubtless also had a number of sons. Forty years later when Moses left Midian, his father-in-law would have been a very old man and very possibly would have already died.

In Exodus 4:18, the name Jethro is used for that of his father-in-law, but most likely refers to Reuel's son who had taken his place as priest by this time The Hebrew word used for father-in-law is the same as that used for brother-in-law or for any one related by marriage, (Genesis 34:9; Deuteronomy 7:3; Joshua 23:12). In Judges 4:11 the reference is to the children of Hobab, the relative by marriage of Moses, and does not refer to Reuel, but to some of his descendants. The time period would have been too great to be either the son of Reuel or his son's son because the time of the judges lasted for 450 years, (Acts 13:20). Adam Clarke, *A Commentary and Critical Notes.* (New York: Abingdon Cokesbury Press, an undated old copy), p. 306.

Reuel is the same name as one of the sons of Esau, and possibly one of his descendants through marriage to a Midianite. Moses' wife's name was Zipporah. She was called an Ethiopian woman (a Cushite) in Numbers 12:1.

There are several possibilities for this word usage of 'an Ethiopian woman'. The area of Arabia from which the Midianites came was often referred to as 'Cush' because of the sons of Cush who had settled there.

(1) She may have been darker in color than the Israelites and was therefore referred to as an 'Ethiopian' as a way to defame her family connections.

(2) Though there is little to suggest the possibility, she may have been Moses' second wife and therefore not a descendant from Midian, but was from Ethiopia in Africa.

(3) Or the term 'an Ethiopian woman' was used in a derogatory way to insult both Moses and his wife. The circumstances surrounding the incident in Numbers may lend more credence to this explanation than the others.

Moses and his wife had been separated for some time when her relative returned her and her sons to Moses in Exodus 18. Jealousy could have been a motive because of her influence on Moses. Miriam and Aaron wanted to be the motivating influence on him and would have resented the presence of his wife at this particular time. They were trying to usurp the leadership God had given to Moses over the nation, and were angry enough to be very petty in reference to both Moses and his wife. God's judgment on them is enough to back up this conclusion.

There is no way of determining for certain, but it seems unlikely Moses would have taken a wife from the line of Ham, since he knew the importance of the Israelite nation in God's plan. The fact that she lived in an Arabian area would indicate she was Arabian by birth, and not from Cush, the son of Ham who formed the Ethiopian nation.

Moses' Preparation (Exodus 2:11-3)

For forty years Moses lived and worked in the desert area of Midian, learning from his father-in-law and from God.

He became a shepherd; a position he had learned to look down upon in Pharaoh's house. But God knew the future and Moses needed firsthand knowledge of the life of a wandering people in order to lead God's people out of Egypt. As a shepherd he learned the ways of the desert; he became stronger physically from the hardships experienced; he had quiet times to think about the lessons from his early childhood and about God; he learned patience, and he became acquainted with the desert through which he was to lead the people.

There is no mention as to whether he had any personal experience with God before the burning-bush episode, but he knew God's voice when He called to him out of the bush, so he had some knowledge of God's workings with men, (which he had learned in his first home).

When God spoke to Moses out of the burning bush He revealed His purpose for both Moses and the nation. In Exodus 3:2 reference is made to the 'angel of the Lord', but the reference word means *Jehovah* and refers to Jesus in the Old Testament, referred to in Malachi 3:1 as the 'Messenger of the covenant'.

Many times in the Scripture fire is associated with God:
- the burning bush,
- the pillar of fire by which He led Israel,
- His appearance on Sinai in clouds and fire (lightnings), (Deuteronomy 4:11,12, 24,33, 36; 5:4; 9:3,10,15),
- the fire of incense in the Tabernacle, (Exodus 30:7; Numbers 3:4),
- the fire of sacrifice and offering, (Exodus 29:41),
- the devouring fire of God, (Exodus 24:17; Leviticus 9:24; 10:2; Numbers 11:1-3), etc.

The association of fire with our Holy God was noted by the pagan nations which adopted fire as an element in their religious ceremonies. This can be observed especially in the Zoroastrian religion; that of the Roman Catholic system, and in the pagan indigenous religions in almost all nations of the world.

God's purpose for Moses was now revealed and Moses' responsibility was made clear. His brothers were still in bondage in Egypt, and God had chosen him to lead them out of Egypt into the land He had promised their ancestors. Moses didn't fully understand God's promise to him. He said in Exodus 3:8, *And I am come down to deliver them out of the hand of the Egyptians, and to bring them up out of that land unto a good land and a large....* God said "I" will deliver them, not you, all you have to do is be an instrument in my hands. It is not your work, it is mine.

How often today do we labor hours on end, neglecting our families and our health, trying to do "God's work" when the work is not ours at all, but His. We do not seem to understand the primary command of God to us is to be faithful. If we are faithful, He will see that His work is accomplished. Our families will not suffer, nor will we 'burn out for God' by ruining our health doing something He never required nor expected us to do. We as Christians need to learn the lesson of Noah. Though he preached 120 years, only his family was saved in the ark. Was he a failure? The destiny of our families should be our primary concern - are we being faithful?

Moses did not feel equipped for the job God had chosen for him. God knew Moses before he was born; He knew his weaknesses and his strengths. Many times our unwilling spirit keeps us from being used by God to accomplish great things.

In today's modern psychological babble it would be said, Moses lacked 'self-esteem'. What he really lacked was an understanding of the power of God to carry out His purpose for His people. Unless we learn to understand 'Christ-esteem' we will never be effective for Him, and will continue to follow the pagan philosophy of the world which offers us an 'out' for all our problems because of our low 'self-esteem'. Each individual must take responsibility for his own actions, and stop blaming someone else for his lack of faith in an

All-knowing God. Paul says in 2 Corinthians 12:10 ...*for when I am weak, then am I strong.* In Christ our weakness is made strong because we rely upon Him and not upon ourselves.

God sent Moses to Pharaoh with the assurance that I AM THAT I AM had sent him. Since Moses was unwilling to trust God completely, God sent Moses' brother Aaron to be the spokesman for him. Moses was correct in saying the people would not believe him nor believe he had been sent by God. He was returning to a people who had been 400 years in servitude, who knew little about the true God, and who knew less about Moses, the messenger sent to them. God empowered Moses to do the things He required of him. ("God's biddings, are God's enablings.")

God told Moses He would harden Pharaoh's heart, (Exodus 4:21), but Moses was not to be discouraged because of this as God would use it to show His power in Egypt. To 'harden' is the word *châzaq* which has several different meanings:

- to make hard or insensible,
- to make heavy, unimpressionable,
- to make firm or stiff, immovable.

Gesenius translates the world to be *obstinate,* Edersheim says *hardened in heart,* (Edersheim, *Bible History*), p. 59. Ten times Pharaoh hardened his own heart; ten times God hardened his heart.

God knew that at this point Moses would lack the faith to carry out His instructions and had therefore already sent Aaron to meet him in the wilderness, (Exodus 4:27). Aaron seems to have had a relationship with God, because he knew when he was spoken to and by Whom, and followed God's instructions to him. He was evidently a man of influence in the nation and was able to gather the elders of the people (the governing council) together to tell them what God had said to Moses. After hearing of God's coming deliverance they "bowed their heads and worshipped", (Exodus 4:31). They still had a knowledge of God and believed in the hope of their deliverance.

In Exodus 4:24-26 there is a verse which continues to be problematic. When Moses left Midian and began his journey to Egypt with his wife and sons, verse 24 says, *And it came to pass by the way in the inn, that the Lord met him, and sought (threatened) to kill him.* (An inn as we understand the word did not exist in those days nor in that area. Travelers tried to stop at a well, or an oasis area where they could refill their water containers and allow their animals to eat the little pasture available. It is easier to follow the events which took place there with the knowledge that they were not enclosed within four walls, but were out in the open.)

Though some writers believe this verse refers to Moses, Clarke gives a more Biblically reasoned view. He says the verse in Genesis 17:14 is key to understanding the full message here. For some reason (probably due to his wife's displeasure), the firstborn son of Moses had not been circumcised and was not included in the Covenant people, circumcision being the outward sign of being part of the covenant. As they began their journey God sought to kill, not Moses, but his uncircumcised son, whose 'soul was to be cut off from his people'. In verse 23 Moses was plainly told that God was going to kill his firstborn son; this was not only a message to Pharaoh but also to Moses; obey or die. The son could not serve God until he was part of the congregation, which required circumcision.

In order to save his life, Moses' wife, Zipporah, took a flint knife, (Joshua 5:2) and circumcised Gershom. She threw the flesh at someone and it 'touched' his feet. Clarke believes the person referred to here is Jehovah and that she was saying to Him, 'I, as well as my son, by this act, do enter into the covenant relationship with You.' Because of the blood shed she admitted to having been joined to Jehovah. But she was so affected by the close-call that she took her children and returned to her home in Midian and did not join the Israelites until Exodus 18. However, verse 2 of Genesis 18, plainly says Moses had sent her back to her home. They were both evidently affected by this event and mutually agreed she should return home to Midian until the Israelites had left Egypt so nothing further would threaten the welfare of the children. (Clarke, *Commentary*, Vol. I), p. 313.

Israel's political government at the time had already been instituted. God had given laws of governing to the early patriarchs and heads (princes) of the 12 clans or tribes from each of the 12 original sons of Jacob, (except Levi and Joseph whose places were taken by the two sons of Joseph, Ephraim and Manasseh). They formed the heads of government called 'rulers of the congregation, (Exodus 34:31; Numbers 7:2, etc.). They were an hereditary aristocracy and together with the two classes of elected officials, the elders and the officers (or scribes), were the representatives of the congregation.

Scribes and elders were already in existence at the time God called Moses to deliver the Israelites. Aaron called all the elders together in Exodus 4:29 to tell them what God had said to Moses. In Numbers 10:4 the princes were called together by blowing one silver trumpet, and when two trumpets were blown the whole assembly was to meet at the door of the Tabernacle.

In Exodus 18:13-27, Jethro, Moses' relative, told Moses in verse 14 that he needed to choose judges from the people so he wouldn't have to do all the judging himself. Israel already had a representative body with two divisions; princes and elders. At that time Moses instituted the judicial arm of Israel's government with men who were 'able, feared God, were truthful, and unselfish' and who were

then placed over the people, (verse 21). Only the most difficult cases were taken to Moses, all others were judged by the lesser judges.

Religion in Israel at the time of the Exodus

Israel, from its inception was surrounded by idolatrous peoples who worshipped all kinds of pagan gods.

Historical records tell of the early religion of Egypt and indicate that it was a monotheistic religion. All nations took with them the idea of and a belief in the true God when they were scattered from Babel. For many nations those beliefs continued for many centuries. Some drifted away from the truth and became idolaters; others retained the knowledge of the Truth and acted upon it; others mixed it with their own particular brand of paganism and became totally corrupt. The later Egyptians fit into the latter nations.

In Egypt the Israelites were influenced by the paganism with which they lived daily. They believed in the true God, Jehovah, but also wanted to incorporate some of the pagan beliefs from Egypt as demonstrated by the golden calf.

As before stated, from the death of Jacob to the calling of Moses, (at least 350 years), God did not communicate directly with any individual.

The Israelites had depended on the knowledge which came from their forefathers as to the existence of a supreme God who was to make of them a great nation. They had no personal knowledge of that God and no written records to consult about Him.

All teaching and knowledge was passed from father to son and both father and mother were responsible for the religious training of the children.

Evidently, some had been faithful in that teaching responsibility because Moses' parents had taught him and his siblings the important promises given to their nation by Jehovah.

Exodus 2:23 points out that the children of Israel collectively cried out for relief from their bondage and God heard them. But it does not say they cried out 'to God', only that He heard them when they cried. It is possible their cry was to God and is supposed to be understood by the text.

In Exodus 2:24, God 'remembered' His covenant with them. That is not to say He had forgotten it, because God cannot forget in the same sense humans can. The time of their refining and training was almost over and God was going to remind them of His covenant with them as a nation. From the beginning of their journey God calls them a 'stiff-necked' people (32:9) , whom He would have destroyed had it not been for Moses' intercession for them. They believed <u>in</u> God, but they didn't believe <u>God</u>.

The Sabbath was still observed among them, as seen in Exodus 16:5. God gave them instructions concerning the gathering of the manna so they would gather twice as much the 6th day in preparation for the Sabbath. The word is first mentioned in verse 23 as 'the rest of the holy Sabbath' which had been observed since the time of creation when God 'rested' from His labor. Some nations continued to observe the Sabbath after the Flood, even some pagan nations at times, but it was mostly kept only by those from the line of Eber.

Sacrifices were also offered by the Israelites as demonstrated by Exodus 3:18; 5:3. When Moses and Aaron asked Pharaoh to allow them to take the people and go into the desert to offer sacrifices to God, Pharaoh knew this to be one of their customs and though not surprised by the request, he still refused to allow them to go. Since the sin of Adam those who had a knowledge of God continued to offer sacrifices for themselves and for their families.

They knew about all these truths: the knowledge of God's promise to their nation; the responsibility of the parents to teach the children; keeping the Sabbath; offering of sacrifices, etc., but not all of them chose to observe the truths. Every man must make his own choices regardless of those of his ancestors, for good or for bad, because each individual is responsible for his own actions before God.

Moses before Pharaoh (Exodus 5-12)

This Pharaoh was Amenhotep II, son of Thotmosis III, who was not a timid man. He had made many successful military campaigns before this time and was a true successor of his famous father.

When Moses arrived in Egypt he was 80 years old and Aaron was 83. They began their appeal to Pharaoh and their demonstration of God's power with the first sign God had instructed them to use, that of the rod turned into a serpent, (Exodus 7:10).

When Pharaoh called his magicians in they were also able to turn their rods into serpents. There are two words used here for serpents; one is *tannîyn* and the other is *nâchâsh*. The first has the meaning of an actual serpent or even of a dragon or large sea creature; the second indicates the hissing of a serpent and a magic spell. If the magicians brought real serpents into the chamber hidden under their garments they were able to cause them to become stiff like rods by using a magic spell much as is used today in charming snakes in the Middle East.

Whatever the case may have been, Moses' rod swallowed up the magician's rods and God's power was manifest, but Pharaoh refused to listen.

In Exodus 8:25 Pharaoh said 'sacrifice here to your God and don't leave'. But Moses said, (8:26), *It is not meet so to do; for we shall sacrifice the abomination of the Egyp-*

tians to the Lord our God: lo, shall we sacrifice the abominations of the Egyptians before their eyes, and will they not stone us?

Meaning, the animals we use to sacrifice to our God are those which are sacred to the Egyptians, and if we try to sacrifice them here in Egypt the people will kill us.

The Ten Plagues sent by God (Exodus 7-12)

The second sign was the first plague sent by God, turning the water to blood, (7:15-25). This plague was against the worship of the Nile, the river god. The plague took place when the Nile was at its highest flood stage and all could see the result of all the water becoming blood. The fish in the river died and this was against their fish-god.

Moses foretold the day it was to take place and it happened on that day. The magicians were able to duplicate the miracle, but they could not take it away as it lasted for seven days, (Exodus 7:25), and Pharaoh refused again to listen.

The second plague was a multitude of frogs on the land, (Exodus 8:1-15). It was against the worship of frogs at Hecka where the god was symbolized by a frog, and represented Osiris. At the time of flooding frogs were hatched and were always present, but never in the numbers seen with the plague. The magicians were also able to duplicate this miracle, but again could not get rid of them, (8:8). Pharaoh said they could leave, but then changed his mind, (8:15).

A specific time was given to take away the frogs and they were taken away as Moses had stated.

The fourth sign and the third plague was 'lice' on the land, (Exodus 8:16-19). The word here is *kinnan* which means some type of insect which could be lice, or gnats, or mosquitoes, etc. Whatever it was it caused the people

to suffer terribly. Gesenius translates the word 'gnat'; a biting gnat which was present in the marshy areas along the Nile and which would have been a great nuisance, even more than the lice, if it had covered the land.

The magicians tried to duplicate this miracle, but were unable to do so, (Exodus 8:18). They acknowledged that the plague had to be 'the finger of God'. The sacred beasts were affected, and it was to show God's power over nature. Pharaoh's heart was hardened and he refused to allow them to leave.

Up until this point the Israelites had been afflicted along with the Egyptians, though not to the same extent because they were farther from the Nile, but from this point on only the Egyptians would suffer from the plagues.

The fourth plague was flies, (Exodus 8:20-32). This meant "divers sort of flies among them, which devoured them", (Psalm 78:45). They included many different kinds of flying insects: bees, wasps, hornets, dog flies, etc., all of which bring great misery with their sting. Israel was not affected, only Egypt and their sacred beasts. Pharaoh said they could leave and sacrifice to their God, but then refused, (Exodus 8:28,32). Pharaoh hardened his heart. This was against their god Baalzebub the god of flies or flying insects.

The fifth plague was a disease of the cattle, (Exodus 9:1-7). This was against the worship of their holy beasts. The sacred bull, Apis of Memphis, would have been affected as well as all others. Though to them he was a god, he was unable to protect himself from the flies.

The ram represented their god Apollo (Jove); the goat represented their god Bacchus, the heifer represented their god Juno and the bull was their god Apis. Because of their extreme superstition they also believed in reincarnation (transmigration of the soul) and feared they might kill a relative or friend if an animal was killed. All cattle were affected.

Clarke's description of the murrain is, "The murrain is a very contagious disease among cattle, the symptoms of which are a hanging down and swelling of the head, abundance of gum in the eyes, rattling in the throat, difficulty of breathing, palpitation of the heart, staggering, a hot breath, and a shining tongue; which symptoms prove that a general inflammation has taken place." (Clarke, *Commentary*, Vol. I), p. 333. The disease was usually fatal.

'All the cattle of Egypt died', (Exodus 9:6). All the cattle that died was owned by the Egyptians, none died which belonged to the Israelites.

The sixth plague was an outbreak of boils, (Exodus 9:8-12). This was to show God's power over the physical body of both men and beasts. God hardened Pharaoh's heart. After the sixth plague there is no more mention of the magicians. They, also, would have suffered from the boils and would not be in the mood to play any more games with a God who could control everything. This was against their healing god, Isis.

In Deuteronomy 28:27, is this warning, *The Lord will smite thee with the botch of Egypt,....* This would have been very well known to the Israelites because they had seen its effect in Egypt.

The seventh plague was hail, (rain, thunder and lightning), (Exodus 9:13-35). This was the time of the barley and flax harvest and those grain crops were destroyed, showing God's power over nature. The source of their food and clothing was destroyed. And Pharaoh hardened his heart, (9:34). Water, (the Nile), earth, (Mother-earth), and air, (the Spirit), were all objects of Egyptian idolatry, and one by one, God used all of them against Egypt to show them all was under the control of Jehovah.

The eighth plague was locusts, (Exodus 10:1-20). This was the time of the wheat and rye harvest which matured later than the barley. What the hail had left the locusts destroyed. All their crops were destroyed which meant no food for livestock or men was left. Pharaoh said they could go, but only the men could go, and the Lord hardened Pharaoh's heart, (10:20).

Locust comes from the Hebrew word *arbeh* meaning 'numerous or multiplied insects; crickets, grasshoppers, locusts, etc'. They covered the earth to a depth of six to eight inches and nothing escaped them.

The ninth plague was darkness on the land of Egypt, (Exodus 10:21-29). This was a loss of confidence in the sun god Ra and showed them again that God controls everything. Pharaoh said the people could go, but not their livestock, (10:24). God hardened his heart, (10:27).

It was a darkness that lasted three days and destroyed their confidence in Typhon, their god of darkness, and their worship of the heavenly bodies which could not give them light. Only Israel had light.

The tenth plague was the most terrible of all, the death of the firstborn, (Exodus 12:29-33). Life and death are in God's hands; man can choose to obey or disobey, but must suffer the consequences of his choice.

God hardened Pharaoh's heart and left him to his own obstinacy without trying to change him anymore.

The death of the firstborn was in retribution for slaying the Israelite babies.

The plagues lasted for a period of 6-10 months.

The reasons for sending the plagues were:

- to demonstrate how God would work through Moses as Israel's leader;

- to show Pharaoh and Egypt who Yahweh was and His power, (Exodus 9:16);
- to give Pharaoh time to see the power of God and believe in Him;
- to make a distinction between Israel and Egypt;
- to show the powerlessness of the magicians;
- to attack the symbols of the Egyptian gods;
- as a witness to the nations of God's power and His presence with Israel, (1 Samuel 4:7-9; 6:5,6);
- that Israel might see God's power and trust in Him.

THE PASSOVER

The word for passover is *pâcach, peçach* which means to spare by skipping over, to leap, to pass over, and is only used in reference to the Jewish Passover. James Strong, S.T.D., LL.D., *Strong's Exhaustive Concordance of the Bible*, (Nashville: Royal Publishers, Inc., n.d.)

Instructions were given beforehand so the people would have everything ready at the moment of departure. Since they did not know the exact time, they had to be prepared at any moment.

The 'borrowing' from their Egyptian neighbors was really 'asking a gift' of them and was a common practice in the East. The gifts were their just due because of their servitude under them without wages, (Exodus 11:2,3).

The Passover instituted:

- The lamb was to be of a year, meaning it could be from 8 days to 12 months old.
- A perfect lamb was to be sacrificed, according to the number in the family, or combined with a neighbor, (Exodus 12:3-6), of the same family to the number of a minimum of ten.
- The lamb was to be kept for four days, from the 10th to the 14th to be sure it was well and without 'blemish', (12:3,5,6).

- It was to be killed in the evening, all of them at the same time, at the ninth hour between the going down of the sun and its actual setting.
- The blood was to be put on the two sideposts and the lintel of each door of the house where the sacrifice was to be eaten.
- The meat was to be roasted with fire and no water added.
- It was to be cooked all together (even with the organs intact, but not the intestines), and eaten with bitter herbs, as a reminder of their experience in Egypt.
- None of the meat was to remain until morning; the leftover was to be burned as a sacrifice to God.
- It was to be eaten standing while being ready to leave quickly.
- It was to be eaten 'in haste', as quickly as possible.

When the blood was applied to the door, the Lord Himself, (Exodus 12:12), would pass over the house and spare the firstborn within, but the person had to remain within the house to receive the protection. The Israelites were sinners as well as the Egyptians, but God chose to redeem them by the blood of the Lamb, (Hebrews 9:11-22).

The death of the firstborn, both of men and animals, was to teach a profound lesson to the pagan Egyptians. The death of the firstborn of their sacred animals would teach them that their holy beasts were powerless to help themselves, and powerless to help the people.

The firstborn of the family was the most important and the most valued of the children, but nothing but the blood of the sacrificial Lamb could save him. The innocent slain lamb was the picture of the perfect Lamb who would come to take away the sin of the world. He was innocent of any sin, he was perfect in all His parts, He shed His blood that others might live; He suffered a hideous death as a sacrifice for sin and as we claim the sacrifice for our own we are spared the penalty of sin and separated for a life of service to Him - the Lamb of God. Everything is dependent upon individual choice and what we will do with Jesus Christ.

The Passover was to be a perpetual covenant as a memorial of God's protection over Israel, (Exodus 12:14,24), and lasted until the Passover Lamb was slain. It is now observed in the ceremony of the Lord's Supper.

The observance of the Passover was as follows:

- It was to take place in the first month of the sacred year. According to the Jewish calendar, their sacred year began with this first Passover and the month was called Abib until the captivity, when it became Nisan. It is our last of March, first of April period and this would be the yearly beginning of the Passover.
- The civil year began in the seventh month of the sacred year. It was called Tisri (September-October). They seem to have had two beginnings in their calendar year, a civil and a sacred.
- The Passover was to begin on day ten of the sacred year. On the 14th day the sacrifice was to be made, but another seven days were required, (Exodus 12:15,18), before it was completed, (this went into effect after the first Passover).
- They were to eat unleavened bread for seven days after the sacrifice; seven being the number of the Covenant.
- An holy assembly was to meet on day one and day seven, (12:16); the word was then given to the elders first, (12:21), and then from them to the congregation.
- It was to continue after they left Egypt in order to remind the people of what God had done for them in bringing them out of Egypt, (12:26).

When the final plague was over Pharaoh told the Israelites to get out of his country and to do it quickly. He also asked them to bless him before leaving because the Egyptians believed worse things were coming if the Israelites did not leave their country, (Exodus 12:32,33). (Edersheim, *Bible History*), pp. 78-82; (Peloubet, 1887), pp. 149-152.

THE EXODUS

The number of the Israelites who left Egypt can be determined as follows:

Taking the numbers in Exodus 12:37 and Numbers 1:46, a nation of 2,500,000 to 3,000,000 is certainly within the realm of certainty and there could have been many more.

There were:

- 603,550 men of military age from 20 years and up
- 603,550 women, probably more because not all would marry
- 1,000,000 children and young people under 20, a very conservative number
- 22,000 Levite males from one month old and up, plus the women and girls of the Levites; all together totalling 2,229,100

This is the total just taking the barest numbers.

A great and mighty people left Egypt that night. God had kept His promise to deliver them, now they had to keep their promise to believe Him and trust Him for all things.

And it came to pass at the end of the four hundred and thirty years, even the selfsame day it came to pass, that all the hosts of the Lord went out from the land of Egypt. It is a night to be much observed unto the Lord for bringing them out from the land of Egypt: this is that night of the Lord to be observed of all the children of Israel in their generations. (Exodus 12:42,43.)

The Departure

They departed from the area of Raamses, ancient Tanis, at the northeastern extreme of Goshen on the Nile Delta, (Exodus 12:37), and traveled to the area of Succoth, (Egyptian, Thukoo), to the southeast which is almost to the northern end of the Bitter Lakes (those above the Gulf of Suez).

Consecration of the Firstborn for religious service (Exodus 13:2-16)

The firstborn male was sanctified because God had spared the firstborn of Israel in the 10th plague. If a girl was born first and a male next, he was not sanctified. Later, God set apart the Levites to serve Him instead of the firstborn males and the child was to be 'redeemed'. This meant five shekels were given to the priest in place of the child. An unclean animal's firstborn was redeemed by the sacrifice of a clean animal.

The Journey

(Moses took the bones of Joseph, (Exodus 13:19), and the other heads of tribes evidently took the bones of the sons of Jacob with them, also, (Acts 7:15-16). (Clarke, *Commentary*, Vol. I), p. 366.

From Succoth they traveled to Etham and had to make a decision as to which route to take. From Etham they were led by the cloud and pillar of God's presence.

There were three possible routes for traveling from Egypt to Palestine: (see map)

The Way of the Sea, (Exodus 13:17), which runs along the Mediterranean and is the shortest and easiest route. It also has more water available to travelers but went directly into the heart of the Philistine nation.

The Wall Road, "The Way of Shur", (Genesis 16:7), the central road, through Hebron and Beersheba. This was the 'Prince's

Wall', and was a series of forts constructed to keep out marauders along the eastern Egyptian border. All the forts were manned by guards, soldiers, and companies.

The Red Sea Road, (Exodus 13:18), which crossed "between the two arms of the Red Sea, from the head of the Gulf of Suez to the head of the Gulf of Akabah". (Peloubet, 1887), p. 156. God had chosen this route for Israel because they were not yet ready to confront a warlike nation like the Philistines. This route gave them time to prepare their hearts to trust God and to learn to rely on Him to fight for them.

They traveled along the western side of the Bitter Lakes where they could avoid the Wall, and pastures were available for their flocks. The cloud and the pillar were leading them, (Exodus 14:19), along the route God had prepared for them - nothing had been left to chance.

From this side of the Exodus the logistical nightmare of trying to lead a group of this size is incomprehensible. Not only were the Israelites an enormous number, but included with them was a 'mixed multitude', (Exodus 12:38), as well as all their animals. It is important to remember that these people were not what we would consider 'mature Christians' and were as 'carnal and worldly-minded' as any people who had ever lived.

Pharaoh had hurried them out of the country in a moment of great anxiety, but quickly realized the significance of what he had done; no more cheap labor, no more great flocks from which to supply them with hides and other products, and a great void had been left in the whole country, (Exodus 14:5). By this time he had also realized they were not coming back and were quickly moving out of his control. He set about to correct his error and bring them back.

When he heard they were still within his borders, though several days had already passed, he was ready to take advantage of the situation and prepared to follow them and return them by force. He took 600 chariots besides horsemen and soldiers, (Exodus 14:7,9), a great number by any reckoning.

In Exodus 14:3, God told Moses, *For Pharaoh will say of the children of Israel, They are entangled in the land, the wilderness hath shut them in.* The word 'entangled' is the Hebrew word *bûwk*, which means 'to be entangled or perplexed'. God knew Pharaoh would take advantage of this imagined problem and try to overtake the Israelites.

As word went out to the soldiers guarding the forts, the Israelites were suddenly fugitives instead of emigrants, and their position changed drastically. They were hemmed in by mountains on the west and the south, and by the sea in front of them. Pharaoh would have come down toward them from the north, so they really had no place to go except the sea and there were no boats to take them to the other side.

In their fear (Exodus 14:10), they cried unto the Lord to save them.

They already began to show their carnal state by rising up against Moses, (Exodus 14:11,12), 'We told you this would happen, and here it comes, we'll all be killed by Pharaoh's army, better to have remained as slaves than to have this happen out here in the wilderness'. A dependent, slave character takes a long time to change.

But Moses believed and knew God would deliver them from Pharaoh. *The Lord shall fight for you, and ye shall hold your peace,* (Exodus 14:14). In other words, be quiet and see God work.

God placed the Lord, Himself, (1 Corinthians 10:9), between Egypt and the Israelites. His presence caused darkness to appear on the side the Egyptians were on, and light where the Israelites were crossing the sea, (Exodus 14:20).

The distance across the sea could not have been more than three or four miles because of the time constraints and the number of people moving across it. (Woods, *Survey*), p. 133.

When God brought them out of Egypt He brought them out 'by their armies', (Exodus 12:51), in an ordered procession. They were evidently lined up in groups which could be controlled more easily and in that way were able to cross the sea more quickly.

God could have delivered Israel by opening the waters without the use of Moses or the rod, but He chose to use both so the people would see and know that Moses was God's instrument to lead them.

Many writers seem to believe that the miracle of parting the waters was a purely natural phenomenon brought about by the ebbing of the tide. However, Exodus 14:29 is very explicit in describing the miracle as to the wall of water on their right and on their left. The law of gravity might allow having a wall on their left, but not on their right where the tide would already have gone out. The east wind mentioned in verse 21 would have functioned to dry the passageway between the two walls and allow the people to pass through on dry ground. Though God used the natural effect of the wind to dry the land, at the same time He performed a miracle in piling up the water above and below the passageway.

When Pharaoh's armies thought they would find the great company of Israelites, all they found was darkness. As the fourth watch of the night began (about 4 a.m.), God sent a terrible storm against them as witnessed by the words in Psalm 77:17-20. The thunder, lightning, and pouring rain caused great alarm to the Egyptians. They could finally begin to see that the Israelites had passed through the sea to the other side and as they tried to pursue them, their chariot wheels became bogged down and some were broken off. The large number of chariots and soldiers became so disoriented that in trying to escape the situation they only became more mired down.

In the midst of the storm they recognized that Jehovah was still fighting Israel's battles and the best thing they could do was to escape, but they were too late.

God told Moses to again stretch out his rod over the waters and the waters returned to their natural place, covering and drowning the Egyptians. The Pharaoh

Egyptian Chariot
(Peloubet, 1913)

was not drowned in this incident as before stated; he lived another twenty-two years and his mummy has been found in the Valley of the Kings. (Wood, *Survey*), p. 134. (For more information on this event go to Section III, on the Sons of Ham, Egypt.)

Clarke believes when the bodies of the Egyptian soldiers washed up on the opposite shore, (Exodus 14:30), that the Israelites stripped them of their clothing, their valuables, and especially of their armaments of war. He says there is no other way to account for them having the weapons with which they fought the native tribes during the course of their journey. (Clarke, *Commentary*, Vol. I), p. 372.

Israel was now a nation in number and God was going to take them into their promised homeland if they chose to obey and follow Him.

In Exodus 15:1-21, Moses, and his sister Miriam, sang the song of deliverance with the Israelites. In the song God was praised for His mighty power in delivering them from Egypt. Recognition was given to God alone and thanksgiving followed for His 'glorious' power. Future difficulties were also referred to in reference to the Edomites, the Moabites, and the Canaanites, who upon hearing of God's care for Israel, would 'melt away' because of fear.

The people had seen the hand of the Lord and recognized Him as great Jehovah; they were walking on the mountain tops, but how quickly the valley follows the mountain top.

As Moses led them from the upper arm of the Suez where they had just crossed over, they went out into 'the wilderness of Shur'. It was not a place of total desert, but a place of little water as they traveled three days and found none, (Exodus 15:22).

When they arrived at Marah (bitter) there was water, but not drinkable water, because of the nitre in the ground, (potassium nitrate used for gunpowder), which caused the water to have an acrid, bitter taste.

The people, ever ready to complain, lost no time in going to Moses about the bitter water, (Exodus 15:24). Some scholars feel that the people who made up the 'mixed multitude' which left Egypt with the Israelites, led the people to complain, but the Israelites themselves were a people who already knew well how to gripe and complain as noted in Exodus 5:21. They didn't need an outside source to lead them. Internally, they were the same people who had been willing to be slaves; they had no understanding of a life of freedom in the sure promises of Jehovah God.

Moses asked the Lord what to do and was directed to a tree, which when cast into the waters, made them sweet. God then began to lay down the conditions of His promises to them, (Exodus 15:26):

- hearken to My voice;
- do right;
- listen to My commandments;
- keep My statutes.

If the people would do these things, God would keep them from the sicknesses He had sent on the Egyptians.

By the time they reached Elim they had been traveling for about a month and had traveled into the wilderness of Sin, (Exodus 16:1; Numbers 33:9).

Manna and Quails, and Water (Exodus 16:4-17:7)

After a month of travel, they had pretty well exhausted their food supply and had very little to eat. The desert is not a place where food could be obtained for a group of their number so, naturally, they went to Moses again and said, "What shall we eat?" The question itself was a valid one, but the murmuring was not.

They began again to talk about how much they had left behind in Egypt and how it would have been better to have stayed and died there rather than in this desert. All they had left in Egypt was servitude and three meals a day. What a trade-off. "But slaves are passive. They submit. They obey. And they expect to be fed." (Weaver, *Mainspring*), p. 80.

Because God is merciful, and loved them, He sent manna and quails to feed them. The manna was something unknown to them, and they called it a name meaning, 'what is it'? It was a miracle from God and after it stopped, it was never known of again. That was the reason God told them to put some in the Ark of the Testimony, (Exodus 16:34), so the later people would become acquainted with the food God had provided. God continued to provide their food for forty years, (Joshua 5:12).

The next leg of their journey took them to Rephidim, (Exodus 17:1-7). When there was no water, and the people became so angry they were on the point of stoning Moses, God told him to strike the rock in Horeb. Again God chose to show the people that Moses was acting for Him in his leadership of the people, (1 Corinthians 10:4).

Battle with the Amalekites (Exodus 17:8-16)

The Amalekites were descendants of Esau, (Genesis 36:12). The reference in Genesis 14:7 to the destruction of 'all the country of the Amalekites' would seem to mean that these people existed before Abraham so could not have been the descendants of Esau. But the canon was not written until many centuries later, and Moses would have known where the Amalekites had settled and would have called the area 'the country of the Amalekites' though they did not exist during the time of Abraham.

Deuteronomy 25:17,18, refers to the Amalekites in this case as having attacked the rear part of the caravan and preying upon those whose progress was slower than the rest. These would have been the old, the sick, mothers with small children, etc. Because of their actions at that time they were to be destroyed, (Exodus 17:14; Deuteronomy 25:19). Joshua was to be informed of God's judgment on Amalek, because he was to follow Moses as leader of Israel and it would be his responsibility to carry out the judgment, (Exodus 17:14).

Our interest in the battle is the way God chose to work in this incident. Joshua was called (first mention of him, Exodus 17:9), and was to gather a group of men to fight the Amalekites. Interestingly, the Israelites had never been warriors, and this was a new concept to them. Had they been men of war, they would never have allowed themselves to become slaves in Egypt.

Fear and the need to protect yourself and your family makes soldiers of us all - and no less so with Israel on this occasion.

This group was not the entire nation of Amalek, but a body of roving thieves who preyed upon the caravans which continually crossed those areas. Many centuries later Marco Polo wrote about wandering tribes that came out of nowhere and stole the trading goods from large caravans.

On this occasion, God would do the fighting for Israel. Joshua collected his men and met the Amalekites in the Valley of Rephidim, and Moses, Aaron, and Hur watched from the top of the hill, (some believe Hur to have been the husband of Miriam, see 1 Chronicles 2:19. He was believed to be co-governor with Aaron; and in Exodus 31:2-5, he is listed as the grandfather of Bezaleel). When Moses held his hands up with the rod in them, in supplication to God, Israel prevailed; when Moses put his hands down, the Amalekites began to win.

Aaron and Hur held up Moses' hands which held the rod, the banner of God. After seating him on a rock, they held his hands up the rest of the day and Israel defeated the Amalekites. The battle was won through obedience to God's commands and the power of prayer.

Again, God could have easily destroyed the Amalekites, but in order to show the Israelites His care for them and to give credence to Moses as their God-given leader, He chose to use this method to teach them. God was the one who gave the victory, but Moses was the vehicle He used to accomplish it.

Moses built an altar to God in thanksgiving and praise and called it Jehovah-nissi, (Exodus 17:15), meaning Jehovah is my ensign or banner. In other words, Moses fought under the banner of Jehovah instead of under a common standard. (Edersheim, *Bible History*), p. 103.

God's message to Israel concerning the Amalekites was due to their continual life of sin, and in 1 Samuel 15:18, God told Saul to carry out this destruction, which he failed to do.

The institution of judges over the people
(Exodus 18; Deuteronomy 1:12-18)

Israel was at this time ruled by God under a theocracy. However, since there was no physical presence of God, a modified republican form of government was instituted to deal with the day-to-day problems of the people.

Moses represented the president or king, who taught them God's law and statutes and ruled under God, the Legislator; the judges represented the judicial system which heard the civil complaints of the people and judged right judgment based on God's laws. It was representative in that the people's desires were re-presented to Moses, and from him to God when the situation warranted it.

It was an exceptional system and worked for Israel as long as the nation obeyed God.

The reference here to Moses' 'father-in-law' has been explained previously, and this was doubtless his brother-in-law, also a priest of the Kenites.

He returned Moses' family to him at this time and suggested the institution of the judges in order to save Moses' physical and emotional strength for more important matters, like speaking for the nation with God.

Those who were to be judges were to be men who were able, (valiant), who feared God, who spoke truth, and who hated covetousness.

The principle of representation is seen to be the most workable because of its benefits: the people were better governed, and Moses was allowed more time to lead the people according to God's command.

Arrival at Sinai (Exodus 19)

Scholars agree that Sinai refers to an entire mountain range of about two miles in length; one of whose main peaks was Horeb and the other Sinai, called Jebel Músa today. Sinai was named for the seneh shrub, a small tree with large thorns and blue flowers.

The Israelites arrived there the third month of their journey and remained there for almost a year, (Numbers 10:11).

God called Moses up into the mountain to hear what He had to say to the nation. God began by reminding them of what He had already done for them in delivering them out of Egypt. He would continue to open the way for them, if they would obey Him. They would be to Him, 'a kingdom of priests, and a holy nation'. Moses was given instructions as to what to tell the people when he descended from the mountain.

He called the elders together and told them, and they in turn told the congregation. The instructions were:

- Demonstrate the willingness to obey the laws God was going to give them.
- Wash their clothes, which had become dirty in their travels.
- Wash themselves physically, for the same reason, and this was a symbol of the internal cleansing which was to come.
- Sanctify themselves spiritually. Sanctify is the Hebrew word *qâdâsh*, which means 'dedicate, set aside for the worship of God'. This meant putting aside all the gods of Egypt which had evidently been a part of their lives, as seen in their willingness to worship the golden calf, the representative of the calf, Mneus, worshipped by the Egyptians.
- Prohibited them going near the mountain on penalty of death.

In Exodus 19:22, the words of the Lord to Moses were: *And let the priests also, which come near* (physically) *to the Lord....* This causes a bit of a problem since there were at that time no formal priests in Israel. The first mention of a priest was Melchizedek, (Genesis 14:18), who was from Salem in the country of the Canaanites.

In ancient times, each individual male (e.g. Cain and Abel), or the head of a family, offered the sacrifice to God. At the time of the patriarchs, the oldest male member of the family offered the sacrifice, and there was no need for a priestly class.

The priests referred to here were likely the heads of families and may have been the heads of tribes.

When they left Egypt, there were 600,000 men of age twenty or over, and it is inconceivable to imagine that a number that large would all be called 'priests'. The smaller hill upon which the priests were to remain while Moses went up the mountain was not large enough for a multitude of people, but would have been sufficient for 12 representative tribal heads.

Sacrifices were made in Egypt, though probably not on a regular basis, and as before noted, when Moses made the request to go into the desert to sacrifice to his God, Pharaoh was not surprised by the request. The Egyptians made continual sacrifices to their gods and the sacrifice was an accepted means of placating one's god or of securing his favor.

Because of their sojourn in a pagan country, it was necessary for the priests to sanctify themselves before they could take their proper position as representatives of the people.

Though the priests were allowed to go nearer the mountain than the people, they were forbidden to go near while God's presence was there, nor were they to touch it, (verse 12).

Sinai appearance (Exodus 19:18-21)

On the third day everything was ready and the Lord descended upon the mountain in a cloud of smoke in which fire could be seen. So awesome was this manifestation of God that even the mountain shook at His presence. The sound of a trumpet whose sound was prolonged and became louder and louder was heard. There was lightning and thunder and smoke.

The Lord called Moses to come up and meet with Him there, (Exodus 19:20). Then God spoke. The order is confusing because chapters 20-23 were spoken by God and in 24:1,2, Moses was called up onto the mountain. The sequence is out of order, but the instructions are the same. Moses was called up and given the 10 Commandments and then all the other stipulations from God vocally (20-23), and then Moses came down (24:3).

The people could see the mountain and could hear the voice, but they could not go near, nor did they wish to, (Exodus 19:16; Deuteronomy 5:5).

First God reaffirmed to Moses Who He is and was - I am the Lord thy God; I brought you out of Egypt where you were in bondage, I did it, not you, nor Aaron; I was the one, (Exodus 20:2).

He then began to give the Ten Commandments, also called the Decalogue, from the Greek word *Deka logoi*, meaning 10 words. These are the only words spoken by God to man and written down by the finger of God Himself, (Exodus 32:16).

Contained in Moses' tables of stone are the basic principles of all modern legal science. Also in Moses' Old Testament writings can be traced the origin of property, society, and government. Principles concerning morals of the people, offices of religion, and judicial governing laws can also be discovered in them.

The Ten Commandments: (Exodus 20:1-17)

1. Thou shalt have no other gods before Me.

2. Thou shalt not make unto thee any graven image, or any likeness of anything that is in heaven above, or that is in the water under the earth.

3. Thou shalt not take the name of the Lord thy God in vain; for the Lord will not hold him guiltless that taken His name in vain.

4. Remember the Sabbath day, to keep it holy.

5. Honour thy father and thy mother; that thy days may be long upon the land which the Lord thy God giveth thee.

6. Thou shalt not kill.

7. Thou shalt not commit adultery.

8. Thou shalt not steal.

9. Thou shalt not bear false witness against thy neighbour.

10. Thou shalt not covet thy neighbour's house, thou shalt not covet thy neighbour's wife, nor his manservant, nor his maidservant, nor his ox nor his ass, nor any thing that is thy neighbour's.

Commandments 1-4 deal with our duty to God:

Men had a Maker to love before he had a neighbor to love. No one who is false to God will be true to his brother.

Commandments 5-10 deal with our duty to ourselves and to others:

"As religion towards God is an essential branch of universal righteousness, so righteousness towards men is an essential branch of true religion." (*Matthew Henry Commentaries,* Vol. I), p. 361.

Commandment 5: Honor thy father and thy mother. A decent respect, an inward esteem is mandated towards our parents regardless of how they might act towards us.

Commandment 6: Thou shalt not kill. This does not forbid 'killing in a lawful war', or in our own defense, nor capital punishment, for these things work for the preservation of life.

Commandment 7: Thou shalt not commit adultery. This forbids all acts of uncleanness. Our chastity should be as dear to us as our life.

Commandment 8: Thou shalt not steal. This forbids us to rob ourselves of what we have by sinful spending; to rob others by invading our neighbor's rights, taking his goods, taking advantage of him in bargains; not paying back what is borrowed or found; not paying just debts, or to rob the public of revenues, or that which belongs to God.

Commandment 9: Thou shalt not bear false witness. This commandment forbids speaking falsely, speaking unjustly, bearing false witness (slandering, backbiting, talebearing, aggravating what is done amiss and making it worse than it is, and any way endeavouring to raise our own reputation upon the ruin of our neighbour's). (Ibid.), p. 366.

Commandment 10: Thou shalt not covet. "Forbids all inordinate desire of having that which will be a gratification to ourselves." Shows discontent of our own lot and envy of our neighbor. How do most minor and major crimes begin? By wanting that which belongs to another. (From Matthew Henry commentary.)

Mr. Grady Weaver understands the profound effects of this body of written laws to society and gives them this interpretation:

"The first commandment tells the individual to reject pagan gods and recognize his own worth as a human being, subject to no power but that of the Creator and Judge.

"The second tells the individual to form no image of abstract rightness, but to direct his reverence toward the divine in truth.

"The third tells the individual not to speak frivolously of the Creator and Judge. Knowledge of fundamental truth - cause and effect - is of first importance and should be taken very seriously.

"The fourth tells the individual to devote some time (one day out of seven) to reflection on the eternal verities.

The fifth recognizes the family as the primary human relationship and establishes the parent's authority over the child as the only authority which a child should accept for his own profit.

"The sixth stresses the sanctity of human life - the individual's right to live, which is a right that must not be violated by any other person.

"The seventh establishes the principle of contract - the inviolability of promises given by persons to each other and the double sanctity of the marriage contract, which is the basis of the family.

"The eighth recognizes the individual's right to own property.

"The ninth recognizes free speech - the individual's control over his own utterances and his responsibility for their truth.

"The tenth emphasizes again the right of ownership. Not even in thought should a person violate the property rights of another." (Weaver, *Mainspring of Human Progress*), pp. 80, 81.

These 10 laws encompass every situation, religious or civil, which could ever exist. They are the answer to all of man's needs, and the only requirement to live well and do right was and is, to obey them.

God's angel

God told Moses He was sending an angel with them to be their guard, to keep them safe, and to observe them, (Exodus 23:20-23).

In Psalm 121:4, the Lord is called the 'keeper,' *shâmar*, of Israel which means to 'guard, protect, keep, observe, save'. In Daniel 10:13,21 Michael is called 'your prince' and 'one of the chief princes' which means the 'foremost keepers'. But this angel in Daniel does not fit the description of the angel-messenger mentioned here in Exodus.

In Exodus 33:2,14,15, are these words: *And I will send an angel before thee; and I will drive out the Canaanite, the Amorite, and the Hittite, and the Perizzite, the Hivite, and the Jebusite... And he said, My presence shall go with thee, and I will give thee rest. And he said unto him If thy presence* (thy face) *go not with me, carry us not up hence.*

Isaiah 63:9,14, *In all their affliction he was afflicted, and the angel of his presence saved them: in his love and in his pity he redeemed them; and he bare them, and carried them all the days of old... As a beast goeth down into the valley, the Spirit of the Lord caused him to rest: so didst thou lead thy people, to make thyself a glorious name.*

From the previous verses it is obvious that the Angel referred to here is Christ Himself. Although Michael was and is the prince of Israel, there is no indication that his voice was ever heard by Israel. On the other hand, the Lord's voice was constantly heard by Moses and His commands were transmitted to the people.

Isaiah 63:10, *But they rebelled, and vexed his Holy Spirit: therefore he was turned,* (the Hebrew word *haphak*, which means to be converted, change, turn [to the contrary]), *to be their enemy, and he fought against them.*

This verse gives a better understanding of Exodus 23:21, *Beware of him, and obey his voice, provoke him not; for he will not pardon your transgressions: for my name is in him.*

It was not that the Lord would not par-

don their sin, it was that they had continued in their sin until their Friend became their Enemy and He determined to destroy them. Only through the intercession of Moses were they spared. Exodus 23:22, if you obey, this will be the result, but if you don't just the opposite will be true.

The Promised defeat of their enemies
(Exodus 23:23-33)

- I will cut them off, (verse 23).
- You will not worship their gods, (verse 24).
- You will destroy their images, (verse 24).
- You will serve the Lord, (verse 25).
- I will provide your physical needs, (verse 25).
- Your animals will be fruitful, (verse 26).
- You will be fruitful, (verse 26).
- I will send the fear of My name before you into the land, (verse 27).
- I will destroy the people who are there, (verse 27).
- I will make your enemies flee, (verse 27).
- I will send hornets to drive out your enemies, (verse 28).
- It will take time to remove them in order that the land might not suffer, ('don't displace before you can replace'), (verse 29).
- You will inherit the land, (verse 30).
- The boundaries were again given, (verse 31).
- Do not make covenants with the people, nor with their gods, (verse 32).

Three Festivals to be observed each year
(Exodus 23:14-19)

God ordained three festivals or feasts for the nation of Israel which were to be observed until the coming of the Messiah:

- The first was the feast of unleavened bread, which had already been given, and was the Passover, (23:15). This was to remind them of their deliverance from Egypt.
- Next was the feast of Harvest, the firstfruits, (verse 16b), which took place at the begin-

ning of the harvest season. The people were to offer the first products taken from their fields, their gardens, their fruit trees, etc. It was the New Testament Pentecost, (Leviticus 23:9-14; Deuteronomy 16:9-12).

- The third was the feast of Ingathering, (23:16), and took place when all the crops had been harvested. It was also called the Feast of Tabernacles, (Leviticus 23:34-43; Nehemiah 8:13-18, etc.).

All the feasts were to remind the people of God's special care over them as a nation. It was a time to give back to God something for which they were thankful, and also to remember that without His presence they would have been nothing but bondservants.

On these three occasions all the males of the nation (from twenty years old and up) were to make a pilgrimage to the sanctuary to appear before the Lord.

The Agreement (Exodus 24:1-3)

In chapters 21-24 God gave Moses the particulars of the application of the commandments to civil law He had just given. Moses then went down from the mountain and wrote down the words God had spoken, (Exodus 24:4).

The next step was to build an altar according to God's specifications, and sacrifices were offered upon the altar. One-half of the blood from the sacrifices was sprinkled on the altar. The young men mentioned in verse 5 were those whose job it was that day to obtain and kill the animals for the sacrifice.

An altar was not a new thing to the Israelites because it had been used since the time of Adam. But God's instructions concerning the altar (Exodus 20:22-26), were to emphasize that though they had just left a country where sacrifices were made on ornate altars which were usually constructed in places elevated above the people, this was not acceptable to God.

After reading the words he had written down from God to the people (the book of the Covenant, (Exodus 24:7), they all agreed to obey God's commands to them.

Moses then sprinkled the people with the remainder of the blood from the sacrifices as a sign of their acceptance of God's law, (Exodus 24:6-8).

After the people had agreed to God's laws, Moses, Aaron, Nadab, Abihu and seventy of the elders of Israel went up into the mountain, (24:9).

When verse 10 of Exodus 24 says, *And they saw the God of Israel,* this did not refer to actually seeing 'Him' physically. They 'saw' an appearance which was like a blue sapphire and over it was a cloud in which lightning could be seen. *No man hath seen God at any time,* (John 1:18), so says John and it is true. Therefore these men did not 'see' God, but saw a manifestation of Him.

To further say in verse 11 that *they saw God, and did eat and drink* was to say that though they had been privileged to see a manifestation of God, it was not God Himself and they were still able to eat and drink because they were not dead, which they would have been had they 'seen' God.

The Tables of Stone (Exodus 24:12-18)

When Moses and the others went back onto the mountain, Joshua also accompanied Moses, possibly as one of the elders. His position of importance was because he was Moses' 'minister', meaning he served Moses however he could. He would be called an apprentice today. He was learning from Moses how to lead the people.

Moses left the elders and the others behind at a particular spot and he and Joshua proceeded to go up higher on the mountain where the cloud and the glory of the Lord covered it. For six days Moses waited for instructions from the Lord and on the seventh day God called to him out of the cloud. He was to go up higher, leaving Joshua at the place they had been on the six previous days, (Exodus 24:16).

From below, the Israelites observed the mountain and saw fire on its peak and heard the thunder rumbling.

Moses remained on the mountain for 40 days and 40 nights and received the ceremonial law and instructions for the building of the Tabernacle and all it's furniture and decoration. He was instructed as to how to make the altar of brass for the burnt offerings and what the priests' clothing was to include. Aaron and his sons (and their descendants, Numbers 3:10; 18:7), were to become the official priests of the nation and were to be set apart and dedicated to the Lord for this service. The laws of the sacrifice were given; the recipe for the oil and the incense was given; and the workmen who were to be in charge of the construction were named.

The Sabbath rest was again explained. It was given only to Israel as a command to keep (Exodus 31:12-17) to remind them that in six days God created the heaven and the earth and on the seventh He rested, or ceased His labor.

Parts of both the civil and ceremonial laws were to last only as long as the conditions required them, but the moral law (i.e. the Ten Commandments) were to continue as long as man himself continued to exist.

God designated at that time a special place where His people would meet with Him.

God gave Moses two tables of stone upon which God Himself had written the ten laws He had already spoken verbally to Moses.

The Golden Calf (Exodus 32)

Because Moses had been gone for such a long time and the people had seen the cloud and the continual fire on the mountain they believed he had died there.

They asked Aaron to make them some 'gods', the kind they had known in Egypt. He took their golden earrings and from them formed a golden calf - the calf-god Mneus, they already knew.

When he presented it to the people he said, *These be thy gods, O Israel, which brought thee up out of the land of Egypt* (Exodus 32:4).

Some scholars believe that Aaron was not actually using the image as a pagan god, but was allowing them to worship the true God through the image. The facts, however, are to the contrary.

The first commandment had forbidden making any kind of 'graven image' by which to worship God. They had just heard the commandment and had agreed to follow it.

Aaron called the image 'thy gods' - not the God of Israel, but pagan 'gods'. He knew Who had brought Israel out of Egypt and it was not a pagan god made of stone. It is easy for sinful man to lose sight of God's power and care when he sets his eyes on earthly things.

From Acts 7:39-41 the picture is clear that they intended to return to Egypt with this 'god' leading them. And they 'rejoiced in the works of their own hand', (verse 41), meaning they were made glad.

Why Aaron consented to their demand is not known, but he was a man prone to sin like any other man. The absence of a physical presence to lead them affected them all. Their dependent character needed a ruler as they were still unable to govern themselves.

Aaron ordered that an altar be built on which sacrifices were offered, supposedly to Jehovah, but their actions showed that thoughts of God were far from their hearts and minds.

"The people sat down to eat and to drink, and rose up to play," (Exodus 32:6). The word 'play' says Clarke, is *letsachek*, which always has a sexual connotation, (fornication and adultery). (Clarke, *Commentary*, Vol. I), p. 464. This is not the picture of a people who are intent upon worshipping God.

When Moses came down from the mountain he heard them singing in a riotous way and saw them dancing, (32:18,19). Their minds were not on the things of God at that time.

Aaron and the Golden Calf
(Peloubet, 1913)

God told Moses what the people were doing and that they had 'corrupted themselves, (32:7), meaning their morals were cast off or destroyed, and for that reason in 32:25 Moses said they 'were naked'.

Because God was so angry with them He told Moses He was going to destroy all of them and form a new nation beginning with Moses. God called the Israelites *thy* people when speaking of them to Moses. God had in that moment forsaken them because they were no longer worthy to be called His people, nor had they ever been, and it was only His grace that had brought them this far.

But Moses said, 'These are *your* people, not mine. Since the calling of Abraham they have been yours; you knew them from the beginning and your mercy has always been enough for even a rebellious group like them. It is You who promised to make them a great nation; it is You who brought them out of Egypt; it is You who will be reproached if You destroy them because the other nations, beginning with Egypt, will say You just took them out into the mountainous desert to destroy them.'

Then Moses asked God to 'repent of the evil' He had determined against them. And God changed His actions because of Moses' intercession for the people.

Moses had a perfect opportunity to rid himself of such a difficult, ungodly group by just allowing God to destroy them, but they were his people, and though unlovely, he still loved them, just as God loves us even when we are unlovely. No doubt God was testing him and he passed the test.

Also, when God called them 'thy' people His idea was to give Moses an opportunity to receive the honor for bringing them out of Egypt, but Moses knew he was not the one who had brought them out. He told God, in 32:11, He was the one who had brought them out and He was responsible for them, not Moses. And that was what God wanted to hear Moses say.

Moses received the written tablets and started down the mountain to where Joshua was still waiting for him. As they neared the camp Joshua heard the people and thought they were at battle with some other tribe, but Moses knew from God what was going on and told Joshua.

When he was within sight of the camp and saw the golden calf and the dancing Moses broke the two tablets in front of the people. He gave them a visual lesson of their disobedience to God, and those who still had a conscience escaped to their tents in shame.

Moses rebuked Aaron for his part in the apostasy of Israel and though he made excuses (as we all do), he knew Moses was right. Aaron said he had cast the gold into the fire and it miraculously came out a calf in 32:24. But in verse 4 the Scripture says he 'fashioned it with a graving tool', or he (or another person), actually sculpted it after it had been molded; it was refined by man's hands, (Deuteronomy 9:20,21). God was very angry with Aaron, but his life was spared because of Moses.

Then Moses called the people to the gate of the camp and asked, "Who is on the Lord's side?" (32:26). Those who chose to follow God (those who had not participated in the idolatry), went to Moses and they were the Levites. At that time they had not yet heard they were to be set apart as priests of Israel, but by this act of faithfulness they proved themselves capable of carrying out God's commands in reference to Israel's worship of God.

Moses told them to go through the camp and slay the 3000 who were 'naked' and had evidently not yet stopped their pagan celebration. The word 'naked', though it certainly can, and many times does, mean unclothed, it seems more true to the text in this case to mean they were spiritually naked without any understanding of God's greatness and His demand that they be a pure nation, totally separated from idolatry. If Aaron had 'made them naked' as in 32:25, he certainly wouldn't have caused them to take off their clothing, but he did participate in constructing an idolatrous pagan symbol which made them even more spiritually naked 'to their shame', (verse 25).

Moses burned the calf image and ground the gold into powder and put it into the water source and made the people drink it, (Deuteronomy 9:21).

The next morning Moses rebuked the people for sinning against God and told them to consecrate themselves to God. He said he would go back up the mountain and speak to God to see if He would pardon them. He still had not completed his time with God, but had been forced to leave in order to stop the people in the midst of their idolatry.

The scene that follows is one of the most telling experiences in the life of Moses. He confessed the sin of the people and then asked God to forgive them. But in mid-sentence he stopped as though he couldn't bear to speak further and after a pause he said, 'and God if you won't forgive them just blot me out of your book, if that will keep Israel from more punishment.' In other words, 'I will bear their sin.'

But God said the individual who sinned had to bear the punishment of his own sin. God always emphasizes the principle of personal accountability.

Besides Moses, only Paul and the Lord Jesus Christ were willing to give their lives for their people. The Lord is the only one whose life was required as the payment for the sins of others, because His was the only life worthy to become their sin-bearer.

Moses was told that God would not go with them as before, but would send an angel with them. It would be God, however, who would drive out the enemy nations who inhabited Palestine, (Exodus 33:2).

When the people heard this pronouncement they took off all their 'ornaments' and mourned; they grieved because of their sin, and they grieved because of the loss of God's presence.

Moses took the tent, (probably his own), and pitched it outside the camp because God would no longer dwell in their midst. God's presence moved outside the camp and moved to the door of the tent when Moses entered into it. God dwelled where Moses dwelled. Moses called the tent the 'Tabernacle of the Congregation', (Exodus 33:7) and those who followed God went there to inquire of Him through Moses.

When the people saw the pillar of cloud rest upon the tent, they rose up collectively and worshipped in their tent doors, (worship: *shâchâh*, literally to bow down, to prostrate one's self). This was an admission of their guilt before God and a beseeching of His forgiveness, (33:10).

The Lord spoke to Moses and he returned to the camp, but Joshua remained in the tent. Evidently, Moses passed on to the people what God had told him and he then returned to the tabernacle where God spoke to him.

Moses told the Lord again that the Israelites were His people (Deuteronomy 3:20; Hebrews 4:8), and asked God whom he was going to send with them. And the Lord told him it would be His presence that would go with them.

Moses said if God was not going to go with them he didn't want to go and only through God's presence would it be known that they were a separated people for the Lord. He asked God to give him some instructions as to how He wished the people to be governed since they were His people and He knew the best way to govern them.

Then Moses asked the Lord to show him His glory and God consented by showing him His after-glory, but not Himself because Moses would not be able to bear that. God hid Moses in a 'cleft of the rock' and covered him with His hand so he would not be destroyed. Then God passed by and Moses saw the glory of His passing.

The Second Tablets of Stone (Exodus 34:1-35)

God told Moses to make two more tablets of stone like the first. The first had been made by God and were written on by God, but Moses was to prepare these two new tablets.

Deuteronomy 10:1-5 says that God wrote on the tablets of stone, and Exodus 34:27 implies that Moses wrote on the tablets. In checking both references this is easily understood. God wrote on the tablets Moses took up with him and they were to be put into the ark where they were to remain. Moses wrote a copy of the tablets which could be kept before the people so they would know them and observe them. All of God's instructions to Israel during that second forty days were written down by Moses so they could be seen by the people.

God instructed Moses to go alone onto the mountain and the people and animals were to remain far away from it. God's presence descended upon the mountain when Moses ascended and He proclaimed Himself to be the Lord Jehovah who was capable of doing everything He said He would do.

He described Himself as:

- merciful,
- gracious,
- long-suffering,
- abundant in goodness,
- abundant in truth,
- keeping mercy,
- forgiving iniquity,
- forgiving transgression,
- forgiving sin,
- because of God's justice there was no forgiveness to the guilty who did not confess, but no guilt was imputed to the innocent.
- He would visit the iniquity of the fathers upon the children to the 3rd and 4th generations.

Upon hearing all these attributes of God's character Moses quickly said, *If now I have found grace in thy sight, O Lord, let my Lord, I pray thee, go among us: for it is a stiffnecked people; and pardon our iniquity and our sin, and take us for thine inheritance.* (Exodus 34:9.)

In 33:5 the Lord had told Moses *Ye are a stiffnecked people* and Moses was agreeing with God's evaluation in 34:9.

In Exodus 33:17 God told Moses he had "found grace in my sight, and I know thee by name". Moses continued this conversation in 34:9 by saying, 'Since (if) I have found grace in thy sight, please do these things (pardon us, go among us), and accept us again as your people.'

God's Covenant (Exodus 34:10-27)

God made a covenant with Moses and Israel which included the promise of what He would do for them:

- I will do marvels such as have not been seen anywhere;
- you will all see the work of the Lord;
- that work will be a terrible thing, (terrible: the Hebrew word *Yârê* which in this case means it will evoke in you a reverential awe, but in your enemies it will cause great fear).

The conditions of the covenant were:

- observe and do all the things I command this day, (verse 11);
- make no covenant with the inhabitants of the land, (verse 12);
- destroy their altars and images, and cut down their groves (to protect yourselves from idol worship) because God will not allow you to live if you follow their pagan gods and practices, (verses 13, 14);
- don't intermarry with the people, so you won't be tempted to worship their gods, (verse 16);
- make no molten images to worship, (verse 17);
- keep the Passover feast of unleavened bread, (verse 18);
- dedicate the firstborn male of man and animals to Me, (verses 19, 20);
- keep the Sabbath, even in harvest when it might not seem convenient, (verse 21);
- keep the feast of Firstfruits, (verse 22);
- keep the feast of Ingathering, (verse 22);
- three times a year all the men are to appear before the Lord at the place appointed, (verse 23);

- while the men are gone to worship the Lord the women and children will be at peace because I will take the desire to possess your land away from the neighboring peoples during that period of time, (verse 24);
- don't offer leaven with any blood sacrifice, (verse 25);
- leave no part of the Passover sacrifice until morning, (verse 25);
- the firstfruit offering was to go to the Lord's house, (verse 26);
- don't seethe the kid in its mother's milk, (verse 26).

Then the Lord instructed Moses to write down all the instructions he had received from the mouth of God.

After spending forty days with the Lord on the mountain Moses descended bringing with him the written down instructions God had given him and the two tablets upon which God had again written the Ten Commandments.

Moses' face shone with the reflected glory of God, and the people, still suffering from the guilt of their rebellion, were unable to look upon that glory. Moses covered his face with a veil and recounted all that had passed between him and God in the last forty days and gave them a copy of the instructions God had instructed him to write down.

When Moses entered into the Tabernacle of the Congregation to speak with the Lord he took his veil off because his shining face had no effect upon the Lord since it was merely a reflection of His own wonderful glory.

There is no indication as to how long this reflected glory lasted, but it was long enough to convince the people that Moses was the man selected by God to lead them to the Promised Land.

Because of disobedience the adults over twenty who began the journey from Egypt were not allowed to enter the Promised Land and forty years in wilderness wandering was the result. When all those people had died, including Moses, those remaining were ready to claim their possession with God's help and guidance.

When the people arrived in Canaan God provided the laws by which they were to be governed. He always provides before we have a need.

On the eve of entering the Promised Land, preparations were made for the new leadership of 2 1/2 millions of people. The leader chosen was Joshua, who had served his apprenticeship under Moses for forty years.

ISRAEL'S HISTORY

Many detailed and trustworthy histories are available on the market and the following is only the basic outline of Israel's remaining Biblical history:

The Theocratic Kingdom was established by God at Sinai and lasted through the period of Joshua's leadership. After the conquest of Canaan, and during his leadership, the land was divided among the sons of Jacob and each one was allotted his territory. After Joshua, unbelief and idolatry led to the Dark Ages of Israel's history when they were without a ruler.

The Dark Ages of Israel's history lasted for 450 years, (Acts 13:20).

During the time of the Judges, God sent angels with specific messages to specific individuals who were to guide the people and deliver them from their oppressors. It was a time of moral and spiritual degeneration of the nation. They were oppressed by many different nations during this period and each time God sent an individual to deliver them.

The individual was without the law, and each man did that 'which was right in his own eyes', (Deuteronomy 12:8; Judges 17:6). The period ended in spiritual darkness and God ceased speaking with the nation.

There were years of transition between the last judge and Eli. The engrafting of a Moabitess into the line of Christ was represented by Ruth during this period.

The United Kingdom

Eli was the last of his family to judge Israel. Then comes the introduction of Samuel as the last prophet.

The loss of the Ark to the Philistines, (1 Samuel 6), takes place when Israel has no leader after the death of Eli. The ark was in the land of the Philistines for seven months, (1 Samuel 6:1), and caused so much trouble that they returned it to Israel where it remained in Kirjath-jearim for twenty years.

The Philistines continued to make war against Israel, and Samuel entreated God for them and He gave them victory over the Philistines, (1 Samuel 7:13); and again under Saul in 1 Samuel 14.

Saul

In 1 Samuel 8:5, Israel asked Samuel to make them a king 'like the other nations', 1120 B.C. This was a rejection of God's government over them and gives an indication of their spiritual condition. Saul was made king and though he started out well and believed God, in a short time he had showed that he was not willing to follow God's commands and rejected God, and was rejected by God, (1 Samuel 15:23).

The "Divine Right of Kings" was established, (Isaiah 33:22). With the establishment of the "divine right of kings" philosophy of government, man willingly or by force, gave to the sovereign ruler a position of supreme importance. By his consent, tacit or overt, he allowed the king to become his absolute ruler with the power of life and death in his hand.

The king, on the other hand, was only too happy to take upon himself this kind of power. He became convinced that his rulings were to be considered the very rulings of God and that no man was empowered to stand against him in any decision. Whatever the king decided was to be carried out regardless of the consequences to the individual or the nation. The individual had no say in the government over him, and this in time led to the writing of the Magna Charta, 1215, and ultimately to the Constitution of the United States in 1787, which guaranteed the liberty of the individual. The Russian Revolution came about as a result of this very philosophy. It's beginning can be seen here with the establishment of the monarchy in Israel.

After the incident with the witch of Endor, Saul lost all his power and was defeated and died.

This period ended in national and individual darkness as demonstrated by Saul's disobedience of, and disregard for, the commands of God. Samuel the last of the judges, anointed Saul and David, but he died before the reign of David.

David

Saul was followed by David, and when David became king the condition of the nation was somewhat changed. He was called 'a man after God's own heart'. He was a great sinner, but he was also a great repenter, (Psalm 51).

David wrote most of the Psalms and throughout his lifetime continued to inquire of God when decisions were to be made.

He reigned as king over Judah in Hebron for seven years and six months, and over the united kingdom of Israel for 33 years; 40 years in all, (2 Samuel 5:5). He conquered Jerusalem and made it his capital, calling it the 'city of David', (2 Samuel 5:9). The nation was unified under David's reign.

After defeating the Philistines in 2 Samuel 5, he called together a large group of men and took the ark of God from Kirjath-jearim to carry it to Jerusalem. But because they put it on a cart instead of carrying it as God had commanded them, Uzzah was killed by God, and they left it in the house of Obed-edom the Gittite where it remained for three months.

David then took the Levites with him to get the ark. They carried it as God had commanded; and it was taken to Jerusalem where David had prepared a tent for it, (2 Samuel 6:17).

God promised to be with David if he would obey Him, and also promised him an eternal kingdom based upon obedience.

Though David desired to build a house for the ark, God refused to allow him that privilege, but told him his son (Solomon) would build the house of God, (2 Samuel 7:12,13).

During the second battle against the Ammonites, David remained in the palace instead of leading Israel into battle. At that time he saw Bathsheba and committed his great sin against God, (2 Samuel 11,12).

He repented of his sin and God accepted him and pardoned him though he still had to reap the bitter harvest of his sin in the death of the child.

This man after God's own heart was still just a man. Because he refused to discipline his children as he should, he found out too late what his lack of interest in them could cause, (i.e. the sin of Amnon against Tamar; the murder of Amnon by Absalom; the exile of David because of Absalom; the sin of Absalom with the concubines of David, and Absalom's death).

God did not allow him to build the Temple because he had been a man of war and had shed so much blood, (1 Chronicles 28:3; 22:8).

He was promised an eternal kingdom which would be carried out through the Lion of the Tribe of Judah, the Lord Jesus Christ, the direct descendant of David. When he died, (1 Kings 2:10,11; 1 Chronicles 29:28) the kingdom went to Solomon, his son by Bathsheba, (1 Kings 1:28-53).

Solomon

God chose Solomon to be king and in the first part of his reign, he asked God for wisdom so he could judge God's people as he should, (2 Chronicles 1:10). Because he had not asked for riches or fame, or the life of his enemies, but was more concerned about the people, God gave him all the rest. Verse 12 says, *Wisdom and knowledge is granted unto thee; and I will give thee riches, and wealth, and honour, such as none of the kings have had that have been before thee, neither shall there any after thee have the like.* (See also 1 Kings 10:6,14-29.)

Solomon was to build the Temple of the Lord, and though David could not build it he gathered together most of the materials necessary with which to build it.

When Solomon took the throne he began the construction. God had stated, (2 Samuel 7:6), that He had never dwelled in houses, but only in tents and tabernacles since the time He delivered Israel from Egypt. But the time had come for the construction of a permanent dwelling place for the Ark of the Covenant.

Solomon called together the greatest workmen of the period and built the Temple from the instructions David had given him. When it was completed it was dedicated to God and after all the sacrifices were offered, the Ark of the Covenant was placed in the holy of Holies in the new Temple and the glory of the Lord filled the place, (2 Chronicles 7:1).

Solomon also built himself a house as God had said, and when it was completed God appeared to him in the night and told him if he would walk before Him as his father had done, He would continue his kingdom as He had promised David. But if he refused and followed other gods, the people would be scattered and sent into other countries.

During the period when Solomon was obeying God he wrote the Proverbs, Ecclesiastes, and the Song of Solomon.

Apostasy was not long in coming, however, and because of his many wives and concubines Solomon's heart was turned from God to the pagan gods of his wives, (1 Kings 11:1-8).

He had married 700 wives, and had 300 concubines, from Ammon, Egypt, Moab, Edom, Sidon, the Hittites, etc., (1 Kings 11:3).

He built an altar to Molech and Chemosh for his wives when he was old and sinned against God. God's judgment was not long in coming, (1 Kings 11:9-13).

God had told him on two occasions that if he refused to keep His commands the kingdom would be taken from him and that was about to occur. However, because God is merciful, He said He would leave him one tribe for 'David's sake' and for 'Jerusalem's sake', (1 Kings 11:13), and that was the tribe of Judah, his own tribe.

Solomon reigned for 40 years over Israel, (1 Kings 11:42). He died in 982 or 939 B.C., (1 Kings 11:43). And the kingdom passed to his son Rehoboam.

The Temple

God had allowed Solomon to build a house for His worship. It was, according to the Scriptural and historical accounts, one of the most beautiful buildings that ever existed, and was the spiritual center for all Jews.

Jerusalem

During the reign of David, Jerusalem became the capital of Israel. It was both the governmental capital and the religious capital. It was the most important city of the kingdom and was the focal point of all Jewish life.

The city was made into a magnificent architectural showplace by both David and Solomon. Water was brought into the city by great aqueducts - no small engineering feat in that time. There was great wealth from the commercial endeavors of Solomon - ships going to Spain and to Africa bringing in gold and different metals, lumber, ivory, exotic animals and slaves. Each caravan crossing this territory was charged a toll and products from the world came into Solomon's kingdom.

Because of the different conditions of the soil in the north and south, (the north had better soil than the south) and the Temple and Jerusalem in the south, there was much jealousy between the two areas.

Solomon had put such an economic burden on the nation that they were close to being bankrupt. The rich were rich and the poor had no hope of ever getting out of their poverty. The individual had no rights.

When Solomon began his building projects he used labor from the nations under his domination. At the end of his reign he put his own people into slavery and this was deeply resented by the nation. This was the situation existing at his death (1 Kings 12:4).

The Divided Kingdom

The division took place at Shechem, the first capital of the northern kingdom, a city of Ephraim, 30 miles north of Jerusalem between Mt. Ebal and Mt. Gerizim, (1 Kings 12:1). This was close to the area where Christ met the Samaritan woman, (John 4).

Extent of the Kingdom

The kingdom extended from the Euphrates on the north to the boundary line of Egypt on the southwest to the Mediterranean on the west except for a small strip of land occupied by the Phoenicians. About 13,000 squares miles, the size of Holland, was the land in which the twelve tribes lived. Solomon had been ruler over an extensive kingdom, however, which included about 60,000 square miles.

The Northern Kingdom

Jeroboam - 10 northern tribes

Causes of the division:

- the sin of Solomon, (1 Kings 11:9);
- Judah took the place of Benjamin in the kingly line, David took the place of Saul;
- Rehoboam's treatment of the people, (1 Kings 12:13);
- the true accusations brought by Jeroboam, (1 Kings 12:3-5).

The Northern Kingdom lasted 250 years, and was taken captive by Sargon, king of Assyria, (722-652), where Israel was kept in captivity for 70 years.

Jeroboam was an Ephraimite and an officer in the court of Solomon. He was banned to Egypt because of his rebellious attitude, (1 Kings 11:26-40), during the reign of Solomon.

He reigned 22 years over Israel and was the northern kingdom's first king, (1 Kings 14:20).

His lineage

His father's name was Zereda, his mother was Zeruah, (1 Kings 11:26).

He was a commoner, but a capable man of great ability. He worked for Solomon and saw the injustice of the treatment of the workmen and slaves. He was personally involved and spoke from his own experience and not as an outsider like Rehoboam.

The prophet Ahijah told him he was chosen by God to be king of the ten northern tribes, (1 Kings 11:38). He was promised a continuing kingdom if he would follow the Lord God and obey Him.

He rebelled against Solomon and tried to take the kingdom and when Solomon stopped him he escaped to Egypt. He is supposed to have married the daughter of Shishak, king of Egypt, who later invaded Judah.

He was called back to be the spokesman for the north at the meeting with Rehoboam at Shechem.

Jeroboam built Shechem ('built' in this case means he added to the already existing small town and made it a royal city), (1 Kings 12:25), and it became his capital city. It was central to the northern kingdom and central to his own tribe of Ephraim. Ephraim was the most powerful of the 10 northern tribes. It was an old city which God had referred to before and because of its historic character was thought to be a city of honor.

The capital was also in Tirzah for some years, and then in 1 Kings 16:24, Omri, father of Ahab, bought the hill of Samaria, and called it Samaria after Shemer, the man from whom he bought it. In 16:29, Ahab began his reign over Israel in Samaria and Samaria from that point on was the capital of the Northern Kingdom.

Jeroboam "said in his heart" - he thought this thought - he did not say it aloud because of the importance of it (1 Kings 12:26). Jerusalem was the religious center of the nation. If they went up (literally Jerusalem was 'up' because it was on a hill) to worship there, the people's hearts would be turned again to the Lord and to Rehoboam, and Jeroboam couldn't

have this happen and succeed as the leader of the northern kingdom, (1 Kings 12:26-33).

When the division of the kingdom came Jeroboam showed his real character by introducing the worship of the golden calves to Israel. He had seen this idolatry in Israel in Baalism and in Egypt in the worship of Apis and other animal gods.

His mind (reason) even went to the extreme that he feared for his life. "They will kill me", (1 Kings 12:27). His advisors and the people were of one accord in his decision to build separate centers of worship for the northern kingdom - one in Bethel, the other in the north, in the territory of Dan.

He had made two calves of gold - reminiscent of the pagan gods of Egypt which God had destroyed before they left there, and another golden calf which was destroyed during the years of wandering, (Exodus 32:4). Then he multiplied the sin by saying "behold thy gods, O Israel, which brought thee up out of the land of Egypt", (1 Kings 12:28). He knew very well it was not gods that brought Israel out of Egypt, but the One and Only God-Jehovah.

Man is always ready to replace the true God with those made by his own hands, be they golden calves or new cars, or splendid homes, or fame or whatever becomes his god.

He put one golden calf in Bethel, in the south on the northern border of Benjamin and one in Dan at the extreme northern border of Israel. Bethel was 12 miles northwest of Jerusalem and was in the direct line of travel used by pilgrims heading for Jerusalem. It was meant to detour them to Bethel.

Bethel had always been known as the 'house of God' because of its association with Abraham and Jacob and the appearance of God to him there twice. This seems to be a direct challenge by Jeroboam to God's presence.

Dan had always been a place associated with idolatry. The area was captured by the Danites when the land was divided and they found their territory too small. The calf was a sin, the sin of idolatry, worshipping a 'thing' instead of God the Spirit. God had forbidden idol worship in Exodus 20 and they chose to disobey the command of God.

The people chose Dan as the place of worship because it was the farthest from Jerusalem and they were less likely to be reminded of their idolatry.

Jeroboam chose priests of the lowest classes of the people because God's chosen priests, the Levites, refused to take part in his idolatry and left to join the southern kingdom. One of the true prophets spoke against Jeroboam as he burned incense before God at Bethel. Jeroboam raised his hand against the prophet and God caused his hand to wither and his arm to stiffen so he could not move it. Only when he repented and called upon God through the priest-prophet was this curse removed, (1 Kings 13:1-6).

Israel was never to be divided, but Jeroboam succeeded in separating the nation. His aim was to advance himself and his agenda; he was only interested in the nation as it reflected power and glory upon him personally. When a leader puts his own personal desires above the good of the nation, calamity is sure to follow.

All nineteen kings of the northern kingdom were evil - the Scripture repeats "they followed the ways of Jeroboam, son of Nebat who caused Israel to sin". What a serious indictment from God.

The boundaries of the Northern Kingdom

The northern kingdom encompassed an area of about 9400 square miles. It was a fertile, well-watered land which yielded good returns in the harvest and provided good pasture land.

Most of Israel's famous historical sites were located there and most of her greatest heroes came from that area.

The inhabitants were an independent, freedom-loving people who chaffed under the servitude instituted by Solomon.

They were influenced by the worldly nations surrounding them and became a nation given over to idolatry.

There was however no national place of religion or government in the northern kingdom.

The Southern Kingdom

Rehoboam - 2 tribes, capital Jerusalem, the kingdom lasted 389 years.

> Judah
> Benjamin

The southern kingdom had periods of revival, and was not as evil as Israel. It was invaded by Shishak, king of Egypt, an ally of Jeroboam, who took many articles from the Temple and the palace. Rehoboam paid tribute to Egypt as one of its vassals.

King Asa hired Ben-hadad, king of Syria to attack Israel on the north. (2 Chronicles 16:2-6.) This was the wrong kind of alliance for Judah, and indicated they didn't trust God to protect them.

The southern kingdom was attacked by Ethiopia, Ammon, Moab and Edom. Each foreign attack brought about a revival for a period of time.

An extensive teaching ministry was carried on in the kingdom especially under the reign of Jehoshaphat. The decline of Judah began under Jehoram with his alliance with Ahab and marriage to Athaliah, the daughter of Ahab.

The captivity of the southern kingdom came from the Babylonian empire, under

Nebuchadnezzar, king of Babylon, (605-535), and lasted for 70 years.

Abraham left Babylon because of his faith and obedience to God; his descendants returned 1500 years later because of their lack of faith and obedience.

Rehoboam meant "Enlarger of the people". Solomon's hope was expressed for this son in his name. He in fact became the 'Diminisher" of his people.

In 2 Chronicles 12:13; 1 Kings 14:21, he is listed as being 41 years of age. The commentators say the Hebrew words are so close that it is probably an error in copying and he was about 21 years of age. If he was 41 years of age, he was still an immature, petulant, and irresponsible young man.

Lineage

He was the son of Solomon and Naamah an Ammonite princess. She was related to Israel through Lot, but represented a pagan culture. Solomon built a temple for Moloch for her on Mt. Olivet, (2 Kings 23:13; 1 Kings 11:1-9).

His Training

Rehoboam was brought up in a harem of the Eastern monarchs. In this setting he would have been in constant rivalry with his half-brothers and sisters. His mother brought him up in her own pagan religion with the same corrupt values she based her life upon. The difficulties which form strong character were missing from the life of Rehoboam.

He was, as the king's chosen son, never allowed to want for anything. His every desire was met and "nobody ever said 'no'." What a great tragedy to never hear the word 'no' in your life. A spoiled, insolent young man became the disgrace of the wisest man who ever lived. This wise man bred a fool.

The importance of the mother in a family cannot be overemphasized. As the mother, so the son.

Individual responsibility

There comes a time in the life of each person when he must decide upon the personal choices he will make. When Rehoboam came to this point in his life he chose to follow his own carnal desires. He was unable or unwilling to follow the advice of the wise counselors of his father and chose rather to listen to the foolish counsel of his young untried companions.

The nation still had a vote in deciding on the successor to the throne. Rehoboam was recognized as the legitimate heir, but the tribes were called to Shechem to present their grievances before a final decision was made. They asked for a hearing and presented their conditions.

Rehoboam asked for three days to consider their requests. The older men said, "Change, and they will follow you faithfully." The young men said, "Pour it on, who do these people think they are trying to tell the king what he can or cannot do," (1 Kings 12:10,11).

His reply to the people was that he would chastise them with scorpions, (these were whips armed with hooks which were used on rebellious criminals), and would add to their work more than his father had ever done.

Rehoboam lost his great opportunity through pride.

Jeroboam lost his great opportunity through worldly policy.

For three years, during which there was spiritual revival, Rehoboam continued to follow the example of his father and he was well established on the throne.

Reason for the revival: the Levites from the north went to Jerusalem because Jeroboam had made priests of the base people and had forsaken the priestly line of the Levites, (2 Chronicles 11:14-17).

After three years Rehoboam left the ways of the Lord, and God sent Shishak, king of Egypt against him. Shishak took the golden shields, made by Solomon, from the Temple, (2 Chronicles 12:2-12), as his prize and Rehoboam had them replaced by shields of brass. Just so the comparison between the two reigns of Solomon and his son, one was of gold, the other of brass.

After this punishment Rehoboam and the people confessed their sins and made a promise to change; it was a humbling experience for a proud king. Because of their change of heart, God delivered them from their enemies. Rehoboam did not follow the Lord with all his heart and continued to do evil.

The divided kingdom severed all the foreign alliances Israel had made and this allowed God to rid them of the pagan influences of those nations, and revival followed.

As God dealt with each nation He gave them an opportunity to obey Him and become a great nation as He had previously promised. Neither was willing to follow Him in obedience to His commands.

Rehoboam sent Adoram as his emissary to the Israelites who still lived in the cities of Judah. Adoram had been the chief officer in charge of forced labor under Solomon, (1 Kings 12:17,18) and was sent to collect tribute for Rehoboam. He was stoned to death by the followers of Jeroboam, adding insult to injury. Rehoboam fled to the royal city of Jerusalem.

Civil war was prevented by the prophet Shemaiah. Rehoboam feared Israel from the north and Egypt from the south. The Egyptians had harbored Jeroboam during his exile and had made an alliance with him. He built many forts to protect Judah, (2 Chronicles 11:5).

A CHART OF THE DIVIDED KINGDOM

EXPLANATIONS.

1. The dates are given according to Prof. Willis J. Beecher in his Dated Events of the Old Testament History, the most thorough and scholarly study of the subject including the Assyrian Canon.

2. But for the period of the Divided Kingdom, there is also given the dates as in Hastings' and other Bible Dictionaries, as they interpret the Assyrian Canon, who make the division of the kingdom to begin at various dates from 939 to 931.

3. The Kings, Prophets and most important Events to be remembered are emphasized.

4. Co-reigns, as of Jehoram for 4 years co-regent with Jehoshaphat, are represented by a lighter parallel line.

The Movement of the History.   Five Great Periods.

I. The United Kingdom.   Three kings. 120 years, 1102-982.

II. The Divided Kingdom. — Judah. One dynasty. 11 kings, 1 queen — 260 years to 720.
Israel. Nine dynasties. 19 kings.

III. Judah. Alone. 8 kings,   David's dynasty 136 years, 722-586.

IV. The Exile. 70 years, 605- 536.

V. The Return. The New Nation. 536-400 and on.

CHRONOLOGY.

JUDAH.			DATES.				ISRAEL.
PROPHETS. CRISES. KINGS.	Years of Reigns.	B.C. Beecher	Years of Division	B.C. Hastings		Years of Reigns.	KINGS. CRISES. PROPHETS.
Rehoboam.	1	982	1	939		1	**Jeroboam.**
RELIGIOUS GROWTH 3 years. Influx of Levites, etc., from Israel. Invasion of Shishak from Egypt. *Decline.*	3	980	3	936		3	Introduces SEMI-IDOLA-TRY. Exodus to Judah of religious people.
	5	978	5	934		5	SHISHAK MONUMENT. AHIJAH.
Abijam.	17 1 2 3	965	18	922		18	SHEMAIAH.
Asa.	1 2	962	21	919		21 22	
Land at rest 10 years.	2 3	961	20	918		1 2	**Nadab.** Parts of 2 years.
War with Israel.		960	23	917		1	**Baasha.** Civil war with Judah.
GREAT REVIVAL AND REFORMATION.	26	947 937	46	894		1 24	**Elah.** Parts of 2 years.
							Zimri. 7 days.
	27	936	47	893		2	
						1	**Omri.** GREAT ENLARGEMENT OF THE KINGDOM. MOABITE STONE.
Decline.	38	925	58	882		12 1	**Ahab.** Marries JEZEBEL. IDOLATRY INTRODUCED. RELIGIOUS PERSECUTION. ELIJAH.
Jehoshaphat.	41 1	921	62	878		5	
WIDE EXTENDED REVIVAL. OUTWARD PROSPERITY.	17	905	78	862		21 1	**Ahaziah.** 2 years with Ahab.
	18	904	79	861		22 2	**Jehoram.**
DECLINE THROUGH ALLI-ANCE WITH JEZEBEL.							ELISHA.
Jehoram. 4 years as Co-regent.	1 22 4 25	900 897	83 86	857 854		5 8	

JUDAH		DATES			ISRAEL	
Prophets. Crises. Kings.	Years of Reigns.	B.C. Beecher	Years of Division	B.C. Hastings	Years of Reigns.	Kings. Crises. Prophets.
Ahaziah (part of 1).	8 / 1	893	90	850	12 / 1	Jehu.
Athaliah.	1	892	91	849		
Temple desecrated. Baal worship.						The zealous reformer. Destroys house of Ahab.
Joash.	6 / 1	886	97	843	7	
					28	BLACK OBELISK.
Temple and its worship restored.	23	864	119	821	1	Jehoahaz.
	37	850	133	807	15 / 1	Jehoash.
	39	848	135		17 / 3	Co-regnant 3 years in addition.
	40	847	136		1	Moabites invade Israel.
Amaziah.	1	846	137	803	2	
Defeated by Israel.	14	833	150		15	Defeats Amaziah of Judah.
Nominal ruler under suzerainty of Israel.	15	832	151	804	16 / 1	Jeroboam II.
Death of Amaziah.	29	817	166		16	JONAH (?). Becomes suzerain of all peoples from Mediterranean to Euphrates.
Interregnum for 11 years.						
Uzziah. Also called Azariah.	1	806	177	801	27	AMOS. HOSEA (?).
Amos.	15	792	191		41	Death of Jeroboam.
						Interregnum for 22 years.
	38	769	214	763		Zechariah (6 mos.).
Leprosy of Uzziah (?).	39	768	215	763		Shallum (1 mo.).
Jotham regent 13 years.	40	767	216	762	1	Menahem.
Eclipse of Sun by which Assyrian dates determined. June 15, 763 B.C.	44	763	220			HOSEA (?).
	50	757	226	752	5 / 10 / 1	Pekahiah.
ISAIAH early prophecies.	52	755	228	750	1	Pekah.
Jotham.	1	754	229	749	2	
Invasion by Israel and by Rezin of Damascus.	15	740	243		16	Successful invasion of Judah with Rezin of Damascus.
	16	741	244		17	
Ahaz.	1	738	245	741	18	
Tributary to Assyria.	3	736	247		20	Deportation by Tiglath-pilezer.
MICAH. HOSEA in Israel, close of his work, 735.	13	726	257	730	1	Hoshea becomes king.
Hezekiah.	16 / 1	723	260	727		TAYLOR CYLINDER.
ISAIAH later prophecies. GREAT PASSOVER of Hezekiah.	2	722	261		5	First siege and capture of Samaria.
	4	720	263		7	**Fall of Samaria** by Assyria.
	6	718	265	722	9	End of Kingdom of Israel.
Invasions of SENNACHERIB.	14	710	273			
	19	705	278			Death of Sargon and Accession of SENNACHERIB in Assyria.
	23	701	282			
Manasseh.	29 / 1	695	288			
		694	289			
DEATH OF ISAIAH. Tribute to Assyria.						Esarhaddon 676.

B.C. Hastings column note: Authorities are practically agreed on these dates.

JUDAH.		DATES.			EVENTS.
Prophets, Crises, Kings.	Years of Reigns.	B. C. Beecher	Years of Division	B. C. Hastings	Contemporaneous History.
Manasseh carried to Babylon.	47	648	335		
Return and reformation.	48	647	336		
NAHUM.					
Amon.	1 / 2 — 55	640 / 639 / 638	343 / 344 / 345		
Josiah.	1				
ZEPHANIAH.	8	631	352		Legislation of Draco at Athens.
JEREMIAH begins prophecy.	13	626			626 Scythian invasion.
Josiah's great reformation begun.	17	622	361		
BOOK OF THE LAW Found.	18	621	363		
REFORMATION Passover.					
Jehoahaz (3 mos.).	31 / 1	608 / 607	373 / 376		Expedition of Pharaoh Necho.
Jehoiakim.					606 DESTRUCTION OF NINEVEH.
Beginning of first captivity.	3, 4	605	378		DANIEL and others taken to Babylon.
HABAKKUK.					
Jehoiachin (3 mos.)	11 / 1	597	386		The great deportation of Jews.
Zedekiah.		596	387		
Beginning of second captivity.					
DANIEL.					Legislation of Solon at Athens.
EZEKIEL.					
TEMPLE DESTROYED.					
Beginning of THIRD CAPTIVITY.	11	586	397		

(vertical note in B. C. Hastings column: Authorities are practically agreed on these dates.)

First Captivity, 605
Second Captivity, 597
Third Captivity and Temple Destroyed, 586

70 Years.
The Seventy Years of Exile foretold by Jeremiah

537, 6 First Return.

516 { Second Temple Completed.

Prophets, Crises, Kings.		B. C. Beecher	Years of Division	B. C. Hastings	Contemporaneous History.
First year of Cyrus.		539 / 538	444 / 445		Cyrus takes Babylon. Cyrus' decree for the return.
First Return. 50,000 under ZERUBBABEL.		537, 6	440.7		CYRUS CYLINDER.
Foundations of Temple laid.		535	448		
HAGGAI. Long delay.					
ZECHARIAH.					
Building of Temple resumed.		520	463		
SECOND TEMPLE COMPLETED.		516	467		
(A Psalm.)		490	493		Battle of Marathon.
		486	497		Accession of Xerxes (Ahasuerus).
		480	503		Thermopylæ and Salamis.
ESTHER becomes Queen.		479	504		Herodotus.
Second Return, under EZRA.		458	525		Pericles. Plato.
					Socrates. Xenophon.
Return under NEHEMIAH. Jerusalem rebuilt.		444	539		
MALACHI. Reforms.					
		336	647		Reign of Alexander the Great.
		323	660		
JUDEA ANNEXED TO EGYPT.		318	665		
		223	760		Accession of Antiochus the Great.
JUDEA ANNEXED TO SYRIA.		198	785		
		175	808		Accession of Antiochus Epiphanes.
		170	813		
Antiochus massacres Jews. The Maccabees lead Jews to revolt.		167	816		
Judea under Roman Power.		63	920		Herod governor of all Syria.
		43	940		Herod king of the Jews under Rome.
Herod takes Jerusalem and is de facto king of Judea.		40	943		
		37	946		Beginning of Roman Empire.
		31	952		

(vertical note in B. C. Hastings column: Authorities are practically agreed on these dates.)

During the seventy years captivity there was no king in Israel. The prophets Zechariah and Haggai prophesied after the captivity, (Haggai 1:1 and Ezra 5:1). Malachi was a contemporary of Nehemiah during the time of the reconstruction of the temple and the walls and city of Jerusalem. Ezra and Nehemiah were governors over Israel and the high priests were Joshua and his sons.

As the Old Testament period ends part of Israel is back in the land under the domination of the Medo-Persian empire. The time of the Greeks and Romans was to come during the 400 silent years between the Old and New Testaments.

Rule of Strangers over Israel

1) Assyria
2) Babylon
3) Persia (Medo-Persian Empire) 536 B.C. restored the Jews to their homeland.
4) Greeks, 332-166 B.C., kingdom divided among Alexander's four generals after his death.
5) Romans (63 B.C.-476 A.D.)

In 70 A.D., under Titus, Jerusalem was razed to the ground and the Jews were scattered, (Jeremiah 24:9). The name Jew became a byword among the nations because of their disobedience, (Deuteronomy 28:37; Psalm 44:14; Jeremiah 24:9, etc.).

The promises made to Israel were eternal promises, (Genesis 17:7; 13:15-17; Deuteronomy 7:6-8, etc.).

Palestine was and is to be theirs, (Genesis 13:14-17). Their history is not yet finished.

CONCLUSIONS

Shem founded the most stable nation in history. He did not wander far from his central position on the earth. He was to have a small numerical increase so he needed less territory. He never disappeared from the world's scene for long periods as did Japheth, and never wandered and was lost like Ham.

The holy oracles were committed to him and he was the teacher of his brothers in religion and letters. The Messiah was to come from him and finally did arrive after a period of many centuries. He would have few famous sons, but among them were some very important people: Moses, David, Solomon and Paul. He had few writings, but through the Bible he covered every important area of letters: science, history, poetry, biography, law and philosophy, and they cannot be equaled in all of literature.

His geographical movements were: in Elam he went southeast to the east of the Persian Gulf. In Asshur he traveled westward to the Caspian. In the Hebrews he traveled and took possession of the land of Canaan. Joktan settled part of the Arabian Peninsula. The only wanderer was his son Lud who left the Armenian mountains and traveled along the Jordan Valley and the Isthmus of Suez. He reached northern Africa where he rested a while between Mizraim and Phut. He intermarried with some of the Libyans and then pushed on across the Sahara to the Canary Islands where he left his traditions and customs and evidently pushed on to the New World to Brazil. His number has dwindled, but his influence is still present in North Africa. His language and customs were adopted by his Hamitic cousins.

Every other nation was founded by man within the boundaries set by God, (Acts 17:26).

Israel was the only nation founded by God. It was promised to Abraham and many hundreds of years later it became a nation at Mt. Sinai.

It is, and always will be, God's special treasure. The years of wilderness wandering, the claiming of the land under Joshua, the 450 years of apostasy under the judges, the united kingdom under Saul, David, and Solomon, the divided kingdom beginning with Rehoboam and Jeroboam, and the seventy years of captivity for each, were used by God in the refining process He continues even today.

Israel will continue, though other nations come and go. The Tribulation period deals with God's judgment of Israel and will culminate with the millennium during which Christ will rule from the throne of David in Jerusalem.

All history must be interpreted in reference to its relationship with Israel. God said to Abraham in Genesis 12:3, "And I will bless them that bless thee, and curse him that curseth thee: and in thee shall all families of the earth be blessed."

This was an eternal promise. Even the disobedience of Israel could not do away with the promise because it was God's promise to them.

In order to understand the events occurring today, all eyes should be on Jerusalem.

"The sceptre of Shem was extended rather over a spiritual and invisible, than over an earthly kingdom. Solomon in his highest glory was rather a master of wise men, than of monarchs; the kings of the earth were his allies, not his vassals. The reign of Shem has been the royalty of Mind, his Scriptures have moulded the development of the nations; the world dates its age to and from the days of the Son of David. Thus Shem has ruled in hearts and brains, and crowningly in his Divine Descendant, who is King of kings, and Lord of Lords." Julia McNair Wright, *Bricks from Babel,* (New York: John B. Alden, Publisher, 1885), pp. 170, 171.

SECTION V

JAPHETH AND HIS SONS

Each son of Noah was given individual and special talents. Ham became the 'Monument-builder', Shem the 'Palace-builder', and Japheth became the 'Mound-builder'. He was called that because his progress can be traced by following his burial mounds through Europe, Media, India, China, the Arctic regions, the New World, North, Central and South America, and down to Patagonia.

Japheth is the "elder" (Genesis 10:21) and the father of the fair-skinned division of the human race. His descendants in general populated Europe, much of Asia, Armenia, and part of Persia. The fact that Japheth is listed first "would seem to indicate that the fair races were the least known to the Jews, it (actually) implies that the latter were well disposed toward them, for Japheth was (ultimately) to dwell in the tents of Shem, and therefore to take part in Shem's spiritual privileges." James Orr, Ed., *International Standard Bible Encyclopedia,* (Wm. B. Eerdmans, 1939), p. 1569.

He is the world's greatest wanderer, a man of unrest and progress; the world's true traveling philosopher. His line of progress is demonstrated through art and he is the world's great artist and architect. He expounded the beautiful and became the father of princes - the founder of kingdoms. The Gospel given to Japheth had a "Go" prefixed to it - his was even a traveling religion, (Matthew 28:19, *"Go ye therefore...."*).

The Japhethites were the ultimate conquerors who built cities and established kingdoms. They have been the most prolific of people and have filled three-quarters of the world.

The **third world empire** was founded by them; the Greek Empire. It was founded by Alexander the Great when he crossed the Hellespont in the spring of 334 B. C.

The Roman Empire succeeded the Greek Empire until its fall in 476 A. D. Since that time every major empire has been founded by the descendants of Japheth.

Migration Impulse

"When Japheth comes to the sea, he builds ships to continue his journey. When he comes to a huge mountain range, he tunnels through it. When he finds an isthmus in his way he cuts it apart and produces a river. He finds the ocean and makes his ship the upper bridge to cross it and the telegraph the lower bridge. He lays a railroad in the jungle, makes a highway in the desert. He conquers air travel to continue his journeys.

"Shem's hand wavers and he lets fall the light of his revelation; Japheth's hand seizes it, and holds it aloft over all the world. Ham's oracles become dumb, his works cease to utter a voice, and Japheth rises up and expounds them.

"He journeyed west, east, and north and made it very difficult to trace the migrations.

"In 'Gomer's bands' there would be a new life of humanity, the breath of liberty, the stride of progress, the primacy of conscience." Julia McNair Wright, *Bricks From Babel,* (New York: John B. Alden Publisher, 1885), p. 77.

Language of the Scriptures

The Old Testament was written in the language of Heber; the New Testament is the language of Javan. The Semitic tongue served at the altars of the old Dispensation; the Japhetic fills the pulpits of the new and carries on the missionary work of the Gospel. It is the Japhethites who are the messengers to prepare for Christ's second coming as a glorious King; it was the Shemites, through the Old Testament, who gave the message of His first coming as a humble servant.

The great family of Japheth spread from the Ganges to the Thames, all geographically of Asiatic origin. The Goths, the Celts, the Slavs, and the Greeks, because of their common beginnings and a common tongue, are called the Indo-Europeans.

Japheth's sons were: Gomer, Magog, Madai, Javan, Tubal, Meshech, and Tiras.

GOMER

The main body of the Gomerites went eastward to the north of India where they lived for many centuries and absorbed much of the language of the Sanskrit, (the ancient literary language of India from which ancient Persian, Greek, and Latin and all present languages of Europe proceed). They are thus called the Indo-European languages.

One group migrated to the Black Forest, the Alps and the Rhine, and became the fathers of the German nation. Morris says they are usually identified as the Cimmeria when they appear north of the Black Sea. Today the name survives as the Crimea in Germany and Cambria or Wales. (Morris, *Genesis Record*), p. 247.

The Celts and the Germans were the two most prominent families of the Gomerites. The Celts filled all of western Europe. They went to Spain and united with the old Iberians. They overrode the Basques in France and prepared Italy for the Gauls. They went into Belgium and Britain.

The Celts were fair-skinned with blue eyes and blond hair. They dyed themselves blue as noted by Lady Callcott, in her book *Little Arthur's History of England,* "In the winter they (the original English settlers who were Celts) used to wrap themselves up in the skins of the beasts they could shoot with their bows and arrows. In the summer they were naked, and instead of clothes they put paint upon their bodies. They were very fond of a fine blue colour, which they made of a plant, called Woad, which they found in their woods. They squeezed out the juice of the Woad, and then stained themselves all over with it, so that in summer they looked as if they were dressed in tight blue clothes." Lady Callcott, *Little Arthur's History of England,* (London: John Murray, 1875), pp. 2,3.

They wore chains and rings of gold and wore their hair in a hundred knots. They had little understanding of the meaning of a home and were not noted for their natural affections. They had no virtue, no pity, no honor. Their one delight was blood. Their souls were full of terrible superstitions and they offered human sacrifices and ate human flesh.

The Celtic priests were the Druids who wore long white beards, and white linen robes. Their religion was very similar to the superstitions they had learned in India.

The Germans had red hair, and if it was not red enough they dyed it redder still. They dressed in plain tunics. The German was a man who loved his family and was faithful in friendships and memories. His tastes were plain.

Both nations bred fierce warriors and lived to fight. When they became too old or too ill to fight they committed suicide rather than live without the honor and glory of battle.

From the Gomerite Celts and Germans come the Franks, Gauls, Normans, Saxons, Belgians, and Frisians. These are the nations God chose to become rulers of the world and take the Gospel message to 'the regions beyond'.

Migrations of the sons of Gomer

Armenia: Part of Gomer's first band goes to northern Armenia, where his son **Togarmah** becomes the father of the Armenians and the nations of the Caucasus. Originally they were in southwestern Armenia and migrated north and west (Genesis 10:3; 1 Chronicles 1:6; Ezekiel 27:14; 38:6). The name Togarama is found in the cuneiform texts near Carchemish. They were the ancient Cimmerians, the Gimirray of the Assyrians in western Russia, (Genesis 10:2,3; 1 Chronicles 1:5, 6; Ezekiel 38:6). The Phrygians were related to, or the same as, the Armenians.

Germany: Ashkenaz, son of Gomer, went westward and settled in modern Germany and the German Jews are still called the Ashkenazi. Originally they were located north of the Black and Caspian Seas in the region of Sarmatia. (Genesis 10:3; 1 Chronicles 1:6; Jeremiah 51:27).

Iberia: According to Josephus the sons of **Riphath** became the Paphlagonians, but others believe they became the Celts. The Iberians had occupied Georgia, by the Black Sea in Russia, and went from there to inhabit Aquitaine, Corsica and Spain. The Biscayans and Basques, relics of the oldest Turanian inhabitants of Europe, still retain their early tongue which is very Russian in sound.

The Iberians moved along the northern coast of the Mediterranean while the Phoenicians, who were children of Ham, traveled along the same coast to the south. The Phoenicians reached the Pillars of Hercules (Gibraltar) and established themselves in southern Spain. The children of Ham and Japheth dwelt in one home and were later joined by the Moors when they invaded Spain in 800 A. D.

The Iberians found enemies in the Ligurians, a very early nation of Gomerites. The Ligurii were Celts who had been displaced by Rosh as he moved westward and they (the Ligurii) had moved to the far west.

Italy: the Umbrians and later the Etruscans went from the east into Italy. Italy was also peopled by many Greek fugitives and explorers. The Greeks taught the Romans to read and write, and to appreciate the arts and to express themselves in song.

Religious beliefs of the Gomerites:

They believed in an all-mighty Father who dwells in the skies. His voice can be heard in the thunder, and can be approached with awe and humility in the silence of the forests, thus his care and interest in the native forests where he lived.

Their supreme God had no visible form but was eternal and unchangeable. He demanded that men be honest and brave and fear the gods and recognize them as the disposers of all events.

There were two states after death; joy for the religious and brave and those who died by the sword; and unending torment for the base.

There were three supreme gods: Odin, Freya, and Thor. (Note how there is always a female deity in pagan religions due to the influence of Semiramis.)

They had an evil deity called Loki who came from a Great Serpent.

The first people in the world were a man and woman who had three sons. A great flood came and everyone except one man and his family perished. They escaped in a small boat.

They had a legend about the end of the world and of heaven. In their traditional stories they had the promise of a coming Redeemer. (McNair, *Bricks from Babel*), pp. 106-107.

(See the last part of this section for the history of the Romans who were Gomerites.)

MAGOG - second son of Japheth, (Ezekiel 38:2,3; 39:1)

The word Gog is used in the Old Testament as the name of a line of princes over Magog, as the word Pharaoh was used for the ruler over Egypt. Later it was used with Magog to denote the nation.

They formed the nation of the Scythes who were a wild, cruel and terrible nation. He was the expression of the wrath of Japheth as Javan was the expression of his genius, Gomer of his endurance, and Madai of his restlessness.

Their first location was above the Black and Caspian Seas. His descendant, Rosh, who is the first tribe of note named, formed the nations of Russia. They were mighty conquerors who destroyed Media, invaded Palestine, took away Egypt's power, conquered Cyaxares, and were the masters of Asia.

The Polar Nations- sons of Magog

The peoples of the North were called *Ichthyophagi*, "Fish-eaters". Their door posts and rafters were enormous whale bones, their mortars were whale vertebrae, and all their domestic utensils, weapons and foods, came from fish. They were also called *Hyperboreans*, dwellers beyond the North-wind. They called themselves men, *par excellence.*

The original people were Finno-Ugrians who stayed close to the coasts and retreated as civilization approached them. Because of this they became known by the name 'Shoremen'.

Their root is Magog. These were from the Scythic Turanians who divided into various families; the most prominent were Mongols, Malays, and original Finns from whom came the Turks. The Turanians were not quite so well developed physically or mentally as the Aryans from Madai.

In their domestic life they were of low character; their language was imperfect, their religious ideas gross. They were hunters and fishermen and had no desire to improve themselves or their lot and could not read or write.

The most widely spread of these peoples were the Ugrians, or Ugorians, which equals Ogres. From them came the stories of the ogres (e.g. Grimm's Fairy Tales). From the Altai mountains they traveled to the east and west and were a wild and savage people who lived in caves and forests and used snares, clubs and weapons made of bone. The Northmen from the Indian region called the Ugrian a *Jotun*; the Greeks called him a *Titan*. (Wright, *Bricks from Babel*), p. 123.

They counted by dozens and sixties using numbers that could be divided by 12 and 60 as the Shumiro-Accads did before them and from whom they took this custom.

Migration of the Ugrians

Some of the Ugrians went southward and intermarried with the Aryans and became more civilized. Many parts of Europe appear to have first been inhabited by the Finns. They were eventually displaced and overpowered by other nations because they had no intention of staying in any one place. They were too savage to have any organized government or leadership, or any systematic warfare or good weapons. "...the Eskimo had no system of government. There were no tribes and no chiefs. But the Eskimos of different regions formed separate cultural groups." (*World Book Encyclopedia*, Vol. 6), p. 278.

The original Ugrians went into the northern regions because they had come from cold country and felt at home there. They settled in Finland, Sweden, Norway, Lapland, and Obi, and were driven farther north as the more civilized Japhetic tribes moved them and took their places.

The more developed of these peoples went to Hungary, and were known as the tribe of Magyars. The entire Slav group of people came from this ethnic root, of which the Magyars are only a small part. Included are the Slavs, Czechs, Bohemians, Poles, etc. These people adopted the ways of the people surrounding them and became a civilized responsible people.

Others migrated to Kamtchatka, to the Siberian plain - to the Obi River, and another group to Lapland. Some went southward to France and apparently helped form the ancient Basque people.

They crossed the Behring Strait and took possession the icebound north. The Esquimaux, the Chuckees, the Kamtchatkans are all from the same root.

Today they are geographically located in Russia, Alaska, Canada, and Greenland.

They are not as physically attractive as other nations, but are hardy, long-lived, and prolific. They are sometimes slow of comprehension, and stubborn, but they are loyal, faithful, and hospitable. When their lives are touched by the Gospel they become faithful followers of Christ.

Religious beliefs

Because they were so far from the cradle of Christianity they lost most of their consciousness of the revelation of God. However, God says in Romans 1 that all men are without excuse and even these people retained a tradition of religious teachings:

The first man, Kallak, rose out of the earth, and a woman was created from his thumb, all other humans came from these two. The woman brought death.

One time the world turned upside down, and everyone was drowned except a few who were transformed into spirits of fire. One man remained, and a woman rose out of the ground; together they repopulated the earth.

They were very superstitious; they believed in Angekoks or wizards; in air, fire, and water spirits, and in demons and ghosts.

Some believed the soul migrates during sleep, and that the soul of the dead could enter the bodies of living animals and humans. They believed the dwelling place of the dead to be in the center of the earth. Some believed the soul was shaped like a body, but was bright and untouchable. Others believed the dwelling place of the dead was above the sky and the soul went there with the speed of a thought.

They believed in 'one mighty, good and supreme god, Torngarsuk,' and when they heard the preaching of the missionaries they recognized Him whom they worshipped in ignorance.

Torngarsuk had a co-deity, his wife or mother (i.e. Semiramis); they lived in bright, unending summer, heat, and sunshine where only the good and industrious could go. The female deity was evil, however.

Torngarsuk kept track of all the deeds of men and when the soul left the body on a dangerous 5-day flight to the isle of light, he reviewed the person's life. When the spirit arrived at the shore of a mighty sea, if he had been evil no kayak awaited him, and demons seized him. (This is very similar to the belief of the Egyptians who believed that a boat would be waiting to take the person to the other side to be judged for his works.) He was enveloped with cold, night, and storms. If he had been good a kayak awaited that took him to a warm snowless island. There were three terraces on this island, for three degrees of goodness in the soul; good, better, best. The best was on the top terrace nearest to Torngarsuk. The edge of the island was circled with fires for cooking. Every fire had a pot full of meat and the good sat around those fires in eternal feasting.

They believed in two states after death, which were determined by one's deeds. Someday the world will be washed clean and a new world made of its pieces. It will be a world of purity, warmth, food, and sunshine, according to their beliefs. (Wright, *Bricks from Babel*), pp. 130-132, excerpts.

MONGOLS AND MALAYS - from the Turanian Scythians.

The headquarters of these peoples was in the Altai Mountains. Mongol was the elder brother and family head. Their chief characteristic was a monosyllabic language. Theirs was one of the ancient centers of civilization; it was the North China plain along the Yellow River. It was the most accessible by land from the West.

Geographic divisions of the Mongols:

East Asia: China, Japan, Korea, Vietnam (to lesser extent) - Mongoloid peoples.

Central Asia: Mongolia, Sinkian (Chinese Turkestan), Tibet

Southeast Asia: Vietnam, Burma, Siam (Thailand), Cambodia, Laos, Malaya, Indonesia, the Philippines

The higher cultures were more from India; both Islam and Christian further distinguished them.

The people of East Asia comprise one-third of the population of mankind.

Language characteristics:

Their language was Sinitic, (the branch of Sino-Tibetan that comprises the Chinese), Mandarin being the main root.

The Altaic was Turkish - from the Mongoloid root.

The Mongolian predominates in central and western Asia - the Mongols.

The Tungusic-Manchus were in Manchuria and Siberia. The Korean and Japanese languages resemble the Altaic, having the same root which was and is a monosyllabic language.

Austronesia is from Malay. The Malaya and Indonesia, the Philippines, aborigines of Taiwan, Madagascar and Melanesia and Polynesia are all from this Austronesian root.

THE CHINESE

The first brother, Chin, surpassed his brothers in pride, ingenuity, and the extent of his territory, and was the greatest of all the children of Mongol. His uncles were the Ogres in the north, the Turks in the west, and the Malays on a long crooked peninsula on the south, and the Hindus in the southwest.

Chin took the **middle kingdom** and claimed it to be the center of the world. The Turk called him Cathay, and told wonderful stories about him. The Hindu called him Chin in contempt of his monosyllabic tongue. In the 17th century the world found out that China and Cathay were the same country.

Chin did not like sea travel so took only one island, Hainan. His younger brother, Japan, was enriched by his civilization.

Geographic characteristics

There is every variety of soil, climate, and vegetation in his kingdom. There are two great mountain ranges and a wonderful river system, with five great lakes. There are excellent and numerous harbors; rich and varied minerals, and a great variety of plants and animals. (Wright, *Bricks from Babel*), pp. 135,136, excerpts.

"A determining influence of East Asian civilization has been its relative isolation from the other great civilizations of mankind. Growing up at the eastern extremity of the Old World and separated from the other major centers of early civilization by great distances and formidable mountains and deserts, it developed distinctive cultural patterns which have been retained in large part until today." Edwin O. Reischauer, John K. Fairbank; *East Asia the*

Great Tradition, (Harvard University, Houghton Mifflin Co., Boston, 1960), p. 8.

Characteristics of Chin

Physically he is a close copy of the Aryan; tawny, black-eyed, nonmuscular, straight-haired, with high cheek bones. Miss Wright calls him "a great imitator, a blend of genius, fortitude, paraphrase, deceit, industry, materialism, literature and acquisitiveness." His is the greatest example of self-contained civilization, national unity, and longevity, in an extensive area, that the world has ever known. (Wright, *Bricks from Babel*), p. 136.

The Chinese were not known of at the time of the Greek Republic and the conquests of Alexander. Alexander believed India to be the eastern limits of the earth. Augustus had not heard of China and not until 140 years after Christ did the first Chinese products reach Rome.

The difficult physical terrain would have limited movement and interrelations with other countries. They had a strong sense of history and an ideal of political unity. They considered China the only civilized land; the border was for the "Four barbarians". They called China the "Central Country" or Chung-Kuo, and it is still called "The Middle Kingdom" by the Chinese. T'ien-hsia meant that 'all under heaven' became 'the empire'.

Early histories were more a mixture of mythological characters than a series of proven facts. The only history that has been proven through archeological evidence is the Shan dynasty (approx. 1400-1100 B. C.). All historical data before that period is a blend of fabulous tales of gods and men and has no basis.

Chinese philosophy was based upon the teachings of Confucius, who taught the Chinese morals, philosophy, astronomy, and civil law. The five famous Confucian relationships were: ruler and subject; father and son; husband and wife; elder brother and younger brother; friend and friend.

However, as evidenced by their language, they had an understanding from the most remote times of the true God and His purpose for man. Many of their logograms use Biblical symbols to form words. For example, the cross is used with the symbols of a man and woman. There are many such examples of God's Word remembered through the centuries in their language. Their logogram for justice has been used for many years to demonstrate that the early Chinese had a concept of God. When the character is taken apart it shows a lamb, over the character for 'me'. How strange that the Chinese should have such a representation. Where would they get such an idea for 'justice'? Could it be that this 'Lamb' has the same significance in this Chinese character as it has in the Judeo-Christian interpretation?

The family was the most important unit in Chinese society and was clan-centered. It provided economic foundation, security, education, social contact, recreation and religion through ancestor worship which began in ancient times. The plan extended backwards and forwards for five generations and the patriarchal father was the center of authority.

The individual was subordinate to the family. His only value was in relationship to his sex, age, and position in the family. The emperor was, in essence, the Great Father.

Personal morality was the basis of society, not the law. And society was held together by Confucianism. There was no church or law to act as a sustaining or controlling force. Because of the 'father image' of the leaders they were able to hold absolute power over the people.

Two-hundred years before Christ a colony of Jews arrived in China and their descendants are still there.

In 94 B.C. the Chinese sent an envoy to seek trade with Arabia and in 61 A.D. Antoninus sent a fruitless embassy to China. In 635 A.D. the Nestorians sent missionaries and in the 13th century missionaries of the Roman Catholic system were sent from Rome during the time of Marco Polo. (Wright, *Bricks*), p. 138.

Early Chinese contributions

They were one of the earliest nations to coin money. Their early writing resembles Egyptian hieroglyphics because they had the same historic source at Babylon. They were ignorant of physical sciences but studied medicine and arithmetic. They began printing, made gunpowder, invented the mariner's compass and the manufacture of silk. They also had an iron-tipped plow, used chopsticks when eating and developed lacquer for painting objects. They had a mail service much like the late pony-express, they used chariots, they worked in bronze and iron casting, had the multiplication tables, built great roads and canals, had standardized weights and measures and a uniform writing system.

Early enemies

Their earliest and greatest enemy was their cousin, Hun, the grandson of Turk. The Huns were a warring nation whose main goal was to conquer. They were almost black in color and according to history, were an extremely violent people. They attacked China toward the end of the second century B.C. and the Great Wall of China was built to try to keep them out. Theirs was a short-lived rule, but they did overrun much of Europe as well as many parts of Asia. At the height of their power Attila was their leader, but their power didn't last very long.

Religious beliefs

The Chinese retained an early tradition of the Noahic family. They had a story of creation and Eden which follows: In the first heaven all creation was happiness and beauty. All beings were perfect; pain, labor, death, want, and vice, were unknown. A covetous attitude began and grew into a mighty tree of wrongs and disasters which has overshadowed the earth. Early men lived very long lives and were taller than pagodas. The earth became so bad that the waters rose and flooded it. Hi was good and was saved, as was his wife, three sons and their wives. (The number three in the first family of the human race is strangely retained in all mythologies; three sons of Adam, three sons of Noah.) These three sons are recalled in eight primary *Konas,* each made up of three.

They believed in one original, all-powerful, universal God, greater than, and before, the gods of their pantheon. This god is called "Y" which is the logogram for three in one. Here it does not refer to the Trinity and Unity of God, but to the three branches of the "race" which God created, (Ham, Shem, and Japheth).

They were indifferent in matters of religion and were materialistic in their beliefs. They had three chief forms of idolatry and had an extreme horror of death and avoided speaking of it directly. They believed in the immortality of the soul, and adored the *manes* (the spirits of the dead) of their ancestors. The majority of their beliefs were a mixture of the ideas they received from the Hindus, the Jews, the Moravians, and the Roman Catholics. They also had, and have, animistic beliefs.

Because they were an agricultural society they placed emphasis on cosmological and cylindrical theories, grades of gods, fertility of the soil, heaven, and later earth.

All authority was strongly religious. The ruler was the chief priest and calendar-maker. (Wright, *Bricks from Babel*), pp. 139-140, excerpts.

The Temple of Heaven in Beijing has no idols and the Shinto shrine has the same floorplan as the tabernacle, which is often seen in pagan religions.

They had an early religion of mother and child worship, which could have come directly from Babylon before they left to find their own place in the world.

The Lunar Christian New Year takes place at the same time as the Passover season and they still put blood on the doorpost and lintel by the use of red tissue paper.

Chinese Language

The Chinese language is one of the most complex of all the languages. "It is one of the most difficult languages to learn to read, because it does not use an alphabet. It also has no standard pronunciation, and may be spoken in as many different ways as there are dialects...The characters in written Chinese each convey a complete idea, and are treated as a single unit. They have only one syllable and are not inflected...A student must learn to recognize about 3,500 different characters before he can read a simple novel. Scholars must know at least 10,000 characters in order to read classic Chinese literature." ("Chinese Language", *World Book Encyclopedia,* 1974 Ed., Vol. 3), p. 394.

Early finds at An-yand show writing in the Chinese language and it is the same form of writing that dominates East Asian civilization.

There are three main characteristics of the Sinitic languages:

(1) the tonal structure (syllables which sound alike are distinguished by the tone in which they are spoken), modern Mandarin has four tones;

(2) the uninflected monosyllables, and

(3) the absence of inflection.

Written words are of great value; prayers are <u>written</u> to the gods, not spoken. There are many famous documents, but few great speeches. Education is the more-honored ability to read and write the 50,000+ characters. The classical Chinese can be read by groups with different dialects. "If they had had a phonetic system of writing they might have broken up into separate national groups, as did the Italian, French, Spanish, and Portuguese." (Reischauer, Fairbank, *East Asia*), p. 43. But that was not God's plan for them and they remained united.

If the ancestors of the Chinese left Babel in a massive emigration to the land of Sinim, they would have had a new language or at least a revised language.

Tradition says the Chinese language was invented by Ts'ang Chieh, a minister and historian of the 'Yellow Emperor', Huang Ti, in a legendary home before the written history of the Hsia Dynasty near 2205 B.C. Ts'ang Chieh used pictographs to form his alphabet. These primitive pictographs were known as 'radicals', and were combined to tell a story or to teach abstract ideas. Combined they formed more complete figures called 'characters' or 'ideographs'.

There are also narratives of certain chapters in Genesis preserved in the ideographic Chinese characters which have changed little since ancient times. Some demonstrate a knowledge of the Hebrew concept of the origin of man and the plan of God for salvation.

Their language has 50 thousand symbols called logograms, each meaning a different word. The word 'civilization' in Chinese is *wenhua* which means 'the transforming influence of writing'. They can understand each other by the written word and thus have brought about civilization to their nation.

This also accounts for the emphasis on beauty and exactness in their writing coming from the brush strokes of their calligraphy.

Their languages:

<u>Mandarin</u> was spoken by the imperial court and is the official language of the Chinese government bureaucracy.

<u>Cantonese</u> is spoken in the south Canton province.

<u>Wu</u> is spoken in Shanghai.

<u>Min</u> is spoken in the Fujian region.

Each language is mutually unintelligible when spoken, but understood when written.

Government

The government was an authoritarian Oriental society. A despotic, absolute monarch was supported by bureaucrats and ruled over a peasant population. The need to keep the Yellow River within its bounds and harness its water for irrigation-water-control caused the implementation of forced labor gangs for public works. This included both public works for water and wall building.

Chon (1122-1027 B.C.) conquered the Shang dynasty. The Chon kings called themselves 'Sons of Heaven'. T'ien, meaning 'heaven' was written with a character originally used as a rough sketch of a man. Many linguists believe this to have been Jesus Christ - the way to heaven.

There were four classes of society: the warrior-administrator; the peasants or primary producers; the artisans or secondary producers; and the merchants.

The Great Wall was constructed by the government to keep out the northern 'barbarians' whose use of horses made them a greater threat.

Horseback riding was adopted by the Chinese and replaced the chariot. They were formidable warriors with horses and crossbow. Horses also speeded communication and brought about a need for trousers instead of flowing robes.

For entering government service one was required to pass an exam about Confucian literature. It was very difficult and only those who could read and were able to receive private tutoring could hope to pass the exam. However, they were allowed to take it as many times as they wanted to and some eventually passed.

Different cultures:

The Zhuang live in the middle of the most populated area of China. They call themselves the <u>Han</u> because they trace their lineage back to the founders of the Han dynasty which ruled China for approximately 400 years beginning in 206 B.C. They spread south and mixed with other ethnic groups, both from the north and south.

The Kazaks, Uygurs, and Tibetans live in the northwest and southwest quadrants of China. They are Buddhists who worship the Dali Lama.

The Uygurs are sedentary farmers who live in adobe houses. There are 5.4 millions in the Zinjiang province.

The Kazaks are nomads who live in the northwest quadrant. There are about 800,000 of them. They are tent-dwellers and were the horsemen bandits on the Silk Road who stole from the merchants. They live in yurts which are the felt tents they construct over a strutwork of tree limbs tied with ropes. These tents have not varied in three thousand years. They put up to eight layers of felt on them in the winter and are able to keep warm. The tents are taken down when they move and are loaded onto carts which are pulled by their animals and are then set up at the next location. They live on the mountain border between the former Soviet Union and China in the northwestern corner of Tibet.

The Tibetans live in the southwestern quadrant called the 'roof of the world'. Its mountains range from 13,000-25,000 feet above sea level. The temperature falls to 40 degrees below Fahrenheit in these areas.

The Golog whose name means, 'head on backward', is one of the fiercest tribes of the Tibetans.

The Tibetans raise yak around Lhasa, and do some farming raising barley. Before 1950 they only ate yak products and barley, no vegetables. They thought the Chinese ate grass like animals because they ate vegetables. Both the Yellow and the Yangtze Rivers begin in Tibet.

Later Religions

Confucianism is based on the philosophy of Confucius who was born in 551 B.C. and died at age 72. He was a wandering scholar who preached moderation and honesty in a time of bloodshed. He left no writings and a century and a half later some of his disciples put together the teachings of Confucius and called them the *Analects*. These teachings taught political principles - how to be a good employee, citizen, father, son, etc. They taught an ethical system of public religion with thousands of rules which had to be kept.

Confucius practiced his ideas of morality and justice in silence. He became the first minister of the State and was reverenced for his wise council. He inspired his disciples to follow his philosophy.

Taoism was begun by Lao Zi in the sixth century. Little is known about him and most of his teachings were stupid tales. Taoism teaches a mystical union with nature and the life of a hermit or life in a simple village. It also teaches an ethical system as does Buddhism, but teaches a private religion.

He introduced a system of myths, superstition and magic which fired the imagination of those who followed him.

There is no omnipotent God in either religion and no hereafter.

Buddhism came from India in the first century A.D. Its founder was a noble called Siddhartha Guatama. His religion provided a hereafter in the form of Nirvana, but like Taoism it taught contemplation and a removal from worldly things. It is composed of mysticism, rituals, ornate temples and monasteries.

For more than 2000 years the Chinese have had these three religions (Buddhism, Confucianism, and Taoism), which have been combined into one. The three founders were contemporaries, and both Confucianism and Taoism are indigenous to China.

But what was the religion of China before these philosophies appeared? With pride the Chinese say their civilization is the oldest in the world, dating back more than 4500 years. This date brings us close to the date of the Tower of Babel.

Confucius, a diligent editor, gathered together what seemed to him the most important details of the history of China (some records to the time of Noah) in a book called "The Book of History." In this book is a story of the Emperor Shun, who lived in legendary history, who sacrificed to Shang Ti, 'the Governor of the Sky'; the name of Shang Ti means 'Emperor above. There is evidence indicating the ancient Chinese were monotheists who worshipped this one God. Also, Shang Ti can be identified with the Supreme Being of the Hebrews when parts of the book of Genesis are compared with the 'recitation scripts' used by the Chinese emperors when they took part as high priests in the national ceremonies of sacrifice. The translation was thus: "In the beginning existed a great chaos, without form and dark. The five elements (the planets) had not begun to revolve, nor the sun and moon to shine. There was no form or sound. You, oh spiritual Sovereign came forth in your power and first divided the pure from the impure. You formed the sky; you formed the earth; you created men. You formed all things with the power to reproduce. You have chosen, O Ti, to hear us because you are our Father, etc."

Historic Progression

The Chinese call their country "The Middle Kingdom" because they say it is the middle of the earth. By the sixth century B.C. it was a large kingdom.

Chinese history begins in 2200 B.C. Before this date there were the five mythical dynasties.

The **Shang** Dynasty 1765-1122 B.C.

The **Xia** (Chou) dynasty - lasted 1000 years to 770 B.C. This dynasty was in North China in the Yellow River Valley. China was mostly small feudal states for six centuries; these ended about 221 B.C.

There was a change in dynasty 221-206 B.C. This was the **Ch'in** Dynasty.

The first emperor of this dynasty united the nation, built the Great Wall, and called the country Qin the name of his home state. The empire lasted fours years after his death.

In 206 B. C. to 222 A. D. an empire (the **Han** dynasty) was founded by Lire Bang a general in the army.

He reduced taxes, and relaxed autocratic rule. He called the empire the Han for the upper valley of the Han River. The empire extended to the limits of modern-day China and its influence reached to the Caspian Sea. The Chinese influence even reached the Roman empire.

It was a form of centralized government:

• paternal benevolence by the ruler,
• a council of ministers backed by a trained bureaucracy;
• the bureaucrats were selected on the basis of passing the exam on Confucian literature.

This empire fell in the third century A.D. During this reign Buddhism arrived from India and became the state religion, and paper was invented.

It was followed by disorder and almost 400 years of anarchy, 222-589 A.D. Buddhism spread and tea began to be used during this period.

Sui dynasty - short lived, 589-618 A.D.

Centralized government. The Grand Canal linked the northern and southern parts of the empire. Buddhism was repressed.

Tang dynasty - 618-907 A.D.

During this dynasty the empire expanded to the south and commerce reached the Indian Ocean. State exams began as did a fast-developing culture.

China began to influence Japan and Korea culturally and economically.

Foot binding began and lasted to the beginning of the 20th century. Printing also began.

Sung dynasty - 960-1127 A.D. The Northern tribes began to threaten and the capital was moved to the south.

Tai Zu (961-1279 A.D.) was the founder.

This was called the Golden Age of the country: great art, poetry, biographies, histories, pottery, and sculptures flourished.

The empire expanded to include Korea and Southeast Asia. Cities grew, government services improved, and contact with the outside world increased.

Science and technology advanced, bureaucracy was refined, foreign trade increased: by ship, the Spice Route was established; overland, the Silk Road became the trade route for merchants.

Silk and porcelain were the most sought after products.

The Sung dynasty was replaced by the **Yuan** dynasty

The Yuan was the first Mongol dynasty. Marco Polo observed China at its peak in 1275 during this dynasty.

Gengis Khan, the grandfather of Kublai, conquered most of the land and after his death, Kublai-Khan, (1278-1368) his grandson, became the first ruler of the Yuan dynasty.

The Mongols were considered to be barbarians - 'they smell so bad one cannot approach them' said the Chinese about them. When they became the rulers they adopted Chinese ways and culture. They continued governmental bureaucracy; and continued artistic freedom; the opera and novels flourished.

The empire reached from the Pacific Ocean to Central Europe and the first Western travelers began arriving in China.

The **Ming** dynasty 1368-1644 A.D.

The Chinese reasserted their superiority after being ruled by the Mongols.

A great time of maritime exploration began, its purpose was to exact tribute. They went as far as the Red Sea and Persia and reached Africa; exploration ended in 1433, but there is no explanation as to why.

They fought with Japan over Korea. Portuguese traders had a post at Macao, and the Lotus Rebellion took place.

Jesuit missionaries were in Peking.

The **Qing** or Ching dynasty - the last imperial dynasty to rule China, 1644-1912 A.D.

This dynasty was founded by the Manchurians who invaded China from the northeast in 1644. They instituted the custom of wearing the hair in a long braid down the back, called a queue.

The height of the empire was under Emperor Chien Lung (1736-1795); the borders were expanded and population increased, but economic problems weakened the empire.

Roman Catholic missionaries arrived in the 13th century.

Advances during the different dynasties:
(early dates are only guesses)

4200-2500 B.C. - pottery, farming

2200-1766 B.C. Xia dynasty - making of silk begins

1766-1122 B.C. Shang dynasty - first verifiable history; perfecting of the wheel for chariots in warfare; carving of jade and ivory, and making of vessels in bronze

1122-221 B.C. Zhou dynasty -iron casting, multiplication tables

600-300 B.C. Philosophers, Confucius 551-479 B.C.

6th century B.C. Meng Tzu, (Mencius) a scholar, 372-289 B.C.

221-206 B. C. Qin dynasty - Shittuang Di - probably the first emperor; built the Great Wall because of the Huns, he built the great canals, roads, and palaces; a uniform writing system and standardized weights and measures were instituted, and book burning was allowed.

202 B.C. - 220 A.D. Han dynasty

Liu Bang was the founder

121-87 B.C. Wu Di conquers South China, North Vietnam and part of Korea; he retreats to southern China when the barbarians from the north conquer the northern part.

The Jürchen founded the Jin dynasty, 1126.

1215-1368 B.C. The Mongol dynasty, or Yuan dynasty.

Genghis Khan - sacks Peking in 1215; in 1234 he conquers the Jin empire. In 1235 he invaded the Song dynasty in the south. In 1271 Genghis Khan's grandson, Kublai Khan founded the Yuan dynasty.

1368-1644 B.C. Zhu Yuanzhang, a Buddhist peasant overthrows the Yuan dynasty and begins the Ming Dynasty; porcelains were invented; the imperial palace was built in Peking, reconstruction of the Great Wall took place; exploration by ship of Southeast Asia was ongoing, and they reached the Red Sea.

1644-1839 B.C. The Manchu invade from the north and found the Qing Dynasty.

1661-1722 B.C. Emperor Kan Xi extends Chinese influence to Mongolia, Central Asia, Tibet, Korea, Annam (Vietnam), Burma, and Thailand. Foreign influence undermined the dynasty.

Chinese Inventions:

Products which originated in China
  silk
  porcelain
  wheelbarrows
  crossbow
  draft-animal harnesses
  cast iron
  mechanical clocks
  printing
  paper, ink, type

800 B.C. - iron ax blades, plow tips, belt buckles and axle fittings

mass production by molds and stack-casting method

105 A.D. - paper, from tree bark, hemp, rags, fishnets - to replace bamboo and silk cloth

130 A.D. - astronomical instruments to track stars/compass for lining up gravesites

First century A.D. - drilled 2000 foot deep holes to tap underground salt resources

3rd century - ink, lampblack and gum molded into sticks

8th century - wooden block printing

931 A.D. began the printing of the Confucian classics

9th century - gunpowder for fireworks

1050 A.D. movable type - not practical for them because of the many symbols, better to use carved wooden blocks

11th Century - compass adapted for ocean navigation

12th century - gunpowder used for military grenades and rockets

MALAY

Though Chin did not leave the mainland, God put the desire for migration in the heart of his uncle Malay.

It has never been determined how the Malays were able to inhabit all the Polynesian islands, but they probably began their migrations soon after the Flood before the oceans were as full as today. This would have allowed them to cross from island to island because many of those islands had not yet been submerged. They could have traveled in much smaller boats and by whatever means they used, those islands have been inhabited by the sons of Malay. The names of the territories inhabited by them are: Malaysia, Polynesia, and Australasia. Their locations are from

Madagascar to the islands near the Western American coast; from the shores of India to islands in the Antarctic Ocean, and a whole line of islands on the Indian and Pacific seas.

Beginnings of their nation

Although anthropologists classify them as southern Mongoloids, it is evident that they were formed from mixing with the Cushites. This explains the great variation of color, skin texture and other physical features which characterize the different peoples of the Malaysian nation. The more powerful Japhethites formed the foundation of the nation and the two branches passed into the islands. Through intermarriage they have produced a family of mixed blood.

The original Malays or Polynesians represented a people who had all but lost the knowledge of the true God. Because of this they did not require an extensive language, nor were they a people of high moral character. Their manners were not those of a civilized people and they were content with the life of an islander. They seem to have branched off from the Altaic family many centuries after Babel and because of the physical conditions under which they lived they became more and more primitive.

MIGRATIONS

They migrated from the Asian continent, on the east of India, to Java, Sumatra, and Borneo. From there they went to all the islands of the oceans, especially to the Indian Archipelago. The Japanese islands are peopled by the younger brothers of the Chinese; Ceylon by the Hindus; all other islands in the Indian and Pacific Ocean, except Bourbon, Mauritius, the little Maldives, Laccadives and Seychelles, are peopled by the Malay-Polynesians. Madagascar and Formosa were also originally peopled by them.

The probable progress of the migration was: from Malacca to Sumatra, Borneo to Banea, to the Philippines, to the Straits of Macassar, from Sumatra to Celebes to New Guinea to Buro, Ceram and other smaller islands. From New Guinea to the New Hebrides, Fiji, Friendlys, Navigators, and Society Islands. Australia lies at Cape York near New Guinea, New Zealand is 1200 miles from Fiji and Tasmania. Between Ladrone, the Sandwich Islands and Fiji there are many smaller islands which they inhabited.

Contributions from other nations

Their culture, arts, and religion came principally from India. Islam overran Malacca and the great islands of the Indian Archipelago. Brahmanism and Buddhism also competed for these peoples. Each religion found them to be people of some refinement in art, literature, and civilization; but cruel, treacherous, superstitious and intolerant. The farthest islands had almost no understanding of the original light given to man. Their superstitions became more gross; their creed more bloody; their manners more brutal.

They have a caste system, taboo, and circumcision, all of these they took from Asia. (Wright, *Bricks from Babel*), pp. 142-145.

Religious beliefs

Their general tradition refers to their ancestors, their gods and their Paradise to the northwest. They have a vague idea of one great creative god, pervading all things. They have many lesser deities, but they deify their ancestors. Their religion is of the baser sort and is superstitious. This includes cannibalism, infanticide, and human sacrifice. The idea of caste regulates the future of the soul.

Their Paradise is a wonderful island where the gods, heroes, and chiefs live. High-caste people are immortal and live with the gods after death. The low-caste people die like the animals. Prayer and sacrifice are needed to ward off wrath and secure the favor of the gods.

They have many traditions concerning the Flood: "Many years ago men were disobedient to the gods and Taorsa, the high god, decided to drown the world. One man in a canoe was spared; when he landed on a mountain he built an altar to his god.

"Another tradition says that one good man was warned to enter a boat with his family and domestic animals." (Wright, *Bricks from Babel*), p. 146,147. Eight people were saved, four men and their wives.

They confuse Creation and the Flood saying that the first man and woman were created from a floating bamboo. The gods created the world and at first there was nothing but water rolling under a dark sky. The gods mingled with men and therefore, some families are of divine origin. The first sin was quarreling between the first man and woman. (Ibid.), p. 147.

Tribal resemblance

There are similarities of language, habits of life and religious ideas.

Some work in agriculture, some are good at various crafts and arts and manufacturing. They are good at fishing and boating. Their tribal weapons, manners, social laws, and life are very similar. (Ibid.), p. 147.

Conclusion

They (the Malays) are the most widely scattered family on the face of the earth, and are the family which has lost more of the original light of God. They are only at present regaining the light of that revelation as missionaries move into these long forgotten islands.

CHILDREN OF THE NEW WORLD

From the earliest ages after the Dispersion these peoples went north and east of the Altaic ranges. They crossed the Behring Strait and the Aleutian Islands to North America. From there they turned southward ignoring the regions their Ugrian relatives would dominate.

Origin of the American tribes (Indians).

They are of a Mongolian root, sometimes called American Mongoloids, (*World Book Encyclopedia*, Vol. 16), p. 53.

Their differences of speech, manners and physique are those common in a single family on two continents. They are the sons of a vanishing civilization; children of a long decline and of a perishing light. Their line of migration has been from north to south between Alaska and Patagonia from which all the tribes of the remaining territories have branched.

The earliest and advancing tribes were builders of mounds closely resembling those of Japheth in the Old World. The various nations of the New World have few monuments, no ancient records, few traditions, and no contemporary testimony to their history. The French Academy says, 'The Indian is an enigma, and the more you study him, the greater the enigma becomes'. (Wright, *Bricks from Babel*), p. 151.

The Northern Indians are connected with those of Mexico, those of Mexico with those of Peru and South America. There are similarities in their pictographs, ideas, worship of the sun and general unity in manners and customs. All speak of a common origin and a common home at the beginning of the nation.

Religious ideas

They believed the world was created from chaos, and believed in a general deluge. There is a good mind and an evil mind who rule the universe. They worshipped the heavenly bodies as types of the Creator.

The Mexicans believe in a serpent which is the source of all evil and is crushed by the great spirit Teotl.

Their traditions include: a belief that America was a great island, under the special care of the Good Spirit, and was the only land in existence. They believed themselves to be indigenous; that they came out of a cave after a general deluge and confusion. But they also stated that long ago their ancestors came from an evil and distant land, over a water full of islands, in a region of ice, cold, and snow, where they endured great hardships until they came by a long journey to a better climate. They said they came from a land beyond the Behring Straits. There is a general tradition pointing to an extinct tribe, Leni or Lenapes, as the original people, or Universal Grandfathers whom they try to contact through the use of peyote. There are further traces of extinct tribes from which other tribes have sprung; the Lanapees, the Eries, the Alleghans; the old mound builders.

They have Old World traditions from many separated nations which were learned when these nations were together before each went his separate way and set up his own kingdom. Examples of these are: "the making of the lintel of a doorway narrower than its threshold in Mexico and Peru; embalming or preserving as mummies the bodies of the dead, both coming from Egypt; the worship of the heavenly bodies and an idea of a future state from the Babylonians; and an idea of the good and bad mind striving in the universe from the Persians. The Mexicans and Peruvians were like the Hindus in caste and in their manner of worshipping the planets; like the Chinese in implicit obedience to a despotic government, skill in imitation, and deep reverence for ancient custom. The Northern tribes had many of the Arab and Ugrian habits and instincts." (Wright, *Bricks from Babel*), p. 153.

Architecture

Their architectural remains were of an early and underdeveloped age; through the length of North and South America can be seen the traces of mound-buildings and tumuli. They did have an understanding of the pyramid though some of them built a circular pyramid. The earliest pottery-making remains are the best examples, and the later remains were much more crude. Indian skills are seen in specimens of shell carvings and carving in hard stone. They had domesticated animals and cultivated plants.

Their legends were much like those in the Old World; Hiawatha, Manco-Capac, Xolotl, and Quetzalcoatl. Their civilization was never one of high culture, in the North, but certainly the cultures of the early Aztecs and the Mayas in Mexico and the Incas in Peru, are exceptions. There is no record of these people until between A.D. 1000 and A.D. 1500. (Ibid.), p. 155.

MEXICO

The most ancient history of this group comes from the Aztecs. Theirs was the highest culture attained among the native American nations; the Peruvians were next in culture. The Toltecs reached a fairly high cultural life, but their nation disappeared.

Among the Aztecs and the other American tribes there is a refinement and philosophy of language not known among the other tribes. They were good farmers and knew how to mine. They became skilled workers in gold and gems and the use of various metals. Their architecture was more than admirable as exemplified by the pyramids in Mexico City and at Chichén-Itzá. They had knowledge of the arts and of astronomy and they grouped their years in cycles as did the people of Eastern Asia.

From their pyramids in Mexico City they studied the planets and the stars and had a pyramid dedicated to the moon and another to the sun.

Migration

The Aztecs passed slowly from the Northwest along the Gila and Colorado Rivers to Anahuac (Mexico). Geographically their location was suited for the empire they were to build. The climate, the fertile soil, the lakes, and the vegetation all worked together to help them become a great nation. Their advanced form of legislation also helped govern them. The same religious notions, style of building and habits of life were found among them, as those found in the Old World.

Religious beliefs

The creation of the world out of chaos was made by the Good Mind. There was a constant conflict between the Good Mind, who was the friend and Maker of man, and the Evil Mind, who was their enemy.

They held traditions of four creations and the destruction of the world similar to those of the Hindus. "India has its four cataclysms, and Hesios writes of the ages of the four metals, so the Aztec mythology tells of four Yongas similar to the four periods of the old Etrurians". (Wright, *Bricks from Babel*), p. 159. This again signifies common ancestry and traditions.

The first cycle of the earth ended in famine; those who did not perish from the famine were eaten by tigers. Giants and enormous monsters lived then. Men lived for many years, and the Cyclops (from Greek mythology) waged war.

The second cycle was closed by fire, only the birds escaped; one man and one woman hid in a cave and repopulated the earth.

The third cycle ended by windstorms; men and beasts were destroyed, but again a man and woman survived by hiding in a cave.

The last destruction was by a deluge. All men and beasts were destroyed except a man and woman who were saved in a hollow log of Cypress wood. (The same wood used in the building of Noah's ark, an interesting remembrance.) The people born to this couple were born without the ability to speak and when they had increased in numbers, and because of their prayers, the birds were sent by the gods to teach them to speak. Because they were scattered they all spoke a different language.

The father who was saved from the deluge was called *Coxcox*. As the water was subsiding he sent out a vulture who did not return but stayed to feed on the decaying corpses. Next he sent a hummingbird which brought back a leaf. Coxcox left his boat on a mountain, then a giant named Xelhua decided to build a hill that would reach the sky. He began a brick pyramid which was destroyed when the angry gods threw fire on it. Many workmen were killed so they stopped building and the temple was dedicated to the god of the air.

The Aztecs had another famous tradition of Quilaztli; the *Woman of our Flesh, the Mother of All Living*. This woman was always represented speaking with a serpent. She was the mother of twin sons, who constantly fought each other about the answer to some long-forgotten question. (Wright, *Bricks from Babel*), pp. 158- 160. (Mormon beliefs fit in here when they teach that Satan and Jesus were warring brothers.)

The Aztecs offered human and animal sacrifices, as did the Peruvians. Both had many gods and cruel religious rites. Their Votan equaled Wodin; Bondha equaled Buddha; Wodin or Odin is Buddha among the Scandinavians and is Bondha with the native Mexicans.

They had cycles and a zodiac, like the Tartars and Tibetans. The Mexicans worshipped one Supreme Being, the Master of all gods. Fifty years before their conquest, a Mexican king wrote 60 hymns to Him. The same king wrote a poem on the *Instability of Human Greatness*, lofty ideas for such a time and people. They, and the Peruvians, believed in the immortality of the soul and in a place of delights and rewards for the spirits of the good and long ages of toil for the souls of the wicked. They believed in the resurrection of the body and for this reason they took special care of their dead.

The sun was their representative of the Chief Divinity. Temples were built to him and human sacrifices were made on his altars.

The greatest Deity was called the "Life-Sustainer of the Universe." He had no temple, no altar, and was too holy to be approached by man. He dwelt in, and above, all things and they were awed by him. He was feared and heard, and the Indian fled from him. This was his answer to the voice of God speaking within him.

Peculiar characteristics

Since they are Mongolian in descent their customs of birth, circumcision and death all point to their Mongolian root. The 'scalp-lock' (the long rope of hair remaining on top of a shaved scalp), was typical of the Japhetic Mongolidae; Scythians, Mantchoas, Chinese, Tartars, and the old Scandinavians possessed this custom.

The coloring of the American Indians varied from tribe to tribe. The Menonimees of Lake Michigan and Green Bay are very light. The Mandans are called 'White Indians' because they are so light. The Zunis had many with light skin, blue eyes, and fair hair, others are copper-colored and others almost black.

Evidence of their Migrations

The Indians of the Aleutian Islands, Alaska, and the Chukehee Peninsula in Asia are the same; those of the Islands call themselves 'Men of the East'. The tribes of Eastern Asia have a distinct tradition of a migration from their ranks over the Behring Strait.

Indications point to another migration from Phoenicia, Northern and Western Africa, and Spain, to America by way of now submerged islands a thousand years before Christ.

South America had five cities with names identical to cities in Asia Minor or North Africa, could this be accidental? On ancient monuments in South America there are pictures of 'bearded men', Negroes and elephants, yet most of the Indian tribal males were beardless. (Wright, *Bricks from Babel*), pp. 160-164, excerpts.

MADAI, The Mede

His kingdom was in Asia, north of Persia, and south of the Caspian Sea between the Caspian and the Zagros Mountains. The home of the Elamites was to the south of them. They are mentioned in the Scripture as follows: Genesis 10:2; 1 Chronicles 1:5; 2 Kings 17:6; 18:11; Ezra 6:2; Esther 1:3, 14, 18, 19; Isaiah 13:17; 21:2; Jeremiah 25:25; 51:11, 28; Daniel 5:28, 31; 6:8,12,15; 8:20; 9:1; 11:1; Acts 2:9.

Ancient Medes
(Rawlinson, Vol. 2)

Ancient Medes
(Rawlinson, Vol. 2)

Before the end of the ancient Assyrian empire Media was a group of divided tribes with no settled form of government. They were dominated by Assyria, and when Assyria's power waned, anarchy ruled in Media. Later they were ruled by their own kings, and ultimately were overrun by the Scythians. They gave a wife to Nebuchadnezzar and that united them with Babylon for the overthrow of Nineveh. Later they seized Babylon and the Medes and Persians united under Cyrus.

Sometime during the second millennium they went into the mountains of India. The great Aryan or Iranic races spread into Asia and were widely dispersed. Their looks and languages were very diverse from tribe to tribe.

Some of the Medes went westward to the Danube.

The Medes were first mentioned by Shalmaneser III of Assyria who raided them in order to obtain their finely bred horses, in 836 B.C. After this Sargon II deported Israelite captives to Media (2 Kings 17:6, 18:11). Media was a part of the Assyrian Empire until 600 B.C., when they rebelled against the weakening Assyrian Empire. They held all lands north of Assyria and invaded Nineveh.

KINGS OF THE MEDES

Dejoces - 708-657 B.C., The first Monarchy

After gaining their freedom from Assyria Media divided into tribes and quickly came to a state of anarchy and lawlessness.

A village judge named Dejoces, saw the need for law and used his local influence to gain a position for himself. He began to arbitrate problems for his village and the surrounding area. Things went well and peace was restored. He then resigned, claiming to have no time for personal affairs.

The surrounding countryside quickly fell into a worse state of anarchy than before. A council was gathered to deliberate a plan of action and Dejoces sent secret emissaries to this assembly. When the time came to suggest a plan of action, they recommended a total change of the state of the republic: a king

should be elected and given the authority to make laws and restrain violence. All agreed to this and since Dejoces was the best candidate, he was elected.

Dejoces reigned 53 years. During that time he selected a personal guard and built a fortified palace. Around this palace he built seven walls, within which grew up the city of Ecbatana.

Dejoces created laws and began to rule the land through emissaries. Judgment was swift and final. Media became an orderly state.

Dejoces' major flaw as a ruler was that he had no contact with his people and because he relied solely on the word of his emissaries there was great opportunity for corruption. (Rollin, *Ancient History*, Vol. I), pp. 293-295.

Phraortes - 657-635 B.C., Son of Dejoces

Phraortes reigned for twenty-two years after his father Dejoces' death. Phraortes was more warlike than his father and attacked and conquered the Persians. With the addition of the Persians to his army he conquered most of Asia Minor. His kingdom encompassed most of Upper Asia from Mt. Taurus to the River Halys in Asia Minor.

He attempted to conquer Assyria but Nebuchadnezzar defeated the Medes and drove them back to Ecbatana, which was blockaded, taken, and sacked. Phraortes was murdered by being wounded by javelins (darts). (Rollin, *Ancient History*, Vol. I), p. 295.

Cyaxares I - 635-594 B.C., Son of Phraortes

Cyaxares reigned for 40 years. He took the throne immediately after his father's murder. The Assyrians, under the general Holofernes, had recently been defeated at Bethulia (a complete account of this battle is found in the Apocryphal book of Judit). Cyaxares took advantage of this and laid siege to Nineveh. During this siege the Scythians were pursuing the Cimmerians across Asia Minor, taking all the land they crossed, and were about to spread throughout Asia.

The Medes returned to their land to protect it from the Scythians but were defeated by them. The Scythians controlled Media and a good portion of Asia Minor for 28 years. The Medes, unable to get rid of them by force, formed an underhanded plan to rid themselves of the Scythians.

They pretended to strengthen their allegiance to them and declared a national holiday in honor of the Scythians. They offered the most prominent Scythians a feast and while they were drunk the Medes killed them. The remaining Scythians fled to Lydia, where king Halyttes took them in.

Cyaxares immediately declared war on Lydia for taking in the Scythians. The war lasted five years with no advantage either way. In the sixth year during a battle there was a full solar eclipse. Both kings took this as a sign of the displeasure of the gods and made their peace. The treaty was furthered by a marriage, when Aryenis, Halyttes' daughter, was married to Astyages, eldest son of Cyaxares.

624 BC - Cyaxares was still seeking revenge for his father's death and laid siege to Nineveh again, this time with the help of the Babylonian king Nabopolassar. He took the city, and killed the king, Saracus, and became the master of Babylon.

NOTE: Prophecy against Nineveh in Nahum two and three is fulfilled here. Nineveh was razed, just as God had spoken through the prophet.

Sometime after this Cyaxares died. (Rollin, *Ancient History,* Vol. I), pp. 296-298.

Astyages - 594-560 B.C., Son of Cyaxares

Astyages ruled 35 years. Many say he is the Ahashuerus of Scripture. His first child, Mandana, was married to the Persian prince Cambyses. From this union came Cyrus the Great.

When Cyrus of Persia went to visit his grandfather Astyages in Media he found:

Pride, luxury and magnificence reigned universally. Astyages himself was richly clothed, had his eyes colored, his face painted and his hair embellished with artificial locks...The Medes had affected an effeminate lifestyle; to be dressed in scarlet and to wear necklaces and bracelets; whereas the habits of the Persians were very plain and coarse. (Rollin, *Ancient History*, Vol. I), p. 309.

The second child of Astyages, Cyaxares II, took the throne of Media. (Ibid.), p. 298.

Cyaxares II - 560-548 BC

He is also considered by some to be the same person as Darius the Mede. He was the brother of Mandana, the wife of Cambyses the Persian king. Cyrus, their son, was one year younger than Cyaxares. Cyrus had come into power by this time and took Babylon. He placed his uncle, Cyaxares II, as ruler of the "Great Satrapy of Babylon." Cyrus married the only daughter of Cyaxares II by his (Cyaxares') request. After the death of Cyaxares II, Cyrus united Media and Persia. (Rollin, *Ancient History*, Vol. I), p. 299.

Darius the Mede and the joining of the empires.

After Cyaxares II there is only one king left to investigate, Darius the Mede, who may in fact be the same Cyaxares. Darius is an historical mystery, as he is only mentioned by this name in the book of Daniel. He is mentioned 28 times in Daniel chapter six. Any conclusion we make as to how the empire of the Medes and Persians was formed will have a great bearing on our identification of Darius the Mede.

Many authors believe that Cyrus conquered the Medes by gaining popularity with them and leading an uprising against Astyages. This is not a conclusion that is consistent with history, especially if we consider the Greek history of the Medes. There is a record that Cyrus went to visit his grandfather, Astyages, for three years. During this time it is likely he was groomed to become a king. Rollin believes that Darius the Mede was Cyrus' uncle, Cyaxares II, and that Cyaxares II was placed over Babylon by Cyrus after he conquered it. This is further supported by the scriptural record of Darius, who was reported to come into power at the age of 63, and seemed to have some experience in government, since he immediately set up 120 satraps (princes) to oversee the land, and three chief satraps over them, one of whom was Daniel.

Although there is no record of any ruler by the name of Darius during this time in the cuneiform texts, there is a ruler mentioned whose powers coincide with those of Darius. He has the powers of a king.

That is, he could create laws which were irreversible and one could commit an offense against him as well as against Cyrus. He is not described as an absolute monarch, rather, indication of a higher human power is evident both in the cuneiform and Scripture. In the cuneitexts he is called Gubaru, and this is the only place where this is mentioned. (For an in depth discussion of this see John C. Whitcomb, *Darius the Mede,* (New Jersey: Presbyterian and Reformed Publishing Co., 1959.)

After the death of Darius, Cyrus became the ruler of Babylon. He allowed the captive Jews to return to Jerusalem and gave money and material to help rebuild the temple. He returned to them the sacred vessels from the temple, which had been taken away by Nebuchadnezzar (Ezra 1:1-11; 4:3,5, etc.).

INDIA

There are two distinct lines of peoples in India.

As before mentioned the northern Japhetic Indians were from Gomer. They lived for a time in India and then began their westward migration dividing into more and more tribes as they moved.

Before the Japhetic migration of Medes a group of Cushites had already gone to India from Babylon.

The Cushite influence is noted in the following:

* their historic interchange with Egypt;

* India was called Oriental Ethiopia;

* the early Indians held sacred the Nilá, a river in Cushdwip (probably Egypt);

* the names of Cush, Mizr, and Rama remain unchanged and are revered by the Hindus;

* the aborigines of India are a distinct group with Hamitic features whose language is not related to the Sanscrit. (Wright, *Bricks*), p. 85.

The Persians and Indians both claim to be Aryans, and their physique and language make good their claim, but the aboriginal mountaineers of India were foreign to the Indian nation, and were reduced to slavery under the caste system.

In the Vedas, (the sacred books of the Indians), it is stated that all these people of the first and second migrations had one origin, and all were the children of one God.

The early Hindu writings were compiled about 1400 years before Christ from ancient documents. In them monotheism is presented as the only Truth. "There is in truth but one Deity, the supreme Spirit, the Lord of the universe, by whom the world was made."

Religious beliefs

At first there was no image and no visible form of worship.

The water was the first element which was worked upon by God so they also identified with it and called the waters, 'His children'.

They believed God created man with an immortal soul, and an internal consciousness of right. After death the soul suffers to make up for the evil done in this life.

God gave man knowledge of writing which He taught to them in an audible voice from the City of God. After this God gave them the Vedas to guide them.

They had a story of the Flood and a story of the sin of Noah and the blessing of Shem and Japheth, and the cursing of Canaan - these facts came to them in the Mosaic language and were practically the same as the Biblical account.

The Hindus believed in the incarnation of the Divinity and they have a Thank-offering which came from a much earlier period when men believed in the only true God. God had not left these early people without a witness. They mixed the Truth of God with the paganism of Babylon. Their later writings contain many of the mythological fables of Greece and Egypt, which would indicate early communication among those nations.

Migrations

For many centuries tribes migrated westward from India taking their own distinct languages with them.

The Medes migrated as far as the Danube and the Thames, following in the paths of the earlier Gomerite migrations.

They rejected their Mongolian ancestors and distinguished themselves by the name, 'Aryans'.

In the 15th century (A.D.) a new group of people migrated into Europe, they called themselves Roma - the *Gypsies*. They were called 'black Hindus' by the Persians. They were actually Bazelgurs of Hindustan. They are a restless, never-halting people who are indicative of the peoples who migrated from the east into Europe.

THE PERSIANS

The Ancient *Persians* were closely related in speech, history, and physical appearance to the Indians, as observed by:

Their early language, Zend, has the same origin as Sanskrit. The language of the Medes and Persians was almost identical and very close to the Indian.

Persian Foot Soldiers

(Rawlinson, Vol. 2)

They were of the same line as the Medes from the line of Japheth. They were Aryans - the word being a Persian word meaning 'noble'. The Persians were the most Aryan of all the line.

Persian Stabbing a Bull

(Rawlinson, Vol. 2)

Their beginnings were in the mountains and they were a hardy, warrior people with simple habits. They drank no wine and their food and dress were of the most basic sort. When Cyrus went to the court of the Medes he was shocked at the display of wealth and luxury because of his simple beginnings.

The Persians were said to have been keen-witted, though not terribly intellectual, probably because of the simple life they led. Poetry and art were important to them as they were to their relatives, the Greeks.

After their empire waned they lost many of their noble character traits and mixed with the Semitic Elamites who lived in the same area, and with the Medes of Japheth to the north, and became just another nation of mixed blood. But during their period of world-greatness they were worthy of the acclaim they received.

Their building and artistic style was learned from the Assyrians and Babylonians who had long centuries of practice before the Persians ever began to build anything settled.

When they began to build they took the ideas of the Assyrians and Babylonians and made them into a new architectural style. Their buildings were mostly palaces and tombs because they had no temples. Their religion was simple and required no place of worship other than the outdoors.

The most famous remains of their architecture are the remains of the royal palaces at Persepolis.

The products they needed they took from other nations; saying they were soldiers and had no need for manufacturing items that could be bought elsewhere.

Religious Beliefs

In their early period they believed in one supreme God, "the Lord God of Heaven". A teaching they had taken with them when they left the Plain of Shinar.

From this teaching they then moved into the "belief of the perpetual conflict of the two great First Principles, that of Light and that of Darkness, personified under the names of Auramazda, or Or'mazd, and Ahriman'." (Swinton, *Outlines of World History)*, p. 61.

Their earliest traditions were like those of the Scripture. (Ormuzd makes one man and woman, who live in peace in a garden. Ahriman, the evil spirit, sends a serpent to persuade them to eat of an evil tree he has planted. Man obeys Ahriman and misery follows as demons interfere with his peace.)

They worshipped the elements, especially fire. The Scythians had taught them these paganistic beliefs.

Fire-worship was called Magianism, the name coming from the name of the priests who led in this worship who were called Magi.

"The Magian religion was of a highly sacerdotal type. No worshipper could perform any religious act except by the intervention of a priest, or Magus, who stood between him and the divinity as a Mediator...The Magi were a priest-caste, apparently holding their office by hereditary succession. They claimed to possess, not only a sacred and mediatorial character, but also supernatural prophetic powers. They explained omens, expounded dreams, and by means of a certain mysterious manipulation of the barsom, or bundle of twigs, arrived at a knowledge of future events, which they communicated to the pious inquirer...

"...they marched in procession to the *pyroetheia*, or fire altars, and standing around them performed for an hour at a time their magical incantations. The credulous multitude, impressed by sights of this kind, and imposed on by the claims to supernatural power which the Magi advanced, paid them a willing homage; the kings and chiefs consulted them; and when the Arian tribes, pressing westward, came into contact with the races [tribes] professing the Magian religion, they found a sacerdotal cast all-powerful in most of the Scythic nations." (Rawlinson, Vol. 2), pp. 61,62.

They had fire-altars on mountain tops which burned continually and were believed to have been lighted from heaven, therefore they were not allowed to go out.

Our word 'magic' comes from them and refers to the practice of the Magi as they attended the perpetual flames. Among the Magi is seen a hope of the world's Deliverer and finds them coming from the East to worship when Christ was born.

Ancient Persians
(Rawlinson, Vol. 3)

The Persians and Medes had the same religion and traditions; they were like two cousins who have learned the same speech, had the same history, and worshipped at the same altar.

There were good spirits, and household genii who were adored.

They had no images.

Government

Their government was good and much less severe to its subjects than most other Oriental empires of the time.

They had leisure time in which to write and read literature, but only one example of their literature has survived. It is called the Zend-Avesta and contains the sacred books of the Persians.

These books were collected by Zoroaster, the religious legislator of the Persians. (His name comes from one of the names of Nimrod, Zero-asta, which referred to fire-worship.)

Their poetry did not equal that of the Hebrews or the Greeks, but was usually based on traditions and songs and stories of the past, or how they remembered the past.

KINGS OF THE PERSIAN PERIOD

Cyaxares I, 633 B.C.

Cyaxares was the first Persian monarch, though he was in fact, a Median king. He destroyed Nineveh in 625 B.C., and pushed westward into Asia Minor.

The Persians had a kingdom in Persis (Persia Proper) at this time, but were under the control of Media.

Cambyses, a Persian

Cambyses followed Cyaxares I and was king of Persia, but under the control of Media to whom he paid tribute.

The daughter of Astyages was married to Cambyses and Cyrus was born to that union.

Cyrus was kept in his grandfather's court at Media as a sort of hostage, though he was also educated at the same time to become a king.

At the death of Astyages, (grandfather of Cyrus), Cyaxares II became king of Media and was no sooner on the throne than Neriglissar, king of Babylon, prepared to go against him with a large army. Cyaxares sent to ask help from Cambyses, the Persian prince, and Cyrus, his son, was to command the Persian troops. Neriglissar was killed during this war.

At the death of Cambyses, Cyrus became king of Persia and united Media and Persia into one kingdom

Cyrus the Great (549-529 B.C., Rollin) (558-529 B.C., Rawlinson)

Note: there is some discussion in reference to the dates of Cyrus. Rawlinson gives the date at 558 B.C., and this seems to coincide with the dates of Cyaxares II. Cyaxares II, Astyages second son, ruled from 560-548 B.C., and it was noted that Cyrus was already in power at this time, so it is possible that the 558 date is the more correct.

Cyrus the Great was the founder of the Persian Empire, he was of the Pasargadae tribe, the most noble of the

Cyrus
(Peloubet, 1893)

Persian tribes. He was able, because of his organizational skill, to take Persia from a group of loosely knit provinces to a well organized united state. They were at that time under the dominion of the Medes and Cyrus freed them from their domination.

Cyrus was a born statesman and used his ability to further the interests of his country. When he conquered other nations he observed, more than any other, the Roman Method of nation making by incorporating the conquered peoples into his nation and leaving them religious freedom and freedom to continue with their own culture.

Cyrus incorporated the new gods of the conquered nations into his own belief-system and honored them also. Because of this attitude the Jews were allowed to continue worshipping God as they had always done. God had foreordained this in order for the Jews to be able to return to Jerusalem with Ezra to begin the rebuilding of the Temple, and later with Nehemiah to rebuild the walls of Jerusalem.

God called Cyrus His 'shepherd' in Isaiah 44:28, and His 'anointed' in Isaiah 45:1. This was all done according to God's plan before Cyrus was born.

Cyrus' first battle appearance was for his grandfather against the Babylonian King, Neriglissar, who wanted to show his bravery and invaded the territories of the Medes.

When Cyrus became king he subdued the northern and western provinces of the Median empire.

The power in Asia, when he took control, was Babylon, (which was declining in power), Media, and Lydia, in Asia Minor.

Croesus was the king of Lydia. He was a very wealthy man and because of his wealth the saying, "Richer that Croesus" exists today, meaning a person of tremendous wealth. He controlled all of Asia Minor west of the Halys River.

Croesus and Cyrus were in a battle for the control of Asia Minor. Croesus and his army crossed the River Halys which formed the boundary between the Lydian and Persian territories and a battle was fought at Sinope, but neither side won. Cyrus quickly followed up this battle and overthrew Croesus and captured his capital city at Sardis. By doing this he added all of Asia Minor west of the Halys to his empire.

He then subdued most of the Greek cities and colonies on the coast of Asia Minor and the history of Greece and Persia became intertwined from that point.

Turning his attention to the East he subdued the tribes in the region between Persia and the Indus, including Parthia, Bactriana, Sogdiana, etc. His only empire left to conquer was Babylon.

Cyrus was king over all the country from the Aegean Sea to the Euphrates until the taking of Babylon.

God called Cyrus to destroy Babylon because of her pride, her cruelty to the Jews especially, and the worship of her kings which was encouraged by the kings themselves.

Jeremiah 51:11 prophesied against Babylon and said it was God's vengeance which would destroy the nation. *Make bright the arrows, gather the shields: the Lord hath raised up the spirit of the kings of the Medes: for his device is against Babylon, to destroy it; because it is the vengeance of the Lord, the vengeance of his temple.* (Isaiah 13:9), *Behold, the day of the Lord cometh, cruel both with wrath and fierce anger, to lay the land desolate....* But God would use Cyrus as His instrument.

And Babylon, the glory of kingdoms, the beauty of the Chaldees' excellency, shall be as when God overthrew Sodom and Gomorrah. It shall never be inhabited, neither shall it be dwelt in from generation to generation: neither shall the Arabian pitch tent there; neither shall the shepherds make their fold there. But wild beasts of the desert shall lie there; and their houses shall be full of doleful creatures, and owls shall dwell there, and satyrs shall dance there. And the wild beasts of the islands shall cry in their desolate houses, and dragons in their pleasant palaces: and her time is near to come, and her days shall not be prolonged. (Isaiah 13:19-22). *I will also make it a possession for the bittern, and pools of water: and I will sweep it with the besom of destruction, saith the Lord of hosts. The Lord of hosts hath sworn, saying, Surely as I have thought, so shall it come to pass; and as I have purposed, so shall it stand.* (Isaiah 14:23,24.)

"Cyrus, whom Divine Providence was to make use of, as an instrument for the executing of his design of goodness and mercy towards his people, as mentioned in the Scripture by his name, above two hundred years before he was born. And, that the world might not be surprised at the prodigious rapidity of his conquests, God was pleased to declare in very lofty and remarkable terms, that he himself would be his guide; and that in all his expeditions He would lead him by the hand, and

would subdue all the princes of the earth before him. *Thus saith the Lord to his anointed, to Cyrus, whose right hand I have holden, to subdue nations before him; and I will loose the loins of kings, to open before him the two-leaved gates; and the gates shall not be shut, I will go before thee, and make the crooked places straight: I will break in pieces the gates of brass, and cut in sunder the bars of iron: And I will give thee the treasures of darkness, and hidden riches of secret places, that thou mayest know that I, the Lord, which call thee by thy name, am the God of Israel. For Jacob my servant's sake, and Israel mine elect, I have even called thee by thy name: I have surnamed thee, though thou hast not known me.* (Isaiah 45:1-4.) (Rollin, *Ancient History,* Vol. I), pp. 336,337.

Conquest of Babylon

After Cyrus had taken control of Asia Minor, he began his conquest of the Babylonian empire. In a fierce battle with Belshazzar, Belshazzar retreated to his palace and prepared for a great feast. He was so sure that his city was impenetrable that he felt secure in its strength.

The city of Babylon had a number of channels for water which flowed beneath it. They were there to take care of flood waters when the Euphrates overflowed. Cyrus posted part of his troops where the river entered the city and another part where the river left the city. His soldiers were to march in as soon as the water was low enough.

Cyrus opened the ditches on both sides of the city, above and below, and the river water ran into them, leaving the channel dry.

The two groups of soldiers entered the channel, marching towards one another and meeting no obstacles.

The gates of brass, which were closed to prevent a descent to the river, had been left open because of the drunkenness and rioting of the night's festival. Had these gates been closed, the city would have been saved.

The two bodies of troops met at the royal palace and surprised the guards, whom they killed. The king came at them with a sword in his hand, at the head of a group who were supporting him, and all were killed by the Persians.

Cyrus Restoring the Vessles of theTemple
(Doré Illustrations)

Belshazzar's mistake was in believing himself to be more important and more powerful than God. As he became more drunken he ordered the sacred vessels, which Nebuchadnezzar had taken from the temple in Jerusalem, to be brought in. He and his princes, and his wives and concubines drank wine from them, all the while praising the pagan gods of 'gold, and of silver, of brass, of iron, of wood, and of stone,' (Daniel 5:4).

God's patience had run out. A man's hand appeared and the fingers began to write on the wall of the palace.

Belshazzar was horrified and the Scripture says, "the joints of his loins were loosed,

and his knees smote one against the other." (Daniel 5:6.)

He called all his wise men, diviners, and astrologers to come and tell him what this meant, but they were unable to do so, fulfilling the prophecy of Isaiah 47:12,13.

The queen mother came into the banqueting hall and told her son to call for Daniel, with whom she was well-acquainted.

Daniel came when he was called. He reminded the king of how God had dealt with Nebuchadnezzar because of his pride, and of how God was going to deal with him because of his pride, (Daniel 5:23).

He then gave the interpretation of the writing, MENE, MENE, TEKEL, UPHARSIN.

MENE: God hath numbered thy kingdom, and finished it.

TEKEL: thou art weighed in the balances and art found wanting.

PERES: thy kingdom is divided, and given to the Medes and Persians.

Daniel was rewarded for his efforts, and the party continued. But though Belshazzar wanted to delay thinking about God's judgment on him, God had everything in place to accomplish His purpose at that moment. The Scripture says, "In that night was Belshazzar the king of the Chaldeans (Babylonians) slain," (Daniel 5:30).

After 210 years the Babylonian empire was ended. Only fifty years previously, Nebuchadnezzar had destroyed Jerusalem and the Temple. The prophecies of Isaiah, Jeremiah, and Daniel were fulfilled.

Cyrus extended the kingdom from the Indus river to the Aegean Sea, from the Caspian and Black Seas to Ethiopia and the Sea of Arabia. He was a great and good king. He was killed in an expedition against the Scythians, after a reign of 29 years.

Persia had become the great imperial power of Asia.

Gambyses or Cambyses (529-521 B.C.), Son of Cyrus

Cyrus was followed by his son Cambyses, a cruel monarch who extended the kingdom to Egypt, and put the Egyptian king to death.

Cambyses did not revoke the edict of Cyrus, but slowed down the rebuilding of Jerusalem.

Before Cyrus' death Smerdis, Cambyses younger brother, had been given several provinces by their father. Shortly after Cambyses became king he secretly ordered Smerdis to be killed.

While Cambyses was putting down a revolt in Egypt a pseudo-Smerdis arose and took the royal title of king. Cambyses considered that his servants might have betrayed him and had not killed his brother as he had ordered and that this might be him.

But it was Smerdis the Magian, who looked a lot like the royal Smerdis who was put on the throne in Cambyses absence. Cambyses had removed the ears of Smerdis the Magian for some offense and those who entered the palace to kill the Magian knew of this. When they found Smerdis, they took off his head-covering and found him earless. They knew he was a phony and he was killed.

Cambyses was either killed or committed suicide on his return from Egypt after hearing of the insurrection in his absence. He reigned for barely 8 years.

Pseudo-Smerdis (521 B.C.), reigned for 8 months

The pseudo-Smerdis never had complete control of the throne. When he died Darius Hystaspes, of the royal line, was given the imperial title because the royal family had become extinct. He was a Persian nobleman. (Ezra 4:5,24; 5:5,6, etc.) It was he who had Smerdis killed, and by leading an insurrection he became king.

He retook Babylon after they revolted against the Persians and made war against the Scythians. (See Rollin, *Ancient History,* Vol. I), pp. 366-368.

Darius I (Hystaspes) (521-485 B.C.)

He was the son of Hystaspes, a Persian by birth, and of the royal family of Achaemenes. (Rollin, *Ancient History*, Vol. I.), p. 369.

Darius was elected king by seven lords of the kingdom, but was elected to a country in revolt. His first job was to put down all the different revolts in the provinces which he did admirably. He was a more noble and just ruler than Gambyses and allowed the Privy Council of each state more input into the government.

King Darius
(Peloubet, 1911)

He organized the kingdom and divided it into 20 provinces (satrapies). The king of each province was dethroned and a Persian official (a satrap) was put in his place to govern the province.

Each province was compelled to pay tribute and a system of royal roads was established to facilitate travel over the empire. A post system was instituted so messages could be taken throughout the kingdom. This is clearly seen in the book of Esther when the king sent messengers all over the kingdom to carry out his commands.

He gave the funds and supplies for the rebuilding project of the Temple and allowed the Israelites who so desired, to return to their land, (Ezra 5 and 6). The Temple construction was completed in 516 B.C. as the tribes of Judah began their return to the Holy Land.

Darius was one of the greatest Persian monarchs after Cyrus.

Persia had become a great power and Darius consolidated the empire in 521 B.C.

Darius began the Persian invasion of Greece. The Ionians under Persian control in Asia Minor revolted and the Athenians encouraged them in their revolt.

Darius tried to conquer the Scythians by crossing the Danube over a bridge of boats. He left his Ionian allies in charge of the boats, saying that if he did not return within three months they were to burn the boats and return to their own country.

When the Sycthians heard of his coming, they sent their families and herds away and practiced a "scorched earth" policy in the land through which the Persians would have to travel. They stopped up the wells and springs and took away anything edible for man or beast.

They then set about to lay an ambush for the Persians.

Willard says Darius received a messenger from the Scythians, who brought him a gift of a bird, a mouse, a frog, and five arrows. The messenger refused to give the meaning of the gift, but one of the Persian officers was able to tell Darius its meaning. "Know," said he, "that unless you can fly in the air like birds, or hide yourself in the earth like mice, or swim the water like frogs, you shall in no wise be able to escape the arrows of the Scythians." (Willard, *Universal History)*, p. 57.

The Persian army became so downhearted because of the enemy and the barrenness of the area that Darius retraced his steps to the Danube without ever fighting with the Scythians.

Scythian soldiers, from a vase found in a Scythian

In the meantime, the Scythians took shortcuts to the river crossing and tried to get the Ionians to destroy the bridge before Darius arrived. They refused, feeling it would be to their advantage to keep on the good side of the Persians. Darius took part of his troops back to Sardis in Asia Minor and finally returned to Persia.

He left his general, Megabysus, with the remainder of the army with instructions to conquer Macedonia and Thrace, which he did in short order.

Aristagoras, one of the kings or *tyrants*, who had been placed in the Persian colonies, led an Ionian revolt against Darius and sent ambassadors throughout Greece asking their help. The Athenians came to their aid, but Sparta refused to help them.

He then traveled throughout Ionia himself, calling on the tyrants to restore the freedom of the cities. He freed his city of Miletus as an example to them.

The Ionians sailed to Ephesus in the third

year of the war and marched to Sardis where they burned the city and drove the Persian governor into the citadel.

They then marched to Ephesus, but were routed by the Persian and Lydian armies and many were killed.

The Athenians backed out of the revolt and took back their ships. The Ionians had a fleet of 353 vessels, and when it was made plain that the Persians intended to destroy Miletus, the most important city of the Ionians, they determined to fight the Persians at sea.

Only by trickery and guile was the Persian commander able to defeat them because the Ionians were far better sailors than the Persians. The Persian captain made a deal with the captains of the enemy ships for them to leave the Ionians, and told them he would destroy the countries of those who refused to leave.

The Samians left with 49 of their 66 ships, but the Samian people condemned the treachery of their leaders. The names of the eleven captains who left the battle were recorded on a pillar which was placed in their territory so all would remember their dishonor.

The battle was lost, Miletus was taken and burned, and the people killed.

The Persians continued to destroy towns and cities all the way to the shores of the Hellespont. (This is a narrow strait between Asia and Europe, later called the Dardanelles and is a part of the passage between the Black and the Aegean Seas.)

The revolt was ended in 494 B.C. and Darius determined to punish the Athenians for their part in it. He sent his son-in-law, Mardonius, with an army to Athens. They were only able to go as far as Macedonia and Thrace which had already been taken by the Persians. His naval fleet was destroyed by a violent storm while sailing around Mt. Athos. Three hundred ships and 20,000 men were lost. Mardonius returned to Asia Minor without a victory.

When Darius sent envoys to the chief Grecian cities to demand tribute in recognition of his right to rule them, most of the cities complied, but Sparta and Athens refused. This caused a meeting of Persia and Greece on the plains of Marathon, north of Athens and east of Thebes, in 490 B.C.

Darius' army was led by Datis. Though the Persians outnumbered them ten to one, the Greeks defeated them, September, 490 B.C.

The death of Darius in 485 B.C., stopped him from returning to Greece to try to defeat them again.

The third empire in the "dream-image of Daniel 2" is Persia.

After the death of Darius, Alexander the Great became master of all the East.

Ahasuerus (Xerxes I, 485-465 B.C.), son of Darius

Xerxes was the father of Artaxerxes I. From the ancient records he was described as 'handsome in person and kingly in bearing; but weak, vain, fickle, and despotic.'

He brought the Egyptians together and united them again into a united political state. He is considered to be "the fourth king of Persia in the prophecy of Daniel (11:2)".

Daniel 11:2, *And now will I show thee the truth, Behold, there shall stand up yet three kings in Persia; and the fourth shall be far richer than they all: and by his strength through his riches he shall stir up all against the realm of Grecia.* He was defeated by Alexander and his kingdom diminished in importance after the Greeks took over the entire area.

He invaded Greece ten years after the battle of Marathon.

During the intervening ten years the Athenians had been preparing for the expected invasion. A navy was created to meet the Persian fleet. The Grecian states met at the Isthmus of Corinth and united against a common enemy. Sparta was at the head of the Grecians, no doubt because of her military prowess.

At Sardis Xerxes collected the greatest army ever seen at that time. He built a double bridge of boats a mile wide, at the Hellespont, in order to allow his 2,500,000 soldiers to enter Greece from Asia Minor. Crossing in two columns, it took seven days and nights for the soldiers to cross.

He also had 1200 ships and many smaller vessels which sailed north and then west toward the coast as backup for the army. Each ship had 200 rowers and 30 fighting men aboard.

In the meantime, the Greeks determined to cut the Persians off in the Pass of Thermopylae, but the battle was lost through treachery and the Greeks were defeated, August, 480 B.C.

At the battle of Mycale, September, 480 B.C. the Persian fleet was destroyed. Xerxes was defeated by the Greeks in the sea battle at Salamis in October, 480 B.C. and retreated into Asia Minor. The Persians never invaded Greece again and were finally driven out of Greece and back to their own country.

We know of Ahaseurus in connection with Israel only from Ezra 4:6 and the book of Esther. During his reign the construction on the wall of Jerusalem was stopped.

Artaxerxes I (Longimanus, 465-425 B.C.), son of Ahasuerus (Xerxes)

Artaxerxes killed his brother Darius, who was evidently older than he, and took the throne.

He was called the 'long-handed' (Longimanus), perhaps because of his ability with his hands. He was a king with an approachable spirit and this helped the Jews. It is very possible that Esther's influence is reflected in this attitude.

Artaxerxes knew little of Jerusalem when he came to the throne, but as time passed he became better acquainted with it and the needs there. His attention was first called to it by Rehum his chancellor who told him it was a dangerous city and that its rebuilding must stop. He called for a stoppage of the work because he trusted his chancellor. (Ezra 4:7-22).

Evidently, Artaxerxes checked the records for the decrees of Cyrus and Darius, and in the seventh year of his reign he gave his support to Ezra's return to Jerusalem. In the twentieth year of his reign he sent Nehemiah back to Jerusalem with the supplies he needed for the reconstruction of the walls of Jerusalem. He was God's instrument to help the Jews at this crucial period of their history.

Other Persian Kings

"Later Persian kings, not referred to in Scriptures were: Xerxes II who reigned two months, Sogdianus who reigned seven months, Darius II (Nothus, 423-405 B.C.), Artaxerxes II (Mnemmon 405-358 B.C.), Artaxerxes III (Ochus, 358-337 B.C.), Arses (337-335 B.C.), and Darius III (Colomanus, or Codomannus, 335-331 B.C.) who was defeated by Alexander the Great at the battle of Issus. (See Rollin, *Ancient History*, Vol. II, pp. 167-170 for information about these kings.)

Favorable Conditions of Persian Rule

"The two hundred years of Persian rule were, in general, favorable to the Jews. The Persian kings were not the absolute monarchs which the Babylonians had been. Most of them were Zoroastrians and adhered or were favorable to monotheism. They adhered to a policy of permitting each province to have its own religion. Through these two centuries the Jews, therefore, were perfectly free to worship God. In fact, other peoples were required to permit them to do so; which meant that they were actually protected in carrying on their worship." Loyal R. Ringenberg, The *Word of God in History*, (Winona Lake: Lambert Huffman Publisher, 1953), pp. 244-246.

JAVAN, (see section beginning below)

TUBAL

He settled in Tibareni, modern day Ordow in Turkey on the Black Sea. In 400 B.C. his descendants were noted to carry leather helmets, nine foot spears and steel battle-axes. They were described as a kingly race and were fond of games and laughter.

MESCHECH (The Moschi, The Muscovites)

Ezekiel 38:2: 39:1 speaks of 'the land of Magog, the Prince of Rosh, Meschech and Tubal.' Rosh (descendant of Magog) became the dominate tribe and gave their name to Russia. Rosh means 'chief'. They settled near Colchis in the mountain district of Kars and Erzroum in Russia.

The Muscovites (Meschech) wore wooden helmets and carried spears and small swords.

About 1000 B. C. they were a nation of considerable power and numbers, holding their principal position in Taurus and Cappadocia.

TIRAS

He and his descendants settled in Thrace, which is located between the Halys, Drave, and Save Rivers in Asia Minor. Later they migrated into the region known as Thracia in northern Greece and southern Bulgaria.

Tiras joined with his brother Gomer to make war and to migrate. From Tiras came the Dacians (modern Romania) and the Goths.

They latter conquered Rome under Alaric in 476 A. D.

These three tribes were great traders and traded slaves in Tyre. In Ezekiel 27:13 they are called manufacturers of brass. They were warlike tribes who fought with Xerxes in 480 B. C.

The Thracians (Tiras) wore skins of foxes on their heads while on their bodies they wore tunics and over those a long cloak of many colors. They also wore buckskin leggings and shoes and carried light javelins and short dirks.

About 700 B. C. they were driven beyond the Caucasus as the Aryans moved westward. There they became known as Moskova; the old capital of Russia, Moscow, takes its name from them.

JAVAN

His four sons, Elishah, Tarshish, Kittim, and Dodanim became the heads and founders of the chief tribes and principal branches of that nation which was renowned for arts and arms.

Genesis 10:5 says, *By these were the isles of the Gentiles divided in their land; everyone after his tongue, after their families, in their nations.*

Javan was also called *Ion,* and made his home in Ionia or Greece, (a part of which is also called Achaia in the Scriptures).

Elishah founded the city of Elis, and the Peloponnesus (the Elysian fields, the river Elissus, or Ilissus refer to their founder, Elishah).

Tarshish, his second son, founded his empire in Cilicia or Tarsus, and perhaps reached southern Spain where the colony known to the Greek-speaking world as Tartessus, was located. It is probable he also settled parts of Achaia.

Kittim, the third son, went to Cyprus which was rich in minerals; gold, silver, and copper. It also had forests for ship-building and great harbors. It abounded in jewels; emerald, jasper, agate, and diamonds. The Assyrians called it the land of Yavnan, 'Isle of the Greeks'. Because of its riches, the Phoenicians, sons of Ham, took control of it, and taught the Kittimites to worship their favorite goddess-Astarte, or Venus. (Alexander the Great was descended from him, as was the Macedonian nation.) The first book of the Maccabees says "Alexander, the son of Philip, the Macedonian, went out of his country, which was that of Cetthim, or Chittim, to make war against Darius, king of Persia." (Rollin, *Ancient History*, Vol. I), p. 410.

The last son, **Dodanim** or **Rodanim** as he is called in 1 Chronicles 1:7, went to Rhodes, "Land of Roses". It was rich in beauty and trade, and was very powerful. He may also have ventured into Italy. He also founded Thessaly and Epirus where the pagan worship of Jupiter of Dodona was observed.

Javan's heritage was that of physical beauty. He was gifted with a richness of imagination and the capacity for refined and accurate speech which would become the language of theology - Greek.

The earliest name for the Ionic peoples was Pelasgi, though this was the name of just one of the tribes. The Egyptians sent colonists to Greece and took possession of the Acropolis at Athens, and introduced the worship of Neith, the Greek Athene or Minerva.

After some time the sons of Hellas (the Greeks) became better navigators than the Phoenicians; better architects than the Egyptians; better warriors than the Assyrians; and had a more beautiful language than the Hindu. They introduced the arts and poetry of beauty.

Religious beliefs of the Ionians

At the time of their beginnings they worshipped one supreme God and had no images or temples. This god was called Zeus.

The attributes ascribed to him were: Supreme, Merciful, Pure, Unchanging, Just, and the Unknown God. Later they adopted the gods of all the other nations with whom they came in contact. They made gods of nature and of their dead heroes, and built many shrines and temples in which to worship them.

THE GREEK NATION

The father of the Greek nation was Javan, the fourth son of Japheth, as before stated.

In some areas the Greeks were some of the most intellectually advanced peoples the world has ever known. In others areas they were a depraved barbarous lot.

Rollin says of Greece: "Of all the countries of antiquity, none have been so highly celebrated, or furnished history with so many valuable monuments and illustrious examples as Greece. In whatever light she is considered, whether for the glory of her arms, the wisdom of her laws, or the study and improvement of arts and sciences, we must allow that she carried them to the utmost degree of perfection; and it may be truly be said, that in all these respects, she has, in some measure been the school of mankind." (Rollin, *Ancient History*, Vol. I), p. 407.

When Paul spoke to the Athenians in Acts 17:16-33, he was overwhelmed with the idolatry of the city. He said "it was wholly given over to idolatry," (verse 16).

On Mar's hill, the highest court in Athens, Paul accused the Athenians of being too superstitious. They had a form of godliness but denied the 'power thereof'. In the Greek religion there was never any claim to unity, and they never recognized themselves as sinners in need of a Savior. They considered the wrong things they did to be 'bad faults' and all they needed to do was try harder and forget the shortcomings as quickly as possible.

Moral striving was not an issue as the Greeks generally were content with their humanness and raised it to the level of the divine.

They were a people who showed the heights to which man can reach intellectually and still be without any knowledge of the true God.

Each major tribal division took the truths of the creation and of God's judgment of the world for sin as they left Sinai, but the Greeks had lost the light of the divine revelation by the time the world began to see them as a civilized people. As yet they were not a nation, but some steps at unification were being taken.

Though they were a people of human genius and excelled in many of the arts and in every major area of life, they were a people totally without religion. Their literature was marvelous for the period; their histories were well told, though given to the fabulous; they were superb dramatists, and the study of philosophy began with them.

The first great orators came from them and some of the greatest teachers of the world were Greeks. The effects of their teaching can be seen in the then-known world under the Roman empire when the whole world spoke Greek and followed Greek principles of life. Those principles had to do with all kinds of noble achievements in every area of human endeavor except religion. Included were architecture, principles of advanced math, medicine, astronomy, the elementary truths of modern science, the arts, etc.

They were advanced intellectually, but they were worse than cave-men spiritually. It is impressive to see the heights and depths man can reach when his life is not founded upon the Solid Rock.

When the Septuagint version of the Bible was translated from Hebrew it was translated into Greek under the sponsorship of the Greek Ptolemy in Egypt. The Greek language still has an effect on us today as many of the words of our Bible are of Greek origin, for example: priest, prophet, Hades, altar, sacrifice, etc. Their language became the language of theology and was extended to more lands than any other except Hindu and English.

The world found at Pompeii the remains of an immoral, degenerate society with no redeeming qualities except those of a civilized human being. When mothers were found with their babies in their arms as they tried to protect them from death, a glimpse of tenderness and love can be seen. In other places the babies were deserted to their fate and the mothers escaped only to be destroyed in another location.

The paintings and implements uncovered by archeologists have told a story not worthy of a people whose beginnings were so hopeful.

Religion - Greek Fables

The Greeks were polytheists but felt that their gods were their friends unlike the religion of fear practiced by the Asiatics.

They recognized three great dwelling places: Olympos, the heavens, home of the gods; Earth, the place of man; and Hades, the place of the dead. Hades had two states: Elysium for the good, and Tartarus for the evil, corresponding to Paradise and Hell in the Bible.

According to them everything in the world began with Chaos, then came the water, which was divided, and then the Earth appeared. The Firmament then appeared to cover the Earth.

The first men were a golden race who dwelt with the gods. But men grew continually worse until Justice withdrew her presence from them.

Eve is the equivalent of their Pandora who opened the box which released all the evils of the world.

They remembered the Flood in the story of Deucalion and Pyrrha. Zeus or Jupiter, their most important god, instructed them to build an ark to save themselves because he was going to destroy the world by water. The ark came to rest on a mountain and Deucalion came out and worshipped Zeus. The Earth was replenished with men because of the prayer of Deucalion.

The story of Babel and the Dispersion are found in their story of the wars of the Titans.

Their legend of Cadmus, who came to them from Asia, refers to the Phoenicians who were Hamites and who taught them to read and write.

They believed they received messages from the gods by means of the oracles. Willard says the oracle at Delphi was a woman seated on a three-legged stool breathing the sulfurous gas fumes that came up out of a cave and whatever she said while under the influence of those fumes was recorded by a priest. He then reported the sayings to the people and used them for his own purposes. The people believed whatever the priests told them and by that means the priests became very wealthy and very powerful because the people were so superstitious.

The two most important locations of the oracles were at Dodona, for Zeus, and Delphi for Apollo.

Their religion consisted mostly of sacrifices to the gods. The offerings could be animals or fruits, wine, milk, etc. They were either offerings of prayer and thanksgiving or sin-offerings. Solemn processions and dances were also part of the worship. Games were an integral part of their worship and were observed frequently.

They had twelve main gods who were worshipped and were called the great Olympian gods, because they were supposed to live on Mt. Olympus. They were:

1. "Zeus, or *Jupiter*, the chief and father of the gods. He is always represented as seated on a throne with the thunderbolts in his right hand, and an eagle by his side.

2. Poseidon, or *Neptune*, the earth-shaker and ruler of the sea; his symbol is a trident.

3. Apollon, or *Apollo* (called also Phoebus Apollo), the divinity of poetical inspiration, of song and music. He was figured as the *beau ideal* of manly beauty.

4. Artemis, or *Diana*, the huntress among the immortals, the divinity of flocks and of the chase. As twin-sister of Apollo, she was the divinity of the moon, [i.e. Semiramis].

5. Hephaistos, or *Vulcan*, the god of terrestrial fire: he is represented as a blacksmith.

6. Hermes, or *Mercury*, the messenger of the gods; the god of eloquence, and the protector of trade: he is marked by his winged sandals, and by his *caducceus*, or wand. [This belief comes from Ham, check section on Cush.]

7. Ares, or *Mars*, the god of war, delighted in the din of battle, the slaughter of men, and the destruction of towns.

8. Hera, or *Juno*, the wife of Jupiter, a beautiful but unpleasant goddess.

9. Athena, or *Minerva* (also *Pallas*), the goddess of wisdom and war.

10. Hestia, or *Vesta*, the goddess of the hearth.

11. Demeter, or *Ceres*, the goddess of agriculture.

12. Aphrodite, or *Venus*, the goddess of love and beauty, is generally represented with her son *Eros*, or Cupid...The Odyssey represents her as the wife of Vulcan...." William Swinton, *Outlines of the World's History*, (American Book Company: New York, 1874), pp. 115-116. (She is the Greek version of Semiramis and Ninus.)

Javan is preserved in their myths of Jason, who is united with Medea, the daughter of the king of Colchis - this goes back to the time when Javan and Madai were together in the tents of Japheth, their father.

They had the story of a serpent who was an enemy of man, and they believed in a race of giants who were evil and were born of the daughters of men.

The Cyclopes represented the early settlers whom they esteemed to be a 'race of surpassing strength and stature.' Their architecture extends into earliest antiquity and is referred to as Cyclopean. This architecture was constructed during the same period as the Chaldean, Assyrian, and early Egyptian monuments. Theirs were huge mounds, constructed without cement, as burial places and monuments to their heroes. Wherever Javan traveled these mounds can be found, therefore the name 'mound-builder' is associated with him.

Jason and the Golden Fleece - the Argonautic Expedition

The Argonauts were purported to be a group of adventurers who went to Colchis in search of the riches of the kingdom - 'the golden fleece'. Jason was the leader of this enterprise and while there he met Medea, the beautiful daughter of the king. She was a sorceress, and with her help he was able to get the riches he sought.

He left a Greek colony planted on the shores of the Black Sea and sailed back to Greece with the riches and the cruel sorceress, now his wife.

He later left her for another woman, Creusa, the daughter of the king of Athens. In revenge Medea killed her own children so their father, Jason, would have to suffer for his actions.

Greek beliefs about their gods

The gods were superior, but were made like men. They did not die and were exempt from mutations. They ruled men and nature and were responsible for the fate of each man. They were in control of both external and internal thought and emotion. They had extraordinary power in both nature and human affairs.

The great king of the gods, was Zeus or Jove who rewarded good and punished evil. Though men and even gods might continue doing things against the will of Zeus, he would eventually bring about a violent punishment on them.

In theory, the gods were omnipotent and omniscient, but they could be fooled. They were excitable, jealous and cruel, and of low moral character. If the individual was good and revered the gods they were tender and bountiful in their dealings with him. They were to be worshipped and sacrifices were to be made to them, especially the thank-offering and the first-fruits offering.

In reference to good and evil in man, man had to bear the burden of his sins, and if he sinned, he would be punished. The soul was thought to be immortal, but crimes committed in this life were to be punished in this world. When they died their spirits were to be purified in Elysium, (reminding one of the Roman Catholic purgatory). Really bad crimes were to be punished in Tartarus.

The geography of Greece

The territory extended to the southern part of Turkey, it was bounded on the east by the Aegean Sea; on the south by the Cretan or Candian Sea; on the west by the Ionian Sea; and on the north by Ilyria and Thrace.

The country itself is divided by various mountains which served to isolate and separate people into little groups or states and allowed them a measure of political freedom.

The peninsula is divided into Northern (Thessaly and Epirus), Central (composed of 11 states), and Southern regions, the Peloponnesus. The most important of the seven principle states was Laconia, (Lacedaemon), whose capital was Sparta. It is surrounded by the Aegean and Ionian Seas, and the Thracian Sea on the northeast.

The Four Divisions of Greek History
(2154 years)

1. From the Dorian migration to the start of the wars with Persia (1100-500 B.C.).

2. From the taking of Troy to the reign of Darius. At that time Grecian history begins to be intermixed with that of the Persians, 663 years.

3. From the beginning of the Persian wars to the time Philip of Macedon conquered Greece, at the battle of Chaeronea, (500-338 B.C.)

4. From the death of Alexander, when the Grecians began to decline, to their final subjection under the Romans. Their downfall dates from the taking and destruction of Corinth, (338-146 B.C.). (Swinton, *Outlines*), p. 81.

The Original Tribes of Greece

The descendants of Javan or Ion (same name), the son of Japheth, all were called Ionians by the Hebrews, the Chaldeans, the Arabians and others. (Isaiah 66:19; Ezekiel 27:13,19.)

The first tribe to enter the land which became Greece were called the Pelasgi, the next tribe to enter were the Hellenes, who came from Elisha, also called Ellas, from whom the word Hellenes comes. They were a more warlike group who went from Thessaly and took over the whole peninsula. Their four divisions were: the Dorians (to the north and south slopes of Mt. Etna), the Aeolians (northern Greece on the west coast of the Peloponnesus), and the Ionians (the narrow strip along the northern coast of the Peloponnesus and eastward into Attica). The Arcadians in the center of the country were the descendants of the Pelasgic people. (Ibid.), p. 78.

They left the Plain of Shinar as a language group and as they traveled westward they divided into more and more tribal groups. At first they covered a more extensive area but later were confined to the peninsula and the Greek islands.

In reality the Scripture is very limited in information about the Greeks and gives us only a hint about their origins and development. However, profane authors are usually not totally trustworthy and many leave gaps concerning their history. It is sufficient to say they had migrated to that location from the East and God's purpose for the nation was about to be revealed.

They began to build homes at a distance from one another in order to defend themselves from 'violence and oppression' and in time these spaces were filled in with more houses and became cities.

The Egyptians and Phoenicians instructed the Grecians in the arts and sciences, navigation, writing, commerce, and the knowledge of laws and polity. (There were colonies of Egyptians and Phoenicians living among them.)

During two centuries of advanced intellectual activity in the city of Athens, the principles and many of the elementary truths of science were formulated. Mathematics, especially astronomy, was taken by the Greeks and furthered from the point where the Hamites had left its study. The Greeks were so accurate in their principles, terminology, and method that there are still no basic changes in them. In a fifty year period the Greeks took geometry from the basics to integral calculus.

Pythagoras (582-507) was the first scientist to hold to the principle that the earth was round. Archimedes invented the whole science of hydrostatics, and Eratosthenes measured the earth so accurately that his figure of 7,850 miles was only 50 miles less than the true polar diameter.

In the study of medicine the Greeks located and understood the importance of the pulse as early as 400 B.C. They also understood that the arteries branched out from the heart and that veins arose from the liver. The physician's Hippocratic oath came from them and is still the ideal of the medical profession in all parts of the world.

During the early days of Greece the principle of 'survival of the fittest' was totally operative and when a stronger person wanted the land of a neighbor he invaded and took it.

In Attica the country was dry and barren and no one cared to take their land from them. Those who lived there distinguished themselves by taking the name meaning, 'men born in the country where they lived,' for nearly all the rest of Greece had been transplanted to other places.

Greece was at first called Hellas (from the Hellenes). It was the Romans who gave it the name of Greece, and the boundaries at that time included the adjacent islands and other settlements on the Mediterranean Sea.

Because of their physical location on the Mediterranean with great inlets and bays, the Greeks were the most civilized early people in Europe. Their social and economic exchanges with many nations gave them an advanced and varied culture from the earliest days. They were the first to give an example to the world of free self-governing states, a principle never thought of before outside of Israel.

The Greeks held parts of the western shores of Asia Minor, and the islands between Asia Minor and Greece were settled by them also. They settled as far west as Sicily and lower Italy, on the north coast of Africa (Cyrene), and along the coast of Thrace and Macedonia.

They "were the first people to show the world what real freedom and real civilization were." (Swinton, *Outlines*), p. 114.

The War of the Heraclidae

This war was supposed to have occurred some 80 years after the fall of Troy. It was between two families, those of Perseus and Pelops who each had for many years been trying to gain the rule of the Peloponnesus.

Hercules was the grandson of Perseus whose family were the Perseid, and were called the Heraclidae.

The tribe of the Pelopidae (Pelops) had driven them out of the Peloponnesus and they had become princes of a small area of land between the mountains of Aoeta and Parnassus called Doris.

The Heraclidae joined with the Dorians and the Aetolians and conquered the Pelopidae and became the masters of the Peloponnesus.

The cities were divided by lot among the main chiefs. Some of the people escaped to Athens seeking refuge from the Heraclidae and their allies; some emigrated (some to Italy, some to Asia Minor where they founded colonies; some went to the Islands of Lesbos and Tenedos), and others became slaves.

About 1000 B.C. the Ionians and Dorians became the most important tribes and it was through them that the country began to develop. The difference between Sparta (Doric) and Athens (Ionians) was a result of these two tribes of people. Sparta became the most important city.

The Ionians were more democratic in spirit and were more materialistic. The Dorians were more simple in their desires and preferred a monarchy. They accepted the practice of slavery, as noted in Ezekiel 27:13 in reference to Tyre.

Because the Athenians had taken in the refugees, the Dorians determined to have their revenge on them and invaded Attica.

They were told by the Oracle of Apollo at Delphi that they would succeed in defeating the Athenians if they would not kill Codrus, the Athenian king. When Codrus heard this he disguised himself as a peasant and entered the Dorian camp where he was killed in a quarrel.

The Dorians quickly left because they believed they would be defeated since Codrus had been killed. No doubt, that was the purpose for the actions of Codrus in entering their camp in the first place, to protect his city.

The office of king was abolished in Athens because of a dispute between the sons of Codrus, and the position of *archon* was put in its place. The eldest son of Codrus, Melon, was elected to serve as the first archon.

The rapid growth of the Greek nation can be attributed to several things:

- they were all descended from the same stock through Javan and were all Hellenes;

- they had a common language and literature;

- their religious rites, temples and festivals were held in common.

In Attica, because they were at peace, they were able to advance toward civilization more quickly and became a refuge for the wealthy of Greece.

Grecian ideas of their beginnings

Unwilling to accept their beginnings as mere savages they invented a fabulous history of their origins. These came from Homer and later from Hesiod who gave them their large pantheon of Olympian deities. Their history during this early period is mostly nonexistent and is so interwoven with the Greek myths that they are inseparable and most unbelievable.

There are some interesting comparisons in Bible history and in the Grecian history of their mythical gods:

- Their god, Zeus, never lived - our God Jehovah lives.

- No mythical god spoke from Mt. Olympus

- our God spoke from Mt. Sinai.

- They spoke of their gods coming down to earth, but no one ever saw them - our God did come to earth where he suffered and died and rose again for our salvation in the person of our Lord Jesus Christ.

- They had the Iliad, often referred to as their Bible - we have the Bible, the inspired Word of God which gives 'light to our path' and leads us in the right way. We never have to wonder if we're doing right, we always have the answer if we care to seek it from the pages of His Book.

- Their religion itself made their gods sinful and evil; it never caused people to want to become more moral individuals - the true religion causes us to want to be more 'perfect' each day as we understand more about the perfection of our Savior.

- Their religion was based on myths - ours is based on an historic reality which changed the course of history and the face of the entire world.

The fundamental failure of this ancient, most brilliant civilization is that its great thinkers so completely failed to determine any positive, complete, assured truth, in matters pertaining to God, to the future state of man, to atonement, to sin, or to any of those matters of religion which are an integral part of our Christian heritage. Could a failure be more complete or more destructive to a civilization?

Time periods of importance

The Fall of Troy

From Homer's epic the Iliad, comes the story of the siege of Troy and there is some indication that the story has at least some historical merit, but there is no conclusive proof that any of it ever occurred. Henry Schliemann wrote a book called *The Greek Treasure* in which he sought to prove by his own archeological finds that Troy did indeed exist and some of his proofs were very convincing. However, at a later period critics seemed to disprove everything he had found as not pertaining to Troy at all.

An abbreviated account is this: At the time Jephtha governed the people of God, 1184 years before Christ, the Greeks took Troy after a siege of 10 years. The daughter of Tyndarus, king of Lacedaemon, was stolen from her husband Menelaus by Alexander or Paris, son of Priam, king of the Trojans. Helen had only lived with her husband three years at this time and the Greeks united to defeat the Trojans. If the account has any truth to it, the world should have begun to have a hint of what the Greeks were able to do with united

strength. This should have served as a warning to Asia as to her future subjection to these awesome nations.

Swinton says the most important information learned from the Iliad and the Odyssey is the observation of the kind of society in which the people lived at the time:

- government by a monarchy

- the tribe or nation was more important than the city

- there was a hereditary nobility

- there was a primitive form of parliament which could hear trials and were privy to information, but could not judge nor offer advice

- there was no polygamy

- there was a high regard for women

- slavery was accepted and considered a 'right'

- there was constant warring between tribes and nations

- military virtues were the most important

- there was a religion, though it was pagan

- polytheism was practiced and there was a belief in 'fate'

- they had respect for the priests

- the temples and religious festivals were held sacred, (Swinton, *Outlines*), p. 79.

The Olympiad

From its beginning, Greece observed the celebration of several different games and each one was associated with a particular form of paganism and was a religious ceremony.

The first were the *Isthmian* games instituted by Theseus in celebration for having stopped the practice of sending seven youths and seven virgins every nine years to the king of Crete to be sacrificed by him. These games were celebrated every four years on the Isthmus of Corinth in honor of Neptune.

The *Nemean* games were instituted by Hercules to celebrate and remember his slaying of a terrible lion that dwelled in the Nemean forest. They were observed every two years in honor of Nemean Jupiter, at Nemea in the Peloponnesus.

The *Pythian* games were celebrated in honor of Apollo Pythius every four years in the third year of the Olympiad near Delphi.

The *Olympic* games were celebrated every four years in honor of Jupiter Olympus in the plain of Olympia in Elis. The prize in the Olympic games was a wreath made of the wild olive tree. But the honor heaped on the winner was the real prize.

The Olympiad is a revolution of four complete years from the celebration of one Olympic game to another.

The common year of the Olympiads began in the summer of the year of the world 776 B.C. and was held every four years from that date. They were the most popular of all the games and came to designate a time period for the Greeks.

Forms of Greek government

Greek government began with a monarchy, which is the oldest form of government, and is from the top down. (All power goes from the monarch to the people, never the opposite way.)

As the nature of man began to degenerate, the system failed as usurpers took the throne and used it for their own selfish ends. Even rightful masters caused injustices to take place through their severity. Because of these problems "a different spirit seized the people, which prevailed throughout Greece, (and) kindled a violent desire of liberty, and brought about a general change of government every where, except in Macedonia; so that monarchy gave way to a republican government" though it, too, was changed from city to city. (Rollin, *Ancient History,* Vol. I), p. 416.

The wise Laws of Minos (who claimed to be descended from Jupiter) were enacted and put into practice in Crete where Minos ruled.

In Athens, their king, Amphictyon III established an assembly called the Amphictyonic Council. This was a group of 12 cities whose princes met twice a year at Delphi to discuss and take measures for the safety of all, and to settle any disputes that might have arisen among them.

None of the city-states belonging to the confederacy was to be destroyed by any other. That any group of people would band together for mutual good and safety is the only legitimate principle of government, and to see that this principle was understood by some at that remote time in history in an interesting phenomenon.

In the United States of America this principle has been carried to a more perfect level and each state forms a part of the confederacy, or the union, for its own peace and protection and that of each of the others.

The Greeks were the first to invent the study of politics. Before the 5th century politics did not exist because the definition of politics and polity, from which the word politics stems, has to do with government *of, for* and *by* the people. Before this time in history the people were not consulted about the kind of government they would have over them and there was no public business.

The sovereign who ruled over each individual kingdom decided how his subjects would be ruled and who would do the ruling. All affairs of government were private and were determined by the sovereign and the ruling class who received their power from him.

Polity, according to Webster's 1828, is (1) *The form or constitution of civil government of a nation or state; and in free states, the frame or fundamental system by which the several branches of government are established, and the powers and duties of each designated and defined. The word seems also to embrace legislation and administration of government.* (2) *The constitution or general fundamental principles of government of any class of citizens, considered in an appropriate character, or as a subordinate state.*

And 'politics' is: *The science of government; that part of ethics which consists in the regulation and government of a nation or state, for the preservation of its safety, peace and prosperity; comprehending the defense of its existence and rights against foreign control or conquest, the augmentation of its strength and resources, and the protection of its citizens in their right, with the preservation and improvement of their morals.* (Webster's 1828).

This being the case, the Greeks had an understanding of the workings of government before the rest of the world even knew there was such a thing.

When the rights of the individual are protected by law, a nation begins to flourish economically, and Greece became a nation the world had to deal with both economically and militarily.

In Europe the study of politics led to the establishment of free, self-governing states, an institution never thought of in the ancient Oriental empires.

By the 8th century B.C. the government had changed into a republican form and people gathered into small free states. Sparta was the only city which retained even the name of 'king'; all the others were ruled by a republican form of government.

Because of the many petty, independent states it was easier for the Persians to conquer the country. The lesson of Federal Union was learned too late to keep the country from being destroyed by the Romans. If the United States were divided into states, with no central point of union, it would also be easily overrun by whatever nation was stronger than the strongest state. For this reason we have a united federal union and government which is supposed to serve the interests and protect the rights of the individual states and citizens.

THE CITY-STATES

Sparta

Lycurgus was of the Heraclidae family, supposed to be the 10th from Hercules.

Because he had refused the crown of Sparta at the death of his brother, and preserved the kingship for his brother's baby son, the people of Sparta paid him great tribute as an honest and generous man. Until the child came of age, Lycurgus governed in his place.

While governing he instituted a new constitution which was to do away with all luxury and instill a public spirit in the people, which would lead to a nation of soldiers.

It was, in practice, a socialistic form of government and the rights of the individual were unimportant, but it accomplished its purpose and Sparta became a great military power.

The Spartans (Dorians) were the dominant power in the Peloponnesus.

Lycurgus was said to have lived about 850 B.C. In order to maintain the power of the small class of lords (around 9000) who were the ruling factor, the Lycurgean constitution was given to 'create and maintain a vigorous and uncorrupted race [nation] of men'. (Swinton, *Outlines of World History*), p. 86.

Sparta was an aggressive military state which was subduing all its neighbors and would have conquered all of Greece and brought it under its power if the Persian invasion had not occurred.

Athens

At the same time Sparta was rising to power another city-state was coming to the forefront. Athens was more interested in intellectual pursuits than in military power.

Thucydides gave an interesting description of the Athenians which the Corinthians had observed:

"The Corinthian allies of Sparta said to the Laodiceans, 'You have never considered what manner of men are these Athenians with whom you will have to fight, and how utterly unlike yourselves. They are revolutionary, equally quick in the conception and in the execution of every new plan; while you are conservative - careful only to keep what you have, originating nothing, and not active even when action is most necessary. They are bold beyond their strength; they run risks which prudence would condemn; and in the midst of misfortunes they are full of hope. Whereas it is your nature, though strong, to act feebly; when your plans are most prudent, to distrust them; and when calamities come upon you, to think that you will never be delivered from them. They are impetuous, and you are dilatory; they are always abroad, and you are always at home. For they hope to gain something by leaving their homes; but you are afraid that any new enterprise may imperil what you have already. When conquerors, they pursue their victory to the utmost; when defeated, they fall back the least. Their bodies they devote to their country as though they belonged to other men; their true self is their mind, which is most truly their own when employed in her service. When they do not carry out an intention which they have formed, they seem to have sustained a personal bereavement; when an enterprise succeeds, they have gained a mere installment of what is to come; but if they fail, they at once conceive new hopes and so fill up the void. With them alone to hope is to have, for they lose not a moment in the execution of an idea. This is the lifelong task, full of anger and toil, which they are always imposing upon themselves. None enjoy their good things less, because they are always seeking for more. To do their duty is their only holiday, and they deem the quiet of inaction to be as disagreeable as the most tiresome business. If a man should say of them, in a word, that they were born neither to have peace themselves nor to allow peace to other men, he would simply speak the truth'." (Wilbur M. Smith, *Therefore Stand: Christian Apologetics,* Michigan: Baker Book House, 1945), pp. 203-245 excerpts.

Athens

(Peloubet, 1893)

Athens was at first governed by kings, but every man was master in his own house. After the death of Codrus, the last king of Athens, the Athenians abolished the regal power and declared that Jupiter was their only king. At the same time the Jews were rejecting the theocracy and demanding a man to rule over them, the Greeks were doing away with their system of kings.

And while the Spartans were becoming more and more a military state under a socialistic government the Athenians were more and more practicing a republican form of government.

After the rule of kings ended, the power was placed in the office of archon, but the archon could only be taken from the royal family and was a lifelong position. Later the position was held for ten years, and was finally opened to any of the nobles, not just the royal line. The number of archons was increased to nine who held office for one year.

The Senate was called the Areopagus, and was made up of nobles. The common people had no part in the government, and as always, this led to abuses of power.

Because of the fierce spirit of independence among the Athenians they even looked upon this power as a threat to their freedom and were never able to come to any agreement on religion or government.

However, after many years of struggle, Athens learned that true liberty consists in a dependence upon justice and reason, and chose for their legislator Draco who published the first written laws of the Greeks, called the 'bloody code'.

In doctrine the laws were Stoical and both the smallest offense and the largest were rewarded with death. These laws did not remain in practice very long as the judges were not so cruel as to demand death sentences for a small crime, and the people would not bring accusations when the penalty was so severe so they faded through disuse. The laws of Draco were so severe that the people began to riot in the beginning of the 6th century.

Those laws were replaced by the philosophies of Solon, one of the seven Greek sages, who was kind and wise in his judgments. He had been chosen by the archons to change the constitution of Athens, in 594 B.C. He repealed the laws of Draco, keeping only the death penalty for murder; freed the poor from slavery to the rich because of debts; formed a three party system for the rich and kept them in control. But he extended to all the people the right to vote, which ultimately gave them the control of all the affairs of the city. He abolished the aristocracy which was oppressing the people and substituted a moderate government which gave all Athenians a share of power, but gave the nobles the most influence. (Swinton, *Outlines*), p. 89.

At this point in the history of Greece, the Persians had already begun to invade the country and had subdued several areas. The Spartans and the Athenians had not submitted to pay tribute to Darius and joined together to stand against the Persians at the battle of Marathon which they won.

After the battle of Plataea and the destruction of the Persian fleet at Mycale by the Greeks, the Greeks were freed from the Persian invasions and the Persians returned to their own land.

The Golden Age of Athenian history.

The Greeks at this juncture found that their ancient mythologies were causing more harm than good to the morals of the people. From this situation came the development of different schools of philosophy.

Athens was the center of these schools and Pericles, who became the ruler for 40 years, was a great patron of the arts and encouraged their development.

He was an aristocrat who joined the democratic party and undermined the influence of Aristides and Cimon. Aristides died and Cimon was banished, leaving Pericles with no rivals.

Though his administration was just and fair, he still was, in all matters, looking out for his own best interests.

As the Romans would do later, he took treasures from Delphos and distributed them to the people in Athens. By his orders the architect Phidias constructed beautiful buildings and statues in order to please the people and keep Pericles in power.

He was very careful in his actions so that he would not be envied by the people, but when he made Athens so beautiful, he provoked the envy of the other Grecian states and in consequence they began to attack Athens.

By making the people satisfied with the material, he weakened their character and the constitutional government, and they were unable to withstand the encroachments of the other city-states.

At this point the Romans had heard of the effectiveness of Greek government and had sent deputies to obtain copies of the laws of Solon. Little did the Greeks suspect that soon that nation would be their conqueror.

The confederacy that had existed during the wars with Persia was broken up and both Athens and Sparta wanted to be the leader. Other states wanted their independence.

The two Peloponnesian wars weakened Greece and opened the way for Philip of Macedon to take over.

Philip of Macedon

A group of people from Argos were supposed to be the first inhabitants of Macedonia. Little was known of the country until the Persian invasion. Though it roots were Greek it was not considered one of the Greek states.

It had been subject to Persia until the battle of Plataea when it became an independent state.

Philip was the father of Alexander. He declared himself to be descended from Hercules, though his ancestors may not have been so auspicious as Hercules and he is said to have been the son of Amyntas II. (He was descended from the tribe of Kittim.) Macedon was a hereditary kingdom situated in what was ancient Thrace, later it was an independent kingdom which took control of a more modern Thrace. It was a tributary which paid tribute to Athens.

Philip was born B.C. 383. His mother was Eurydice, and his brothers were Alexander, and Perdiccas. Another son of Amyntas, Ptolemy, was illegitimate. Philip's father died after having reigned 24 years and his brother Alexander succeeded his father as the eldest son, but reigned only one year and was followed by Perdiccas the next son, after a plot to overthrow him was squelched. Ptolemy felt he was entitled to the throne, but upon what basis one can only conjecture. The decision as to whose right it was to claim the throne was given to Pelopidas, the general of Thebes, who was supposed to be a man of good judgment. He ruled in favor of Perdiccas.

However, in order to get Perdiccas and Ptolemy to agree to live by the treaty agreed upon by both, Pelopidas took Philip as a hostage to Thebes. At that time Philip was only 10 years old. His mother begged Pelopidas to give Philip a good education and he was placed with Epaminondas who was a military man. He had in his house, for the education of his own son, a Pythagorean philosopher who taught Philip. Epaminondas was a wise and virtuous man, and a great commander and statesman. Philip learned as much from his example as from his teacher, though later history would prove he did not take these lessons to heart.

Rollin says, "The Thebans did not know that they were then forming and educating the most dangerous enemy of Greece." (Rollin, *Ancient History*, Vol. III), p. 31.

After he had been in Thebes for nine or 10 years Philip heard that Macedonia was in revolution and slipped away secretly to his homeland. Perdiccas was killed in battle and several intrigues were in operation for replacing him. He had a young son who was the rightful heir, and when Philip arrived home, he governed the kingdom through the child for some time. The Macedonians, alarmed by the hostility of their neighbors, deposed the rightful heir and placed Philip on the throne.

Philip wanted to be considered a Greek so he could have Macedonia admitted to the Greek union, of which he determined Macedonia would be the head. The Sacred or Phocian War was his opportunity to do this. He became ruler of Macedon in 358 B.C., and ruled for 23 years.

He married Olympias, the daughter of Neoplotemus, the son of the king of Epirus, one of the Greek states to the west of Macedonia. She was the mother of Alexander, who was born at Pella, capital of Macedonia, in the first year of the 106th Olympiad.

Philip was forty-seven years old at his death, 336 A.D. He had reigned 24 years.

When he died the barbarians of the north who had been under his control, revolted. Then the Greeks rebelled and his kingdom began to fall apart.

Philip has been described in various ways by historians, but M. de Tourreil gives this description of his character in Rollin: "Deceit, craft, fraud, falsehood, perfidy and perjury. Are these the weapons of virtue? We see in this prince a boundless ambition, conducted by an artful insinuating, subtle genius; but we do not find him possessed of the qualities which formed the truly great man. Philip had neither faith nor honour, every thing that could con-

tribute to the aggrandizing of his power, was in his sense just and lawful. He gave his word with a firm resolution to break it; and made promises that he would have been very sorry to keep. He thought himself skillful in proportion as he was perfidious, and made his glory consist in deceiving all with whom he treated. He did not blush to say, 'That children were amused with playthings, and men with oaths.'

"How shameful was it for a prince to be distinguished by being more artful, a greater dissembler, more profound in malice, and more a knave, than any other person of his age, and to leave so infamous an idea of himself to all posterity! What idea could we form to ourselves...of a man who should value himself for tricking others, and rank insincerity and fraud among the virtues? Such a character in private life, is detested as the bane and ruin of society. How then can it become an object of esteem and admiration in princes and ministers of state, persons who are bound by stronger ties than the rest of men, because of the eminence of their stations, and the importance of the employments they fill, to revere sincerity, justice, and, above all, the sanctity of treaties and oaths; to bind which, they invoke the name and majesty of a God, the inexorable avenger of perfidy and impiety! A bare promise among private persons ought to be sacred and inviolable, if they have the least sense of honour; but how much more ought it to be so among princes! 'We are bound,' says a celebrated writer, 'to speak truth to our neighbour; for the use and application of speech implies a tacit promise of truth; speech having been given us for no other purpose. It is not a compact between one private man and another; it is a common compact of mankind in general, and kind of right of nations, or rather a law of nature. Now whoever tells an untruth, violates this law and common compact.' How greatly is the enormity of violating the sanctity of an oath increased, when we call upon the name of God to witness it, as is the custom always in treaties? 'Were sincerity and truth banished from every other part of the earth,' said John I. king of France, upon his being solicited to violate a treaty, 'they ought to be found in the hearts and in the mouths of kings'." (Rollin, *Ancient History*, Vol. III), p. 75 (excerpts). Proverbs 17:7, *Excellent speech becometh not a fool:* **much less do lying lips a prince.**

ALEXANDER THE GREAT

The ram which thou sawest having two horns are the kings of Media and Persia. And the rough goat is the king of Grecia: and the great horn that is between his eyes is the first king. (Daniel 8:20,21.)

The prophet Daniel saw four beasts rising from the sea. Each of the beasts represents an empire and each empire was to follow the other successively. Babylon, the lioness; the Medo-Persians, the bear constantly seeking his prey; the Grecian, the spotted leopard with four heads and four wings; and last the Roman as the beast with ten horns and feet of iron. The Grecian empire was to play a large part in the history of the world and Alexander was to be the greatest player.

"To this picture the prophet adds, elsewhere, other touches. He enumerates the order of the succession of the kings of Persia; he declares, in precise terms that after the three first kings, viz. Cyrus, Cambyses, and Darius, a fourth monarch will arise, who is Xerxes; and that he will exceed all his predecessors in power and in riches; that this prince, puffed up with the idea of his own grandeur, which shall have risen to its highest pitch, will assemble all the people in his boundless dominions, and lead them to the conquest of Greece. But as the prophet takes notice only of the march of this multitude, and does not tell us what success they met with, he thereby gives

us pretty clearly to understand that Xerxes, a soft, injudicious, and fearful prince, will not have the least success in any of his projects...On the contrary, from among the Greeks in question, attacked unsuccessfully by the Persians, there will arise a king, of a genius and turn of mind quite different from that of Xerxes; and this is Alexander the Great. He shall be a bold, valiant monarch; he shall succeed in all his enterprises; he shall extend his dominions far and wide, and shall establish an irresistible power on the ruins of the vanquished nations: but, at a time when he shall imagine himself to be most firmly seated on the throne, he shall lose his life with the legal dignity, and not leave any posterity to succeed him in it. This new monarchy, losing on a sudden the splendour and power for which it was so renowned under Alexander, shall divide itself towards the four winds of heaven. From its ruins there shall arise, not only four great kingdoms, Egypt, Syria, Asia Minor, and Macedon, but also several other foreigners, or barbarians, shall usurp its provinces, and form kingdoms out of these." (Rollin, *Ancient History*, Vol. III), p. 125.

Early life

On the day Alexander was born, in the first year of the 106th Olympiad, the temple of Diana at Ephesus, was burned. It was considered to be one of the seven wonders of the ancient world. It was purported to have burned because the goddess Diana was away attending the mother of Alexander, though actually it was set fire by a man who merely wanted his name to be remembered throughout history.

Alexander, even more than his father, was obsessed with ambition and an inordinate desire for glory. While others, his father included, sought honors at the Olympic games, Alexander said he would only compete if his opponents were kings.

When news was brought to him that his father had taken another city or won another battle, he said to his companions, "My friends, my father will possess himself of every thing, and leave us nothing to do." (Rollin, *Ancient History*, Vol. III), p. 76.

At the time Alexander became king, he was 20 years old. He was already acquainted with war and government having accompanied his father on the campaign to Boeotia and commanding the cavalry at Chaeronea.

He was an intelligent young man, interested in all kinds of learning with an open, generous nature.

Philip had been a very sensible and intelligent person about his son's education, and had provided the best teachers of his time for his son. Alexander was very intelligent and wise partly because of the wisdom imparted to him by his teachers. Two teachers were provided: Leonidas, a person of rigid morals, and Aristotle the most famous and learned philosopher of the day.

At sixteen, when his father was absent in wars, he was appointed regent of Macedonia and invested with absolute authority and ruled with great wisdom and bravery.

Reign of Alexander - Greek Supremacy 335-323 B. C.

Alexander and Darius III (Codomannus) of Persia, began to reign the same year, A. D. 336. When he came to the throne the barbarian nations saw an opportunity to obtain their liberty and united against him. The Greeks also felt he was too young to offer them resistance and set about to restore their boundaries. Alexander realized that he had to subdue both fronts immediately or lose all of them and be totally confined to Macedon.

He took his armies and subdued the barbarians making his name a terror to them, and then marched against the Greeks at Thebes. They had been stirred up by Demosthenes to revolt.

Demosthenes had called Alexander a 'child and a hair-brained boy' from whom they had nothing to fear and who did not dare stir out of his kingdom. Alexander said, "Demosthenes called me a boy, but I will show him before the gates of Athens, that I am a man."

Demosthenes approached Attalus, a lieutenant in Alexander's army, the uncle of Cleopatra, Philip's second wife, to try to get him to rebel. Attalus was not in good standing with Alexander and tried to get in better standing by sending the letters of Demosthenes to him and declaring his loyalty to Alexander. Alexander saw through his plans and he was later assassinated for treason on orders from Alexander.

At a meeting of the states and free cities of Greece, held at Corinth, Alexander was elected the generalissimo against the Persians. The armies of Greece and Macedon were preparing to make good their ancient oath to do away with that nation.

Only two years after the death of his father, in 334 B.C. Alexander set out on his expedition against Persia with an army numbering between 20 and 30 thousand men, most of them Macedonians. He never returned to Macedonia or Greece.

The Conquest of the East

He appointed Antipater as viceroy and left him 12,000 soldiers and about 12,000 cavalry to keep the peace.

Before Alexander left Europe he divided all his lands and all his goods among his friends as a person would do who did not expect to return. His friend Perdiccas asked him what he had left for himself and he replied, 'Hope.' Perdiccas refused to accept his own portion, saying that the portion of those who were going with him to fight needed only to share in his hope, not in his earthly goods. Such was the enthusiasm with which Alexander inspired the friends who shared his enterprises.

When Alexander began his march into Asia Minor after crossing the river Granicus, he moved with great rapidity. The prophet Daniel referred to his movement as being so fast he seemed to only skim the ground. He moved quickly into Asia Minor, then to the Near East taking the city of Tyre as was prophesied in God's Word, (Zechariah 9:1-4; Jeremiah 47:4; Ezekiel 28:1-19 and Isaiah 23.)

He also destroyed Gaza as God had prophesied in Zechariah 9:5; Jeremiah 47:5; Zephaniah 2:4.

He then moved eastward to Jerusalem where he met with the high priest and his entourage. Both Josephus and the Talmud state that Jaddua the high priest was given instructions in a dream as to how to meet Alexander. He went out at the head of a procession of priests all clothed in their priestly garments. Other citizens who were dressed in white followed them. When Alexander saw the priest with his fine clothing of purple and scarlet with the mitre on his head and the golden plate with the name of God on his forehead, he was astonished and he went near them and spoke to the high priest and worshipped the God of the Jews.

He said that while still in Macedonia he had a dream in which he had seen the high priest in his royal robes. Because of his dream he spared Jerusalem and claimed to worship the God of the Jews. Jaddua showed him the passage in Daniel which predicted that the first king of Greece would destroy the Persian empire, and of course, Alexander took that to mean him. From this point on Alexander was a friend to the Jews and encouraged them to settle in the territories he subdued.

From Jerusalem he went down to Egypt and across to part of Lybia, back through Egypt and up through Samaria into Asia.

He chased Darius III out of Babylonia and sent him back towards Persia. After subduing Babylonia he continued on to Persia and took control of that country. He went north into Media and Bactria (where he found Darius had been taken and murdered), then into Sogdiana, and even tried to take part of Scythia where he was rebuked by their emissaries and left them in peace.

Not content with having subdued the before mentioned countries, he determined to march into India since Semiramis had reached that country before turning back. It was his desire to excel her in everything she had done as he considered her a great general and conqueror.

He reached India and took many of the western areas captive and passed the Indus, but did not reach the Ganges because his troops refused to go any further. From there he returned to Persia.

On the return trip many of the soldiers (a quarter of the army) died from lack of food and water.

Several more places were subdued in Persia on their return. The army then moved into Media and then on to Babylon, (323 B.C.).

Alexander determined to rebuild Babylon and the temple of Belus and put his army to work removing the rubble, but the project was never completed.

While in the middle of this, and several other projects he had undertaken, he continued to live a life of terrible excess in feasting and drinking.

The Magi and Chaldeans had told him not to enter Babylon or he would die and though he said he put no faith in them, he continued to allow the thought of his death to occupy his mind. Because of this he offered many sacrifices to appease his pagan gods and drank himself senseless time after time to escape his thoughts of death.

Finally, at one of his banquets, he had drunk himself into a stupor and a second night of drinking was proposed. The second night he exceeded even his limit and passed out. He had a terrible fever and was carried to the palace already half dead. He died not many days afterward. He was 32 years and 8 months old when he died in the first year of the 114th Olympiad, and had reigned for 12 years.

He left the empire without an heir, saying only that it should go to the most worthy.

The Character of Alexander

He introduced polygamy to the Macedonians by encouraging them to take wives of the captured nations. Until this time the Macedonians and Greeks had always been monogamous.

He had previously married Roxana, a princess from Sogdiana, but one of his other wives, Statira, the daughter of Darius, was expecting a child in about a month's time. He made no provision for the empire to be passed to that child and it wasn't. According to the prophesy in the book of Daniel the kingdom was divided among four of his generals.

Alexander started out as a man with a noble purpose, and a generous nature. He was a man of many personalities, depending upon the situation and his turn of mind at the moment.

After training his troops to be the fiercest and most disciplined in history, at the end of his life he led them into the degenerate lifestyle of the Persian court.

After conquering Asia Minor and part of Asia proper as a great general, he demanded that his men and his subjects worship him as a god, declaring himself to be the son of Jupiter-Apollo, but they refused him this order.

He was kind when he captured the mother of Darius, Sysigambis, and his wife and daughters. He kept them in the royal manner to which they were accustomed, but was so cruel he had his closest friend killed on pure hearsay.

After the death of another friend he had a fabulous temple built to honor him and declared him to be a god who was to be worshipped. Another of his generals who had been with both him and his father and had reached the age of 70 in his service, was murdered on his orders just because the man's son had been falsely accused

His soldiers and his people loved him, and his soldiers would follow him into any kind of battle, but the people whom he conquered hated him because of his cruelty.

He planned well and executed his plans brilliantly, but other than Memnon the Rhodian, who fought for Darius, he never met a general worthy of his fighting abilities. Had Memnon lived it is doubtful Alexander could have continued across Asia, and had he marched against the Romans he would have been defeated immediately. The countries he subdued were not strong militarily and did not put up a defense which could have stopped him.

He was a well-educated young man, but his vices were many and in the end they took precedence over his education.

He was a great friend and cultivated many sincere and close friendships, but he was a formidable enemy and could be swayed easily in his opinions of even his friends.

To many of the cities he conquered he immediately gave total freedom, but others, (e.g. Helicarnassus), he completely destroyed without reason.

He tried to rule some of the kingdoms he conquered, but he never ruled the kingdom that was his by right of birth and took no interest in it whatever.

He was not a good ruler, only a good warrior.

"Was ever ambition more extravagant or rather, more furious, than that of this prince? Coming from a little spot of ground, and forgetting the narrow limits of his paternal domains, after he had far extended his conquests, has subdued not only the Persians, but also the Bactrians and Indians, has added kingdom to kingdom; after all this, he still finds himself pent up; and, determined to force, if possible, the barriers of nature, he endeavors to discover a new world, and does not scruple to sacrifice millions of men to his ambition or curiosity. It is related that Alexander, upon being told by Anaxarchus the philosopher, that there was an infinite number of worlds, wept to think that it would be impossible for him to conquer them all, since he had not yet conquered one....

"It must be confessed, that the actions of this prince diffuse a splendour that dazzles and astonishes the imagination, which is ever fond of the great and marvelous. His enthusiastic courage raises and transports all who read his history, as it transported himself. But, should we give the name of bravery and valour to a boldness that is equally blind, rash, and impetuous; a boldness void of all rule, that will never listen to the voice of reason, and has no other guide than a senseless ardour for false glory, and a wild desire of distinguishing itself, be the methods ever so unlawful?...True valour is not desirous of displaying itself, is no ways anxious about its own reputation, but is solely intent in preserving the army. It holds its course equally between a fearful wisdom,

that forsees and confronts dangers of every kind. In a word, to form an accomplished general, prudence must soften and direct the too fiery temper of valour; and this latter must animate and warm the coldness and slowness of prudence." (Rollin, *Ancient History*, Vol. III), pp. 218,219. (Excerpts.) None of which pertained to Alexander.

Daniel showed the leopard intermixed with good and bad qualities and that is how the world saw Alexander - a paradox of good and bad.

God's Purpose for Alexander

- He spread the Hellenic culture (Greek ideas and Greek civilization), and the Greek language into Asia and Egypt where the language became universal and was used later to translate the Scriptures.

- He was used to fulfill the prophecy concerning the destruction of Tyre.

- He was used to fulfill the prophecy concerning the destruction Gaza.

- He broke down the cultural differences between the Greek and the barbarian and prepared the way for the Gospel.

- The sea route from Europe to India was rediscovered.

- Increased trade and colonization made the spread of the Gospel easier and more rapid.

- The Jews were encouraged to settle in the newly founded cities of his empire and their influence spread the Gospel into those new areas.

THE DIVISION OF ALEXANDER'S EMPIRE

And I saw in a vision; and it came to pass, when I saw, that I was at Shushan in the palace, which is in the province of Elam; and I saw in a vision, and I was by the river of Ulai. Then I lifted up mine eyes, and saw, and be-

hold, there stood before the river a ram which had two horns: and the two horns were high; but one was higher than the other, and the higher came up last. I saw the ram pushing westward, and northward, and southward; so that no beasts might stand before him, neither was there any that could deliver out of his hand; but he did according to his will, and became great. And as I was considering, behold, an he goat came from the west on the face of the whole earth, and touched not the ground: and the goat had a notable horn between his eyes. And he came to the ram that had two horns, which I had seen standing before the river, and ran unto him in the fury of his power. And I saw him come close unto the ram, and he was moved to choler against him, and smote the ram, and brake his two horns: and there was no power in the ram to stand before him, but he cast him down to the ground, and stamped upon him: and there was none that could deliver the ram out of his hand. Therefore the he goat waxed very great: and when he was strong, the great horn was broken; and for it came up four notable ones toward the four winds of heaven. (Daniel 8:2-8, see also 8:20-22).

Daniel said: The kingdom was to be divided when this king was at the height of his power. It was to be divided into four parts; north, south, east and west. The divided kingdom would not be as large as Alexander had ruled over, because of the many divisions which would take place, besides the four main divisions.

Alexander's son was born shortly after his death and since there was no heir of an age to rule, Perdiccas, one of Alexander's chief generals, ruled as regent. On his deathbed Alexander had given Perdiccas his signet, which gave him the authority to rule. After the death of Perdiccas, this position was taken by Seleucus.

Alexander's half brother, who was mentally deficient, was made titular king until Alexander's son was old enough to rule. But there was a fight in progress for the throne.

Ptolemy suggested that the greatest generals should be sent to rule the provinces and be given absolute military power. Of course, Ptolemy was one of those generals.

Ptolemy took Egypt; Antipater took Macedonia; Laomedon took Syria, and Seleucus Nicanor took Babylon and points eastward, (Susiana, Media, and Persia).

The Ptolomies ruled Egypt, Cyrene, Cyprus and a protectorate of the seacoast cities of Asia Minor to the Black Sea. The last ruler of the Ptolomies was Queen Cleopatra, and in 30 B.C. at her death, Egypt became a Roman province.

Antipater and his descendants ruled the area under Macedonia until 168 B.C. when the Romans took possession of it. This included Thrace, Thessaly, the protectorate over Greece, and other areas of the seacoast.

Laomedon was quickly dispossessed of Syria by Antigonus who had been given Lycia, Pamphylia and Phrygia in Asia Minor. Antigonus was in a continual battle for power with Ptolemy until Antigonus' death in 301 B. C.

Seleucus added all the countries between the Indus and the Euphrates and the Jaxartes and the Indian Ocean to his domain. He then took Phoenicia and Syria besides Babylon. He founded the city of Antioch and moved his capital from Babylon to that city. He took the title of *king* in 306 B.C. His son, Antiochus, became king in 293 B.C. His line of the Seleucidae ruled until taken over by the Romans, in 65 B.C. by Pompey.

Antigonus kept trying to bring the whole empire under his rule, but the other leaders joined together against him and he was killed at Ipsus in Phrygia in 301 B.C. at the age of 81.

Those who had joined together to defeat him: Ptolemy, Seleucus, Lysimachus and Cassander of Macedon, divided the remainder of Alexander's empire. Phoenicia and Syria fell to Seleucus at this time.

In 281 B.C. Lysimachus was killed in a battle against Seleucus and his possessions in Asia Minor went to Seleucus who had already become a very powerful king in the Mid- and Far East.

The Macedonians ruled Syrian and Egypt from 301-125 B.C.

For about 120 years Palestine was an Egyptian possession (319-198 B.C.). During that time the Jews prospered financially, but were constantly caught between the two armies of the Ptolemies and the Seleucidae as they each tried to take the other's territory.

The Ptolemies ruled 116 years, (Daniel 11:6). During the reign of Ptolemy II, called Philadelphus (*lover of his brother*), Alexandria was established as a center of learning. Under his direction the Hebrew Scriptures were translated into the Greek, and were known as the Septuagint because 70 Hebrew scholars were said to have had a part in the work. This is the version which would be used during the 1400-1500's to translate the Scriptures into English.

"This was nothing less than the gift of God's providence to bring to the world, through the widely diffused Greek tongue, the Word of God. Thus, in a measure, which many do not realize, the world was being prepared for the coming of its Redeemer. (Ringenberg, *The Word of God in History)*, p. 267.

Greek became the language of all government and literature throughout many countries where the people were not Greek by birth. It was thus at the very moment that Greece began to lose her political freedom that she made an intellectual conquest of a large part of the world.

The evil effects of Alexander's conquests

The worst effects were the demoralization of the Greeks through the acquisition of the enormous wealth of the Persian Empire, and through contact with the vices and effeminate luxury of the Oriental nations.

The Kingdom of the Seleucidae

And when he shall stand up, his kingdom shall be broken, and shall be divided toward the four winds of heaven; and not to his posterity, nor according to his dominion which he ruled: for his kingdom shall be plucked up, even for others beside those. (Daniel 11:4.)

The king of Syria is designated as 'the king of the north' (Daniel 11:6-35). If the Syrian kingdom is 'the north' then certainly it is not the portion 'divided toward' the east wind. These directional terms are to be understood in relation to Israel: Syria toward the north; Babylon and the lands east of the Euphrates, toward the east; Egypt to the south, and Macedon to the West. (Daniel 11:6-35.)

Seleucus became king of Syria and founded Antioch, which he named for his father (Antiochus I). He made Antioch a huge, magnificent city of several hundred thousand inhabitants, and later it was the third city in the Roman Empire.

The king at this time was Antiochus II, (also called Epiphanes), son of Seleucus, who was bitterly opposed to the Jews. His rule lasted thirty-nine years, and was a time of almost continual persecution for the Jews.

The Jewish priest Onias was replaced by his brother Jason in an attempt to displace the Hebrew spirit with the Greek spirit. Jason sent a group of Hebrews to Tyre to take part in the Greek games and to offer a sacrifice to Hercules. The Jewish nation at this time was experiencing a period of national degeneracy.

During a period when Antiochus was at war with Egypt, he was reported to have died. The Jews rejoiced when they heard the news, but when Antiochus heard of their attitude he became so angry he killed 40,000 of them.

He took a sow into the Temple (some say an entire herd of swine), and offered it upon the altar and sprinkled the blood throughout the Temple.

THE MACCABEES

The Asmonians were a family from the priestly line of the Jews. Mattathias was the son of John, and grandson of Simon, whose father was named Asmoneus from whom came the family name of Asmonians.

Mattathias had five sons, all as zealous for God and His law as their father. They were: Joannan, surnamed Gaddis; Simon, surnamed Thasi; Judas, surnamed Maccabeus; Eleazar, called Abaron; and Jonathan, called Apphus.

Antiochus sent Apelles, one of his officers, to Modin, the city of Mattathias, and tried to persuade him to follow the king's command to forsake their own religion and profess the same pagan religion as the king. Apelles believed if Mattathias would follow the king's religion all the rest of the people would follow also. He also offered positions of importance to Mattathias and his family if they would follow the king.

However, Mattathias told Apelles in a loud voice so all could hear, that though the entire Jewish nation chose to forsake God, he and his family would continue to serve Him and His statutes forever.

At that moment he saw an apostate Jew going to sacrifice on the pagan altar placed there by Antiochus, and Mattathias killed him. His sons joined him and together they killed the king's commissioner and all his followers.

Mattathias had effectively thrown down the gauntlet and issued a call to those Jews who continued to follow God. They all fled to the mountains with their wives, children and cattle. Others continued to follow them and Rollin says, "so that all the deserts of Judea were filled, in a little time, with people who fled from the persecution." (Vol. IV,) p. 132. This was the same region where David hid from the pursuit of Saul. They hid in the mountains and deserts and caves.

The Jews who had been attacked by Apollonius in Jerusalem on the Sabbath, did not fight back because it was the Sabbath, but the Jews quickly learned that people in such danger had to fight whenever and wherever to save themselves. In the attack on Jerusalem, all the men the troops could find were killed, and the women and children were caught and sold as slaves.

The city was plundered and parts of it were burned.

When Antiochus was told that the Jews would not obey his decrees as the other nations had, he went to Judea himself and began to persecute them in terrible ways.

At this time an elderly man of 90 years, a doctor of the law, who had been faithful to God his whole life, was taken and commanded to eat pork. When he refused he was cruelly tortured and put to death.

Also seized were a mother and her seven sons who were also commanded to eat pork. They all refused and each son was tortured; their tongues torn out because of their testimony for God; their skin torn from their heads, and their hands and feet cut off. They were then fried in the pans Antiochus had ordered heated, and each died with a testimony of God's faithfulness on his lips, expressed before their tongues were removed.

The words of the youngest son to Antiochus were: "What is it you expect from me? I do not obey the king's command, but the law which was given us by Moses. As to you, from whom flow all the calamities with which the Hebrews have been afflicted, you shall not escape the hand of the Almighty. Our sufferings, indeed, are owing to our sins: but, if the Lord our God, to punish us, was for a little time angry with us, he at last will be appeased, and be reconciled to his servants. But as for you, the most wicked, the most impious of men, do not flatter yourself with vain hopes. You shall not escape the judgment of the Creator, who is all-seeing, and omnipotent. As to my brothers, after having suffered for a moment the most cruel torments, they taste eternal joys. In imitation of the example they have set me, I freely give up my body and life for the laws of my forefathers: and I beseech God to extend his mercy soon to our nation; to force you, by wounds and tortures of every kind, to confess that he is the only God; and that his anger, which has justly fallen on the Hebrews, may end by my death, and that of my brethren." (Rollin, *Ancient History*, Vol. IV), p. 135.

The king was furious on hearing his words and the last brother was more cruelly tortured than the others before he died.

It is clear that Antiochus' purpose was to exterminate all the faithful Jews. He prohibited circumcision and two women who were said to have circumcised their children were thrown from the highest part of the city wall with their children clinging to their necks.

He built a statue of Jupiter Olympus on the altar of burnt sacrifice and consecrated the Temple in Jerusalem to his pagan gods. For three and one-half years Antiochus continued with his tortures and blasphemies until Judas Maccabaeus retook the Temple and cleansed it and began his retaking of Judea.

Mattathias was already an old man when all this occurred and before his death in 167 B.C. (at age 145), he appointed Judas as their general and Simon as 'father' of the refugees. At his death Mattathias was buried in Modin with his ancestors, greatly mourned by the faithful of Israel.

Judas raised an army and defeated two of Antiochus' generals and fortified the whole country. He then killed the Jews who were following the king's paganism.

The Syrians came many times with thousands of soldiers, but because he believed God was in charge of the battle Judas was victorious, and his victories are said to have inspired the Syrians with awe because they were humanly impossible.

He fought the Syrian yoke for six years, (166-161 B.C.).

John Lord says of him: "He bore the brunt of six years' successful war against the most powerful monarchy in Asia bent on the extermination of his countrymen. And amid all his labors he had kept the Law; being revered for his virtues as much as for his heroism. Not a single crime sullied his glorious name and when he fell at last, exhausted, the nation lamented him as David mourned for Jonathan, saying, 'How is the valiant fallen!' A greater hero than he never adorned an age of heroism." John Lord, LL.D., *Beacon Lights of History,* Vol. 3, (New York: Fords, Howard and Hulbert, 1913), p. 21.

Because of the continued warring with Syria, he sent to Rome (162 B.C.) to make an alliance with them for protection; little did he understand the consequences of his action. In 161 B.C. he was killed in battle.

Jonathan, his brother, succeeded him and after fighting several battles against the Syrians, the Jewish Commonwealth was recognized by Syria in 153 B.C., though they continued as a tributary until 143 B.C. Jonathan was betrayed and killed in 143 B.C. and his brother, Simon, became the head of the Jewish state from 143-135 B.C.

Simon sent a golden shield worth fifty talents and weighing 1000 pounds to Rome as a token of their friendly alliance. He became Rome's appointee and this marks the beginning of the supremacy of the Roman state in Palestine.

During his reign he put the Mosaic Law back into effect, repaired the Temple and restored the land. Prosperity increased and after a period of 23 years of warfare, comparative peace reigned. He was betrayed and murdered (135 B.C.) by his son-in-law who wanted to become the high priest. The rule of the Maccabees lasted 30 years. He was followed by his son John Hyrcanus.

During his reign the two-party system of the Pharisees and Sadducees came into being.

John Lord says of the Pharisees: "They multiplied fasts and ritualistic observances as the superstitious monks of the Middle Ages did after them; they extended the payment of tithes to the most minute and unimportant things, like herbs which they grew in their gardens; they began the Sabbath on Friday evening, and kept it so vigorously that no one was permitted to walk beyond one thousand steps from his own door." (Lord, *Beacon Lights*), p. 22.

The Pharisees took a stand against Hyrcanus and the Roman government that supported him; they interpreted the Law in the 'most minute fashion', but failed to understand the spirit of the Law. They held a Messianic doctrine, but this was to be an earthly king who would free them from Roman bondage, not a spiritual king who would free them from moral degeneracy and eternal damnation.

Hyrcanus belonged to the Sadducees. This sect was composed of the wealthy, aristocratic, and worldly Jews. According to the Scripture they did not believe in the resurrection, nor in retribution or rewards in a future life. They were able to follow their own desires in reference to political power and worldly pursuits. The family whose members had begun as spiritual giants were reduced to mere materialists.

From the year 105 B.C. the Jewish condition worsened and the line of the Maccabees continued to decline.

When a dispute arose between the two grandsons of Hyrcanus about who would rule Palestine, Pompey took advantage of the situation and took possession of Jerusalem in 63 B.C. when he entered the temple enclosure at Jerusalem and killed twelve thousand Jews.

The fourth world power, (Daniel 2), was now in control of Palestine.

THE ROMANS, sons of Gomer, son of Japheth

The Romans were part of the four principle tribes who first inhabited the Italian peninsula. They were the Gauls, Etruscans, Iapygians, and the Italians. The first three have little importance in Italy, the Italians being the most powerful tribe.

The Gauls were mostly in the north and were from the same Japhetic tribe as the Gauls in France.

The Etruscans lived in the area between the Arno and Tiber rivers. They were also descendants of Japheth; they were great builders and were skilled in many of the arts.

The Iapygians were in the southern part of the boot and were considered to be a very primitive people, though they were also Japhethites.

There were also many Greeks in Italy as seen from the previous history of Greece.

The Italians were mostly in the central part of Italy. They were related to the Hellenes and many similarities can be seen in their languages of Greek and Latin.

They were divided into two groups, the Latins and the Umbro-Sabelleans, (Umbrians, Sabines, Samnites, etc). The Latins were the branch of the Italians who were the founders of Rome.

At a later period the Gauls were in Lombardy, the Ligurians in Genoa, the Venetians in the territory of the Adige, and the Etruscans and Umbrians in Tuscany. In the area of Rome were the Sabines, Latins, and Volsci, the Capua and Campania were in Naples, and in the remainder of the kingdom were the Marsi, the Samnites, the Apulians, Lucanians, and the Greeks, as well as lesser tribes. (Swinton, *Outlines*), pp. 131,132.

Their early history is a collection of legends which have no truth. The early records of the city of Rome were destroyed by a fire in 390 B.C. when the Gauls burned the city. The earliest history they possess was written by Livy 750 years after the founding of Rome.

Alba Longa was the head of a 30 city confederacy. A group of people went from that city in 753 B.C. to found "Rome" - a word meaning 'a march' or 'border'. Most of the people were shepherds and farmers. In time an Etruscan village and a Sabine village joined with them as their equals, and the size of the city was increased.

From the beginning the Romans were divided into two classes; the Patricians, who could trace their lineage to royal birth or to ancestors of free birth; and the rest of the people, called Plebeians. The Patricians were the upper class and formed part of the government and all the priesthood. They had ownership of public lands and were allowed to use a family name. The Plebeians were subject to both the Patricians and the king.

The Plebeians had no political importance, but were freemen and were personally independent, being no one's slaves.

The fifth king of Rome changed the constitution and gave the Plebeians a voice in the government through a national assembly called the Assembly of the Hundreds. In the Assembly Plebeians and Patricians could both vote. However, the richest and oldest families still held most of the power.

The sixth king tried to do away with the new form of government, but was driven from office and the position of king was ended and never renewed in Rome.

There were four important periods in Roman history encompassing a period of 482 years:

1. From the establishment of the republic to the invasion of the Gauls, 509-390 B. C.

2. From the invasion of the Gauls to the taking of the peninsula by the Gauls, 390-266 B.C.

3. From the beginning of the foreign conquests of the Romans (the Punic and Macedonian wars), to the beginning of civil strife under Gracchi, 266-133 B. C.

4. From the beginning of civil strife to the establishment of the empire under Augustus, 133-27 B.C. (Ibid.), p. 136.

After the removal of the king Rome became a republic. Elections were held each year to elect two magistrates (Consuls) and the constitution remained the same.

The limits of Roman power extended along the whole coast of the Tyrrhenian Sea from Ostia to Terracina. They also traded with Sicily, Sardinia and Africa.

By the middle of the fourth century B. C. Rome had become a true republic after many battles between the Patricians and the Plebeians. The Patricians wanted to hold all the power and the Plebeians demanded their fair share.

What had been essentially an aristocratic republic finally became a true republic of the people and with that liberty the Romans began their 'wars for dominion'. These were fought with their Latin relatives, with the other Italian nations, with the Greek settlements in southern Italy, and with the Gauls in northern Italy.

By 290 B. C. the Romans had become the masters of central Italy; and by 266 B. C. they had conquered the Greeks and were masters of the whole peninsula. Rome consolidated its power and formed the Roman nation ruled by the *populus Romanus*, the Roman people.

The *populus Romanus* were the free citizens of the thirty-three tribes living in Roman territory, as well as individuals living in other parts of Italy who had been born Romans or had become Roman citizens. All of those had the right of going to Rome and voting at the Assembly. This was actually a small group of men, but their votes decided the 'destinies of the whole population of Italy', about five millions of people. (Ibid.), pp. 136-147.

The dependent and allied states (those who had surrendered to the Romans) were allowed to keep their own laws and practice their own form of government, but they had no say in the political decisions of Rome.

The Roman Method of Nation-Making - "Conquest with incorporation"

1. The conquered peoples were given privileges and protection by law as citizens.

   a. The majority of the people were not slaves.

   b. The Romans were unable to hold on to large extensive regions.

   c. They eventually slipped into Oriental despotism.

2. The conquered peoples were held by force by generals who represented the Roman authority; no local self-government was exercised; the flow of power was still from the top down.

"The secret of Rome's wonderful strength lay in the fact that she incorporated the vanquished peoples into her own body politic. In the early times there was a fusion of tribes going on in Latium, which if it had gone no further, would have been similar to the early fusion of Ionic tribes in Attika or of Iranian tribes in Media... Never before had so many people been brought under one government without making slaves of most of them... Now liberty and union were for the first time joined together, with consequences enduring and stupendous. The whole Mediterranean world was brought under one government; ancient barriers of religion, speech, and custom were overthrown in every direction; and innumerable barbarian tribes, from the Alps to the wilds of northern Britain, from the Bay of Biscay to the Carpathian Mountains, were more or less completely transformed into Roman citizens, protected by Roman law, and sharing in the material and spiritual benefits of Roman civilization. Gradually the whole vast structure became permeated by Hellenic and Jewish thought, and thus were laid the lasting foundations of modern society, of a common Christendom, furnished with a common stock of ideas concerning man's relation to God and the World, and acknowledging a common standard of right and wrong. This was a prodigious work, which raised human life to a much higher plane than that which it had formerly occupied, and endless gratitude is due to the thousands of steadfast men who in one way or another devoted their lives to its accomplishment.

"This Roman method of nation-making had its fatal shortcomings, and it was only very slowly, that it wrought out its own best result. It was but gradually that the rights and privileges of Roman citizenship were extended over the whole Roman world, and in the meantime there were numerous instances where conquered provinces seemed destined to no better fate than had awaited the victims of Egyptian or Assyrian conquest....

"What was needed was the introduction of a fierce spirit of personal liberty and local self-government. The essential vice of the Roman system was that it had been unable to avoid weakening the spirit of personal independence and crushing out local self-government among the peoples to whom it had been applied.... It owed its wonderful success to joining Liberty with Union, but as it went on it found itself compelled gradually to sacrifice Liberty to Union, strengthening the hands of the central government and enlarging its functions more and more, until by and by the political life of the several parts had so far died away that, under the pressure of attack from without, the Union fell to pieces and the whole political system had to be slowly and painfully reconstructed...Now if we ask why the Roman government found itself thus obliged to sacrifice personal liberty and local independence to the paramount necessity of holding the empire together, the answer will point us to the essential and fundamental vice of the Roman method of nation-making. It lacked the principle of representation. There was no notion of such a thing as political power delegated by the people to representatives who were to wield it away from home and out of sight of their constituents. The Roman's only notion of delegated power was that of authority delegated by the government to its generals and prefects who discharged at a distance its military and civil functions...

"Even could the device of representation have occurred to the mind of some statesman trained in Roman methods, it would probably have made no difference. Nobody would have known how to use it. You cannot invent an institution as you would invent a plough. Such a notion as that of representative government must needs start from small beginnings and grow in men's minds until it should become part and parcel of their mental habits. For the want of it the home government at Rome became more and more unmanageable until it fell into the hands of the army, while at the same time the administration of the empire became more and more centralized; the people of its various provinces, even while their social condition was in some respects improved, had less and less voice in the management of their local affairs, and thus the spirit of personal independence was gradually weakened." John Fiske, *The Historical Writings of John Fiske,* Volume VI, *The Beginnings of New England.* (Boston: Houghton, Mifflin and Company, 1902), pp. 14-19 excerpts.

Advantages of the Roman domination

Many nations were united in language, manners, and customs and this led to a more united empire and prepared the way for the extension of the Gospel as the church was dispersed after the death of Christ.

Commerce flourished and by it routes were opened into the remotest parts of the empire. All roads truly did lead to Rome as it was the capital of the world at that time. The Romans were great road builders and were able to keep the empire united in communication because of their system of roads over which messengers and soldiers could move rapidly.

They invented the swiveling front axle for four-wheeled vehicles and this helped them to travel more widely.

Their ships had a capacity of 400 tons and traveled widely over the oceans. A ship of this size was not duplicated until the 19th century. The emperors allowed full freedom of commerce and kept government interference out of industry so it was able to flourish and meet the needs of the empire. The Mediterranean shipping routes connected the various peoples, and trading increased.

There were also camel caravans making trips into India and Ceylon.

Nations were civilized by the laws and commerce of the Romans and their philosophy of government was spread throughout the Empire.

The Preparation of the World for the coming of Christ

"God endowed the Greeks and Romans with the richest natural gifts, that they might reach the highest civilization possible without the aid of Christianity, and thus provide the instruments of human science, art, and law for the use of the church, and yet at the same time show the utter impotence of these alone to bless and save the world.

"Rome was the practical and political nation of antiquity. Their calling was to carry out the idea of the state and civil law, and to unite the nations of the world in a colossal empire, stretching from the Euphrates to the Atlantic, and from the Libyan desert to the banks of the Rhine; about one hundred millions of people. The Romans from the first believed themselves called to govern the world, and having conquered it they organized it by law. Heathen Rome lived quite a while in this opulent state, yet before our Lord appears the causes of decay are at work. Domestic and civil virtues were diminishing; the worship of their gods had sunk to mere form, running either into absurd superstitions, or giving place to unbelief. Man must believe something, and worship either God or the devil. Magicians and necromancers abounded, as did vice and debauchery, and amusement came to be sought in barbarous fights of beasts and gladiators, which could consume 20,000 in a month.

"Thus, Rome was in a hopeless misery, and the world was on the verge of despair.

"It was at this time, when God in His patience had allowed the three most important nations of antiquity to try to provide peace and individual freedom to mankind, without Christ, religion, intellectual and cultural prowess, and civil government, as represented by Judaism, Greece, and Rome. All failed, for religion, philosophy, history, literature, science, fine arts, economics, civil government - without Christ are hollow shells. But with Christ, they become aspects or outworkings of the abundant life.

"For two thousand years, from the time of Abraham, God had allowed mankind to try to achieve salvation without Christ, and mankind utterly failed, and knew it had failed, and knew not what to do - it had tried everything, and everything failed. 'Christ entered a dying world as the author of a new and imperishable life'." Verna Hall, unpublished speech. FACE, San Francisco, CA. (Used by permission of the author before her death.)

As Rome becomes the ruler of the world, God is setting the stage for the coming of Christ.

The influence of the Greeks on the Romans

The Greek rhetoricians, scholars, tragedians, flute-players, and philosophers, teachers, physicians, merchants and artists came to Rome to live. Because theirs was an older culture and more respected, they became the schoolmasters, but were still considered to be servants. They brought literature with them and the Romans began to write.

The Greeks brought with them both good and bad. The people became effeminate, luxurious, and corrupt in morals. ("Give me for a few years the direction of education, and I will undertake to transform the world," said Leibniz. And, of course, that is what was taking place in Rome during this period.)

As a direct result of Greek education, marriage was not respected, the old Roman faith waned, politics became corrupt, bribery and corruption were common, and slave-trade flourished.

During this period the Romans also adopted many of the gods of the Greeks. One of the most important characters, as far as later history is concerned, came into the Roman system in 204 B.C. This was the cult of the Great Mother which came from Asia with a Hellenistic covering. This cult would later develop into the mariolatry of the Roman Catholic system.

Religion

The religion of Rome never rose above the lower stages of animism, (i.e. the belief that natural objects are the abode of spirits more powerful than man, and that all natural forces and processes are the expression of the activity of similar spirits). Thorndike says:

"The main thing was to repeat certain magic words and names, or to perform certain ceremonies connected with the hearth-fire, door, and threshold in order to safeguard family life and the home, or agricultural magic to ensure good crops, or public rites to preserve the state." Lynne Thorndike, *A Short History of Civilization,* (New York: F.S. Crofts and Company, 1937), p. 175.

Their gods lacked human attributes; they inspired no loyalty and inspired no personal devotion.

If man observed all proper ritual in his worship, the god was duty bound to act propitiously: if the god granted man's desire he must be rewarded with an offering. If man failed in his duty, the god punished him: if the god refused to hearken, man was not bound to continue his worship. Arthur E. R. Boak, *A History of Rome,* (New York: The Macmillan Company, 1925), p. 61.

The power of the gods could affect the community as well as the individual and the State was obliged to exercise extreme care in relation to them. This religion was crude, but shows their strong sense of law. The knowledge of the obligations of pacifying the gods and their willingness to meet the requirements constituted a large portion of their civil law. Thorndike concludes in this manner:

"Since their religion was primitive and, as time went on, became increasingly behind the times, they came more and more to adopt the attitude of observing merely the letter of the religious law. This also became true of their attitude to the civil law where,...they pretended to continue the old rules and customs while really reading a new spirit into them. In religion, however, the new spirit did not seem to be forthcoming, until finally the empty shell of outward paganism gave way to a new religious attitude from the orient and then to Christianity in particular. But the Roman government was so intimately connected with the old religious forms that it clung to them until a very late date." (Thorndike, *History of Civilization),* p. 176.

From the Roman practice of appeasing the spirits of the departed, came the custom of remembering the dead with offerings at special times in the year. This was not ancestor-worship, but has a definite carry-over into today's society.

The religion of the Romans did not act as a moralizing influence on them, but it did unite them. It brought about the unity of the family, and the unity of the state. It gave them a sense of responsibility to perform the duties required of them in the observance of their worship, and helped to develop the conservatism of the Roman people.

There were no answers to be found in the religions of Rome; there was no peace, no hope, just a 'hoping' for a better life - that life would not be possible until Rome had united the world and thus prepared the way for the coming of the Son of Man.

Summary

The Roman people, from the beginning, were trained to be obedient and docile. Later the result of this inbred apathy is seen - there is a continuous parallel between modern America and ancient Rome. It is necessary to become alert, thinking Americans if we are to stop the present trend to follow Rome to destruction. The class-system has existed in every country of the world except America, democracy has also existed in many countries, but America is the first Christian Republic which has ever existed.

ROME AS A REPUBLIC (509-27 B.C.)

In place of a king, two consuls were elected each year. In the middle of the 4th century internal strife was ended and Rome began its 'wars for dominion'. It was necessary that it become a great nation before it could play its part in history.

It is a striking fact that there was not yet even a dawning Roman literature: in arts, science, philosophy, Rome had done - absolutely nothing. But, in fact, it was in the art of governing mankind that Roman genius was to appear; and it was this that showed itself in those early years, - it was their valor, their probity, their patriotism, their political tact, and not speculation or literary culture, that distinguished them. (Swinton, *Outlines*), p. 61.

At the close of the period Rome was the sole Great Power left in the then known world.

The Provincial government

Provincial government was instituted in the areas which were conquered, but the people were allowed to retain their native habits, and their religion and laws.

The inhabitants were governed by a military president sent from Rome with a staff of officials. Those who had taken an active part for the cause of Rome were extended certain liberties, the others were treated as subjects. All were required to pay taxes or tribute to a Roman citizen called a publican, (Matthew 10:3). It is easier to understand and appreciate the scandal caused by the calling of Matthew, by an understanding of the system of tax-collecting. Boak describes it this way:

"...the Roman state did not collect its taxes in the provinces through public officials but leased for a period of five years the right to collect each particular tax to the private corporation of tax collectors which made the highest bid for the privilege. These corporations were joint stock companies, with a central office at Rome and agencies in the provinces in which they were interested. It was this system which was responsible for the greatest evils of Roman provincial administration. For the *publicani* were usually corporations of Romans, bent on making a profit from their speculation, and practiced under the guise of raising the revenue, all manner of extortion upon the provincials." (Boak, *History of Rome*), p. 113.

The magistrates from Rome had charge of all Roman interests in the province. The people were made 'Roman citizens' politically and legally.

Civil strife (133-27 B.C.).

There followed an intense period of civil strife. There were only two levels of society during this period, the rich and the poor.

The ruling force of government was divided into four factions: the oligarchical, the aristocratic, the Marian, and the military.

Pompey represented the oligarchical faction. When Pompey was in Asia this faction was taken over by Cicero. Pompey was the dominant figure because of his military prowess and political influence.

Crassus represented the aristocratic faction. He was himself an extremely wealthy man, said to have been worth $10 million at his death.

Julius Caesar represented the Marian faction and would soon become a force to deal with.

Catiline represented the military faction. He plotted to have Cicero murdered but was himself betrayed and killed.

As a result of these four divisions the First Triumvirate was formed.

The First Triumvirate

Pompey joined forces with Caesar and they admitted Crassus to form the First Triumvirate, or rule by three. (Palestine came under Roman rule at this time.)

During this period Caesar conquered the three-hundred tribes beyond the Alps, and Britain.

In the course of time Crassus was murdered and Caesar and Pompey became bitter enemies. Pompey was made sole consul for the aristocratic faction in 52 B.C. and began to use his power against Caesar.

Caesar wanted to obtain the consulship for the year 48 B.C., but under the influence of Pompey it was proposed that he give up his command and return to Rome (he was in Gaul at this time), by November 13, 50 B.C. While Caesar was in Gaul he had treated the people fairly and had won them over. He also developed his "unusual military talents and created a veteran army devoted to himself." Because of these events he had become very powerful and Pompey knew that he was a tremendous threat; he therefore set out to destroy Caesar.

Caesar still had another year left in his term to govern and would doubtless have been murdered had he returned to Rome.

He offered to give up his command at the beginning of 49 B.C. if Pompey would also give up his. The senate refused this proposal and passed a motion that Caesar was to disband his army by a certain day and if he did not follow their proposal he would be regarded as an enemy of the state.

Caesar, however, had a distinct advantage over Pompey, in that he possessed a large army which would follow him on command. Pompey did not possess any veteran troops in Italy where the deciding battle was to take place. Caesar advanced toward the river Rubicron which separated Gaul and Italy.

Crossing the Rubicron

The crossing of this river was in reality a declaration of war against the republic, and it is related that, upon arriving at the Rubicron, Caesar long hesitated whether he should take this irrevocable step. After pondering many hours he at length exclaimed, "The die is cast!" and plunged into the river.

Supreme ruler

Pompey did not attempt to defend Italy because there was not enough time to raise an army. He fled to Greece where he was successful in raising a great army and returned to "overwhelm the 'usurper'."

Caesar marched on Pompey's armies and a great battle was waged at Pharsalia in 48 B.C. in which Pompey was totally defeated. He fled to Egypt and was murdered there on the order of Ptolemy.

Caesar pursued him to Egypt and learned of his death in Alexandria when Ptolemy sent him the head of Pompey. History tells us that Caesar was a compassionate man and was much moved; though Pompey had been his enemy, he ordered that the head be embalmed with the costliest spices.

While Caesar was in Alexandria he became involved in the internal strife taking place between the twenty-year-old Cleopatra (descendant of the Greek Ptolomies) and her thirteen-year-old husband-brother. Caesar took Cleopatra back to Alexandria where the people had driven her from the city, and a time of intense struggle followed. The people of Alexandria were united against Caesar but he managed to keep the seaports open and finally received help from Mithradates of Pergamon. The young king was killed as he tried to flee and the people of Alexandria gave up. Cleopatra was, by custom, married to an even younger brother and given the rule of Egypt. During this period Caesar set fire to the Egyptian fleet and inadvertently destroyed the library of Alexandria, and with it a major part of the manuscripts of the period.

Caesar was enchanted with Cleopatra and stayed the winter at Alexandria to be near her.

After several more battles in Africa he returned home and became Master of the Roman dominion. He became the Imperator for life, a perpetual dictator. He ruled well and was fair with the people.

He was assassinated only two year later by Cassius and Marcus Brutus. They were both jealous of his greatness though they had both been honored by him. The plot and assassination were vividly portrayed by Swinton:

"The plot ripened into a determination to assassinate Caesar, and the conspirators fixed on the Ides (15th) of March as the time of putting the design into execution. Rumors of the plot got abroad, and Caesar was strongly urged not to attend the senate. But he disregarded the warnings which were given him. As soon as Caesar had taken his place, he was surrounded by the senatorial conspirators, one of whom, pretending to urge some request, seized his toga with both hands and pulled it violently over his arms. Then Casca, who was behind, drew a weapon and grazed his shoulder with an ill-directed stroke. Caesar disengaged one hand and snatched at the hilt, exclaiming, "Cursed Casca, what means this?" "Help!" cried Casca, and at the same moment the conspirators aimed each his dagger at the victim. Caesar for an instant defended himself; but when he perceived the steel flashing in the hand of Brutus he exclaimed, "What! thou too, Brutus!" (Et tu, Brute!) and drawing his robe over his face he made no further resistance. The assassins stabbed him through and through; and, pierced with twenty-three wounds, Caesar fell dead at the foot of the statue of his great rival, Pompey." (Swinton, *Outlines of History*), pp. 173,174.

Contributions of Caesar

In his lifetime he fought over fifty battles in which over one million men fell. He conquered the major part of the then known world for Rome. He was an intellectual genius, a general, a statesman, a lawgiver, an orator, an historian, a mathematician, (he brought in the Roman calendar based on the equations of the Egyptian solar year), and an architect. He tried to improve the political, social, intellectual and moral degeneration of the decayed Roman nation. Boak sums up his life in this way:

"His claim to greatness lies not in his ability to outwit his rivals in the political arena or out general his enemies on the field of battle, but in his realization, when the fate of the civilized world was in his hands, that the old order was beyond remedy and in his courage in attempting to set up a new order which promised to give peace and security both to Roman citizens and to the provincials." (Boak, *History of Rome*), p. 184.

What a propitious time for God to work! Caesar left a united world to be ruled by Augustus; it was a world which would soon witness the most significant event in 4000 years of history.

A new ruling force.

After the death of Caesar, Mark Antony, a representative of the Caesarian principles, seemed the likely successor. A claim was made, however, by Caesar's great-nephew, Caius Octavius, a young man of nineteen. Caesar had adopted him in his will and made him heir to three-quarters of his estate; he took the name Caius Julius Caesar Octavianus.

At first Antony and Octavius were opposed to each other, but they later became reconciled, and with Lepidus, they formed the Second Triumvirate. Many people were killed during this period, including Cicero, who had spoken out against Mark Antony.

Brutus and Cassius had fled from Rome and had raised an army 100,000 strong. Octavius and Antony marched on them and the two armies met at Philippi. The forces of Brutus and Cassius were defeated and both of them committed suicide.

The Roman territory was divided among Antony, Lepidus, and Octavius. Lepidus was soon robbed of his share and Antony made his headquarters in Alexandria. While there he fell in love with Cleopatra and lost all regard for anything except being with her. He divorced his wife, the sister of Octavius, and married Cleopatra. He then gave her several Roman provinces as gifts.

Octavius regarded this as treason and used it as a pretext for declaring war on Antony.

Cleopatra and Antony went to sea with the Egyptian fleet to fight the Romans. About half way through the battle she left and Antony followed her. The fleet surrendered to Octavius and some months later he marched on Alexandria where Antony and Cleopatra were waiting. Antony's troops abandoned him and Cleopatra withdrew to a monument and had the news spread that she was dead. Antony was so grieved when he heard this news that he stabbed himself with a mortal wound. He then heard that Cleopatra was still alive and had himself taken to her and died in her presence.

Cleopatra tried to bewitch the young Caesar as she had the elder, but he would have nothing to do with her. Rather than become a captive, Cleopatra killed herself by allowing an asp to bite her, or according to some sources, by the scratch of a poisoned needle.

Many times in history it is stated that she died for love, but it is more true that she died because her own selfish plans had failed and she could not face the responsibility of her own actions.

Octavius Caesar

Octavius Caesar became the ruler of the great dominion which Julius had prepared for him. He became Emperor of the Roman world and was saluted with the new title of Augustus, (Luke 2). He was elected the head of state religion and Roman Catholicism began to better organize into a system.

Rome under Caesar Augustus

Agustus,
the Emperor of Rome
at the birth of Christ.
(Peloubet, 1913)

Augustus began to rule when he was only 36 years of age. He was declared to be Imperator, "father of the country", and prince, meaning the first. Augustus ruled for 44 years of Roman history and witnessed the greatest historical event of all times - the birth of Christ in 4 A.D.

When Augustus came to the throne the world was in very bad condition and the people were extremely wicked, a quote from Thorndike concerning the slaves will suffice to point out this fact:

"Good heavens! What stunted little men met my eye, their skin all striped with livid scars, their backs a mass of sores, with tattered patchwork clothing that gave them shade rather than shelter...their foreheads branded, heads half-shaven, ankles pierced with rings,...eyelids ulcerated." (Thorndike, *A Short History of Civilization*), p. 189.

Suffering was widespread and one-half of the people were slaves.

Men had lost faith in the old gods and there was no satisfaction, and no hope. They believed in no god, and no life after death. This view led to extreme superstition and faithlessness which ultimately led to emperor worship.

In the city of Rome itself over 500,000 people were supported by public charity and the distribution of free grain was also under the authority of Augustus. Public welfare systems are always the result of a democratic form of government. As Augustus took more and more governmental control and 'big government' got bigger, more and more people became dependent on the state for their livelihood, demonstrating a direct parallel to today.

Blood spectacles were very popular in the amphitheaters and were loved by the people because they made them forget their misery and hopelessness. Is it not also possible to compare the obsession for violence in today's T.V. programs and movies to this period of Roman history?

Such was the state of the people that even suicide was bitterly commended. Is this another parallel to today? Suicide in the teenage years is up 100%; for the twenties age group it is up 300%.

Augustus' part in God's plan

Augustus was to organize and unify the world from the Atlantic to the Caspian Sea, and from Britain to the Nile River in Egypt. He was to make of the world of these diverse peoples one big neighborhood.

He was the first to determine the population and the total value of property in each province so that the assessment of taxes could be made upon a fair basis. He compiled careful census lists:

And it came to pass, in those days, that there went out a decree from Caesar Augustus, that all the world should be taxed (registered). (Luke 2:1.)

Because of this registering Joseph went to Bethlehem to be registered for the imperial census and to thus fulfill Old Testament prophecy as to the place of the birth of the Messiah:

And Joseph also went up from Galilee, out of the city of Nazareth, into Judaea, unto the city of David, which is called Bethlehem; (because he was of the house and lineage of David;) To be taxed with Mary his espoused wife, being great with child. (Luke 2:4,5.)

But thou, Bethlehem Ephratah, though thou be little among the thousands of Judah, yet out of thee shall he come forth unto me that is to be ruler in Israel; whose goings forth have been from of old, from everlasting. (Micah 5:2.)

The calendar at that moment in history was in error, and it was found ten centuries afterward to be lacking four years of the true period; but since changing a system that had then been adopted by nearly all of Europe would have caused great confusion in civil and ecclesiastical affairs, the error was, by general consent, allowed to remain, and we continue to reckon from this era (A.D., anno domini, that is, "in the year of our Lord"), which, however, lacks four years and six days of the real Christian epoch, (our method of counting time was not introduced till the year 532 A.D.).

THE BIRTH OF CHRIST

While Augustus was ruling over an hundred millions of his fellow-polytheists, there took place in an obscure corner of the Roman dominion an event the importance of which the wisest Roman could not have foreseen. This was the birth of Christ, the founder of a religion which was to overspread the polytheistic nations, dissolve ancient creeds and philosophies, and renovate the faith, the thoughts, the whole life of the civilized world. Now the diffusion of Christianity was powerfully aided by the fact of the Roman Empire, - by the unity of government under that empire; hence it has been truly said that 'the Roman empire may be defined as a compulsory assemblage of polytheistic nations in order that Christianity might operate over a large surface at once of that polytheism which it was to supersede and destroy'. (Swinton, *Outlines*), pp. 194,195.

The reign of Augustus was one of comparative peace and tranquillity. There were fewer wars and revolutions than there had been for many years. As seen from previous statements this facilitated the ministers of Christ in carrying out the Great Commission and taking the Gospel to the whole race of men.

Augustus died in 14 A.D., after ruling for 44 years and was succeeded by his step-son Tiberias Claudius Nero.

Roman boundaries.

The northern borders of the empire extended to the British Channel, the North Sea, the Rhine River, the Danube River and the Black Sea.

The eastern borders took in the Euphrates River and the Syrian Desert.

The southern border extended to the Sa-

hara Desert and the western border to the Atlantic Ocean.

Nations included within the interior of the empire were:

Portugal	France	W. Holland
Spain	Belgium	Bavaria
Switzerland	Greece	Tripoli
Italy	Asia Minor	Tunis
Austria	Syria	Algeria
W. Hungary	Palestine	Turkey
Egypt	Most of Morocco	
Britain		

The territories included three civilizations:

Latin, from the Atlantic to the Adriatic Sea, which brought a united government; Greek, from the Adriatic Sea to

Roman Library

(Peloubet, 1893)

the Taurus Mountains, which brought about a united language, and Oriental, beyond the Euphrates River, which brought both true and false religions, but most importantly it brought the world the Savior.

Condition of the empire under Augustus.

The Roman empire spread throughout the major part of the civilized world and there were an approximate 100 millions of people, not less than half of whom were slaves.

Peace was kept in the city of Rome by a special group of soldiers of tested valor who were paid double wages by Augustus. There were 350,000 regular soldiers throughout the empire to keep the peace.

While the conquered nations were left with their independent municipal constitutions and officers, the central authority remained in Rome.

The population of Rome was about two and one-half millions. The city was 20 miles wide and had 30 gates in its walls. It was the site of the Coliseum, the Capitol, and its temples, the Senate-House, and the Forum. Augustus boasted that "he found the city brick and left it marble".

Roman Soldier
(Peloubet, 1893)

Entertainment

The Circus Maximus (the great circus) was used for public games, races, and shows. It had a 200,000 spectator capacity.

The Coliseum, which had an 80-100,000 person capacity, was used for fights and races of the gladiators and for combat with wild animals.

There were theaters and public baths which were constructed by the emperors to makeup for the loss of liberty. Public shows and entertainments were also instituted to deaden the pain, at least momentarily, of the miserable and wretched condition of the people.

The Forum was a place of public assembly and the great market place of the city. It was adorned with the statues of warriors and statesmen.

The Temple of Janus was constructed entirely of bronze. The custom was to close the gates only during periods of peace, it was closed only three times in 800 years. Emma Willard says:

"...the temple of Janus, which was shut only in profound peace, and which had remained continually open since the reign of Numa Pompilius, was closed, and at this period the 'Desire of Nations', the 'Prince of Peace', was born." Emma Willard, *A System of Universal History in Perspective*, (Philadelphia: A.S. Barnes and Company, 1843), p. 129.

Summary

"It would seem that the government of Rome under the Republic had become so corrupt, and the Roman populace so debased and so disorderly that, in the providence of God, a monarchy was the only thing that could prolong the life of the nation. It was to establish order, to enforce law, and thus, in its degree, to 'prepare the way of the Lord'." Dorothy Ruth Miller, *A Handbook of Ancient History in Bible Light*, (New York: Fleming H. Revell Company, 1937), p. 248.

It is important to not lose sight of the workings of God in Roman history; He was preparing a united world, a world government, and a time of comparative peace for the coming of the Messiah.

Roman supremacy (63 B. C.)

Rome began to rule Palestine during the First Triumvirate consisting of Julius Caesar, Pompey, and Crassus.

When Caesar died, Antony was left in charge of the area which included Palestine. He appointed Herod ruler of Judea.

Herod was not a Jew by birth, but an Edomite. (Judas Maccabees retook Hebron from the Edomites, and John Hyrcanus forced them to submit to the rite of circumcision and incorporated them into the Jewish people.

They took part in the defense of Jerusalem against the Romans, many were Zealots, but were almost as dangerous to the Israelites as the enemy. They are heard of very few times after this.) He was a descendant of Esau.

Caesar had intended that the kingship of Jerusalem should continue with the Hyrcanus family, but Herod took the status of king, becoming the king in 37 B.C. Through a series of well-planned events he gained some acceptance among the Jews.

Herod was afraid of the Asmonean (Hyrcanus family) party, (the Maccabees), and had Antigonus executed. Aristobulus was high priest and Herod had him drowned by "accident". Hyrcanus, in exile, was brought back from Parthia and was executed. Then to finish his bloody work, Herod had his wife Miriamne, whom he loved, executed. She was from the Asmonean line. He killed his own two sons, and many Jews were slain during this period because of his fear of losing the throne.

During the infancy of Christ he had all the boy babies slain because of his fear that a Jewish king had been born.

He tried to appease the Jews though, and those who were worldly-minded were happy to be appeased.

He built an amphitheater at Jerusalem, and built the city of Cæsarea to give Palestine a seaport for profit and pleasure.

His most important act was rebuilding the temple at Jerusalem. The Jews told Jesus in John 2:20 that it took forty-six years to finish this great work. Those who worked on the construction of the temple were said to have been specially consecrated for this work.

God will accomplish His purpose. He used an ungodly, wicked man to rebuild the temple and to prepare the world for the coming of the Messiah.

Government at the time of Christ

The Sanhedrin.

The Sanhedrin was formed by Ezra and was the highest Jewish governing body in Judea. There were 70 members, (some say 71), and only those Jews whose descent was above question were eligible to become members.

They were the rabbis or teachers of the nation. They dictated the standards of religious faith and life in the temple.

When Jesus' mother finds Him in the temple at the age of twelve, He is instructing this group of men concerning His heavenly Father. The Sanhedrin tried and condemned Him to death.

The Sanhedrin took the lead in the administration of all public affairs, except those that were under the authority of the tribunal of the governor at Cæsarea.

Schools of Interpretation.

Hillel, a Babylonian Jew recognized the importance of freedom of the individual conscience in the interpretation and application of the Law. Gamaliel, who taught Saul of Tarsus, was a grandson of Hillel.

Shammai, a rabbi, taught the letter of the Law, and the strict adherence to traditions. He carried this to such an extent that he often contradicted himself.

Religion at the time of Christ

Jewish Parties

The three Jewish sects which brought about the division of the Jewish nation represent the three human tendencies of formalism, skepticism, and mysticism. They were the Pharisees, the Sadducees, and the Essenes. By the time of the coming of Christ they were all actively operating in the Holy land.

The Pharisees.

When the exiles returned from Babylonian captivity they practiced a very strict morality. The Law and the ceremonies of Moses were rigidly kept. The Sabbath was kept with a strictness unknown to their ancestors, (as already noted with the observance of the Sabbath by the Maccabees).

From this group there arose the sect known as the Pharisees. They were fanatic in their observance of the Law, but were very popular and powerful.

Formal learning was held in very high regard, but they lacked common sense.

Almsgiving was stressed to the point of self-righteousness; these strict observances developed an overbearing arrogance, and a spirit of hypocrisy, but they were the ruling class of the Jewish nation.

Christ rebuked them for their formalism, their pretended holiness, their self-seeking, and their enslavement to tradition.

They were enemies of Christ; their hypocrisy was revealed in Matthew 12:14 and Luke 11:44. They were called blind guides in Matthew 23:16, and fools, (Matthew 23:17, and Luke 11:40); full of dead men's bones within, and of all uncleanness and iniquity, (Matthew 23:27,28); sons of them who killed the prophets, (Matthew 23:31); serpents, and a generation of vipers, (Matthew 23:33). They loved the chief seats in the synagogues, and the greetings in the market places, (Luke 11:43).

They took counsel against Christ in Matthew 12:14 and Mark 3:6.

The Sadducees.

The fanaticism of the Pharisees gave rise to another party - the Sadducees. They were a revolutionary party with a very progressive spirit, though small in number they were influential, wealthy, talented and were men of much learning. Included among them were the nobility and the gentry.

They refused to acknowledge the oral law of Moses and said they were only bound by written law.

They were indifferent to tradition and had no belief in the resurrection of the dead, the spiritual world, and a future life, (Matthew 22:23-33).

In their habits of life they were more given to luxury than the Pharisees. They also had more social pride and were less religious.

The moral law, the prophets, and the Messianic hope were practically despised.

A talmudic account says of them, "They are high priests and their sons are treasurers of the temple, and their sons-in-law assistant treasurers; and their servants beat the people with sticks."

Edersheim says they sold temple necessities, changed money, and made a great profit.

When the resurrection of Christ became an issue they persecuted the Church.

The Essenes.

The ascetics of Judea numbered approximately 4000 at the time of Christ. They isolated themselves from society and formed colonies. Each colony had its own synagogue, a common hall for meals and assemblies, and provision for daily baths in running water.

The members gave up all they possessed and led a communistic life-style. They read the law of Moses daily and nightly and regulated their lives accordingly.

Their food and clothing were plain. They had no need for money as all their needs were raised through agriculture. Slaves, war, and commerce were held in contempt. They abstained from marriage though they felt it was all right for others.

Morality was lofty and in their oath they promised 'to honor God, to be righteous toward man, to injure no one, either at the bidding of another or of their own accord, to hate evil, to promote good, to be faithful to everyone (especially to those in authority), to love truth, to unmask liars, and to keep the hand from theft and the conscience from unrighteous gain.'

Some historians say that John the Baptist was a member of this sect, though it is probably more a traditional view than an actual fact

They are purported to have been the sect that hid the Dead Sea Scrolls. Modern archeology has given us the story of the tragic end of the Essenes in 68 A.D. The Roman troops, under the leadership of Vespasian, came into Palestine to put down a rebellion among the Jews.

The Essenes seem to have foreseen the Roman invasion and in preparation they hid their sacred library. The scrolls, mostly of leather, as was the custom in those days, were put into clay pots and sealed. These were then hidden in the caves high up in the limestone cliffs; these caves were almost inaccessible and were originally invisible from the plain below. Evidently, the Romans advanced more quickly than they had anticipated and many of the scrolls were hurriedly thrown into the caves where they disintegrated.

The Essenes had doubtless planned to reclaim the precious scrolls, but none seems to have survived to return.

In 1947, seven of these scrolls were found by a Bedouin goatherder, and others have been recovered since that time. Thousands of fragments of other scrolls have been found and are probably the remains of those thrown into the caves at the Roman advancement.

The first reference to these scrolls was made by Origen, one of the great scholars of the early church, when he compiled a book of the various Greek versions of the Old Testament, called the Hexalpa. This was in the third century A.D. and in it he wrote of the discovery of Biblical manuscripts in a jar near Jericho. No one can prove that Origen was referring to a finding in his time similar to the recent discovery of the Dead Sea Scrolls, but the parallel is too striking to permit any other reasonable interpretation. Origen's statement is further corroborated by the fact that the Masorites, the Jews who edited the authoritative Hebrew Old Testament, sometimes cited the "Jericho Pentateuch" as an authority. Eusebius and Jerome also mention it. No one knew what the Jericho Pentateuch was, but it now seems likely that it was an Essene work.

All eleven caves in and around Qumran (where the scrolls were found), yielded the remains of hundreds of rolled manuscripts. Among them were parts of every book of the Hebrew Bible except the book of Esther. Some of these dated from the second century B.C., or earlier, pre-dating by a thousand years the oldest previously known copies of the Biblical books in Hebrew. Since most of these manuscripts show only minor variations from today's Old Testament, the Dead Sea Scrolls conformed to the scrupulous accuracy of Biblical scribes over the centuries.

It seems to the world coincidental that God chose this particular sect at this particular spot to preserve the Scriptures. To the Christian this is only another example of God's care in His design for man. This spot was especially chosen at the northern end of the Dead Sea because weather conditions were ideal for the preservation of the scrolls. The manuscripts had been preserved in the clay pots for nearly two thousand years by the Dead Sea region's extreme dryness.

The Herodians.

These were usually Jews who obtained

some personal benefit from supporting the Herodian arm of the Roman government. They were not of proper Jewish descent as they had supplanted a royal family and priesthood and were in direct antagonism to the Pharisees.

They united with the Pharisees to try to ensnare Jesus about paying tribute to Caesar, (Matthew 22:16; Mark 12:13) and plotted to murder the Lord, (Mark 3:6; Mark 12:13).

Places of Worship During the Time of Christ

The Temple.

The temple was reserved for great ceremonies and celebrations, it was an object of pride and awe, adorned and glorious, but was not for the common man.

The synagogue.

The synagogue was established on the return of the Jews from captivity. All towns had a synagogue or a *proseucha* - place of prayer, which was a sort of church. It was humble and modest for use by the people in ordinary worship.

It was a place of religious instruction (Luke 11:1; Acts 15:21), and constituted a school for the children.

Those who could read and teach were allowed to stand up and speak and this represented the democratic element in Judaism.

It was used in God's providence so the world, through the dispersion of the Jews, might hear the message of God, particularly of the coming of the Messiah.

Summary

"All this appears to have been most singularly and wisely directed by the adorable hand of an interposing providence, to the end that this people, which was the sole repository of the true religion, and of the knowledge of one Supreme God, being spread abroad through the whole earth, might be every where, by their example, a reproach to superstition, contribute in some measure to check it and thus prepare the way for that yet fuller discovery of divine truth, which was to shine upon the world from the ministry and gospel of the Son of God." Verna Hall, *Self-Government with Union*, (San Francisco: The American Christian Constitution Press, 1962), p. 103.

Philosophy of Rome

God brought about a united government to facilitate the spread of the Gospel throughout the world.

Much of the philosophy of Rome came from the Greeks because of their instruction in the Greek language and Greek eloquence. During this period of time the sciences flourished.

There were two main divisions of philosophy: the Epicureans and the Academics. The Epicurean favored the great men, and established a false security in the present. They indulged in their sin without repentance and continued in their wicked undertakings without the fear of coming judgment.

The Epicureans derived their name from the philosopher Epicurus who was born 341 B.C. in the island of Samos, but was an Athenian.

He founded a school in 306 B.C. which continued until his death in 270 B.C. He did not recognize a Creator but in his system of belief were many gods who did not take part in the affairs of man.

"With regard to his ethics a popular misconception prevails. He desires that pleasure shall be pursued and pain avoided; but the notion that by pleasure he meant only sensual gratification is erroneous. He included under the term the pleasure derived from the exercise of the intellect and the moral faculty. Personally he was so pure that some thought he was destitute of passions." John D. Davis, *Davis Bible Dictionary,* (The Varsity Company, Nashville, 1973), pp. 226,227.

The Epicureans were the opposite of the Stoics in physical expression.

The Academics were those who belonged to the school or adhered to the philosophy of Socrates and Plato. The latter is considered the founder of the academic philosophy in Greece. He taught that matter is eternal and infinite but without form, unmanageable, and tending to disorder (Second Law of Thermodynamics). He also taught that there is an intelligent cause, the author of spiritual beings, and of the material world.

Rome's view of Christianity

As the Gospel went out to the Gentile nations Rome took a very different view of Christianity.

They looked upon Christianity as a newly formed club since their own clubs included the worship of local deities, giving divine honors to men, and various religious customs. They could not see any difference in this religion and their own. They felt this was just a new deity to worship, as they always worshipped the divinity of the reigning emperor and could add a new deity at will.

They saw in this religion new rites to be observed: Christian baptism, common meals, and the Lord's Supper, but these were all considered as they considered the secret rites of the other clubs.

They had not been touched by the power of the Gospel so viewed it much as those of the world view Christianity today.

Beginning of Persecution in Palestine

Pharisaic Judaism.

Christianity brought a contrast to the law.

It brought a contrast between "the image of a Jewish Messiah coming in glory", and the form of the crucified One who called Gentiles and Jews without distinction into his heavenly kingdom.

Pharisaism meant the completion of national Judaism; Christianity meant the abolition of national Judaism. It can easily be understood why this might be viewed as a threat and would cause some severe reactions in Palestine.

The stoning of Stephen was one of the first outward signs of the reaction to Christianity. Stephen taught that Jesus had come to destroy temple worship and to do away with the law of Moses, and this was what Pharisaism was built upon.

Stephen was accused of speaking blasphemous words against Moses, and saying to the Sanhedrin that Jesus of Nazareth would destroy the temple, and 'change the customs' which Moses had delivered.

He was the first martyr for the faith at the hands of a Jewish mob, and this incident began the dispersion of the Jerusalem church. It was one more step towards the admission of the Gentiles into Christ and His oracles.

James, the brother of John, was beheaded by Herod Agrippa for his stand for Christ.

Peter was imprisoned and finally martyred. Judaism vented its hatred of Christianity by violence, and only the Apostles dared remain in Jerusalem. This, of course, hastened the spread of Christianity to accomplish God's purpose.

RULERS OF ROME

Rome had many rulers who ruled only a short time and nothing significant was recorded about their reign; these will only be listed with no comment.

Augustus reigned through 14 A.D., the significant events of his reign are listed under the life of Christ.

Tiberius - 14 A.D. to 37 A.D. During his reign Christ was crucified.

Caligula - 37 A.D. to 41 A.D. He made Herod Agrippa king of Judea.

Claudius - 41 A.D. to 54 A.D.

Nero - 54 A.D. to 68 A.D.

"In the reign of the brutal Nero the first persecution took place, but it was confined to the city of Rome. A great fire, which consumed a large part of the city, took place. Men said that the emperor's own hand had kindled the flame, out of mere madness, and that while the burning continued, he sat calmly looking on, singing verses to the music of his lyre. To divert suspicion from himself, Nero resolved to direct it upon the Christians. Tacitus writes, 'With this view (that is to divert suspicion), Nero inflicted the most exquisite tortures on those men who, under the vulgar appellation of Christians, were already branded with deserved infamy. They derived their name and origin from one Christ, who in the reign of Tiberius had suffered death by the sentence of the procurator Pontius Pilate. For a while this dire superstition was checked, but it again burst forth; and not only spread itself over Judea, the first seat of this mischievous sect, but was even introduced into Rome, the common asylum which receives and protects whatever is impure, whatever is atrocious. The confessions of those who were seized discovered a great multitude of their accomplices, and they were all convicted, not so much for the crime of setting fire to the city, as for their hatred of human kind. Some were nailed on crosses, others sewn up in the skins of wild beasts and exposed to the fury of dogs; others, again, smeared over with combustible materials, were used as torches to illuminate the darkness of the night. The gardens of Nero were destined for the melancholy spectacle, which was accompanied with a horse-race, and honored with the presence of the emperor, who mingled with the populace in the dress and attitude of a charioteer. The guilt of the Christians deserved indeed the most exemplary punishment, but the public abhorrence was changed into commiseration, from the opinion that those unhappy wretches were sacrificed, not so much to the public welfare, as to the cruelty of a jealous tyrant'." (Swinton, *Outlines of History*), p. 195,196. (Hebrews 11:35-38.)

"The flames of the burning of the world's capital, together with those living torches, the bodies of the martyrs flaring in the gardens of the Emperor Nero, lit up the Church's entry into the world's history. Hitherto the Christians had been confused by the populace with the Jews. Now, for the first time, the distinction became generally recognized - the Christians alone, not the Jews, were charged with the burning of Rome." Rudolf Sohm, *Outlines of Church History,* (London: MacMillan and Company, 1895), p. 9.

Galba - 68 A.D. to 69 A.D.

Vitellius - 69 A.D.

Vespasian - 69 A.D. to 79 A.D.

He was sent to Palestine to put down the Jews who were in revolt, and subdued Galilee. It was during this siege, led by Vespasian, that the Dead Sea Scrolls are believed to have been hidden by the Essenes, again demonstrating the hand of God in history.

He was proclaimed emperor by the army at the death of Nero.

Titus - 79 A.D. to 81 A.D.

He took over the subjugation of Palestine from his father, Vespasian. He destroyed Jerusalem in 70 A.D. He tried to preserve the

Temple, but the soldiers destroyed it anyway (that the Scriptures might be fulfilled, Matthew 24:1,2).

Domitian - 81 A.D. to 96 A.D.

Nerva - 96 A.D. to 98 A.D.

Trajan - 98 A.D. to 117 A.D.

This emperor instituted proceedings against the Christians in 112 A.D. If they refused to offer incense to the Emperor they were sentenced to death. Trajan declared war on Christians.

"The Roman Emperor was the incarnation of the idea of the State. The altar raised to him was consecrated to the worship of that which, for Paganism, was the highest moral force, the power of the State. To the new views which the Christians put forward with reckless determination, the worship not only of idols, but of the emperor (that is, of the State), was irreconcilable. To the Christian the highest of all things was not the almighty Caesar, not the Roman Empire, not the Roman nation. To the Christian the Highest was, before all, not of the world, for his longing was fixed upon a better. With Christianity a new theory of the world came into history, challenging all others to open combat, a theory which insisted on the worthlessness of all earthly things when compared with heavenly things; which rendered unto Caesar the things that are Caesar's, but at the same time desired to give God the things that are God's. And this theory of the world made in Christianity its claim to be the only universally valid one. While Judaism shut itself in from the outer world, and claimed its promises, as it guarded its beliefs, for itself alone; while the philosophical systems appealed only to the learned, Christianity claimed from the very first to conquer the world. It went out into the highways and marketplaces for the very purpose of gaining a decisive influence over those modes of popular thought on which the commonwealth now depended.

"For this reason Christianity was dangerous to the State, in the old pagan sense. It struck at the very foundations of the ancient State - that State which, with its unlimited and illimitable power, claimed to regulate the whole outer and inner life of man." (Sohm, *Outlines of Church History*), pp. 10,11.

To sacrifice to the Emperor the Christians renounced their Christianity and escaped death; they were accused of treason if they refused. They were persecuted because they refused to worship the state. Polycarp, bishop of Smyrna was martyred during his reign.

Hadrian - 117 A.D. to 138 A.D. He was a Spaniard.

He was probably the only genius among the Roman rulers. He rebuilt Jerusalem and named it Aelia Capitolina. He built a pagan temple to Jupiter on the former temple site and made Jerusalem a Roman colony.

Antoninus Pius - 138 A.D. to 161 A.D.

Followed by several co-rulers.

Marcus Aurelius - 161 A.D. to 180 A.D. and **L. Verus** 161 A.D. to 169 A.D.

Persecution of the church in southern Gaul (later France) was carried out and many Christians from the church at Lyons were killed (177 A.D.).

Commodus - 180 A.D. to 192 A.D.

Pertinas - 193 A.D. co-ruled with Julianus 193 A.D.

Septimium Severus - 193 A.D. to 211 A.D.

Laws were enacted that forbid anyone to become a Christian. Christians in Egypt, and the Latin provinces of Africa were persecuted.

Caracalla - 211 A.D. to 217 A.D. co-ruled with Geta 211 A.D. to 212 A.D.

Macrinus - 217 A.D. to 218 A.D.

Elagabalus - 218 A.D. to 235 A.D. co-ruled with Alexander Severus - 222 A.D. to 235 A.D.

Maximus - 235 A.D. to 238 A.D.

Gordianus I and **Gordianus II** co-ruled 238 A.D.

Philippus - 244 A.D. to 249 A.D.

Decius - 249 A.D. to 251 A.D.

He gave orders for the general persecution of Christians. All authorities were to force the Christians to sacrifice to the Emperor without waiting for any special charges against them.

Trebonianus Gallus - 251 A.D. to 253 A.D.

He issued fresh edicts against the Christians and continued the persecution.

Aemilianus - 253 A.D.

Valerian - 253 A.D. to 260 A.D.

Valerian took up the work of Decius and commanded all bishops, priests, and deacons of the church, as well as Christian senators and judges, to be put to death if they refused to recant. His persecution was aimed at destroying the organization of the church.

Gallienus - 260 A.D. to 268 A.D.

The son of Valerian, he repealed the edicts of persecution. The profession of the Christian faith was still punishable by death and the law could be put into effect at any instant when anyone refused to offer incense to the imperial image. A state of practical toleration existed and the law was only carried out in isolated cases.

Claudius II - 268 A.D. to 270 A.D.

Aurebian - 270 A.D. to 275 A.D.

Tacitus - 275 A.D. to 276 A.D.

Forianus - 276 A.D.

Probus - 276 A.D. to 282 A.D.

Carus - 282 A.D. to 283 A.D.

Carinus and **Numerianus** co-rulers - 283 A.D. to 284 A.D.

Diocletian - 284 A.D. to 305 A.D.

During his reign the Roman empire rose up in hatred against the Christians. The absolute monarchy of the state was sought and the bitterest persecution of the church began. Diocletian and his son-in-law Galerius were both enemies of the church. God inflicted an incurable disease upon him.

Maximian - 286 A.D. to 305 A.D.

Constantius I - 305 A.D. to 306 A.D.

He was the father of Constantine.

Galerius - 305 A.D. to 311 A.D., co-ruler.

Galerius was the son-in-law of Diocletian. He urged the attack on Christians. All Christian churches were to be destroyed; all sacred books confiscated and burned; all clergy put in prison and forced to sacrifice. He commanded all Christians to sacrifice under penalty of death. Galerius was an insane butcher. The food for sale in the market places was drenched with sacrificial wine in order to compel the Christians to sacrifice.

On his death-bed he issued an edict of general toleration; he had to confess that Christianity had won.

The Church has remained unconquerable even during all the persecution of the first centuries. "The marvel of its greatest achievement is just this: that it could not be destroyed, that it won the victory although so miserably represented by its followers...The church conquered, not because of the Christians, but in spite of them and through the power of the Gospel." (Sohm, *Outlines of Church History*), pp. 21,22.

Constantine I, The Great - 306 A.D. to 337 A.D.

He fought under the banner of a cross which he claimed to have seen in a vision, but it was what was later known as the Crusader's cross and more particularly that of the Templars, not the cross of Christ.

In 313 he issued an edict of toleration and placed Christianity on the same level as paganism. Every man was at liberty to choose his own divinity and to worship whom he would. He built new churches and repaired old ones. The clergy was freed from taxes and Sunday was proclaimed a day of rest.

He moved the seat of government to Constantinople, a mainly Catholic city. This was the beginning of the separation of the Latin and Greek churches.

The edicts of toleration "...prepared the way for the legal recognition of Christianity, as the religion of the empire. It ordered the full restoration of all confiscated church property at the expense of the imperial treasury, and directed the provincial magistrates to execute this order at once with all energy, so that peace might be fully established and the continuance of the Divine favor secured to the emperors and their subjects.

"This was the first proclamation of the great principle that every man had a right to choose his religion according to the dictates of his own conscience and honest conviction, without compulsion and interference from the government. Religion is worth nothing except as an act of freedom. A forced religion is no religion at all." Philip Schaff, *History of the Christian Church,* (New York: Charles Scribner's Sons, 1883), pp. 72, 73.

This edict was issued in 313, but did not reach its fulfillment until 1787 with the establishment of the Constitution of the United States of America; notice how long it took to gain freedom for the individual.

Constantine is believed by many to have been a Christian, but was in reality a Roman Catholic. He allowed a certain amount of freedom to worship, but he actually only put Christianity and paganism on an equal footing.

Constantine acted as a wise statesman and saw the political benefits of making himself a friend to Christianity after the horrendous acts of the former Roman emperors.

He called for the Council of Nicea which was attended by many of those who had been tortured and maimed, and who still carried the marks of that torture in their bodies.

But to call him a great Christian emperor is a mistake. He allowed the Gospel to continue moving westward and allowed a measure of religious freedom never seen before in the Roman empire, and that was how God used him for His purpose.

CONCLUSIONS

"The flower of paganism appears in the two great nations of antiquity, Greece and Rome. These, with the Jews were the chosen nations of the ancient world. The Jews were chosen for things eternal; the Greeks prepared the elements of natural culture, of science and art, for the use of the church; and the Romans developed the idea of law, and organized the civilized world. Both Greeks and Romans were unconscious servants of Jesus Christ." (Verna M. Hall, unpublished speech, *Preparation for Christianity in the History of the Jewish and Heathen World,* used by permission of the author.)

The sons of Japheth have been used of God to continue the westward movement of the Gospel. When the Jewish nation lost its way and rejected its Messiah God moved the Gentiles to continue the spread of the Gospel. (Gentile meaning the Japhethites.)

As the Gospel moved across Europe there were always signs, (internal and external) following both nationally and individually in the lives of those whom God had chosen for His purpose. Alexander was one of the non-Christian men of the Japhetic line used by God. He spread the Greek language into both the East and the West and it was the language used by God to spread the Gospel.

After him God used the Roman empire to continue the spread of the Gospel by the early Christians as they were dispersed throughout the empire. As the Romans moved westward many missionaries followed into the newly conquered countries and gave the heathen peoples there the message of a Savior who had died for them also and Who promised them life eternal if they would accept Him as their Savior.

As before stated Constantine put Christianity and paganism on an equal footing and allowed the individual the right to choose which one he would follow without coercion by the State.

The continued westward movement after the fall of the Roman empire continued to reach more and more of Europe for Christ. They were not easy times, and many gave their lives to spread the message, but most did so willingly.

All during this period the Roman Catholic system continued to try to stop the spread of the Gospel by allowing only those rites and ceremonies which it considered valid and worthwhile to their system. The Bible was suppressed and only the clergy had access to it. This led to the Dark Ages, a time when the Word was not accessible to the common man.

As the Middle Ages approached individuals began to confront the teachings of the Roman Catholic system and give the truth to the world. For their efforts they were many times imprisoned and upon threat of death told to either believe the way the system believed or stop propounding their ideas.

Among them can be listed Copernicus, Galileo, Kepler, and many others in the scientific world.

The Reformation/Renaissance period brought about a revival of interest in the Greek classics and scholars again learned the Greek language. This enabled them to translate the Scriptures from the Greek Septuagint into the English language. The printing press made the Bible cheap enough that anyone who wanted one could buy one. The Word liberated the individual and also liberated any nation that chose to follow its principles of truth.

The descendants of Japheth continue to carry the Gospel from the shores of the United States of America around the world. Only America has a form of government that allows the free expression of religion and only if American Christians are watchful will it continue.

God allowed the Japhethites to do a marvelous work in founding the first Christian nation in the world (the United States of America) and giving them the command to "Go into all the world with the Gospel".

Many great missionaries from the line of Japheth have been sent into the world and have been able to change entire nations for Christ. Among those would be, Adoniram Judson, Hudson Taylor, John Hyde, Fred Donnelson, Carrie Ten Boom, Lottie Moon, Bob Hughes, Jim Eliot, etc. And the work they began is being carried on by thousands of missionaries around the world who have gone from the shores of America to take the wonderful "good news" of the King of Kings.

Japheth's work is not finished. God still has a great work for him to do. And the Japhethites will continue to be a force for good in the world as long as they are true to the mission God has given them.

SECTION VI
CONCLUSIONS:
REIGN OF THE THREE SONS OF NOAH

Through the ages many earthly monarchs have desired with all their hearts to rule a world-wide kingdom. Among them were Nebuchadnezzar, Babylonia; Cyrus, Medo-Persia; Alexander the Great, Greece; Caesar, Rome; Charlemagne, the Holy Roman Empire; Philip II of Spain; and Napoleon, France. And, of course, those who ruled the enormous Soviet Union and still lusted for more territory. All were disappointed because it was not in God's plan for any of them to become world-wide rulers as it is not, nor ever will be, His will to have an earthly world-wide government ruled by one man.

The sons of Noah refused to leave the plains of Shinar after arriving there from the Armenian mountains where the ark had landed. The fear of another judgment from God served to fill them with the terror of being alone and one group would not leave without the other. From this fear came the construction of the Tower of Babel. Until God 'came down' and confused their languages, they were unwilling to leave their homes and venture out into new territory.

Nimrod, son of Ham through Cush, was the first to develop a thirst for world-empire before the dispersion. For this reason, the Tower of Babel was to be the Mecca of religion and government to which all men would voluntarily return from time to time. But when God gave the command to leave, Noah's descendants left, not willingly, nor with picked companions, but with those who were of the same speech as they. In all of this, however, God was leading men to the place He had destined for their different homes, just as He would later lead Moses and Israel by fire and cloud to the land He had prepared for them.

Acts 17:26, *And hath made of one blood all nations of men for to dwell on all the face of the earth, and hath determined the times before appointed, and the bounds of their habitation.*

SHEM

Shem was to be the fixed element in history: always moving toward the climax of the Semitic line in Christ. All the world was to look backward for two thousand years to this Light of the World as all eyes are to turn, in all the generations to come. Therefore Shem, the founder of the central nation in history, was to keep his place in a central position in the earth. He was not to have long periods of disappearance like Japheth, nor to wander and be lost, like Ham. Shem was to "dwell in the presence of his brethren"; the place of his tent was always to be known. Shem was to have a numerically small increase; and would only need a small physical area in which to live. To him were committed the holy oracles, he was the schoolmaster of his brethren in religion and letters. The illustrious sons of Shem were to be few in number, but among them were to be Moses, Solomon, and Paul. Shem's writings would not be extensive; yet in the Bible they were to cover every aspect of letters—science, history, poetry, biography, law, philosophy, and in their perfection, would be the unequaled crown of literature. (Wright, *Bricks from Babel*), pp. 167, 168.

A look at the tents of Shem tells an unexpected story: He goes, in Elam, southeast as far as the Persian Gulf. He moves north in Asshur, and reaches the head waters of the Tigris. Then traveling westward through Asia Minor, he rests upon the Caspian. In the Hebrews he has Palestine for a possession; in Joktan the hot deserts of the Arabian Peninsula. It would seem that the command to wander did not come to the Shemites, but there is one great wanderer in this family. Lud, who had rested awhile in the Armenian mountains, suddenly left his home. He traveled along the Jordan valley and over the Isthmus of Suez. Everywhere he goes he causes a disturbance in the native peoples. He camps in Barca, and waters his caravans at every oasis. He enters the Canaries and leaves his mark there. As the ages have passed, his host has dwindled to a handful; but he has written his story on all Northern Africa, and impressed his language, and his customs on his Hamitic cousins. (Ibid.), p. 167.

HAM

"Ham had a wider empire; hot southern suns suited his blood; a warm land, where food would grow with little cultivation; where easily-built habitations would suffice; lands where there would be but few stimulants to lofty achievements pleased the majority of the nation of Ham. But there were in this nation widely differing capacities, and they had an inheritance where all their possibilities could be developed. There were traders among the Hamites, and they shared Arabia with Shem. There were builders of rare genius, and they received Egypt, the land of architecture. There was ability for world-rule which was displayed in Babylon. Thus we see Ham getting the first kingdom of Chaldea, part of Arabia and nearly all of Africa. Aram held the coast and Lud had a part of the central and western northernmost area." (Wright, *Bricks from Babel*), p. 168.

But we find the Hamites also in Palestine, until they are either destroyed or are absorbed through marriage by the Hebrews; and then there is yet another colony whose history can never be written. Obscure glimpses come of those Cushites who departed from Babylonia, went eastward, entered India, and were pushed downward into Malacca by the advancing Japetidae. These sons of Cush were carried along on the forefront of the Malayan wave as it inhabited the Polynesian Islands, and together they became the dark and mixed tribes of the Archipelagoes. The lightest hued of the Hamitic nations, the Libyans, also were sprinkled along the Mediterranean Islands, and mixed with the Iberians on the European coast of the Mediterranean. (Ibid.), p. 169.

JAPHETH

Japheth's good fortune was to receive all that his two brothers had left. He was especially adapted for the Temperate Zone; but was capable of accommodating himself to all climates, and to all methods of life. Japheth therefore has possession of Europe, of at least seven-ninths of Asia, and of the whole of America, with nine-tenths of the islands. Africa alone gave him no inheritance. Japheth had three great resting places—Media, Greece, and India. After his first flight at Babel, he had two other grand points of departure, Persia, where the term Aryan comes from and the Altai Mountains, where constant streams of population flowed for ages into the Asian plains, and then into America and Polynesia over land and water routes.

Immediately after the Dispersion, Japheth's son, Javan, began his journey toward Greece, but did not reach his homeland until many centuries had passed. In Magog the Scythians were established in the north; and Madai occupied Media. Long periods of time were to pass before the Japetidae were even comparatively settled in their homes. Wave after wave of migration rolled forward, and receded. The earliest tribes were absorbed into the nations of a later growth. The great body of the Indo-European families, lying across the North Temperate Zone in the Old World are observed; the Ugrians, wandering around the Pole; the Mongolians in America, giving way to a late emigration of Europeans coming over the Atlantic; and the Malayans of Oceanica, followed by their happier brethren, who brought them the light of life. (Ibid.), pp. 169, 170, excerpts.

"The contribution of Japheth has been in the application of philosophy to technology and the consequent development of the scientific method. As the application of Japheth's philosophy to the technology of Ham produced science, so the application of his philosophy to the religious insights of Shem produced theology. The Hamitic people never developed science and the Semitic people did not develop theology, until the influence of Japhetic philosophy was brought to bear...most of us have been brought up to believe that we Indo-Europeans, are the most inventive people in the world. It is exceedingly difficult to escape from this culturally conditional prejudice to take a fresh objective look at the origins of our technological achievements. One may take almost any essential element of our highly complex civilization - aircraft, paper, weaving, metallurgy, propulsion of various kinds, painting, explosives, medical techniques, mechanical principles, food, the use of electricity, virtually anything technological in nature - and an examination of the history of its development leads us surely and certainly back to a Hamitic people and exceedingly rarely to Japheth or Shem. The basic inventions which have been contributed by Shem or Japheth can, it seems, be numbered on the fingers of one hand. This seems so contrary to popular opinion, yet it is a thesis which can be supported - and has been documented - from close to 1000 authoritative sources." (Willmington's Bible Commentary), p. 34.

CONCLUSIONS

"The reign of Ham was a brief, tumultuous reign which brought agony to the peoples of the then-known world. Egypt, Ethiopia, Babylonia perished,—and the reign of Ham was ended.

"The scepter of Shem was extended over a spiritual and invisible world rather than over an earthly kingdom. Solomon in his highest glory was a master of wise men, not of monarchs; the kings of the earth were his allies, not his vassals. The reign of Shem has been the royalty of Mind, his Scriptures have shaped the development of nations and the world dates its age to and from the days of the Son of David. Thus Shem has ruled in hearts and brains, and most importantly in his Divine Descendant, the Lord Jesus Christ." (Wright, *Bricks from Babel*), pp. 170,171.

When Ham had failed, and Shem had fulfilled his primary destiny, the empire was given to Japheth. The great accomplishments of Japheth are then seen; the length of his dominion, the vast extent of his territory, and the great multitudes of his children. He is admired for his inventions, for his successes, his learning, and for his gift of combining utility and beauty. In Japheth, the world was intellectually blessed, and is presently blessed through him by his great missionary zeal to take the Gospel message of salvation around the world. His understanding and application of politics has changed the face of the world and continues to do so, freeing many nations of the world from totalitarian governments and giving them freedoms never before imagined.

"Is there not a day to come, when Japheth shall do yet better than in his past? when Ham shall retrieve his disasters: when Shem shall reach shining heights yet untrodden? and a long and glorious destiny shall stretch before the three sons of Noah?" (Ibid.), pp. 169-171, excerpts above.

"What we have been trying to show is that the historical process reflects the interaction between three families of people descended respectively from the three sons of Noah whom God appears to have apportioned specific responsibilities and equally specific capabilities for the fulfillment of them; to Shem, responsibility for man's religious and spiritual well-being; to Japheth, his mental well-being; and to Ham, his physical well-being...all the great religions of the world - true and false - had their roots in the family of Shem, all true philosophical systems have originated within the family of Japheth, and the world's basic technology is a Hamitic contribution... When these three work together in balanced harmony, civilization as a whole has advanced.

"It is important to observe that all three are necessary for this. If any one element is given overemphasis the ultimate effect is detrimental! No society prospers which is over materialistic, or overly intellectual, or overly spiritual." (*Noah's Three Sons*, Dr. Arthur Custance, as cited in *Wilmington's Guide to the Bible)*, p. 34.

APPENDIX I

Chart of the 'supposed' Geological Ages

ERAS	PERIODS	CHAR. OF LIFE	EST. YRS. AGO
	Quaternary: Recent Epoch Pleistocene Epoch	Rise of modern plants and animals, and man	25,000 975,000
CENOZOIC	Tertiary: Pliocene Epoch Miocene " Oligocene " Eocene "	 Rise of mammals and development of highest plants	12,000,000 25,000,000 35,000,000 60,000,000 70,000,000
	Cretaceous	Modernized angio- sperms and insects abundant. Foraminifers profuse. Extinction of dinosaurs, flying reptiles, and ammonites.	
MESOZOIC	Jurassic	First (reptilian) birds. First of highest forms of insects. First (primitive) angiosperms.	70,000,000 to 200,000,000
	Triassic	Earliest dinosaurs, flying reptiles, marine reptiles, and primitive mammals. Cycads and conifers Modern corals common Earliest ammonites	
	Permian	Rise of primitive reptiles. Earliest cycads and conifers. Extinction of trilobites. First modern corals.	

PALEOZOIC	Pennsylvanian	Earliest known insects. Spore plants abundant.	
	Mississippian	Rise of amphibians. Culmination of crinoids.	
	Devonian	First known seed plants Great variety of boneless fishes. First evidence of amphibians.	
	Silurian	Earliest known land animals. Primitive land plants. Rise of fishes. Brachiopods, trilobites, and corals abundant.	200,000,000 to 500,000,000
	Ordovician	Earliest known vertebrates. Grap-tolites, corals, bra-chiopods, cephalopods and trilobites abundant. Oldest primitive land plants.	
	Cambrian	All subkingdoms of invertebrate animals represented. Brachiopods and trilobites common.	
PROTEROZOIC	Keweenawan		500,000,000 to
	Huronian	Primitive water-dwelling plants and	
	animals.	1,000,000,000	
ARCHEOZOIC	Timiskaming	Oldest known life (mostly indirect	1,000,000,000 to
	Keewatin	evidence).	1,800,000,000

APPENDIX II

The Human Ear

When sound vibrations enter the auricle (the ear we see), they move along the auditory canal to the middle ear to the little window (eardrum) which separates the outer ear from the middle ear. The middle ear is filled with air and consists of three tiny bones; the hammer, (attached to the eardrum), the anvil, (attached to the hammer), and the stirrup, (attached to the anvil), which all vibrate with sound waves. The stirrup in turn is attached to the footplate which is attached to a small oval, skin-covered window and connects the footplate to the bones of the inner ear. The Eustachian tube connects the middle ear with the throat.

The main part of the inner ear is the cochlea which looks like a snail shell. It has three coils, the latter ending in another skin-covered window (the round window) which acts as a safety valve for the inner ear, between the cochlea and the middle ear.

The semicircular canals are three small curved bony tubes attached to the cochlea. They are to help you keep your balance and do not contribute to hearing.

The cochlea and semicircular canals are filled with liquid. The cochlea has to do with hearing and the semicircular canal (and its accompanying bony tubes) help with your sense of balance.

Sound (vibrating air) enters the outer ear and passes into the eardrum. These vibrations are weak but cause the eardrum to move slightly. The vibration of the eardrum pushes the hammer, which pushes the anvil, which pushes the stirrup. The footplate of the stirrup pushes the oval window of the inner ear. Each phase makes the vibrations stronger. The push on the oval window is 22 times greater than the push on the eardrum.

The cochlea changes the vibrations of the footplate into electrical signals which move the liquid in the cochlea. The auditory nerve carries the electrical signals to the brain which changes the signals into sound. And all this took place in an instant when God breathed into Adam the breath of life.

APPENDIX III

The Uniqueness of the Human Eye

The human eye is shaped like a ball and is about one inch across and weighs about .25 of an ounce.

The outer layer of the eyeball (the white of the eye) is tough, white, fibrous tissue called the sclera. In the middle it becomes transparent allowing light to pass through. This part is called the cornea.

The cornea is covered by a delicate transparent membrane, the conjunctiva. It produces fluid which washes the eye in conjunction with the tear glands keeping the eye clean and moist.

Inside the sclera (the white) is a dark red layer called the choroid which contains blood vessels that nourish the eye. It also contains pigmented cells which absorb light and prevent it from being reflected back to the light-sensitive layer of the eye. The iris, (which gives the eye color), at the front of the eye, is part of the choroid layer. The iris is actually a muscle which opens and closes to control the light entering the eye through the pupil. In the center of the iris is the pupil, a hole through which the light passes into the eye.

Inside the choroid is another layer called the retina. Cells in the retina detect light and turn it into electrical nerve messages. These messages are carried by the nerves in the back of the eye to the optic nerve, and then to the brain. There is a blind spot in the back of the eye, where the nerves leave the eye, and no light is detected.

Two chambers of liquid are contained in the eye. In the front of the eye, behind the cornea is the aqueous humor. The iris is located at the back of this chamber, and behind the iris is the lens. The lens is transparent and focuses light onto the retina. Behind the lens is the vitreous humor, a clear jelly-like substance which makes up most of the eyeball.

The lens is suspended between the cornea and the retina by ligaments which are joined to the ciliary muscles. When light rays enter the eye they must be 'bent' in order to form a clear, sharp image on the retina. This is done by the curved cornea, the front tear film layer, and the lens. One-quarter of the focusing and fine adjustments of focusing these light rays are done by the lens which is about the size of a pea and is located just behind the iris. It is clear and yellowish in appearance and is made up of layers of cells like an onion. It is biconvex - thicker in the center than on the edges; flatter in the front than at the back. It is surrounded by an elastic capsule. It appears to rest in a clear plastic bag of yellowish jelly. The capsule is suspended by thread-like ligaments from the ciliary muscles which are attached to the sclera.

The ciliary muscles relax and the sclera, stretched by the pressure of the vitreous humor, pulls the lens into a thin, flat shape to bring distant objects into focus. To focus on nearby objects the ciliary muscles contract and shorten. Thus the lens is released from the pull of the sclera and it bulges outward allowing you to see close objects.

The tear glands wash a watery liquid over the conjunctiva and cornea, cleaning and disinfecting the surface of the eye. This liquid then drains down the eye and collects in the inner corners of the eyelid. It passes through the tiny holes in the inside corners of the eyes and is carried through them to the tear sac then to the back of the nose where it is swallowed. The eye is one of the most intriguing of God's creations and the evolutionist still can not explain its make-up or how it can work with such wonderful precision as a result of the evolutionary process. When Adam became a living soul all these processes began instantaneously. Only an omnipotent God can account for this.

BIBLIOGRAPHY

The Internet: Barnett, Lincoln. The Universe and Dr. Einstein.

The Internet: Moon and Spencer. Binary Stars and the Velocity of Light.

The Internet: Jueneman, Frederic B. Industrial Research and Development.

The Internet: Stansfield, Dr. Biblical Age of the Earth.

The Internet: Brown, Walt, Center for Scientific Creation.

The Internet: Jopling, Allan V. Journal of Sedimentary Petrology, Vol. 36, No. 4.

The Internet: Charles, Robert W. Ph.D. Los Alamos National Laboratory.

————ABC Documentary. China the Land and the People. New York: Gallery Books, 1988.

Adler, Irving and Ruth. Your Ears. New York: The John Day Co., 1963.

Aling, Charles F. Egypt and Bible History. Grand Rapids: Baker Book House, 1981.

Allen, Richard Hinckley. Star Names, their Lore and Meaning. New York: Dover Publishers, Inc., 1963.

Anderson, Bernhard W. Understanding the Old Testament. Englewood Cliffs, New Jersey: Prentice-Hall, Inc., 1957.

Anderson, Neil T. Rompiendo Las Cadenas. Oregon: Harvest House Publishers, 1990.

Austin, Steven A., Ph.D., Grand Canyon, Monument to Catastrophe. California: Institute for Creation Research, 1994..

Biblical Archaeology Review, Publication. Washington, D.C. (3000 Connecticut Ave., N.W., Suite 300, 20008.

Bengston, Hermann; Bresciani, Edda; Caskel, Werner; Smith, Morton. The Greeks and the Persians, From the Sixth to the Fourth Centuries. London: Weidinfield and Nicolson, n.d.

Blundan, Caroline, Elvin, Mark. Cultural Atlas of China. New York: Facts on File, Inc., 1983.

Blunt, A.W.F., B.d. Israel in World History. London: Oxford University Press, 1927.

Boak, E. R. A History of Rome. New York: The Macmillan Co., 1925.

Botsford, George Willis, Ph.D. and Lillie Shaw Botsford. A Source Book of Ancient History. New York: The Macmillan Co., 1913.

Broderick, Mary, translator and editor. Outlines of Ancient Egyptian History. London: 1892.

Bryant, Jacob. Observations and Inquiries; Relating to Various Parts of Ancient History Containing Dissertations on the Wind Euroclydon, and on the island Melite, together with an Account of Egypt in Its Most Early State, and of the Shepherd Kings (The time of Their coming, the Province which They Particularly Possessed, and to Which the Israelites Afterwards Succeeded, is Endeavoured to be Stated. The Whole Calculated to Throw Light on the History of that Ancient Kingdom, as Well As On the Histories of the Assyrians, Chaldeans, Babylonians, Edomites, and Other nations.). Cambridge, 1767.

Bullinger, E. W. The Witness of the Stars. Grand Rapids: Kregel Publishers, 1976.

Callcott, Lady. Little Arthur's History of England, London: John Murray, 1875.

Cannop, Thirlwall, D.D. A History of Greece. Volumes I, II, London, 1835.

Clarke, Adam, LL.D. Clarke's Commentary on the Old Testament, Vol. I. New York: Abingdon-Cokesbury Press, n. d.

Cooke, Josiah Parsons. Religion and Chemistry. New York: Charles Scribners Sons, 1880.

Cotterill, H.G., M.A. Ancient Greece. New York: Frederick A. Stokes Co., 1913.

Coye, Molly Joel, Livingston, Jon, and Highland, Jean, editors. China Yesterday and Today. New York: Bantam Books, 1984.

Cox, Rev. George W. A General History of Greece. New York: Harper and Brothers, 1876.

Cox, Rev. George W. Lives of Greek Statesman, Volumes I and II. London: Longmans, Green and Co., 1885.

Cramer, Rev. J.A., M.A. A Geographical and Historical Description of Ancient Greece, Volumes I, II, and III. Oxford: Clarendon Press, 1828.

Creasy, Sir Edward S., The Fifteen Decisive Battles of the World. New York: Everyman's Library, 1962.

Curtius, Ernst, Ph.D., History of Greece, Vol. I-III. New York: Scribner's Sons, 1867.

Davidson, A. B. & Streane, Q. W. The Book of the Prophet Ezekiel. London, Great Britain: Cambridge: at the University Press, 1916.

Davis, John D. Davis Dictionary of the Bible. Tennessee: The Varsity Company, 1973.

Davis, William Stearns. Readings in Ancient History. Vol. I, Boston, New York, Chicago: Allyn and Bacon, 1912.

de Vaux, Roland, O. P., Translated by John McHugh. Ancient Israel: Its Life and Institutions. New York: McGraw-Hill Book Company, 1961.

Dods, Marcus, D.D. Genesis. Edinburgh: Morrison and Gibb Limited, for T. & T. Clark, 1900.

Dods, Marcus, D. D. The Book of Genesis. The Expositor's Bible, Armstrongs, n.d. (pages are missing).

Duruy, Victor. History of Greece, Vol. I-III. Boston: Estes and Lauriat, 1890.

Edersheim, Alfred. The Old Testament Bible History. Grand Rapids, Michigan: William B. Eerdman's Publishing Co., 1972.

Edersheim, Alfred. Prophecy and History in Relation to the Messiah. Grand Rapids: Longmans, Green, and Co., 1901 original printers, reprint 1980.

Eliot, Samuel. History of Liberty, Vols. I, II. Boston: Little, Brown and Co., 1853.

Ellicot, John, D. D., editor. Layman's Handy Commentary on the Bible: Genesis. Grand Rapids: Zondervan Publishing House, 1957, original publication 1903.

Edwards, Jonathan. The History of Redemption. Grand Rapids, Michigan: Associated Publishers and Authors Inc.

Feinberg, Charles Lee. The Prophecy of Ezekiel. Chicago, Illinois: Moody Press, 1984.

Fisher, George Park, D.D., LL. D., Outlines of Universal History, New York and Chicago: Ivison, Blakeman, and Co., 1885.

Fiske, John. The Historical Writings of John Fiske, Volume VI, The Beginnings of New England. Boston: Houghton, Mifflin and Company, 1902.

Gesenius, H. W. F. Hebrew-Chaldee Lexicon to the Old Testament. Grand Rapids: Baker Book House, 1979 reprint.

Gibbon, Edward. The History of the Decline and Fall of the Roman Empire, Vol. 1. London: The Folio Society, 1983, reprinted from the 1910 edition.

Gillies, John, LL.D., F.A.S. The History of Ancient Greece. Philadelphia: Thomas Wardle, 1835.

Gish, Duane T. Dinosaurs by Design. China: Master Books, 1998.

Goldsmith. The Grecian History, From the Earliest State to the Death of Alexander the Great. Philadelphia: Grigg, Eliot and Co., 1847.

Grant, Michael. The History of Ancient Israel. New York: Charles Scribner's Sons, 1984.

Greenridge, A.H.J., M.A. A Handbook of Greek Constitutional History. New York: Macmillan and Co., 1896.

Grimal, Pierre, Ed. Larousse World Mythology. Prometheus Press, N. Y., 1965.

Grote, George. History of Greece, in four volumes. New York: W.L. Allison Co., 1849.

Hall, Verna M. Self-Government with Union. San Francisco: The American Christian Constitution Press, 1962.

Hebbe, G.C., LL. D. Universal History. New York: DeWitt and Davenport, 1848.

Heeren, A.H.L. A Sketch of the Political History of Ancient Greece. Oxford: D.A. Talboys, 1834.

Henderson, George. Studies in the Book of Genesis. Great Britain: Stanley L. Hunt Ltd., n.d.

Hislop, Rev. Alexander. The Two Babylons. Neptune, New Jersey: Loizeaux Brothers, 1959, originally published in 1916.

Hunt, Dave. Beyond Seduction. Eugene, Oregon: Harvest House Publisher, 1987.

Hutchinson, Horace G. The Greatest Story in the World. New York: D. Appleton and Co., 1928.

Joppie, A. S. The Ministry of Angels. Grand Rapids: Baker Book House, 1963.

Kagan, Donald, editor. Botsford and Robinson's Hellenic History. New York: Macmillan Co., 1969.

Keller, Werner, translated by William Neil. The Bible as History. New York: William Morrow and Co., 1956.

Kirk, Russell. The Roots of American Order. La Salle, Illinois: Open Court, 1974.

Kofahl, Robert E. Handy Dandy Evolution Refuter. San Diego: Beta Books, 1977.

Lattimore, Richmond, translator. The Iliad of Homer. Chicago and London: The University of Chicago Press, 1967.

Life Application Bible, KJV. Illinois: Tyndale House Publishers, Inc., 1989.

Locke, John. Treatise of Civil Government and a Letter Concerning Toleration. New York: Appleton-Century Company, Inc., 1937, renewed by Meredith Publishing Co., 1965.

Lord, John, LL.D. The Old Pagan Civilizations and Jewish Heroes and Prophets, Volume I. of Beacon Lights of History. New York: William H. Wise and Co., Inc., 1920.

Lord, John, LL.D. Jewish Heroes and Prophets, Volume II. of Beacon Lights of History (The World's Heroes and Master Minds). New York: Fords, Howard, and Hulbert, 1913.

Lord John, LL.D. <u>Ancient Achievements,</u> Volume III. of <u>Beacon Lights of History</u> (The World's Heroes and Master Minds). New York: Fords, Howard, and Hulbert, 1913

Margalit, Baruch. Article on "Mesha, the King of Moab". Biblical Archaeology Review, November/December, 1986.

Miller, Dorothy Ruth. <u>A Handbook of Ancient History in Bible Light.</u> New York, London, and Edinburgh: Fleming H. Revell Co., 1937.

Morris, Henry M. and Whitcomb, John C. <u>The Genesis Flood.</u> The Presbyterian and Reformed Publishing Company, 1982.

Morris, John D. <u>The Young Earth.</u> Colorado Springs: Creation-Life Publishers, Inc., 1994.

Morris, Henry M. <u>The Genesis Record.</u> Grand Rapids: Baker Book House, 1976.

Morris, Henry, M. <u>Scientific Creationism</u>. San Diego: Creation-Life Publishers, 1974.

Muller, Herbert J. <u>The Loom of History</u>. New York: Harper and Brothers, 1958.

Nelson, Byron C. <u>The Deluge Story in Stone</u>. Minneapolis: Bethany Fellowship, Inc., 1968, originally published in 1931.

Orr, James, E.d. <u>International Standard Bible Encyclopedi</u>a, Wm. B. Eerdmans, 1939.

Parker, Steve, editor. <u>The Eye and Seeing</u>. New York: Franklin Watts, 1989.

Peloubet, Rev. F. N. D.D., and Peloubet, M. A. <u>Select Notes, A Commentary of the International lessons for 1887.</u> Boston: W. A. Wilde and Company, 1886.

Phillips, John. <u>Exploring Genesis</u>. Chicago: Moody Press, 1980.

Phillips, John. <u>Exploring the World of the Jew</u>. Neptune, New Jersey: Loizeaux Brothers, 1993.

Prideaux, Humphrey. <u>The Old and New Testament Connected in the History of the Jews and Neighboring Nations From the Declension of the Kingdoms of Israel and Judah to the Time of Christ,</u> Volumes I, II. London: Strand and H. Lintot, 1719.

Ragozin, Zenaide A. <u>The Story of Assyria</u>. New York: G.P. Putnam's Sons, 1889.

Ragozin, Zenaide A. <u>The Story of Chaldea</u>. New York: G. P. Putnam's Sons, 1909.

Ragozin, Zenaide A. <u>Media, Babylon, and Persia.</u> New York: G. P. Putnam's Sons, 1903.

Rawlinson, George, M.A., F.R.G.S. <u>Ancient History</u>. New York: The Colonial Press, 1900.

Rawlinson, George, M.A. <u>Ancient Egypt.</u> New York: G. P. Putnam's Sons, 1887.

Rawlinson, George, M. A. <u>Phoenicia</u>. New York: G. P. Putnam's Sons, 1908.

Rawlinson, George, M.A. <u>The Five Great Monarchies of the Ancient Eastern World,</u> in Three volumes. New York: Dodd, Mead, and Co., 1862.

Rawlinson, George. <u>The Seven Great Monarchies of the Ancient Eastern World</u>, in three volumes. New York: H. L. Burt Company, 1870.

Rehwinkel, Alfred M. <u>The Wonders of Creation.</u> Minneapolis: Bethany Fellowship, Inc., 1974, original publication 1887.

Rehwinkel, Alfred M. <u>The Flood</u>. Illinois: Good News Publishers, n.d.

Reischauer, Edwin O. and Fairbank, John K. East Asia the Great Tradition, Harvard University Boston: Houghton Mifflin Co., 1960.

Ringenberg, Loyal R. The Living Word in History. Winona Lake: Lambert Huffman, Publisher, 1953.

Rollin, Charles. The Ancient History of the Egyptians, Carthaginians, Assyrians, Babylonians, Medes and Persians, Grecians, and Macedonians, in two volumes. Derby and Jackson, 1857.

Ross, Allen P. Creation and Blessing, A Guide to the Study and Exposition of Genesis. Grand Rapids: Baker Book House, 1988.

Rushdoony, Rousas John. The Institutes of Biblical Law. U.S.A: The Presbyterian and Reformed Publishing Company, 1973.

Ryrie, Charles C. Biblia de Estudio Ryrie. Illinois: Moody Press, 1991.

Schaff, Philip. History of the Christian Church. New York: Charles Scribner's Sons, 1883.

Seiss, Joseph A. The Gospel in the Stars. Grand Rapids: Kregel Publishers, 1972.

Shuckburg, E.S., Litt.D. Greece. New York: Putnam's Sons, 1905.

Shuckford, Samuel, D.D. The Sacred and Profane History of the World Connected, in three volumes. London: 1743.

Silverstein, Dr. Alvin, and Silverstein, Virginia B. The Story of Your Ear. New Yord: Coward, McCann and Geoghegan, 1981.

Sinclair, Kevin. The Yellow River. Los Angeles: Knapp Press, 1987.

Smith, Wilbur. Therefore, Stand: Christian Apologetics. Michigan: Baker Book House, 1945.

Sohm, Rudolf. Outlines of Church History. London: MacMillan and Company, 1895.

Stager, Lawrence E. "Why were Hundreds of Dogs Buried at Ashkelon?" BAR, May/June, 1991, Vol. XVII, No. 3.

Strong, James, S.T.D., LL.D. Strong's Exhaustive Concordance of the Bible, Nashville: Royal Publishers, Inc., n.d.

Süssman, Bethsabée and Roland. Beijing Photos. New York: Adama Books, 1987.

Swinton, William. Outlines of the world's History. New York, Cincinnati, Chicago: American Book Co., 1874..

Thalheimer, M.E. A Manual of Ancient History. Cincinnati and New York: Wilson, Hinkle and Co., 1872..

Thatcher, Oliver J., Editor-in-chief. The Library of Original Sources, in eight volumes. Milwaukee, Wisconsin: University Research Extension Co., 1907.

The Origin of Laws, Arts, and Sciences Among the Most Ancient Nations, in three volumes. Edinburgh: 1775.

Thompson, J. A. The Bible and Archaeology. Grand Rapids: Wm. B. Eerdmans Publishing Co., 1972.

Thorndike, Lynne. A Short History of Civilization. New York: F. S. Crofts and Co., 1937.

Unger, Merrill F. Unger's Bible Dictionary. Chicago: Moody Press, 1957.

Vila, Samuel, and Santa María, Darío A. Diccionario Bíblico Ilustrado. Barcelona Spain: Talleres Gráficos de la M.C.E. Horeb, A.C., 1981.

Voegelin, Eric. Order and History, Vol. I, Israel and Revelation. Louisiana State University Press. (Vail-Ballon Press, Inc.), 1961.

Walker, A.H., M.A. A Primer In Greek Constitutional History. Oxford, 1902.

Walton, Rus. Fundamentals for American Christians. Plymouth: Plymouth Rock Foundation, n.d.

Walvoord, John F. The Beginnings of the Nations. Grand Rapids: Zondervan Pub. House, 1967.

Weaver, Grady. The Mainspring of Human Progress. New York: The Foundation for Economic Education, 1974.

Webster, Noah, LL. D. An American Dictionary of the English Language. New York: S. Converse, 1828, republished by F.A.C.E., Anaheim, Ca., 1967.

Whibley, Leonard, M.A. A Companion to Greek Studies. Cambridge: 1916.

Whiston, William, translator. Josephus Complete Works. Grand Rapids, Michigan: Kregel Publications, 1969.

Whitcomb, John C., Darius the Mede. New Jersey: Presbyterian and Reformed Publishing Co., 1959.

Willard, Emma. Ancient Geography. Hartford: Wm. Jas. Hamersley, 1852.

Willard, Emma. A System of Universal History in Perspective. Philadelphia: A. S. Barnes and Company, 1843.

Willmington, Dr. H. L. Willmington's Guide to the Bible. Illinois: Tyndale House Publishers, Inc., 1984.

Wood, Leon. A Survey of Israel's History. Grand Rapids, Michigan: Zondervan Publishing House, 1970.

Woodbridge, William Channing, and Emma Willard. Universal Geography. Hartford: Wm. Jas. Hamersley, 1852.

Woodrow, Ralph. Babilonia, Misterio Religioso. Riverside: Evangelistic Association, 1977.

World Book Encyclopedia. 1974 Edition, Vol. 3.

Wright, Julia McNair. Bricks From Babel. New York: John B. Alden, Publisher, 1885.

Youngblood, Ronald, ed. The Genesis Debate. Nashville: Thomas Nelson Publisher, 1986.

Zodhiates, Spiros, Th.D., compiler and editor. The Hebrew-Greek Key Study Bible, KJV version. Tennessee: AMG Publishers, 1984.

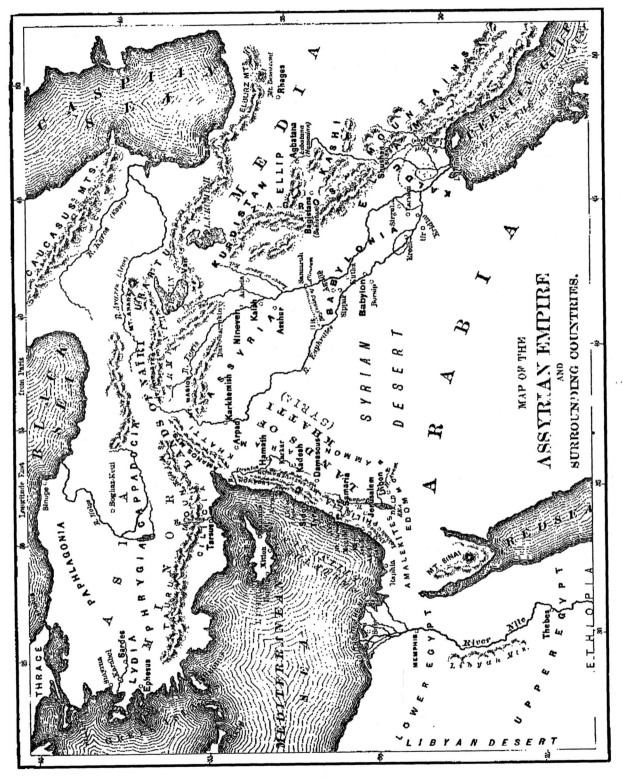

MAP OF THE
ASSYRIAN EMPIRE
AND
SURROUNDING COUNTRIES.

Assyrian Empire

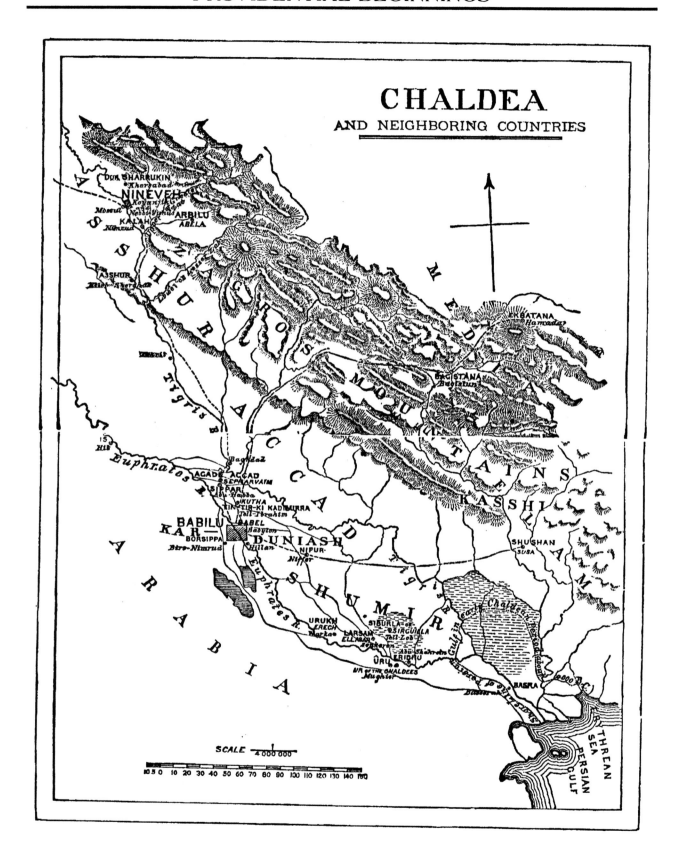

CHALDEA
AND NEIGHBORING COUNTRIES

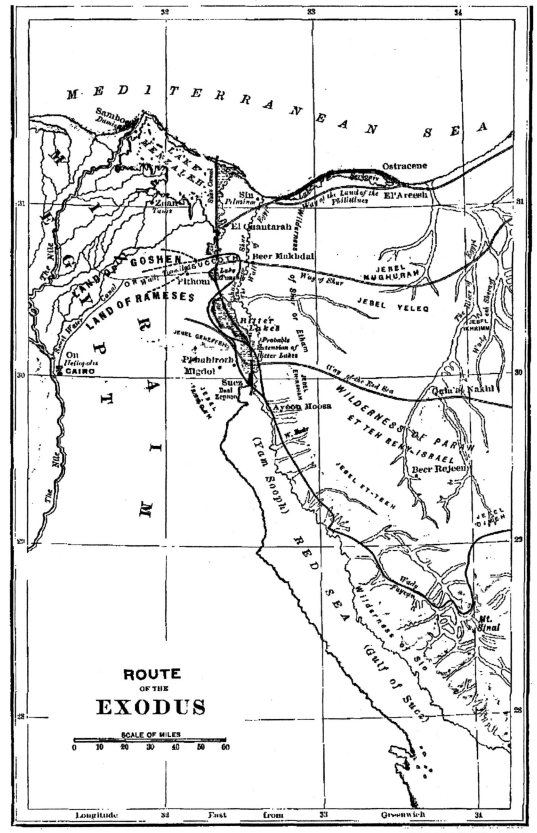

ROUTE
OF THE
EXODUS

(PELOUBETS, 1894)

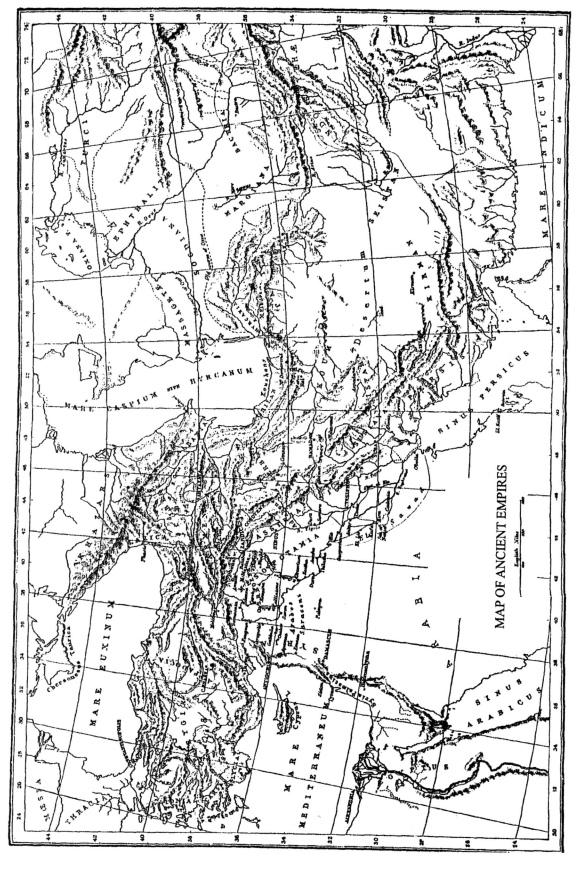

MAP OF ANCIENT EMPIRES

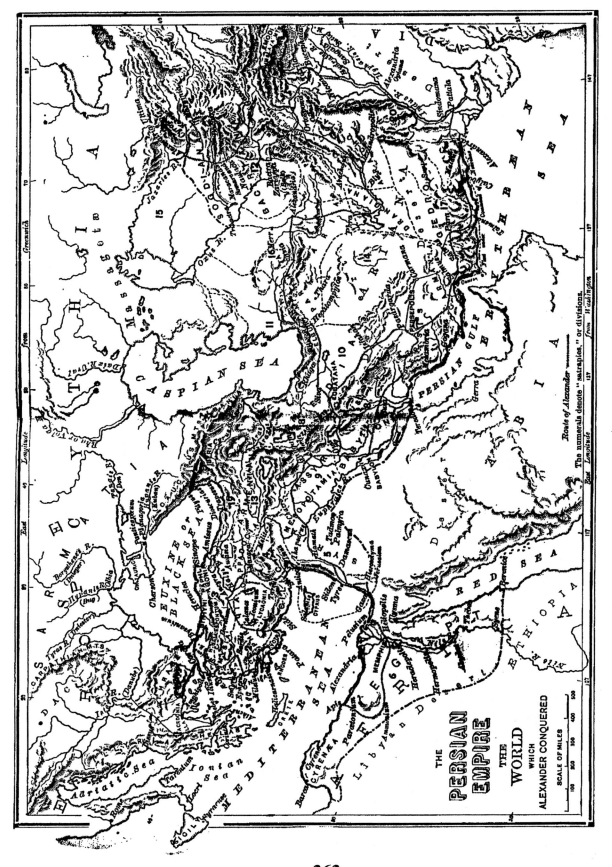

THE
PERSIAN
EMPIRE
THE
WORLD
WHICH
ALEXANDER CONQUERED

SCALE OF MILES

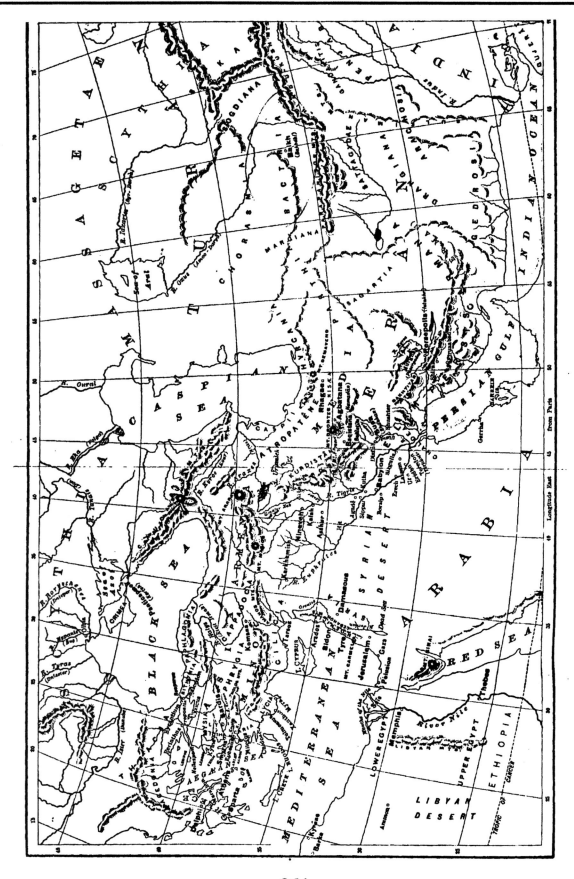

THE PERSIAN EMPIRE AND BORDERLANDS

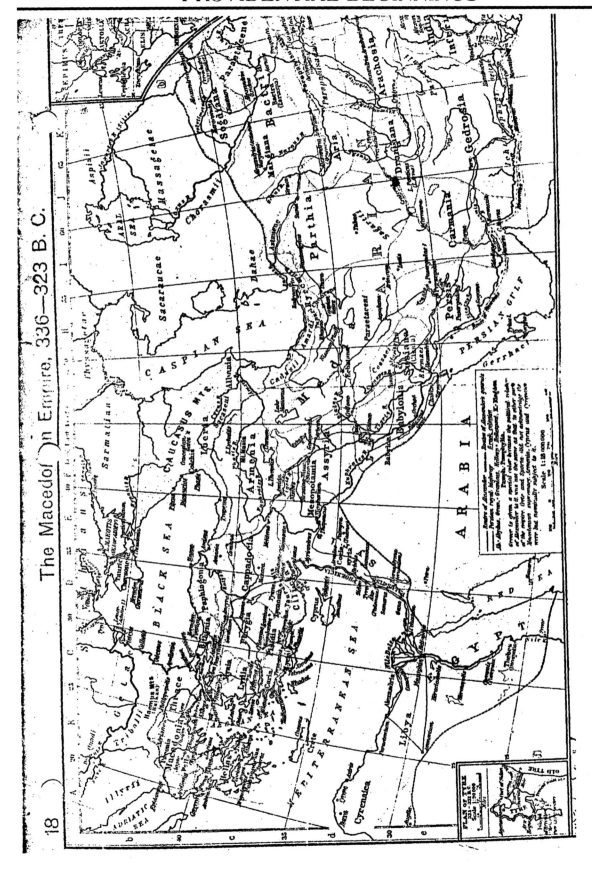

THE MACEDONIAN EMPIRE

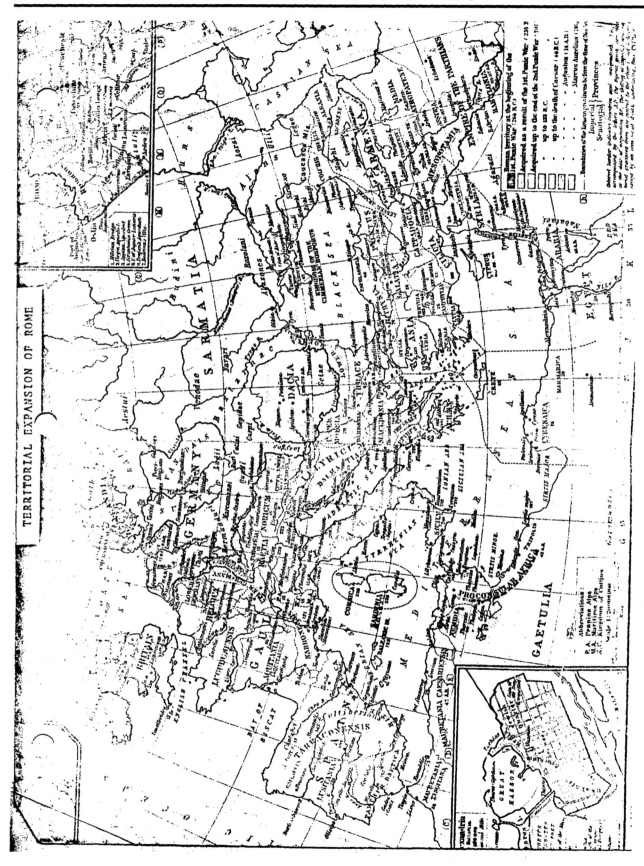

TERRITORIAL EXPANSION OF ROME

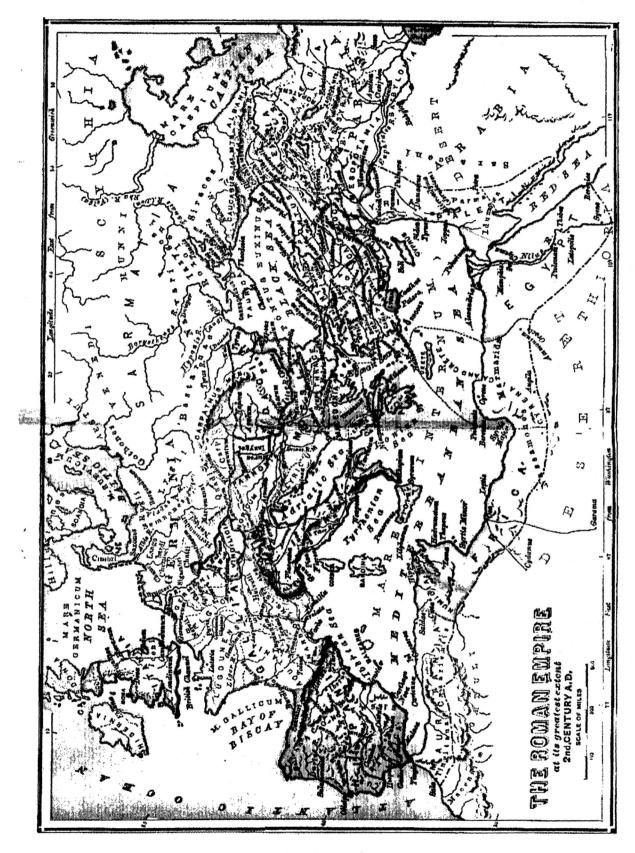

THE ROMAN EMPIRE
at its greatest extent
2nd CENTURY A.D.
SCALE OF MILES

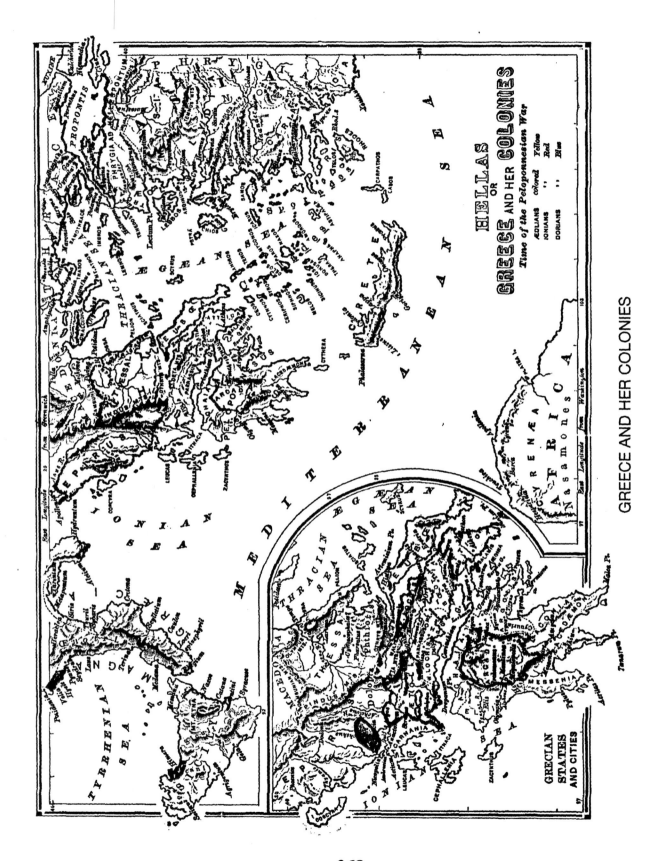

GREECE AND HER COLONIES

INDEX

Aaron 227,229-231,240,242,246-249
Abel 49,50,241
Abimelech 167,176,177,180,183,184,199
Abram 50,113,125,132,133,157-171,178
 Abraham 11,76,86,104,115,118,122,125,132-134,156,160-173,
 75-181,183-185,187,198,200,201,204,219,223,225-227,229,242,
 250,262,263,325
Abyssinia 76,112
Accad 78,91,129,138,143,154,165,167
 Akkadians
Adam 2,29,31,36,37,3943,45,47,55,101,164,231,245,272
Africa 34,58,7577,84,108,109,111,112114,122,134,136,175,227,254,
262,272,277, 283,303,340,343
Alexander the Great 30,97,265,295,296,298,312,319
Altai-Ural Mtns. 268,270
Amalekites 113,136,239,240
Ammon 76,113,140,148,175,253,256
 Ammonites 113,176,252
Amorite (s) 113,121,168
Anak 113
 Anakim 113
Angel (s) 2-5,6,13-21,44,51,52,89,175,228,243,244,248
Animal(s) 35,95,101103,130,131,138,168,176,179,185,190,192,193,
195,200,210,213,229,232,233,234,244,245,249,250,254,255,283
 Animal psychology 36
Anthracite coal 28,67
Antarctica 67
Arab (s)76,108,112,122,135,139,155,158,161,169,178,181,198,281
 Semitic Arabs 76
 Hamitic Arabs 76
 Japhetic Arabs 133
Arabia 63,76,90,93,134-136,142,226,227,272,293
Ararat 58
Arctic Ocean 63
Ark 53,54,56-58,62,68,69,138,228,239,249,251,252,253,300
Aram 119,125,136,138,139,142,180,187,228,239,249,251,252,253,
 Aramaeans 119,136,139,152
Armenia 58,112,118,126,136,138,139,141,151
Arphaxad 51,125,129,130,133,160,180
 son of 129
Ashkelon 10,115-117
Ashtoreth 115,116,118
Asia 84,125,126,265,268,270-273,277-279,282-285,290,293,300-304
Asia Minor 118,119,125,136,139,175,283-285,289-291,294-297,313-
316
Asshur 78,112,119,125-128,137-139,150,151,160,262
Assyria(an) 78,79,83,84,89,90-93,97,109,110,114,118,119,121,122,
126,129,137,139,140,142-146,148,149,151,152-156,167,254,262,284
 Assyrian Empire 77,78,82,90,98,125,126,137139,142,143,152,
 284
 Assyro-Babylonian Empire 77
Atmosphere 2,14,21,22,58,61,62,66,103,128

Baal 79-81,115,116,126,152,181,232
 Baalism 255
Babel
70,78,79,80,81,98,100,104,121,132,134,137,157,173,230,273,275,279,300
Babylon 30,75,77,78-81,83-86,88-98,109,110,115,116,118,121,122,
125,129,130,136-139,141-143,146-154,257,262,272,273,284-287,290,
291,293,312,315,317-319
 Babylonian 77,79-81,84,85,87-90,92,93,97,104,105,110,114,
 120,126,127,129,140,142,149,156,158,164,285, 290,293,335
 Babylonian Empire 77,91,92,98,110,256,291,293
Bactriana 79,291
Basalt 63,64,66

Beasts 11,35,40,95,97,139,155,192,232234,266,282,291,312,317,
325,341
Beersheba 181,214,215,236
Behring, Strait of 62,269,280,281,283
Belshazzar 97,121,129,291-293
Belus 79,81,315
 Temple of 79,81
Benjamin 121,189,197,199,209-213
 tribe of
Beth-el (Bethel) 167,168,188,189,197,198,200,219,256,257
Big-bang 6
Birds 10,11,21,33,34,95,282,294
Black Sea 266,267,297,301,317,333
Brazil 76,136,262
Burbank, Luther 271

Caesar 328-332,334,337,340
 Julius 328,330,334
 Augustus 330-332
Cain 42,48-51,166,241
Calendar 88,89,142,215,235,273,330,332
Canaan 4,69,75,113,115-
118,121,125,166,184,189,217,218,220,221,223,251,262,287
Canaanites
52,70,112,113,117,121,164,167,169,172,196,201,221,238,241
 Sons of 113,115,116,118
Capital punishment 39,54,68,243
Canary Islands 136,262
 Canaries 136
Carthaginians 136,142
Caspian Sea 276,283,331
Celts 266,267
Cenozoic 59
Chaldea 93,119,122,126,129,130,140-142,152,163,164,166
 Chaldean 78-80, 84,85,92,116,126,129,132,143,146-
149,152,155,158,165,170,196,301
China 63,84,121,159,265,270-272,274-278
 Chinese 121,270-279,281,283
Christ 47,48,58,83,85,86,88,94,112,120,121,269,271,272,274,283,
287, 289,305, 325,326,331,332,334-337,339,342,343
Chromosomes 40,41,50
Circumcision 168,170,171,195,229,279,283,320,334
Civil Government 49,54,68,165,307,326
Cleopatra 100,110,313,318,320-331
Comets 5,31
Confucius 271,275,277
 Confucianism 272,275
Constantine I 88, 342,343
Copper 98,99,100,114,120,133,161,227
Council of Nicea 85,343
Creation of Man 36-40,88
Creation of Woman 40
Creatures of the Deep 34
Curse (ed) 9,47,55,68,163,176-178,181,185,204,256,263
Cush 75-79,80,81,98,99,134,227,286,301
 Cushites 76,98,125,136,279,286
Cycles 29,57,121
 Times and seasons 10
 Day and night 11,35,68
Cyrus 90-92,97,98,110,130,284-286,288-294,296,312

Dagon 78,87,116,149
Daniel 16,17,86,93-95,97,244,286,292,293,296,312,314-319
Dark Ages 134,251,343
Darius the Mede 130,285,286,
Darwin, Charles 7,64
Demons 20,52,87,131-133,191,269,288

Deposition 63,64,67
Dinosaurs 6,35,55,64
Dispersion 2,70,75,104,118,133-135,280,300,337,339
Divine Right of Kings 78,251
Dragons 35,86,291

Earthquake (s) 26,61,64,175
Eber 129,133,134,157,160,161,205,231
Egypt 28,31,41-43,53,63,67,75,76,79,81,83,84,93-95,100,102, 113,
114,118,119,122,123,128,137,139,140,142,144,148,152-154,161,
167,169,170,176,178,183,199-201,205-207,209-211,213-218,220-
225,228-242,245-248,251,253, 258,262,268,286,287,293,299,313,
314,316-319,329,332,333,341
    Egyptian (s) 52,76,80,84,98-104,106-108,110,112,113, 118,
    119,127,128,136,142,144,145,149,153,161,164,167,169, 204-
    212,215-217,221-226,228,230-235,272,293,301,318,324,329
Elam 113,125,146-150,152,154-156,159,160,317
    Elamites 125,147-151,155,159,160,268,283
Elohim 3,45,126,127,162,189,
Embalm (-ers, -ing) 101,102,136,220,221,281
Emim (s) 113
Equator 25,27,30,64,76,105
Erosion 10,26,32,62
Esarhaddon 152,153
Esau 119,181-187,189,192-194,197,198,201,203,227,239,334
    Edom (-ites)
117,136,146,148,186,187,194,197,198,238,253,256,334
    Idumeans 187,198
Essenes 335,336,340
Ethiopia
43,75,76,99,108,109,112,123,135,137,144,146148,152,153,227,256,
286,293
Evolution 1,2,5,6,7-11,29,32,33,57,59,63,64
Euphrates
79,93,109,110,126,129,130,136,138,147,149,157,162,180,254,291,
292,318,319,325,333
Europe
25,63,86,108,115,119,122,125,134,295,303,307,314,317,332,343,
332,343
Evolution 1,2,5,6,7-11,29,32,33,57,59,63,64
Exodus (the) 2,111,113,198,222,225,230,235,236

Fall (the) 1,20,43-48,50,54,55,58
Feast of Unleavened Bread 244
Feast of Harvest 244
Feast of Ingathering 245,250
Firmament 21,28,130,300
Fish 33,34,67,78,87,102,114-116,118,131,149,175,216,232,268
Flood 1,5,6,15,24,27-29,31,35,46,50,53-70,75,77,79,87,99,101,111,
113,156,161,173,231,232,267,279,280,287,292,300
Fossils 5-7,11,26,32,55,58,59,60-64,68
Foundation (s) 3,7,13,26,38,62,63,151,198,271-279
Fowls 40,58,59,95

Gap Theory 4,6
Garden of Eden 7,85
Geologic 4,5,7,11,26,32,55,59,64
Germans 266
    Germany 63,266,267
Giants 52,113
Gibraltar, Strait of 109,115
Golden Calf 84,230,241,246,247,255
    Mneus 101,241,246
Gomer 286,297,322
    Gomerites 266,267
Gomorrah 88,89,160,167,172,173,175,291
Goshen 201,215-217,223-225,236

Grand Canyon 65
Granite 6,26,62-64,66,134
Greek 28,80,84,100,103,104,109,113,114,116,117,120,242,298,299
    Greece 83,84,106,287,301-304,306-312,314,318,322,326,329,
    333,338,343
    Grecians 296,302,303
    Grecian Empire 312

Hagar 169,172,177,178,181
Ham 54,69,70,75,76,80,87,90,98,101,107,122,123,125,128,136-138,
156,157,167-169,172,177,227,238,262,265,267,272,298,301
    Hamites 69,122,181,201,300,303
    Hamitic tribes 75,130,139,152,195,201,262
Hammurabi (Laws of) 91,92,121,159,169
Haran 160,162,165,167,180,186,188,195,197,199
Hebrews 1-3,12-17,19,21,36,41-43,48,49,70,80,83,94,110,111,118,
121,125,127,132,136,149,157,160,162,169,181,183,192,199,204-206,
208,212,217,223,224,227,233,237,241,244,276,289,302,319,320
Hebron 119,167,180,181,197,199,209,214,236,252,334
Hellenes 302-304,322
Hieroglyphics 76,99,119,167,272
Hittites 84,113,118-120,137-139,142,152,165,167,180,186,255
Holy Spirit 2,8,12,13,38,48,83-85,116,244
Horus 84,102-104
Hyksos 104,108,110,111,114,119,215,223,225,226

Ice Age 66
India 79,82,84,114,115,122,135,137,265,266,275,276,279,282,284,
286, 287, 314,315,325
Indus River 159,293
Isaac 119,161,165,167,169-171,177-187,194,197,198,201,222,223,
226
Ishmael 76,134,161,167,169-171,178,181,186,198,214,230
    Ishmaelites
Ishtar 19,78,81,116,119-121
Israel 1,18,41,53,70,82,85,89,94,96,108-112,116-118,121,122,291,
296,303,319,320,332
    Israelites 70,75,78,84,102,111-113,117,118,121,122,294,334

Jacob 107,121,156,161,163-165,181-201,203,209-211,214-218,220-
223,226,230,236,251,255
Japheth 69,77,122,125,130,148,152,156,157,169,262,265-268,272,
280,287,288,298,301,302,322,343
    Japhethites 69,122,265,279,322,343
Javan 265,297,298,301,302,304
Jeroboam 109,254-258,263
Jerusalem 12,89,93,94,96,109,110,112,121,138,140,143,148,149,151,
164,197,201,252,254,258,262,263,286,290,292,293,296, 314,319,320,
322,334,339-341
Jews 52,70,84,9193,97,125,133,138,139,145,151,157,163,164,170,
171,207,254,262,265,267,272,286,290,291,296,297,309,314, 317-
322,334-337,339,340,343
Joktan 76,129,133-135,169,262
    Joktan Araba
Joseph 52,107,108,110,170,187,189,194,195,197-201,203-218,220-
223,230,236,332
Judah 93,94,97,109,110,113,142,143,145-147,149,152,163,189,197,
200-203, 211,213,215,218,219,252,256,258,294,332

Kaldu (land of) 140,150
Kar-Dunyash (Babylon) 137,143,148
Kasshi 148
Katti 148
Kenite(s) 226,240
Keturah 76,134,169,185,204,206

Laban 161,186-192,199

Latin (s) 266,322,323,333,341,342
Leah 188,189,210,218
Limestone 65,66
Logograms 271,274
Lot 53,125,160,165-167,174-176
Lybia 109,136,314
    Libyans 136

Maccabees 298,319,321,334,335
Macedonia (-ans) 295,303,306,310,311,313-315,317,318
Macpelah 119
Magi 79,388,389,315
    Magians
Malay (s) 122,268,270,278,279,280
Manna 231,239
Mantle 26,61
Mariolatry 85,326
Mammal (s) 35,36,59
Marriage 48,49,50,76,82,111,113,118,121,174,180,181,183,189,195,
202 ,208,227,243,263,283,336
Mede (s) 88,89,90,93,97,98,109,110,130,283-292
    Madai, 75,266,268,283,301
Memphis 101-103,105,107,112
Mendel, Gregory 6
Merodach 80
    Merodach Baladan 143,146-150,152,155
    (King of bit Yakin)
Mesopotamia 120,121,126,129,130,139,142,157,160,165,180
Messiah 1,48,50,51,53,61,84,85,97,125,161,163-165,176,244,262
Meteor 4,5,32,61
Midian 226,227,229,230
    Midianites 181,201,207
Mizraim 75,98,99,101,107,111-113,136,221,262
    son of Ham 75
    founder of Egypt 75
    sons of 111
Moab 113,117,143,146,148,175,253,256
    Moabites 52,113,176,238
Mohammed 86
    Moslem 171
    Mohammedanism 86
    Mahomet 139
Mohorovic Discontinuity 26
Moon 28,79,87,88,100,103,109,116,120,122,124,128,131,133,135,
139,159,171, 199,276,282,300,339,301
Mongols 268,270,277
    Mongolian 270,280,283,287
Morgan, Thomas 6
Moses 2,52,91,111,156,170,180,215,222,225-232,234,236-242,244-
251,262,320
Mutations 6,7,55,335,336,339
Mythology 80,101,102,118,282

Nahor 133,160,161,165,180,192
Nebuchadnezzar 92-97,110,114,257
Necho 93,109,110,152,153
New Age 9,50,85,104
Nile River 98,104,105,108,109,111,112,168,178,206,209,215,216,
224, 232, 233,236
Nimrod 75,77-83,80-82,86,87,89,91,93,98,100,101,107,120,125,
128,129,133,137,289
Nineveh 75,78,91-93,120,126,128,130,137,138,142,144,148,149-
156,160
Ninus 78,80,83,87,91,142
Noah 10,11,13,24,28,30,34,42,43,53,56,58, 60-63,68,100,101,107,
162,228,265,272,275,287

Olympiad 305,306,311,312,315
On 208
    city of Egypt 208
    priests of 208
Osiris 84,103,104

Palestine 29,93,112,113,118,121,122,152
Passover 234,235,244,250
Pasteur 8
Pathros 112
Persecution 319,338,339,341,342
Persia 115,117,158,162
    Persian 81,84,88,89,92,98,114,115,262
    Persian Empire 30,97,98,155,262
    Persian kings
    Persian Gulf 76,113,114,118,129,136,141,146,147,149, 157,
    178,262
Peleg 129,133,134,160
Petroleum 67,90,175
Pharaoh (s) 101,102,104,106-110,118,127,167,199,204,206-211,215,
216,218,219,223-225,228,229,231,232,234-236,238,241
Pharisees 320,333,342
Philip II 50,345
Philip of Macedon
Philistines 52,94,112,138,140,144,146,164,169,184,220,236,251
Phoenicia 98,113,114,142
    Phoenician(s) 102,109,113-118,121,122
    Religion of 115
Phut 75,112,113,118,136,262
Plague (s) 133,149,181,232,233,235,236
Plants 12,27,80,103,133,270,281
Plesiosaur 64
Population rates 33,143,224
Potiphar 107,201,203,204
Promised Land
70,89,133,164,194,215,219,221,222,230,233,250,251,263,264
Ptolemy (-ies) 28,136,299,310,311,317,318,329
Pyramid (s) 75,81,104-106,108,139,224, 226,281,282

Rachel 160,161,181,176,188,189-193
Rainbow 60,68
Rebekah 119,180,195-200,202,211
Red Sea 75,109,111,113,115,135,224,238,277,278
Rehoboam 109,112,253, 256,263
Reuben
Rome 84,86,105,106,115,321-323,325-331,333,334,338-340,343
    Roman (s) 302,303,307,310,316,318,322,323,325-
328,330,334,336,343,367,369
    Roman Empire 17, 86
    Roman Emperors 338-342
Roman Catholicism 28, 44,83,85,86,88,128,228,132,330
Rosetta Stone 100
Russia 50, 252,267-269,297

Sabbath 41-43,164,231,242,246,250,319-321,335
Sabeans 135
Sacrifice 77,80,102,117,120,139,141,178-180,192,196,211,215,219,
228, 231,232,234,236,241,245,246,250,276,280,299,316,320,324,
341,342
    human 117,178,179,280
Sadducees 320,321,333-335,342
Samaria 140,144,145,199,255,314
Saracen (s) 123
Sarai 165,167,169,170
    Sarah 167,169,170,172,176,177,178,180,181,183,199,218
Sargon 78,92,119,126,144-148,151,158-160,284
Satan 2,6,9,18-20,84,85,87,104,120,131,174,176,177,282

Saul 127,138,220,226,240,251,252,254,263,319,335
Savior 53,84,88,166,179,180,189,201,299,305,332,343
Scythians 153,156,161,163,270,282-284,287,293,294
Sea 25,75,88,109,112-115,119,120,122,131,135,138,140,141,146,
148,152,154,155,158,175,178,194,219,224,231,236238,265,269,270,275,295,296,
300,312,317,330
    content 25,125
    tides 25
    paths in the sea 25,26
Seleucus 316,317
    Seleucidae 316,317
Semiramis 82-84,87,104,137,267,301,314
Sennacherib 128,138,148-152
Septuagint 112,223,299,318
Serpent 44,45,56,77,82,83,103,104,121,190,231,267,280,282,288,301
Seth 2,50-52
Sheba 76,134,135,184
Shechem 167,195,196,199,211,218
Shem 51,54,69,75,87,102,112,113,119,122,125,133,136,137,156-158,
160,262,263,265,272,287
    Shemite (s) 76,87,112,113,119,130,153,159,160,180,265,
    sons of 122,125
    Semitic 265,288
Shinar (Plain of) 51,78,79,82,89,98,101,129,288,302
Shumiro-Accads 132,133,160,268
Siberia 61, 63,64,270
Sidon 94,113,114,118,140,141,148,152,253
    Sidonians 94,114,118
Sinai 100,121,161,228,241,299,305
Sodom 53,88,89,160,166,167,172,173-176,291
Solomon 76,94,108,114,118,122,135,139,153,160,170,252-
258,262,262
Soul 37-39,41,47,77,101,102,104,182,210,229,232,269,272,279,283,
287,301
Soviet Union 275
Spain 25,50,134,254,266,267,283,298,333
Spirit 12,36,38,39,77,83,84,86,101,131,132,145,163,168,179,180,
182,187,204,207,211,212,214,219,228,233,244,256,291,296,304,
306,308,310,319,322,325,326,328
Stars 29,100,130,133,168,199,215,278,282
    numbers 29
    for signs 29,30
    names 30
    groups 30
    the Zodiac 30,83,88,133
    the twelve signs 31
Sumeria 120
    Sumerian (s) 78,87,121,159
Sun 80,83,85,88,98,100-104,115,116,128,130,133,134,138,193,199,
208,215,233, 234,276,280,282,289
Syria 82,84,93,94,97,98,117,118,119,120-122,126,159,168,256
    Damascus, capital of 119,122,136,139,140,142,143,145,168

Tabernacle 41,85,102,219,228,230,246,248-250,273
Taurus (Mountains) 118,119,136,161,175
Temple of Janus 333,334
Ten Commandments 142,146,250
    Tables of Stone242, 245,246
    Second Tables of Stone 249
Terah 132,133,156,160-163
Teraphim 191,196
Thebes 103,107,153
Thermodynamics 9,10
    First Law 9
    Second Law 7,9,55,338
Tigris River 78,119
Totalitarian (-ism) 78

Tower of Babel 70,79-81,100,132,137,173,275
Turanian (s) 94,110,111,113-116,122,140,141,146,152,267,270
Tyre 94,110,111,113-116,122,140,141,146,152,297,304,314,317,319

Uniformitarian (-ism) 5,10,11,29,60,
United States 67,78,171,174,225,252,307,342
Ur 87,103,122,152,180
    Ur of the Chaldees 133,157,165,167,168
Ural-Altai Mountains
    Ural Altaic 99

Vapor 43,88
Vapor Canopy 23,24,55,56,58
Virgin Mary 85
Volcano (-es) 61,175

Water (s) 6,22,65,79,87,91,130,132,133,139,140,147,148,151,154,
156,157,163,165,175,184,188,212,219,229,232,234,236-239, 242,
248,269,274,280-282,287,293,294,296,302,317,329
Water cycle 10
Wine 68,69,92,100,176,196,287,292,300,341
Woman 40,43,48,78,85,89,92,104,116,118,145,172,176-178,188,
189,191,195,197,201,224, 227,254,280,282,288,300,301
Xerxes 82,295-297,312

Yahweh 234
Young Earth 31

Zagros Mountains
Zipporah
Zodiac 30,31, 83,85,282
Zoroaster 289
    Zoroastrian (s, -ism) 295

Printed in the United States
16535LVS00002B/39-254